Munich Studies on Innovation and Competition

Volume 13

The Munich Studies on Innovation and Competition present fundamental research on legal systems that have been created with the objective of promoting and safeguarding innovation and competition as the most important factors for economic growth and prosperity. Accordingly, this series will include monographic works in English in the different fields of intellectual property and competition law such as patent, trademark and copyright law, as well as unfair competition and antitrust law. Rather than describing what the law is, the series strives to contribute to the scholarship on how these legal systems should develop so as to promote innovation and competition. Therefore, its outlook is both international, by not focussing on any specific national legal system, and interdisciplinary. In particular, studies are encouraged that also incorporate the methods and findings of other disciplines such as economics, sociology and anthropology.

More information about this series at http://www.springer.com/series/13275

Korbinian Reiter

Market Design Powers of the European Commission?

Remedies under Articles 7 and 9 Regulation 1/03

Springer

Korbinian Reiter
Berlin, Germany

ISSN 2199-7462 ISSN 2199-7470 (electronic)
Munich Studies on Innovation and Competition
ISBN 978-3-662-60710-7 ISBN 978-3-662-60711-4 (eBook)
https://doi.org/10.1007/978-3-662-60711-4

This Springer imprint is published by the registered company Springer-Verlag GmbH, DE, part of Springer Nature.
The registered company address is: Heidelberger Platz 3, 14197 Berlin, Germany

Preface

This book constitutes an updated version of my doctoral thesis, written mostly in 2014 at the Max Planck Institute for Innovation and Competition and the Faculty of Law of the Ludwig-Maximilians-University in Munich. The decisional practice of the European Commission and the EU Courts as well as relevant literature have been taken into account until September 2019.

I want to express my very special gratitude to Professor Thomas Ackermann, my supervisor, and to Professor Josef Drexl, who reviewed the thesis as a second referee. They have provided me with invaluable help and inspiration, both academically and personally. I would also like to thank the Max Planck Institute for Innovation and Competition for the grant of a generous scholarship and for offering me unique working conditions.

I am deeply indebted to Dorothea, Josephine and Arthur for the many hours they sacrificed to let me advance my work and, foremost, for providing me with the encouragement and distraction necessary to carry on. The result is dedicated to my parents, without whose endless support throughout all of my life this book could never have been written.

Luxemburg
October 2019

Korbinian Reiter

Contents

Chapter 1
Introduction

The present work analyses remedies that may be adopted by the Commission on the basis of Articles 7 and 9 Regulation 1/03.[1] Broadly speaking, such remedies constitute measures by which a firm that is found or suspected to violate Articles 101 or 102 TFEU can be obliged to act in a way that puts the infringement to an end. Such remedies can for instance consist of a simple obligation to cease and desist anticompetitive conduct, of an obligation to grant access, an obligation to respect a certain minimum or maximum price—or even of an obligation to break up a company. While Article 7 empowers the Commission to impose injunctions against the will of the concerned undertaking subsequent to the finding of an infringement, Article 9 provides the Commission with the opportunity to make binding commitments that are offered by the concerned undertakings with a view to eliminate the Commission's concerns.

The interest pursued by the study is twofold. Its first objective consists in assessing whether the criticism that is levelled in the literature at the Commission's use of the Article 9 procedure is justified. In a nutshell, this criticism posits that the Commission's recourse to Article 9 instead of Article 7 leads to overbroad remedies, undermines procedural safeguards and reduces legal certainty. The debate does, in this regard, not merely concern a simple interpretation of the provisions of the enforcement regulation, but has a more worrying, rather dramatic undertone. In view of the frequency with which the Commission uses commitment instead of infringement decisions, critics see a risk for the orientation of the enforcement of Articles 101 and 102 TFEU as such. They fear that this enforcement no longer serves its legitimate purpose to protect competition, but as an instrument to restructure—or "design"—markets according to the will of the enforcer, unconstrained by the rule of law. To a large extent, this criticism was fuelled by the Alrosa judgment of the Court of Justice, overturning a judgment of the General Court in which the latter had established rigorous criteria for the use of commitment decisions. Perceived as a lost

[1] I will refer to these two provisions as Article 7 and Article 9 hereafter.

K. Reiter, *Market Design Powers of the European Commission?*, Munich Studies on Innovation and Competition 13, https://doi.org/10.1007/978-3-662-60711-4_1

opportunity to set limits to the Commission's powers under Article 9, the judgment of the Court of Justice has been described as its "worst decision".[2]

In order to assess the pertinence of the criticism of the Article 9 procedure, the present work uses Article 7 as a normative benchmark. It examines, on the one hand, whether and to what extent the Commission's commitment practice is inconsistent with the standards of Article 7 decisions in terms of scope of the remedy, procedural safeguards, and legal certainty. On the other hand, it asks whether and to what extent inconsistencies can be justified with the two particularities that distinguish the Article 9 from the Article 7 procedure: The goal of procedural economy that underlies commitment decisions and their consensual nature. Using Article 7 as a normative benchmark for the Commission's commitment practice presupposes, however, a clarification of the standards that apply under this provision. This clarification is hence the second objective of the present work.

The gist of the thesis submitted is that most of the criticism of the Commission's use of commitment decisions and of the legal standards applicable to the article 9 procedure is not justified. There is in principle no need for reform. Critics tend to overstate the degree to which the Commission's commitment practice lags behind the standards of infringement decisions by emphasising both the rigour of the Article 7 procedure and the laxness of the Article 9 procedure. The present work reverses the argument: It underlines the amount of flexibility enjoyed by the Commission in Article 7 procedures and the existence of limitations in Article 9 procedures. The remaining inconsistencies between the Commission's commitment practice and the standards for Article 7 decisions can, it is submitted, be justified with the consensual nature of commitment decisions and their underlying goal of procedural economy. This conclusion applies all the more in view of the broadly accepted need for some sort of consensual mechanism to close antitrust investigations and in view of the lack of convincing proposals to improve the current legal framework for the adoption of remedies.

A more detailed introduction to the background of the present study will be provided in its second chapter. Beforehand, some brief remarks are, however, called for regarding the delimitation of the subject matter, the terminology employed, and the importance of soft law for the analysis. These will be followed by a succinct outline of the general structure of the present work.

1.1 Delimitation of the Subject Matter

The narrow confinement of the subject matter to remedies adopted by the Commission on the basis of Articles 7 and 9 calls for some explanations. On the one hand, it may seem attractive to analyse these measures in the broader context of other means to enforce Articles 101 and 102 TFEU. This could not only include other instruments

---

[2] Jenny (2015).

in the Commission's toolbox such as interim measures,[3] findings of inapplicability,[4] fines[5] and periodic penalty payments.[6] In view of the decentralised enforcement of competition law, a truly comprehensive perspective on the enforcement mechanisms for Articles 101 and 102 TFEU would also have to encompass the enforcement tools at the disposal of the competition authorities and courts of the Member States.[7] On the other hand, even if one were in principle ready to limit the analysis to measures adopted by the Commission that resemble the ones taken on the basis of Article 7 and 9, one might still be tempted to extend the perspective beyond the enforcement of Articles 101 and 102 TFEU. In fact, also in related areas of EU law, namely in particular in the areas of Article 106 TFEU, merger control,[8] state aid[9] and anti-dumping law,[10] the Commission has the power to adopt measures that are to a certain extent comparable to the remedies adopted on the basis of Articles 7 and 9. In the fields of antitrust, Article 106 TFEU, merger, state aid and anti-dumping the Commission is equally exposed to the—well known—criticism that it enjoys too much leeway and instrumentalises the respective procedures for purposes of industrial policy. This criticism could in principle serve as a tertium comparationis that would permit a broader approach.[11]

---

[3]Article 8 Regulation 1/03.

[4]Article 10 Regulation 1/03.

[5]Article 23 Regulation 1/03.

[6]Article 24 Regulation 1/03.

[7]Pursuant to Articles 5 and 6 Regulation 1/03, the competition authorities and courts of the Member States have the power to apply Articles 101 and 102 TFEU in individual cases. See generally on the decentralised enforcement system of EU antitrust law eg Ortiz Blanco/Jörgens (2013), 1.41ff; De Smijter/Sinclair (2014), 2.05ff; Jones/Sufrin (2014), 923.

[8]See Articles 6(2) and 8(2) Merger Regulation and the Commission's Merger Remedies Notice (2008). Generally on merger remedies see eg Whish/Bailey (2012), 884ff; Jones/Sufrin (2014), 1245ff; Hoeg (2014).

[9]See Article 7(4) Regulation 659/1999. Generally on the Commission's use of conditions and obligations in state aid decisions see Bleckmann (2004); Ehricke (2006); Becker (2010); critically Ackermann (2014), 152f.

[10]Article 8 Regulation 1225/2009. Generally on anti-dumping undertakings see Stegemann (1990); Vermulst (2010), 3-002ff; Van Bael/Bellis (2011), § 6.10ff.

See also Temple Lang (2009), 133: "As the case law [on Article 9 decisions develops], practising lawyers should remember that there is another part of the Commission that also has regularly to consider whether to accept what are in effect commitments when they are offered, in anti-dumping cases. The Community Courts are likely to see similarities".

[11]See Messina/Ho (2011), 747, who argue that the Alrosa judgment of the CJ will influence the commitment practice in merger control and state aid, "especially with regard to the discretionary power of the Commission, and the consequent effects for the proportionality check and the intensity of judicial review".

See also the state aid case ING [GC, T-29/10 (2012)]: During the financial crisis, the Commission declared aid granted by the Netherlands to the bank ING compatible with the common market subject to compliance with certain restructuring commitments. These commitments comprised in particular a reduction of ING's balance sheets by 45%, a three-year ban on acquisitions, and a prohibition for ING to act as a price leader. In its appeal against the decision, ING argued inter alia

Various commentators have indeed analysed remedies pursuant to Article 7 or 9 in a broader context: Hjelmeng confines himself to the enforcement of Articles 101 and 102 TFEU, but includes fines and private enforcement[12]; Lianos extends this approach also to the Merger Regulation.[13] Frese provides a general account of the enforcement powers of competition authorities of the Commission and some competition authorities of the Member States with a view to the enforcement of Articles 101 and 102 TFEU.[14] Kellezi analyses remedies adopted under the Merger Regulation and on the basis of Articles 7 and 9; she confines her analysis of the latter to Article 102 TFEU.[15] A comparable approach that extended also to Article 101 TFEU was already undertaken by Müller-Tautphaeus prior to the modernisation of the EU competition rules.[16] Sofianatos covers the enforcement of Articles 101 and 102 TFEU and of the Merger Regulation by means of injunctions and commitments—thus including in particular injunctions granted by national courts, but excluding fines and claims for damages.[17] Finally, some commentators have also tried to draw parallels between, on the one hand, the Commission's remedies practice under Regulation 1/03 and the Merger Regulation, and, on the other hand, the Commission's practice to subject state aid decisions to conditions and obligations.[18]

Without prejudice to the merits of such broader perspectives, the present approach is deliberately more restricted. While the pragmatic desire to limit the subject matter of the study may be one reason, the more important one are the considerable differences that separate remedies adopted on the basis of Articles 7 and 9 from the mentioned related areas. These differences justify a more restricted perspective. In fact, they imply that a broader approach would have to come at the cost of a higher level of abstraction than is intended in the present work. Regarding the said differences, it suffices to sketch the major points:

that the restructuring requirements infringed the principle of proportionality. The GC did not have to decide the issue because it annulled the Commission's decision for different reasons. The GC's judgment was confirmed by CJ, C-224/12 P (ING, 2014).

[12]Hjelmeng (2013).

[13]Lianos (2012, 2013).

[14]Frese (2014).

[15]Kellezi (2010).

[16]Müller-Tautphaeus (2003).

[17]Sofianatos (2009).

[18]See Immenga (2011, 2012); Anestis (2012).

1.1.1 Distinction from Other Means to Enforce Articles 101 and 102 TFEU

Sofianatos has rightly emphasised that the central distinction between injunctions and commitments, on the one hand, and fines and damages claims, on the other, is that, unlike the latter, the former constitute a direct intervention on the market.[19] Moreover, injunctions and commitments pursue neither a punitive nor a compensatory goal. At the same time, the injunctions and commitments adopted by competition authorities should also be distinguished from injunctions and settlements before the civil law courts of the Member States. While the former focus on the general interest in the maintenance of competition on the market, the latter focus on the individual interest of the respective plaintiff. Also interim measures and findings of inapplicability follow their own logic. Although an interim measure certainly constitutes a direct intervention on the market, its effects are from the outset temporary. A finding of inapplicability merely confirms the compatibility of a practice with the competition rules; it does, however, not involve an obligation to act in a certain manner.

1.1.2 Distinction from Similar Powers in the Fields of Anti-dumping, State Aid and Article 106 TFEU

As far as the distinction of remedies adopted on the basis of Article 7 and 9 from similar powers of the Commission in the fields of anti-dumping, state aid and Article 106 TFEU is concerned, the following aspects bear mention: Anti-dumping measures fall under the EU's external action.[20] Unlike antitrust and merger remedies, undertakings given by companies to avert the imposition of an anti-dumping duty do not pursue the overall goal of lowering prices, but the exact opposite, namely a price increase by foreign producers to protect producers within the EU.[21] Price undertakings are often considered to entail the risk of facilitating collusion rather than promoting competition.[22]

---

[19]Sofianatos (2009), 12: "Contrairement aux autres instruments qui n'opèrent qu'une intervention indirecte sur le marché, les injonctions et les engagements mettent en place une intervention directe. Ils influent sur le comportement des opérateurs [...] C'est pour cette raison qu'ils acquièrent la qualité de mesures correctives".

An exception from this rule must however be made for remedies that involve the disgorgement of illicit profits or restitution; these will be discussed below (Sect. 3.3.4.1.3).

[20]See Article 207(1) TFEU.

[21]See Wessely (1999), 2.

[22]See Stegemann (1990); Kulms (1990), 286f and 303ff; Wessely (1999), 143ff; Theuringer (2003), 40 fn 4; Van Bael/Bellis (2011), § 6.15.

State aid procedures are procedures against Member States. They typically leave more room for negotiation and compromise between the Commission and the State in question than procedures under Regulation 1/03.[23] Unlike antitrust and merger remedies, conditions and obligations attached to a positive state aid decision do not directly bind the concerned undertakings vis-à-vis the Commission, but only the concerned Member State. If such a condition or obligation is violated, the Commission cannot take action directly against the infringing undertaking, but only against the concerned Member State.[24]

Also Article 106(3) TFEU allows the Commission to address decisions directly only to Member States.[25] If the Commission wants to proceed directly against a public undertaking for infringement of Article 106(1) or (2) TFEU, it must use its powers under Regulation 1/03.[26] The Commission's discretion in deciding whether to take action on the basis of Article 106(3) TFEU is greater than under Regulation 1/03: The Court of Justice has held that the Commission's refusal to act under Article 106(3) TFEU is not amenable to judicial review.[27]

[23]See Temple Lang (2011), 214; see also the opinion of AG Kokott in C-547/16 (Gasorba, 2017), 24f, pointing to the differences regarding the respective enforcement systems of antitrust and state aid rules.

[24]See GC, T-371/94 (British Airways, 1998), 290: "[...] the legal and practical utility of such conditions of authorisation lies in the fact that, if the recipient undertaking were to fail to observe them, it would be for the Member State concerned to ensure proper implementation of the authorisation decision and for the Commission to assess whether it was appropriate to demand that the aid be repaid [...]. It should be borne in mind that [...], the Court of Justice held that, if a State does not comply with the conditions imposed by the Commission in a decision approving aid, the Commission is entitled, under the second subparagraph of Article [108(2) TFEU], to refer the matter directly to the Court of Justice by way of derogation from Articles [258 and 259 TFEU]"; Ehricke (2006), 241f; Becker (2010), 213; Sinnaeve (2010), § 31, 52.

[25]The Greek Lignite case constitutes a more recent example in which the Commission relied on Article 106(3) TFEU in order to impose specific measures on Greece to remedy the anticompetitive effects of an infringement of Article 106(1) TFEU read in conjunction with Article 102 TFEU. The General Court annulled the decision in which the Commission had found that Greece had infringed Article 106(1) TFEU. In the view of the General Court, the Commission had not shown that there was an abuse [GC, T-169/08 (DEI, 2012)]. Consequently, the General Court also nullified the decision in which the Commission had imposed specific remedies on Greece to stop the abuse [GC, T-421/09 (DEI, 2012)]. Both judgments were reversed by the Court of Justice and referred back to the General Court [CJ, C-553/12 P (DEI, 2014) and C-554/12 P (DEI, 2014)]. For a discussion of the case see eg Graham (2013), 144; Frenz (2014); Kipiani (2014), 423; Sadowska (2014), 30ff.

[26]See Jones/Sufrin (2014), 653.

[27]CJ, C-141/02 P (max.mobil, 2005), 69; Jones/Sufrin (2014), 653.

1.1.3 Distinction from Merger Remedies

Remedies adopted by the Commission under the Merger Regulation are the ones that resemble those adopted on the basis of Article 7 and 9 the most.[28] Nonetheless, also merger remedies follow their own logic. The difference between merger and antitrust remedies predicates to some extent already on the dichotomy between structure and behaviour. However, in the view defended here, this dichotomy is not decisive: The statement that Articles 101 and 102 TFEU address behaviour and that therefore only behavioural remedies are admissible, while the Merger Regulation protects the structure of the market and therefore requests structural remedies, is at best true as a general rule with plenty of room for exceptions.[29] The convergence of the types of remedies that are adopted by the Commission on the basis of the Merger Regulation and on the basis of Regulation 1/03 has been emphasised repeatedly in the recent past.[30] This convergence, which is additionally spurred by the more economic approach with its emphasis on concrete effects instead of abstract categories of conduct, militates in principle for an analysis that encompasses both antitrust and merger remedies.

However, while the types of remedies used in antitrust and merger control converge, the ways in which they are adopted still differ to a significant extent. Two aspects shall be mentioned: First, under Regulation 1/03, the conduct of the undertakings is at the outset free. It does not require prior authorisation by the Commission. The Commission intervenes only if it suspects or finds an infringement. By contrast, a concentration that falls under the scope of the Merger Regulation must be notified to and approved by the Commission before it can be implemented. This difference regarding the ways in which Articles 101 and 102 TFEU and the substantive rules of merger control are enforced is commonly described by contrasting an ex post to an ex ante control. It leads to differences regarding the ways in which remedies are adopted: Under the Merger Regulation, the Commission is not empowered to impose unilateral injunctions in order to make a notified concentration compatible with the common market. The Commission can only either prohibit the notified concentration in its entirety or accept commitments offered by the parties.[31] Such commitment offers seek merely to enable the clearance of a concentration which would otherwise be prohibited. By contrast, under

---

[28]The section of the Manual of Procedures (2012) that deals with the content of commitment decisions (Module 16, 45) includes references to the Commission's Merger Remedies Notice (2008) and to the model texts the Commission has adopted for divestiture remedies and monitoring trustees.

[29]The dichotomy between structural and behavioural remedies will be discussed in more detail below (Sect. 3.4).

[30]Commission, Ten Years of Antitrust Enforcement under Regulation 1/2003, SWD(2014) 230/2, 188; Italianer (2012); Alexiadis/Sependa (2013), 4; Gerard (2013), 21; more carefully Lübking (2011), who points also to the limits of this convergence.

[31]See Merger Remedies Notice (2008), 6: "The Commission is not in a position to impose unilaterally any conditions to an authorisation decision, but only on the basis of the parties'

Regulation 1/03, the Commission has the power to impose unilateral injunctions. Moreover, commitment offers are made by the concerned undertakings with a view to prevent the imposition of an infringement decision, which facilitates follow-on damages actions before the national courts and which may be accompanied by a fine. Second, the Merger Regulation exposes all actors involved in the examination of a notified concentration to much higher time pressure than Regulation 1/03. The EU Courts have repeatedly emphasised that the general scheme of the Merger Regulation is characterised by a particular "need for speed [...] which requires the Commission to comply with strict time-limits for the adoption of the final decision".[32]

1.1.4 No Comparative Study

The present work does not endeavour a systematic comparison of remedies adopted by the Commission on the basis of Articles 7 and 9 with similar instruments used by other competition authorities. In that regard, reference is made to the existing literature that compares the EU practice with the practice both in the US[33] and the EU Member States.[34] It bears mention, however, that within the EU, directive 2019/1 now considerably harmonises the remedial powers of the competition authorities within the ECN: articles 10 and 12 of directive 2019/1 oblige the Member States to vest their competition authorities with powers similar to those enjoyed by the Commission under articles 7 and 9 of Regulation 1/03.[35]

Throughout the present study, examples from other legal orders and in particular from German law will be used on an occasional basis. The German practice can

commitments. [...] If [...] the parties do not validly propose remedies adequate to eliminate the competition concerns, the only option for the Commission will be to adopt a prohibition decision".

For the sake of completeness, it should be pointed out that Article 8(4) Merger Regulation empowers the Commission to adopt unilateral injunctions where a concentration has been implemented prior to having been declared incompatible with the common market or where it has been implemented in contravention of a condition, which has found that, in the absence of the condition, the concentration would be incompatible with the common market.

[32]CJ, C-413/06 P (Impala, 2008), 49; see also eg C-202/06 P (Cementbouw, 2007), 39; GC, T-151/05 (NVV, 2009), 166; T-79/12 (Cisco, 2013), 109.

[33]Eg Oehler (1976); Müller-Tautphaeus (2003); Ducore (2006); Georgiev (2007); Hennig (2010); Kipiani (2014).

[34]Eg Pera/Carpagnano (2008); Falconi (2011); Schweitzer (2012); Hinds/Eaton (2014); Frese (2014), 238f. See also, for an international overview of the use of commitment decisions, OECD (2016).

[35]See also the corresponding recitals 37 and 39 of directive 2019/1.

provide useful insights since the German rules on unilateral injunctions[36] and commitment decisions[37] were modelled after the European system.[38]

1.1.5 No Study of General Usefulness of Remedies, nor of Political or Economic Expediency

Finally, a last reservation is called for. In particular in the US literature, a fair amount of scepticism can be observed as regards the overall usefulness of antitrust remedies. The effect of the latter on the market is sometimes considered to be at best non-existent and in the worst case even negative. The absence of any remedy is hence occasionally perceived as the least unfavourable solution.[39] Such scepticism may serve as a healthy counterweight to potential over-enthusiasm on the side of competition authorities. Nevertheless, it will not further be addressed here. As will be explained in more detail below, any assessment of the overall effects of a remedy on the market is from the outset exposed to serious methodological problems.[40] The ambition of the present work is more limited. It focuses on the legal boundaries for the imposition of injunctions pursuant to Article 7 and for the acceptance of commitments pursuant to Article 9. It does, however, not attempt an evaluation of the overall usefulness of these measures. Nor should statements made throughout the following sections that a certain remedy was or could have been lawfully adopted on the basis of Article 7 be understood as implying an opinion with a view to the more general questions of economic or political expediency.

1.2 Terminology

Trying to avoid cumbersome and unnecessary terminological discussions as far as possible, I will limit myself to two clarifications regarding the use, for the purpose of the present study, of the term "remedy" and the dichotomy between "structural" and "behavioural" remedies.

---

[36]§ 32 ARC.

[37]§ 32b ARC.

[38]The Bundesgerichtshof [KVZ 55/07 (Nord KS, 2008), 18] has ruled that Article 7 Regulation 1/03 provides guidance as regards the interpretation of § 32 ARC.

[39]See Bougette/Marty (2012), 14, 18 and 56 with references; also Hovenkamp (2008), 300: "Finding the right remedy for antitrust violations is never easy, and we have never been particularly good at it. . . .".

[40]See Sect. 3.4.1.2.2.1.2 below.

1.2.1 Remedy

The term "remedy" is ambiguous, even when confined to its legal meanings.[41] It is often used simply as umbrella term for the various means to prevent or correct a legal wrong.[42] Also in the context of EU competition law, the use of the term varies. Some commentators employ a broad understanding that extends to the imposition fines and the various means to enforce competition law before national courts, in particular the attribution of damages.[43] Others insist on the distinction between measures that aim at putting an infringement to an end, on the one hand, and, fines and damages, on the other; they exclude the latter from their definition of remedies.[44] Yet another approach uses the term to describe the actions that can be brought in competition matters before the EU Courts.[45] The present study will not further address this terminological question. In view of the delimitation of the subject matter and without prejudice to a possible broader understanding in other contexts, the present use of the term remedy will generally denominate decisions that are adopted by the Commission on the basis of Articles 7 and 9. In addition, the term remedy will be used where the present work includes references to the Commission's commitment practice under the Merger Regulation.

1.2.2 Structural and Behavioural Remedies

A paramount claim of the present work is that the categorisation of remedies along the lines of the structure—behaviour dichotomy should be given up, because it is difficult to make and legally irrelevant. It is submitted that the assignment of a remedy to either category does not permit any conclusion as regards the admissibility of the remedy under Regulation 1/03.[46] Despite the lack of conceptual clarity, the terms structural and behavioural remedy will, however, occasionally be used throughout the present study. This is consistent with the wording of Article 7 and with the universal practice in the literature. However, according to the view defended here, no legal consequences are associated with either concept.

---

41 See Zakrewski (2005), 7ff; Lianos (2012), 180ff; Lianos (2013), 372ff.

42 See Zakrewski (2005), 9f: "[The term] remedy is often used in legal discourse simply to refer to any means provided by the law for obtaining redress or relief from a grievance. Where a grievance arises from an actual breach of duty, that which removes the grievance is a *corrective* remedy. Where it arises from a threatened or apprehended breach of duty, that which makes the claimant better is a *preventive* remedy"; Van Gerven (2000), 502: "remedies [...] are classes of action, intended to make good infringements of the rights concerned".

43 Lianos (2012), 189ff; Lianos (2013), 376ff; Hjelmeng (2013).

44 Lowe/Maier-Rigaud (2008), 598 and 600; Hellström/Maier-Rigaud/Bulst (2009), 44f.

45 Gray/Lester/Darbon/Facenna/Brown/Holmes (2006).

46 See Sect. 3.4 below.

1.3 The Importance of Soft-Law

In 2011 the Commission published a Notice on Best Practices for the conduct of proceedings concerning Articles 101 and 102 TFEU. In 2012, the publication of the Commission's Antitrust Manual of Procedures followed.[47] Both of these soft-law documents contain clarifications as regards the Commission's powers to adopt remedies under Articles 7 and 9. They will frequently be referred to throughout the present study.

The EU Courts have consistently ruled that the principles of equal treatment and legitimate expectations confer an indirect binding effect on soft law instruments such as notices, guidelines and communications.[48] The Commission may only depart from such measures, if it gives reasons that are compatible with the said principles.[49] As far as can be ascertained, it is not contested that this indirect binding effect applies also to the Best Practices.[50] However, it has been suggested that the Manual of Procedures should be considered only as "purely internal guidance" of the Commission.[51] This suggestion is not fully convincing in so far as it could imply that the principles of equal treatment and legitimate expectations do not confer any indirect binding effect at all on the Manual of Procedures.

It is true that the Manual of Procedures contains a disclaimer in which the Commission states inter alia that the document constitutes an "internal working tool intended to give practical guidance to staff"; that the document "does not contain binding instructions for staff"; that the "fact that the modules [contained in the Manual] are in the public domain does not change their character as purely internal guidance to staff"; and that "the published modules therefore do not create or alter any rights or obligations arising under the competition rules of the Treaty".[52] Nonetheless, the Commission states also that it publishes the Manual "in order to provide greater transparency about the Commission's procedures in applying the competition rules".[53] In Expedia, the Court of Justice considered the purpose of the De Minimis Notice to create transparency in applying the competition rules to be a reason why the principles of equal treatment and legitimate expectations confer an

[47]Temple Lang (2013), 2 fn 1, reports that the Commission at first refused to publish the Manual of Procedures and only agreed to do so subsequent to a ruling by the European Ombudsman. The latter held that the Commission was obliged to grant access to the Manual under the rules on access to documents (Regulation 1049/2001).

[48]See, for the fining guidelines: CJ, C-189/02 P (Dansk Rørindustri, 2005), 211; for the de minimis notice: CJ, C-226/11 (Expedia, 2012), 28; generally on the Commission's use of soft-law in the area of competition law eg Ackermann (2010), 10f; Jones/Sufrin (2014), 118f.

[49]CJ, C-397/03 P (Archer Daniels Midland, 2006), 91.

[50]See also GC, T-297/11 (Buzzi Unicem, 2014), 140f.

[51]Wagner-von Papp (2012), 932.

[52]See the Notice at the beginning of the Manual of Procedures (2012).

[53]Ibid.

indirect binding effect on the said Notice.[54] Even if the disclaimer that the Manual of Procedures constitutes "purely internal guidance to staff" could prevent the creation of legitimate expectations on the part of the undertakings, the principle of equal treatment would nevertheless confer an indirect binding effect on the Manual of Procedures to the extent that the Commission follows it in its actual practice. It is hence submitted that the Manual of Procedure has at least some indirect binding effect which can be relied upon by the concerned undertakings—even if the latter may be weaker than that of other soft-law instruments used by the Commission.[55]

In any event, it goes without saying that the Manual of Procedure has de facto an important impact on the Commission's practice. Therefore, it cannot be neglected throughout the course of this study, regardless of its precise legal effects.

1.4 Outline

The outline of the following chapters can at this stage be kept short. Additional explanations regarding the structure of the present study will be provided where necessary. As already stated, the primary goal of the work is to assess against the normative benchmark of Article 7 whether the criticism that is levelled at the Commission's use of Article 9 is justified. For this purpose, this criticism has been structured along the lines of the following three topics: The relaxation of the link between harm and remedy; the relaxation of procedural safeguards; and the impact of commitments on legal certainty. The three chapters that deal with these topics constitute the core of the present study. They are enclosed by an introductory chapter that prepares the basis for the following analysis and a concluding chapter that discusses proposals that have been made to improve the current practice.

[54]CJ, C-226/11 (Expedia, 2012), 28: "[. . .] the purpose of that notice is to make transparent the manner in which the Commission [. . .] will itself apply Article 101 TFEU. Consequently, by the *de minimis* notice, the Commission imposes a limit on the exercise of its discretion and must not depart from the content of that notice without being in breach of the general principles of law, in particular the principles of equal treatment and the protection of legitimate expectations".

[55]See also Temple Lang (2013), 15f, who argues that the Manual of Procedures binds the Commission in the same way as its other soft-law instruments. In his view, the fact that the Manual is formally designed as a set of instructions to Commission officials "does not seem relevant to the principle of legitimate expectations or the principle of equal treatment".

Bibliography

Ackermann (2010): Europäisches Kartellrecht, in: Riesenhuber (Ed.), Europäische Methodenlehre, 2nd edition, 2010

Ackermann (2014): State Aid for Banks in the Financial Crisis: The Commission's New and Stronger Role, in: Ringe/Huber (Eds.), Legal challenges in the global financial crisis. Bail-outs, the Euro, and regulation, 2014, p. 149

Alexiadis/Sependa (2013): Structural remedies under European Union antitrust rules, Concurrences 2013/2, 21

Anestis (2012): State Aid and Antitrust Remedies: Anything in Common?, EStAL 2012, 551

Becker (2010): Nebenbestimmungen im europäischen Beihilfenrecht, 2010

Bleckmann (2004): Zur Auflage im Beihilferecht, NVwZ 2004, 11

Bougette/Marty (2012): Quels remèdes pour les abus de position dominante? Une analyse économique des décisions de la Commission européenne, Concurrences 2012/3, 30

De Smijter/Sinclair (2014): The Enforcement System under Regulation 1/2003, in: Faull/Nikpay (Eds.), The EU Law of Competition, 3rd edition, 2014

Ducore (2006): Settlement of competition conduct violations at the United States antitrust agencies and at the European Commission – Some observations, in: Hawk (Ed), Annual proceedings of the Fordham Competition Law Institute 2005, 2006

Ehricke (2006): Auflagen und Bedingungen in Beihilfeentscheidungen der Europäischen Kommission, EWS 2006, 241

Falconi (2011): Commitment decisions in the EU and UK – Developments, open issues and considerations for companies and competition authorities, Competition Law 2011, 41

Frenz (2014): Genehmigungen zur Braunkohlegewinnung zugunsten der DIE verstoßen gegen europäisches Wettbewerbsrecht, DVBl 2014, 1455

Frese (2014): Sanctions in EU competition law. Principles and practice, 2014

Georgiev (2007): Contagious Efficiency: The growing reliance on U.S.-style antitrust settlements in EU law, 2007 Utah L. Rev. 971

Gerard (2013): Negotiated remedies in the modernization era: the limits of effectiveness, available online

Graham (2013): Abuse of Dominant Position in the Context of Exclusive Rights Granted by Authorities, JECLP 2013, 144

Gray/Lester/Darbon/Facenna/Brown/Holmes (2006): EU Competition Law. Procedures and Remedies, 2006

Hellström/Maier-Rigaud/Bulst (2009): Remedies in European antitrust law, 76 Antitrust L. J. 43 (2009)

Hennig (2010): Settlements im Europäischen Kartellverfahren, 2010

Hinds/Eaton (2014): Commitment issues - new developments in EU and Irish competition law, ECLR 2014, 33

Hjelmeng (2013): Competition Law Remedies: Striving for Coherence or Finding New Ways, CMLR 2013, 1007

Hoeg (2014): European Merger Remedies, 2014

Hovenkamp (2008): The Antitrust Enterprise, paperback edition, 2008

Immenga (2011): Zusagen, Auflagen und Bedingungen der Kommission – Herausforderungen im Beihilferecht und nach Art. 9 VO 1/2003, in: Albach/Bechtold (Eds.), Recht, Ordnung und Wettbewerb, Festschrift zum 70. Geburtstag von Wernhard Möschel, 2011

Immenga (2012): Gestaltungsspielräume der Kommission, in: Immenga/Körber (Eds.): Die Kommission zwischen zwischen Gestaltungsmacht und Rechtsbindung, 2012, p. 9

Italianer (2012): Legal certainty, proportionality, effectiveness: the Commission's practice on remedies, Speech given in December 2012, available online

Jenny (2015): Worst decision of the EU Court of Justice: The Alrosa judgment in context and the future of commitment decisions, Fordham Int'l L.J. 2015, 701

Jones/Sufrin (2014): EU Competition Law, 5th edition, 2014

Kellezi (2010): Les mesures correctives dans les cas de concentrations d'entreprises et d'abus de position dominante, 2010
Kipiani (2014): Les engagements en matière de pratiques anticoncurrentielles. Analyse des droits français, européen et américain, 2014
Kulms (1990): Competition, Trade Policy and Competition Policy in the EEC: The Example of Antidumping, CMLR 1990, 285
Lianos (2012): Competition Law Remedies. In Search of a Theory, in: Lianos/Sokol (Eds.), The Global Limits of Competition Law, 2012
Lianos (2013): Competition law remedies in Europe, in: Lianos/Geradin (Eds.), Handbook on European Competition Law. Enforcement and Procedure, 2013
Lowe/Maier-Rigaud (2008): Quo vadis antitrust remedies, in: Hawk (Ed.), Annual proceedings of the Fordham Competition Law Institute 2007, 2008, p. 597
Lübking (2011): Konvergenz und ihre Grenzen bei Zusagen in der EU-Fusionskontrolle und nach Artikel 9 VO 1/2003, WuW 2011, 1223
Messina/Ho (2011): Re-establishing the Orthodoxy of Commitment Decisions under Article 9 of Regulation 1/2003: Comment on Commission v Alrosa, ELR 2011, 737
Müller-Tautphaeus (2003): Abhilfebefugnisse der Europäischen Kommission im Wettbewerbsrecht, 2003
OECD (2016): Commitment decisions in antitrust cases, OECD Policy Roundtables, 2016, available online
Oehler (1976): Entflechtung und Kontrahierungszwang. Methoden und Erfahrungen im amerikanischen Recht der Wettbewerbsbeschränkungen, 1976
Ortiz Blanco/Jörgens (2013): in: Ortiz Blanco (Ed.), EU Competition Procedure, 3rd Edition, 2013
Pera/Carpagnano (2008): The law and practice of commitment decisions: a comparative analysis, ECLR 2008, 669
Sadowska (2014): Committed to Reform? Pragmatic Antitrust Enforcement in Electricity Markets, 2014
Schweitzer (2012): Commitment Decisions in the EU and in the Member States: Functions and Risks of a New Instrument of Competition Law Enforcement within a Federal Enforcement Regime, available online
Sinnaeve (2010): in: Heidenhain (Ed.), European State Aid Law, 2010
Sofianatos (2009): Injonctions et engagements en droit de la concurrence: étude de droit communautaire, français et grec, 2009
Stegemann (1990): EC Anti-Dumping Policy: Are Price-Undertakings a Legal Substitute for Illegal Price Fixing, Weltwirtschaftliches Archiv 1990, 268
Temple Lang (2009): Commitment decisions under Regulation 1/2003, in: Gheur/Petit (Eds.), Alternative enforcement techniques in EC competition law, 2009
Temple Lang (2011): Three Possibilities for Reform of the Procedure of the European Commission in Competition Cases under Regulation 1/2003, CEPS Special Report, available online
Temple Lang (2013): The strengths and weaknesses of the DG Competition Manual of Procedure, JAE 2013, 1
Theuringer (2003): Antidumping und wettbewerbsbeschränkendes Verhalten, 2003
Van Bael/Bellis (2011): EU Anti-Dumping and Other Trade Defence Instruments, 5th edition, 2011
Van Gerven (2000): Of Rights, Remedies and Procedures, CMLR 2000, 501
Vermulst (2010): EU Anti-Dumping Law and Practice, 2nd edition, 2010
Wagner-Von Papp (2012): Best and even better practices in commitment procedures after Alrosa: the dangers of abandoning the "struggle for competition law", CMLR 2012, 929
Wessely (1999): Das Verhältnis von Antidumping- und Kartellrecht in der Europäischen Gemeinschaft. Eine Untersuchung der wettbewerbsrechtlichen Schranken des EG-Handelsschutzrechts, 1999
Whish/Bailey (2012): Competition Law, 7th edition, 2012
Zakrewski (2005): Remedies reclassified, 2005

Chapter 2
Prolegomena

In order to prepare the basis for the following discussion, it is useful, first, to highlight the main features that distinguish Article 7 and Article 9 as legal bases for the adoption of remedies. In that regard, the first section of the present chapter shall only provide an overview. In so far as the features are problematic, they will be addressed in more detail below. Second, in view of its paramount importance for the present study, the Alrosa case will be presented in detail; a first comment on the criticism that relates directly to the judgment shall also be made. The full importance of the questions addressed in this study will become apparent in the third section of the present chapter: It will place the Alrosa case in the broader context of the overall development of the Commission's practice.

2.1 Fundamentals Regarding Article 7 and Article 9 as Legal Bases for the Adoption of a Remedy

2.1.1 Article 7

Where the Commission finds that there is an infringement of Articles 101 or 102 TFEU, Article 7(1) Regulation 1/03 empowers it to put the infringement to an end. For this purpose, the provision enables the Commission to impose any remedy on the infringing undertaking that meets the threshold of the principle of proportionality. For the current purpose of a brief comparative overview over Article 7 and Article 9, it suffices to highlight three distinct features of an Article 7 remedy. First, any Article 7 remedy predicates on a finding of an infringement, which the Commission must prove to the requisite legal standard. The fact that the remedy predicates on a finding of an infringement has at least two important implications. On the

K. Reiter, *Market Design Powers of the European Commission?*, Munich Studies on Innovation and Competition 13, https://doi.org/10.1007/978-3-662-60711-4_2

one hand, it means that the remedy can be combined with a fine.[1] On the other hand, to the extent that an Article 7 decision contains a finding of an infringement, it is binding for the competition authorities and the courts of the member states.[2] Article 7 decisions may therefore serve as a basis for private damages actions. Second, any Article 7 decision is preceded by an elaborate administrative procedure with relatively far reaching rights of defence. In particular, the Commission must give the concerned undertakings the opportunity to present their views on the intended decision. For this purpose, the Commission has to communicate a detailed statement of objections to them and grant them access to its file. Third, the Commission imposes Article 7 remedies unilaterally. The concerned undertakings merely have the possibility to present their views. The final decision about the remedy lies, however, with the Commission.

2.1.2 *Article 9*

In the run up to an Article 7 decision, the Commission can also opt for an Article 9 decision to close an investigation. The latter provision empowers the Commission to make commitments binding that are offered by a concerned undertaking to meet the Commission's concerns. Such commitments differ from Article 7 remedies under the three aspects mentioned above. First, an Article 9 decision does not contain a finding of an infringement.[3] In view of the absence of a finding of an infringement, commitment decisions cannot serve as the basis for the imposition of a fine or for a private damages action. Second, depending on the point of time when the decision is taken, the administrative procedure that leads to an Article 9 decision can be less elaborate than the one leading to an Article 7 decision. The Commission may accept commitments already before it notifies a statement of objections to the concerned undertakings. In such a case, the Commission adopts an Article 9 remedy on the sole basis of a "preliminary assessment" of the case. The concerned undertakings usually waive their right of access to the file. Pursuant to Article 27(4) Regulation 1/03, the Commission must, however, give third parties the opportunity to submit comments on proposed commitments by means of a so-called "market-test"[4] before it makes the commitments binding. No mandatory market test is prescribed for the adoption of an Article 7 decision. Third, an Article 9 remedy predicates always on the consensual will of the Commission and the undertaking. The Commission is

[1]Pursuant to Article 23(2)(a) Regulation 1/03 the imposition of a fine is possible if the Commission finds that an undertaking infringes Article 101 or 102 TFEU at least negligently.

[2]Article 16 Regulation 1/03.

[3]Pursuant to recital 13, 2nd sentence, Regulation 1/03, "[c]ommitment decisions should find that there are no longer grounds for action by the Commission without concluding whether or not there has been or still is an infringement." Instead of all see only Schweitzer (2010), 547, and AG Kokott, opinion in C-547/16 (Gasorba, 2017), 32.

[4]Best Practices (2011), 129ff; Manual of Procedures (2012), Module 16, 56ff.

normally not obliged to make a remedy offer binding under Article 9 instead of adopting an Article 7 decision. Similarly, the undertaking concerned is never obliged to meet the Commission's requests for a particular remedy.[5]

2.1.3 Distinction of the Article 9 Procedure from the Settlement Procedure in Cartel Cases

On a side note, it bears mention that the commitment procedure pursuant to Article 9 must be distinguished from the settlement procedure in cartel cases pursuant to Article 10a Regulation 773/2004.[6] This distinction will be addressed in more detail below.[7] For the present purposes, it suffices to highlight the major points: The settlement procedure applies only to cartel cases. By contrast, cartel cases are excluded from the scope of application of the Article 9 procedure. The core feature of the settlement procedure is that the parties of a cartel investigation acknowledge their involvement in the cartel and their liability for it. In return, the Commission reduces the fine that it would otherwise have imposed on them.[8] Unlike an Article 9 decision, the settlement procedure hence leads to an infringement decision pursuant to Article 7 and to the imposition of a fine pursuant to Article 23(2) Regulation 1/03.

2.2 The Alrosa Case and Its Criticism

The distinction between Article 7 and Article 9 procedures was emphasised by the Court of Justice in its landmark ruling in Alrosa, handed down in 2010. The Court of Justice overturned a judgment of the General Court, in which the latter had assimilated the two procedures in order to quash a decision that made binding commitments entered into by De Beers. Setting to date the legal standard for the interpretation of Article 9, the case will frequently be referred to again throughout the course of the present study. For this reason, both the case and its criticism merit a detailed and coherent presentation already at this early stage.[9]

---

[5]See Kellerbauer (2011), 8.

[6]For this distinction see eg Metha/Centella (2010), 396ff; Schweitzer (2010), 549; Richter (2012), 640f; Kellerbauer/Ortiz Blanco/Jörgens/Centella (2013), 10.117ff; Laina/Laurinen (2013), 306; Colombani/Kloub/Sakkers (2014), 8.715.

[7]See Sect. 6.2.3.1.2 below.

[8]Whish/Bailey (2012), 262; similarly Kellerbauer/Ortiz Blanco/Jörgens/Centella (2013), 10.109.

[9]The literature on the case is abundant: see only eg Le More (2007); Temple Lang (2009); Schweitzer (2010); Frenz/Ehlenz (2010); Körber (2010); Klees (2010); Hennig (2010b); Brenner (2010); Idot (2010); Muguet-Poullennec/Barbier de La Serre (2010); Cavicchi (2011); Cengiz (2011); Kellerbauer (2011); Messina/Ho (2011); Wagner-Von Papp (2012); Jones/Sufrin (2014), 983ff.

2.2.1 The Case

2.2.1.1 The Facts

The case concerned an exclusive purchase agreement between Alrosa and De Beers. De Beers occupied at the time the number one position on the world market for the production and supply of rough diamonds. Alrosa occupied the number two position on that market. Both undertakings were active in the entire supply chain for diamonds, including the exploration, mining, trading, manufacturing and the jewellery business. Geographically, De Beers' activities were focused on South Africa, Botswana, Namibia, Tanzania and the United Kingdom. Alrosa's activities concentrated on the Community of Independent States (CIS). Against the background of long standing trading relations, the two undertakings notified an agreement to the Commission, under which Alrosa undertook to supply De Beers with quantities of rough diamonds that accounted for one half of Alrosa's annual production and for the entire production exported outside the CIS.[10] The Commission opened two separate procedures and sent two statements of objections to the parties. In the first one, which was addressed jointly to De Beers and Alrosa, the Commission expressed the opinion that the agreement might violate Article 101 TFEU. In the second one, which was addressed only to De Beers, the Commission expressed the opinion that the agreement might also violate Article 102 TFEU.

At first, Alrosa reacted by offering a commitment that consisted of the obligation to discontinue the supply of rough diamonds to De Beers completely after a 10-year transition period during which the supply was to be continuously reduced. However, Alrosa subsequently withdrew that offer.[11] Next, Alrosa and De Beers proposed joint commitments which consisted of the obligation to cap the supply at a certain maximum level after a 6-year transition period during which the supply was to be continuously reduced.[12] The Commission market-tested those commitments. In view of the negative responses it received, the Commission invited Alrosa and De Beers to submit new commitments.[13] Subsequently, De Beers offered an individual commitment that consisted of the obligation to discontinue the purchase of rough diamonds from Alrosa completely after a transitional period of 3 years during which the purchase was to be continuously reduced.[14] The Commission sent Alrosa a copy of the commitments proposed by De Beers, together with non-confidential versions of the comments received during the market test. After an exchange of views with Alrosa, the Commission made De Beers' individual commitments binding pursuant to Article 9.[15]

---

[10]See GC, T-170/06 (Alrosa, 2007), 8ff.

[11]See GC, T-170/06 (Alrosa, 2007), 18.

[12]See GC, T-170/06 (Alrosa, 2007), 19.

[13]See GC, T-170/06 (Alrosa, 2007), 20f.

[14]See GC, T-170/06 (Alrosa, 2007), 22.

[15]See GC, T-170/06 (Alrosa, 2007), 23ff.

2.2.1.2 The Judgment of the General Court

Upon appeal by Alrosa, the General Court annulled the decision for two independent reasons: First, the Court found that the decision violated Article 9 and the principle of proportionality. Second, in the view of the Court, the Commission had infringed Alrosa's rights of defence.

2.2.1.2.1 Violation of Article 9 and the Principle of Proportionality

As regards the violation of Article 9 and of the principle of proportionality, the Court argued that the principle of proportionality applied to Article 9 decisions essentially in the same way it applied to Article 7 decisions.[16] The Court acknowledged that decisions adopted on the basis of Article 9 differed from those adopted on the basis of Article 7 in that the former do not require the formal establishment of an infringement. The Court also accepted that the Commission's obligation to analyse the market and to identify the infringement were therefore "less definitive" in the context of Article 9 than in the context of Article 7. Nonetheless, in the view of the Court, the Commission was obliged to establish the reality of the competition concerns also in the context of Article 9 to a degree that was sufficient to allow a review of the proportionality of the commitment.[17] Moreover, the Court found that the voluntary character of commitments did not relieve the Commission of its duty to respect the principle of proportionality, because it was the Commission's decision that made the commitments binding.[18] In that regard, the Court ruled that compliance with the principle of proportionality required the Commission to examine whether any of the measures known to it were less onerous than the commitment under scrutiny and also capable of eliminating the concerns.[19] Finally, the Court argued that the Commission could only rely on a margin of discretion regarding the proportionality of the commitments, if it had effectively engaged into a complex economic assessment.[20]

When applying those standards, the Court found that the Commission's decision did not meet up to them. The Commission had admitted during the procedure that there was a grey zone between the joint commitments and the ones that had been offered individually by De Beers. In this respect, the Commission had stated that the identification of alternatives to the commitments made binding would have required a complex economic assessment that Article 9 was intended to avoid and that its endorsement of a complete discontinuance of all supplies was based on the difficulty of establishing alternative commitments.[21] The Court inferred from these statements

---

[16]See GC, T-170/06 (Alrosa, 2007), 92ff.

[17]See GC, T-170/06 (Alrosa, 2007), 100f.

[18]See GC, T-170/06 (Alrosa, 2007), 105.

[19]See GC, T-170/06 (Alrosa, 2007), 131.

[20]See GC, T-170/06 (Alrosa, 2007), 108ff.

[21]See GC, T-170/06 (Alrosa, 2007), 124.

that the Commission had not carried out complex economic assessments and therefore applied a standard of full review.[22] The Court found that the commitment made binding was disproportionate, because several other solutions existed that were less onerous, but equally capable of eliminating the Commission's concerns. First, the Court referred to a simple prohibition for the parties from entering into any agreement allowing De Beers to reserve to itself the whole or a material part of Alrosa's production exported outside the CIS.[23] Second, the Court held that the Commission had failed to explain why the joint commitments were not capable of eliminating its concerns. According to the Court, a complete and indefinite prohibition to enter into contract could only be justified in exceptional circumstances, for instance in oligopoly constellations. However, the Commission had only referred to an oligopoly in the statement of objections regarding the Article 101 TFEU procedure, but not in the statement of objections regarding the Article 102 TFEU procedure.[24] Moreover, the Court considered that the cap provided for in the joint commitments ensured the sale of sufficient quantities of diamonds to third parties to make a coordination of Alrosa's and De Beers' pricing policy at least difficult.[25] Third, the Court argued that even if the joint commitments were insufficient, the Commission could have amended them along the lines of a proposal made by Alrosa during the administrative procedure. According to that proposal, Alrosa was to be allowed to sell a limited quantity of diamonds to De Beers on an ad hoc basis at open auctions. The Court found that such an amendment would have enabled third parties to gain full access to Alrosa's output whilst preserving the opportunity for Alrosa to sell a limited quantity also to De Beers.[26] In that regard, the Court rejected the Commission's concerns that Alrosa and De Beers could abuse the possibility of open auctions. The Court argued that the possibilities to reopen proceedings pursuant to Article 9(2) and to impose fines pursuant to Article 23(2) were sufficient to ensure compliance.[27]

2.2.1.2.2 Violation of Alrosa's Rights of Defence

As regards the violation of Alrosa's rights of defence, the Court acknowledged that Alrosa was formally not an "undertaking concerned" in the sense of Article 27(2) for the purpose of the procedure regarding Article 102 TFEU.[28] However, since Alrosa had the status of a concerned undertaking for the purpose of the procedure regarding Article 101 TFEU and since the Commission and the parties had at all times de facto treated the two procedures as a single one, Alrosa should have been accorded the

[22]See GC, T-170/06 (Alrosa, 2007), 125.
[23]See GC, T-170/06 (Alrosa, 2007), 128.
[24]See GC, T-170/06 (Alrosa, 2007), 141.
[25]See GC, T-170/06 (Alrosa, 2007), 134.
[26]See GC, T-170/06 (Alrosa, 2007), 138.
[27]See GC, T-170/06 (Alrosa, 2007), 146 and 150ff.
[28]See GC, T-170/06 (Alrosa, 2007), 176.

rights of a concerned undertaking also with respect to the procedure regarding Article 102 TFEU.[29] The Court objected to the facts that the Commission had provided Alrosa with a non-confidential version of the comments received in response to the market test only 6 weeks after Alrosa's written request and only simultaneously with the copy of De Beer's individual commitments. The Court found that, under those conditions, Alrosa had been prevented from presenting an effective reply and from proposing new joint commitments with De Beers.[30]

2.2.1.3 The Opinion of Advocate General Kokott

Advocate General Kokott proposed to set aside the judgment of the General Court and to uphold the decision.

2.2.1.3.1 Violation of Article 9 and of the Principle of Proportionality

In the view of the Advocate General, the conclusion of the General Court that the Commission had violated Article 9 and the principle of proportionality was deficient for two reasons: First, the General Court applied a too strict proportionality test. Second, the General Court exceeded the limits of judicial review by substituting its own assessment for that of the Commission.

2.2.1.3.1.1 Too Strict Proportionality Test

The Advocate General agreed with the General Court that, as a general principle of EU law, the principle of proportionality was applicable also in the context of Article 9. In her view, this meant in principle that the Commission could not make disproportionate commitments binding. Instead, the Commission had to point out to the undertaking that the commitments were disproportionate and, if necessary, suggest changes. If the commitments were divisible, the Commission could make them binding only in part.[31] However, according to the Advocate General, there were fundamental differences between Article 7 and Article 9 as regards the concrete modalities of the proportionality test that the General Court had failed to recognise.[32] The Advocate General argued that the concerns of procedural economy that characterised Article 9 affected the examination of the proportionality in two ways: First, demands regarding the appropriateness were higher under Article 9 than under Article 7. Under the former provision, the Commission could reject a commitment, if it was not manifestly appropriate.[33] Second, as regards the necessity,

[29]See GC, T-170/06 (Alrosa, 2007), 186f.

[30]See GC, T-170/06 (Alrosa, 2007), 201.

[31]See opinion of AG Kokott in C-441/07 P (Alrosa, 2009), 43.

[32]See opinion of AG Kokott in C-441/07 P (Alrosa, 2009), 49.

[33]See opinion of AG Kokott in C-441/07 P (Alrosa, 2009), 53.

the Advocate General proposed to make a distinction between the interests of the undertaking having offered the commitment and the interests of third parties. In relation to the undertaking having offered the commitment the necessity could be presumed, because the undertaking offered the commitment voluntarily.[34] On the other hand, such a presumption could not be made where the interests of third parties were affected. According to the Advocate General, in the latter case, the Commission was still not required to seek itself less onerous alternatives to an offered commitment. Similar to the General Court,[35] the Advocate General was of the opinion that the Commission was obliged to review all the alternatives known to it in order to ascertain whether they constituted means of resolving the competition problems that were less onerous for the affected third party.[36] However, different from the General Court, the Advocate General emphasised that the Commission was only required to take alternatives known to it into consideration that were equally appropriate as the commitment under scrutiny. Since the reasons of procedural economy that underlie Article 9 required that a commitment be manifestly appropriate, the same requirement had to be met also by any potential alternative.[37] In the view of the Advocate General, the General Court had therefore committed an error, when it criticised the Commission for not taking less onerous alternative solutions into consideration on the basis of the alleged difficulty in determining them. According to the Advocate General, the Commission could rely on the fact that the appropriateness of the alternatives could not be established with sufficient certainty without further investigations or evaluations.[38]

2.2.1.3.1.2 Excess of the Limits of Judicial Review

The Advocate General also concluded that the General Court had committed an error by substituting its own assessment for that of the Commission, thereby exceeding the limits of its powers of judicial review. In that regard, the Advocate General rejected the proposition of the General Court that the Commission had not carried out complex economic assessments. In her view, the adoption of any commitment required a future-oriented, prospective economic analysis of the expected effects of the commitment and its alternatives on market activities and an assessment whether the alternatives were equally appropriate to address the competition concerns. This alone required an appraisal of complex economic matters.[39]

---

[34]See opinion of AG Kokott in C-441/07 P (Alrosa, 2009), 55 and 60.

[35]See Sect. 2.2.1.2.1 with footnote 19 above.

[36]See opinion of AG Kokott in C-441/07 P (Alrosa, 2009), 56 and 79.

[37]See opinion of AG Kokott in C-441/07 P (Alrosa, 2009), 57.

[38]See opinion of AG Kokott in C-441/07 P (Alrosa, 2009), 58f.

[39]See opinion of AG Kokott in C-441/07 P (Alrosa, 2009), 71 and 74.

Under the limited standard of review that was hence applicable, the General Court was entitled to examine whether the facts ascertained by the Commission were capable of substantiating the conclusion drawn by it.[40] However, according to the Advocate General, the General Court had not found that the Commission's conclusion regarding the inappropriateness of the alternative solutions was not ascertained by facts. Instead, the General Court had substituted its own assessment for that of the Commission.[41] In this connection, the Advocate General took offence at the opinion of the General Court that the joint commitments or amended commitments allowing for a limited sale of diamonds in open auctions would have been sufficient to prevent Alrosa and De Beers from coordinating their pricing policies.[42] According to the Advocate General, the General Court had in particular failed to recognise that De Beers was not only a buyer, but also a seller of rough diamonds. The relation between Alrosa and De Beers was therefore not merely a vertical one, but also a horizontal, competitive one. In such a constellation, the Commission could lawfully assume that letting De Beers buy up parts of the production of Alrosa would influence prices to the detriment of consumers.[43] Moreover, the Commission could also conclude that there was an incentive for De Beers to abuse an auction procedure to artificially push up prices.[44]

2.2.1.3.2 Violation of Alrosa's Rights of Defence

The Advocate General also saw an error in the conclusion of the General Court that the Commission had violated Alrosa's rights of defence. She took the view that, since the Commission had not acted arbitrarily in conducting two separate procedures, Alrosa enjoyed only the status of an interested third party in the Article 102 TFEU procedure.[45] As an interested third party, Alrosa had from the outset no right of access to the file.[46] According to the Advocate General, it followed nonetheless from Alrosa's general right to be heard that the Commission had to inform it about the substance of the unilateral commitments offered by De Beers and explain that the joint commitments were not sufficient.[47] However, since the Commission had orally informed Alrosa at a meeting about the insufficiency of the joint commitments and of its plan to accept only commitments leading to a complete cessation of the trading relations, the Advocate General was of the opinion that the Commission had met those requirements.[48]

[40] See opinion of AG Kokott in C-441/07 P (Alrosa, 2009), 78.

[41] See opinion of AG Kokott in C-441/07 P (Alrosa, 2009), 83.

[42] See opinion of AG Kokott in C-441/07 P (Alrosa, 2009), 85 and 88.

[43] See opinion of AG Kokott in C-441/07 P (Alrosa, 2009), 122 and 233ff.

[44] See opinion of AG Kokott in C-441/07 P (Alrosa, 2009), 128f.

[45] See opinion of AG Kokott in C-441/07 P (Alrosa, 2009), 175f.

[46] See opinion of AG Kokott in C-441/07 P (Alrosa, 2009), 182 and 192.

[47] See opinion of AG Kokott in C-441/07 P (Alrosa, 2009), 199f.

[48] See opinion of AG Kokott in C-441/07 P (Alrosa, 2009), 203ff.

2.2.1.4 The Judgment of the Court of Justice

In a grand chamber judgment, the Court of Justice set aside the judgement of the General Court and confirmed the Commission's decision.

2.2.1.4.1 Violation of Article 9 and of the Principle of Proportionality

As far as the conclusion of the General Court that the Commission had violated Article 9 and the principle of proportionality is concerned, also the Court of Justice distinguished between questions of proportionality and judicial review.[49]

2.2.1.4.1.1 Too Strict Proportionality Test

The Court of Justice essentially shared the Advocate General's opinion that the General Court had carried out an erroneous proportionality test. The Court of Justice confirmed that, in the context of Article 9, the generally applicable proportionality test had to be adapted to the provision's underlying goal of procedural economy.[50] Moreover, in the view of the Court of Justice, an undertaking offering a commitment consciously accepts that the concessions it makes may go beyond what the Commission could have imposed pursuant to Article 7 after a thorough investigation.[51] Therefore, in the context of Article 9, the Commission is not required itself to seek out less onerous or more moderate solutions than the commitments offered to it.[52] Rather, "application of the principle of proportionality by the Commission in the context of Article 9 [. . .] is confined to verifying that the commitments in question address the concerns it expressed to the undertakings concerned and that they have not offered less onerous commitments that also address those concerns adequately. When carrying out that assessment, the Commission must, however, take into consideration the interests of third parties".[53]

2.2.1.4.1.2 Excess of the Limits of Judicial Review

The Court of Justice also ruled that the judicial review of an Article 9 decision related solely to whether the Commission's assessment was manifestly incorrect.[54] Expressly referring to the reasons set out by the Advocate General, the Court of Justice found that the General Court had erroneously substituted its own assessment for that of the Commission. According to the Court of Justice, when the General

[49] CJ, C-441/07 P (Alrosa, 2010), 37.

[50] CJ, C-441/07 P (Alrosa, 2010), 35ff and 47.

[51] CJ, C-441/07 P (Alrosa, 2010), 48.

[52] CJ, C-441/07 P (Alrosa, 2010), 61.

[53] CJ, C-441/07 P (Alrosa, 2010), 41.

[54] CJ, C-441/07 P (Alrosa, 2010), 42.

Court evaluated whether the alternative solutions were appropriate to resolve the identified competition concerns, it had incorrectly not confined itself to evaluating whether the Commission's conclusion was obviously unfounded, having regard to the facts established by it.[55] Alrosa had not succeeded in showing that the commitments made binding by the Commission went manifestly beyond what was necessary to address the concerns identified by the Commission.[56]

2.2.1.4.2 Violation of Alrosa's Rights of Defence

As far as the violation of Alrosa's rights of defence was concerned, the Court of Justice sided with the Advocate General's opinion that, since the Commission had not acted arbitrarily in conducting two separate procedures, Alrosa enjoyed only the status of an interested third party in the Article 102 TFEU procedure.[57] Different from the Advocate General, the Court of Justice did not hold that the Commission had to inform Alrosa about the substance of the unilateral commitments offered by De Beers and explain that the joint commitments were not sufficient. Rather, the Court of Justice took the view that the Commission was not required to state to Alrosa the reasons for rejecting the joint commitments and to suggest to Alrosa that it offer new joint commitments with De Beers. According to the Court of Justice, it followed from the Commission's discretion in regard of Article 9 decisions that the Commission's acceptance of the individual commitments offered by De Beers did not depend on the position of Alrosa or any other undertaking.[58]

2.2.2 Essential Criticism and Preliminary Comment

The Alrosa judgment of the Court of Justice prompted mostly critical reactions in the literature.[59] Apart from the Commission[60] and members of its services,[61] only few voices welcomed the Court's emphasis on the distinction between the Article 7 and the Article 9 procedure as realignment with the intent of the legislator to promote procedural economy.[62] The following section is not meant to give a comprehensive

---

[55] CJ, C-441/07 P (Alrosa, 2010), 62ff.

[56] CJ, C-441/07 P (Alrosa, 2010), 120.

[57] CJ, C-441/07 P (Alrosa, 2010), 88ff.

[58] CJ, C-441/07 P (Alrosa, 2010), 88ff.

[59] See the references in Sect. 2.2, footnote 9 above; moreover Barbier de la Serre (2012), 99: "big cause for concern"; Jenny (2015): "worst decision of the EU Court of Justice".

[60] See MEMO/10/285.

[61] See Mische/Višnar (2010), 22.

[62] Messina/Ho (2011), 750; similarly also Hennig (2010a), 141f and 180f and (2010b), 448 and 450f.

account of all the arguments that have been exchanged over the Court's judgment. Many of those arguments will be addressed later in this work during the broader discussion of the criticism that is levelled at the Article 9 procedure in general. In particular questions that relate to the scope of judicial review and the rights of defence shall only be addressed further below. However, already at this stage, some clarifying remarks are called for that concern the focus of the criticism levelled at the judgment: The Court's modification of the proportionality test for the purpose of Article 9.

2.2.2.1 Summary of the Criticism Regarding the Modified Proportionality Test

In this regard, commentators take offence, first, at the Court's justification of reduced proportionality requirements with the qualification of a commitment offer as conscious acceptance that the commitment may go beyond what the Commission could have imposed pursuant to Article 7. They argue either that commitment offers are not made voluntarily[63] or at least that the consensual nature of a commitment does not constitute a sufficient guarantee for its proportionality.[64] The threat of an infringement decision, accompanied by heavy fines[65] and possibly private follow-on actions,[66] discriminatory treatment of a company refusing to comply with the Commission's commitment requests in other procedures,[67] the Commission's active role during the negotiation of the commitments,[68] the lack of access to the file that prevents an informed decision[69] and the absence of a full investigation of the facts

[63]See Klees (2009), 379; Muguet-Poullennec/Barbier de la Serre (2010), 40; Hennig (2010b), 452; Gerard (2013b), 15f; Botteman/Patsa (2013), 362f; Jenny (2015), 713ff and 760.

[64]Wils (2006), 352; Brenner (2010), 1336; Frenz/Ehlenz (2010), 308; Klees (2011), 18; Schweitzer (2011), 646f; Wagner-Von Papp (2012), 943ff and 949; Lugard/Möllmann (2013), 9; Gerard (2013b), 30; von Kalben (2018), 66ff.

[65]Eg Waelbroeck (2009), 235f; Klees (2009), 379; Körber (2010), 82; Muguet-Poullennec/Barbier de la Serre (2010), 40; Hennig (2010b), 452; Waelbroeck/Frisch (2013), 683; Gerard (2013b), 16.

[66]See Hennig (2010b), 452; Wagner-Von Papp (2012), 948.

[67]See Wagner-Von Papp (2012), 948. Wagner-Von Papp disputes the standard argument that the power to impose fines allows the Commission to extract disproportionate commitments (944ff). In his view, the decisive factors that may lead to disproportionate commitments are the Commission's "power to vary sanctions outside the procedure at hand" (948) and the Commission's ability "to transform any deterrent effect of future private litigation into a bargaining chip for extracting further-reaching commitments" (949).

See also Budzinski/Kuchinke (2012), 274, who refer to speculations that E.On's commitment to divest its transmission grid [COMP/39.388 (German electricity wholesale and balancing market, 2008)] was the result of a "cross policy deal", in which the Commission closed two other procedures "in spite of an excellent state of evidence" in consideration for E.On's commitment.

[68]Frenz/Ehlenz (2010), 308.

[69]Wils (2006), 352.

and of a precise circumscription of the accusation[70] are all considered factors that deprive a commitment offer of its voluntary nature or at least provide incentives for the concerned undertakings to offer overbroad commitments.

Second, several critics of the judgment claim that the proportionality test advanced by the Court of Justice fails to offer sufficient protection for third parties. In support of the latter allegation, they rely on the Court's dictum that, in the context of Article 9, the Commission is only required to verify that the offered commitments address its concerns and that the undertakings have not offered less onerous commitments that also address those concerns adequately.[71] The critics underline that the proportionality test of the Court remains behind the one suggested by Advocate General Kokott, according to whom the Commission was obliged to review not only the commitments offered by the concerned undertakings, but all the alternatives "known to it".[72] From the fact that the Court did not absorb the latter terms into its judgment, the critics infer that, if the concerned undertakings have not offered any alternatives, the proportionality test applied by the Court is reduced to an evaluation whether a commitment eliminates the Commission's concerns.[73] It is argued that this modification of the proportionality test disadvantages third parties, because the Commission is not obliged to take less onerous alternatives into account that are put forward during the market test pursuant to Article 27 Regulation 1/03.[74]

Third, some commentators have claimed that the Court's modified proportionality standard would in any event not suffice to protect the public interest in the competitive process, even on the assumption that the interests of the concerned undertakings and third parties were satisfactorily protected.[75]

---

[70]See Waelbroeck (2009), 233f; Schweitzer (2011), 646f and 657; Wagner-Von Papp (2012), 950; Botteman/Patsa (2013), 362.

[71]See Sect. 2.2.1.4.1.1, footnote 53 above.

[72]See Sect. 2.2.1.3.1.1, footnote 36 above.

[73]Frenz/Ehlenz (2010), 307: "Damit sind auch keine offensichtlich geeigneten oder der Kommission bekannten Alternativen neben den Zusagen mit in die Bewertung einzustellen [. . .] Eine elegantere Lösung bieten hingegen die Schlussanträge von GA Kokott, welche eine Einbeziehung offensichtlicher oder bekannter Alternativen offenlassen, die neben den Zusagen der Unternehmen Berücksichtigung finden können"; Klees (2011), 19: "Gibt es keine alternativen Zusagen, entfällt die Prüfung der Erforderlichkeit; die Verhältnismäßigkeitsprüfung reduziert sich dann auf eine bloße Geeignetheitsprüfung"; Wagner-Von Papp (2012), 939f: "Where the Commission is faced with only one offer of commitments, the residual proportionality review under the ECJ's Alrosa judgment is completely eliminated"; see also Muguet-Poullennec/Barbier de la Serre (2010), 39: "si la Commission n'est pas tenue d'examiner les solutions alternatives moins contraignantes que celles qui lui sont proposées par les parties, comment le Tribunal peut-il exercer un contrôle de proportionnalité minimal?"; Prek/Lefèvre (2016), 90: "the Commission is under a duty to examine the necessity of commitments only if the undertakings concerned offer less burdensome commitments that are equally appropriate."

[74]See Hennig (2010b), 449 and 450f; Klees (2010), 691 and 693.

[75]See Schweitzer (2011), 647; Wagner-Von Papp (2012), 950.

2.2.2.2 Comment

At least the core of the described criticism must be taken seriously, in particular when considered in the broader context of the arguments that are advanced against Article 9 commitments in general. An in-depth evaluation of these arguments shall, however, be reserved to the subsequent parts of this work. At this stage, only some moderating remarks regarding the judgment of the Court of Justice will be made.

2.2.2.2.1 The Judgment Is Generalisable Only to a Limited Extent

Although Alrosa remains a "landmark ruling",[76] the importance of the judgment for the general interpretation of the Article 9 procedure should not be overstated. Certainly, the case was decided by a grand chamber. Nonetheless, far reaching generalisations of the judgment should be encountered with caution, given that also a grand chamber decides only individual cases.

First, as several observers acknowledge,[77] the case concerned a very particular constellation that is difficult to generalise: Alrosa tried to enforce rights similar to those which it would have enjoyed as a concerned undertaking in the procedure regarding Article 101 TFEU also in respect of the procedure regarding Article 102 TFEU. Alrosa's situation therefore differed from that of complainants or "normal" interested third parties who present comments during the market test pursuant to Article 27(4) Regulation 1/03.

Second, the judgment of the Court of Justice has rightly been criticised for its succinct reasoning.[78] The latter leaves too much room for interpretations and exposes the judgment to misunderstandings.

Third, there is a certain likeliness that the abstract formulations of the Alrosa judgment were coined by the outcome the Court of Justice wanted to achieve in the concrete case at hand: A confirmation of the commitments made binding by the Commission. Certainly, the substantive question whether this outcome is correct is controversial.[79] The question cannot be treated here in detail. However, at least at

---

[76]Eg Kellerbauer (2011), 1.

[77]Temple Lang (2009), 133; Brenner (2010), 1335; Falconi (2011), 45; Lianos (2013), 445.

[78]Hennig (2010b), 448; Kellerbauer (2011), 6.

[79]See, on the one hand, Schweitzer (2011), 645: "Eine Kritik am Alrosa-Urteil setzt [. . .] nicht notwendig am Ausgang des Verfahrens an. Viel spricht dafür, dass die Kommission auf der Grundlage der ihr vorliegenden Informationen ohne offenkundigen Beurteilungsfehler davon ausgehen durfte, dass die vollständige Beendigung der vertraglichen Beziehungen zwischen De Beers und Alrosa unter dem Gesichtspunkt von Art. 102 AEUV, insbes. zur Beseitigung der aus den Vertragsbeziehungen folgenden Marktabschottung, geboten war". On the other hand, see O'Donoghue/Padilla (2013), 907: "It is difficult to see how a general restriction on Alrosa having any trading relationship with De Beers for the affected products would be compatible with proportionality in a final infringement decision under Article 7". See also Gyselen (2014), 255 together with fn 21, who mentions the Alrosa-case as an example in which the Commission makes binding commitments "although it knows full well that they are not (all) necessary but

first blush, the better arguments militate for the Commission's strict approach to request a complete cessation of all purchases of rough diamonds by De Beers from Alrosa. In fact, as is apparent from the opinion of Advocate General Kokott, in view of the particular constellation that the market relation between De Beers and Alrosa was not merely a vertical, but also a horizontal one, the Commission had reasonable concerns that letting de Beers buy up only a limited amount of Alrosa's production, even in open auctions, would amount to a prohibited restriction of competition.[80] If this is true, then the Commission could also legitimately assume that neither the joint commitments, which provided merely for a cap of the supplies, nor Alrosa's suggestion to allow limited purchases in open auctions would have eliminated its concerns. Rather, the complete cessation of all supplies was necessary. It is true and deplorable that the judgment of the Court of Justice does not contain a detailed discussion of the substantive justification of the Commission's concerns. However, by referring to the more comprehensive opinion of the Advocate General and by stating that the General Court had unlawfully substituted its own assessment for that of the Commission and that Alrosa had not succeeded in proving a manifest error in the Commission's appraisal, the Court of Justice indicated its view that the Commission's concerns were not lacking a reasonable basis.[81] If one accepts that the outcome of the case is correct, the fact that the Court of Justice had to demarcate its

---

certainly (more than) sufficient to address its concerns"; Jenny (2015), 741f: "It could have been difficult for the Commission [. . .] to justify [under Article 7] that the complete cessation of all commercial transactions for an indefinite period was the minimum remedy acceptable to alleviate the competition problem identified". The position of Wagner-von Papp (2012) on the substance of the case is not clear to me: On the one hand, he is of the opinion that the commitment to discontinue all purchases of rough diamonds constituted an "overkill" for a theory of harm under Article 102 TFEU and that such a commitment would only have been justified to meet a theory of harm under Article 101 TFEU (963f). On the other hand, he acknowledges that the Commission was right to prohibit even limited ad hoc sales of diamonds by Alrosa to DeBeers in auctions, because these would have amounted to infringements of Article 102 TFEU (969 fn 158).

[80]See Sect. 2.2.1.3.1.2 with footnote 42 above.

[81]See Sect. 2.2.1.4.1.2 with footnote 55 above. See also Brenner (2010), 1335, who rightly argues that the failure of Alrosa's action was mostly due not to the discretion granted by the Court of Justice to the Commission, but to the fact that Alrosa's interest in maintaining some of its supplies to De Beers caused anticompetitive concerns.

Wagner-von Papp (2012), 969 fn 158, criticises the silence of the judgment of the CJ on the question whether ad hoc sales of diamonds by Alrosa to DeBeers in auctions would have amounted to an infringement of Article 102 TFEU. According to Wagner-von Papp, this silence "could be interpreted as implying [. . .] that a commitment decision could be based on a theory of harm that is erroneous as a matter of law, provided only that the undertaking offers commitments". In my view, this criticism is justified only to the extent that it is directed against the ambiguity of the CJ's judgment. On the substance, I think that the judgment should not be interpreted in the way suggested by Wagner-von Papp. According to my interpretation, the CJ followed AG Kokott's reasoning that ad hoc sales would have amounted to infringements of Article 102 TFEU.

own approach from that followed by the General Court in order to achieve the desired result may explain some of the rather unbalanced language used in the judgment.[82]

2.2.2.2.2 The Modification of the Proportionality Test Applied by the Court Raises at Most Limited Concerns Regarding the Interest of the General Public in the Protection of the Competitive Process

Although it is hence submitted here that the judgment of the Court of Justice is only generalisable to a limited extent, it shall not be disputed that the judgment places an emphasis on the distinction between the legal standards that must be applied to an Article 7 decision and those that must be applied to an Article 9 decision. The essential feature of the Court's modification of the proportionality test for the purpose of Article 9 is a maceration of the necessity requirement.[83] However, the judgment remains ambiguous as regards the precise meaning of this maceration and in particular the consequences for the rights of third parties. In order to preserve the rationale of procedural economy that underlies Article 9, the Court of Justice makes it clear that the Commission is not required to seek itself less onerous alternatives to a commitment offer. The Court shifts the responsibility for the necessity of a commitment thus from the Commission to the concerned undertaking.[84] Nonetheless, if a concerned undertaking offers more than one commitment, the Commission may only make the least onerous of all equally effective solutions binding. Moreover, the Commission must take the interests of third parties into account.[85] Unfortunately, these statements of the Court of Justice do neither expressly reject nor confirm the suggestion of Advocate General Kokott that the protection of the rights of third parties requires the Commission also to take alternative solutions into account that are known by the Commission, but have not been offered by the concerned undertaking.[86]

In order to comment on the criticism that is raised against the described modification of the proportionality test, it is useful to distinguish between the interests of the concerned undertakings, the interests of third parties and the interest of the general public in the protection of the competitive process. It will be submitted that the modification applied by the Court does not raise any concerns as regards the rights of the concerned undertakings. As far as the rights of third parties are concerned, the judgment can and must be construed in the light of the opinion of

[82]See the apposite remark of Muguet-Poullennec/Barbier de la Serre (2010), 39: "Peut-être la Cour s'est-elle un peu laissée emporter par la volonté d'étayer sa thèse, en contrepoint de celle qui avait été exposée par le Tribunal".

[83]See eg Hennig (2010a), 179f; Kellerbauer (2011), 8.

[84]See Kellerbauer (2011), 8; Ortiz Blanco/Jörgens/Kellerbauer (2013), 13.31.

[85]See Sect. 2.2.1.4.1.1 with footnotes 52 and 53 above.

[86]See Sect. 2.2.1.3.1.1 with footnote 36 above.

Advocate General Kokott. If this done, also the rights of third parties can be considered as guaranteed in a sufficient manner. With respect to the interest of the general public in the protection of the competitive process, the modification of the proportionality test by the Court causes only limited concerns.

2.2.2.2.2.1 Interests of Concerned Undertakings

As regards the interests of the concerned undertakings, it should be recalled that the Court qualified a commitment offer as a conscious acceptance that the commitment may go beyond what the Commission could have imposed under Article 7 after an in-depth investigation.[87] This statement must be read in the light of the opinion of the Advocate General who suggested that, in view of the voluntary nature of the offer, the necessity of a commitment could be presumed in relation to the undertaking having offered it.[88] This reasoning must be approved. In that connection, it is not expedient to ponder over the difference between a "conscious" and a "voluntary" offer.[89] The decisive question is whether the proportionality test should be used to protect an undertaking offering a commitment against its own offer.[90] This question must be answered in the negative.[91] The concerned undertakings, typically represented by qualified legal counsel, are sufficiently able to weigh the respective pros and cons of the commitment they offer against those of a potential infringement decision. The counterargument that a company's defence capacities do not relieve the Commission of its responsibility to respect the rule of law[92] cannot call this conclusion into question. The rule of law does not exclude mechanisms that, for

---

[87]See Sect. 2.2.1.4.1.1 with footnote 51 above.

[88]See Sect. 2.2.1.3.1.1 with footnote 34 above.

[89]But see Muguet-Poullennec/Barbier de la Serre (2010), 40: "[. . .] le fait de savoir que l'on propose des engagements allant au-delà de ce que pourrait imposer la Commission ne signifie pas qu'ils sont soumis de façon volontaire. La conscience d'être forcé à faire quelque chose n'affecte pas la réalité de la contrainte exercée".

[90]See also Bueren (2011), 753, who rightly underlines that the question of voluntariness is not a psychological, but a normative question: "Freiwilligkeit in diesem Sinne bedeutet also, dass eine [Erklärung] dem Rechtsinhaber normativ zugerechnet werden kann".

[91]See also Georgiev (2007), 1019: "the defendant is not required to enter into settlement proceedings and has voluntarily surrendered some of the regular procedural guarantees"; Sadowska (2014), text after figure 1: "By entering into a settlement (voluntarily) and offering the commitments, the firm implicitly agrees on their final shape. Its active role in the settlement means there is a questionable role for the principle of proportionality"; Podszun (2012), 64: "Die regelmäßig durch versierte Anwälte vertretenen Unternehmen sind in ihrer Entscheidung rechtlich ebenso wie wirtschaftlich frei, sich gegen den Vorwurf eines Kartellrechtsverstoßes nach Belieben zu wehren"; Schweitzer (2011), 647: "[Das Abstellen des EuGH auf die Freiwilligkeit der Zusagen] ist in dem Maße überzeugend, in dem der Verhältnismäßigkeitsgrundsatz allein die Interessen der beteiligten Unternehmen schützen soll"; Kreße (2014), 26: "Weshalb die Unternehmen [. . .] nicht mehr in der Lage sein sollen, Chancen und Risiken der möglichen Verhaltensweisen gegeneinander abzuwägen und sich für die wirtschaftlich sinnvollere Verhaltensweise zu entscheiden, ist nicht ersichtlich"; Kipiani (2014), 623.

[92]Dunne (2014), 437.

reasons of procedural economy, entrust the subjects of an investigation with the responsibility to safeguard their interests themselves. Moreover, the concerned undertakings also have the possibility to resort to so-called "salami tactics"[93]: If an undertaking presents a limited commitment in a first step and, at a later stage of the procedure, increases its concessions, the modified proportionality test obliges the Commission to engage into a comparative analysis of the alternatives that have been offered. Certainly, the undertaking faces the risk that the Commission may switch to the infringement procedure.[94] However, in view of the Commission's own interest in an Article 9 decision, such a switch seems most likely, if the Commission gets the impression that the salami tactics are used to protract the procedure.

2.2.2.2.2.2 Interests of Third Parties

As far as the interests of third parties are concerned, it is useful to make a further distinction between, on the one hand, complainants and other third parties for whom the commitment made binding does not reach far enough, and, on the other hand, third parties who consider a commitment overbroad.

Since the Alrosa case did not concern the former, the judgment is from the outset only of limited bearing in that regard.[95] In any event, the Court's modification of the proportionality test for the purpose of Article 9 does not entail any disadvantage for complainants and other third parties for whom a commitment that has been made binding does not reach far enough. Under the modified test, the Commission must still verify whether the commitment that it intends to make binding adequately addresses its concerns.[96] Complainants and third parties who consider that the Commission has violated that obligation can bring an action before the General Court. If they meet the admissibility requirements, they can claim that the Commission violated the discretion it has when it sets its priorities in dealing with the cases before it.[97] The applicable standard is the ordinary one that has first been developed by the General Court in the Automec II case.[98] Whether this standard is in general permissive enough to safeguard the interests of complainants and other third parties

---

[93]See for the term and a critical discussion Wagner-Von Papp (2012), 937ff; generally on the remaining possibility for the concerned undertakings to offer several sets of commitments see Muguet-Poullennec/Barbier de la Serre (2010), 40; Klees (2010), 692; Hennig (2010b), 452f; Lianos (2013), 445.

[94]Klees (2010), 692; Hennig (2010b), 452f.

[95]See Sadowska (2014), 55, and Sect. 2.2.2.2.1 with footnote 77 above.

[96]See Sect. 2.2.1.4.1.1 with footnote 53 above; also Schweitzer (2011), 646.

[97]See Wagner-Von Papp (2012), 940 fn 47.

[98]GC, T-24/90 (Automec II, 1992); see also eg Jones/Sufrin (2014), 1071ff.

may of course be questioned.[99] However, the threshold that must be met in order to show that the Commission violated its discretion in prioritising cases is in any event the same, irrespective of whether a decision has been adopted on the basis of Article 7 or of Article 9 or whether the Commission has closed the file without addressing a decision to the investigated company at all. The standard is not affected by the Court's proportionality test.

On the other hand, as far as the interests of third parties who consider a commitment overbroad are concerned, the lack of clarity of the Alrosa judgment of the Court of Justice is certainly deplorable.[100] Furthermore, if the judgment really relieved the Commission of an obligation to consider alternatives that have been put forward by third parties,[101] such an approach would have to be rejected. It is, however, submitted that the judgment can and must be construed in the light of the opinion of the Advocate General. This implies that the Commission is obliged to take into account alternative solutions that are known by it and in particular those that have been proposed by third parties.[102] The Court's unambiguous statement that the

[99]See Wagner-Von Papp (2012), 940 fn 47, who argues that such a challenge of a commitment decision is deemed to fail due to the broadness of the Commission's discretion in prioritising cases. But see M. Jaeger (2011), 302, who relies on GC, T-427/08 (CEAHR, 2010) to illustrate that the General Court exercises intense control over the Commission's discretion in prioritising cases. See also GC, T-108/07 (Spira, 2013), as a further example that demonstrates the intensity of the control exercised by the General Court over the Commission's discretion in prioritising complaints.

[100]Critically in particular Klees (2010), 693.

[101]See Sect. 2.2.2.1 with footnote 71 above.

[102]In spite of the Court's mistakable formulation that the Commission is only obliged to take the commitments that have been offered to it by the concerned undertakings into account, some commentators interpret the judgment as requiring the Commission to take also the market test observations of third parties into account:

See Brenner (2010), 1335: "Nach den Ausführungen des EuGH beschränkt sich zwar die Prüfung der Kommission auf die vorgebrachten Verpflichtungszusagen und die Kommission muss nicht selbstständig weniger belastende Optionen prüfen; ausdrücklich ausgenommen von dieser Beschränkung der Prüfungspflicht sind indes die Interessen Dritter. Mit der Erfassung der Drittinteressen über den Markttest dürften diese ebenso wie die vorgebrachten Verpflichtungszusagen zum berücksichtigungspflichtigen Sachstand gehören".

Kellerbauer (2011), 7, who interprets the CJ's Alrosa judgment as meaning that the Commission must take less onerous proposals of third parties into account, but has discretion in rejecting them.

De Bronnet (2012), Art. 9, 11: "Die Kommission ist zwar nicht gehalten, selbst nach weniger einschneidenden Alternativen zu den bei ihr eingereichten Zusagen zu suchen. Gleichwohl hat die Kommission alle ihr bekannten Alternativen mit gleicher Eignung, die von ihr angenommenen Wettbewerbsprobleme auszuräumen, daraufhin zu überprüfen, ob sie mildere Mittel zur Lösung der fraglichen Wettbewerbsprobleme darstellen, mit denen die Interessen des die Verpflichtungszusage anbietenden Unternehmens und Dritter nicht oder weniger stark beeinträchtigt werden".

Sadowska (2014), 49: "Under Article 9, the Commission needs only to make sure that accepted commitments address its concerns [. . .] and that they do not manifestly go beyond what is necessary to address these concerns. However, the Commission is under no obligation to seek out less onerous solutions than the ones proposed to it". Similarly also ibid, 190.

As will be explained below, the Commission appears to interpret the judgment in the same way.

Commission must consider the interests of third parties[103] at the same time permits and calls for such an interpretation. In fact, the contrary interpretation would deprive this statement of any meaningful content.

Two further specifications are, however, called for. First, as the Advocate General rightly underlines, the Commission's obligation to consider alternative solutions that have been put forward by third parties exists only, if these alternatives are manifestly equally effective[104] as the commitment under scrutiny.[105] Second, it must be borne in mind that the Commission cannot force a concerned undertaking to align a commitment offer with the proposal of a third party. The Commission can only suggest adopting the offer or, at most, make the offer binding only in part if it is divisible.[106] Should the concerned undertaking refuse to adapt its offer, the Commission must balance the pros and cons of imposing the solution that was proposed by the third party unilaterally in an Article 7 decision against those of accepting the commitment offered by the concerned undertaking. If the advantages of an Article 9 decision outweigh those of an Article 7 decision and the commitment offered by the concerned undertaking is not disproportionate in the narrow sense from the perspective of the third party, the Commission may make the commitment binding.

Overall, it is submitted that if the Alrosa judgment is construed in the suggested way, the interests of third parties are sufficiently protected.

2.2.2.2.2.3 Interest of the General Public in the Protection of the Competitive Process

Third, as far as the interest of the general public in the protection of the competitive process is concerned, it is useful to distinguish between under- and over-enforcement errors.[107] The modified proportionality test of the Court of Justice entails a risk of over-enforcement, because it allows the Commission to make commitments binding that go beyond what is necessary to eliminate the Commission's concerns. On the other hand, given that the Court obliges the Commission to ensure that a commitment eliminates the existing concerns, the modified proportionality test does not increase the risk of under-enforcement.[108] Certainly, each Article 9 decision fosters the risk of both types of enforcement errors through the fact that the Commission is not obliged to investigate the case as thoroughly as it would have

---

[103]See Sect. 2.2.1.4.1.1 with footnote 53 above.

[104]Critically Klees (2010), 691 fn 35, who is of the opinion that an alternative solution only needs to be sufficiently effective. The question will be further discussed below (Sect. 3.2.1.2 with footnote 104 and Sect. 3.4.1.2.2 with footnotes 891ff).

[105]See Sect. 2.2.1.3.1.1 with footnote 37 above.

[106]See the opinion of AG Kokott, Sect. 2.2.1.3.1.1 with footnote 31 above.

[107]In the literature, under- and over-enforcement errors are also referred to either as Type I and Type II errors or as false negatives and false positives; see Whish/Bailey (2012), 193; in the context of remedies Gautier/Petit (2014), 5.

[108]See Sect. 2.2.1.4.1.1 with footnote 53 above.

to in order to adopt a decision pursuant to Article 7.[109] However, the latter risks are not caused by the Court's maceration of the necessity requirement. Rather, they result directly from the shape the legislator has given Article 9 for reasons of procedural economy. Overall, it is thus submitted that the modification of the proportionality test by the Court of Justice for the purpose of applying Article 9 causes only limited concerns as regards the interest of the general public in the protection of the competitive process: The concerns relate only to a risk of over-enforcement.

2.2.2.2.3 Intermediate Conclusion on the Modification of the Proportionality Test in the Alrosa Judgment

Overall, it is submitted that despite the relaxation of the proportionality test in the Alrosa judgment, proportionality issues still play an important role for decisions adopted pursuant to Article 9.[110] Criticism claiming that the Court mutilated the principle of proportionality beyond recognition,[111] that it would have been more consistent if the Court had completely abandoned the principle of proportionality in the context of Article 9[112] or that the Alrosa judgment is the "worst decision"[113] of the Court of Justice clearly overshoots the mark. This conclusion is further supported by the way the Commission has construed the proportionality test for the purpose of Article 9 in the wake of the Alrosa judgment. In the Best Practices, the Commission states the following:

> In light of the principle of proportionality, the Commission must verify that the commitments address the identified competition concerns and that the commitments offered do not manifestly go beyond what is necessary to address these concerns. When carrying out that assessment, the Commission will take into consideration the interests of third parties.

---

[109] See Schweitzer (2011), 647.

[110] See Hjelmeng (2013), 1029: "[Despite the rather broad limits for the Commission's discretion drawn up by the Court] there can [...] be no doubt that the principle of proportionality plays an important role in the context of Article 9 decisions, and that the concerns of the Commission in this respect must be related to at least potential infringements of Article 101 or 102."

[111] Klees (2010), 693 ("bis zur Unkenntlichkeit verstümmelt").

[112] Klees (2010), 693: "Vor diesem Hintergrund muss sich der Gerichtshof fragen lassen, ob es nicht die systematisch sauberere Lösung gewesen wäre, sich gleich ganz von dem Verhältnismäßigkeitsgrundsatz im Rahmen des Art. 9 VO Nr. 1/2003 zu lösen." See also Wagner-Von Papp (2012), 943, who speaks of "the ECJ's *de facto* elimination of judicial review of the proportionality of commitments"; similarly Jenny (2015), 762.

[113] Jenny (2015).

> However, it is not obliged to compare such voluntary commitments with measures it could impose under Article 7 [. . .] and to regard as disproportionate any commitments which go beyond such measures.[114]

Certainly, a non-comprehensive glance at the Commission's actual practice under Article 9 following the Alrosa judgment of the Court of Justice yields a heterogeneous picture as regards the abstract formulae the Commission uses in its decisions to describe the requirements of the proportionality test. Many decisions simply reproduce the statement of the Court of Justice[115] according to which the Commission must ensure that the commitment addresses its concerns, verify whether the concerned undertakings have not offered any less onerous commitments, and take the interests of third parties into account.[116] Other decisions expressly add the evaluation whether the commitment does not go manifestly beyond what is necessary to address the concerns as an independent requirement.[117] In yet another decision, the Commission examines whether the commitment addresses its concerns "without being excessive".[118] The importance of such abstract formulations is of course from the outset limited. Nonetheless, they can at least serve as indicia that the Commission applies a meaningful proportionality test to Article 9 decisions also in the wake of the Alrosa judgment.

More importantly, the fact that the Commission applies a meaningful proportionality test to Article 9 decisions is also confirmed by the concrete way in which the Commission assesses the proportionality of commitments. The Commission's practice is replete with examples of cases in which the Commission rejected third parties' or complainants' requests for a further reaching remedy, thus ensuring that the

[114]Commission Best Practices (2011), 115. See also the Antitrust Manual of Procedures (2012), Module 16, 45: "[c]ommitments which are not related to the concerns [. . .] will not be accepted by the Commission". For the sake of completeness, it should, however, be added that in the Antitrust Manual of Procedures (2012), Module 16, 46, the Commission refers yet again to a less comprehensive proportionality test that does not expressly take the interests of third parties into account: "The Commission should [. . .] verify that: (a) the commitments are sufficient to address its competition concerns; and (b) the undertakings have not offered less onerous commitments that also address the concerns adequately." However, the less comprehensive version of the proportionality test in the Manual of Procedures can be explained with the fact that interests of third parties are being dealt with in the sections of the Manual that concern the market test pursuant to Article 27 (4) Regulation 1/03 (Module 16, 56ff). Moreover, the Commission states expressly in the Manual (Module 16, 3) that the Manual must be construed in the light of the Best Practices and that the latter takes priority in all respects.

[115]See Sect. 2.2.1.4.1.1, footnote 53 above.

[116]See eg COMP/39.592 (Standard & Poor's, 2011), 78; COMP/39.654 (Reuters, 2012), 93; COMP/39.847 (E-Books, 2013), 121; COMP/39.678 (Deutsche Bahn I, 2013), 98; COMP/39.939 (Samsung, 2014), 120; COMP/39.398 (Visa, 2014), 101.

[117]See COMP/39.230 (Rio Tinto, 2012), 130; COMP/39.595 (Continental/United/Lufthansa/Air Canada, 2013), 141. The former decision derives that additional requirement from the Alrosa judgment of the Court of Justice.

[118]COMP/39.736 (Siemens/Areeva, 2012), 102.

commitments did not go beyond what was necessary to eliminate the Commission's concerns.[119] In that connection, the Microsoft Internet Explorer decision provides a good example in which the Commission explicitly took account of the interests of third parties: The Commission concluded that Microsoft's obligation to provide a browser choice screen did not unduly affect the interests of OEMs or vendors of web browsers.[120]

2.3 The Broader Context: The Development of the Commission's Practice and the Explanations for the Frequent Occurrence of Commitment Decisions

Voices that cautioned against the disadvantages of commitments existed in the literature long before the Alrosa judgments of the General Court and the Court of Justice.[121] Already during the modernisation process, Mestmäcker emphasised the "abuse potential"[122] of the envisaged Article 9. He argued in particular that the provision would place the Commission in a position "to organize markets and to implement policy objectives even in violation of Articles 81 and 82".[123] K. Schmidt spoke of the "flight into informality" that was made possible by the new Article 9 procedure[124]—a term that was readily picked up by other observers.[125] Later, it was in particular the Alrosa case that sparked the increasing interest in Article 9 and the evolving commitment practice of the Commission. At the time of writing, the amount of literature that deals with the commitment procedure is almost unmanageable. It is probably fair to say that the preponderant view on the Commission's commitment practice is a rather critical one.[126]

---

[119]Eg COMP/37.966 (Distrigaz, 2007), 29; COMP/39.388 (German electricity wholesale and balancing market, 2008), 60; COMP/38.636 (Rambus, 2009), 54ff; COMP/39.386 (Long-term electricity contracts France, 2010), 70; COMP/39.596 (BA/AA/IB, 2010), 153ff; COMP/39.316 (GdF, 2010), 58, 66 and 82ff; COMP/39.317 (E.ON Gas, 2010), 57; COMP/39.654 (Reuters, 2012), 78, 85, 87 and 90; COMP/39.727 (CEZ, 2013), 40ff; COMP/39.767 (BEH, 2015), 114ff; COMP/40.153 (Amazon, 2017), 183ff; see also Gerard (2013b), 29f.

[120]COMP/39.530 (Microsoft – tying, 2009), 108ff.

[121]See for the criticism of the Commission's use of undertakings under Regulation 17/62 the references in Sect. 2.3.1.2, footnote 195 below.

[122]Mestmäcker (2000), 441; see also Mestmäcker/Schweitzer (2014), § 21, 60.

[123]Mestmäcker (2000), 441.

[124]K. Schmidt (2003), 1242 ("Flucht in die Formlosigkeit").

[125]Eg Klees (2009), 377; Brenner (2010), fn 39; Körber (2010), 82 and 91; Wagner-von Papp (2012), 961 fn 123.

[126]For a different overall assessment of the literature on commitments see Sadowska (2014), 37: "Generally speaking, most commentators view the introduction of Article 9 commitment decisions as a positive development in the EU competition enforcement, considering all the benefits of this mechanism".

As already indicated above, three lines of argument can be identified on a rough and generalising scale: First, Article 9 is criticised for leading to a relaxation of the link between harm and remedy. The main thrust of the argument is that the Commission can and does use commitment decisions in order to extract overbroad remedies which it could not have imposed unilaterally on the basis of Article 7. Second, commentators decry that Article 9 restricts the due process requirements that exist in the context of Article 7, namely the rights of the concerned undertakings, complainants and other third parties to participate in the administrative procedure and their right to effective judicial review. Third, the commitment procedure is criticised for its negative impact on legal certainty. In that regard, critics emphasise above all that the use of commitments leads to a dearth of judicial precedents which would otherwise contribute to the clarification of the law.

It should, however, be emphasised from the outset that most of the critics of the Article 9 procedure and the Alrosa judgment of the Court of Justice do not call into question the existence of the commitment procedure as such. They merely strive to improve it. It is broadly accepted that in particular reasons of procedural economy justify the existence of a possibility for the Commission to adopt decisions that involve consensual elements.[127] The concerns relate rather to the risk of an "overuse" of commitment decisions[128] and to a lack of judicial control than to the existence of the commitment procedure as such. In particular Schweitzer has argued that the dangers that are associated with the use of commitments might possibly be acceptable if Article 9 were used only occasionally. However, in her view, these dangers become intolerable as soon as commitment decisions become the predominant enforcement tool of the Commission.[129] Against this backdrop, it becomes clear that the concerns that are being raised in the literature against the use of commitment decisions cannot be assessed solely by commenting on the Alrosa case and its criticism. It is necessary to have a look at the broader context of the

---

[127]See eg Georgiev (2007), 1033: "Settlements have a role to play in the modern administrative state"; Podszun (2012), 62: "[...] Entwicklung hin zu einer modernen, flexiblen Rechtsdurchsetzung. Durch Kooperation können Maßnahmen von denjenigen, die die Folgen zu tragen haben, besser beeinflusst werden. Das ist grundsätzlich begrüßenswert [...] Die lautstarke Kritik am Vorgehen der Behörden in der Fachöffentlichkeit scheint demgegenüber zum Teil überzogen"; Botteman/Patsa (2013), 373: "necessary component of any mature antitrust system"; Lugard/Möllmann (2013), 3: "An antitrust enforcement system based solely on infringement procedures without any room for negotiated outcomes would undoubtedly be inefficient and inappropriate"; Gerard (2013b), 27: "Even if the commitment procedure requires adjustments, that possibility should be preserved, it is submitted, because it responds to a concrete need to guarantee the effectiveness of antitrust enforcement in highly (or increasingly) dynamic markets".

[128]Wils (2006), 349f; Botteman/Patsa (2013), 367; Sadowska (2014), 38.

[129]Schweitzer (2011), 647: "Bliebe die Verplichtungsentscheidung gemäß Art. 9 Abs. 1 VO 1/2003 ein Instrument von dem – entsprechend den ursprünglichen Vorstellungen – nur vereinzelt Gebrauch gemacht würde, so wäre die Lockerung der wettbewerbsrechtlichen Bindungen mit Blick auf die verfahrensökonomischen Zielsetzungen unter Umständen hinzunehmen. [...] Die Rechtsförmigkeit der europäischen Wettbewerbspolitik scheint aber in dem Maße gefährdet, in dem die Verpflichtungsentscheidung zum dominanten Instrument der Rechtsdurchsetzung wird". Similarly already Gippini-Fournier (2008), 411.

overall development of the Commission's practice.[130] First, this look will reveal that, although commitment decisions play indeed a paramount role in the Commission's enforcement practice, the instrument is not as revolutionary as is sometimes contended. Second, the reasons for the frequent occurrence of commitment decisions will be presented.

2.3.1 Development of the Practice: A Shift Towards a "Culture of Consent"?

Regulation 17/62, the predecessor of Regulation 1/03, did not contain a provision that could be compared to Article 9. De facto, so-called "undertakings" given by companies with a view to align their practices with the competition rules had nevertheless often played a role in competition procedures already prior to the enactment of Regulation 1/03. Despite this existing practice, according to a statement made by John Temple Lang, a former Director of DG COMP, "[t]he Commission initially believed that commitment decisions would be unusual and rare, and has been rather surprised that, for various reasons, there have been so many cases in which commitments have already been suggested either by companies or by Commission officials".[131] This statement has become the standard reference in the literature to substantiate that the quantitative success of the Article 9 procedure was unexpected.[132] To what extent this was actually the case and whether the frequent use of commitment decisions could at least have been predicted in view of the Commission's existing practice shall not further be discussed here. Rather, the following two points will be addressed: First, some empirical observations will be made as regards the frequency of commitment decisions and of appeals against such decisions. Second, a brief look at the Commission's practice under Regulation 17/62 will permit some relativising comments on the contention that the introduction of Article 9 constituted a "paradigm shift" from a more adversarial towards a more negotiated approach.

[130] Overviews over the Commission's decisional practice can be found eg in Rab/Monnoyeur/Sukhtankar (2010), 171ff; Schweitzer (2011), 659ff; Falconi (2011), 45f; Whish/Bailey (2012), 259f; Gyselen (2014); Lugard/Möllmann (2013), 5f; Hjelmeng (2013), 1019f; Dunne (2014), 406ff; Kipiani (2014), annexe 2.

[131] Temple Lang (2006), 270.

[132] See eg Georgiev (2007), 997 fn 119; Schweitzer (2010), 551 fn 23 and (2012), 2 fn 2; Cengiz (2011), 137 fn 44; Lugard/Möllmann (2013), 2 fn 3; Botteman/Patsa (2013), 348 fn 5; Gerard (2013b), 1 fn 4; Sadowska (2014), 11 fn 43; see also, albeit with a reference to Botteman/Patsa instead of to Temple Lang, Marsden (2013), 3 fn 6, and, without any reference, Rab/Monnoyeur/Sukhtankar (2010), 171; Dunne (2014), 406; Jenny (2015), 709.

2.3.1.1 Empirical Observations

2.3.1.1.1 Regarding Commission Decisions

Many commentators emphasise the quantitative importance of the commitment procedure outside the area of hardcore cartels.[133] Also the Commission accepts that Article 9 decisions "quickly obtained a prominent position in [its] enforcement practice".[134] More precise quantitative assessments about the ratio between infringement and commitment decisions in the Commission's practice vary over time and depend on which decisions are taken into account. Inter alia the following figures have been mentioned; all of them exclude the area of hardcore cartels[135]: Up to September 2010, 9 prohibition decisions and 24 commitment decisions (=73% commitments)[136]; up to July 2011: 9 prohibition decisions and 18 commitment decisions (=66% commitments)[137]; up to December 2011: 16 prohibition decisions and 23 commitment decisions (=59% commitments)[138]; up to December 2012: 14 prohibition decisions and 26 commitment decisions (=65% commitments)[139]; up to March 2013: 15 prohibition decisions and 26 commitment decisions (=63% commitments)[140]; up to July 2013: 7 prohibition decisions and 31 commitment decisions (=82% commitments)[141]; up to December 2013: either 18 prohibition decisions and 29 commitment decisions (=62% commitments)[142] or 17 prohibition

[133]Schweitzer (2012), 2: "almost all infringement proceedings outside the hardcore-cartel arena ultimately end with a commitment decision"; Barbier de la Serre (2012), 98 and 99: commitment procedure has become "the normal procedure"; Gerard (2013b): "enforcement mechanism of choice in the modernization era" (1) and "default mechanism to enforce antitrust principles in the EU" (22); Botteman/Patsa (2013), 347: "tool of choice"; Podszun (2012), 52: "Lieblingskind der Behördenmitarbeiter"; Jones/Sufrin (2014), Preface vi: "outside the cartel area, Commission infringement decisions under Article 7 Regulation 1/2003 are now a rarity"; Prek/Lefèvre (2016), 66: "Outside the field of cartels [. . .] there are now far more commitment decisions than prohibition decisions"; Jenny (2015), 702: "enforcement decisions have become the exception [. . .] and commitment decisions have become the norm"; von Kalben (2018), 106: "außerhalb der [. . .] Hardcore Kartelle das Hauptinstrument der EU-Wettbewerbsrechtsdurchsetzung".

[134]Commission, Ten Years of Antitrust Enforcement under Regulation 1/2003, SWD(2014) 230/2, 179.

[135]Further statistical overviews have been provided eg by Klees (2010), 688f and (2011), 15 fn 9; Bougette/Marty (2012), 25f; Podszun (2012), 51; Botteman/Patsa (2013), 349f; Gyselen (2014), 248; Commission, Ten Years of Antitrust Enforcement under Regulation 1/2003, SWD(2014) 230/2, 184ff.

[136]Barbier de la Serre (2012), 98f fn 31 and 32: He mentions also that three quarters of Article 102 cases and two thirds of Article 101 cases were decided applying the commitment procedure.

[137]Schweitzer (2011), 639. Schweitzer does not mention which is the last decision she took into account. Since the Article was published in July 2011, I took that date.

[138]Lübking/von Koppenfels (2012), 68.

[139]Lugard/Möllmann (2013), 3f.

[140]Almunia (2013), 2.

[141]Gerard (2013b), 6f.

[142]Mariniello (2014), 2.

decisions and 32 commitment decisions (=65% commitments)[143]; up to February 2014: either 11 prohibition decisions and 29 commitment decisions (=73% commitments)[144] or 19 prohibition decisions and 34 commitment decisions (=64% commitments)[145]; up to December 2014: 17 prohibition decisions and 29 commitment decisions (=63% commitments)[146]; up to march 2018: 15 prohibition decisions and 41 commitment decisions (=73% commitments).[147]

The overview clearly attests the lack of a universally accepted method how to count prohibition and commitment decisions respectively.[148] The present work will not further address this issue. Nor will it provide a new quantitative assessment. It must suffice to state that the emphasis that critics of the Article 9 procedure place on its quantitative importance[149] is probably slightly exaggerated. Without any claim to statistical accuracy: The simple average of the various just mentioned proportions of infringement and commitment decisions amounts to about two thirds commitments. The importance of that number is relativised if one bears in mind that the prosecution of cartels, which is not captured by the said number, constitutes the overall priority of the Commission's enforcement practice.[150] It is also noteworthy that the percentage of commitment decisions in the Commissions practice seems to remain to date below the level of consent orders and consent decrees entered into in the U.S. by the FTC and the DoJ[151]: The latter are reported to settle around 90% of

---

[143]Italianer (2013), 3. See also Gerard (2013b), 8 fn 33, who incorrectly depicts Italianer's numbers as including cartels. In the speech, Italianer expressly stated that these numbers relate to "cases other than cartels" and that the Commission had taken 60 decisions in cartel cases in the same period. Sadowska (2014), 11f, arrives at the same figures as Italianer.

[144]Gautier/Petit (2014), 3 and 21.

[145]Commission, Policy Brief 3/2014, 3; Brenner (2014), 672 fn 3; OECD (2016), 14.

[146]Wils (2015), 3f.

[147]Von Kalben (2018), 106f.

[148]See also Budzinski/Kuchinke (2012), 268: "there is a lack of empirical evidence concerning the increasing number of deals". See also Wagner-Von Papp (2012), 941 fn 51, who suggests – albeit in a different context – that statistical problems may be caused by the coding of the non hard-core decisions. Moreover, approaches may diverge as regards the question what counts as one decision and what counts as several decisions.

[149]See the references in Sect. 2.3.1.1.1, footnote 133 above.

[150]See Commission, Ten Years of Antitrust Enforcement under Regulation 1/2003, SWD(2014) 230/2, 10, where the Commission emphasises the priority given to the prosecution of cartels by stating that almost 50% of its antitrust decisions concern cartels.

[151]See also Kipiani (2014), 508: "En Europe, nous sommes encore loin du schéma américain où les autorités de concurrence négocient en tout point avec les entreprises. Cette culture du "plea bargaining" n'est pas encore d'actualité"; Wils (2015), 9: "Compared to the more than 90 % of civil antitrust cases brought by the Department of Justice and the Federal Trade Commission that are resolved through consent decrees, the European Commission's 63 % figure for commitment decisions does not appear particularly high."

their cases.[152] Nevertheless, it is undeniable that the commitment procedure plays a paramount role in the Commission's enforcement practice.

2.3.1.1.2 Regarding Court Procedures

Compared with the important number of commitments made binding by the Commission, there are relatively few court cases that concern Article 9 decisions. Nonetheless, such cases exist. If Alrosa remains, at the time of writing, the only case in which the Court of Justice effectively dealt with the substantive scope of an Article 9 decision, the issue will soon have to be addressed by the Court of Justice again in the pending appeal in Canal+.[153] The Court of Justice also had to interpret Article 9 in Gasorba,[154] but this case concerned only the procedural question of the impact of a commitment decision adopted by the Commission on the powers of the competition authorities and courts of the Member States.[155] Several actions have been filed with the General Court in which third parties have claimed that the contested commitment did not eliminate the competition concerns in a sufficient manner. Some of these cases were not decided on their substance. The General Court rejected two actions brought against the Repsol commitment decision[156] as inadmissible. Both applicants failed to comply with the limitation period imposed by Article 263(6) TFEU.[157] Hynix withdrew two further actions that it had brought against the Rambus commitment and the related rejection of its complaint.[158] That withdrawal happened as a consequence of a settlement between Rambus and Hynix.[159] However, another appeal brought by Morningstar against the Reuters commitment was declared admissible and rejected on the substance.[160] Alrosa is, in the meantime, also no longer the only case in which the Courts had to assess whether a remedy did not go too far. Called upon to address the issue again in Canal

[152] Ducore (2006), 228 fn 2; Georgiev (2007), 999; Hennig (2010a), 48 fn 139 and 95; Forrester (2010), 640; Ginsburg/Wright (2013), 1; OECD (2016), 13, all report that both the DoJ and the FTC settle around 90% of their respective cases. I have not verified whether these figures are correct. Gerard (2013b), 7 fn 30, refers to only 60% or 70% consent decrees. These figures seem, however, to be outdated: In support of the 60% figure, Gerard cites Epstein (2007), 1, who on his part relies on articles that date from 1992 and 1984. In support of the 70% figure, Gerard cites an article that dates from 1995.

[153] C-132/19 P, Canal+ (pending).

[154] CJ, C-547/16 (Gasorba, 2017).

[155] See Sect. 5.1.4 below.

[156] COMP/38.348 (REPSOL, 2006).

[157] GC, T-274/06 (El Mareny, 2007); T-45/08 (Evarista Molina, 2008). The latter case was confirmed on appeal, CJ, C-36/09 P (2010).

[158] GC, T-148/10 (Hynix, 2013).

[159] See Botteman/Patsa (2013), 359f.

[160] GC, T-76/14 (Morningstar, 2016).

+, the General Court rejected the appeal brought against an allegedly over-broad commitment by a contracting partner of the concerned undertaking.[161]

Besides those actions, which were instituted directly against the adoption of a commitment decision, there have also been two appeals related to refusals of the Commission to reopen proceedings after the adoption of a commitment decision. In CEES, the General Court upheld the Commission's refusal to reopen proceedings against Repsol despite allegations that that company had failed to comply with its commitment.[162] The second appeal concerned the Commission's refusal to reopen proceedings in reaction to Visa's request to amend the commitment it had entered into vis-à-vis the Commission.[163] Visa later withdrew its application,[164] most likely due to the fact that the Commission had in the meantime accepted amended commitments offered by Visa in reaction to a supplementary statement of objections.[165] Finally, it bears mention that in Cartes Bancaires, the General Court had to deal with the question whether a commitment offer that was not accepted by the Commission could serve as a point of reference for the examination of the proportionality of an Article 7 decision.[166]

2.3.1.2 A Change of Paradigm?

The important role played by the Article 9 procedure in the Commission's enforcement practice and the lack of subsequent litigation in court have prompted some commentators to speak of a "paradigm shift"[167] from an adversarial to a more negotiated approach. In view of the inflationary use that term has experienced in the wake of the influential work of Thomas Kuhn,[168] also its use in the context of the commitment procedure is, however, very likely little more than a catchy

[161]GC, T-873/16 (Canal+, 2018).

[162]GC, T-342/11 (CEES, 2014).

[163]COMP/39.398 (Visa, 2010).

[164]GC, T-447/12.

[165]COMP/39.398 (Visa, 2014). The amended commitments were made binding on 26 February 2014; Visa's appeal was removed from the register of the General Court on 30 April 2014.

[166]GC, T-491/07 (Cartes Bancaires, 2012), 427ff. On appeal, the CJ set aside the judgment and referred the case back to the General Court. The judgment of the CJ does, however, not deal with the remedy, see CJ, C-67/13 P (Cartes Bancaires, 2014). The findings of the General Court regarding the remedy will be discussed in more detail below (Sect. 3.3.1.5.1.2 with footnotes 396ff).

[167]Podszun (2012), 48, 49, 54f; Lugard/Möllmann (2013), 4 and 11; see also Gerard (2013b), 19: "paradigmatic shift".

[168]On the popularisation of the term "paradigm" in the wake of Kuhn's work "The structure of scientific revolution" (1962) see Rose (2004), 30ff: "Trotz zahlreicher Erläuterungen und Präzisierung des Paradigmabegriffes und schließlich eines weitgehenden Verzichts auf diesen Begriff, hat Kuhn die explosionsartige und inflationäre Ausbreitung und Popularisierung dieses Begriffes in nahezu allen Bereichen des geistigen und kulturellen Lebens und die damit einhergehenden Mißdeutungen nicht verhindern oder abwenden können." Rose (30 fn 78) also refers to an anecdote about an ice cream that was sold in the U.S. under the name "paradigm shift".

buzzword.[169] The same is true for the "emergence of a culture of consent".[170] The significance of the use the Commission makes of the commitment procedure shall not be downplayed here. Nonetheless, in addition to the remarks that have just been made with a view to the quantitative importance of the Article 9 procedure, also some moderating observations regarding the novelty of the instrument are called for.

Already under the old enforcement system of Regulation 17/62, negotiated solutions[171] were at least not uncommon.[172] They played a role under Articles 101 and 102 TFEU and both in the context of formal and informal decisions.[173] As far as formal decisions are concerned, the Commission was ready to reduce the amount of a fine[174] or to adopt another formal decision that had positive effects for the concerned undertaking, such as a negative clearance decision[175] or an

[169]But see Podszun (2012), 54f, who interprets the Commission's use of the commitment procedure as an expression of a fundamental change of the questions guiding the Commission's action. According to Podszun, those guiding questions have changed from whether the Commission's action is lawful and in particular proportionate to whether the Commission's action is efficient and leads to more competition, in particular consumer welfare.

[170]See Gerard (2013b), 17, who borrows the term from Ginsburg/Wright (2013). See also Waelbroeck (2009), who speaks of "a new settlement culture".

[171]By "negotiated solutions" I understand not only the cases in which a company gives a "commitment" or an "undertaking" to act in a determined way, but generally all the cases in which the company modifies its practices in agreement with the Commission in order to eliminate concerns that have been raised. Such "genuine settlements" must be distinguished from an informal closure of a file for other reasons: For instance, the Commission may find that the practice is compatible with the competition rules; the practices or agreements may be completely abandoned or expire, so that a decision becomes superfluous. For that distinction see Waelbroeck (2009), 225; Bourgeois (1993), 90. Van Bael (1986), 64, suggested to restrict the term settlements "to situations where something is actually being settled in consideration of concessions that are made".

[172]See Gippini-Fournier (2008), 399: "cases were often settled on account of commitments under Regulation 17/62"; Schweitzer (2010), 548 fn 7: "[. . .] practice of informal settlements, which the Commission frequently made conditional on commitments offered by the undertakings concerned"; Hennig (2010a), 111: "Bereits unter der [VO 17/62] hat die Kommission nicht selten Verpflichtungszusagen von Unternehmen informell entgegengenommen"; Bueren (2011), 445f: "Unter der VO 17/62 wurden zahlreiche Fälle auf informeller Ebene durch Verhandlungen über Abstellungsmaßnahmen [. . .] beendet. [. . .] gängige Praxis der Kommission, [. . .] Verpflichtungserklärungen entgegenzunehmen"; Ortiz Blanco/Jörgens/Kellerbauer (2013), 13.01: "[. . .] a high number of cases were indeed resolved by way of a settlement"; ibid., 13.08: "For a long time, the Commission has accepted commitments to settle antitrust proceedings on an informal basis"; O'Donoghue/Padilla (2013), 918f; Wils (2015), 9f; Blockx (2018), 96f.

[173]See for the following remarks in particular the more detailed accounts of Bourgeois (1993), 93f; Müller-Tautphaeus (2003), 300ff and 418; Saitzek (2008), 5ff; Sofianatos (2009), 79ff; Hennig (2010a), 111ff and 339ff; Bueren (2011), 446f, all with references to the Commission's practice. Moreover eg Temple Lang (2006), 267f; Wils (2006), 346f; Georgiev (2007), 992 and 995f; Falconi (2011), 42; McGeown/Orologas (2013), 2f; Jenny (2015), 703ff. For numerous examples of the Commissions practice to accept undertakings under Regulation 17/62 see also Temple Lang (1993), 368 fn 90.

[174]OJ 1985 L 85/1 (Woodpulp, 1984), 149; OJ 1988 L 65/19 (Hilti, 1987), 103; OJ 1988 L 284/41 (Napier Brown, 1988), 85f.

[175]Eg COMP/35.473 (Argev, 2003).

exemption, if the concerned undertakings offered commitments or otherwise modified their practices to comply with the competition rules. Conditions and obligations that were attached to an exemption decision pursuant to Article 8(1) Regulation 17/62 were often not designed unilaterally by the Commission, but based on proposals made by the concerned undertakings.[176] This was promoted by the Court's jurisprudence that, in the context of an application for exemption, it was in the first place for the concerned undertakings to submit alternatives, if the Commission raised concerns regarding the initial notification. In the view of the Court, the Commission was allowed to give the undertakings indications as regards any possible solutions, but the Commission was not legally required to do so.[177] Negotiated solutions also played a role in the context of informal decisions: They led to comfort letters, to non-opposition in opposition procedures[178] or to the simple decision not to continue a procedure or not to open it in the first place.

Also for the pre-modernisation era, there seem to be no reliable figures that would allow a precise quantitative assessment of the ratio of decisions in which the alignment of a practice with Articles 101 and 102 TFEU was unilaterally imposed, i.e. "adversarial", to decisions in which that alignment predicated on negotiated solutions.[179] Such figures would, however, be useful to substantiate the claim that the introduction of Article 9 has significantly increased the consensual proportion of such decisions. With a view to the area outside hardcore cartels that is of interest here, Georgiev mentions that, "between September 1997 and May 2004, the ratio of informal settlements to prohibition decisions was less than 1 to 4, whereas [between May 2004 and August 2007], the ratio of settlement decisions to prohibition decisions [was] almost 1 to 1".[180] However, the 20% ratio that Georgiev makes out for the pre-modernisation era appears to be too low, in particular for two reasons. First, Georgiev neglects a significant amount of decisions that should in my view be counted as negotiated solutions. On the one hand, he does not at all take formal decisions into account.[181] He thereby misses all the reductions of a fine, negative clearances and exemptions with or without conditions that were granted as a result of

---

[176]Eg OJ 1989 L 226/25 (UIP, 1989); COMP/37.398 (UEFA, 2003); COMP/38.284 (Air France/ Alitalia, 2004); Sofianatos (2009), 79: "La Commission a fait une utilisation importante [d'engagements] en subordonnant l'exemption d'une entente à des conditions et charges détaillées dans sa décision"; Saitzek (2008), 23; Hennig (2010a), 346.

[177]CJ, C-43/82 (VBVB, 1984), 52; see also C-142/84 (BAT Reynolds, 1987), 23; opinion of AG Lenz in C-360/92 P (Publishers Association, 1994), 35f; GC, T-395/94 (Transatlantic Container Line, 2002), 264.

[178]On commitments in opposition procedures see Saitzek (2008), 23f; generally on the opposition procedure see Waelbroeck (1986), 272ff.

[179]For the lack of statistics regarding the adoption of commitments under regulation 17/62 also Blockx (2018), 96.

[180]Georgiev (2007), 1000; Botteman/Patsa (2013), 349 rely on Georgiev in order to claim that, since the entry into force of Regulation 1/03, the Commission has "relied on commitments to a much greater extent than it had relied on informal settlements under the previous regime".

[181]Georgiev (2007), 1000.

a negotiated solution. On the other hand, Georgiev does not take comfort letters into account, although these can also be the result of a negotiated solution.[182] Second, Georgiev's numbers predicate solely on public information.[183] However, a large part of the Commission's informal decisions has never been published.[184] If one considers that, according to the Commission's own figures, prior to the modernisation more than 90% of all cases were closed informally,[185] Georgiev's ratio of 1–4 seems unlikely.[186] It would mean that only a negligible number of all informal closures were the result of a negotiated solution. It appears, however, more likely that there is a number of unpublished informal closures that were the result of a negotiated solution that Georgiev fails to take into account.[187]

Against this backdrop, it may be doubted that the shift from an adversarial to a more negotiated approach caused by the introduction of Article 9 Regulation 1/03 is really as "pronounced"[188] as is often claimed.[189] Indeed, in a more recent article, Wils claims that the ratio between commitment and prohibition decisions has not changed with the introduction of Article 9.[190] It appears thus more appropriate to consider the consensuality inherent to Article 9 decisions as old wine in new bottles.[191] In fact, the major novelty brought about by the provision does not seem

---

[182]See the references in Sect. 2.3.1.2, footnote 173 above. Examples from the Commission's practice are Amadeus/Sabre (XXIst Report on Competition Policy, 95); Baccarat (XXIst Report on Competition Policy, 98); ETSI (XXVth Report on Competition Policy, 131); MD Foods (XXVth Report on Competition Policy, 136).

[183]Georgiev (2007), 1000.

[184]See van Bael (1986), 64f, who mentioned that at the time less than 5% of the Commission's settlements were published; Sofianatos (2009), 81; Hennig (2010a), 112f and 345.

[185]XXIXth Report on Competition Policy (1999), 25; see also van Bael (1986), 62. As has been rightly pointed out by Hennig (2010a), 112 fn 562, this figure comprises all informal settlements. It is not limited to cases in which the closure of the proceedings was conditional on a commitment or other negotiated solution.

[186]See also Forrester (2010), 639, who states with regard to the system of Regulation 17/62 that "[i]f notifications received express or informal endorsement from the Commission, such approval was usually conditioned upon the making of concessions".

[187]But see Wils (2006), 346, who reports that "[s]ettlements were usually described in the Commission's annual Report on Competition Policy, but often without much detail"; also Jones/ Sufrin (2014), 993, who state that settlements "were frequently publicised".

[188]Schweitzer (2012), 2: "[. . .] a pronounced shift can be observed since the entry into force of Regulation 1/03, away from adversarial competition law enforcement towards negotiated deals".

[189]See also Wils (2014a), 7, who presents figures showing that under Regulation 17/62, the Commission adopted on average 7.5 prohibition decisions and 2 exemption decisions with conditions or obligations per year, while under Regulation 1/03 it has adopted on average 7 prohibition decisions and 3 commitment decisions per year. Wils' figures comprise hardcore cartel decisions.

[190]Wils (2015), 12; see also OECD (2016), 14.

[191]See Barbier de la Serre (2006), 133f: "[En ce qui concerne la procédure d'engagements introduite par l'article 9], cela consiste un peu pour la Commission à faire du neuf avec du vieux"; consenting Sofianatos (2009), 82; see also Hennig (2010a), 114: "Im Grunde wurde [. . .] das bereits vor der Reform seitens der Kommission praktizierte [. . .] Verfahren des informellen Settlements auf eine gesetzliche Grundlage gestellt".

to be the possibility to resolve competition cases in a consensual way. Rather, it appears to lie in the fact that there is now a formal basis also for the negotiated solutions that were earlier on arrived at informally. With regard to these cases, the introduction of the Article 9 procedure brought about two changes that are broadly accepted as improvements.[192] First, it enabled the Commission to impose fines and penalties in case of non-compliance with a commitment.[193] Second, it improved transparency.[194] On a sidenote, it should be added that also the criticism that was levelled at the Commission's recourse to negotiated solutions prior to the modernisation[195] anticipated much of the concerns that are voiced today.[196]

2.3.2 Explanations for the Frequent Occurrence of Commitment Decisions

The facts that the Article 9 procedure is not as revolutionary as is sometimes contended and that the undeniable quantitative success may merely be a continuation of the Commission's prior practice do not discharge of the necessity to search for reasons that can explain the frequent occurrence of commitment decisions. These reasons will hence constitute the subject of the following section. It will focus on three possible explanations: First, the incentives and disincentives for a commitment decision. Second, the fact that commitment decisions may replace the exemption procedure that existed under Regulation 17/62. Third, the influence of the more economic approach.

Before these three issues will be addressed in more detail, one further potential explanation for the frequent use of the commitment procedure shall be mentioned. Its actual importance is, however, difficult to assess. It shall therefore only briefly be touched upon for the sake of completeness: It has been suggested that the Alrosa judgment of the Court of Justice may have led to an increased use of commitment

[192] Eg Whish (2006), 564 and 571; Georgiev (2007), 1033; Wils (2015), 12.

[193] See Articles 23(2)(c) and 24(1)(c) Regulation 1/03. Also eg Temple Lang (2006), 286; Wils (2006), 346; Schweitzer (2010), 548; Rab/Monnoyeur/Sukhtankar (2010), 173; Hennig (2010a), 114; Ritter (2012), Art. 9, 1f; Sadowska (2014), 10. Prior to the modernisation, the Commission was confined to a reopening of the procedure. Choné/Souam/Vialfont (2014), 169, consider the Commission's power to render a commitment legally binding and to impose fines for non-compliance as "the major innovation compared to the earlier framework".

[194] Eg Wils (2006), 346; Ritter (2012), Art. 9, 2.

[195] See in particular van Bael (1986), 82ff; Bourgeois (1993), 98ff; von Winterfeld (1995); Van Bael (1995), 242.

[196] According to Sousa Ferro (2005), 459, one can oppose concerns that the Commission uses the Article 9 procedure to extract overbroad remedies by stating that the introduction of the Article 9 procedure has not changed anything in that respect, since the same problem existed with merely informal undertakings.

decisions.[197] However, as long as there is a lack of a universally accepted method on how to count infringement and commitment decisions respectively,[198] such a claim is impossible to verify.[199] Moreover, even if one could statistically observe an increased use of commitment decisions after Alrosa, it does not necessarily reflect causality, but may also only be a correlation.[200]

2.3.2.1 Incentives and Disincentives for a Commitment Decision

The most obvious explanation for the frequent use of the Article 9 procedure lies in the incentives and disincentives for the concerned undertakings and the Commission to follow the path of a commitment decision.

2.3.2.1.1 Incentives

2.3.2.1.1.1 Commitments Are Speedier and Less Costly Than Infringement Decisions

Along the lines of the discussion about consensual dispute resolution in general,[201] the standard argument advanced in favour of commitment decisions is that they are speedier and less costly than Article 7 decisions.[202] This is advantageous not only for the Commission, but also for the concerned undertakings and the general public.[203] Both the Commission and the concerned undertaking can reallocate the liberated resources to other activities, which in turn is of benefit to the general welfare. A speedy resolution is also advantageous for the competitive process, in particular in

---

[197] See Botteman/Patsa (2013), 351f: They observe that the Commission "made noticeably more use of commitment decisions, relative to prohibition decisions, to conclude Article 102 TFEU investigations" after the delivery of the opinion of AG Kokott. Jenny (2015) claims that the Commission's use of commitment decisions "slowed down" after the Alrosa judgment of the General Court (751), but that the judgment of the Court of Justice is "one of the major reasons" for the – alleged – overall increase in commitment decisions (702 and 762).

[198] See Sect. 2.3.1.1.1 with footnote 148 above.

[199] Against the possibility of quantitative statements about the impact of the Alrosa judgement on the Commission's commitment practice also Wagner-Von Papp (2012), 940, with further reasons. It must, however, be acknowledged that subsequent to the Alrosa judgment of the General Court and prior to the Alrosa judgment of the Court of Justice, members of the Commission's services stated that the Commission would "continue to mainly rely on Article 7 prohibition decisions" [Lowe/ Maier-Rigaud (2008), 611].

[200] Botteman/Patsa (2013), 351f expressly acknowledge this by stating that the increase in commitments after AG Kokott's opinion "may be purely coincidental". See also Wagner-Von Papp (2012), 942, who cautions against the fallacy of the "post hoc, ergo propter hoc" argument for causation.

[201] See Budzinski/Kuchinke (2012), 279 fn 29; Wagner-Von Papp (2012), 959.

[202] Instead of all see only O'Donoghue/Padilla (2013), 896ff; Wagner-Von Papp (2012), 959; OECD (2016), 25ff, all with further references.

[203] Wagner-Von Papp (2012), 959.

dynamic markets, because it allows preserving competition that might otherwise have been stifled. Several facets of the argument that Article 9 decisions are speedier and less costly can be distinguished.

First, the procedure that leads up to an Article 9 decision at least bears the potential of being streamlined in comparison to the procedure that leads to an Article 7 decision. The Commission is relieved of the burden of having to collect evidence that meets the requisite standard for an infringement decision. Moreover, in particular if the commitment is made binding before the Commission issues a statement of objections, both the Commission and the concerned undertaking can save time and resources, if the undertaking concerned waives its rights of defence, in particular the right of access to the file.[204] However, there are arguments that call into question the extent to which these features really accelerate the procedure.[205] The process of negotiating the commitment may require additional resources that must be taken into account,[206] in particular if a case proves "complicated to settle".[207] Empirically, recourse to Article 9 reduces the duration of a procedure from its formal opening until the adoption of a decision on average only to a limited extent.[208] This applies also with a view to dynamic markets. Commentators have criticised that, with a respective duration of 29, 24 and 17 months, the Rambus, Microsoft and IBM commitments were not reached particularly swiftly.[209] The adoption of the unilateral prohibition decision imposed on Motorola regarding the enforcement of standard essential patents[210] lasted 2 months less than the adoption of the commitment decision in the comparable proceedings against Samsung.[211] In Gazprom, even more than 5.5 years lie between the opening of procedures and the adoption of the commitment decision.[212] Overall, the saving of resources that is entailed by the

[204]For the discussion whether there is a right of access to the file under the Article 9 procedure see Sect. 4.1.1.2.2.2.1 with footnote 24 below.

[205]See Jenny (2015), 732ff; OECD (2016), 31; Botta/Wiedemann (2018), 72; von Kalben (2018), 152ff.

[206]Budzinski/Kuchinke (2012), 280; Sadowska (2014), 6.

[207]Falconi (2011), 47; OECD (2016), 31: "It could well be that for complex negotiations the cost increases and the whole enforcement action might take longer than a regular investigation."

[208]See Mariniello (2014), 4, according to whom Article 7 procedures are on average only 17% slower than Article 9 procedures (28.5 versus 24.3 months) and even 15% faster where Article 102 TFEU cases are concerned (26 against 22.7 months). According to Lugard/Möllmann (2013), 7, the overall difference in duration is even less significant. They state that on average, a commitment procedure lasts approximately 22 months and an infringement procedure approximately 23 months. But see also Gerard (2013b), 9, who presents a chart indicating that the duration of commitment procedures is less long than that of infringement procedures; von Kalben (2018), 154, presents figures indicating that the commitment procedure is 25% faster than the infringement procedure.

[209]Lugard/Möllmann (2013), 7; Marsden (2013), 2 fn 5.

[210]COMP/39.985 (Motorola, 2014): 25 months.

[211]COMP/39.939 (Samsung, 2014): 27 months.

[212]COMP/39.816 (Gazprom, 2018): The Commission opened proceedings in September 2012 and adopted the commitment decision in May 2018.

procedure that leads up to an Article 9 decision may hence be less important than is often assumed.[213]

Second, if one extends the perspective to the period after the adoption of the decision, an Article 9 decision nevertheless brings about important advantages over an Article 7 decision in terms of speed and cost. Due to its consensual nature, a commitment is unlikely to be challenged by the concerned undertaking in court.[214] The Commission and the concerned undertaking hence save the time and resources of litigation. Due to the reduced likeliness of a challenge in court, the commitment is also more likely to produce effects on the market immediately. For an infringement decision, this is not necessarily the case. Although an appeal does in principle not display a suspensory effect,[215] the concerned undertaking may apply to the Court for interim relief. In this connection, commentators have pointed out that the General Court has often suspended prohibition decisions and that the refusal to suspend the Commission's decision in Microsoft I[216] was the exception rather than the rule.[217]

Third, from the perspective of the concerned undertakings, a commitment is less costly than an infringement decision in that it cannot serve as the basis for the imposition of a fine, does not facilitate follow-on action and avoids the negative reputation associated with an infringement decision. The incentive to avoid a fine is particularly strong in view of the "dramatic rise in antitrust fines over the last decade".[218] From a rational choice perspective, reputation related incentives may also be of relevance from the perspective of the Commission,[219] in particular if the Commission's chances for proving an infringement to the requisite standard are weak. In such a case, a commitment may create positive reputation by enabling the Commission to take at least some kind of enforcement action.[220] At the same time, it reduces the risk of negative reputation caused by a defeat in court.[221]

---

[213]See also the Commission's staff working document accompanying the report on the functioning of Regulation 1/03, COM(2009)206 final, 104, where the Commission explains the long duration of some commitment procedures with the fact that the procedures in question were initiated under Regulation 17/62.

[214]To date, no commitment decision has been challenged by the undertaking that offered the commitment; see also Kellerbauer (2011), 3 fn 24; Wagner-Von Papp (2012), 959 fn 114.

[215]Article 278 TFEU and Article 60 of the Statute of the Court of Justice.

[216]GC, T-201/04 R (Microsoft I, 2004).

[217]Temple Lang (2006), 274; O'Donoghue/Padilla (2013), 897 together with fn 72; I have not verified whether statistic evidence supports this conclusion.

[218]Sadowska (2014), 54.

[219]See Budzinski/Kuchinke (2012), 282: They point out that the "self-interest factors [of a competition authority] can be boiled down to (i) demonstrating activity by frequent interventions, and (ii) showcasing interventions as being a success". See also Forrester (2010), 649, who emphasises that competition authorities "are accountable to the outside world, and need to show results".

[220]See Rab/Monnoyeur/Sukhtankar (2010), 175: "In a situation where the Commission's investigation into a suspected infringement does not produce sufficiently strong and convincing evidence to support the finding of an infringement, Article 9 provides an alternative process for resolving the case and addressing competition concerns".

[221]See Budzinski/Kuchinke (2012), 284.

2.3.2.1.1.2 Commitments Are More Effective Than Infringement Decisions

Commitments may also be considered to be more attractive than infringement decisions due to their increased effectiveness. Again, at least two aspects of the argument can be distinguished.

The first reason why commitments can be more effective than infringement decisions is their consensual nature.[222] As the Court of Justice emphasised in Alrosa, Article 9 "enables undertakings to participate fully in the procedure, by putting forward the solutions which appear to them to be the most appropriate and capable of addressing the Commission's concerns".[223] The consensuality is attractive both for the Commission and the concerned undertakings. From the perspective of the Commission, the stronger involvement of the concerned undertakings in the remedy design may help to overcome information asymmetries.[224] Moreover, it may promote the concerned undertaking's identification with the remedy and thereby contribute to a more effective implementation.[225] From the perspective of the undertaking, the commitment procedure presents an opportunity to gain greater insight in the Commission's views and to retain some control over the design of the remedy.[226]

A second argument that is sometimes advanced in support of the higher effectiveness of commitments is their "flexibility"—understood as regulatory potential to improve the competitive structure of the market.[227] With good reason, this argument

---

[222]See eg Podszun (2012), 52f: "sachnähere und in der Regel angemessene Entscheidungen"; Cengiz (2011), 135: "superior in terms of their problem-solving capacity"; Sadowska (2014), 7: "Negotiations over commitments bring together the Commission's expertise in competition law compliance and the undertaking's sector specific knowledge".

[223]CJ, C-441/07 P (Alrosa, 2010), 35; see also Hennig (2010b), 450.

[224]Budzinski/Kuchinke (2012), 275.

[225]See the Commission's staff working document accompanying the report on the functioning of Regulation 1/03, COM(2009)206 final, 102: "As commitment decisions result from the parties' initiative and willingness to offer commitments, the same parties tend to be more readily inclined to implement their own voluntary commitments"; Manual of Procedures (2012), Module 16, 8: "The fact that the commitments are not imposed by the Commission but voluntarily submitted and implemented only after discussions with the parties as well as a market test may also facilitate the later implementation of the commitments". See also Budzinski/Kuchinke (2012), 279; McGeown/Orologas (2013), 5; Wathelet (2015), 554: "it is a truism that undertakings are more likely to adhere to a negotiated solution rather than one that has been imposed upon them".

[226]See Forrester (2010), 645; Rab/Monnoyeur/Sukhtankar (2010), 175; Schweitzer (2012), 2; O'Donoghue/Padilla (2013), 896f.

[227]See in particular Mariniello (2014), 6: "From the Commission's perspective, proactive remedies can be a useful tool. Despite the criticism of proactive remedies in the legal literature [...], they might be justifiable on economic grounds. Proactive remedies allow the Commission to offer the elimination of a fine in exchange for remedies that can affect market structure, increase competition and therefore potentially lead to higher welfare levels of consumers". See also Botteman/Patsa (2013), 357: "The commitment procedure may provide scope for the formulation of remedies that are more successful at resolving the EC's concerns and restoring effective competition in the market to the benefit of consumers. [In fact], remedies imposed through commitment decisions may be more creative and go further than what the EC could have imposed under infringement proceedings"; similarly also Cook (2006), 211f; Hjelmeng (2013), 1030 and 1036f; O'Donoghue/Padilla (2013), 898; Sadowska (2014), 7; OECD (2016), 32.

has been described as a "double-edged sword".[228] In fact, "flexibility" constitutes a euphemism for remedies that the Commission could not have lawfully obtained under Article 7.[229] The benefit of a positive effect on competition comes at the cost of a loss of rule based competition policy. Nonetheless, irrespective of whether one conceives the flexibility argument as something positive or negative, it must be admitted that the regulatory potential may provide an incentive for the Commission to resort to the Article 9 procedure.

2.3.2.1.2 Disincentives

From the perspective of the Commission, the major disincentive of a commitment decision is its inferiority to an infringement decision in terms of deterrence. This inferiority is broadly acknowledged.[230] It predicates in particular on two reasons. On the one hand, from an ex ante perspective, an undertaking has a lower incentive to comply with the competition rules when it knows that it can later avoid or at least mitigate the consequences of breaking the law by means of a settlement.[231] On the other hand, deterrence decreases with a decline in infringement decisions that serve as precedents.[232] Compliance with rules depends on the predictability of their application. An Article 9 decision reduces the predictability of the application of the competition rules, because a commitment decision only expresses the Commission's concerns. It does not contain an authoritative statement whether a certain conduct amounts to an infringement.

A further reason that cautions against the use of the commitment procedure from the perspective of the Commission is the possible protraction of the procedure due to unsuccessful negotiations. Concerned undertakings may withdraw a commitment until the adoption of the commitment decision or the market test may show that the commitments are not appropriate to eliminate the existing concerns.[233]

[228] See Wagner-Von Papp (2012), 959; Dunne (2014), 401.

[229] Wagner-Von Papp (2012), 959.

[230] Eg Budzinski/Kuchinke (2012), 281f; Hjelmeng (2013), 1030; Mariniello (2014), 5; Choné/Souam/Vialfont (2014), 170 and 177.

[231] See Edwards/Padilla (2010), 673; Budzinski/Kuchinke (2012), 281f; Hjelmeng (2013), 1030: "under-deterrence may occur because infringements are perceived as less risky in light of the prospects of settling the case". But see also Gerard (2013b), 12: "[T]he loss in repressive utility resulting from the Commission's acceptance of commitments appears relative, notably as it is able to maintain a high level of general deterrence by adopting a tough stance in remaining infringement cases".

[232] Hjelmeng (2013), 1030; Mariniello (2014), 5.

[233] See Manual of Procedures (2012), Module 16, 10.

Another potential disincentive for the Commission to resort to the commitment procedure is the loss of the fine.[234] If the Commission levies a fine on an undertaking, the paid amounts contribute to the central budget of the EU.[235] Where the Commission adopts a commitment decision, it cannot impose a fine and thus forfeits an additional source of income. The importance of this disincentive to resort to the commitment procedure is, however, at best limited. Primarily, fines are punishments and not sources of revenue. Their contribution to the budget of the Union is merely a side effect that should not play a role for the decision whether a fine is imposed or not. At least officially, this will likely also be the position of the Commission. Nonetheless, it cannot be excluded that, at least unofficially, the loss of a fine plays a role for the decision whether to adopt a commitment decision.

From the perspective of the concerned undertakings, two reasons are advanced in the literature that allegedly militate against a commitment.[236] On the one hand, the undertakings' inclination to enter into a commitment is said to be negatively affected by the risk of having to make concessions that go beyond what the Commission could lawfully impose in an infringement decision. On the other hand, the undertaking is said to be discouraged from using the Article 9 procedure by the fact that the commitment decision does not offer a safe harbour against prosecution by national competition authorities and private litigation in national courts. The first reason must be approved of. As regards the second, it is submitted that the fact that a commitment does not provide a safe harbour cannot be considered as a disadvantage for the concerned undertaking when compared with the infringement procedure. Also a successful defence in an Article 7 procedure does not shield the undertaking from prosecution by national competition authorities or private litigation. This would only be the case, if the Commission made a finding of inapplicability pursuant to Article 10 Regulation 1/03. Hence, although the fact that an infringement decision facilitates private litigation constitutes an incentive to engage into the commitment procedure, the fact that a commitment does not provide for a safe harbour cannot be considered as a disincentive.

[234] Edwards/Padilla (2010), 669: "[...] the competition authority will be willing to settle when the potential sacrifice in consumer welfare resulting from litigation [...] and the litigation costs [...] exceed the cost of settling in terms of lost fines and diminished deterrence"; similarly at 674f.

[235] See eg Commission, MEMO/09/235 (Intel, 2009); Engelsing/Schneider (2008), 4-23-168.

[236] Rab/Monnoyeur/Sukhtankar (2010), 175f.

2.3.2.1.3 Intermediate Conclusion

It has been argued that undertakings have a "systemic bias in favour of commitment decisions rather than infringement decisions".[237] A similar claim has also been made for the Commission.[238] If both allegations were true and if one also assumes that there are no legal constraints to prevent the adoption of a commitment decision, the continued existence of infringement decisions outside the area of hardcore cartels[239] would have to come as a surprise. Conversely, the subsistence of infringement decisions outside the area of hardcore cartels shows that the bias of the concerned undertakings, the Commission, or both, is not as systemic as expected, even if one maintains the assumption that there are no legal constraints to prevent the adoption of a commitment decision.

Statements about whether a potential bias in favour of commitment decisions has a systemic character or not are difficult to make. Such statements predicate on implicit assumptions that are hard to generalise. For example, the proclivity of an undertaking to enter into a commitment will be influenced by its individual risk aversion[240] and the chances the undertaking sees for successfully defending itself against the Commission, national competition authorities or private litigation.[241] Similarly, also the Commission's disposition in favour of commitments is not axiomatic. One might also argue that some members of the Commission's services may have a biased preference for infringement decisions, because "successful litigation and high fines may do more to foster a professional career within the authority than a settlement".[242] More importantly, there is good reason to assume

[237]Wils (2006), 349. In his view, this systemic bias stems from the fact that "the benefits of infringement decisions for the enforcement of Articles [101 and 102 TFEU], namely the public censure, deterrence, disgorgement of illicit gains and punishment, and facilitation of follow-on actions for compensation, are strictly negative from the perspective of the undertakings that are the addressees of the infringement decisions".

[238]Budzinski/Kuchinke (2012), 284f: "[...] consensual arrangements are well-suited to the self-interest of competition authorities, in particular if the threat of unfavourable court decisions is prevalent. Thus, if a competition authority does not act completely altruistic and unselfish, it should be prone to enter such arrangements". See also Sadowska (2014), 47: "potential bias on the part of the Commission in favour of commitment decisions".

[239]For the area of hardcore cartels, there is a legal constraint: The last sentence of Recital 13 of Regulation 1/03 provides that "[c]ommitment decisions are not appropriate in cases where the Commission intends to impose a fine". In the Manual of Procedures (2012) (Module 16, 13), the Commission expressly acknowledges this legal constraint and states that "[c]onsequently, [it] does not apply the Article 9 procedure to secret cartels that fall under the Notice on immunity from fines and reduction of fines in cartel cases".

[240]For the argument that an undertaking's inclination to enter into a disproportionate commitment depends on its risk aversion see Wils (2006), 351; Cengiz (2011), 136; Wagner-Von Papp (2012), 944.

[241]Sadowska (2014), 9.

[242]Edwards/Padilla (2010), 670f.

that, as a public authority, the Commission will take the inferiority of commitment decisions in terms of deterrence and legal certainty into account.[243]

Overall, it is undeniable that there are strong incentives for the concerned undertakings and the Commission to resort to the commitment procedure. Nonetheless, even in the absence of legal constraints, the existing disincentives continue to preserve space for infringement decisions, also outside the area of hardcore cartels. A consensual outcome is no predestined certainty. Rather, it depends on the weight the concerned undertaking and the Commission assign to the respective incentives and disincentives in an individual case.

2.3.2.2 Replacement of Exemption Decisions That Existed Under Regulation 17/62

It is broadly acknowledged that Article 9 shares certain features with the grant of exemption decisions pursuant to Article 101(3) TFEU that was possible under the notification system of Regulation 17/62.[244] The two procedures are certainly not identical.[245] However, they resemble each other in particular in that they address existing needs for "fine-tuning"[246] of practices with ambiguous effects on competition. Under the old system, the Commission provided at least some guidance how an agreement could be made compatible with Article 101 TFEU.[247] Since the enactment of Regulation 1/03, an undertaking must self-assess its practices. There is good reason to assume that Article 9 compensates at least for some of the resulting loss of guidance.[248]

---

[243]In the Manual of Procedures (2012), Module 16, 11f, the Commission indicates that, when deciding on whether to adopt a commitment decision, it will take the necessity to deter other undertakings or to establish a strong precedent into account.

[244]See Temple Lang (2006), 290f; Whish (2006), 564; Georgiev (2007), 1030; Sofianatos (2009), 82; Rab/Monnoyeur/Sukhtankar (2010), 176; Schweitzer (2010), 548f, (2011), 649 and (2012), 11 and 15f; Cengiz (2011), 138; Falconi (2011), 47; Lugard/Möllmann (2013), 7; Dunne (2014), 406f; Whish/Bailey (2012), 167f; Jones/Sufrin (2014), 989; Brenner (2014), 676.

[245]For an emphasis of the differences see in particular Whish (2006), 564; Schweitzer (2011), 649; Whish/Bailey (2012), 168; AG Kokott, opinion in C-547/16 (Gasorba, 2017), 45ff. But see Georgiev (2007), 1030: "settling with the Commission is equivalent to receiving an individual exemption of the kind that was available under Regulation 17/62".

[246]Rab/Monnoyeur/Sukhtankar (2010), 176; Cengiz (2011), 138; Schweitzer (2012), 11.

[247]See Forrester (2010), 639: "The system of notification committed the Commission to be ready to consider, to react, and to advise in response to requests for guidance by the private sector". But see also the strand of case law cited in Sect. 2.3.1.2, footnote 177 above, according to which it was in the first place for the concerned undertakings to submit alternatives, if the Commission raised concerns regarding the initial notification.

[248]See Sofianatos (2009), 82: "les décisions d'engagements [...] sont vouées à remplir le vide que laisse la suppression de la négociation au stade de l'exemption"; Dunne (2014), 407: "guiding role that [the notification procedure] granted to the Commission [...] [is] discernible in within many commitment decisions"; also Forrester (2010), 639 and Whish/Bailey (2012), 167.

The "fine-tuning" argument does not need to be confined to the formal grant of an exemption pursuant to Article 101(3) TFEU.[249] As explained above, under the old system, the Commission relied on consensual solutions in a variety of constellations that concerned formal and informal decisions and both Article 101 TFEU and Article 102 TFEU.[250] In principle, there is no reason why these cases should not also be perceived as an expression of an existing need for fine-tuning. Thus understood, the current frequent use of Article 9 can be explained with the general need to bring practices that have ambiguous effects on competition fully in line with Articles 101 and 102 TFEU.

The Commission will nonetheless have to be and be vigilant against letting the Article 9 procedure become a full-scale surrogate—or in respect of Article 101 (1) and Article 102 TFEU even an extension—of the old notification system.[251] The primary goal of Article 9 Regulation 1/03 is procedural economy, not legal certainty for the concerned undertakings.[252] As will be explained in more detail below,[253] a concerned undertaking does in principle not have a right to a commitment decision. This circumstance enables the Commission to apply the Article 9 procedure selectively.[254]

2.3.2.3 The Impact of the More Economic Approach

It has been argued convincingly that the "more economic"—or "more effects based"[255]—approach to competition law reinforces the proclivity of the Commission and the concerned undertakings to resort to commitment decisions.[256] The many and often diverse understandings that are assigned to the concept of the "more

---

[249]See Sofianatos (2009), 82, who extends the argument also to negative clearance decisions pursuant to Article 2 Regulation 17/62; also Schweitzer (2011), 649: "nicht ein bloßes Äquivalent der früheren Genehmigungsentscheidungen und Negativatteste".

[250]See Sect. 2.3.1.2 with footnote 172 above.

[251]See Whish (2006), 564; consenting Sofianatos (2009), 82.

[252]Schweitzer (2011), 649: "Keineswegs soll [das Instrument der Verpflichtungsentscheidungen] zu einem Ersatz für das frühere Notifizierungsverfahren werden. Es dient nicht primär dem Interesse der Unternehmen an Rechtssicherheit, sondern dem Interesse der Kommission an der zügigen Beilegung von Wettbewerbsproblemen"; AG Kokott, opinion in C-547/16 (Gasorba, 2017), 36ff.

[253]See Sect. 5.1.2 with footnote 49 below.

[254]See Schweitzer (2011), 649, who emphasises that the Commission applies the commitment procedure only selectively.

[255]The terminology is not consistent. Without expressing a preference for either term, I will use the term "more economic approach".

[256]Cengiz (2011), 136; Wagner-Von Papp (2012), 964; Botteman/Patsa (2013), 352f; Gerard (2013b), 13; Mestmäcker/Schweitzer (2014), § 21, 54; Sadowska (2014), 180; Jenny (2015), 734, who goes as far as to argue that the Commission uses the Article 9 procedure to "bypass the constraints of a more economic approach in the name of enforcement effectiveness" (703).

economic" approach shall not be presented here in detail.[257] For the present purposes, it suffices to mention two of its characteristics that are broadly accepted: First, the shift from broad per se rules to a more refined contextual analysis of a given practice according to the circumstances of the individual case at hand. Second, an increased use of complex economic models, empirical evidence and econometric studies that require the input of important amounts of data.

The said characteristics entail two consequences that foster the inclination of the concerned undertakings and the Commission to resort to the Article 9 procedure. On the one hand, they both cause additional costs for the enforcement of and the compliance with the competition rules.[258] The avoidance of cost is, however, a paramount incentive for the Commission and the concerned undertaking to settle a case. On the other hand, in particular the shift towards a case-by-case analysis reduces legal certainty and hence the predictability of the outcome of a case.[259] Yet again, a lack of predictability constitutes an incentive to settle.

2.3.3 Conclusion

It follows from the above that the alleged "shift" from an adversarial to a consensual paradigm in the enforcement of competition law is probably less significant than is often contended. Also under Regulation 17/62, consensual means to close an investigation were nothing extraordinary. It remains that—outside the cartel area—the commitment procedure plays an important role and constitutes even the predominant enforcement tool. The frequent use of commitments already under Regulation 17/62, the incentives that exist both for the Commission and the concerned undertakings to choose the path of an Article 9 instead of an Article 7 procedure, the impact of the more economic approach, and the use of commitment decisions as a mechanism to fine-tune practices with ambiguous effects even outside the area of Article 101(3) TFEU all provide explanations for the frequent occurrence of commitment decisions in the Commission's practice. It is submitted that besides providing merely an explanation, the said aspects demonstrate also that there is a genuine need for commitment decisions. A complete abolishment of the Article 9 procedure is therefore out of question. Nevertheless, the question remains whether the criticism that is levelled at the Commission's practice is justified and whether and to what extent there is room for improvements.

---

[257] See only the contributions in Schmidtchen/Albert/Voigt (2007); Drexl/Podszun/Kerber (2011); Basedow/Wurmnest (2011); Bourgeois/Waelbroeck (2013); also Ackermann (2010), 22, Kersten (2010), 297ff, and Podszun (2012), 53f.

[258] See Wagner-Von Papp (2012), 964; Gerard (2013b), 13; (2013a), 33f; Perrot (2013), 294; Botteman/Patsa (2013), 352f; Wils (2014b), 7f with further references in fn 58.

[259] On the potential negative effects of the more economic approach on legal certainty see eg Kerber/Christiansen (2006), 217ff; Drexl (2009), 679; de Hautecloque (2009), 95f; Hancher/de Hautecloque (2010), 329.

It is important to keep the extent to which commitment decisions determine the Commission's actual practice outside the cartel area in mind throughout the following discussions. At the same time, it is also clear that an assessment whether the Commission uses the Article 9 procedure more often than optimal cannot rely solely on a quantitative evaluation of the overall proportion of commitment and infringement decisions. The following three chapters of the present work set therefore more concretely out to assess whether the criticism that is levied at the Article 9 procedure is justified. According to the three lines of argument described above, it will be analysed in more detail to what extent the commitment procedure leads to a relaxation of the link between harm and remedy, to a relaxation of the procedural safeguards and to reduced legal certainty when compared to the Article 7 procedure and in how far these aspects constitute compelling arguments against the use of commitment decisions.

Bibliography

Ackermann (2010): Europäisches Kartellrecht, in: Riesenhuber (Ed.), Europäische Methodenlehre, 2nd edition, 2010

Almunia (2013): Remedies, commitments and settlements in antitrust, Speech given in March 2013, available online

Barbier de la Serre (2006): Actualité du droit processuel, RLC 2006/7, 131

Barbier de la Serre (2012): Competition law cases before the EU Courts: Is the well running dry?, in: Merola/Derenne (2012): The Role of the Court of Justice of the European Union in Competition Law Cases. GCLC Annual Conference Series, 2012

Basedow/Wurmnest (2011): Structure and Effects in EU Competition Law. Studies on Exclusionary Conduct and State Aid, 2011

Blockx (2018): The Impact of EU Antitrust Procedure on the Role of the EU Courts (1997-2016), JECLP 2018, 92

Botta/Wiedemann (2018): EU Competition Law Enforcement vis-à-vis Exploitative Conducts in the Data Economy. Exploring the Terra Incognita, Max Planck Institute for Innovation and Competition Research Paper No. 18-08, available online

Botteman/Patsa (2013): Towards a more sustainable use of commitment decisions in Article 102 TFEU cases, JAE 2013, 347

Bougette/Marty (2012): Quels remèdes pour les abus de position dominante? Une analyse économique des décisions de la Commission européenne, Concurrences 2012/3, 30

Bourgeois (1993): Undertakings in E.C. competition law, in: Slot/McDonnell (Eds.), Procedure and Enforcement in EC and US Competition Law, 1993, p. 90

Bourgeois/Waelbroeck (2013): Ten years of effects-based approach in EU competition law, 2013

Brenner (2010): Wer freut sich, wenn zwei sich nicht streiten?, WRP 2010, 1333

Brenner (2014): Regulierung mithilfe des Kartellrechts – Verpflichtungszusagen der Europäischen Kommission, EuR 2014, 671

Budzinski/Kuchinke (2012): Deal or No Deal? Consensual arrangements as an Instrument of European Competition Policy, Review of Economics 2012, 265

Bueren (2011): Verständigungen – Settlements in Kartelbußgeldverfahren, 2011

Cavicchi (2011): The European Commission's discretion as to the adoption of Article 9 commitment decisions: Lessons from Alrosa, Europa-Kolleg Hamburg, Institute for European Integration, Discussion paper 3/11, available online

Cengiz (2011): Judicial review and the rule of law in the EU competition law regime after Alrosa, ECJ 2011, 127
Choné/Souam/Vialfont (2014): On the optimal use of commitment decisions under European competition law, IRLE 2014, 169
Colombani/Kloub/Sakkers (2014): Cartels, in: Faull/Nikpay (Eds.), The EU Law of Competition, 3rd edition, 2014
Cook (2006): Commitment Decisions: The Law and Practice under Article 9, World Competition 2006, 209
De Bronnet (2012): Europäisches Kartellverfahrensrecht. Kommentar zur VO 1/2003, 2nd edition, 2012
De Hautecloque (2009): Legal Uncertainty and Competition Policy in European Deregulated Electricity Markets: the Case of Long-term Exclusive Supply Contracts, World Competition 2009, 91
Drexl (2009): Competition Law as Part of the European Constitution, in: von Bogdandy/Bast, Principles of European Constitutional Law, 2nd Edition, 2009
Drexl/Podszun/Kerber (2011): Competition Policy and the Economic Approach, 2011
Ducore (2006): Settlement of competition conduct violations at the United States antitrust agencies and at the European Commission – Some observations, in: Hawk (Ed), Annual proceedings of the Fordham Competition Law Institute 2005, 2006
Dunne (2014): Commitment decisions in EU competition law, JCLE 2014, 399
Edwards/Padilla (2010): Antitrust Settlements in the EU: Private Incentives and Enforcement Policy, in: Ehlermann/Marquis (Eds.), European Competition Law Annual 2008, 2010, p. 661
Engelsing/Schneider (2008): in: Hirsch/Montag/Säcker (Eds.), Competition Law: European Community Practice and Procedure. Article-by-Article Commentary, 2008
Epstein (2007): Antitrust Consent Decrees in Theory and Practice. Why less is More, 2007
Falconi (2011): Commitment decisions in the EU and UK – Developments, open issues and considerations for companies and competition authorities, Competition Law 2011, 41
Forrester (2010): Creating New Rules or Closing Easy Cases? Policy Consequences for Public Enforcement of Settlements under Article 9 or Regulation 1/2003, in: Ehlermann/Marquis (Eds.), European Competition Law Annual 2008, 2010, p. 637
Frenz/Ehlenz (2010): Die Verhältnismäßigkeit im Wettbewerbsrecht – Alrosa, EWS 2010, 305
Gautier/Petit (2014): Optimal Enforcement of Competition Policy. The Commitments Procedure under Uncertainty, October 2014, available online
Georgiev (2007): Contagious Efficiency: The growing reliance on U.S.-style antitrust settlements in EU law, 2007 Utah L. Rev. 971
Gerard (2013a): The effects-based approach under Article 101 TFEU and its paradoxes: Modernisation at war with itself, in: Bourgeois/Waelbroeck (Eds.), Ten years of effects-based approach in EU competition law, 2013
Gerard (2013b): Negotiated remedies in the modernization era: the limits of effectiveness, available online
Ginsburg/Wright (2013): Antitrust Settlements: The Culture of Consent, Concurrences 2013/2, 56
Gippini-Fournier (2008): The Modernisation of European Competition Law: First Experiences with Regulation 1/2003, in: Köck/Karollus (Eds.), The Modernisation of European Competition Law. FIDE Congress, 2008
Gyselen (2014): The European Commission's commitments decisions in abuse of dominance cases, in: Hawk (Ed), Annual proceedings of the Fordham Competition Law Institute 2012, 2014
Hancher/De Hautecloque (2010): Manufacturing the EU energy markets: The current dynamics of regulatory practice, 11 Competition & Reg. Network Indus. 307 (2010)
Hennig (2010a): Settlements im Europäischen Kartellverfahren, 2010
Hennig (2010b): Die Bedeutung des Verhältnismäßigkeitsgrundsatzes bei der Annahme von Verpflichtungszusagen durch die Kommission nach Art. 9 VO (EG) Nr. 1/2003, ZWeR 2010, 440

Hjelmeng (2013): Competition Law Remedies: Striving for Coherence or Finding New Ways, CMLR 2013, 1007
Idot (2010): Droit spécial du contrat - Importantes précisions de la Cour de justice de l'Union européenne sur le contrôle des engagements, Revue des contrats 2010, 1276
Italianer (2013): To commit or not to commit, that is the question, Speech given in December 2013, available online
Jaeger, M. (2011): The Standard of Review in Competition Cases Involving Complex Economic Assessments: Towards the Marginalisation of the Marginal Review?, JECLP 2011, 295
Jenny (2015): Worst decision of the EU Court of Justice: The Alrosa judgment in context and the future of commitment decisions, Fordham Int'l L.J. 2015, 701
Jones/Sufrin (2014): EU Competition Law, 5th edition, 2014
Kellerbauer (2011): Playground instead of playpen: The Court of Justice of the European Union's Alrosa judgment on Art. 9 of Regulation 1/2003, ECLR 2011, 1
Kellerbauer/Ortiz Blanco/Jörgens/Centella (2013): in: Ortiz Blanco (Ed.), EU Competition Procedure, 3rd Edition, 2013
Kerber/Christiansen (2006): Competition policy with optimally differentiated rules instead of "per se rules vs rule of reason", JCLE 2006, 215
Kersten (2010): Herstellung von Wettbewerb als Verwaltungsaufgabe, in: Veröffentlichungen der Vereinigung der Deutschen Staatsrechtslehrer (VVDStRL) 69 (2010)
Kipiani (2014): Les engagements en matière de pratiques anticoncurrentielles. Analyse des droits français, européen et américain, 2014
Klees (2009): Das Instrument der Zusagenentscheidung der Kommission und der Fall E.On – Ein (weiterer) Sündenfall, WuW 2009, 374
Klees (2010): Freie Bahn für die Kommission in Kartellverfahren bei Anwendung des Art. 9 VO Nr. 1/2003, RIW 2010, 688
Klees (2011): Die Zusagenpraxis der Europäischen Kommission in Kartellverfahren – Eine kritische Analyse, EWS 2011, 14
Kreße (2014): Die Verpflichtungszusage als Instrument der europäischen Wettbewerbsaufsicht, WRP 2014, 1261
Körber (2010): Rechtliches Gehör, Verpflichtungszusagen nach Art. 9 VO 1/2003 und die Alrosa-Entscheidung, in: Weiß, Tagungsband zum 1. Speyerer Kartellrechtsforum, 2010, p. 73
Laina/Laurinen (2013): The EU Cartel Settlement Procedure: Current Status and Challenges, JECLP 2013, 302
Le More (2007): Kartellbekämpfung, Verpflichtungszusagen und Grundrechte: eine schwierige "Ménage à trois", EuZW 2007, 722
Lianos (2013): Competition law remedies in Europe, in: Lianos/Geradin (Eds.), Handbook on European Competition Law. Enforcement and Procedure, 2013
Lowe/Maier-Rigaud (2008): Quo vadis antitrust remedies, in: Hawk (Ed.), Annual proceedings of the Fordham Competition Law Institute 2007, 2008, p. 597
Lübking/von Koppenfels (2012): Effektive Durchsetzung des EU-Wettbewerbsrechts und Verfahrensgarantien – Die Kommission zwischen Gestaltungsmacht und Rechtsbindung, in: Immenga/Körber (Eds.): Die Kommission zwischen zwischen Gestaltungsmacht und Rechtsbindung, 2012
Lugard/Möllmann (2013): The European Commission's Practice Under Article 9 Regulation 1/2003: A Commitment a Day Keeps the Court away?, CPI Antitrust Chronicle, March 2013(3)
Mariniello (2014): Commitments or prohibition. The EU antitrust dilemma, Bruegel Policy Brief, 2014/01, available online
Marsden (2013): The Emperor's Clothes Laid Bare: Commitments Creating the Appearance of Law, While Denying Access to Law, CPI Antitrust Chronicle, October 2013 (1)
McGeown/Orologas (2013): You made a pledge, then keep your promise: Article 9 commitments decisions in European antitrust law, CPI Antitrust Chronicle, March 2013(3)
Messina/Ho (2011): Re-establishing the Orthodoxy of Commitment Decisions under Article 9 of Regulation 1/2003: Comment on Commission v Alrosa, ELR 2011, 737

Mestmäcker (2000): The E.C. Commission's Modernization of Competition Policy: A Challenge to the Community's Constitutional Order, EBOR 200, 401

Mestmäcker/Schweitzer (2014): Europäisches Wettbewerbsrecht, 3rd edition, 2014

Metha/Centella (2010): EU Settlement Procedure: Public Enforcement Policy Perspective, in: Ehlermann/Marquis (Eds.), European Competition Law Annual 2008, 2010

Mische/Višnar (2010): The European Court of Justice confirms approach in De Beers commitment decision, CPN 2010/3, 17

Muguet-Poullennec/Barbier de La Serre (2010): La procédure d'engagements en droit de l'Union: à la recherche du juste équilibre entre efficacité administrative et protection des entreprises, RLC 2010 n° 25, 36

Müller-Tautphaeus (2003): Abhilfebefugnisse der Europäischen Kommission im Wettbewerbsrecht, 2003

O'Donoghue/Padilla (2013): The law and economics of Article 102 TFEU, 2nd edition, 2013

OECD (2016): Commitment decisions in antitrust cases, OECD Policy Roundtables, 2016, available online

Ortiz Blanco/Jörgens/Kellerbauer (2013): in: Ortiz Blanco (Ed.), EU Competition Procedure, 3rd Edition, 2013

Perrot (2013): Managing cases under the effects-based approach: The experience of the French competition authority, in: Bourgeois/Waelbroeck (Eds.), Ten years of effects-based approach in EU competition law, 2013, p. 293

Podszun (2012): Paradigmenwechsel in der kartellbehördlichen Befugnisausübung. Grundlagen, Gefahren, Grenzen, ZWeR 2012, 48

Prek/Lefèvre (2016): Competition litigation before the General Court: Quality if not quantity, CMLR 2016, 65

Rab/Monnoyeur/Sukhtankar (2010): Commitments in EU competition cases. Article 9 of Regulation 1/2003, its application, and the challenges ahead, JECLP 2010, 171

Richter (2012): The settlement procedure in the context of the enforcement tools of European competition law - a comparison and impact analysis, ECLR 2012, 537

Ritter (2012): in: Immenga/Mestmäcker (Eds.), EU-Wettbewerbsrecht, 5th Edition, 2012

Rose (2004): Thomas S. Kuhn: Verständnis und Mißverständnis. Zur Geschichte seiner Rezeption, 2004, available online

Sadowska (2014): Committed to Reform? Pragmatic Antitrust Enforcement in Electricity Markets, 2014

Saitzek (2008): Verpflichtungszusagen im europäischen Kartellrecht, 2008

Schmidt, K. (2003): Umdenken um Kartellverfahrensrecht! Gedanken zur Europäischen VO Nr. 1/2003, Betriebs-Berater 2003, 1237

Schmidtchen/Albert/Voigt (2007): The more economic approach to European competition law, 2007

Schweitzer (2010): Commitment Decisions under Article 9 of Regulation 1/2003. The Developing EC Practice and Case Law, in: Ehlermann/Marquis (Eds.), European Competition Law Annual 2008, 2010, p. 547

Schweitzer (2011): Verpflichtungszusagen im Gemeinschaftsrecht, in: Albach/Bechthold (Eds.), Recht, Ordnung und Wettbewerb, Festschrift zum 70. Geburtstag von Wernhard Möschel, 2011

Schweitzer (2012): Commitment Decisions in the EU and in the Member States: Functions and Risks of a New Instrument of Competition Law Enforcement within a Federal Enforcement Regime, available online

Sofianatos (2009): Injonctions et engagements en droit de la concurrence: étude de droit communautaire, français et grec, 2009

Sousa Ferro (2005): Committing to commitment decisions - unanswered questions on Article 9 decisions, ECLR 2005, 451

Temple Lang (1993): Air Transport in the EEC – Community Antitrust Law Aspects, in: Hawk (Ed.), Annual proceedings of the Fordham Competition Law Institute 1992, 1993

Temple Lang (2006): Commitment decisions and settlements with antitrust authorities and private parties under European antitrust law, in: Hawk (Ed.), Annual proceedings of the Fordham Competition Law Institute 2005, 2006
Temple Lang (2009): Commitment decisions under Regulation 1/2003, in: Gheur/Petit (Eds.), Alternative enforcement techniques in EC competition law, 2009
Van Bael (1986): The antitrust settlement practice of the EC Commission, CMLR 1986, 61
Van Bael (1995): Fining a la carte: the lottery of EU competition law, ECLR 1995, 237
Von Kalben (2018): Verpflichtungszusagen im EU-Wettbewerbsrecht. Eine Untersuchung der Funktionen und Grenzen von Verpflichtungsbeschlüssen nach Art. 9 VO 1/2003 unter besonderer Berücksichtigung des Energiesektors, 2017
Von Winterfeld (1995): Verpflichtungserklärungen in europäischen Kartellverfahren, in: Due/Lutter/Schwarze (Eds.), Festschrift für Everling, Volume II, 1995, p. 1689
Waelbroeck (1986): New forms of settlement of antitrust cases and procedural safeguards: is Regulation 17 falling into abeyance?, ELR 1986, 268
Waelbroeck (2009): The development of a new "settlement culture" in competition cases. What is left to the Courts?, in: Gheur/Petit (Eds.), Alternative enforcement techniques in EC competition law. Settlements, commitments and other novel instruments, 2009
Waelbroeck/Frisch (2013): Après l'arrêt Menarini: l'impact de la Convention européenne de sauvegarde des droits de l'homme et des libertés fondamentales sur les procédures en droit de la concurrence, in: Govaere/Hanf (Eds.), Scrutinizing internal and external dimensions of European law. Les dimensions internes et externes du droit européen à l'épreuve. Liber amicorum Paul Demaret. Vol. II (2013), p. 663
Wagner-Von Papp (2012): Best and even better practices in commitment procedures after Alrosa: the dangers of abandoning the "struggle for competition law", CMLR 2012, 929
Wathelet (2015): Commitment Decisions and the Paucity of Precedent. Editorial, JECLP 2015, 553
Whish (2006): Commitment Decisions under Article 9 of the EC Modernisation Regulation: Some Unanswered Questions, in: Johansson/Wahl/Bernitz (Eds.), Liber Amicorum in Honour of Sven Norberg, A European For All Seasons, 2006, p. 555
Whish/Bailey (2012): Competition Law, 7th edition, 2012
Wils (2006): Settlements of EU Antitrust Investigations: Commitment Decisions under Article 9 of Regulation No. 1/2003, World Competition 2006, 345
Wils (2014a): Ten Years of Regulation 1/2003 – A Retrospective, NZKart 2014, 2
Wils (2014b): The Compatibility with Fundamental Rights of the EU Antitrust Enforcement System in which the European Commission Acts both as Investigator and as First-instance Decision Maker, World Competition 2014, 5
Wils (2015): Ten years of commitment decisions under Article 9 of Regulation 1/2003: Too much of a good thing?, available on www.ssrn.com

Chapter 3
The Relaxation of the Link Between Harm and Remedy

The present chapter deals with the relaxation of the link between harm and remedy brought about by the use of the Article 9 instead of the Article 7 procedure. In a nutshell, it aims at assessing whether and to what extent the allegation that the recourse to consensual commitments leads to remedies that go beyond what could have been imposed unilaterally is correct.

3.1 Introduction

Some introductory remarks are called for. First, it will be explained why the link between harm and remedy constitutes a particularly important limitation to the Commission's powers in the context of Article 7. In that regard, the "general clause" character of the said provision and the necessity to distinguish competition law remedies from regulatory remedies will be emphasised. Second, a more detailed presentation of the criticism according to which the Article 9 procedure entails a shift towards increased enforcement errors and regulatory remedies is necessary. This will, third, pave the way for a preliminary comment and for an outline of the structure of the remainder of the present chapter.

3.1.1 The Importance of the Link Between Harm and Remedy in the Context of Article 7: A Barrier Against the Blurring of the Boundaries Between Competition Law and Regulation

In the context of Article 7, the requirement to respect a link between harm—or infringement—and remedy is of particular importance. This importance can be

K. Reiter, *Market Design Powers of the European Commission?*, Munich Studies on Innovation and Competition 13, https://doi.org/10.1007/978-3-662-60711-4_3

explained with the fact that the said requirement has to compensate for the lack of other constraints that results from the "general clause" character of Article 7 and hence to provide the major safeguard against the imposition of a regulatory remedy.

3.1.1.1 The "General Clause" Character of Article 7 and the Difficulties of Defining Limits for the Content of an Article 7 Remedy

Article 7(1) defines the possible content of remedies in general and abstract terms that give the Commission a broad margin of manoeuvre. Besides the open wording, this result is also fostered by the governance mechanism of the provision. The latter restricts only the ends of the Commission's action, but not its means. In fact, while it follows from Article 7(1) that the sole legitimate purpose of a remedy is to put an infringement of Articles 101 or 102 TFEU to an end, the provision also makes it clear that the means at the Commission's disposal in order to achieve this end are not limited: In principle, the Commission may impose any remedy unilaterally, regardless of whether it has a structural or a behavioural character.[1] There is no exhaustive set of types of remedies to which the Commission is confined. Certainly, by means of a rather long-winded phrasing, Article 7(1) also confirms that any remedy must meet the requirements of the principle of proportionality. However, the latter result follows already from the nature of the principle of proportionality as a general principle of law and its codification in Article 5 TEU. The incorporation of the principle of proportionality into the wording of Article 7(1) has only a declaratory nature.[2] Overall, albeit phrased in a more lavish manner, Article 7(1) hence does not provide for more restrictions to the Commission's remedial actions than its predecessor, Article 3(1) Regulation 17/62, which stipulated simply that the Commission had the power to put infringements to an end.[3]

---

[1]See Recital 12: "[...] Commission's power to impose any remedy, whether behavioural or structural [...]". See also Hjelmeng (2013), 1008: "[...] Article 7 is focused on terminating the infringement [...]. However, there is a certain flexibility in Article 7 with regard to the type of remedies (structural or behavioural), the form of remedy (positive or negative orders) and the purpose of the remedy (termination of infringements, prevention of future infringements and restoration of competition)".

[2]See Klees (2005), § 6, 81; Hauser (2009), 186; Krings (2012), 230ff, 241; Petzold (2012), 200.

[3]See Article 3(1) Regulation 17/62: "Where the Commission, upon application or upon its own initiative, finds that there is infringement of Article 85 or Article 86 of the Treaty, it may by decision require the undertakings or associations of undertakings concerned to bring such infringement to an end."

On the fact that Article 7 Regulation 1/03 does not impose stricter limits on the Commission than Article 3 Regulation 17, see Mestmäcker/Schweitzer (2004), § 20, 1: "[Artikel 7 VO 1/03] entspricht dem bisherigen Artikel 3 der VO 17. Auch die in Art. 7 VO 1/03 neu hervorgehobenen strukturellen Abhilfen sind schon bisher geltendes Recht. Die zu Art. 3 VO 17 ergangene Rechtsprechung und Literatur behalten ihre Bedeutung." O'Donoghue/Padilla (2006), 676, fn 2: "The legal powers conferred by Regulation 1/2003 are either identical to or broader than those conferred by Regulation 17." See also GC, T-491/07 (Cartes Bancaires, 2012), 437: "Selon la

The open wording and governance mechanism of Article 3(1) Regulation 17/62 and Article 7(1) Regulation 1/03 corresponds to the open textured nature of Articles 101 and 102 TFEU. The difficulty of providing an exhaustive list of prohibited anticompetitive practices and the resulting need for general and abstract formulations on the infringement side warrants the use of an equally open structured provision also with a view to the remedies that can be imposed by the Commission. This reasoning is nicely captured by the following words of Advocate General Warner, taken from his opinion in Commercial Solvents:

> I would accept the argument of the Commission that the reason why Article 3 (1) [of Regulation 17/62] was left in general terms was that infringements of Article 85 and 86 can take so many forms that it would have been impossible for the authors of the Regulation to provide a catalogue of the measures capable of being ordered by the Commission in order to bring such infringements to an end.[4]

The necessary openness of Article 7 makes it hard to determine the admissible content of remedies in advance and in the abstract. An attempt to seize this content positively is from the outset doomed to fail. It is only possible to delimit the outer boundaries of the Commission's powers. However, even these boundaries can mostly not be determined in the abstract, but must be defined by reference to the concrete infringement in question.[5]

3.1.1.2 The Link Between Harm and Remedy As a Barrier Against the Blurring of the Boundaries Between Competition Law and Regulation

Against the backdrop of the general openness of Article 7, the role of the link between harm and remedy as requirement that puts a limit to the Commission's remedial powers becomes paramount. One particular function of this limitation may be seen in the prevention of the imposition of a regulatory remedy that would blur the boundaries between competition law and regulation.

It is notoriously difficult to define "regulation".[6] For the present purpose, it suffices to employ a negative and formal definition according to which "regulation"

---

jurisprudence relative à l'article 3, paragraphe 1, du règlement n° 17, applicable, par analogie, à l'article 7, paragraphe 1, du règlement n° 1/2003 [. . .]".

[4]AG Warner, opinion in CJ, 6/73 (Commercial Solvents, 1974), 272. The same considerations apply for Article 7 Regulation 1/03.

[5]See Mestmäcker (1974), 529: "Die Verpflichtung der Unternehmen, die festgestellte Zuwiderhandlung abzustellen, konkretisiert den Verbotsgehalt im Einzelfall. Demgemäß entscheiden Inhalt und Zweck der in Bezug genommenen Verbotsnorm über den zulässigen Inhalt der Verbotsentscheidung. Die Grenzen des zulässigen Entscheidungsinhalts lassen sich deshalb nicht generell bestimmen. Die Verpflichtungsentscheidung muss sich auf die festgestellte Zuwiderhandlung beziehen." Similarly Hauser (2009), 116.

[6]See eg Masing (2003), 1ff; (2006), 9; von Danwitz (2004), 977; Ruffert (2010), § 7; Ackermann/ Petzold (2011), 4; Dunne (2014a), 229.

describes any public intervention on the market that pursues goals that go beyond those of competition law. The differences and overlaps between competition law and regulation have been abundantly discussed and shall not be repeated here in all detail.[7] Only one particular aspect shall be emphasised: Even if one employs a narrow definition of regulation that relates only to a society's handling of market power and does not extend to further goals like the provision of universal services, environmental protection or redistribution of wealth,[8] it remains possible to draw a useful distinction between competition law and regulation. This distinction is expressed in the contrast of pairs of words such as "keeping markets open" and "opening up of markets" or "preserving" and "creating" competition. From an ideal point of view, competition law predicates on the premise that markets are functioning and competition is self-supporting as long as certain limited rules are respected. The competition rules thus merely serve the goal to keep markets open that are in principle functioning and to preserve competition of which the conditions are at the outset present. On the contrary, regulation rests on the assumption of inexistent or failed markets and a resulting lack of competition. Regulatory rules thus serve the goal to open up those markets and to introduce, create and maintain competition of which the conditions are at the outset absent.[9]

---

[7]See eg Motta (2004), xviii; Kirchner (2004); Masing (2006), 47ff; Ibanez Colomo (2010); Ackermann/Petzold (2011), 6ff; O'Donoghue/Padilla (2013), 44ff; Sofianatos (2009), 355f; Jones/Sufrin (2011), 54ff; Dunne (2014b), 411ff and (2014a), 228ff; Kipiani (2014), 413f; von Kalben (2018), 198ff. For numerous further references regarding the "competition versus regulation debate" see Sadowska (2014), 2 fn 9.

[8]Against such a narrow definition see eg Lepsius (2010), § 19, 27f, who emphasises that regulation is precisely characterised by the fact that is pursues broader social goals than the control of market power. See also Masing (2006), D 155, who contrasts the "one-dimensionality" of competition law and the "multi-dimensionality" of regulation; Kersten (2010), 316 fn 114: "Regulierung ist die zielplurale Gestaltung von Marktprozessen".

[9]See O'Donoghue/Padilla (2013), 46f: "Competition law is a set of principles which protects competition from anticompetitive conduct. [. . .] By contrast, [. . .] sector-specific regimes can in some cases take pro-active measures to effectively create competition on downstream markets. Incumbents may be, for instance, forced to divest their upstream operations even in the absence of any proven abuse of dominance. In the case of margin squeeze, an NRA may also be tempted to adopt wholesale rates that are favourable to the incumbent's competitors to stimulate entry."

Masing (2006), 48f: "So geht das allgemeine Wettbewerbsrecht von einem bestehenden, sich selbst herstellenden und tragenden Wettbewerb aus. [. . .] Demgegenüber obliegt der Regulierungsverwaltung die Aufgabe, Wettbewerb erst zu schaffen (bzw. zu ermöglichen). Ihr Ausgangspunkt liegt darin, dass sich selbst tragender Wettbewerb in den Netzwirtschaften gerade nicht von selbst einstellt [. . .] Er muss erst strukturiert und abgesichert werden, wofür besondere Interventionsmöglichkeiten erforderlich sind. Regulierung hat das Ziel, die Liberalisierungsagenda durch nach vorn blickend wettbewerbsfördernde Entscheidungen durchzusetzen und eine monopolbestimmte Marktsituation, wie sie sich als folge der ehemals staatlichen Monopole ergeben hat, in Wettbewerbsstrukturen zu überführen."

Sofianatos (2009), 355f: "[. . .] la régulation désigne une forme d'intervention [. . .] qui a pour objet de créer les conditions d'une concurrence souhaitable [. . .] Le droit de la concurrence n'adopte pas, du moins en ce qu'il sanctionne les comportements anticoncurrentiels, une perspective de régulation; il ne s'agit que, au coup par coup, de ramener à l'ordre ordinaire de l'offre et de la

Despite an undeniable proximity between competition law and regulation, the distinction between the two areas is important. If the Commission were allowed to use its powers under Regulation 1/03 for regulatory purposes, it could circumvent the specific "safeguards and limitations that control the enactment and implementation of regulation".[10] In that regard, it shall for the present purposes suffice to emphasise one particular point[11]: The danger that a regulatory use of competition law represents for the separation of powers.[12]

If the Commission were allowed to use its powers under Regulation 1/03 for regulatory purposes, it could circumvent the requirements of the legal bases that are provided by the TFEU for the adoption of regulatory acts. Such acts can be based in particular either on Article 114 TFEU, or, to a more limited extent, also on Article 106(3) TFEU. The adoption of regulatory acts on the basis of Article 114 TFEU takes place in accordance with the ordinary legislative procedure pursuant to Articles 289(1) and 294 TFEU. It hence requires in particular the approval of the Parliament and the Council. Article 106(3) TFEU enables the Commission to act alone. However, the provision has a limited scope of application[13]; moreover it allows only for addressing directives or decisions to the Member States. The liberalisation measures adopted in the sectors of energy, telecommunications and postal services were mostly based on Article 114 TFEU.[14] Also Regulation 2015/751 on

---

demande des comportements déviants". Idem, 385: "L'intervention des régulateurs sectoriels est une intervention ex ante, visant la construction et le maintien d'équilibres dans des secteurs partiellement ouverts à la concurrence, tandis que celle des autorités de concurrence se met plutôt en place ex post, avec pour objectif de préserver la concurrence en l'état."

Similar thoughts about the distinction of regulation from competition law underly also the opinion of the US Supreme Court delivered by Justice Scalia in the Trinko case (2004): "The [Telecommunications Act] is in an important respect much more ambitious than the antitrust laws. It attempts "*to eliminate the monopolies* enjoyed by the inheritors of AT&T's local franchises." *[...]* Section 2 of the Sherman Act, by contrast, seeks merely to prevent *unlawful monopolization*. It would be a serious mistake to conflate the two goals. The Sherman Act is indeed the "Magna Carta of free enterprise," *[...]* but it does not give judges *carte blanche* to insist that a monopolist alter its way of doing business whenever some other approach might yield greater competition."

[10]Dunne (2014b), 443.

[11]For other aspects of the problem see Dunne (2014b), 443f. In the context of a potential use of Article 9 for regulatory purposes, Dunne underlines that "the need for sufficient political support, the use of regulatory impact assessment tools, the skilled market-specific expertise of enforcers, the high degree of stakeholder involvement in all aspects of the regulatory process, plus the typically robust opportunities for judicial review together enable a relatively high level of outside scrutiny and supervision of the regulatory enterprise". According to her, the same is not true for Article 9 Regulation 1/03.

[12]See on the separation of powers doctrine as an argument against a regulatory use of competition law also Dunne (2014b), 435f with further references.

[13]According to consistent case law, the provision empowers the Commission only "to lay down general rules specifying the obligations arising from the Treaty which are binding on the Member States as regards the undertakings referred to in Article [106(1) and (2)]; see eg CJ, C-202/88 (Telecommunications terminals equipment, 1991), 14; Mestmäcker/Schweitzer (2012), Art. 106(3), 2 with further references in fn 5.

[14]For overviews see Wernicke (2011), Art. 106, 90ff; Immenga/Mestmäcker (2012), A.V., 36ff.

interchange fees for card-based payment transactions was adopted on the basis of this provision. If regulatory measures were adopted by the Commission on the basis of Regulation 1/03 instead of by the Parliament and the Council upon proposal by the Commission on the basis of Article 114 TFEU, such measures would lack the democratic legitimation that is ensured by the ordinary legislative procedure.[15] This is problematic, not least because the regulatory "creation" of competition constitutes normally a more intrusive intervention than the "preservation" of competition that is the goal of competition law. The decision about whether a market should be subjected to such an increased intervention hence needs a higher degree of democratic legitimation.[16]

Consequently, contrary to a regulatory remedy, a competition law remedy should not pursue the general goal of opening up a market or creating more competition.[17] It should only "restore" competition to the extent that it is disturbed by an infringement of the competition rules. A fortiori, a competition law remedy should not aim at other potential regulatory goals such as the provision of universal services, environmental protection or redistribution of wealth. For the sake of completeness, it must still be underlined that this does not mean that regulatory intervention is generally undesirable. It only should not be based on competition law. Moreover, the statement that a competition law remedy should not aim at regulatory goals does not mean that the goals of competition law and regulation never overlap and that regulatory goals cannot be taken into account in a competition law context as a positive side effect of a remedy that remains still within the boundaries of competition law.

---

[15]The importance of the distinction between competition law and regulation for the separation of powers can be illustrated with the action taken by the EU against high roaming charges: Competition law did not allow the Commission to intervene alone. However, with the approval of the Council and the Parliament, the Commission was able to introduce price regulation. See Ackermann (2010); Dunne (2014b), 436 with further references.

[16]See Sofianatos (2009), 388: "L'emploi de mesures correctives, non seulement pour protéger la concurrence mais également pour structurer le marché et y introduire la compétition inquiète. L'ouverture des marchés est une tâche traditionnellement dévolue au législateur. Il s'agit d'une question politique [. . .]".

See also Dunne (2014b), 435: "The determination of whether breach of the competition rules has occurred is properly considered a judicial or adjudicative function [. . .]. By contrast, the enactment of regulation is a legislative task, whereas its implementation is typically a delegated executive one. In formulating regulation, the legislature makes political choices [. . .] Thus, it has been argued that competition authorities enforcing the competition rules should not apply or sanction use of competition law to create de facto regulation within a sector, given that this is a legislative rather than an executive or judicial function".

[17]See also Bueren (2011), 473: "Das allgemeine Wettbewerbsrecht dient lediglich dazu, (mutmaßlich) rechtswidriges Verhalten zu unterbinden, grundsätzlich aber nicht dazu, einen Markt durch darüber hinausgehende Maßnahmen wettbewerblich zu gestalten"; Podszun (2012), 65: "Ein staatlicher Gestaltungswille ist hier fehl am Platz. Kartellrecht erhebt nicht den Anspruch der Marktlenkung oder Regulierung. Es ist vielmehr gerade der Koordinierungsfunktion des Marktes [. . .] verpflichtet"; von Kalben (2018), 164f and 207f.

3.1.2 *The Criticism Regarding the Relaxation of the Link Between Harm and Remedy in the Context of the Article 9 Procedure: A Shift Towards Increased Enforcement Errors and Regulation*

3.1.2.1 Abstract Risk of Enforcement Errors

Critics of the Article 9 procedure emphasise the risk of enforcement errors.[18] The potential sources of such errors are manifold and can either lead to under- or over-enforcement.[19] Under- and over-enforcement must in this connection be understood as remedies that either stay behind or go beyond restoring compliance with Article 101 and 102 TFEU, or, in other words, as remedies that stay behind or go beyond what the Commission could or would have imposed on the basis of Article 7. A first potential source of error that may lead to either under- or over-enforcement is the "shift of focus" from the infringement to the remedy.[20] In that connection, commentators decry, on the one hand, the lack of a thorough investigation and circumscription of the alleged infringement.[21] On the other hand, they condemn that the theory of harm is developed to fit the remedy and not vice-versa. In that regard, the critics denounce the fact that the negotiations about the remedy take place simultaneously with or even prior to the issuance of the preliminary assessment.[22]

With a view to further potential sources of error, it is useful to distinguish between under- and over-enforcement. On the one hand, strategic abuse of the negotiation process by the concerned undertaking[23] or regulatory capture of the Commission in favour of the concerned undertaking and to the detriment of third parties and the competitive process[24] are considered to result in insufficient

[18]Generally on enforcement errors in the context of commitment decisions see eg Cengiz (2011), 135f and 150f; Dunne (2014b), 439; Gautier/Petit (2014), 5.

[19]On that distinction see already Sect. 2.2.2.2.2.3 with footnote 107 above.

[20]See Melamed (1995), 15; Gerard (2013) 2 and 13; OECD (2016), 38.

[21]See eg Cengiz (2011), 136f; Schweitzer (2011), 647 and (2012), 3; Wagner-Von Papp (2012), 950; Mariniello (2014), 4.

[22]See eg Cook (2006), 215f; Georgiev (2007), 1019f; Gerard (2013), 13f; Botteman/Patsa (2013), 369f; Sadowska (2014), 50 with fn 185; Jenny (2015), 736. But see Schweitzer (2010), 557: "It appears that the Coca-Cola practice of publishing the preliminary assessment only after the commitments have been agreed remains the exception".

[23]See Budzinski/Kuchinke (2012), 275f: "incentives to propose ineffective remedies"; Podszun (2012), 66: "Verhandlungen sind [. . .] für die einseitige Prägung durch das sündige Unternehmen anfällig"; McGeown/Orologas (2013), 5: "excessive leeway [for the parties offering the commitments] in designing the proposal"; Botteman/Patsa (2013), 360: "the investigated company's incentive to secure commitments with the narrowest possible scope [. . .] may render the final commitments ineffective".

[24]See Wagner-Von Papp (2012), 951: "The introduction of negotiations between the opponents brings with it the spectre of transforming the adversarial procedure [. . .] into a common quest for a mutually acceptable solution, in which the interests of the authority and the undertakings concerned become more and more aligned"; Budzinski/Kuchinke (2012), 281: "there is vital danger that

remedies. On the other hand, in particular the influence of third parties on the Commission[25] and the strong incentives for the concerned undertaking to prevent an infringement decision[26] are said to constitute reasons for overbroad remedies. Which of the two kinds of error risks prevails remains unclear. On the one hand, the strength of the Commission's negotiation power vis-à-vis the concerned undertakings could make under-enforcement unlikely.[27] On the other hand, commentators have underlined the likeliness of under-enforcement in view of past experiences with ineffective remedies.[28]

With a view to both types of enforcement errors, it is recalled that "competition has no lobby".[29] Critics thereby stress that, even where the Commission, the concerned undertaking and third parties participating in the market test agree, the remedy may still be inadequate to protect the competitive process as such.[30] In support of that conclusion, they rely either on the lack of a thorough investigation[31]; on the fact that private incentives for remedial action are too disperse to provide for a sufficient protection of the competitive process[32]; or on the compromise that is inherent in any negotiated solution.[33] The Commission is considered to defend the public interest in the protection of the competitive process in a sufficient manner in adversarial procedures. However, as regards negotiated procedures, commentators see a significant risk that the Commission fails to fulfil this task.[34]

---

competition authorities and anticompetitive companies become 'partners in crime'"; Mariniello (2014), 6: the win-win situation for the Commission and the concerned undertakings "does not mitigate the harm to a plethora of losers".

[25]Botteman/Patsa (2013), 361: "Third parties' incentives to secure the broadest commitments possible [...] may also render the final commitments inadequate"; Gerard (2013), 14f: "[The market test] opens up space for building constituencies promoting specific business interests"; Gyselen (2014), 254, who states that inter alia due to third parties' right to sue if the remedy does not go far enough, "it is tempting for the EC to use the Alrosa comfort zone to err on the safe side and over-enforce the antitrust rules".

[26]Georgiev (2007), 1028: "[The concerned undertakings are] willing to accept broader or unorthodox remedies in exchange for the more efficient procedure and the avoidance of fines and negative publicity"; see also MK (2009), 499; Cengiz (2011), 136 and the references in Sect. 2.2.2.1 with footnotes 65ff above.

[27]In that direction Cengiz (2011), 136 and 151.

[28]See Podszun (2012), 66 and Botteman/Patsa (2013), 360f, who rely on results of the Commission's Merger Remedies Study (2005) that show that the Commission accepted commitments that did not go far enough.

[29]Wagner-Von Papp (2012), 951, with the hint (fn 84) that this adage is attributed to Franz Böhm.

[30]See Schweitzer (2011), 647; Wagner-Von Papp (2012), 950f; Dunne (2014b), 440; OECD (2016), 34; also Cengiz (2011), 151, who mentions a "strong public interest in the correct application of competition rules in each individual case and the imposition of proportionate remedies which go beyond the specific interests and incentives the parties involved in proceedings may have".

[31]Schweitzer (2011), 647.

[32]See Wagner-Von Papp (2012), 950 and 951.

[33]See Dunne (2014b), 440.

[34]See in particular Wagner-Von Papp (2012), 950f; similarly also Schweitzer (2011), 647.

3.1.2.2 Abstract Risk of Abuse of Commitments for Regulatory Purposes

In so far as the discomfort caused by the risk of enforcement errors concerns the risk of over-enforcement, it overlaps with a further point of critique that is levied at the relaxation of the link between harm and remedy in the context of Article 9: The potential instrumentalisation of commitments for regulatory purposes.[35] The gist of the argument is that the commitment procedure allows the Commission to extract remedies that do not merely put an infringement to an end, but go beyond in that they strive to open up a market or generally improve the conditions for competition. The criticism echoes similar concerns that continue to be raised in the U.S. against an excessive use of consent decrees.[36] It is argued that commitments run the risk of creating the typical inefficiencies of regulation. These are said to result from subjecting private action to government approval, which does not keep pace with changing market conditions.[37] Other commentators infer support for their warnings against an instrumentalisation of commitments for regulatory purposes from Hayek's concept of competition as a discovery procedure and the resulting need for a rule-oriented competition policy. In essence, they argue that the use of commitments enables the Commission to proceed to active market design according to its own imaginations. In view of the Commission's necessary knowledge deficit, such market design is, however, considered prone to error and inferior to the solutions that are found by the market participants themselves.[38]

---

[35]See eg Georgiev (2007), 1026ff; Muguet-Poullennec/Barbier de la Serre (2010), 36; Klees (2010), 694; Ibanez Colomo (2010), 286f; Cengiz (2011), 136; Schweitzer (2011), 656f and (2012), 3; Bueren (2011), 473ff; Hjelmeng (2013), 1021 and 1030; Gerard (2013), 18ff; Lianos (2013), 448f; Dunne (2014b), 400 and 429; Kipiani (2014), 433; Brenner (2014), 672; Sadowska (2014), 43ff; Jenny (2015), 763; Schulz (2018).

[36]See eg First (1995); Melamed (1995); Epstein (2007); Ginsburg/Wright (2013).

[37]Georgiev (2007), 1028: He warns against the risk of "economy-wide inefficiency created by subjecting companies to (imperfect) prospective regulation through commitments or consent decrees; by definition these tools require that companies seek the government's approval when economic conditions change and an adjustment of behavior is needed. This leads to economic inefficiencies both in the case when approval is not forthcoming and even when it is merely slow".

[38]Budzinski/Kuchinke (2012), 282f: "[T]he trend towards more complex and more 'constructive' [– in the sense of actively designing and moulding the new structures –] interventions into the market structure and situation in the course of the remedy deals becomes rather obvious. [. . .] [N]either does it fit the idea of rule-based competition policy, nor the concept of limiting intervention into competitive markets in order to restrict the authority to the task of preventing the self-erosion of competition by anticompetitive arrangements and conduct. Eventually, the perspective of economic theory raises doubts as to whether the competition authority – with or without cooperation of the industry in question – possess[es] sufficient knowledge and competence to design and configurate competitive markets (*Hayek [. . .]*)".

Podszun (2012), 49: "[D]as Entdeckungsverfahren der Marktteilnehmer wird in einzelnen Entscheidungen durch eine gezielte Steuerung seitens der Behörden ersetzt (Gefahr des market engineering)"; ibid, 65: "Wer mit von Hayek vom Entdeckungsverfahren Wettbewerb überzeugt ist, muss zukunftsorientierten, behördlichen Vorgaben an unternehmerische Entscheider skeptisch

3.1.2.3 The Materialisation of the Risks of Enforcement Errors and Instrumentalisation of the Commitment Procedure for Regulatory Purposes

To what extent the previously described abstract risks of enforcement errors and of the abuse of the commitment procedure for regulatory purposes actually materialise in the Commission's practice remains largely unclear. There is widespread agreement that some decisions give rise to concerns. The standard quote[39] for a decision in which the Commission is considered to have gone beyond what it could have imposed under Article 7 is Coca-Cola.[40] In order to substantiate the claim that the Commission instrumentalises the Article 9 procedure for regulatory purposes, commentators typically refer to the commitments accepted in the energy sector, either more in general[41] or more particularly to the ones that resulted in the divestiture of transmission grids by vertically integrated companies.[42] While these two examples are at least widely agreed on as cases in which the Commission overstepped its competences, commentators seem more reluctant to make the same statement also in regard of other commitment decisions.[43] Rather, the critics often confine themselves to emphasising that the Commission accepted commitments in cases involving complex facts or novel questions of law—without claiming expressly, however, that in these cases the Commission's preliminary assessment was wrong.[44] At least

---

gegenüber stehen. Ökonomisch ist die Rationalität der Marktteilnehmer derjenigen der Fachbehörde stets überlegen, rechtlich bedeutet dies einen Verzicht auf market engineering".

[39]Eg Cook (2006), 212 fn 6; Rab/Monnoyeur/Sukhtankar (2010), 181 and 183; Forrester (2010), 659; Schweitzer (2010), 555f and 560 fn 71; Cavicchi (2011), 14; Kellerbauer (2011), 4 fn 41; Falconi (2011), 52 fn 45 together with fn 23; Wagner-Von Papp (2012), 955 fn 100; O'Donoghue/Padilla (2013), 898 fn 74; Botteman/Patsa (2013), 360 fn 63; Jenny (2015), 724ff; von Kalben (2018), 129.

[40]COMP/39.116 (Coca-Cola, 2005).

[41]Eg Ibanez Colomo (2010), 298ff; Sadowska (2011); Hancher/de Hauteclocque (2010), 322ff; Schweitzer (2011), 649; O'Donoghue/Padilla (2013), 901; Gerard (2013), 9f with fn 41; Dunne (2014b), 408 and 421; Jones/Sufrin (2014), 983; Kipiani (2014), 3419ff; Jenny (2015), 727ff; for recent detailed studies of whether the Commission instrumentalises the article 9 procedure for regulatory purposes in the energy sector also von Kalben (2018), 210ff and Schulz (2018).

[42]Eg Klees (2009), 381f and (2011), 17f; Cengiz (2011), 137f; Podszun (2012), 63; Gerard (2013), 19f; von Kalben (2018), 281ff; Botteman/Patsa (2013), 353f; for a good overview of the criticism levelled at the E.On and RWE decisions see also Bueren (2011), 474f.

[43]See eg Podszun (2012), 66: He states with regard to the Rambus decision (COMP/38636, 2009) that the commitments may have been appropriate in view of the particular constellation of a patent ambush. Nonetheless, he is "surprised" by the "ease" with which the Commission approaches price regulation ("Mag es in dieser besonderen Konstellation eines patent ambush auch angemessen gewesen sein, eine [. . .] Zusage [mit Kappungsgrenzen] für bindend zu erklären, so überrascht doch die Leichtigkeit, mit der sich die Kommission hier in die Nähe einer Preisregulierung begibt"). Moreover Wagner-von Papp (2012), 969, who emphasises that his article should not be understood as a "criticism of the Commission's actual practice", but merely of the "institutional set-up", which he considers insufficient to "ensure the continued high quality of commitment decisions".

[44]See eg Gerard (2013), 20; Dunne (2014b), 437.

some commentators seem to concede that excesses do not occur systematically.[45] Nonetheless, the possibility that the potential risks of enforcement errors or a regulatory instrumentalisation of commitments materialise is said to be "more then merely theoretical"[46] or "non-negligible".[47]

3.1.3 *Preliminary Comment and Outline of the Remainder of the Present Chapter*

The present chapter endeavours to assess the pertinence of the criticism that is levied at the relaxation of the link between harm and remedy in the context of Article 9 in more detail. For this purpose, a concrete research agenda will be developed below. Beforehand, it is still necessary to address one particular point: The alleged risk that Article 9 increases the risk of under-enforcement, i.e. of remedies that stay behind what the Commission could or would have imposed in an Article 7 decision.

3.1.3.1 Article 9 Only Increases the Abstract Risk of Over-Enforcement

It is submitted that, when compared to Article 7 decisions, Article 9 decisions do not increase the risk of under-enforcement.[48] They only increase the risk of over-enforcement.[49]

---

[45]Schweitzer (2011), 657: "sich mitunter abzeichnende Tendenz der Kommission, über das Mandat zum Schutz des auf einem Markt möglichen Wettbewerbs auf die Herstellung abweichender wettbewerblicher Strukturen zu dringen"; Dunne (2014b): "It is not contended here that the Commission uses the Article 9 procedure only in circumstances where the necessary elements for liability in the context of an Article 7 infringement decision cannot be made out on the facts" (425); "Although our case survey clarifies that [the risk of a regulatory instrumentalisation of commitment decisions] is not a wholesale criticism of current practice, certain more questionable quasi-regulatory applications of Article 9 are discernible" (443).

See with a view to Article 102 TFEU cases also Gyselen (2014), 255f: After reviewing the Commission's post Guidance Paper commitment practice, he concludes that "all in all, the EC does not seem to have relaxed the proportionality standard in Article 9 cases". Gyselen exempts only the structural remedies accepted by the Commission from his conclusion.

[46]Cengiz (2011), 137 and 151.

[47]Dunne (2014b), 431.

[48]But see Sadowska (2014), 55f, who emphasises that the "potential mismatch between commitments and anticompetitive concerns" entails the risk "that the Commission accepts less than is required to remedy an anticompetitive problem". As will be argued immediately below, in my view, Sadowska fails to see that this risk exists to the same extent also under Article 7.

[49]See for a similar conclusion also Botteman/Patsa (2013), 361: "While the [investigated company's incentive to secure commitments with the narrowest possible scope and third parties incentives to secure the broadest commitments possible] are to a certain extent balanced during the Market Test stage, the risk that the EC goes beyond what is strictly necessary to restore competitive conditions in the relevant market remains largely unchecked. This is principally owed to the

3.1.3.1.1 No Increase in Risk of Under-Enforcement

An increase in the risk of under-enforcement can with a high likeliness be excluded. In that connection, it is useful to distinguish between the interests of third parties who are capable of ensuring their rights themselves and the broader interest of the general public in the protection of the competitive process. With respect to both, two thinkable sources of under-enforcement errors exist in the context of Article 9 when compared to Article 7: On the one hand, the fact that the Commission does not have to find that there is an infringement; on the other hand, the consensuality of the Article 9 procedure, as opposed to the adversarial nature of Article 7. Consensuality may lead to errors of under-enforcement where it promotes the capacity of the concerned undertaking to strategically abuse the Article 9 procedure or where it leads to an alignment of the interests of the Commission with those of the concerned undertaking.

3.1.3.1.1.1 The Interests of Third Parties Who Are Capable of Ensuring Their Rights Themselves

In comparison with Article 7, Article 9 does not curtail the rights of third parties who claim that the Commission should have imposed a further reaching remedy.

On the one hand, an increase in the risk of under-enforcement of the rights of third parties cannot be derived from the relaxation of the Commission's investigative duties. In fact, it is submitted that the relaxation of the Commission's investigative duties under Article 9 is unidirectional. The Commission is relieved of the obligation to prove the infringement. It is, however, not dispensed of the duty to ensure that the principles laid down by Articles 101 and 102 TFEU are applied. Certainly, the Commission's obligation to investigate a case is subject to the Commission's right to prioritise cases. However, third parties and in particular complainants can challenge an Article 9 decision by claiming that the Commission has violated the discretion it has in prioritising cases.[50] Since the relaxation of the Commission's investigative duties under Article 9 is unidirectional, the same standard applies for such an appeal regardless of whether the decision has been adopted on the basis of Article 7 or of Article 9.[51]

On the other hand, an increase in the risk of under-enforcement of the rights of third parties can also not be derived from the risks brought about by the consensual nature of the Article 9 procedure. First, the market test that must be carried out before any commitment may be adopted acts as a counterbalance to risks stemming from a

---

simplified proportionality test that applies under the commitment procedure, as established by the CoJ's ruling in Alrosa".

[50] See for the possibility of third parties to challenge commitment decisions on grounds of under-enforcement, GC, T-76/14 (Morningstar, 2016); for a discussion of the judgment see Idot (2016), 31, and Paemen/Baltrusch (2017), 99.

[51] See also Sect. 2.2.2.2.2.2 with footnotes 96ff above and Sect. 5.1.3.1 with footnotes 81ff below.

potential strategic abuse of the Article 9 procedure by the concerned undertaking. Since such a market test is not prescribed for an Article 7 decision, its benefits cancel out the disadvantage of a potential strategic abuse of Article 9. Second, the rights of third parties and complainants to challenge the decision for violation of the discretion to prioritise cases prevent the Commission from unlawfully aligning its interest with those of the undertakings concerned. In that regard, it must once more be emphasised that the Court of Justice insisted in Alrosa on the Commission's obligation to verify whether the commitment that it intends to make binding adequately addresses its concerns.[52] The standard for challenging a remedy because it does not adequately address the Commission's concerns is the one for violation of the discretion to prioritise cases. As pointed out above that standard is the same, regardless of whether a decision has been adopted on the basis of Article 7 or of Article 9.

3.1.3.1.1.2 The Interest of the General Public in the Protection of the Competitive Process

It is true that the interests which are represented in the market test or in potential challenges of the Commission's decision in court do not necessarily fully depict the interest of the general public in the protection of the competitive process.[53] In particular, the stakes of some of the parties who are affected by a remedy may not be important enough to provide a sufficient incentive to participate in the market test or to challenge a commitment. There is hence a risk that such "dispersed interests" will not be taken into account. However, this risk exists also in the context of Article 7. The reasons why a remedy may be under-enforcing the competition rules in that it fails to satisfy dispersed interests may be different under Article 7 and Article 9. It is submitted, however, that there is no good reason to assume that the risk is greater under Article 9 than under Article 7.

On the one hand, Article 7 does not provide for a stricter obligation for the Commission to ensure that the principles laid down by Articles 101 and 102 TFEU are applied than Article 9. Also in the context of Article 7, the risk that under-enforcement errors are caused by a lack of thoroughness of the investigation is checked for only by the right of third parties to challenge the Commission's decision for violation of its discretion to prioritise cases. Moreover, the investigative resources that are needed to meet the requirement of Article 7 regarding the finding of an infringement may prompt the Commission to concentrate on certain aspects of a case. It may therefore contribute to neglecting dispersed interests that are not the focus of the Commission's investigation. On the contrary, the reduced standard of prove available under Article 9 may enable the Commission to take also dispersed interests into account.

---

[52]See Sect. 2.2.1.4.1.1 with footnote 53 above.

[53]See Sect. 3.1.2.1 with footnote 30 above.

On the other hand, it is true that the consensual nature of commitments increases the risk of under-enforcement of dispersed interests in so far as the risks of a strategic abuse of the procedure by the concerned undertaking or of an alignment of the interest of the Commission with that of the concerned undertaking do not or not to the same extent exist in the context of Article 7. However, the adversarial nature of Article 7 displays independent weaknesses that may themselves lead to under-enforcement of dispersed interests. On balance, these weaknesses will even out the deficits of Article 9. First, the adversarial nature of an Article 7 remedy increases the likelihood of an appeal by the concerned undertaking. In order to avoid a potential defeat in court, the Commission may be inclined to impose a less far-reaching remedy that does not suffice to satisfy all dispersed interests. Second, the adversarial nature of an injunction lacks the benefits that may result from the involvement of the investigated company in the design of the remedy. As explained above, such an involvement may reduce information asymmetries and also lead to a more effective implementation of the remedy.[54] For the sake of completeness, one final remark should still be added. The major advantage of the adversarial nature of the Article 7 procedure for dispersed interests is that the investigated company may itself raise dispersed interests in defence against a remedy. However, this advantage over the Article 9 procedure does not offer protection against under-enforcement of Articles 101 and 102 TFEU. The investigated company will only raise dispersed interests before the Commission or in court, if this corresponds to its own interest. This is, however, only the case if a remedy threatens to over-enforce the competition rules.

3.1.3.1.2 There Is an Increase in Risk of Over-Enforcement

Even if the Alrosa judgment of the Court of Justice is interpreted restrictively, as was suggested above,[55] Article 9 still increases the risk of over-enforcement. The major sources of the risk of over-enforcement are the fact that the Commission is relieved from proving the existence of an infringement; the fact that the Commission only needs to take less burdensome alternative remedies into account if they are known by it and manifestly as appropriate to resolve the Commission concerns as the commitment under scrutiny; and the strong incentives for the investigated company to avoid an infringement decision. Certainly, the consent of the investigated company to a commitment provides a sufficient justification for not counting potential over-enforcement errors as a decisive concern from the perspective of the concerned undertaking.[56] Nonetheless, the interests of third parties and the general public in the avoidance of over-enforcement errors must also be taken into account.

First, as regards the rights of third parties who may claim that a remedy is overbroad, it must be stated that the risks of over-enforcement that result from the

[54] See Sect. 2.3.2.1.1.2 with footnotes 222ff above.

[55] See Sect. 2.2.2.2.2.2 with footnotes 101ff above.

[56] See Sect. 2.2.2.2.2.1 with footnotes 87ff above.

relaxation of Commission's investigative duties and from the strong incentives of the investigated company to avoid an infringement decision are not completely unchecked. This applies all the more, if one follows the restrictive interpretation of the Alrosa judgment that was suggested above. The market test provides also third parties who claim that a remedy is overbroad with an opportunity to present their observations. Since no market test is prescribed for infringement decisions, this opportunity even constitutes an advantage of the commitment procedure. Moreover, third parties can challenge a commitment on the ground that it is overbroad. Nonetheless, the rights of third parties to defend themselves against an overbroad remedy are less strong where a remedy is based on Article 9 than where it is based on Article 7.

In the first place, it is true that even under Article 9, the Commission is not completely exempted from substantiating its "concerns". The fact that the Commission must carry out a "preliminary assessment" means that minimum requirements as regards the Commission's duty to substantiate its concerns exist also in the context of Article 9. It is submitted that a third party could rely on these minimum requirements in support of action against an overbroad remedy. However, while the precise contours of the Commission's duty to substantiate its concerns in the context of Article 9 remain to date largely obscure,[57] it is clear that that duty reaches less far than the obligation under Article 7 to prove an infringement.[58] Unlike in the context of Article 7, in the context of Article 9, a third party could not challenge an overbroad remedy on the ground that the Commission did not prove the infringement to the requisite standard. This increases the risk of errors of over-enforcement.

In the second place, Article 9 increases the risk of errors of over-enforcement by relaxing the necessity requirement of the proportionality test. The Commission can confine itself to an assessment of the solutions that are known by it. It is not required to seek itself less onerous solutions. Moreover, the Commission must only make a less burdensome alternative binding, if it is manifestly as effective in resolving the competition concerns as the commitment under scrutiny. It should be emphasised

[57]In Alrosa, the GC accepted that the Commission's obligation to analyse the market and to identify the infringement were "less definitive" in the context of Article 9 than in the context of Article 7. Nonetheless, in the view of the Court, the Commission was obliged to establish the reality of the competition concerns also in the context of Article 9 to a degree that was sufficient to allow a review of the proportionality of the commitment (Sect. 2.2.1.2.1 with footnote 17 above). The Court of Justice did neither expressly contradict nor confirm this statement. See also Hennig (2010), 142, who suggests that the Commission's obligation to substantiate its concerns under Article 9 should vary according to the gravity of the remedy. He suggests also that the standard of a "prima facie finding of infringement" that applies in the context of the Commission's power to order interim measures pursuant to Article 8 Regulation 1/03 could serve as the minimum threshold.

[58]But see Lowe/Maier-Rigaud (2008), 603: "a preliminary assessment under Article 9 can only contain concerns that would reach the standard for objections if the Commission pursued an Article 7 procedure"; by contrast see ibid. (608): "The preliminary nature of the reasoning is comparable to the prima facie element in the reasoning of an Article 8 decision: while the standard of evidence is lower than under Article 7, the Commission can only act where its concern relates to a possible infringement [...]".

once more that—according to my interpretation of the Alrosa judgment of the Court of Justice—the relaxation of the necessity requirement in the context of Article 9 does not completely eliminate the rights of third parties as regards the necessity requirement. It is submitted that, if a third party puts forward a less burdensome equally effective remedy in the context of the market test, the Commission must take this proposal into account—without prejudice to the fact that the Commission cannot make the proposal of a third party binding without the approval of the investigated company.[59] Nonetheless, it remains that, in the context of Article 9, the Commission's obligation to verify the existence of less onerous solutions remains less strict than in the context of Article 7. Where the Commission's preliminary assessment results in reasonable doubts regarding the appropriateness of the alternative solutions proposed by the third party, the Commission may refrain from investing further resources into an in-depth investigation. Rather, in such a case it may make the commitments offered by the concerned undertaking binding, even though they are more burdensome for the third party.

Second, as regards the interest of the general public, it goes without saying that the risks of over-enforcement described above are magnified where the interests in preventing an overbroad remedy are so dispersed that they are not represented in the market test or in a challenge of the commitment in court. In that regard, the adversarial nature of the Article 7 procedure displays the advantage that the investigated company may with some likeliness raise the dispersed interests of third parties in its own defence. Certainly, in principle the investigated company may raise the dispersed interests of third parties that may be impaired by an overbroad remedy also in the course of the negotiations of a commitment. However, where it cannot easily convince the Commission, the strong incentives to avoid an infringement decision, in particular the possibility to evade a fine and the facilitation of follow-on actions, will prevent the investigated company from insisting too much on its point of view. The incentives to avoid an infringement decision thus let the individual interest of the concerned undertaking diverge from the interest of the general public.

Overall, the increase in risk of over-enforcement errors in the context of Article 9 decisions manifests itself clearly in the language of the Court of Justice and the Commission. Both emphasise that a commitment cannot be considered as unlawful for the sole reason that it goes beyond what the Commission could lawfully have unilaterally imposed under Article 7.[60]

---

[59]See Sect. 2.2.2.2.2.2 with footnote 106 above.

[60]CJ, C-441/07 P (Alrosa, 2010), 47; Commission, Best Practices (2011), 115; see also Sect. 2.2.2.2.3 with footnote 114 above.

3.1.3.2 Development of a Research Agenda

The fact that the Article 9 procedure only increases the potential for over-enforcement errors, whilst it leaves the potential for under-enforcement unaffected, relativises the criticism that is levied at commitments to a certain extent. The pertinence of the criticism is further attenuated, if one follows the interpretation of the Alrosa judgment of the Court of Justice suggested above and accepts that the rights of third parties to defend themselves against an overbroad remedy are not completely eliminated in the context of Article 9. Finally, it should be recalled that the undeniably remaining increase in risk of over-enforcement errors must be balanced against the benefits brought about by the Article 9 procedure.

In order to assess the importance that the remaining risk of an increase in over-enforcement errors should play in the overall assessment of the Article 9 procedure, it is necessary to seize that risk in more concrete terms. In that regard, it appears useful to ask when exactly a commitment goes beyond what the Commission could have unilaterally imposed by virtue of Article 7. Moreover, one must have a closer look at the Commission's decisional practice and evaluate whether the commitments made binding by the Commission actually exceeded what the Commission could have imposed unilaterally. These questions will be the leitmotif of the present chapter. However, before an answer can be attempted, three preliminary remarks are still called for. They concern the importance of clarifying the boundaries of Article 7; the inferences that can be drawn from the Commission's use of novel theories of harm or its pursuit of regulatory objectives; and the limitations and the outline of the following analysis.

3.1.3.2.1 Importance of Clarifying the Boundaries of Article 7

The question whether a commitment decision goes beyond what the Commission could have imposed under Article 7 cannot be answered without knowing what powers Article 7 confers upon the Commission.[61] In that regard, the EU Courts have consistently emphasised that Article 7 must be applied "according to the nature of the infringement"[62] and that, "in the context of the application of [Article 7], the principle of proportionality means that the burdens imposed on undertakings in order to bring an infringement of competition law to an end must not exceed what is appropriate and necessary to attain the objective sought, namely reestablishment of compliance with the rules infringed".[63] The same idea underlies the statement that

[61]See Temple Lang (2009), 140: "If commitment decisions cannot go further than prohibition decisions to provide remedies for infringement, it becomes necessary to clarify how far prohibition decisions can go".

[62]See eg CJ, 6/73 (Commercial Solvents, 1974), 45; C-241/91 P (ITP, 1995), 90; C-279/95 P (Langnese, 1998), 74; GC, T-410/03 (Hoechst, 2008), 198; T-491/07 (Cartes bancaires, 2012), 437.

[63]CJ, C-241/91 P (ITP, 1995), 91; GC, T-491/07 (Cartes bancaires, 2012), 438.

"[t]he prohibition [contained in a remedy] may cover only practices that are incompatible with the [Treaty]".[64] These formulas do, however, leave room for interpretation. It is therefore little surprising that it is controversial, how close exactly the universally conjured nexus between harm and remedy must be under Article 7. While the voices that request a close link seem to prevail,[65] some less strict views can also be found.[66] Overall, the precise boundaries of Article 7 remain to date still rather nebulous. According to Temple Lang, it is for instance unclear whether an Article 7 remedy may go beyond a termination of the anticompetitive conduct and also "take away some or all of the market power or advantages illegally obtained by the companies in question".[67] Similarly, the Commission's power to unilaterally impose structural remedies remains highly controversial.[68]

Against the background of the uncertainty that exists in regard of the scope of the Commission's powers under Article 7, it is surprising to see how little attention the critics of the Article 9 procedure pay to the former provision.[69] Moreover, where commentators endeavour at all to look at the Commission's unilateral powers, they mostly construe those powers restrictively.[70] For instance, Article 7 is said to provide a legal basis only for remedies that ensure "corrective justice", i.e. such remedies that restore the status quo ante. The provision is said not to allow for forward-looking remedies that aim at preventing the recurrence of anticompetitive conduct.[71] In a similar vein, commentators deny that Article 7 allows the

[64]GC, T-7/93 (Langnese, 1995), 205; T-228/97 (Irish Sugar, 1999), 298.

[65]See eg Hauser (2009), 116f: "Kongruenz im Sinne einer wesensmäßigen Gleichartigkeit"; Economides/Lianos (2010), 414f; Rab/Monnoyeur/Sukhtankar (2010), 181: "direct and indispensible link"; Sadowska (2011), text following fn 41: "clear and direct link between the infringement [...] and the remedy [...]"; Podszun (2012), 57 and 63: "Konnex, der eng zu ziehen ist"; Krings (2012), 439: "Unmittelbarkeitszusammenhang"; Petzold (2012), 201: "Kongruenzerfordernis"; Lianos (2013), 406: "close fit".

[66]See Petit/Neyrinck (2011), 120, fn 32, who claim that, "subject to the proportionality principle [...], EU competition law does not ascribe specific remedies to particular types of [infringements]", so that there is no "formal nexus" between infringement and remedy. See also, with respect to structural remedies, Prümmer (2007), 164: "Die strukturelle Abhilfemaßnahme nach Art. 7 VO 1/2003 geht über die bloße Abstellung der Zuwiederhandlung hinaus und erlaubt strukturelle Korrekturen bei grundsätzlich allen Verstößen gegen Art. 81 EGV und Formen des Marktmissbrauchs (Art. 82 EGV)".

[67]Temple Lang (2009), 140; see also Maier-Rigaud (2014), 9, according to whom the Commission's power to eliminate subsisting effects of a terminated practice "is not evidently grounded in Regulation 1/2003".

[68]See only the contributions of Koch (2008a); Hauser (2009); Krings (2012); Maier-Rigaud (2012) and (2014); Voell (2014).

[69]Exceptions are for example Lianos (2013), 406ff and Hjelmeng (2013).

[70]See eg Sadowska (2014), 7: "negotiated outcomes might prove to be useful [...] where unilaterally devising effective remedies under Article 7 would be [...] problematic given the Court's rather conservative stance on remedies".

[71]See Gerard (2013), who claims that, historically, "the EU Courts have sanctioned the imposition of remedies that were found to go beyond the restoration of the *status quo ante*, notably as they were designed to prevent the possible recurrence of the infringement in the future" and that today Article

Commission to impose positive obligations for infringements of Article 101 TFEU. Others emphasise the difficulty to impose structural remedies on the basis of Article 7. Such restrictive interpretations of the Commission's power to issue injunctions facilitate the claim that the Commission's commitment practice goes beyond what the Commission could have imposed under Article 7. If, however, it could be shown that the Commission's powers under Article 7 are broader than is generally contended by the critics of the Article 9 procedure, this would again take away some of the pertinence of the criticism. In the present chapter, the Commission's powers under Article 7 will hence play a much more prominent role than is usually the case in works dealing with Article 9.

3.1.3.2.2 The Commission's Use of Novel Theories of Harm or the Pursuit of Regulatory Objectives Prove As Such Neither Over-Enforcement Errors Nor a Regulatory Instrumentalisation of Competition Law

It has been pointed out above that critics of the Article 9 procedure often avoid definitive statements whether the Commission could have imposed the remedy in question also unilaterally on the basis of Article 7. Rather, they confine themselves to expressing doubts or to criticising that the Commission relied on novel theories of harm for which it is unclear whether the Courts would have followed the Commission's approach.[72] In a similar vein, commentators that criticise the Commission for a regulatory instrumentalisation of commitments do not always state that the remedies in question could not lawfully have been obtained under Article 7. Rather, they confine themselves to criticising that the Commission adopted the commitments "in support of liberalisation".[73] It is, however, submitted that neither does the Commission reliance on novel theories of harm in commitment decisions prove the existence of errors of over-enforcement. Nor does the adoption of commitments in support of liberalisation demonstrate that the Commission abuses commitments for regulatory purposes.

On the one hand, it goes without saying that a novel theory of harm is not necessarily inconsistent with Articles 101 and 102 TFEU. It would therefore be erroneous to infer from the fact that the Commission relied on a novel theory of harm

---

7 "follows the same approach". See also Wagner-Von Papp (2012), 966f: "To date, the Courts have reacted in a hostile manner to any attempts by the Commission to take a proactive stance in devising remedies".

[72]See Sect. 3.1.2.3 with footnotes 43ff above.

[73]See Schweitzer (2011), 649: "Der Gebrauch, den die Kommission im Anschluss an ihre Sektoruntersuchung insbes. im Energiesektor von Art. 9 VO 1/2003 gemacht hat, spricht dafür dass sie Verpflichtungsentscheidungen auch und gerade als wettbewerbspolitisches Instrument zur Unterstützung ihrer Liberalisierungsziele nutzt". Also Dunne (2014b), 408: "The Commission has [adopted the commitments in the energy sector], quite overtly, in order to support and supplement the liberalization of EU energy markets". See also Sadowska (2014), 57f.

in a commitment decision that the Commission exceeded the powers it would have had under Article 7. Where the Commission relies on a novel theory of harm in a commitment decision, one simply cannot tell whether the Courts would have endorsed the Commission's approach in the context of an infringement decision.[74] Not imposing a remedy in a case involving a novel question may as much lead to under-enforcement as imposing a remedy may lead to over-enforcement. Certainly, there are disadvantages in terms of legal certainty associated with the lack of testing novel theories in court. However, the question whether Article 9 reduces legal certainty should not be conflated with the question whether the provision leads to disproportionate remedies.

On the other hand, also the fact that the Commission imposes a commitment in pursuit of a regulatory agenda does not as such mean that the Commission could not lawfully have imposed the remedy in question unilaterally on the basis of Article 7. The proximity between EU competition law and sector specific regulation is broadly accepted.[75] It can be illustrated with cases in which enforcement of competition rules paved the way for subsequent regulatory acts.[76] The obvious examples of an overlap between the two areas are the "essential facilities" doctrine and the control for exploitative pricing. Both have been endorsed by the EU Courts in the context of competition law. Albeit only in the context of merger control, the General Court has expressly acknowledged that a remedy's goal to resolve competition concerns and the broader goal to open a market to competition may co-exist.[77]

---

[74]On a sidenote, one must add that also the result found by the Courts may be incorrect.

[75]See eg Ibanez Colomo (2010), 262; Ackermann/Petzold (2011), 8ff; Ackermann (2012); Dunne (2014b), 419ff.

[76]In order to tackle problems in the market for ground-handling services, the Commission initially relied on a policy of competition enforcement against individual airport operators. This approach was confirmed by the CJ (C-82/01 P [Aéroports de Paris, 2002]). Subsequently, a EU-wide directive (OJ 1996 L 272/36) on the regulation of such services was introduced; see Dunne (2014b), 436 with further references.

In a similar vein, with respect to problems caused by Multilateral Interbank Exchange Fees (MIFs), the Commission initially relied on a policy of competition enforcement. Again, the Commission's approach was confirmed by the Courts [CJ, C-382/12 P (Mastercard, 2014)]. Later on, the Commission proposed a directive to introduce price regulation; see the Commission's proposal for a Regulation on interchange fees for card-based payment transactions (COM/2013/0550 final) and the Commission's press release STATEMENT/14/2767.

[77]GC, T-87/05 (EDP, 2005), 92: "the resolution by the commitments of the competition concerns raised by the concentration and the pursuit of the opening of the markets to competition may co-exist".

The use of the term "opening" of markets is in my view unfortunate. As explained above (Sect. 3.1.1.2 with footnote 17), strictly speaking, competition law – including merger control – does not serve the goal to "open" up failed markets, but merely to keep markets open that are in principle self-supporting. Nonetheless, even in the abstract ideal, the areas of competition law and regulation intersect in that they both aim at "maintaining" competition. As is apparent from the context of the EDP judgment, the General Court merely meant that a remedy's purpose of resolving competition law concerns could legitimately coincide with regulatory goals. To the extent that competition law and regulation overlap, this cannot be objected to. See also Ibanez Colomo (2010), 277, according to whom "the General Court made it clear that the use of competition law as regulation would not be

Certainly, the proximity between competition law and regulation does not mean that the Commission can at will substitute the two instruments for one another. Otherwise, it could circumvent the specific requirements that exist for the typically more burdensome regulatory actions.[78] However, to the extent that the areas of competition law and regulation overlap, the fact that a competition remedy pursues—also—a regulatory goal can as such not be criticised.

For the sake of completeness, it bears still mention that also remedies that were adopted on the basis of Article 7 and that were confirmed by the Courts have been criticised for their regulatory nature. The remedies that were unilaterally imposed by the Commission on Microsoft in the 2004 decision illustrate this well.[79] Such criticism resounds the fundamental debate about whether competition law should pursue a "hands-on" or "hands-off" approach. It is, however, important to distinguish between the criticism that is levied at a regulatory approach of the Commission and the Courts in the context of Article 7 and the criticism directed at the instrumentalisation of the commitment procedure for regulatory purposes. Not persevering this distinction consistently risks the fallacy of inferring an instrumentalisation of the commitment procedure for regulatory purposes from a general disapproval of the approach of the Commission and the Courts in the context of Article 7.

3.1.3.2.3 Limitations and Outline of the Following Analysis

As explained above, the leading questions of the present chapter will be when exactly a commitment goes beyond what the Commission could have unilaterally imposed by virtue of Article 7 and how frequently such "excessive" commitments appear in the Commission's decisional practice. In order to attempt an answer, the scope of the Commission's powers under Article 7 must first be clarified. The results gained from the study of Article 7 can then serve as a normative benchmark for the assessment of Article 9.

3.1.3.2.3.1 Limitations

The envisaged analysis is subject to important limitations, both as regards Article 7 and Article 9. First, with respect to the assessment of the Commission's unilateral powers, as explained above,[80] the openness of Article 7 makes it impossible to

---

problematic in itself, but only in so far as it would amount to an error in law or in fact on the part of the Commission".

[78]See Sect. 3.1.1.2 with footnote 10 above.

[79]See Forrester (2005), 169; Ibanez Colomo (2010), 292ff; Gerard (2013), 19, according to whom the "regulatory approach to the design of remedies in the EU [. . .] also appears to extend beyond negotiated procedures".

[80]See Sect. 3.1.1.1 with footnote 4 above.

provide an exhaustive catalogue of types of remedies that are admissible under the latter provision. The open textured nature of Articles 101 and 102 TFEU, the general clause character of Article 7, and the fact that each remedy must be linked to the corresponding infringement all imply that, at least in theory, there is an infinite number of remedies. Even if the analysis were confined to remedies for established theories of harm, their comprehensive presentation would surpass the limitations of the present work. The following discussion of the Commission's powers under Article 7 must therefore remain selective. Moreover, the link between infringement and remedy implies that a contentious theory of harm renders also the remedy controversial. It can, however, not be the purpose of the present work to reassess the many and often highly disputed theories of harm of competition law. Rather, at least in the context of Article 7, the following analysis must accept the theories of harm relied upon by the Commission or the EU Courts as set. Taking these as the point of departure, the analysis can only ask whether a particular remedy fits the theory of harm that has been applied by the Commission or the Courts.[81]

Second, as regards the comparison of Article 9 decisions with the Commission's powers under Article 7, two ways in which a commitment may go beyond an injunction must be distinguished. On the one hand, the theory of harm applied in a commitment decision may exceed the boundaries of what could have been established as an infringement under Article 7. On the other hand, the remedy may not match the theory of harm. The present analysis will place an emphasis on the latter question, although the former will not be completely neglected. This focus has in particular two reasons. In the first place, commitment decisions frequently predicate on complex or novel theories of harm. Where this is the case, it is difficult to assess whether the Commission could successfully have relied on the same theories of harm in an Article 7 decision. This is, however, the decisive question. A more general discussion of whether an employed theory of harm is generally correct would risk the already mentioned fallacy of inferring the disproportionate character of a commitment from a general disapproval of a theory of harm. In any event, in view of the quantitative amount of commitment decision that have in the meantime been adopted by the Commission, a comprehensive general assessment of the employed theories of harm would surpass the limits of the present work. In the second place, the "shift of focus"[82] from the infringement to the remedy entailed by Article 9 necessarily makes it difficult to assess the Commission's theories of harm. The information regarding the Commission's theory of harm that is contained in a

[81] See also Lowe/Maier-Rigaud (2008), 598f, who rightly stress the importance of drawing "a clear distinction between the finding of an infringement, i.e. liability, and remedies". In their view, "these two aspects are confused [all to often] and allegedly softer [. . .] remedies are considered more appropriate to accommodate more general doubts relating not to the remedy but to the question of liability and whether the conduct should be considered a competition law infringement to begin with".

Forrester (2005) and Andreangeli (2010) provide symptomatic examples of the conflation of liability and remedies.

[82] See Sect. 3.1.2.1 with footnote 20 above.

commitment is typically more succinct than in an infringement decision. The lack of subsequent discussion in court and the corresponding reduced attention in the literature additionally compound the development of an informed position. Overall, the following analysis to what extent the Commission's commitment practice surpasses the limits of Article 7 must hence remain confined essentially to a plausibility check of whether the EU Courts would have endorsed the Commission's theory of harm if the decision had been adopted on the basis of Article 7. Taking the theories of harm as point of departure, it can then be questioned whether the link between harm and remedy is relaxed in the context of Article 9.

Obviously, the renunciation to engage into a more profound evaluation of the theories of harm employed in commitment decisions constitutes a major weakness of the present analysis. It is mostly due to this lacuna that the excessive nature of commitments "cannot be excluded".[83] However, in the absence of a positive finding that the theories of harm employed in commitment decisions could not have been used under Article 7, the opposite cannot be excluded either. While the resulting uncertainty has to be acknowledged as a disadvantage of the commitment procedure, it must be emphasised once again that this disadvantage is one of legal certainty. It should not be conflated with the question whether the Commission uses Article 9 to adopt excessive remedies. Moreover, it must be recalled that the purpose of Article 9 is precisely to attain procedural economies by relieving the Commission of the obligation to prove an infringement.

Finally, it must be pointed out that the present work does not provide a comprehensive analysis of all decisions that have to date been adopted on the basis of Article 9. Rather, it takes a selective perspective that looks at some commitment decisions that have been particularly controversial or that can for other reasons be considered to be particularly illustrative. Since the commitments that were adopted in the energy sector are to date often perceived as the most critical ones,[84] a strong emphasis will be placed on their analysis.[85]

3.1.3.2.3.2 Outline

In order to facilitate the reading, I refrain from contrasting the Commission's powers under Article 7 and those under Article 9 in two coherent blocks. Rather, I structure the comparison of those powers mostly according to types of remedies. Recalling the reference to Borges' "Chinese encyclopaedia" in the preface to Foucault's Order of

[83]See Schweitzer (2012), 3: "It cannot [...] be excluded that commitments go beyond a tailored remedy for the alleged infringement and restrict competition themselves".

[84]Dunne (2014b), 430: "The clearest example of the overreaching of existing regulation via Article 9 is seen in the strategic deployment of commitment decisions to restructure EU energy markets"; see also the references in Sect. 3.1.2.3, footnotes 41f above.

[85]For a similar approach that is, however, limited to the analysis of two decisions in the energy sector see Sadowska (2014).

Things,[86] I decided, however, not to invest too much energy into the development of a taxonomy of types of remedies. Moreover, for the reasons set out below, I decided to include also some "alien elements" in the present chapter. It cannot be denied that the lack of taxonomic effort and the inclusion of those alien elements have resulted in a certain arbitrariness of its structure.

First, some preliminary general observations on the principle of proportionality are necessary to provide the basis for the following analysis (Sect. 3.2). Second, under the headline "the link between harm and remedy in general" (Sect. 3.3), I distinguish between remedies that terminate on-going anticompetitive conduct; remedies that address imminent anticompetitive conduct; remedies that eliminate the causes of anticompetitive conduct; and remedies that remove the subsisting effects of past anticompetitive conduct. This categorisation follows at least partially the classic distinction between the various functions of remedies.[87] The respective categories are, where necessary, divided into sub-categories. Third, I dedicate an independent section (Sect. 3.4) to the so-called "structural" remedies.

Furthermore, the present chapter comprises several elements that can be considered as alien, because they do not directly analyse the relaxation of the link between harm and remedy. Nevertheless, I decided to include them into the present chapter. A fourth section (Sect. 3.5) will address ancillary remedies. These comprise in

---

[86]"This book first arose out of a passage in [Jorge Luis] Borges, out of the laughter that shattered, as I read the passage, all the familiar landmarks of my thought – *our* thought that bears the stamp of our age and our geography – breaking up all the ordered surfaces and all the planes with which we are accustomed to tame the wild profusion of existing things, and continuing long afterwards to disturb and threaten with collapse our age-old distinction between the Same and the Other. This passage quotes a 'certain Chinese encyclopaedia' in which it is written that 'animals are divided into: (a) belonging to the Emperor, (b) embalmed, (c) tame, (d) suckling pigs, (e) sirens, (f) fabulous, (g) stray dogs, (h) included in the present classification, (i) frenzied, (j) innumerable, (k) drawn with a very fine camelhair brush, (l) *et cetera,* (m) having just broken the water pitcher, (n) that from a long way off look like flies'. In the wonderment of this taxonomy, the thing we apprehend in one great leap, the thing that, by means of the fable, is demonstrated as the exotic charm of another system of thought, is the limitation of our own, the stark impossibility of thinking *that.*"

[87]See eg Lowe/Maier-Rigaud (2008), 599: "Bringing an infringement effectively to an end entails: to make good the conduct at stake, by prohibiting the infringing conduct; to eliminate its consequences, i.e. preventing the undertakings concerned from continuing to enjoy the fruits of their illegal behaviour and re-establishing effective competition on the market; to prevent its repetition – whether in the form of a repetition of the same conduct or conduct having an equivalent effect on the market".

Hjelmeng (2013), 1007f, according to whom "remedies and sanctions" for infringements of Articles 101 and 102 TFEU in general may fulfil the following functions: (1) termination of on-going infringements; (2) compensation to victims; (3) deterrence or prevention of future/repeat infringements; (4) restoration of the status quo ante; Lianos (2012), 189: "Competition law remedies are adopted with the principle aim to restore competition in the market. This includes first the micro goals of putting the infringement to an end, compensating the victims, and curing the particular problem to competition, but also the macro goal of putting incentives in place so as to minimize the recurrence of just such anticompetitive conduct". As explained above (Sect. 1.1.1 with footnote 19 and Sect. 1.2.1 with footnotes 42ff above) my definition of remedies does, however, not comprise sanctions and remedies available under private enforcement in national courts.

particular external monitoring and alternative dispute resolution mechanisms. Although ancillary remedies do from the outset not "mirror" the respective infringement, they have been included into the present chapter, because, also in their regard, it seems worthwhile to investigate to what extent commitment decisions may "go beyond" what the Commission could have imposed under Article 7. In a similar vein, a further section (Sect. 3.6) groups two subjects that are neither structured according to a type of remedy, nor directly related to the question of the link between harm and remedy. Nonetheless, they both relate to the question how far injunctions and commitments may respectively go. The two subjects are: The importance of fundamental rights and the applicability of EU law. Finally, both in the context of Article 7 and Article 9, a lapse of time and the corresponding change in circumstances may let the remedy and the underlying competition concerns drift apart. A final section (Sect. 3.7) has therefore been included in the present chapter that deals with the duration and modification of injunctions and commitments.

3.2 General Remarks on Proportionality

The Court of Justice elaborated the principle of proportionality as a general principle of EU law.[88] Today, the principle is codified, on the one hand, as a general limitation of the competences of the Union in Article 5(4) TEU and, on the other hand, more specifically, as a limitation of any restriction of fundamental rights in Article 52 (1) Charter. The EU version of the principle of proportionality has over time emancipated itself from its roots in German constitutional law and become a genuine principle of European law.[89]

As far as competition remedies are concerned, the requirement of proportionality overlaps to a large extent with that of the link between infringement and remedy. Most of the topics that will be addressed below under the heading "link between infringement and remedy" could equally be discussed under the heading "proportionality". For instance, one might ask whether besides putting the anticompetitive conduct itself to an end, also the elimination of its causes or of its subsisting effects can be considered as legitimate objectives of a remedy. These discussions shall, however, not be anticipated here. Nonetheless, the principle of proportionality also raises several general questions that are independent of the link between harm and remedy and therefore merit to be dealt with in advance. These shall be addressed in the following section.

[88] See CJ, 11/70 (Internationale Handelsgesellschaft, 1970), 4 and 15.

[89] See von Danwitz (2012), 367.

3.2.1 In the Context of Article 7

3.2.1.1 The Structure of the Test: Two or Three Steps?

To date there is still some uncertainty as regards the question whether the test for examining the compatibility of a legal act with the principle of proportionality consists of two or three steps.[90] This uncertainty exists also with respect to competition law remedies. Several statements of the Courts seem to imply a two-step test that examines only whether the remedy is suitable and necessary to attain the objective sought, namely re-establishment of compliance with the rules infringed.[91] The suitability step of the test asks whether the remedy is able and likely to achieve its purpose.[92] The necessity criterion is met, if no less burdensome remedy of equivalent effectiveness can be identified.[93] A different strand of case law adds a third limb to the test, asking whether the remedy is also proportionate in a narrow sense.[94] A remedy passes this third threshold, if an overall balancing leads to the conclusion that the burden entailed by the remedy is adequate when compared to the benefits secured.[95]

Along the lines of a strong opinion in the literature,[96] it is submitted that the correct test for assessing whether a legal act complies with the principle of proportionality includes all three steps mentioned above. The fact that the Courts examine often only the first two steps can, on the one hand, be explained with the procedural particularity that, with the exception of matters of public policy, the assessment of the Courts is from the outset limited to substantiated challenges, so-called "pleas in law", that must be raised by the applicant.[97] Where an applicant abstains from putting forward an argument as regards the third step of the proportionality test, the Courts will not examine it of their own motion.[98] On the other hand, the Courts sometimes address the arguments that belong to the third step of the proportionality test when assessing the first two steps.[99] As far as competition remedies are concerned, this means that, upon substantiated challenge by the applicant, the Courts must and will evaluate the overall adequacy of the burden entailed by the remedy in

---

[90]See eg Messina/Ho (2011), 744; Craig (2012), 591 and 601ff; Hofmann/Rowe/Türk (2012), 129; von Danwitz (2012), 371ff.

[91]Eg CJ, C-241/91 P (ITP, 1995), 93; GC, T-201/04 (Microsoft I, 2007), 1223 and 1276; T-395/94 (Atlantic Container Line, 2002), 410; T-354/94 (Stora Kopperbergs, 1998), 98.

[92]See Hofmann/Rowe/Türk (2012), 129; von Danwitz (2012), 371f.

[93]See von Danwitz (2012), 371f.

[94]GC, T-177/04 (Easyjet, 2006), 133; T-170/06 (Alrosa, 2007), 98 and 112; T-491/07 (Cartes Bancaires, 2012), 428; see also the opinion of AG Kokott in C-441/07 P (Alrosa, 2009), 46.

[95]See Craig (2012), 602; von Danwitz (2012), 372.

[96]See Cengiz (2011), 144; Craig (2012), 601ff; von Danwitz (2012), 371ff; Trstenjak/Beysen (2012), 269f.

[97]See Sect. 4.2.2.1.2.1, footnotes 273f below.

[98]See Hofmann/Rowe/Türk (2012), 130; Craig (2012), 602; von Danwitz (2012), 373.

[99]See Craig (2012), 602; Trstenjak/Beysen (2012), 270.

comparison to the benefits secured.[100] In extreme cases, even the least burdensome of all effective remedies may hence be disproportionate.[101]

3.2.1.2 Relation Between the Intrusiveness of a Remedy and Its Effectiveness

As will be shown in more detail below in the context of the discussion of the admissibility of the so-called structural remedies, there is a controversy whether the principle of proportionality forbids the imposition of a more effective, but also more burdensome remedy where a less burdensome, but still sufficiently effective remedy is available. The controversy resembles a dispute in German constitutional law that concerns the question whether the effectiveness of a measure must be put in relation with its intrusiveness in order to assess its necessity. Some authors favour such an approach. They claim that a measure fails the necessity test, if it is only slightly more effective, but at the same time significantly more burdensome than its alternative.[102] The counterview argues that the lower intrusiveness of an alternative may only be taken into account, if the alternative is as effective as the more burdensome measure.[103] The latter view appears more persuasive. As long as the more burdensome measure meets the third step of the proportionality test, the decision maker cannot be compelled to pursue its goal with a less effective alternative, even if the latter is less burdensome.[104]

For the same reason, the conclusion that only equally effective alternatives need to be taken into account for the assessment whether a remedy is necessary applies also to the principle of proportionality under EU law.[105] This result is also supported by the Sky Österreich judgment of the Court of Justice. In that case, the Court confirmed the proportionality of Article 15(6) of the Audiovisual Media Services Directive,[106] which imposes an obligation on holders of exclusive broadcasting

[100] For a three-step test in the context of competition law remedies see also eg Sullivan (2003), 414f and 417f; Müller-Tautphaeus (2003), 283; von Rosenberg (2009), 239; Messina/Ho (2011), 476; Lianos (2013), 404. For only a two-step test see Hellström/Maier-Rigaud/Bulst (2009), 49; Andreangeli (2010), 248; Gerard (2013), 24f; Sauer (2013), 11.07. See, generally in the context of competition law, also Steenbergen (2008), 265f, and Sauter (2014), 327.

[101] See with respect to § 32 ARC and the principle of proportionality under German law Fuchs (2009), fn 113; Jaeger (2010), § 32 ARC, 24.

[102] See Sachs (2011), Art. 20 GG, 153; similarly Schulze-Fielitz (2006), Art. 20 GG, 183.

[103] See Grzeszick (2006), Art. 20 GG, 116 with further references.

[104] See Grzeszick (2006), Art. 20 GG, 116, who emphasises that the relation between the effectiveness and the intrusiveness of a measure is solely a question of the third step of the proportionality test. See also von Rosenberg (2009), 239, who is of the opinion that the Commission only has to resort to a less burdensome and less effective behavioural remedy, if the more burdensome and more effective structural remedy does not meet the third step of the proportionality test.

[105] See for the same result, albeit without further explanation, von Danwitz (Sect. 3.2.1.1, footnote 93 above).

[106] N° 2010/13/EU.

rights to permit other broadcasters to show short extracts from events of high interest in exchange for remuneration that does not exceed the additional costs incurred by the rights holders in providing access. When assessing the necessity of the provision, the Court found that the less restrictive alternative of providing for higher remuneration for the rights holders was not equally effective. In the view of the Court, a higher remuneration could endanger the goal of Article 15(6) of the Directive to safeguard the freedom to receive information and to promote pluralism of the media by deterring or even preventing certain broadcasters from requesting access. The Court examined whether the less restrictive alternative would have attained the pursued objective "as effectively" as the provision under scrutiny, not whether it would have done so in a "sufficient" manner.[107]

3.2.1.3 Importance of Monitoring Costs

Several commentators argue that the proportionality of a structural remedy cannot be justified with potentially lower monitoring costs for the Commission when compared to the monitoring costs of a behavioural remedy.[108] Proponents of such an argument rely in particular on the wording of Article 7(1), 3rd sentence, Regulation 1/03, according to which "[s]tructural remedies can only be imposed either where there is no equally effective behavioural remedy or where any equally effective behavioural remedy would be more burdensome for the undertaking concerned than the structural remedy". They infer from the fact that the term "burdensome" relates only to "the undertaking concerned" that monitoring costs can only be taken into account as a burden for the concerned undertaking, but not as a burden for the Commission.[109] If this argument were pertinent, there would be no reason—besides possibly the mentioned wording—to limit it to the comparison of a structural with a behavioural remedy. One could argue equally well that lower monitoring costs of a given remedy for the Commission must also not be taken into account when comparing two behavioural or two structural remedies.

The argument is, however, from the outset not convincing. It is submitted that monitoring costs can be taken into account when assessing the proportionality of a remedy, irrespective of whether they constitute a burden for the Commission or the undertaking and regardless of the remedy's classification as structural or behavioural. The wording of Article 7(1), 3rd sentence, Regulation 1/03 allows for this conclusion, because the monitoring costs for the Commission can be taken into

[107]See CJ, C-283/11 (Sky Österreich, 2013), 50ff, in particular 55 and 57.

[108]Eg Koch (2008a), 111; Hauser (2009), 228; Kellezi (2010), 140f; Ritter (2012), Art. 7, 48 fn 150; Sofianatos (2009), 374: "le principe de proportionnalité oblige les autorités à accepter des mesures comportementales, quelle que soit la difficulté d'en contrôler l'application".

[109]Eg Hauser (2009), 228; Sadowska (2011), fn 46 = Sadowska (2014), fn 347.

account when assessing how "effective" a remedy is.[110] Also more generally, the imperative to impose effective remedies necessitates the consideration of the monitoring costs for the Commission. The conclusion that monitoring costs of the Commission can be taken into account when assessing the proportionality of a remedy is further backed up by a look at the interpretation of the principle of proportionality under German constitutional law. The Bundesverfassungsgericht has ruled that an alternative measure that implies significantly increased costs for the public treasury can be neglected when assessing the proportionality of a legal act.[111]

3.2.1.4 Remedies Addressing a Market or Conduct That Is Not Covered by the Found Infringement

The only legitimate goal of a remedy is to put the identified infringement to an end. Therefore, the Commission can, as a general rule, not extend a remedy to a market or to conduct that is not covered by the found infringement.[112] Nor can the Commission impose compensatory remedies that leave the identified infringement partially or fully unaddressed, but improve the competitive conditions in areas for which no anticompetitive behaviour has been found.[113] For instance, the Commission cannot use the finding of predatory pricing on one market as an opportunity to impose price reductions on different markets.[114] The remedy addresses neither the conduct that has been identified as infringement, nor the market on which the infringement took place.

There is, however, one exception to the just mentioned general rule. A remedy can be extended to conduct or a market that is not covered by the identified infringement, if this is necessary to put the identified infringement to an end. For instance, as far as divestiture remedies are concerned, the Commission states in the 2008 Merger Remedies Notice that it may also be necessary to include activities which are related to markets where the Commission did not identify competition concerns, if this is required to ensure the viability of the divested business.[115] Similar considerations may for instance also apply where the Commission orders a horizontal or vertical break up of a company pursuant to Article 7 Regulation 1/03. It must, however, be emphasised that the third step of the proportionality test imposes a limit

[110] See also the approach of Koch (2008a), 134, according to whom costs for the general public may not be taken into account during the necessity step of the proportionality test, but during the general balancing of costs and benefits in the third step of the proportionality test.

[111] See Bundesverfassungsgericht, 1 BvR 1276/84 (Rückkehrgebot für Funkmietwagen, 1989), 66; 1 BvR 1045/89 (Vergütung des Konkursverwalters, 1993), 60; Grzeszick (2006), 114; Sachs (2011), Art. 20, 152.

[112] See, in the context of merger remedies, GC, T-177/04 (Easyjet, 2006), 133.

[113] See Podszun (2012), 57.

[114] The example will be discussed in more detail below (Sect. 3.3.1.6.1.1.1.4 with footnote 453).

[115] Merger Remedies Notice (2008), 23.

to the extension of a remedy to conduct or a market that is not covered by the identified infringement, even where such an extension can be considered as necessary: The costs of the extension of the remedy must stand in an adequate relation to the benefits of putting the infringement to an end.

3.2.2 In the Context of Article 9

3.2.2.1 General Observations

The modifications of the proportionality test under Article 9 have already been discussed above[116] in the context of the assessment of the criticism levied at the Alrosa judgment of the Court of Justice. They shall in principle not be repeated here. It should, however, be recalled that, according to the view defended here, the Alrosa judgment can and must be construed as meaning that the Commission must take the submissions of third parties who consider a commitment overbroad into account. This implies not only that, in the context of the control of the necessity of a given remedy, the Commission must consider alternative proposals submitted by such parties.[117] Rather, it is also submitted that third parties can rely on the fact that the commitment offered by the investigated company violates the third step of the proportionality test. Since the proportionality of a commitment cannot be presumed with a view to third parties, the third step of the proportionality test remains applicable. At least in theory, a third party could therefore argue that the overall benefits of the commitment that was offered by the investigated company do not outweigh the costs for the third party. In practice, such an argument will, however, succeed only in very exceptional circumstances, due to the significance of the public interest in the protection of competition. In Alrosa, AG Kokott explicitly rejected Alrosa's claim that the commitments made binding by the Commission would violate the third step of the proportionality test.[118]

3.2.2.2 Coca-Cola

As pointed out above, the Coca-Cola commitment is the standard example used in the literature to demonstrate that the Commission really uses the Article 9 procedure to extract remedies which go beyond what it could have imposed under Article 7.[119] Commentators criticise the said decision in particular for allegedly extending to markets that were not covered by the Commission's investigation. In that

[116]See Sect. 2.2.2.2.2 with footnote 83 above.

[117]See Sect. 2.2.2.2.2.2 with footnote 102 above.

[118]Opinion of AG Kokott in C-441/07 P (Alrosa, 2009), 260f together with 224ff.

[119]See Sect. 3.1.2.3 with footnote 39 above.

connection, the decision fits the present context: As pointed out above, under Article 7, the principle of proportionality prohibits the Commission from extending the scope of a remedy to a market that is not covered by the found infringement. The following observations will, however, show that the criticism that is levied at the decision is unfounded. Coca-Cola does not support the claim that the Commission uses the Article 9 procedure to extract remedies that it could not have imposed under Article 7.

3.2.2.2.1 The Case

The Commission was concerned that The Coca-Cola Company (TCCC) and its three anchor bottlers[120] violated Article 102 TFEU and Article 54 EEA by restricting competition throughout the EU and in Iceland and Norway on the respective national take-home and on-premise markets for carbonated soft-drinks. The Commission considered that TCCC and the three bottlers collectively held a dominant position.[121] The concerns related to three categories of abusive practices: Exclusivity, growth and target rebates, and bundling practices.[122]

In order to offset the concerns, TCCC and its three bottlers committed in essence to abstain in the future from the three practices that had raised the concerns.[123] The commitment provided for a particular definition regarding the geographic scope of application. It was to apply in all Member States of the EU and in Iceland and Norway subject to the condition that TCCC-branded carbonated soft-drinks accounted for more than 40%, and more than twice the share of the nearest competitor, of national sales in the previous year.[124] Moreover, the commitment contained also specific provisions regarding its implementation. The investigated parties undertook to bring their agreements with their respective customers in line with the commitment by a certain date. However, there were some territories concerned by the investigation that were not served by the three bottlers to which the commitment decision was addressed. In those territories, TCCC worked with other bottlers. With a view to those other bottlers, TCCC undertook to use its best efforts to attain compliance with the commitment. As a means of last resort for

[120]According to M.833 (Coca-Cola/Carlsberg, 1997), 10, "[t]he term anchor bottler identifies certain bottling companies in which TCCC holds a minority equity interest and which are strongly committed to the strategic goals of TCCC and to furthering the interests of TCCC's worldwide production, distribution and marketing systems".

[121]COMP/39.116 (Coca-Cola, 2005), 23.

[122]COMP/39.116 (Coca-Cola, 2005), 26ff; for a more detailed description of the case see Gasparon/ Višnar (2005); Schweitzer (2010), 555f.

[123]See, as regards the details of the commitments that shall not further be discussed here, COMP/ 39.116 (Coca-Cola, 2005), 42ff.

[124]COMP/39.116 (Coca-Cola, 2005), 41.

ensuring the other bottlers' compliance, TCCC engaged itself to terminate the agreements with any bottlers that refuse to adhere to the commitments.[125]

3.2.2.2.2 The Criticism

As far as can be ascertained, the critical reliance on the Coca-Cola decision in the literature in support of the claim that the Commission extracts overbroad remedies goes back to an observation made by Cook in an article published in 2006.[126] Cook stated the following:

> The competition authority may be able to obtain a more wide-reaching remedy through commitments than it could impose after an infringement decision. For example, as an inducement to settlement discussions or for reasons of convenience, a company may offer to apply a commitment in geographic or product markets that did not form part of the competition authority's investigation or in which it is not (or may not be) dominant. With such a commitment, the competition authority is obtaining something that it would not have been able to impose on its own. The clearest example of this to date is the Coca-Cola decision under Article 9. Notwithstanding the fact that the Commission's investigation covered only four Member States, the negotiated commitments potentially apply in all EU Member States in which TCCC's carbonated soft drinks account for more than 40% of sales and more than twice the share of the nearest competitor. In addition, TCCC is required to use its best efforts to ensure that all of its EU bottlers—including those that were not part of the Commission's investigation – agree to abide by the commitments.

Cook hence seems to take offence at three aspects of the Coca-Cola decision: First, that the decision extended to markets that were not covered by the investigation; second, that the decision extended to markets on which the investigated companies did not hold a dominant position; third, that the decision contained provisions that concerned bottlers that were not addressees of the decision.

3.2.2.2.3 Comment

None of the prongs of Cook's criticism is convincing. First, the Commission's investigation did not cover only four Member States.[127] As is apparent from the decision, the subject matter of the procedure was "the supply of carbonated soft drinks [...] in the Community, Iceland and Norway". Moreover, according to the decision, evidence indicated that one or more of the practices existed in all Member

---

[125]COMP/39.116 (Coca-Cola, 2005), 47ff.

[126]Cook (2006), 212 fn 6.

[127]Schweitzer (2010) seems to accept this in principle. She formulates more carefully than Cook that "the commitments offered by Coca-Cola are not limited to the Member States in which anticompetitive practices had mainly been investigated" (556). Nevertheless, she follows Cook's allegation that the Commission made binding commitments in markets that did not form part of its investigation (560).

States, Iceland and Norway.[128] The fact that not all practices were identified in all the States to which the remedy was in principle applicable would not have excluded the geographic scope of the remedy under Article 7. As will be explained in more detail below, the EU Courts apply a rather lax standard as regards the necessity to establish a risk that the investigated company will commit the conduct from which it is enjoined.[129] In view of the fact that at least one of the practices raising concerns had been implemented in each State that was concerned by the investigation and that the other practices had been implemented in a large number of other States that were concerned by the investigation, there would have been a sufficient risk that the investigated companies could extend all of their practices over the entire territory covered by the investigation. The fact that the Coca-Cola commitment applied to all Member States, Iceland and Norway does therefore not permit the conclusion that the Commission extracted a remedy that exceeded its powers under Article 7.

Second, there was also no risk that the Coca-Cola commitment would cover markets on which the investigated companies did not hold a dominant position.[130] As is apparent from the decision, the commitment should apply only in markets where TCCC's carbonated soft-drinks occupied a very strong position compared to the rivals and for as long as that strong position continued to exist. In order to attain that goal, the applicability of the commitment was made subject to the condition that TCCC-branded carbonated soft-drinks had to account for more than 40%, and more than twice the share of the nearest competitor, of national sales in the previous year. These proxies for dominance are consistent with the case law of the Courts.[131] The

[128]In the decision, the Commission expressly stated that, during its investigation, it gathered evidence of the practices raising concern "in several EEA Contracting Parties, indicating that one or more of the practices have been implemented in all Member States, Iceland and Norway" (11). The Commission also stated that "the evidence gathered on the investigated markets and practices covered the 25 Member States, Norway and Iceland" (13). Finally, the parts of the decision that deal with the respective practices raising concerns refer to the concrete territories in which the practices were identified (fn 7ff). See also Gasparon/Višnar (2005), 61: "Evidence indicated that one or more of the [. . .] practices existed in all the EC Member States, Iceland and Norway".

[129]See Sect. 3.3.1.3, footnote 151 below.

[130]But see Wagner-Von Papp (2012), 955 fn 100, who seems to share Cook's criticism of the Coca-Cola decision in that regard: Wagner-Von Papp cites the Coca-Cola decision to substantiate the reality of the risk that the Commission extends a commitment that addresses Article 102 TFEU concerns to a market on which the investigated company is not dominant, thereby preventing the investigated company "from engaging in legitimate competitive conduct to the detriment of the consumers that could have profited from rebates and discounts by a non-dominant undertaking".

[131]See CJ, 85/76 (Hoffmann-LaRoche, 1979), 39 and 48, where the Court of Justice held that large market shares in combination with lower market shares of competitors could indicate dominance. The GC, T-219/99 (British Airways, 2003), 210ff, has confirmed the existence of a dominant position where the market shares of the investigated company amounted to only 40%, but were considerably larger than those of its rivals; see Whish/Bailey (2012), 183; Bellis (2013), 11. In the (2008) Guidance, 14, the Commission states that dominance is not likely if the undertaking's market share is below 40%. The Commission used similar proxies for dominance as in Coca-Cola again in the commitment decisions COMP/37.966 (Distrigaz, 2007), 27, and COMP/39.386 (Long-term electricity contracts France, 2010), 47; de Hautecloque (2009), 108 underlines this similarity.

condition provided a flexible mechanism that enabled the commitment "to adapt to potential evolutions of Coca-Cola's market power".[132]

Third, the Commission did also not go beyond what it could have imposed under Article 7 by making the provisions binding that concerned the bottlers that were not addressees of the decision. It follows from the decision that the subject of the investigation covered the three categories of anticompetitive conduct mentioned above also where these practices were applied by bottlers that were not addressees of the decision.[133] Certainly, under Article 7 the Commission could not have directly enjoined the other bottlers from applying anticompetitive practices without addressing a decision to them. However, in the Coca-Cola decision, the Commission and the addressees of the decision did not create any direct obligations for the other bottlers to refrain from the practices raising concerns.[134] Rather, the Coca-Cola commitment contained an obligation for TCCC to use its best efforts to attain compliance with the commitment. As a means of last resort, this included the obligation to terminate the agreements with any bottlers that refuse to adhere to the commitments. The said obligations engaged only TCCC vis-à-vis the Commission. Any effects of these obligations on the bottlers that were not addressees of the commitment decision constituted hence merely a reflex.[135] Such a reflex would not have excluded the imposition of the remedy on the basis of Article 7.[136]

---

[132]Gasparon/Višnar (2005), 63.

[133]COMP/39.116 (Coca-Cola, 2005), 7 and 48.

[134]Contracts at the expense of third parties are generally inadmissible. See also Hjelmeng (2012), 888: "a commitment decision is not capable of rendering contracts with third parties null and void, if this is to the detriment of the third party".

[135]See the opinion of AG Kokott in C-441/07 P (Alrosa, 2009), 180, where the AG considered that the termination of the sales relation between Alrosa and DeBeers was merely a reflex of DeBeers commitment vis-à-vis the Commission. Similarly already Gippini-Fournier (2008), 416f, who criticises the Alrosa judgment of the General Court for not having given sufficient consideration to the fact that Alrosa was not legally bound by the commitments finally accepted by the Commission.

Under German civil law, inadmissible contracts at the expense of a third party must be distinguished from admissible contracts where the negative effect on a third party constitutes merely a reflex of the contractual obligations entered into by the parties of the contract: see Bundesgerichtshof, VI ZR 211/03 (Personenbezogenes Entgelt, 2004), under II.2.

[136]As will be explained in more detail further below (Sect. 4.1.3.1 with footnote 105), the Court of Justice confirmed in Consten Grundig that reflex effects do not prevent the imposition of a remedy.

3.3 The Link Between Harm and Remedy Under Article 7 and Article 9 in General

Critics of the Article 9 procedure sometimes claim that the Commission does not have the power under Article 7 to impose forward-looking remedies that aim at preventing the recurrence of anticompetitive conduct.[137] This alleged restriction of the Commission's powers under Article 7 is then contrasted with the broad use the Commission makes of forward-looking remedies under Article 9. In a similar vein, it is contended that Article 9 entails a shift from "proscriptive" to "prescriptive" remedies, i.e. from those that merely prohibit discrete forms of anticompetitive behaviour to those that entail affirmative obligations.[138]

Contrasting the "prescriptive" and "prospective" use of commitments with allegedly merely "proscriptive" and "retrospective" powers under Article 7 is, however, not convincing. The depiction of the Commission's powers under Article 7 as merely "proscriptive" and "retrospective" is flawed. Such a portrayal may correspond to a stylized ideal of competition enforcement where authorities are confined to ex post findings of an infringement and the imposition of fines. It may also, at least to a certain extent, correspond to the actual use the Commission makes of the powers it has under Article 7.[139] However, the fact that the Commission does not fully exploit its potential powers under Article 7 does not mean that these powers do not exist.

The following section will show in more detail that Article 7 remedies are not merely proscriptive and retrospective. Already an abstract cease and desist order pursues a prospective goal, namely to suppress the future continuation of the anticompetitive conduct that was found to constitute an infringement. The same is true for more precise negative or positive orders. In particular the admissibility of positive orders also shows that the Commission's powers under Article 7 are not merely proscriptive. Moreover, under Article 7, the Commission can also issue so called "like-effects" orders that enjoin the concerned undertakings for the future from practices that are similar to the one that was found to constitute an infringement. Such like effects orders do not necessarily have to remain abstract, but can be precisely formulated—yet again demonstrating the prescriptive and prospective

---

[137] See Wagner-Von Papp (2012), 966f: He considers that Article 7 gives the Commission only the power to order a "backward looking termination of the infringement". He also claims that "[t]o date, the Courts have reacted in a hostile manner to any attempts by the Commission to take a proactive stance in devising remedies"; Gerard (2013), 18: "[. . .] the EU Courts have sanctioned the imposition of remedies that were found to go beyond the restoration of the *status quo ante*, notably as they were designed to prevent the possible recurrence of the infringement in the future".

[138] See Dunne (2014b), 417 and 419ff.

[139] See Dunne (2014b), 426: She emphasises that "[i]n practice, the Commission generally limits its remedial actions in infringement proceedings to express obligations to comply with competition law, plus what can amount to very high fines". The limited remedial actions in infringement proceedings are then contrasted to "(often substantial) modifications of their structure or market behavior" that "undertakings must agree to" in the context of Article 9.

potential of Article 7. Article 7 allows the Commission also to issue orders that address not the anticompetitive conduct that was found to constitute an infringement as such, but rather the underlying causes for the occurrence of anticompetitive conduct. All these remedies clearly aim at preventing the recurrence of the anticompetitive conduct that was found to constitute an infringement; they thus have a prospective nature.[140] At the same time, also "backward-looking" remedies may be adopted on the basis of both Article 7 and Article 9. As will be shown in more detail below, under both provisions, the Commission has the power to adopt remedies that aim at eliminating the subsisting effects of past anticompetitive conduct.

3.3.1 Terminating On-Going Anticompetitive Conduct

3.3.1.1 Abstract Cease and Desist Orders

The simplest and most widespread Article 7 remedy is an abstract cease and desist order, typically accompanied by a "like effects" order.[141] The EU Courts have consistently accepted that the Commission may require undertakings that have infringed the competition rules in abstract terms "to put the infringement to an end".[142] Strictly speaking, such abstract cease and desist orders are, like all other termination orders, only necessary, if the concerned undertakings have not yet put an end to the anticompetitive practices before the decision is issued. However, the Commission interprets this requirement extensively and makes use of cease and desist orders wherever there is a risk that the anticompetitive practices continue.[143] Cease and desist orders are not problematic as regards the link between infringement and remedy. They only require the undertakings to stop precisely the conduct that has been found to constitute an infringement. Abstract cease and desist orders are normally not used in Article 9 commitments. If they were, this would be as unproblematic as in the context of Article 7.

---

[140]See also Hjelmeng (2013), 1012: "[I]t remains a fact that remedies aimed at terminating an infringement apply prospectively, in that they restrain or impose specific future courses of conduct. Therefore, in particular with regard to Article 102 remedies, it is not possible to draw a clear distinction between remedies aimed at preventing future recurrences of the infringement and mere termination of past infringements".

[141]See Schwarze/Weitbrecht (2004), 19.

[142]See eg CJ, 40/73 (Suiker Unie, 1975), 606; Müller-Tautphaeus (2003), 360; Jaeger (2008), Art. 7, 11; Kerse/Khan (2012), 6-042; Ritter (2012), Art. 7, 37.

[143]See Dalheimer (2005), 8; Kerse/Khan (2012), 6-042 with plenty of examples.

3.3.1.2 Concrete Negative Orders

Besides abstract cease and desist orders, the Commission may also formulate more precise prohibitions. For instance, in Gema I,[144] Tetra Pak II[145] and AAMS,[146] the Commission ordered the concerned undertakings to amend or delete certain precisely determined contractual clauses, which the Commission had qualified as abusive. The VW decision constitutes a further example concerning Article 101 TFEU.[147] Like abstract cease and desist orders, also these more precise prohibitions do not raise concerns as regards the link between infringement and remedy, as long as they merely prohibit the anticompetitive conduct that was found to constitute an infringement.[148] The same conclusion applies also where more precisely formulated obligations to abstain from the conduct that raised anticompetitive concerns are included in an Article 9 remedy.[149]

3.3.1.3 Similar Conduct

In order to prevent the circumvention of a remedy that merely addresses precisely the conduct that was found to constitute an infringement, the Commission may prohibit conduct that, by its nature or its effects, is identical or similar to the one for which the Commission has established an infringement.[150] Strictly speaking, also such remedies are only necessary, if there is a risk that an identical or a similar infringement will be committed in the future. The Courts are, however, not exigent in this respect. In Hoechst, the Commission imposed a like effects order, the scope of which was limited to the market for which the Commission had found an infringement, although the concerned undertaking had already left the said market. On appeal,

---

[144]OJ 1971 L 134/15 (Gema I, 1971); see also Mestmäcker (1974), 531; Müller-Tautphaeus (2003), 261.

[145]1992 OJ L 72/1 (Tetra Pak II, 1991), 172 and the operative part of the decision. See also Schwarze/Weitbrecht (2004), 28.

[146]1998 OJ L 252/47 (AAMS, 1998).

[147]1998 OJ L 124/60 (VW, 1998).

[148]See Hjelmeng (2013), 1012: "In most cases, the required obligation will be that undertakings refrain from certain conduct which is contrary to Article 101 or 102. Such termination orders will "mirror" the infringement, in that parties are restrained from continuing the course of conduct which is outlawed by the substantive Treaty provisions".

[149]COMP/39.736 (Siemens/Areva, 2012) constitutes an example. The Commission was concerned that a non-compete obligation in the joint venture agreement that covered also the period after the cessation of the joint venture violated Article 101 TFEU. The two companies committed to eliminate the respective clause and to replace it by certain more precisely determined rules. Similarly also COMP/40.153 (Amazon, 2017), where Amazon committed to ban certain MFN clauses that raised the Commission's concerns.

[150]See Müller-Tautphaeus (2003), 262; Dreher/Thomas (2008), 1560, who justify the Commission's power to issue like effects orders with the need to prevent circumvention; also O'Donoghue/Padilla (2006), 680, who rely on the "requirement that a remedy must be effective".

the General Court upheld the order, stating that the injunction was "by nature preventive and [did] not depend on the situation of the undertakings concerned at the time of adoption of the [d]ecision".[151]

3.3.1.3.1 Abstract Like Effects Orders

The simplest form of orders to prevent circumvention is an abstractly formulated "like effects" order, by which the Commission requests the concerned undertakings to refrain from "any act or conduct having the same or similar object or effect" as the identified infringement.[152] The EU Courts interpret like effects orders restrictively "in the light of the grounds" of the decision.[153] This allows them to find that abstract like effects orders merely aim "at preventing a repetition of the practices, which have been identified as infringements in the decision" and that such orders are hence not disproportionate.[154] Abstract like effects orders are problematic only as regards their compatibility with the principle of legal certainty. In this respect, they will be discussed in more detail below. Most likely due to their lack of legal certainty, abstract like effects orders only play a role in the context of Article 7.

3.3.1.3.2 Concrete Obligations That Aim at Preventing Similar Conduct

Concrete obligations that aim at preventing the recurrence of conduct that is similar to the one that was identified as infringement or competition concern play a role both in the context of Article 7 and Article 9. The following section shall first discuss two examples from the Commission's practice under Article 7. Thereafter, the Commission's adoption of several Article 9 remedies that address the anticompetitive use of single branding obligations shall provide an occasion to assess whether the prescriptive and prospective obligations contained in these commitments could also have been imposed under Article 7.

3.3.1.3.2.1 Exchange of Information

In the Cartonboard cases,[155] the Commission found that suppliers of cartonboard had exchanged commercial information on deliveries, prices, plant standstills, order

---

[151] GC, T-410/03 (Hoechst, 2008), 200; see Jones/Sufrin (2014), 980 fn 334.

[152] Eg COMP/38698 (CISAC, 2008); Manual of Procedures (2012), Module 25, 25; Kerse/Khan (2012), 6-041 and 6-043; Sauer (2013), 11.06.

[153] See GC, T-491/07 (Cartes bancaires, 2012), 439, 440, 445 and 448.

[154] See GC, T-491/07 (Cartes bancaires, 2012), 439, 440.

[155] GC (1998), T-310/94 (Gruber + Weber), 177; T-311/94 (BPB de Eendracht), 286; T-334/94 (Sarrió), 280; T-352/94 (Mo och Domsjo), 256; T-354/94 (Stora Kopparbergs), 112; see for a discussion of the remedies eg Müller-Tautphaeus (2003), 257f; Wagner-von Papp (2012), 965; Kerse/Khan (2012), 6-052; Hjelmeng (2013), 1016; Lianos (2013), 409f.

backlogs and machine utilisation rates in support of various measures infringing Article 101 TFEU.[156] In reaction to this, the Commission did not only prohibit the exchange of the individual information, which it had found to be unlawful, but also the exchange of certain aggregated statistical information that was not covered by the decision.[157] The General Court annulled the respective parts of the decision, because they went beyond what was necessary to put the identified infringement to an end.[158]

The Cartonboard cases need to be compared to PVC II, which concerned a price fixing cartel. The like effects order imposed by the Commission expressly included the concrete obligation to abstain from "any exchange of information of the kind normally covered by business secrecy by which the participants are directly or indirectly informed of the output, deliveries, stock levels, selling prices, costs or investment plans of other individual producers, or by which they might be able to monitor adherence to any express or tacit agreement or to any concerted practice covering price or market-sharing. Any scheme for the exchange of general information to which the producers subscribe [had to] be so conducted as to exclude any information from which the behaviour of individual producers can be identified, and in particular the undertakings [had to] refrain from exchanging between themselves any additional information of competitive significance not covered by such a system".[159] The General Court upheld the order. It stated, first, that the Commission was not only allowed to prohibit the exchange of information on sales and prices, which were covered by the findings of infringement in the contested decision. Rather, the Commission was also entitled to prohibit the exchange of information which indirectly allowed for identical results to be achieved. In this respect, the Court referred to the example that a prohibition to exchange sales data could be circumvented by exchanging output and stock-level information, from which the sales data could then be easily deduced.[160] Second, according to the Court, the prohibition of the exchange of information that allowed the undertakings to monitor their illicit agreements directly related to the findings of the Decision concerning the implementation of illegal monitoring mechanisms.[161] Third, the Court made it clear that, contrary to the Cartonboard cases, the obligation to conduct any information scheme so as to exclude any information from which the behaviour of individual producers could be identified, did not cover the exchange of data in aggregated form.[162]

The two cases show that the Commission may only prohibit certain future practices in order to prevent the circumvention of the prohibition of a found infringement, if these practices amount themselves to anticompetitive behaviour.

---

[156]Eg GC, T-311/94 (BPB De Eendracht, 2008), 12 and 278 to 281.

[157]Eg GC, T-311/94 (BPB De Eendracht, 2008), 285.

[158]Cf. eg GC, T-311/94 (BPB De Eendracht, 2008), 286.

[159]See GC, T-305/94 (PVC II, 1999), 11.

[160]See GC, T-305/94 (PVC II, 1999), 1254.

[161]See GC, T-305/94 (PVC II, 1999), 1255.

[162]See GC, T-305/94 (PVC II, 1999), 1256ff.

In the Cartonboard cases, the Commission had not shown in the decision that the exchange of aggregated statistical information was anticompetitive and, although it did not decide the matter, the General Court seems to have had doubts in this respect.[163] The Commission therefore could not prohibit the exchange of aggregated statistical information for the future without demonstrating that this amounted to an infringement of Article 101 TFEU. By contrast, in PVC II, the General Court does not seem to have had any doubts as regards the anticompetitive nature of the practices that were prohibited in the like effects order. The major reason for this appears to be that the order did not extend to aggregated statistical information. Both cases are rather unspectacular illustrations of the link between harm and remedy. The problem lies mostly on the infringement side and consists of determining precisely which practices must be considered as anticompetitive. Once this task has been achieved, the delimitation of the scope of the remedy follows logically from the scope of the infringement. Such a straightforward relation between harm and remedy is also illustrated by the Court of Justice's Woodpulp judgment, in which the Court annulled parts of a remedy "in so far as they impose[d] obligations other than those resulting from findings of infringements made by the Commission which ha[d] not been declared void by the Court".[164]

Contrary to what is claimed in the literature,[165] the Cartonboard jurisprudence cannot be interpreted as a prohibition for the Commission to impose forward-looking injunctions that aim at preventing the recurrence of anticompetitive conduct. The Cartonboard cases merely show that the Commission cannot rely on Article 7 without showing that the conduct that it prohibits would amount to an infringement of the competition rules. PVC II clearly confirms that the Commission may impose forward-looking prohibitions that extend to behaviour that is similar to the one identified as infringement, as long as the prohibited similar behaviour still amounts to an infringement.

3.3.1.3.2.2 Microsoft Tying

In its 2004 decision, the Commission did not only require Microsoft to offer a version of Windows without the Media Player. To prevent a circumvention of the remedy, the Commission also imposed an abstractly formulated like effects order in the operative part of the decision.[166] The content of the like effects order was

---

[163]The General Court merely held that the fact that the exchange of statistical information might be used for anticompetitive purposes did not make it anticompetitive; rather, it was necessary to establish the actual anticompetitive effect; see GC, T-311/94 (BPB De Eendracht, 2008), 286.

[164]CJ, C-89/85 (Wood Pulp, 1993), 185. See also Kellezi (2010), 134, who also relies on the Wood Pulp judgement: "Les mesures correctives n'ont pas lieu d'être en absence d'infraction aux règles de la concurrence".

[165]See Wagner-Von Papp and Gerard, cited in Sect. 3.3, footnote 137 above, who both invoke the Cartonboard cases in support of their allegation that Article 7 does not allow the Commission to impose forward-looking remedies that aim at preventing the recurrence of anticompetitive conduct.

[166]COMP/37.792 (Microsoft, 2004), Article 4(2).

specified more precisely in a non exhaustive list of prohibited practices provided in the grounds of the decision. For instance, Microsoft had to abstain from reserving privileged interoperability with Windows to the Media Player, from providing a download link only for the Media Player or from providing a financial incentive for OEMs or consumers to obtain Windows together with the Media Player.[167] Microsoft did not contest those obligations imposed on it under Article 7 before the General Court.[168]

3.3.1.3.2.3 Single Branding Obligations

Remedies that address single branding obligations provide a good occasion to discuss whether the Commission uses the Article 9 procedure to adopt prescriptive and prospective remedies that it could not have imposed under Article 7. On the one hand, in Distrigaz, Long-term electricity contracts France, and Repsol, the Commission made binding commitments that contained rather precise prescriptions regarding the concerned undertakings' future use of single branding obligations. On the other hand, the Langnese case provides an example where the EU Courts set a limit to the Commission's power to address single branding obligations by means of unilateral injunctions. In the literature, the Langnese jurisprudence is invoked in support of the allegation that the EU Courts sanction the imposition of remedies that are designed to prevent the possible recurrence of an infringement in the future.[169] The following section will in a first step analyse the Commission's powers to address single branding obligations under Article 7. In that connection, I will argue in essence that the Langnese jurisprudence should not be construed as prohibiting the Commission from making prospective and prescriptive injunctions. In support of this argument, I will rely on an order that was used by the Bundeskartellamt in the Langfristige Gaslieferverträge case and confirmed by the Bundesgerichtshof. In a second step, I will then argue that the Distrigaz and Long-term electricity contracts France commitments do not go beyond what the Commission could have imposed under Article 7. Finally, some remarks regarding the Repsol commitment are called for.

3.3.1.3.2.3.1 In the Context of Article 7 Regulation 1/03

3.3.1.3.2.3.1.1 Langnese

In Langnese, the Commission found that a network of exclusive purchase contracts infringed Article 101 TFEU and ordered Langnese not to conclude any such contracts for a period of 5 years.[170] The General Court quashed the order: Relying

[167]COMP/37.792 (Microsoft, 2004), 1013. See also O'Donoghue/Padilla (2006), 680.

[168]See GC, T-201/04 (Microsoft I, 2007), 1194ff.

[169]Gerard (2013), 18 together with fn 87.

[170]See GC, T-7/93 (Langnese, 1995), 5.

on the bundle theory developed by the Court of Justice in the Delimitis judgment,[171] the General Court recalled that Article 101 TFEU precludes the conclusion of exclusive purchase agreements only where they contribute significantly to any partitioning of the market.[172] The Commission could therefore only prohibit the currently existing bundle of exclusive purchase contracts, which was found to have such an effect. It could, however, not generally prohibit the future conclusion of any exclusive purchase contracts.[173] On appeal, the Court of Justice confirmed the General Court's approach, which it considered consistent with the fact that Article 7 must be applied according to the nature of the infringement.[174]

3.3.1.3.2.3.1.2 Langfristige Gaslieferverträge

The General Court's Langnese judgment must be contrasted to the German case Langfristige Gaslieferverträge,[175] in which the Bundesgerichtshof clarified that a competition authority is not necessarily confined to a simple cease and desist order, if a bundle of exclusive purchase contracts infringes Article 101 TFEU. The Bundeskartellamt found that E.On had violated Article 101 TFEU by concluding a network of long-term exclusive gas purchase contracts with regional or local gas suppliers.[176] The remedy imposed by the Bundeskartellamt consisted not only in an obligation to terminate the existing contracts, but also in a prohibition to conclude certain purchase contracts in the future. Simplified, for a period of around 4 years, E. On was required to limit the duration of newly concluded purchase contracts to 4 years, where the contracts covered between 50 and 80% of a customers demand, and to 2 years, where the contracts covered more than 80% of a customers demand.[177]

The Bundesgerichtshof confirmed the remedy. It expressly rejected the argument that an order to terminate the existing contracts would have been sufficient.[178] According to the Bundesgerichtshof, it was necessary to make a prescription with respect to E.On's future conduct in order to guarantee that E.On did not anew infringe Article 101 TFEU through the conclusion of gas purchase contracts.[179]

---

[171] CJ, C-234/89 (Delimitis, 1991); cf. Jones/Sufrin (2011), 218ff and 663ff.

[172] GC, T-7/93 (Langnese, 1995), 207.

[173] See for a discussion of the remedy also Müller-Tautphaeus (2003), 250f; Jaeger (2008), Art. 7, 12; Sauer (2013), 11.06 fn 24; Lianos (2013), 410.

[174] Cf. CJ, C-279/95 P (Langnese, 1998), 74.

[175] BGH, KVR 67/07 (Gaslieferverträge, 2009); for a discussion see Jaeger (2008), Art. 7, 12; idem (2010), § 32 ARC, 19f and 27f; von Kalben (2018), 224ff; for a general evaluation of the effectiveness of the remedy see Zapfe/Mecke (2011).

[176] See BGH, KVR 67/07 (Gaslieferverträge, 2009), 6 and 26.

[177] See BGH, KVR 67/07 (Gaslieferverträge, 2009), 6.

[178] This argument had been raised in the literature against the preceding judgment of the appellate court by Dreher/Thomas (2008), 1559.

[179] See BGH, KVR 67/07 (Gaslieferverträge, 2009), 28: "Zur Beseitigung des festgestellten Verstoßes gegen Art. 81 EG war es nicht ausreichend, die Altverträge [. . .] zu beenden [. . .]. Mit

The Court inferred this necessity from a concrete prognosis of the likeliness that future gas purchase contracts concluded by E.On would again lead to an infringement of Article 101 TFEU, unless they were limited to the thresholds provided for in the order of the Bundeskartellamt. For this prognosis, the Court took account of the individual circumstances of the case. These included the structure of the gas market, the structure of the undertaking E.On[180] and the fact that E.On had reserved its right to conclude long-term purchase contracts covering all or most of a customer's demand vis-à-vis the Bundeskartellamt in the course of the proceedings.[181] The Court expressly rejected E.On's argument that an order could not prohibit the conclusion of individual contracts, where the finding of an infringement relied on the cumulative effect of a bundle of contracts.[182] In this respect, it held that it was not necessary to include the circumstances of the market, which made a certain practice anticompetitive, into an order. According to the Court, the addressee of an order was sufficiently protected by the possibility for the competition authority to withdraw the order in case of a change of the market conditions.[183]

3.3.1.3.2.3.1.3 Discussion

Dreher and Thomas have criticised the termination order of the Bundeskartellamt as illegitimate market design.[184] They argue inter alia that the order is contrary to the Langnese judgments of the EU Courts.[185] Their criticism must, however, be rejected. It is submitted that the order is not inconsistent with the Langnese rulings of the EU Courts, that it is in line with the Commission's Guidelines on vertical restraints and that the Commission has or at least should have the same powers under Article 7 Regulation 1/03.

---

der Beendigung der bisherigen langfristigen Lieferverträge wurde zwar das bisherige Netz paralleler langfristiger Verträge beseitigt. Die Abstellungsverfügung musste aber auch eine Verhaltensvorgabe für die Zukunft geben, um zu gewährleisten, dass die Betroffene nicht durch den Neuabschluss von Lieferverträgen erneut gegen Art. 81 EG verstößt. Wäre dies unterblieben, wäre angesichts der festgestellten Verhältnisse auf dem relevanten Markt nicht auszuschließen gewesen, dass die Betroffene die beendeten Verträge zu Bedingungen fortsetzt, die keine wesentliche Öffnung des Marktes für Wettbewerber bewirken".

180 See BGH, KVR 67/07 (Gaslieferverträge, 2009), 29, 30 and 51.

181 See BGH, KVR 67/07 (Gaslieferverträge, 2009), 31 and 51.

182 See BGH, KVR 67/07 (Gaslieferverträge, 2009), 48.

183 See BGH, KVR 67/07 (Gaslieferverträge, 2009), 49.

184 See Dreher/Thomas (2008) and Dreher (2009): "Verfügung mit weitreichenden marktstrukturellen Gestaltungsvorgaben"; "unzulässige[...] hoheitliche[...] Marktsteuerung". More carefully Podszun (2012), 65: "In der Entscheidung zu langfristigen Gaslieferverträgen und den genauen Vorgaben hinsichtlich Laufzeit und Bezugsquote liegt ein extremer Eingriff in die Vertragsfreiheit der Parteien, der nur durch die äußerst angespannte Situation im Energiesektor erklärt werden kann".

185 See Dreher/Thomas (2008), 1560f.

3.3.1.3.2.3.1.3.1. The Conditions for a Prohibition of Single Branding Agreements The starting point of the discussion must be the conditions under which Article 101(1) TFEU prohibits single branding agreements.[186] It follows from the principles that underlie the case law of the EU Courts, the Block Exemption Regulation and the Guidelines on vertical restraints, which for their part can be considered as consistent with the case law of the EU Courts,[187] that such agreements are not per se prohibited. Rather, it must be assessed on a case-by-case basis whether the respective agreement leads to market foreclosure. Two constellations must be distinguished: Either the agreement itself leads to market foreclosure. Or, it constitutes part of a bundle of similar agreements that have a cumulative foreclosure effect. In the latter case, an individual agreement is only prohibited if it contributes to an appreciable extent[188] to the cumulative foreclosure effect. The criteria for assessing whether an agreement leads in itself to market foreclosure or whether an agreement contributes appreciably to the cumulative foreclosure effect of a bundle of similar agreements overlap to a large extent. Albeit not exhaustive, the following three criteria are of particular relevance: The market position of the parties of the agreement, i.e. their market power or their market shares[189]; the size of the tied part of the buyer's purchases[190]; and finally the duration of the agreement.[191] The foreclosure effect of a single branding obligation or its contribution to the overall foreclosure effect of a bundle of similar agreements is a function of these three criteria. A shorter duration or a lower level of the tied part of the buyer's purchases can compensate a

---

[186]For the conditions under which single branding agreements are prohibited by Article 101 (1) TFEU see eg Jones/Sufrin (2011), 663ff; Whish/Bailey (2012), 638f; as regards long-term energy supply contracts see eg Saecker/Jaecks (2002), 22f and 29ff; Ehricke/Pellmann (2005), 1107f; Laumann (2007), 56ff; Roth (2007), 167; de Hauteclоque (2013), 81ff.

In the following discussion, I will not treat Article 101(3) TFEU. The arguments made under β) regarding the admissible scope of the termination order apply in principle mutatis mutandis. Since, by virtue of Article 2 Regulation 1/03, the burden of proof is in this respect on the undertaking, the competition authority is, however, not obliged to make a prognosis whether the conditions of Article 101(3) TFEU will also be absent in the future.

[187]See Jones/Sufrin (2011), 665: "The Commission's approach in the Guidelines is consistent with the Court's case law"; Whish/Bailey (2012), 638: "consistent with the many judgments of the EU courts".

[188]CJ, C-234/89 (Delimitis, 1991), 24 (appreciable contribution) and 27 (significant contribution).

[189]According to the Guidelines, the likeliness that an agreement containing a vertical restraint is anticompetitive scales with the market power of the concerned undertakings, in particular of the supplier; see Guidelines on vertical restraints (2010), 97, 132, 133. In the absence of barriers to entry, market shares are an important indicator of market power; see Guidelines on vertical restraints (2010), 112.

[190]See Guidelines on vertical restraints (2010), 103 and 133. 133 of the Guidelines does not refer to the tied part of one single branding agreement. Rather it refers to "the market coverage" of a plurality of single branding "obligations" or the (overall) "market share that is sold under a single branding obligation". However, the overall market share of the supplier that is sold under a plurality of single branding obligations depends itself on the size of the part of a buyers purchases that is tied in each individual agreement applied by the supplier.

[191]See Guidelines on vertical restraints (2010), 133.

higher degree of market power. Similarly, a shorter duration or a lower degree of market power will justify a higher level of the tied part of the buyer's purchases.

The Block Exemption Regulation provides for certain thresholds regarding each of the mentioned three criteria. First, Article 1(1)(d) defines "non compete obligations" as such that cover more than 80% of the buyer's purchases.[192] Second, Article 3(1) provides that such non compete obligations are, as a rule, exempted as long as the market shares of both concerned parties are below 30%. Third, Article 5(1)(a) excludes an exemption for non-compete obligations with a duration of over 5 years.

3.3.1.3.2.3.1.3.2. The Consequences for the Admissible Scope of a Termination Order It follows from the above that, even on the assumption that there is a bundle of agreements that leads to an overall foreclosure effect, an individual "exclusive" supply agreement, i.e. one that ties a very large part (i.e. more than 80%) or all of a buyer's purchases,[193] is not necessarily prohibited under Article 101(1) TFEU. Its contribution to the overall foreclosure effect of the bundle and thus its prohibition depend not solely on the tied share of the buyer's purchases, but also on its duration and the market shares of the concerned parties. This explains, why, in the Langnese case, the EU Courts held that the Commission could not generally prohibit the future conclusion of any exclusive supply contracts, independently of the duration of the contracts and the development of the concerned parties market shares.

However, contrary to the Commission's approach, the approach of the Bundeskartellamt did not consist of an across the board prohibition of all exclusive supply agreements. Rather, the Bundeskartellamt applied a more nuanced solution that took account of the duration of the respective agreement and the level of the tied part of the buyer's purchases. Under the approach of the Bundeskartellamt, E.On was not categorically enjoined from tying important shares of the purchases of a buyer. It only had to limit the duration of the contracts accordingly.[194] The order imposed by the Bundeskartellamt was thus in any event less intrusive than the one used by the Commission in the Langnese case.

Certainly, despite this fact, the order of the Bundeskartellamt is still problematic in so far as it disregards two further criteria that are in principle of relevance: On the one hand, the necessity of the subsistence of a bundle of agreements that leads to an overall foreclosure effect and, on the other hand, the market power or the market

---

[192]"Non compete" obligations are only a subcategory of "single branding" obligations. While the former are limited to obligations for a customer to source at least 80% of its demand from the supplier, the latter encompass also "quantity forcing" below that threshold; see Guidelines on vertical restraints (2010), 103 and 129.

[193]See Guidelines on vertical restraints (2010), 103: "Exclusive arrangements [. . .] result in one party sourcing all or practically all of its demand from another party."

[194]See the judgment of the court of appeal, OLG Düsseldorf, 2 Kart 1/06 (V) (2007), 146: "Die Betroffene ist nicht gehindert, sich an einem Wettbewerb um den gesamten Bedarf (100%) eines Regional- und Ortsgasunternehmens für die Lieferdauer von zwei Jahren zu beteiligen und einen entsprechenden Vertrag abzuschließen. [. . .] Die Laufzeit [. . .] des Vertrages darf bei einer vollen Deckung des Bedarfs insgesamt die Dauer von zwei Jahren jedoch nicht überschreiten."

shares of the concerned parties.[195] This begs the question whether the order of the Bundeskartellamt can be considered as lawful, although it does not take these two criteria into account. Moreover, it is questionable whether the exact thresholds applied by the Bundeskartellamt are consistent with the Commission's Guidelines.

As regards the first question, it must be pointed out that termination orders typically depend on market circumstances that, for their part, do not directly belong to the conduct addressed in the termination order.[196] For instance, the imposition of a supply obligation in order to put a refusal to deal abuse to an end hinges on the dominant position of the concerned undertaking. Although such external circumstances do not constitute the object of the termination order, their presence is nevertheless a necessary condition for it, because, in their absence, the conduct that constitutes the object of the termination order is not prohibited.[197] If a termination order aims not solely at current, but also at future conduct, a competition authority cannot simply rely on the presence of the external circumstances that contribute to the anticompetitive character of the conduct that the authority wants to address at the time of the adoption of the decision. Rather, the authority must make a prognosis of whether these circumstances and hence the conditions for a termination order will also be present in the future.[198] The competition authority can only issue a termination order regarding future conduct, if its prognosis results in the finding that the external circumstances that contribute to the anticompetitive character of the conduct that the competition authority wants to address will also be present in the future. Nevertheless, this does not mean that the external circumstances that contribute to the anticompetitive character of a certain practice must be included into the termination order itself. As the Bundesgerichtshof argued convincingly, the addressee of the order is sufficiently protected by the obligation of the competition authority to withdraw the order in case of a change of the market

[195]Before the Bundeskartellamt issued its E.On decision, it had published a general discussion paper regarding the assessment of long-term gas supply contracts. In this paper, the Bundeskartellamt suggested that such contracts should be considered as anticompetitive whenever they had either a duration of more than two years and tied more than 80% of a customer's demand or a duration of more than four years and tied more than 50% of a customer's demand; see Ehricke/Pellmann (2005), 1105. This approach was criticised for not taking the market shares of the concerned parties and the existence of an overall foreclosure effect into account: see Ehricke/Pellmann (2005), 1109; Roth (2007), 167; Laumann (2007), 86. Where the market shares of the concerned parties are below 30%, the Block Exemption Regulation for Vertical restraints exempts non compete obligations of a duration up to five years. It was therefore discussed, whether the Bundeskartellamt could have withdrawn this benefit pursuant to Article 29(2) Regulation 1/03 and imposed the stricter conditions suggested in its discussion paper; see Ehricke/Pellmann (2005), 1110f.

[196]See BGH, KVR 67/07 (Gaslieferverträge, 2009), 50.

[197]For instance, in a refusal to deal case, the object of the termination order is not the dominant position, but the obligation to supply. However, in the absence of a dominant position, an obligation to supply cannot be imposed.

[198]For the necessity of such a prognosis see Jaeger (2010), § 32 ARC, 19.

conditions.[199] In fact, it follows from the principle of legality and general principles of administrative law that an authority must revoke or modify an order in case a change of the external circumstances makes its original form illegal.[200]

In the E.On case, the Bundeskartellamt had not only found that, at the time of the decision, E.On had a market share of 75% and a dominant position and that there was an overall foreclosure effect brought about by a bundle of single branding contracts. Rather, as is apparent from the judgments of the court of appeal and the Bundesgerichtshof, a concrete prognosis also showed that it was likely that E.On's market position was not going to change in the near future and that future purchase contracts concluded by E.On would again lead to a cumulative foreclosure effect, unless they were limited by the order of the Bundeskartellamt.[201] Under these conditions, the termination order of the Bundeskartellamt must be regarded as in principle lawful, even though it does not expressly take account of E.On's market position and the subsistence of a bundle of agreements that leads to an overall foreclosure effect.

This leaves only the second question, namely whether the exact thresholds regarding the duration and the tied part of a buyer's purchases used by the Bundeskartellamt are consistent with the Commission's Guidelines. It is submitted that also this question must be answered in the affirmative. In fact, the Guidelines provide that, in the presence of a market share of the supplier of above 30% and in the resulting absence of an exemption pursuant to Articles 2(1) and 3(1) of the Block Exemption Regulation, single branding obligations exceeding 5 years are generally anticompetitive.[202] This applies not only to non-compete obligations, i.e. those that tie 80% or more of a buyer's purchases, but also to minimum purchase requirements below that threshold. However, if the duration of any minimum purchase requirement, i.e. also one that amounts to only, for instance, 35%, must be limited to 5 years and the foreclosure effect depends on the level of the purchase requirement and its duration, than it is at least plausible to limit the duration of a 50% purchase requirement to 4 years and the duration of an 80% purchase requirement to 2 years.

At the time of the decision, E.On had a market share of 75% and a dominant position. It exceeded hence the 30% market share threshold, so that its single branding agreements did not fall under the Block Exemption Regulation.[203]

---

[199] See Sect. 3.3.1.3.2.3.1.2 with footnote 183 above; also Jaeger (2010), § 32 ARC, 20.

[200] The principle of legality requires that a decision that is no longer lawful must in principle be revoked or modified, unless there are contrary legitimate expectations. However, typically legitimate expectations only cause problems where the addressee benefits from a decision, but not where he is burdened by the latter. See also the more detailed discussion below (Sect. 3.7.2 below).

[201] BGH, KVR 67/07 (Gasliefervertäge, 2009), 49; see also the judgment of the court of appeal, OLG Düsseldorf, 2 Kart 1/06 (V) (2007), 109f and 124.

[202] See Guidelines on vertical restraints (2010), 133: "Single branding obligations between one and five years entered into by non-dominant companies usually require a proper balancing of pro- and anticompetitive effects, while single branding obligations exceeding five years are for most types of investments not considered necessary to achieve the claimed efficiencies or the efficiencies are not sufficient to outweigh their foreclosure effect."

[203] See OLG Düsseldorf, 2 Kart 1/06 (V) (2007), 124.

A prognosis showed that this was also likely to be the case in the future. The approach of the Bundeskartellamt to limit the duration of newly concluded purchase contracts to 4 years, where the contracts covered between 50 and 80% of a buyer's purchases, and to 2 years, where the contracts covered more than 80% of a buyer's purchases is thus consistent with the Commission's Guidelines. The Commission could impose an identical order under Article 7 Regulation 1/03.

3.3.1.3.2.3.1.3.3. Single Branding Agreements and Dominance It follows from the previous remarks that Article 7 empowers the Commission to use thresholds identical to the ones used by the Bundeskartellamt, as soon as the market shares of one of the parties exceed 30% so that the block exemption does not apply. However, at least in the Gasliefervertr̈age case, E.On held a dominant position at the time of the decision and the prognosis showed that this was unlikely to change in the future. This begs the question whether such a finding of dominance enables the Commission to go even further and enjoin the dominant undertaking from entering into any exclusive purchase obligations, i.e. such that exceed 80%, at all, independently of their duration. In other words, would the EU Courts have had to consider the Commission's order in Langnese as lawful, if the Commission had established that Langnese held a dominant position[204]?

This would be the case, if there was a general prohibition to use exclusive purchase agreements for dominant undertakings—at least in the context of Article 102 TFEU.[205] The controversy about this question cannot be treated in detail here.[206] Suffice it to say that up to the Intel judgment of the Court of Justice, the EU Courts had taken a restrictive stance and more or less consistently applied a general prohibition, unless the dominant undertaking shows that the use of the exclusive purchase agreement is objectively justified.[207] A strong doctrinal trend criticised this approach and called for a case-by-case analysis.[208] The position of the Commission was ambiguous. While the Article 82 Guidance Paper points towards a

[204]In Langnese, the General Court merely found that Langnese had a market share of above 45% and held a "strong position"; see GC, T-7/93 (Langnese, 1995), 96.

[205]For the present purposes, it is in principle not necessary to distinguish between Articles 101 and 102 TFEU. The provisions are not mutually exclusive (see Jones/Sufrin [2011], 279f) and a general prohibition of exclusive purchase agreements for dominant undertakings might also follow from Article 101 TFEU.

[206]See for a more detailed discussion eg Jones/Sufrin (2011), 419ff; Whish/Bailey (2012), 682ff; O'Donoghue/Padilla (2013), 423ff.

[207]See CJ, 85/76 (Hoffmann-LaRoche, 1979), 89f; GC, T-65/89 (British Gypsum, 1993), 65ff; T-286/09 (Intel, 2014), 72ff.

[208]Eg Eilmansberger (2008), 2-15-454; Jones/Sufrin (2011), 420; Whish/Bailey (2012), 199ff and 684; O'Donoghue/Padilla (2013), 69 and 423ff. More restrictively, agreeing with the case law of the EU Courts, eg Jung (2011), Art. 102, 201; Fuchs/Möschel (2012), Art. 102, 217.

The debate was revived by the Intel judgment of the General Court, GC, T-286/09 (Intel, 2014), in which the GC confirmed the prior case law according to which the grant of exclusivity rebates by a dominant operator that is not objectively justified violates Article 102 TFEU. Agreeing with the approach of the GC eg Whish (2015), 1f; Wernicke (2015), 21f and 23; Wils (2014); critically eg Ibanez Colomo (2014).

case-by-case analysis,[209] the Commission nevertheless used the broad prohibition applied by the EU Courts at least as an alternative base for its decisions and defends its decisions in court accordingly.[210] At least under the approach applied by the EU Courts in the context of Article 102 TFEU up to the Intel judgment of the Court of Justice, the Commission could thus enjoin a dominant operator from concluding any exclusive purchase contracts at all, as long as these were not objectively justified.[211]

In Intel, the Grand Chamber of the Court of Justice reversed the previous case law on exclusivity agreements and opened the door up for a more circumstantial analysis of the case at hand.[212] The judgment of the Court of Justice remains, however, enigmatic and its precise implications to date largely unclear. It remains to be seen whether the appeals pending before the General Court against the Commission's Qualcomm[213] and Google Android[214] decisions will be able to bring about further clarifications. At this stage, it is submitted that the Intel judgment is arguably best understood as having only slightly macerated the prohibition for a dominant undertaking to apply exclusivity agreements unless they are objectively justified, by transforming this prohibition procedurally into a rebuttable presumption.[215] Following such an interpretation, the consequences of the judgment for the remedies side appear limited: As long as the dominant undertaking cannot rebut the presumption of the anticompetitive nature of the exclusivity agreements, the Commission can enjoin it from concluding any such agreements at all, as long as these are not objectively justified.

The same or at least a similar result can also be reached by reference to the Guidelines on vertical restraints. It was argued above that, as soon as the market share of the supplier exceeds 30%—and thus already below the level of dominance, these Guidelines allow to limit the duration of a single branding agreement to 4 years, where the agreement covers between 50% and 80% of a buyer's purchases, and to 2 years, where the agreement covers more than 80% of a buyer's purchases. However, where the market position of the supplier amounts to dominance, the increased foreclosure effect must somehow be compensated. Exclusive purchase contracts, i.e. those that tie more than 80% of a buyer's purchases, must thus either be generally be prohibited. Or their duration must at least be limited to a very short duration, for instance 1 year.[216] On the other hand, this does not mean that the same

---

[209]See Commission Guidance Article 82, 20 and 33ff.

[210]Eg COMP/37990 (Intel, 2009), 924f. See also O'Donoghue/Padilla (2013), 424: "[T]he Commission's translation of its policy into the decisional practice remains somewhat schizophrenic [...]"; similarly at 432f.

[211]See de Hautecloque (2009), 107: "E.On Ruhrgas [author's note: the Langfristige Gaslieferverträge case] could have entailed a *quasi*-automatic per se prohibition".

[212]CJ, C-413/14 P (Intel, 2017), 133ff.

[213]COMP/40.099 (Google Android, 2018), under appeal in GC, T-604/18, pending.

[214]COMP/40.220 (Qualcomm, 2018), under appeal in GC, T-235/18, pending.

[215]See Dittert (2017), 587; Kadar (2019); Hajnovicova/Lang/Usai (2019), 145.

[216]The Guidelines on vertical restraints (2000), 141 and (2010), 133, leave the question open whether "single branding obligations" with a duration of less than a year may be used by a dominant

applies also for all single branding agreements. Where the tied part of the buyer's purchases lies only between 50% and 80%, such agreements can be permitted up to a duration of 2 years. Where the tied part of the buyer's purchases lies below 50% or even below 35%, a duration of four or even 5 years is admissible.

3.3.1.3.2.3.2 In the Context of Article 9 Regulation 1/03

3.3.1.3.2.3.2.1 Distrigaz and Long-Term Electricity Contracts in France

3.3.1.3.2.3.2.1.1. The Cases The Commission accused Distrigaz of having violated Article 102 TFEU by concluding a bundle of exclusive gas supply contracts. According to the statement of objections, Distrigaz's supply contracts provided for de jure or de facto exclusivity.[217] The duration of the contracts exceeded 1 year.[218] A calculation of the proportion of the relevant market tied to Distrigaz for various dates in the future showed that Distrigaz tied 50–60% for 6 months ahead, 35–45% for 1 year ahead and 20–30% for 2 and 3 years ahead.[219] On that basis, and in view of Distrigaz' dominant position, the Commission considered that there was a significant foreclosure effect.[220]

In order to offset the Commission's concerns, Distrigaz committed to ensure that for each calendar year a minimum of 65% and on average for all calendar years a minimum of 70% of the gas volumes supplied by itself would return to the market. Moreover, Distrigaz committed to limit the contract duration to 5 years. In that regard, the company undertook to grant unilateral termination rights for existing contracts and to abstain from concluding new contracts exceeding that threshold.[221] Supplies to new gas fired power plants were exempted from Distrigaz's commitment in order to allow for efficiency enhancing investments in new generation.[222] The duration of the commitment was limited to the moment when Distrigaz would lose its dominant position and to a maximum of 4 years.[223] As regards the proportionality of the commitment, the Commission considered in particular that Distrigaz's obligation not to tie on average more than 30% of its sales more than 1 year ahead offset

---

undertaking: "Single branding obligations shorter than one year entered into by non-dominant companies are generally not considered to give rise to appreciable anti-competitive effects or net negative effects". As opposed to the term "non-compete obligation", the term "single branding obligation" covers also tied shares of a customer's demand below 80%. Since the positive statement about single branding obligations with a duration of less than a year applies only to non-dominant undertakings, one could at least argue that the Guidelines point toward a complete prohibition of arrangements by which a dominant operator ties more than 80% of a customer's demand.

[217]COMP/37.966 (Distrigaz, 2007), 19f.

[218]COMP/37.966 (Distrigaz, 2007), 21f.

[219]COMP/37.966 (Distrigaz, 2007), 23.

[220]COMP/37.966 (Distrigaz, 2007), 24.

[221]COMP/37.966 (Distrigaz, 2007), 27.

[222]COMP/37.966 (Distrigaz, 2007), 27 and 37; Gauer/Kjølbye (2014), 12.77.

[223]COMP/37.966 (Distrigaz, 2007), 27; Gauer/Kjølbye (2014), 12.77.

the identified foreclosure effect. At the same time, the Commission emphasised that the commitment still left Distrigaz considerable flexibility in how to contract with its customers.[224] The additional obligation to limit the contract duration to 5 years was justified with the need to prevent Distrigaz from undermining the effects of the commitment by tying the most attractive customers, for example the largest with the most stable demand.[225]

The Long-term electricity contracts in France decision[226] resembles the Distrigaz decision both with a view to the theory of harm and the remedy employed.[227] It shall in principle not be discussed here separately. It seems noteworthy, however, that competing suppliers had requested during the market test to limit the contract duration to three instead of 5 years. They argued that it was impossible for them to plan their supplies over a 5-year time horizon. The Commission rejected that argument. In its view, it was the responsibility of the competing suppliers to manage their sources of supply in a manner that allowed them to propose long-term supply contracts. In that connection, the Commission stated that the competing suppliers could either buy in the wholesale market or invest in generating capacity.[228]

3.3.1.3.2.3.2.1.2. Discussion Commentators invoke the two described decisions as examples for remedies that the Commission could not have imposed under Article 7 and for the instrumentalisation of the Article 9 procedure for regulatory purposes.[229] This criticism is not convincing. It is submitted that the Commission could have imposed the remedies adopted in Distrigaz and Long-term electricity contracts France also on the basis of Article 7. It was argued above that under the strict standard applied by the EU Courts until the Intel judgment of the Court of Justice, the Commission could even have prohibited the use of exclusive dealing agreements by the two dominant undertakings completely—at least to the extent that the companies could not prove that the use of exclusive dealing agreements was objectively justified. Even after Intel, such a complete prohibition appears to remain possible as long as the concerned undertaking cannot rebut the presumption of the anticompetitive nature of the exclusivity agreements.[230]

In any event, it was argued above that the Commission should have the power under Article 7 to impose an order like the one that was used by the

[224] COMP/37.966 (Distrigaz, 2007), 35.

[225] COMP/37.966 (Distrigaz, 2007), 36.

[226] COMP/39.386 (Long-term electricity contracts France, 2010).

[227] See Gauer/Kjølbye (2014), 12.78; Kipiani (2014), 421.

[228] COMP/39.386 (Long-term electricity contracts France, 2010), 80.

[229] See Lugard/Möllmann (2013), 7, who cite the Long-term electricity contracts France decision in support of the allegation that the Article 9 procedure "allows the Commission to impose desirable market conduct, which it [. . .] otherwise could not"; Dunne (2014b), 417, who cites both decisions as examples for "the Commission's willingness to participate in the prospective structuring of markets".

[230] See Sect. 3.3.1.3.2.3.1.3.3 with footnote 205ff above; de Hautecloque (2009), 107: "Distrigaz [. . .] could have entailed a *quasi*-automatic per se prohibition".

Bundeskartellamt in Gasliefervertäge. If one accepts that premise, it follows a fortiori that also the remedies adopted in Distrigaz and Long-term electricity contracts France meet the requirements of Article 7. The latter remedies are less intrusive than the order of the Bundeskartellamt. In that order, E.On was required to limit the duration of newly concluded purchase contracts to 4 years, where the contracts covered between 50 and 80% of a customers demand, and to 2 years, where the contracts covered more than 80% of a customers demand. The Bundeskartellamt made thus precise prescriptions as regards the maximum duration and tied market share of each individual contract. The two remedies adopted by the Commission provided the concerned undertakings with more flexibility for the design of their individual contracts.[231] Under the Commission's remedies, the concerned undertakings retained the possibility to conclude exclusive dealing agreements, i.e. agreements that cover 80–100% of a customer's demand, up to a duration of 5 years as long as the companies did not on the whole tie more than a pre-determined percentage of their sales. In contrast, the order of the Bundeskartellamt permitted exclusive dealing agreements only up to a duration of 2 years. For the sake of completeness, it should be added that, unlike the order of the Bundeskartellamt, the remedies adopted by the Commission were explicitly conditional on the subsistence of the dominant position of the concerned undertakings. Compared to the order of the Bundeskartellamt, they were hence also less burdensome in that the concerned undertakings did not have to apply for a withdrawal should they lose their dominant positions.[232]

The remedies adopted in Distrigaz and Long-term electricity contracts France can therefore not be invoked as examples in which the Commission exceeded the powers it would have had under Article 7.[233] Rather, if one wants to call the Commission's approach into question, one may ponder whether the said remedies were strict enough. As explained above, according to the case law of the EU Courts, the Commission could in principle have prohibited the future use of exclusive dealing agreements by the two dominant undertakings completely. Critics of the Article 9 procedure might therefore perceive the two commitments as a manifestation of an alignment of the Commission with the interests of the investigated companies.[234]

The tension between the approach of the EU Courts and the Commission is difficult to resolve. It can probably best be explained with the Commission's efforts to reform Article 102 TFEU.[235] However, even if one rejects the reformed approach of the Commission and follows the more rigid stance of the Courts, there remain

[231]De Hautecloque (2009), 102 and (2013), 92, contrasts the flexible approach of the Commission with an allegedly "rather form-based" approach of the Bundeskartellamt; see for a contrasting of the two approaches also Gauer/Kjølbye (2014), 12.80.

[232]On that question see Sect. 3.3.1.3.2.3.1.3.2 with footnotes 195ff above.

[233]For such a conclusion also von Kalben (2018), 244ff.

[234]See for such arguments in an abstract context Sect. 3.1.2.1 with footnote 24 above.

[235]See Sect. 3.3.1.3.2.3.1.3.3 with footnote 209 above. See also de Hautecloque (2009), 107ff: He argues convincingly that the approach followed by the Commission in Distrigaz consists of transferring the standards that have been developed for the modernised application of Article

ways to reconcile the remedies adopted in Distrigaz and Long-term electricity contracts France with the standard of Article 7. On the one hand, even under the rigid stance of the Courts, a dominant operator may use exclusive dealing obligations, if this is objectively justified. Although the Commission did not treat the question that way in the two decisions, it cannot be excluded that, within the limits provided for in the two remedies, the use of exclusive dealing obligations was objectively justified.[236] On the other hand, the remedies may also have sufficed to bring the exclusive dealing agreements in question outside the scope of the Commission's priorities.[237] For the purposes of the present work, the latter questions need not be discussed in more detail. It is submitted that in any event the tension between the approach of the Courts and the Commission is not a question of the relaxation of the link between harm and remedy in the context of Article 9. Rather, it is a general question of the substantive interpretation of the competition rules. To what extent the use of exclusive dealing agreements should be prohibited for dominant undertakings depends on the substantive interpretation of Article 102 TFEU. In Distrigaz and Long-term electricity contracts France, the Commission followed the less rigid interpretation associated with the reform of the said provision. There is hence at least a likeliness that the Commission would have adopted the less rigid reformed approach also under Article 7.

On a sidenote, one interesting aspect bears still mention. The remedies adopted in Distrigaz and Long-term electricity contracts France did not limit the share of the market that could be tied by the dominant undertakings. Rather, they limited the share of the sales of the dominant undertakings that could be tied.[238] This might be considered as problematic, given that the two companies could not automatically tie a larger part of their sales if they lost market shares. However, there is a justification for the reliance on shares of sales instead of overall market shares: The size of the overall market was difficult to assess.[239] While this may have been an industry specific problem, it points to a general aspect that is important for the design of a remedy. Not least in view of the sanctions that may be imposed on an undertaking for violation of a remedy, the principle of legal certainty requires that the remedy is designed in a way that the undertaking can assess whether it complies with its obligations.

---

101 TFEU to Article 102 TFEU and that this anticipates the 2008 Guidance Paper. See also de Hautecloque (2013), 94f.

[236]See for an overview of the potential procompetitive effects of exclusive dealing arrangements in the energy sector only de Hautecloque (2013), 27ff with further references.

[237]See on the relation between commitments and the Commission's right to prioritise also Sect. 5. 1.3 with footnotes 80ff below.

[238]In principle, the tied share of the sales of the dominant undertaking is linked to the tied share of the overall market through the market share of the dominant undertaking. For instance, Distrigaz had a market share of around 70%. The 30% cap regarding the tied share of the sales of the dominant undertaking hence corresponded to a maximum tie of 20% of the relevant market; see COMP/37.966 (Distrigaz, 2007), 14 and 35; Gauer/Kjølbye (2014), 12.80.

[239]Gauer/Kjølbye (2014), 12.80 fn 147.

3.3.1.3.2.3.2.2 Repsol

3.3.1.3.2.3.2.2.1. The Case In Repsol, the Commission was concerned that the Spanish refiner and distributor of fuel for motor vehicles violated Article 101 TFEU through a bundle of long-term exclusive supply agreements concluded with service stations. The agreements were concluded with 1430 operators of stations that were owned by Repsol, 770 operators of stations that were owned by the operator himself, and 460 stations for which the owner had granted Repsol a right in rem to the usufruct. The latter stations were leased back by Repsol to the owner or a third party linked to him.[240] The Commission considered that in particular the agreements concluded with operators that owned a station and those that had granted Repsol a right in rem to the usufruct contributed significantly to create a foreclosure effect on the fuel retail market in Spain. According to the Commission, Repsol had a market share of around 35% to 50%. The tied share of Repsol's sales amounted to 25–35%. The usufruct agreements had a duration between 25 and 40 years. Moreover, the contracts were concluded in a context where market access was difficult due to the significant vertical integration of operators, the cumulative effect of the parallel networks of vertical restraints, difficulties in setting up an alternative network, the saturation of the market and the nature of the product.[241]

In order to meet the Commission's concerns, Repsol committed, first, to offer the operators of the usufruct stations the possibility to terminate their agreements early and to buy those stations back at market value. Second, Repsol undertook to observe a 5-year maximum duration for new fuel distribution agreements containing non-compete clauses. The 5-year limitation period was not to apply to operators of service stations owned by Repsol or leased by it from third parties unconnected with the operators. Third, during a certain period, Repsol would not buy existing service stations that were not tied to its network from their operators. Fourth, Repsol committed to ensure that stations would be free to grant discounts on the recommended price.[242]

3.3.1.3.2.3.2.2.2. Discussion The first three of the just mentioned obligations address the competition concerns that result from Repsol's bundle of exclusivity arrangements. The grant of early termination rights eliminated the overall foreclosure effect produced by the bundle. The limitation of non-compete clauses to a maximum duration of 5 years and the exception for stations that were owned or leased by Respol corresponded to Article 5(a) of the Vertical Block Exemption Regulation.[243] The obligation to refrain from buying service stations prevented

[240] I follow the description of the case in Gauer/Kjølbye (2014), 12.80.

[241] COMP/38.348 (Repsol, 2006), 20ff; see also Chauve (2006); de Hautecloque (2009), 102; Gauer/Kjølbye (2014), 12.80; Kipiani (2014), 288.

[242] COMP/38.348 (Repsol, 2006), 20.

[243] See COMP/38.348 (Repsol, 2006), Annex B.1.a). Article 5(a) of the old Block Exemption Regulation for Vertical Agreements (2790/99) provided in essence that no block exemption was granted for non-compete clauses the duration of which exceeded five years. However, the time limitation of five years did not apply where the contract goods were sold by the buyer from land

Repsol for a certain period from circumventing the limitation of the exclusivity contracts through forward integration. There is at least no apparent reason to doubt that the Commission could have imposed those obligations also on the basis of Article 7.[244]

However, one may ask whether such doubts must be raised with a view to the fourth obligation described above: The commitment to ensure that stations would be free to grant discounts on the recommended price. As far as is apparent from the decision, the Commission's preliminary assessment did not raise any concerns regarding the maintenance of retail prices.[245] Only during the market test, third parties submitted that service stations were de facto not able to grant discounts.[246] The Commission stated in a footnote of the decision that further analysis would be required to assess whether stations were able to grant discounts. The Commission also mentioned that the Spanish competition tribunal had held Repsol liable for price fixing and enjoined the company from doing so, and that the Spanish competition authority was monitoring the compliance with that injunction.[247] Since the Commission did not form a definitive opinion on whether it had concerns regarding retail price maintenance, one might argue that the acceptance of Repsol's commitment to ensure that stations would be free to grant discounts went beyond what the Commission could have imposed under Article 7. In principle, such a view seems correct. As explained above,[248] the principle of proportionality opposes remedies that extend to conduct which is not covered by the suspected infringement.

Nevertheless, a relativising observation is called for. Article 101 TFEU prohibits the imposition of minimum or fixed resale prices, unless the concerned undertakings prove that the criteria of Article 101(3) TFEU are fulfilled.[249] Repsol's commitment to ensure that stations would be free to grant discounts on the recommended price therefore did not go beyond the substantive prohibitions of the competition rules. The way in which the commitment went beyond what the Commission could have imposed under Article 7 was different. It was shown above that, under the latter provision, the Commission may only impose a termination order if there is a risk that the concerned undertaking will commit the action which the Commission wants to

owned by the supplier or leased by the supplier from third parties not connected with the buyer. The new Block Exemption Regulation for Vertical Agreements, N° 330/2010, contains essentially the same provision in Article 5(1)(a), (2).

[244]Repsol had notified its agreements to the Commission already in 2001 and applied for a negative clearance or an individual exemption. One might therefore also reflect whether the Commission could have imposed the three obligations also as conditions or obligations pursuant to Article 8 (1) Regulation 17/62. In my view, this question must be answered in the affirmative.

[245]Chauve (2006), 27, mentions even that "in its preliminary assessment, the Commission had noted that the provisions of the contracts signed by Repsol did not prevent service stations from granting discounts on the price recommended by Repsol".

[246]COMP/38.348 (Repsol, 2006), 36.

[247]COMP/38.348 (Repsol, 2006), fn 10.

[248]See Sect. 3.2.1.4 with footnote 112 above.

[249]See Whish/Bailey (2012), 647f; Jones/Sufrin (2014), 789.

prohibit.[250] Strictly speaking, given that the Commission did not conclude whether it considered that there was such a risk, it could not have imposed the remedy in question under Article 7. However, it is submitted that this way of exceeding the powers established by Article 7 is less worrying than an over-enforcement of the substantive competition rules.

For the sake of completeness, it should still be pointed out that an association of service station operators later complained to the Commission that Repsol failed to comply with its commitment to ensure that stations would be free to grant discounts on the recommended price. The association requested that the Commission reopen the procedure pursuant to Article 9(2) and impose a fine on Repsol. The Commission rejected the complaint. The rejection was inter alia based on the fact that the Spanish competition authority had already imposed a fine on Repsol in 2009 for having violated Article 101 TFEU by resale price maintenance. The General Court dismissed the appeal that was brought against the rejection decision.[251]

3.3.1.4 Positive Orders and the Freedom of Choice of the Concerned Undertakings

3.3.1.4.1 In the Context of Article 7 Regulation 1/03

According to a widespread perception, Article 7 remedies for infringements of Article 101 TFEU are in principle limited to negative orders, while positive orders can only be imposed for certain infringements of Article 102 TFEU.[252] The distinction is sometimes explained with a "different logic" of Articles 101 and 102 TFEU.[253] Followers of such a view underline that Article 101 TFEU prohibits only agreements or cooperation, but does not regulate market conduct as such. From this, they infer that remedies for Article 101 TFEU are, in general, limited to negative orders to terminate the agreement or cooperation and that "the scope for imposing positive duties is limited to measures aimed at making the termination order effective".[254] At the same time, Article 102 TFEU is said to regulate market conduct directly, thus allowing for remedies that "require specific adjustments to the market

[250]See Sect. 3.3.1.1 with footnote 143 and 3.3.1.3 with footnote 151 above.

[251]GC, T-342/11 (CEES, 2014).

[252]Koska (2008), 248; Kellezi (2010), 364; Whish/Bailey (2012), 253f; Hjelmeng (2013), 1013. Similar arguments were already put forward by the Commission in GC, T-24/90 (Automec II, 1992), 40 to 42. See also Sorinas/Moretti (2012), 4.8: "[T]he Commission's power to require positive actions is different for infringements of Article 101(1) and for those of Article 102 TFEU. Whereas an undertaking that has infringed Article 102 can be ordered, eg., to supply a customer, to grant a license, or to grant access to an essential facility, this cannot be done following an infringement of Article 101"; Komninos (2013), 231: "[. . .] the European Commission [. . .] cannot issue orders imposing positive measures to undertakings in Article 101 TFEU cases".

[253]Whish/Bailey (2012), 253.

[254]Hjelmeng (2013), 1012.

conduct of the dominant undertaking".[255] Supporters of the described distinction between remedies for Articles 101 and 102 TFEU typically rely on the Automec judgment,[256] which will be discussed in more detail below. In essence, the Court used the broadly accepted view that, where several ways to put an infringement to an end exist, a competition authority must leave the choice between them to the concerned parties, as an argument in order to rule that the Commission did not have the power to impose a duty to supply in order to render a selective distribution system compatible with Article 101 TFEU. According to the Court, an order to supply would have deprived the concerned undertakings of the possibility to terminate or modify the agreement.

In the following section, it will be argued that the suggested distinction between remedies for Articles 101 and 102 TFEU is oversimplified.[257] On the one hand, it is not persuasive to limit termination orders for infringements of Article 101 TFEU to a negative content. In this respect, it will be shown that, contrary to what might be inferred from the Automec judgment, the imposition of a positive obligation to put an infringement of Article 101 TFEU to an end is not necessarily incompatible with the requirement to leave the choice between several admissible remedies to the parties. On the other hand, it will be argued that the latter requirement applies also with respect to infringements of Article 102 TFEU. The contention that Article 102 TFEU allows for remedies that "dictate the conditions for a further relationship with the aggrieved party" or "require specific adjustments to the market conduct of the dominant undertaking"[258] cannot be upheld without further reservations.

3.3.1.4.1.1 Positive Orders for Infringements of Article 101 TFEU

Before it will be shown that it is not persuasive to limit termination orders for infringements of Article 101 TFEU to a negative content, it is useful to recapitulate the relevant case law in more detail.

---

[255]Hjelmeng (2013), 1013f. It is true that Hjelmeng acknowledges that "[a]t the outset, the Automec limitation applies also to Article 102 cases". Nevertheless, he expresses the opinion that "in practice, this does not rule out the possibility of ordering positive measures" and that, "[i]f the infringement of Article 102 consists in a refusal to act, [...] the Commission has the power to dictate the conditions for a further relationship with the aggrieved party".

[256]GC, T-24/90 (Automec II, 1992). For a discussion of the remedy see eg Müller-Tautphaeus (2003), 254ff; Sofianatos (2009), 294f; Lianos (2013), 412; Hjelmeng (2013), 1012ff; Whish/Bailey (2012), 253.

[257]Critically also Jaeger (2010), § 32 ARC 28, who considers the Automec doctrine as unsatisfactory: "unbefriedigend, [...] zumal da der Grundsatz der Vertragsfreiheit die europäische Rechtsprechung bei einer Lieferverweigerung, die einen Verstoß gegen Art. 102 AEUV [...] darstellt, nicht hindert, die Befugnis der Kommission anzuerkennen, das zuwiderhandelnde Unternehmen zur Belieferung zu verpflichten".

[258]See Sect. 3.3.1.4.1 with footnote 255 above.

3.3.1.4.1.1.1 Case Law

As pointed out above, the Automec judgment constitutes the typical reference for supporters of the view that positive obligations cannot be imposed for infringements of Article 101 TFEU. In spite of the existence of earlier judgments on the matter, this is not surprising, given that, up to the Automec judgment, the position of the EU Courts was ambiguous. While the Ford I judgment of the Court of Justice pointed already in the same direction as Automec, the General Court initially seems to have taken a different stance in Peugeot. The Automec judgment can thus be seen as a correction of the Peugeot ruling and as an alignment of the General Court with the case law of the Court of Justice. In Germany, the Bundesgerichtshof later followed the approach of the General Court in Automec.

As a preliminary caveat, it must be highlighted that all of the judgments discussed below were taken under the old exemption system. While some details of the reasoning of the Courts might therefore no longer be valid after the system change,[259] the gist of their argumentation remains still applicable and must thus serve as basis for the following discussion.

3.3.1.4.1.1.1.1 Ford I

In Ford I, Ford applied to the Commission for an exemption of a selective distribution system for the German market, which was comparable to other distribution systems for which the Commission had granted exemptions.[260] While the Commission still examined the application, an increasing number of British customers bought right-hand drive cars in Germany due to monetary fluctuations.[261] In order to protect its British distribution system, Ford reacted by addressing a circular to its German distributors, in which it announced that it would no longer provide them with right-hand drive cars.[262] In an interim order, the Commission required Ford to continue the supply of right-hand drive cars to German distributors.[263] The Court of Justice annulled that order. It argued, in essence, that the Commission could not have imposed an order to supply in its final decision regarding the exemption for the selective distribution system either. According to the Court, the fact that the Commission could subject the grant of an exemption for the selective distribution system to a condition to continue the supply of right-hand drive cars did not mean that the Commission was empowered "to convert that requirement [. . .] into a separate, enforceable order which [left] no choice to [Ford]".[264] This reasoning of the Court of Justice must be read in conjunction with the more explicit explanations of

---

[259]Article 1(1) and (2) Regulation 1/03 provide for the direct applicability of Article 101(3) TFEU. On the "system change" see eg Jones/Sufrin (2011), 197; Whish/Bailey (2012), 166ff.

[260]See CJ, 228/82 (Ford I, 1984), 5; for a discussion of the remedy see Ullrich (1984), 589ff.

[261]See CJ, 228/82 (Ford I, 1984), 6.

[262]See CJ, 228/82 (Ford I, 1984), 7.

[263]See CJ, 228/82 (Ford I, 1984), 9.

[264]See CJ, 228/82 (Ford I, 1984), 19 to 22.

Advocate General Slynn. He noted that, in a final decision, the Commission could in particular "make the grant of an exemption conditional on Ford [. . .] restoring the supply of [right-hand drive] cars [or] require Ford [. . .] not to operate the [selective distribution] agreement whilst right-hand drive cars were not being supplied". However, what the Commission could not do was to require Ford "in positive terms [to] supply right-hand drive cars to ist dealers".[265] Advocate General Slynn went on as follows:

> It may well be that, as a result of one of the final orders which could be made, Ford would be driven commercially to renew supply. The essential difference, however, is that it would have the choice, however difficult in practice to operate, of abandoning the agreement, persuading its dealers to modify it or renewing the supply. The present order does not give any such choice.[266]

3.3.1.4.1.1.1.2 Peugeot

Eco System sold Peugeot cars in Luxemburg and Belgium to French final consumers. Peugeot distributed a circular, asking approved resellers to suspend deliveries to Eco System. In an interim order, the Commission required Peugeot to suspend the circular and fixed a maximum quota of cars that had to be delivered to Eco System.[267] On appeal, Peugeot relied on the Ford I judgment, arguing that the Commission had gone beyond what it could have imposed in a final decision, because the order did not leave it a choice.[268] The General Court nevertheless confirmed the order. Skipping the question of whether the order left a choice to Peugeot, the Court argued that the order stayed within the framework of a potential final decision. The Court demarcated the case from the Ford I judgment by holding that, contrary to the Ford case, Peugeot's circular itself—and not the distribution system as such—constituted the subject matter of the main proceedings.[269] Moreover, the Court found that the order merely required Peugeot "to refrain [. . .] from complying with [the] circular [. . .], in other words [. . .] to return to the previous situation as regards [. . .] the supply of vehicles to Eco System".[270]

It seems at least questionable whether this rather formalistic trick to restrict the "subject matter of the main proceedings" to the circular and thus to the refusal to supply really warrants the result of the General Court's judgment, in so far as it is diametrically opposed to the result of the Ford I case.[271] Whether the subject matter

---

[265]See opinion of AG Slynn, 228/82 (Ford I, 1984), 1170.

[266]See opinion of AG Slynn, 228/82 (Ford I, 1984), 1170.

[267]See GC, T-23/90 (Peugeot, 1991), 1 to 4.

[268]See GC, T-23/90 (Peugeot, 1991), 50.

[269]See GC, T-23/90 (Peugeot, 1991), 56.

[270]GC, T-23/90 (Peugeot, 1991), 55.

[271]But see Müller-Tautphaeus (2003), 253f, Sofianatos (2009), 293, and Lianos (2013), 411, who all approve the distinction made by the General Court. They all infer from the judgment that, where the refusal to deal – i.e. the circular – constitutes itself the object of the anticompetitive agreement, an order to supply can be adopted. This view seems to be contested by Whish/Bailey (2012), 254:

of the main proceedings was really restricted to the circular appears doubtful in particular in view of the final decision taken: The Commission did not only order the withdrawal of the circular and thus the supply of Eco System, but also withdrew the block exemption for the entire distribution system unless the parties complied with the obligation to withdraw the circular.[272] Ultimately, the question can be left open. In the following Automec judgment, the General Court aligned its position with that of the Court of Justice.[273]

3.3.1.4.1.1.1.3 Automec

In Automec, an Italian distributor of BMW cars complained to the Commission that BMW had infringed Article 101 TFEU by refusing to supply him as a distributor in BMW's selective distribution network, which had previously been approved by the Commission and of which he satisfied the requisite criteria.[274] Automec requested the Commission to put the infringement to an end and to impose an order to supply on BMW.[275] The Commission rejected the complaint, in essence for two reasons.[276] On the one hand, the Commission argued that it had no power under Article 101 TFEU to issue an order to supply and that Automec had not provided evidence for an infringement of Article 102 TFEU, under which the Commission could issue such orders.[277] On the other hand, with respect to the request to order BMW to put the infringement to an end, the Commission found that the question whether BMW's implementation of its selective distribution system infringed Article 101 TFEU could be left to the Italian civil courts.[278] The General Court endorsed both of the Commission's arguments and rejected Automec's appeal. Only the reasoning of the General Court regarding the first argument of the Commission is of importance here. The Commission's second argument does not relate to the question whether the Commission can impose positive orders for infringements of Article 101 TFEU, but merely to the question under which conditions the Commission can reject a complaint on the ground that the complainant can assert its rights before national Courts.[279]

"The Commission could order an undertaking to terminate an agreement not to supply, but it does not follow that it can also make an order to supply".

[272]See OJ 1992 L 66, 1; Müller-Tautphaeus (2003), 254 fn 87.

[273]The assumption that the Automec judgment constitutes a clarification of the General Court's position in view of divergent earlier case law is supported by the increased importance assigned to the case by the General Court. That importance is demonstrated by the referral of the case to the "full court" and the appointment of an Advocate General (17).

[274]See GC, T-24/90 (Automec II, 1992), 1 and 5.

[275]See GC, T-24/90 (Automec II, 1992), 6 and 7.

[276]See the opinion of judge Edwards acting as AG, T-24/90 (Automec II, 1992), 101, and the judgment of the General Court, 27f.

[277]See GC, T-24/90 (Automec II, 1992), 13.

[278]See GC, T-24/90 (Automec II, 1992), 13.

[279]Generally on the conditions for rejecting a complaint see eg Jones/Sufrin (2011), 1174ff; Whish/Bailey (2012), 286.

With respect to the first argument, i.e. the request to impose an order to supply, the General Court found that the civil law consequences of an infringement of Article 101 TFEU were a matter of national law, with the exception of the nullity provided for in Article 101(2) TFEU. According to the Court, the question whether an infringement of Article 101 TFEU could lead to an obligation to enter into contract, was hence a matter of national law.[280] The Court went on as follows:

> As freedom of contract must remain the rule, the Commission cannot in principle be considered to have, among the powers to issue orders which are available to it for the purpose of bringing to an end infringements of Article [101(1) TFEU], the power to order a party to enter into contractual relations, since in general the Commission has suitable remedies at its disposal for the purpose of requiring an undertaking to terminate an infringement. In particular, there cannot be held to be any justification for such a restriction on freedom of contract where several remedies exist for bringing an infringement to an end. This is true of infringements of Article [101(1) TFEU] arising out of the application of a distribution system. Such infringements can also be eliminated by the abandonment or amendment of the distribution system. Consequently, the Commission undoubtedly has the power to find that an infringement exists and to order the parties concerned to bring it to an end, but it is not for the Commission to impose upon the parties its own choice from among all the various potential courses of action which are in conformity with the Treaty.[281]

Already at this point, a brief observation is called for. Some commentators infer from the quoted passage of the Automec judgment that the Commission can require an undertaking "to terminate an agreement", whilst it cannot require compliance with a positive obligation.[282] The first part of this contention is incorrect. In Automec, the General Court did not state that the Commission could require an undertaking to terminate an agreement. Rather, the Court limited the Commission's powers to an abstract order "to bring the infringement to an end". Indeed, allowing the Commission to require the termination of an agreement would be contrary to the Court's own reasoning. Since the Court explicitly acknowledged that the amendment of the distribution system or the supply of the excluded party constitute other admissible ways of bringing the infringement to an end, an order to terminate the distribution agreement would mean "to impose upon the parties [the Commission's] own choice from among all the various potential courses of action which are in conformity with the Treaty". This is, however, precisely what the Court wanted to prevent. It is hence submitted that the content of the Automec judgment is not well captured in the contrasting of admissible negative termination orders to inadmissible positive orders to supply. It is better expressed in the confrontation of, on the one hand, admissible unspecific orders that leave a choice to the concerned undertakings,

---

[280] See GC, T-24/90 (Automec II, 1992), 50.

[281] GC, T-24/90 (Automec II, 1992), 51f.

[282] See Whish/Bailey (2012), 253f: "Article 101 prohibits agreements, and the Commission may make an order to terminate them [. . .] The Commission can order an undertaking to terminate an agreement not to supply, but it does not follow that it can also make an order to supply".

Hjelmeng (2013), 1012f: "Under Article 101, an infringement is brought to an end by an order to terminate the contract [. . .] orders terminating an infringement of Article 101 must be limited to a duty to discontinue the cooperation, or to remove offensive clauses in a contract".

and, on the other hand, inadmissible specific orders that deprive the concerned undertakings of a potential choice.[283]

3.3.1.4.1.1.1.4 Depotkosmetik

In so far as the General Court left it in Automec to national law whether an infringement of Article 101 TFEU could lead to an obligation to enter into contract, it is interesting to note that, under German law, the Bundesgerichtshof denies a distributor, who is excluded from a selective distribution system in contravention of Article 101 TFEU, a right to be supplied. Expressly referring to the Automec case law of the General Court, the Bundesgerichtshof argues that, in order to put the infringement to an end, the undertaking applying the selective distribution has the choice between supplying the distributor or amending or abandoning the distribution system.[284] The illegally excluded distributor must hence rely on a claim for damages.[285] Regardless of the merits of the substance of the Bundesgerichtshof's judgment, it must be stated that the reference to the Automec judgment is in any event not persuasive. Since the General Court had explicitly left it to national law to decide whether an infringement of Article 101 TFEU could lead to an obligation to enter into contract, the Automec judgment cannot serve as authority to deny such an obligation under national law.

3.3.1.4.1.1.2 Discussion

With the exception of the Peugeot case, the described judgments all clearly militate against the admission of specific positive orders to ensure compliance with Article 101 TFEU. The paramount concern of the courts is to guarantee that, where several ways to put an infringement to an end exist, a competition authority leaves the choice between them to the concerned parties. This endeavour must in principle be approved.

However, the courts also assume that the imposition of a positive obligation to modify an agreement and comply with a positive obligation is incompatible with a preservation of the freedom of choice, because such an obligation deprives the

---

[283] See the interpretation of the Automec judgment of Mestmäcker/Schweitzer (2004), § 20, 35: "Bestehen verschiedene den Wettbewerbsregeln entsprechende Möglichkeiten, den Verstoß abzustellen, so darf die Kommission die Unternehmen nicht zu einer bestimmten, in die Vertragsfreiheit eingreifenden Abstellung zwingen." Similarly Koska (2008), 249: "[Dem Automec Urteil] ist zu entnehmen, dass die Kommission [...] befugt ist, die Zuwiderhandlung festzustellen und den betroffenen Parteien die Abstellung aufzugeben, ohne jedoch den Parteien bezüglich der verschiedenen möglichen und mit dem EWG-Vertrag zu vereinbarenden Verhaltensweisen eine bestimmte Wahl vorzuschreiben".

[284] BGH, KZR 23/96 (Depotkosmetik, 1998), 20. The judgment is very controversial in Germany. For a discussion and further references see eg Papadimitriou (2005), 125ff; Jaecks/Säcker (2008), 2-8-184ff; Jaeger (2009), Art. 81, 54 fn 172 and 173, Rheinländer (2007a, b, c), Liesegang (2013) and Emde (2013).

[285] See Jaeger (2009), 54.

parties of the possibility to terminate the agreement entirely. The paramount point of the following section is, however, that the latter argument is not convincing. After a closer look at the potential field of application for positive orders for infringements of Article 101 TFEU, it will be shown that the imposition of an obligation to modify an agreement and comply with a positive obligation is not incompatible with the requirement to preserve the parties' freedom of choice, since it does not deprive the parties of the possibility to acquit themselves of the positive obligation by terminating the entire agreement. Finally, it will also be pointed out that the imposition of a positive obligation may also be justified where it serves to eliminate the subsisting effects of an infringement of Article 101 TFEU.

3.3.1.4.1.1.2.1 The Potential Field of Application of Positive Orders for Infringements of Article 101 TFEU: Constellations in Which the Anticompetitive Character of an Agreement Stems from an Omission

There are numerous constellations where the prohibition of an agreement depends precisely on the question whether the parties comply with positive obligations vis-à-vis each other or third parties.[286] For example, Article 3(2) of Regulation 1217/2010 makes the grant of a block exemption for a research and development agreement dependent on the fact that the parties have access to the final result of the joint research and development. Article 3(5) of the same Regulation provides that "[p]arties charged with the manufacture of the contract products by way of specialisation must [under certain conditions] be required to fulfil orders for supplies of the contract products from the other parties". According to the Guidelines on Horizontal Cooperation Agreements, standardisation agreements only fall outside the scope of Article 101(1), if participation in the standard setting is unrestricted and if there is effective access to the standard on fair, reasonable and non-discriminatory terms.[287] In the insurance sector, pursuant to Article 3(2) lit. d) and e) of Regulation 267/2010, the grant of a block exemption for agreements relating to the joint compilation and distribution of certain information requires that the information is "made available on reasonable, affordable and non-discriminatory terms, to any insurance undertaking which requests a copy" and, under certain conditions, also to consumer and customer organisations. As regards distribution agreements in the motor vehicle sector, Article 4(2) of Regulation 1400/2002 made the grant of a block exemption dependent on the supplier granting independent operators "access to [. . .] technical information, diagnostic and other equipment, tools, including any relevant software, or training required for the repair and maintenance of [. . .] motor vehicles".[288] The Guidelines for motor vehicle distribution contracts now provide that a qualitative

[286] See also Fletcher/Jardine (2008), 540, with the hint that "fair and reasonable pricing may in some cases be necessary to justify the application of Article [101(3) TFEU]".

[287] Guidelines on horizontal cooperation agreements (2010), 280ff.

[288] Regulation 1400/2002 is no longer in force.

selective distribution agreement will fall under the prohibition of Article 101 TFEU, "if, within the context of the agreement, one of the parties acts in a way that forecloses independent operators from the market, for instance by failing to release technical repair and maintenance information to them".[289] All these constellations confirm that the question of whether a positive order can be imposed for an infringement of Article 101 TFEU is not limited to the field of selective distribution systems. In view of the rather broad potential field of application, the question is of paramount significance for the interpretation of Article 7.

3.3.1.4.1.1.2.2 The Compatibility of Positive Orders with the Freedom of Choice of the Concerned Undertakings

In the following section, it will be shown that the abstract order "to put the infringement to an end", to which the General Court confined the Commission in the Automec judgment, does not constitute the only order that preserves the concerned parties' freedom of choice as regards the various means to restore compliance with Article 101 TFEU. First, it will be demonstrated from a general perspective that also the more precise orders to terminate the entire agreement or to comply with a positive obligation allow to preserve the parties' freedom of choice, since these orders must be considered as being respectively conditional on the compliance with the positive obligation or the termination of the entire agreement. Thereafter, the impact of the three different types of orders—i.e. the abstract order "to put the infringement to an end" and the two more precise orders to terminate the entire infringement or to comply with the positive obligation—on the concerned parties freedom of choice will be discussed in more detail. In this respect, it is useful to distinguish between constellations in which the concerned parties agree whether they prefer compliance with the positive obligation to abandoning the entire agreement and constellations in which there is a dispute between the parties in that regard.

3.3.1.4.1.1.2.2.1. Three Ways to Put an Infringement to an End Wherever the anticompetitive character of an agreement depends on compliance with positive obligations like the ones just mentioned above, it is correct that the parties to the agreement must, in principle, have the choice whether they want to completely abandon their agreement, for instance because compliance with the positive obligations makes it unattractive for them, or whether they want to modify the agreement in order to comply with the positive obligations.[290] However, as has been pointed out above, it is erroneous to assume that a negative prohibition of the entire agreement leaves that choice to the parties. In Automec, the General Court did not state that the Commission could prohibit the entire agreement, but limited the Commission to the imposition of an abstract order "to put the infringement to an end". In so far as commentators claim that the Commission cannot impose a positive obligation to

[289] Supplementary guidelines on vertical restraints in agreements for the sale and repair of motor vehicles and for the distribution of spare parts for motor vehicles (2010), 62.

[290] See also Deselaers (1992), 89ff.

make an agreement compatible with Article 101 TFEU, but that it can require the termination of the agreement, their views must hence be rejected.[291]

At the same time, the Automec approach to confine the Commission to an abstract order "to put the infringement to an end" is also little persuasive. Although such an abstract order certainly constitutes one possible means to preserve the concerned parties' freedom of choice, it is not the only one. Rather, there are two further possibilities: The Commission can either "prohibit the entire agreement as long as the parties do not comply with the positive obligation". Or, the Commission can order the parties to "comply with the positive obligation as long as they implement the agreement". On the one hand, an unconditional prohibition of the entire agreement is impossible, because the agreement loses its anticompetitive character as soon as the positive obligation is complied with. An unrestricted order to terminate the entire agreement must thus be considered as disproportionate. On the other hand, also the order to comply with a positive obligation must be conditional, namely on the continuity of the otherwise anticompetitive agreement, in which the order to comply with the positive obligation has its sole justification.

Several commentators have expressed a favourable stance as regards orders containing specified alternate courses of conduct.[292] The conditional orders just mentioned belong in this category.[293] In Ford I, the Court of Justice had no problem in accepting that the Commission could subject the grant of an exemption for the selective distribution system to a condition to continue the supply of right-hand drive cars to German distributors.[294] This amounts to admitting that the Commission could "prohibit the entire agreement as long as the parties do not comply with the positive obligation". If this is the case, then it is difficult to see, why the exact opposite, i.e. the order to "comply with the positive obligation as long as the parties implement the agreement", should not be admitted. Indeed, the reason why, in Ford I and Automec, the EU Courts excluded positive orders for infringements of Article 101 TFEU, does not seem to be the consideration that an order to "comply with the positive obligation as long as the parties implement the agreement" would unduly encroach on the parties freedom of choice. Rather, the reason seems to lie in the refusal of the Courts to accept that also positive orders are actually conditional, i.e. dependent on the continuity of the otherwise anticompetitive agreement.[295]

[291] See Sect. 3.3.1.4.1.1.1.3 with footnotes 282 and 283 above.

[292] Eg Wertheimer (1984), 738; Deselaers (1992), 91f; Koska (2008), 250; Jaeger (2010), § 32 ARC, 23.

[293] See Deselaers (1992), 91f: He insists that a termination order must respect the concerned undertaking's freedom of choice; nevertheless, he also suggests that an order to comply with a positive obligation under the condition of the maintenance of the agreement would meet this requirement.

[294] See Sect. 3.3.1.4.1.1.1.1, footnote 264 above.

[295] See CJ, 228/82 (Ford I, 1984), 21: In view of its "unequivocal wording" and the accompanying like effects order, the CJ refused to interpret the Commission's order to supply as being conditional on the cessation of the selective distribution agreement.

In Automec, the General Court did not even treat the question whether the Commission could have issued an order to supply on the condition of the subsistence of the distribution agreement.

This refusal to take the actual conditionality of positive obligations into account seems, however, mistaken. Even if the condition of a continuity of the agreement is not considered an integral part of any order to comply with a positive obligation, the Commission can nevertheless explicitly provide for such a condition in the decision. Where this does not happen, the addressee of such an order to comply with a positive obligation has in any event the right to demand its revocation, if the entire agreement is abandoned. In this respect, the arguments that have been made above in the context of the discussion of termination orders for single branding infringements apply mutatis mutandis.[296]

3.3.1.4.1.1.2.2.2. The Impact of the Three Types of Orders on the Parties Freedom of Choice Where the Parties Have Shared Preferences as Regards the Continuation of the Agreement If the parties agree whether they want to abandon their agreement or modify it in order to comply with the positive obligation, a comparison of the three described types of orders shows that they do not have a significantly different impact on the party's freedom of choice. An abstract order to "put the infringement to an end" is in this case from the outset unproblematic, since, besides the prohibition to continue the status quo, it does not contain any prescriptions regarding the future behaviour of the parties at all. The situation is similar also as regards the two more specific orders: If the Commission prohibits the entire and the parties prefer modifying the agreement, they can do this in order to avoid the complete prohibition of the agreement. If the Commission orders the compliance with the positive obligation, the parties can abandon the agreement in order to acquit themselves of the obligation to comply with the positive obligation.

Certainly, in comparison to an abstract order to put an infringement to an end, the two more specific orders comprise the disadvantage of requiring the parties to go through a revocation procedure, where the respective condition is not inherent in the respective order. In such a case, if the Commission prohibits the entire agreement, the parties must apply to the Commission for a revocation of the order once they have rendered the agreement compatible with Article 101 TFEU by complying with the positive obligation. In the same vein, if the Commission has ordered compliance with the positive obligation, the parties must apply to the Commission for a revocation of the order once the agreement has been terminated. For the following three reasons, this additional burden of a revocation procedure constitutes, however, at best a weak argument in favour of an abstract termination order.

First, it must be underlined that this additional burden does not exist, if the respective condition is already inherent in the respective order. This would be the case if the order provided explicitly for a condition or if the order were at least interpreted in that sense. In such a case, the fulfilment of the condition, e.g. the termination of the agreement, would lead automatically to the elimination of the corresponding order, e.g. the compliance with a positive obligation. Second, even where the respective condition is not inherent in the respective order, the additional

[296]See Sect. 3.3.1.3.2.3.1.3.2 with footnote 199f above; moreover Jaeger (2010), § 32 ARC, 28.

burden brought about by the necessity of a revocation procedure can in any event be reduced through reliance on a prognosis at the time the order is taken. If, up to the time the decision is taken, the parties have indicated a preference for maintaining their agreement and the Commission therefore orders them to comply with a positive obligation, the burden of a revocation procedure in case the parties later change their mind and agree to abandon the entire agreement does not seem unreasonable. The right to be heard guarantees that the Commission makes such a prognosis. As will be shown in more detail below,[297] the Commission must indicate to the parties during the administrative procedure with sufficient clarity, which remedies it intends to impose. Thus, the parties have in any event an opportunity to inform the Commission about their preference for an alternate way to stop the infringement. The Commission must respect such a preference, as long as the remedy proposed by the parties is equally effective in putting the infringement to an end. Third, at least where the order rests on a prognosis, the remaining burden brought about by the necessity of a revocation procedure is balanced, if not even outweighed, by the fact that the parties gain legal certainty about what they have to do in order to render their agreement compatible with Article 101 TFEU.[298] A mere abstract order "to put an infringement to an end", eventually accompanied by an equally abstract like effects order, does not provide guidance for the concerned parties how they should behave in order to avoid that their agreement is anew considered as an infringement. This is different, if the Commission orders compliance with certain precisely formulated obligations.

3.3.1.4.1.1.2.2.3. The Impact of the Three Types of Orders on the Parties' Freedom of Choice Where the Parties Disagree About the Continuation of the Agreement Albeit more complex, the situation must be assessed similarly, when the parties disagree whether to abandon or modify the agreement.

According to settled case law of the Court of Justice, the nullity provided for by Article 101(2) TFEU extends only to the concrete clause of an agreement which is affected by the Article 101(1) TFEU prohibition; only where an affected clause is not severable from the rest of the agreement, the latter is void in its entirety; for the rest, it is a question of national law whether the nullity of a severable clause pursuant to Article 101(2) entails the voidness of the entire agreement.[299] This case law confirms that EU competition law prohibits only the anticompetitive part of an agreement. The impact of the anticompetitive part on the remainder of the agreement is a question of national law. Also if the anticompetitive part of an agreement consists in an omission, it is therefore a question of national law whether this entails the nullity of the agreement in its entirety or whether the parties have an obligation to eliminate

[297] See Sect. 4.1.1.1.1 with footnotes 10ff below.

[298] See also Koska (2008), 250, who underlines that orders that prescribe specific alternate ways of conduct have the advantage of being more precise than an abstract order to put the infringement to an end.

[299] See CJ, 56/65 (Société La Technique Minière, 1966); 319/82 (Société de Vente de Ciments, 1983), 11; Jones/Sufrin (2011), 1197; K. Schmidt (2012), Art. 101 Abs. 2, 21.

the omission by taking positive action.[300] It is submitted that an order of the Commission must respect this autonomy of national law.

In Automec, the General Court relied on the described strand of case law in support of its finding that the question whether an infringement of Article 101 TFEU could lead to an obligation to enter into contract was a matter of national law.[301] This is, in principle, correct. However, at the same time, the Court also used this argument to restrict the Commission's powers to mere abstract orders "to put the infringement to an end". The latter approach must be rejected. The necessary respect for national law does not require a confinement of the Commission's powers to such abstract orders. In fact, it was pointed out above that the more specific orders to terminate the entire agreement or to modify it in order to comply with a positive obligation must be regarded as depending respectively on the compliance with the positive obligation or the termination of the entire agreement. Even if such conditions are not inherent in the respective order, the concerned parties can, in any event, request a revocation, if the respective condition is fulfilled. Both orders therefore leave enough room for the respect of national law in that they allow for maintaining the agreement in a modified form or for abandoning the agreement, should national law provide for the respective solution.[302]

Certainly, at least at the outset, an order to terminate the agreement favours the party that prefers abandoning the agreement to complying with the positive obligation. In the same vein, an order to comply with the positive obligation at least initially favours the party that prefers maintaining the agreement. Both orders can thus create a

---

[300]See CJ, 10/86 (VAG France, 1986), 15f, where the CJ held that it was a question a national law to determine whether the incompatibility of a part of an agreement with Article 101 TFEU had "the effect of obliging the contracting parties to amend the content of their agreement in order to prevent it from being void". See also CJ, C-377/05 (BMW, 2007), 48ff: The CJ confirmed that the consequences of the prohibition of contractual terms under Article 101 TFEU for the remaining parts of an agreement were a question of national law. Moreover, the CJ specified that EU law did not preclude national law from providing for the invalidity of the entire agreement.

For possible solutions under German law see Schmidt (2012), Art. 101 Abs. 2, 23ff: § 139 BGB provides that "[i]f a part of a legal transaction is void, then the entire legal transaction is void, unless it is to be assumed that it would have been undertaken even without the void part." Where standard terms are concerned, § 306 BGB provides that, as a rule, "the remainder of the contract remains in effect". Besides §§ 139 and 306 BGB, contractual severability clauses and statutory or contractual obligations to adapt the contract play a role.

[301]See Sect. 3.3.1.4.1.1.1.3, footnote 280 above.

[302]It is submitted that the binding effect of Commission decisions provided for by Article 16 (1) Regulation 1/03 does not undermine this conclusion. If the Commission orders the parties to comply with a positive obligation in order to make their agreement compatible with Article 101 TFEU, a national court may still rule that the agreement is void in its entirety, which would then lead to either the automatic elimination of the order to comply with the positive obligation or to the revocation of the order. As the question whether an agreement is void in its entirety is a question of national law, the Commission has no competences in making a finding in this respect. The Commission's order to comply with the positive obligation hence does not encompass an implicit finding that the agreement is not void in its entirety. The order therefore cannot have a binding effect in this respect.

tension with national law: The party that is initially disfavoured by the order, but whose preference corresponds to what is provided for by national law, must tolerate the undesired order until the party has asserted its position before the national courts, which then leads to an automatic elimination of the Commission's order or at least to the revocation of the latter. In such a situation, an abstract order "to put the infringement to an end" has the advantage of being neutral. One might therefore consider it as "more respectful" of national law than both of the two more precise orders.

Yet again, the latter advantage of an abstract order constitutes at most a weak argument against the use of the two more precise orders. First, also in case of dispute between the parties about the maintenance of the agreement, the Commission will in some cases be able to make a prognosis. If the Commission can foresee that in a dispute the party preferring to modify the agreement and to comply with the positive obligation would prevail, e.g. because the agreement itself or the general rules of national law provide for an obligation to amend the agreement and comply with the positive obligation, then there is no reason why the Commission should not be able to order the compliance with the positive obligation already from the outset. Second, even where such a prognosis is exposed to obstacles, for instance because the solution provided for by national law is difficult or even impossible to predict, a precise order may still be warranted by reasons of effectiveness. In fact, in case of a dispute between the parties about whether to abandon or modify the agreement, an abstract order "to put the infringement to an end" runs the risk of leading to a mutual blockade of the parties and a perpetuation of the anticompetitive situation until a decision has been taken under national law. In order to avoid this, it seems preferable to adopt either of the two more precise orders and to accept the potential disadvantage that one of the parties may eventually turn out to have—at the outset—been unduly disfavoured by the order, until the decision under national law led to the order's automatic elimination or its revocation upon request.

3.3.1.4.1.1.2.2.4. Intermediate Conclusion The analysis so far reveals that the Commission should be allowed to make positive orders also with respect to infringements of Article 101 TFEU. This is in particular the case where a prognosis shows that the parties unanimously prefer the compliance with the positive obligation to the abandonment of the entire agreement or that, in case of a dispute between the parties, the party preferring the compliance with the positive obligation would be able to assert its position before the national courts. In both cases, the parties are sufficiently protected against an undue limitation of their freedom of choice by the fact that the order to comply with the positive obligation is in any event conditional on the continuity of the agreement. With respect to the first constellation, i.e. the one in which the parties agree, the following needs to be added: As far as infringements of Article 102 TFEU are concerned, it is broadly accepted that the Commission can require the infringing undertaking to make proposals how to put the infringement to an end.[303] There is no reason why this power of the Commission should not extend

[303]CJ, 6/73 (Commercial Solvents, 1974), 45; see also GC, T-201/04 (Microsoft I, 2007), 1255; Dalheimer (2005), 10; Bauer (2008), 4-7-028; Sauer (2013), 11.07; Hjelmeng (2013), 1014.

to infringements of Article 101 TFEU.[304] However, if the parties propose the compliance with a positive obligation to the Commission in reaction to an order to make proposals, the Commission must also have the power to make that proposal binding pursuant to Article 7 Regulation 1/03.[305]

3.3.1.4.1.1.2.3 Positive Orders to Eliminate the Subsisting Effects of an Infringement of Article 101 TFEU

Even where the parties agree that they would prefer abandoning their anticompetitive agreement to making it compatible with Article 101 TFEU by complying with a positive obligation, or where the party that prefers abandoning the agreement would prevail in case of a dispute, the imposition of a positive order may nevertheless be justified in order to eliminate the subsisting effects that result from the illegal implementation of the agreement before the intervention of the Commission.[306] Some of the examples mentioned above[307] illustrate this very well: If the parties contravene against Article 3(2) of Regulation 1217/2010 by implementing a research and development agreement that does not provide for their access to the final result of the joint research and development, the termination of the agreement may not suffice to restore competition between the parties. Similarly, where the implementation of a standardisation agreement that does not provide for access to the standard on fair, reasonable and non-discriminatory terms has led to the evolution of an industry standard, the mere termination of the agreement may not suffice to ensure that all parties to the agreement and third parties have access to the evolved standard. If insurance companies agree to share information without making the shared information also available to other insurance companies, thereby infringing Article 3(2) lit. d) of Regulation 267/2010, the mere termination of the agreement will not eliminate the competitive advantage the companies have created by sharing the information. In all those cases the imposition of an access obligation may be

---

[304]With respect to German law Jaeger (2010), § 32 ARC, 23 in conjunction with 28, expressly states that the competition authority can order the undertakings to make proposals how to put an infringement of Article 101 TFEU to an end.

[305]One might also consider that Article 9 of Regulation 1703 could serve as the legal basis for the acceptance of such a proposal. However, there are several objections: First, where the order to make proposals was based on Article 7, the Commission has made a finding as regards the infringement. This is not required for an Article 9 decision. Second, according to Recital 13 of Regulation 1/03, Article 9 commitments are incompatible with fines. However, the Commission can impose a fine together with an Article 7 order to make proposals how to put an infringement to an end. Third, where the order to make proposals to put the infringement to an end is based on Article 7, the parties have not made the proposals voluntarily. It is therefore submitted that Article 7 is the correct legal basis, if the Commission makes a proposal binding that has been made by the parties in reply to an Article 7 order.

[306]For the general discussion of measures aiming at the eliminating of the subsisting effects of an infringement see Sect. 3.3.4 with footnotes 600ff below.

[307]See Sect. 3.3.1.4.1.1.2.1 with footnotes 286 to 289 above.

indispensable to eliminate the subsisting effects of the respective infringements of Article 101 TFEU.

3.3.1.4.1.1.2.4 Conclusion: A Look Back at Selective Distribution Systems

Summing up, positive orders should not be excluded for infringements of Article 101 TFEU. This shall be illustrated once more by a critical look back at the example of the anticompetitive exclusion of a distributor from a selective distribution system. If one accepts that a refusal to supply a distributor who fulfils the criteria of an otherwise legal selective distribution agreement can bring the agreement under the head of Article 101(1),[308] it is difficult to see why the Commission should not be allowed to address this concrete cause of the anticompetitive character of the selective distribution agreement.[309] The emphasis of the freedom of choice of the supplier to abandon its distribution system, which underlies the Ford I and Automec rulings, is in this respect not persuasive. On the one hand, there is a likeliness that the supplier will either not be willing to abandon the distribution system anyway or that he will at least not be able to assert the abandoning of the distribution system vis-à-vis the other distributors under national law. The nullity provided for by Article 101(2) TFEU does not cover the entirety of the contracts with the other distributors and these contracts are not automatically void under national law.[310] On the other hand, even if the supplier prefers the abandoning of the distribution system and succeeds in asserting this position vis-à-vis his contractual partners, the freedom of

[308]In order to be captured by Article 101(1) TFEU, the refusal may not merely constitute a unilateral act, cf. Deselaers (1992), 27ff; Jones/Sufrin (2011), 672 and 147ff; Whish/Bailey (2012), 643 fn 191 and 105ff.

[309]See the annotation of Ullrich (1984), 591, to the Ford I judgement: "If it is only the refusal to sell which renders the selective distribution system unlawful, and if, as is generally acknowledged, it is only the restrictive element of an enterprises conduct which may be enjoined by virtue of Article [7 of Regulation 1/03], then it is surprising to see that the Court and its Advocate General would allow the Commission to issue an order enjoining Ford to operate the distribution system whilst refusing to sell right-hand cars in Germany rather than to enjoin Ford's refusing sales whilst operating a selective distribution system! As a matter of fact, Ford continued to apply its selective distribution system, and there was no question that it might or should stop doing so nor had the Commission any reason or right to block the operation of the entire system in order to enjoin the practice of its unlawful features. This would have been out of proportion to the end to be achieved." See also Jaeger (2010), § 32 ARC, 28: "Wenn [. . .] – im Beispiel des selektiven Vertriebssystems – bei realistischer Prognose nicht damit zu rechnen ist, dass das betreffende Unternehmen sein Vertriebssystem von Grund auf ändern wird und die Beibehaltung des Vertriebssystems nur bei einer Belieferung auch des bisher abgewiesenen Nachfragers kartellrechtmäßig ist, ist § 32 Abs. 2 [GWB] dahin auszulegen, dass die Kartellbehörde dem Unternehmen diese Belieferung auferlegen kann."

[310]See Sect. 3.3.1.4.1.1.2.2.3, footnotes 299f above. Deselaers (1992), 29, Papadimitriou (2005), 189f, and Koska (2008), 250, point out that an isolated non-admittance to a distribution system does not entail the voidance of the entire system; only a systematic discrimination may do this. More generally, Liesegang (2013), 238, and Emde (2013), 360, point out that under German law, the entire distribution system will only be void in exceptional circumstances. See also Jaecks/Säcker (2008), 2-8-187.

choice of the supplier to abandon its distribution system is sufficiently assured by the fact that the order to supply is necessarily conditional on the maintenance of the distribution system.[311] Similar arguments militate also against the approach of the Bundesgerichtshof in the Depotkosmetik judgment.[312]

3.3.1.4.1.2 Positive Orders for Infringements of Article 102 TFEU

While, in the context of Article 101 TFEU, already the basic admissibility of positive orders is controversial, the same cannot be said for Article 102 TFEU. As regards the latter provision, it is well established since the Commercial Solvents judgment that the Commission can issue "an order to do certain acts or provide certain advantages which have been wrongfully withheld".[313] Nevertheless, this should not lead to the conclusion that, in the context of Article 102 TFEU, the Commission is relieved from the obligation to respect the freedom of choice of the concerned dominant undertaking. As regards infringements of Article 102 TFEU in general, it can be stated that, just as under Article 101 TFEU, there are normally several ways to put an infringement to an end. In fact, although Article 102 TFEU goes beyond Article 101 TFEU in that it imposes a "special responsibility",[314] the provision nevertheless does not predetermine the conduct of a dominant operator down to the last detail.[315] Rather, through the various prohibitions enshrined in it, Article 102 TFEU establishes merely a legal framework for the conduct of the dominant undertaking. As long as the latter does not overstep the boundaries drawn by that framework, it enjoys a freedom to act, which must also be respected by the Commission when imposing a remedy.

As regards more particularly the relation between the Commission's power to issue positive orders and its obligation to respect a dominant undertaking's freedom of choice, the following section will distinguish between two constellations: On the one hand, also in the context of Article 102 TFEU, positive action may in some cases be merely one among several ways to put an infringement to an end. With respect to

---

[311] See Sect. 3.3.1.4.1.1.2.2.1, footnote 296 above.

[312] See Sect. 3.3.1.4.1.1.1.4, footnote 284 above; Papadimitriou (2005), 188ff; Rheinländer (2007c), 384ff; Jaeger (2009), 55; Emde (2013), 359.

[313] CJ, 6/73 (Commercial Solvents, 1974), 45.

[314] CJ, 322/81 (Michelin I, 1983), 57; see Jones/Sufrin (2011), 366 and Whish/Bailey (2012), 192 for further references.

[315] Where the Courts refer to the "special responsibility" formula, they merely mean that a conduct that is permitted for a non-dominant operator can be qualified as abusive where it is applied by a dominant one. See the paraphrasing of the "special responsibility" formula in GC, T-111/96 (ITT), 139: "It follows from the nature of the obligations imposed by Article 86 of the Treaty that, in specific circumstances, undertakings in a dominant position may be deprived of the right to adopt a course of conduct or take measures which are not in themselves abuses and which would even be unobjectionable if adopted or taken by non-dominant undertakings ". In the Atlantic Container Line judgment (T-191/98, 1460), the GC was even more explicit: "special responsibility means only that a dominant undertaking may be prohibited from conduct which is legitimate where it is carried out by non-dominant undertakings"; see also Jones/Sufrin (2011), 366.

these cases, it will be argued below that the principles that have been developed in the context of Article 101 TFEU should be applied mutatis mutandis. On the other hand, there are cases in which the positive action constitutes in principle the only way to put the abuse to an end. Nevertheless, as will be argued below, even in these cases, the Commission must still respect the freedom of choice of the concerned undertaking with respect to the details of the implementation of the remedy.

3.3.1.4.1.2.1 Orders Requiring Positive Action Where There Are Several Ways to Put the Abuse to an End

There are abuse cases, in which the imposition of an order requiring positive action is only one among several ways to put the infringement to an end. On a rather general level, one can for instance say that an abusive discrimination can be stopped either by withdrawing the benefit in question from those to whom it was granted in a discriminatory manner or by granting the same benefit also to others. Moreover, discriminatory practices can be put to an end by rendering the criteria for discrimination objectively justified. In Aéroports de Paris (ADP), the General Court acknowledged that, in such a case, the Commission must respect the concerned undertaking's freedom of choice also in the context of Article 102 TFEU. The Commission found that ADP had infringed Article 102 TFEU by applying discriminatory commercial fees in the Paris airports of Orly and Charles de Gaulle on suppliers of certain types of groundhandling services. As remedy, the Commission ordered ADP to put an end to that infringement by applying a non-discriminatory scheme of commercial fees. On appeal, ADP complained that the order did not indicate what it was required to do.[316] Referring to the Automec judgment, the Court emphasised that, in exercising its power to issue directions under Article 7 Regulation 1/03, the Commission had to observe the principle of freedom of contract.[317]

The abuse procedures against Microsoft for tying the Media Player and the Internet Explorer to Windows can serve as another example. The various remedies that were debated in this context will be discussed in more detail below.[318] At this point, it suffices to say that the two procedures show that a tying abuse can be brought to an end in at least two different ways: Either by a "negative" order to untie the tied products. This was the way that was followed in the decision regarding the Media Player, in which the Commission required Microsoft to offer not only an integrated version of Windows with the Media Player, but also a fully functioning version of Windows without the Media Player. The tying abuse could, however, also be stopped by a "positive" order to include not only the own products of the dominant undertaking, but also the products of competitors into the bundle. This was the way that was followed in the decision regarding the Internet Explorer, in

[316]GC, T-128/98 (Aéroports de Paris, 2000), 81.

[317]GC, T-128/98 (Aéroports de Paris, 2000), 82.

[318]See, also for references, Sect. 3.3.1.7 with footnotes 550ff below.

which Microsoft committed to update Windows with a choice screen software that allowed users to pick their preferred browser.

Finally, further examples of situations in which positive action is merely one among several ways to stop an abuse may be found in the various constellations mentioned above in the context of Article 101 TFEU, in which an omission may make an agreement anticompetitive. It is not entirely clear whether such infringements of Article 101 TFEU would also be captured by Article 102 TFEU, if at least one of the parties holds a dominant position.[319] However, if one assumes that this is the case,[320] then the termination of the agreement and the compliance with the positive obligation are alternate ways to put the infringement to an end—also where a dominant undertaking is concerned.

Wherever an order to take specific positive action constitutes merely one among several ways to put an abuse of a dominant position to an end, the same principles that have been developed above in the context of Article 101 TFEU should be applied. The mere fact that the case is treated under Article 102 TFEU does not warrant a deviation. This means that, although it is true that the choice regarding the remedy must in principle be left to the dominant undertaking, the latter requirement does not hinder the imposition of the order to take specific positive action. The dominant undertaking is sufficiently protected by the fact that the order to take specific positive action is conditional on compliance with the alternate way to stop the abuse. If the Commission orders to take positive action, the dominant undertaking can in any event request a revocation of that order as soon as it complies with an alternate way to stop the abuse.

3.3.1.4.1.2.2 Orders Requiring Positive Action Where the Latter Constitutes the Only Way to Put the Abuse to an End: The Typical Refusal to Deal Cases

There are other types of infringements of Article 102 TFEU in which positive action constitutes the only way to put the abuse to an end. Typical examples are refusal to deal cases in general and in particular the so-called "essential facilities cases".[321] As regards the latter, the theory of abuse is based on the withholding of an input that is indispensable for another market participant. If this is the case, the abuse can only be

---

[319] In principle, Article 101 and 102 TFEU are not mutually exclusive. Article 102 TFEU may therefore also capture restrictive agreements that fall already under Article 101 TFEU. The typical example are exclusive dealing arrangements (see GC, T-65/98 [Van den Bergh, 2003]). On the other hand, not all restrictive agreements concluded by a dominant undertaking amount to an abuse of a dominant position (see Commission, [2004] Notice on application of Article 101[3], 106; Jones/Sufrin (2011), 280; O'Donoghue/Padilla [2013], 36).

[320] For a discussion when refusals to deal in the context of cooperation agreements may amount to a violation of Article 102 TFEU, see O'Donoghue/Padilla (2013), 573f.

[321] The essential facilities cases constitute only one of several subcategories of refusal to deal cases; for an overview see eg Jones/Sufrin (2011), 479ff; Fuchs/Möschel (2012), Art. 102, 305ff; Whish/Bailey (2012), 697ff; O'Donoghue/Padilla (2013), 509ff.

put to an end by providing the indispensable input. Nevertheless, the fact that, in such refusal to deal cases, an order to supply constitutes the only way to stop the abuse should not lead to the conclusion that the Commission may "dictate the conditions for a further relationship with the aggrieved party" or "require specific adjustments to the market conduct of the dominant undertaking".[322] That an order to supply constitutes the only way to stop an abuse does not mean that the Commission has the power to precisely determine the conduct of the concerned parties. Rather, the Commission must still respect the concerned undertakings' freedom of choice as regards the details of the implementation.[323] Certainly, through the various prohibitions enshrined in it, Article 102 TFEU establishes a framework within which these details must be set. For instance, the remuneration charged for access may not be abusively high, must be non-discriminatory and cannot lead to a margin squeeze; access may not be granted exclusively and not be illegally tied to another product or service. However, within that framework, also the dominant operator maintains a freedom to act, which must be respected by the Commission when imposing a remedy.

It will be shown below, first, that both the Commission's practice and the case law of the EU Court's contain clear indications that, even where the imposition of a positive obligation constitutes the only way to put an abuse to an end, the Commission must nevertheless respect the parties' freedom of choice as regards the implementation. Second, it will be argued that this does not only apply in cases where the dominant undertaking refuses to start supplying a new customer, but also at least in some cases concerning the abusive ruptures of pre-existing supply relations. Finally, it will be argued that the Commission's obligation to respect the concerned parties' freedom of choice does not categorically preclude more detailed prescriptions as regards the implementation of the obligation to supply. More detailed prescriptions can be made, as long as they do not go further than the prohibitions enshrined in Article 102 TFEU.

[322]See Sect. 3.3.1.4.1 with footnote 255 above.

[323]With respect to German law, the Bundesverfassungsgericht, 1 BvR 1627/95 (Arzneimittelimport, 2000), 38, has held that the imposition of a duty to supply on a dominant undertaking only becomes problematic, where the order is not confined to a general obligation to enter into contract, but also stipulates all the essential details of the contractual relation: "problematisch wird ein solches Gebot erst dann, wenn es sich nicht nur darauf beschränkt, die grundsätzliche unternehmerische Entscheidung über die Aufnahme von Geschäftsbeziehungen zu korrigieren, sondern auch alle wesentlichen Einzelheiten dieser Beziehungen festlegt und damit den Adressaten der Verfügung darauf beschränkt, die behördlicherseits getroffene Entscheidung umzusetzen sowie die hieraus resultierenden wirtschaftlichen Konsequenzen zu tragen." See also Jaeger (2010), § 32 ARC, 29.

3.3.1.4.1.2.2.1 The Commission Must Respect the Parties' Freedom of Choice As Regards the Implementation of an Obligation to Deal

Several commentators express the opinion that, in view of the deficits of generalised courts and competition authorities to act as regulators, the details regarding the implementation of an obligation to deal should, at least in a first step, be left to negotiation between the concerned parties.[324] The following cases show that the practice of the Commission is generally in line with such an approach. At the latest in the Microsoft penalties judgment, the General Court explicitly construed the concerned parties' freedom of choice as a limitation to the Commission's powers in the context of refusals to supply under Article 102 TFEU.

3.3.1.4.1.2.2.1.1.Commercial Solvents[325] Commercial Solvents decided to extend its business from the production of certain raw materials also to the derivative products. In this context, the company announced to its customer Zoja, who was active on the derivative market, that it would stop supplying it with the raw materials, save for quantities that Commercial Solvents had committed to in the past. The Commission considered the rupture of supply to amount to an abuse of a dominant position. In order to cover Zoja's most urgent needs, the Commission ordered Commercial Solvents to supply Zoja once with certain quantities of the raw materials at the maximum price charged for those within a certain period of time. As regards the subsequent supply of Zoja, Commercial Solvents was required to submit proposals to the Commission.[326] On appeal, Commercial Solvents argued inter alia that the Commission did not have power to order it to supply within a given time a given quantity of a given product at a maximum price, but only to require it in general terms to put the infringement to an end.[327] The Court of Justice rejected that argument with the following words:

> [H]aving established a refusal to sell incompatible with Article [102], the Commission was entitled to order certain quantities of raw material to be supplied to make good the refusal of supplies as well as to order that proposals to prevent a repetition of the conduct complained of be put forward. In order to ensure that its decision was effective, the Commission was entitled to determine the minimum requirements to ensure that the infringement was made good and that Zoja was protected from the consequences of it. In choosing as a guide to the needs of Zoja the quantity of previous supplies the Commission has not exceeded its discretionary power.[328]

At first blush, the just cited passage might be understood as a precedent to support the generalised allegation that the Commission has the power to impose precisely

[324]See Jaeger (2010), § 32 ARC, 29; Podszun (2012), 56f and 68; O'Donoghue/Padilla (2013), 932f and 941.

[325]For descriptions of the case see eg Jones/Sufrin (2011), 481ff; O'Donoghue/Padilla (2013), 527. For a discussion of the remedy see eg Müller-Tautphaeus (2003), 238ff; Kellezi (2010), 277; Podszun (2012), 50; Lianos (2013), 366f.

[326]See CJ, 6/73 (Commercial Solvents, 1974), p. 227.

[327]See the opinion of AG Warner in CJ, 6/73 (Commercial Solvents, 1974), p. 271.

[328]CJ, 6/73 (Commercial Solvents, 1974), 46.

determined quantities or prices.[329] Such an interpretation would, however, go too far. A closer look at the passage reveals that the Court distinguished between the Commission's power to order "certain quantities" on the one hand and its power to require the dominant undertaking to put forward "proposals" on the other hand. In this respect, it is apparent from the submissions of the Commission that its order contained specific prescriptions as regards the supply only to the extent that this was necessary to cover Zoja's most urgent needs. On the contrary, the Commission submitted itself that, for the longer-term supplies, it had deliberately "relied on the presentation of proposals that would be open to discussion".[330] The Commercial Solvents judgment can therefore only be interpreted as a confirmation that the Commission may make prescriptions regarding the details of an order to supply, in so far as these are necessary to ensure the customer's survival in the short term. The judgment does, however, not contain any statement regarding the question whether the Commission is also entitled to make such precise prescriptions regarding a long-term supply.

3.3.1.4.1.2.2.1.2. Magill In Magill,[331] the Commission found that the TV companies ITP, BBC and RTE had infringed Article 102 TFEU by refusing access to their copyright protected program listings. The Commission imposed the following remedy:

> ITP, BBC and RTE shall bring the infringements [. . .] to an end forthwith by supplying each other and third parties on request and on a non-discriminatory basis with their [. . .] program listings and by permitting reproduction of those listings [. . .]. If they choose to supply and permit reproduction of the listings by means of licences, any royalties requested [. . .] should be reasonable. Moreover, ITP, BBC and RTE may include in any licences granted to third parties such terms as are considered necessary to ensure comprehensive high-quality coverage of all their programmes, including those of minority and/or regional appeal, and those of cultural, historical and educational significance. The parties are therefore required [. . .] to submit proposals for approval by the Commission of the terms upon which they consider third parties should be permitted to publish [. . .] programme listings [. . .].[332]

On appeal, RTE and ITP challenged the order.[333] They complained in particular that the Commission did not merely require them to put the infringement to an end, "but laid down the precise manner in which that was to be brought about, by requiring [them] to grant compulsory licences of the protected works".[334] The General Court upheld the order. In reply to the described argument, it stated that requiring the supply with the program listings on a non-discriminatory basis was "the only means of bringing [the] infringement to an end". However, according to

[329]For such an interpretation of the Commercial Solvents case see Kellezi (2010), 276f and 363, and the remarks in Sect. 3.3.1.4.1.2.2.2, footnote 353 below.

[330]See the opinion of AG Warner in CJ, 6/73 (Commercial Solvents, 1974), p. 273.

[331]OJ 1989 L 78/43 (Magill, 1988). For a description of the case see eg Jones/Sufrin (2011), 499.

[332]See GC, T-76/89 (ITP, 1991), 11.

[333]See GC (1991), T-69/89 (RTE), 86ff, and T-76/89 (ITP), 67ff.

[334]GC (1991), T-69/89 (RTE), 95, and T-76/89 (ITP), 68.

the Court, by imposing such an obligation, "the Commission did not deprive [RTE and ITP] of [their] choice between the various measures which could bring the infringement to an end".[335] The Court of Justice endorsed the judgments of the General Court and agreed in particular with the reasoning that the imposition of the general obligation to supply the program listings was "the only way of bringing the infringement to an end", while the licensing of the programs constituted merely a "possibility".[336]

The major importance of the Magill judgment regarding remedies is sometimes seen in the statement of the EU Courts that the order to supply constituted the "only means" to stop the abuse.[337] Nevertheless, by this statement, the Courts merely referred to the general imposition of an obligation to supply. The second aspect of the judgment is at least equally important: The Courts highlighted that the Commission's order did not deprive the infringing undertakings of their choice how to implement the obligation to supply. In this respect, the undertakings were again only required to submit proposals to the Commission.[338]

3.3.1.4.1.2.2.1.3. IMS Health In the IMS case,[339] the Commission considered that the refusal to license a copyright protected compilation of sales data, the so called "1860 brick structure", violated Article 102 TFEU. In an interim measure, the Commission required IMS to grant licenses "on request and on a non-discriminatory basis". The operative part of the decision expressly provided that it was in principle up to the parties to agree on the royalties. Only if no agreement was reached, an independent expert was to determine the royalties.[340] During the administrative procedure leading to the decision, IMS had argued that the Commission was obliged "to specify how any license fees were to be calculated and the terms of the license". The Commission rejected the argument, stating that "allowing the parties to reach a mutual agreement, and failing that, to engage an expert, [was] entirely appropriate".[341] For reasons that shall not further be discussed here, the President of the General Court subsequently suspended the order.[342] The order was ultimately withdrawn by the Commission.[343]

---

[335]GC (1991), T-69/89 (RTE), 98, and T-76/89 (ITP), 71. This reasoning of the General Court must be considered in the light of the Commission's argument that its order did not "impose a single solution but propose[d], in a flexible manner, certain courses of conduct designed to bring the infringement to an end". According to the Commission, the order merely "suggest[ed] two ways of bringing the infringement to an end: the supply [. . .] on a non-discriminatory basis of the listings concerned [. . .] or the grant of licences on conditions which take account of the parties' legitimate preoccupations"; cf. GC (1991), T-69/89 (RTE), 96, and T-76/89 (ITP), 69.

[336]Cf. CJ, C-241/91 P (ITP, 1995), 91.

[337]Lowe/Maier-Rigaud (2008), 606; Lianos (2013), 368.

[338]See Sect. 3.3.1.4.1.1.2.2.4 with footnotes 303ff above; consenting Kellezi (2010), 280.

[339]For descriptions of the case see Jones/Sufrin (2014), 532ff; O'Donoghue/Padilla (2013), 532f.

[340]2002 OJ L 59, 18.

[341]2002 OJ L 59, 18, 218.

[342]GC, T-184/01 R (IMS, 2001).

[343]OJ L 268/69 (IMS, 2003).

3.3.1.4.1.2.2.1.4. Microsoft Penalties In its 2004 decision, the Commission found inter alia that Microsoft had violated Article 102 TFEU by refusing to grant access to certain interoperability information. In order to put the abuse to an end, the Commission ordered Microsoft to make the interoperability information available and to allow for its use on reasonable and non-discriminatory terms.[344] The Commission later inflicted penalties on Microsoft, because the latter had disregarded the 2004 decision by charging unreasonable remuneration rates. On appeal, Microsoft argued in particular that the Commission had "infringed its obligation to specify positively what Microsoft had to do in order to comply with [the order contained in the 2004 decision]".[345] The Court rejected this argument. One of the reasons it used was that several remuneration rates conformed to the requirements of Article 102 TFEU, so that, in line with the Automec judgment, it was "not for the Commission to impose [. . .] its own choice from among all the various potential courses of action which are in conformity with the Treaty or with a decision imposing behavioural remedies".[346]

The Microsoft penalties judgment will be discussed in more detail below with respect to its conformity with the principle of legal certainty. At this point, it suffices to state that, like in Aéroports de Paris mentioned above,[347] the General Court explicitly applied the Automec principles in the context of Article 102 TFEU. While the Commercial Solvents, Magill and IMS Health cases all point already in a similar direction, they are different in so far as none of them contain a wording that draws such clear limitations to the Commission's powers. In order to reject Microsoft's argument, the Court could have contented itself with stating that the Commission was free to abstain from determining the precise details for the supply of the interoperability information in order to preserve the parties freedom of choice. However, the Court went beyond such an approach and chose a wording and a precedent that explicitly limit the Commission's power. Hence, the approach followed by the General Court in Microsoft makes it unmistakeably clear that, even in refusal to deal cases, in which the imposition of a general order to supply constitutes the "only means"[348] to stop the abuse, the Commission must respect the concerned parties' freedom of choice as regards the details of the implementation of the order to supply.

3.3.1.4.1.2.2.2 A Distinction Between Rupture of On-Going Supply and Refusal to Supply a New Customer?

Kellezi has suggested gradating the level of detail with which competition authorities can define the conditions of a duty to supply according to whether the abuse consists in the rupture of on-going commercial relations or in the refusal to supply a

[344]COMP/C-3/37.792 (Microsoft, 2004), Article 5 a) of the operative part.

[345]GC, T-167/08 (Microsoft II, 2012), 74.

[346]GC, T-167/08 (Microsoft II, 2012), 95.

[347]See Sect. 3.3.1.4.1.2.1 with footnotes 316f above.

[348]See Sect. 3.3.1.4.1.2.2.1.2 with footnote 335 above.

new customer.[349] She is of the opinion that in the former case, competition authorities can order the continuation of the commercial relation under the conditions of the relation before the rupture of supply and hence determine quantity, quality and price.[350] Only in the latter case, priority is to be given to a negotiated solution, in which proposals of the parties play an important role.[351]

However, Kellezi's distinction needs to be refined. Certainly, a competition authority can order the continuation of a commercial relation under the previous conditions where the rupture of supply infringes a running contract. This may, for instance, be the case, if the contract has been cancelled with a too short notice.[352] However, a rupture of supply may also go hand in hand with an expiry or a termination of the previous supply agreement that are legal under general civil law. In such a case, the freedom left to the dominant undertaking for the determination of the supply conditions must be the same as if the case concerned the refusal to supply a new customer.[353]

3.3.1.4.1.2.2.3 Scope for Specific Orders Regarding the Implementation of a Positive Obligation

As is apparent from the decisional practice described above, the Commission meets the requirement to respect the concerned parties freedom of choice regarding the implementation of a duty to deal often by resorting to broad and abstract terms, such as an order to supply "on reasonable terms". The problems thus caused from the point of view of the principle of legal certainty will be discussed in a different section below. At this point, it should only briefly be pointed out that such abstract orders are not the only ones that are compatible with the Commission's duty to respect the concerned parties freedom of choice. Ultimately, everything depends on the scope of

---

[349]Kellezi (2010), 276ff.

[350]Kellezi (2010), 276f: "[L]'autorité [. . .] peut ordonner à l'entreprise condamnée de continuer les relations commerciales sous les mêmes conditions qu'avant la rupture de celles-ci, ou avec des changements minimes. [. . .] Les éléments essentiels à déterminer sont la quantité, le prix ainsi que la qualité".

[351]Kellezi (2010), 279ff, 282: "Lorsque le refus d'entretenir des relations commerciales concerne des nouveaux clients, la priorité doit être donnée à une solution négociée où les parties, de par leurs propositions, ont un rôle important".

[352]See Eilmansberger (2008), 2-15-433, who argues that a rupture of supply may constitute an abuse if the period of cancellation is inadequate, i.e. if it does not allow the retailer "to amortise product specific investments [. . .] and to switch to the distribution of other products".

[353]This can be illustrated with the Commercial Solvents case, in which Commercial Solvent's refused to supply Zoja save for quantities that it had already committed to in the past, cf. CJ, 6/73 (Commercial Solvents, 1974), 7 and 23. The Commission therefore correctly limited its principle order to requiring Commercial Solvents to make proposals for the conditions of supply in the future. Contrary to what Kellezi (2010), 276f, seems to suggest, the fact the Commission also ordered a one time supply of certain quantities at a maximum price was not justified by the fact that the case concerned a rupture of previous supply, but rather by the "urgent needs" of the customer, cf. CJ, 6/73 (Commercial Solvents, 1974), p. 227.

the prohibitions enshrined in Article 102 TFEU. As long as the Commission's orders do not go beyond these prohibitions, it can also make more detailed prescriptions. For example, since the dominant undertaking may neither charge an excessively high, nor a predatory price for the supply, the Commission could make more detailed prescriptions in this respect, for instance by providing for a maximum or minimum price. Such orders are compatible with the requirement to respect the parties' freedom of choice, since the latter only applies within the boundaries of what is lawful.

3.3.1.4.2 In the Context of Article 9 Regulation 1/03

In the Commission's commitment practice, positive obligations appear frequently. With a view to Article 101 TFEU, the following examples shall be mentioned: In order to offset concerns regarding the joint marketing of media rights, football associations committed inter alia to auction off the rights in several more precisely determined packages in a transparent and non-discriminatory procedure.[354] Four major car manufacturers undertook to provide technical information about car repairs to independent garages.[355] Parties to airline alliance agreements engaged themselves to release slots and to enter into certain agreements with competitors.[356] The International Association of Classification Societies (IACS) committed inter alia to enable classification societies that were not IACS members to participate in its working groups and to grant access to IACS' technical resolutions and related background documents.[357] Container liner shipping companies committed to modify their pricing announcements to include at least certain elements regarding the total price and to make these announcements binding as maximum prices.[358] ISDA and Markits engaged themselves to license IP rights on FRAND terms on the market for credit default swaps.[359]

Also in the context of Article 102, positive obligations are rather the rule than the exception. Examples are the obligations of dominant energy companies to divest generation capacity or transmission grids[360]; Microsoft's obligation to provide for a

---

[354] COMP/37.214 (Bundesliga, 2005), 27ff; COMP/38.173 (Premier League, 2006), 32ff; similarly already COMP/37.398 (UEFA, 2003), 27ff.

[355] COMP/39.140 (Daimler, 2007); COMP/39.141 (Fiat, 2007); COMP/39.142 (Toyota, 2007); COMP/39.143 (Opel, 2007); see also Schweitzer (2010), 554f, who states that these commitments "essentially amount to a specification of the requirements under Article 4(2) Regulation 1400/2002".

[356] COMP/39.596 (BA/AA/IB, 2010); COMP/39.595 (Continental/United/Lufthansa/Air Canada, 2013); COMP/39.964 (Air France-KLM/Delta/Alitalia, 2017).

[357] COMP/39.416 (Ship Classification, 2009); for a description of the case see Derenne (2010), 162; Dohms/Rieder (2010), 41.

[358] COMP/39.850 (Container Shipping, 2016).

[359] COMP/39.745 (CDS, 2016).

[360] See the discussion below (Sect. 3.4.2.1 with footnotes 946ff).

browser choice screen[361]; IBM's obligation to make spare parts and technical information available to independent mainframe maintainers[362]; Thomson Reuters' obligation to create a licence allowing customers the use of its instrument code for data sourced from Thomson Reuters' competitors[363]; BEH's obligation to set up a power exchange market[364]; Gazprom's obligation to offer to some of its customers the possibility to change the delivery destination of the procured gas[365]; TenneT's obligation to increase electricity trading capacity between Denmark and Germany.[366]

The details of these decisions shall not be discussed here. However, as a matter of principle, it can be stated that, if one follows the opinion defended above that Article 7 allows for positive orders both with respect to Article 101 TFEU and Article 102 TFEU, the fact that the Commission makes positive obligations binding under Article 9 does not indicate that the Commission uses the latter provision to extract excessive remedies. A further aspect provides an even stronger legitimisation for the inclusion of positive obligations in commitment decisions, regardless of whether the remedy in question addresses concerns relating to Article 101 TFEU or Article 102 TFEU. In the context of Article 7, the central argument against the use of any or at least more specific positive orders is the necessity to preserve the concerned undertaking's freedom of choice how to put an infringement to an end. As long as there are several equally effective ways how to comply with the competition rules, the Commission should not unilaterally substitute its assessment for that of the concerned undertakings. However, due to the consensual nature of commitments, this argument is of limited importance in the context of Article 9. Given that commitments are offered by the concerned undertakings, they express the undertakings' preference of how to put an infringement to an end. As explained above, Article 7 empowers the Commission to require the concerned undertakings to submit proposals how to put an infringement to the end and to make such proposals binding, regardless of whether they contain positive obligations.[367] If one accepts this premise, then there is no reason why an Article 9 commitment containing positive obligations should be considered as going beyond what the Commission could have imposed under Article 7.

[361] See the discussion below (Sect. 3.3.1.7 with footnotes 550ff).

[362] COMP/39.692 (IBM, 2011).

[363] COMP/39.654 (Reuters, 2012). The appeal by which Morningstar claimed that the final commitments did not go far enough was rejected on its substance in GC, T-76/14 (Morningstar, 2016); for a discussion of the judgment see Idot (2016), 31, and Paemen/Baltrusch (2017), 99.

[364] COMP/39.767 (BEH, 2015).

[365] COMP/39.816 (Gazprom, 2018), in particular 163: "the Commitments, in addition to being strictly prohibitive in respect of certain types of behaviour (e.g. territorial restrictions), also impose positive forward-looking obligations on Gazprom to facilitate the free flow of gas across CEE". For a discussion of the case see Lübking (2019), 434.

[366] COMP/40.461 (DE/DK Interconnector, 2017).

[367] Section 3.3.1.4.1.1.2.2.4 above.

3.3.1.5 The Scope of Remedies and Article 101(3) TFEU

3.3.1.5.1 In the Context of Article 7

Every practice that falls under the head of Article 101(1) TFEU can potentially be justified pursuant to Article 101(3) TFEU.[368] In exceptional cases, even a restriction of competition by object may therefore be lawful.[369] A remedy may only cover practices that are incompatible with the competition rules. Hence, a remedy can, in principle, not prohibit a practice that fulfils the requirements of Article 101(3) TFEU. This is not problematic, if the Commission limits the scope of a prohibition order to the particular form of the practice that it investigates. If the investigated form does not fulfil the requirements of Article 101(3) TFEU, it can be prohibited. Problems arise, however, if the Commission extends the scope of a prohibition order also to similar practices for which it is not yet clear, whether the concerned undertakings will be able to show that the conditions of Article 101(3) TFEU are met. In Mastercard and Cartes Bancaires, the General Court was confronted with the question whether such far-reaching prohibitions are lawful. Before the two cases will be discussed below, some introductory explanations regarding the treatment of so-called Multilateral Interchange Fees (MIFs) under EU competition law are called for in order to provide the basis for the following discussion.

3.3.1.5.1.1 MIFs and the Remedy Imposed in Mastercard

3.3.1.5.1.1.1 General Remarks Regarding the Treatment of MIFs Under EU Competition Law

For a sales transaction with a payment card, the cardholder's bank can charge the merchant's bank a so-called interchange fee. If the level of that fee is fixed by means of a decision binding all banks participating in the payment card scheme, this is called a MIF.[370] Such MIFs restrict competition between merchant's banks, because they set a price floor for the fees charged by the merchant's banks to merchants.[371] MIFs therefore fall under the head of Article 101(1) TFEU. Like any practice captured by Article 101(1) TFEU, MIFs are nevertheless not prohibited, if they meet the requirements of Article 101(3) TFEU.[372] A potential justification of MIFs is that they redress cost imbalances between the cardholder's banks, which bear the main cost of the card payment system, and the merchant's banks, which have revenues from fees paid by merchants.[373] Similarly, it can be argued that MIFs

[368]GC, T-17/93 (Matra Hachette, 1994), 85; T-168/01 (Glaxo Smith Kline, 2006), 233.

[369]Jones/Sufrin (2011), 203 fn 73, 240 and 814f; Whish/Bailey (2012), 153ff.

[370]Commission, MEMO/07/590; see also Commission MEMO/13/719; Lista (2013), 150.

[371]See COMP/34579 (Mastercard, 2007), 404; Commission, MEMO/07/590; GC, T-111/08 (Mastercard, 2012), 143; opinion of AG Mengozzi in C-382/12 P (Mastercard, 2014), 69.

[372]See Commission, MEMO/07/590 and Sect. 3.3.1.5.1, footnotes 368 and 369 above.

[373]See the sector enquiry of the Commission: Communication from the Commission COM(2007) 33 final, 15; Commission staff working document, 115 and 117.

stimulate card issuing and use, because the cardholder's banks use the MIFs to incentivise card use through certain bonuses. The stimulation of card use is particularly relevant, because payment card schemes involve two sided markets characterised by indirect network externalities: An increase in card use will lead to more merchants accepting the card, which in turn will increase the utility of the card for users and lead to more users.[374] The Commission's decisional practice regarding the application of Article 101(3) TFEU to MIFs is mixed. It depends to a large extent on the circumstances of the individual case.[375]

In 2002, the Commission granted an exemption for certain MIFs fixed by Visa until the end of 2007. The exemption was granted only after Visa had modified the relevant MIF schemes, resulting in a progressive reduction of the MIFs down to a weighted average of 0.7% of a transaction.[376] In 2007, the Commission found that certain MIFs fixed by Mastercard did not meet the requirements of Article 101 (3) TFEU and ordered Mastercard to repeal the relevant MIFs.[377] Following the decision, Mastercard at first provisionally repealed the MIFs.[378] When Mastercard reimposed modified MIFs in 2008, the Commission was concerned that this would constitute a violation of the 2007 decision or of the competition rules. Only after Mastercard informally undertook in 2009 to cut the MIFs down to a weighted average of 0.2% of a transaction for debit cards and of 0.3% for credit cards, the Commission decided informally not to pursue Mastercard "either for non-compliance with the 2007 decision, or for infringing the antitrust rules".[379] In 2010, the Commission made binding commitments by Visa to cut its MIF for debit cards down to a weighted average of 0.2% of a transaction for 4 years.[380] In 2014, the Commission made again binding commitments by Visa to maintain the MIF for debit cards at 0.2% and to cut down the MIF for credit cards to 0.3%.[381] Also several national competition authorities within the ECN issued decisions regarding MIFs.[382] In 2015, the European Parliament and the Council adopted the Interchange Fee Regulation,[383] which from December 2015 capped interchange fees for cards issued and used in Europe at 0.2% for debit cards and 0.3% for credit cards. The caps of this

[374]See Commission, MEMO/07/590; MEMO/13/719. For a more detailed discussion of payment card schemes as two sided markets see Gyselen (2005); Evans/Schmalensee (2005); Lista (2013), 166.

[375]See Commission, MEMO/07/590. For a detailed account of the Commission's decisional practice regarding MIFs, also before the first Visa decision, see Lista (2013), 153ff.

[376]See OJ 2002 L 318/17, 16ff; Lista (2013), 159f.

[377]COMP/34579 (Mastercard, 2007); see also Hellström/Maier-Rigaud/Bulst (2009), 51f; Jones/Sufrin (2011), 1023f; Lista (2013), 161f.

[378]See Commission, MEMO/08/397.

[379]See Commission, IP/09/515.

[380]See Commission, IP/10/1684.

[381]See Commission, IP/14/197.

[382]For an overview, see ECN Sub-group Banking and Payments, Information Paper on Competition Enforcement in the Payments Sector, May 2012.

[383]Regulation 2015/751 on interchange fees for card-based payment transactions.

regulation do, however, not apply to inter-regional transactions, as the Regulation does not apply to cards issued outside the EEA. Regarding the latter transactions, the Commission made in 2019 again binding commitments by Visa and Mastercard to cap the level of inter-regional interchange fees.[384]

3.3.1.5.1.1.2 The Remedy Imposed in Mastercard

As stated above, in the 2007 decision, the Commission found that certain MIFs applied by Mastercard infringed Article 101 TFEU. The Commission required Mastercard to put the infringement to an end and to refrain from conduct having an identical or similar object or effect. For this purpose, the Commission explicitly required Mastercard to repeal all decisions on MIFs within a transitional period of 6 months. To ensure compliance with the remedy, the Commission imposed penalties.[385]

On appeal, Mastercard complained that the remedy was disproportionate and that the Commission had violated its obligation to state reasons in that it required the MIFs to be repealed completely or set at zero. According to Mastercard, since the Commission accepted that a MIF could generally be justified under Article 101 (3) TFEU, the Commission rather ought to have determined the methodology by which the MIF should be calculated in order to make it compatible with the competition rules.[386] The General Court upheld the Commission's order. As regards the alleged violation of the principle of proportionality, the Court argued that it was for Mastercard to prove compliance with the conditions of Article 101(3) TFEU and to put forward a method of setting the MIF that would meet those conditions. According to the Court, "in the absence of such proof, the Commission [had to] ensure that the infringement of Article [101 TFEU] which it ha[d] properly identified [was] brought to an end".[387] With respect to the alleged failure to state reasons, the Court argued that the general acceptance by the Commission that MIFs could meet the requirements of Article 101(3) TFEU was "irrelevant" for the remedy, which the Court found to be a "direct consequence of the finding that the MIF [was] unlawful".[388] Mastercard did not raise a plea in law regarding the remedy in its appeal to the Court of Justice. However, in the context of his analysis of the conditions of Article 101(3) TFEU, AG Mengozzi considered Mastercard's argument that the Commission had "not provided the slightest guidance" as to the precise methodology that Mastercard should follow in setting the MIF "ineffective", because it was not capable of identifying any error or law by the General Court.[389]

---

[384] COMP/39.398 (Visa, 2019); COMP/40.049 (Mastercard II, 2019); Commission, IP/19/2311.

[385] See GC, T-111/08 (Mastercard, 2012), 44 and 304.

[386] See GC, T-111/08 (Mastercard, 2012), 314 and 326.

[387] See GC, T-111/08 (Mastercard, 2012), 327.

[388] See GC, T-111/08 (Mastercard, 2012), 313f.

[389] Opinion of AG Mengozzi in C-382/12 P (Mastercard, 2014), 166.

3.3.1.5.1.2 The Remedy Imposed in Cartes Bancaires

In Cartes Bancaires, the Commission found that certain fees adopted by the "Groupement des Cartes Bancaires", managing the CB card system, infringed Article 101 TFEU. The Commission's major concerns related to the so-called MERFA ("Mécanisme Régulateur de la Fonction Acquéreur"), a formula that determined whether a fee of up to 11 Euro on each card issued should be paid by member banks that were not sufficiently active in terms of acquisition of merchants or installation of automated teller machines (ATMs).[390] The Groupement argued that the disputed fees were at least justified under Article 101(3) TFEU. Allegedly, the fees were necessary to stimulate contracts between banks and merchants for card acceptance services and to stimulate the installation of ATMs, thus levelling out an imbalance in the CB card system. Moreover, the fees allegedly helped to prevent new entrants from free riding on the investments made by other members.[391] However, the Commission found that the Groupement had not succeeded in proving that the fees were necessary for the said purposes.[392] During the administrative procedure, the Commission rejected commitments proposed by the Groupement, because the latter insisted that any potential commitments should include a reservation allowing the Groupement to take measures that were necessary to level out an imbalance in the CB card system.[393] The Commission considered this reservation capable of being interpreted as allowing the adoption of measures similar to the MERFA. However, in the Commission's view, any such commitments were unacceptable.[394] As remedy, the Commission ordered the Groupement to bring the infringement to an end and to refrain from measures having an identical or similar object or effect. The Commission did not impose penalties.[395]

On appeal, the Groupement complained that the like effects order was disproportionate and violated the principle of legal certainty. According to the Groupement, the order was imprecise and went beyond the Commission's finding of an infringement in so far as it prohibited "similar conduct".[396] The Groupement argued in particular that the order prohibited also any future fees that were necessary to level out imbalances of the CB card system and to reinforce its competitive position.[397] The General Court confirmed the order, which it interpreted restrictively "in the light of the grounds" of the decision.[398] According to the Court, the grounds of the decision "define [. . .] clearly the scope and limits"[399] of a like effects order and

[390]See Commission, IP/07/1522.

[391]See Commission, MEMO/07/413.

[392]COMP/38606 (Cartes Bancaires, 2007), 379ff; Commission, MEMO/07/413.

[393]See GC, T-491/07 (Cartes bancaires, 2012), 448.

[394]See Commission, MEMO/07/413.

[395]COMP/38606 (Cartes Bancaires, 2007).

[396]GC, T-491/07 (Cartes bancaires, 2012), 436.

[397]GC, T-491/07 (Cartes bancaires, 2012), 442.

[398]See GC, T-491/07 (Cartes bancaires, 2012), 439, 440, 445 and 448.

[399]GC, T-491/07 (Cartes bancaires, 2012), 445.

such an order merely aims at preventing a repetition of the practices that have been identified as infringements in the decision.[400] The Court explicitly stated that the Commission's use of the term "similar" did not mean that the Groupement was enjoined from adopting measures that were necessary to level out imbalances in the CB card system or to reinforce its competitive position.[401] In the Court's view, the latter conclusion was not invalidated by the fact that the Commission had refused to accept commitments in which the Groupement had reserved its right to take measures that were necessary to level out imbalances of the CB card system and to reinforce its competitive position. In this respect, the Court argued in essence that the Commission's order had to be interpreted only in the light of the grounds of the decision, which did not contain an uncertainty regarding the practices that had been identified as infringements in the decision; the order could not be interpreted in the light of the negotiations of the commitments.[402] Given that it considered the order sufficiently precise, the Court also saw no undue risk for the Groupement to get fined for recidivism.[403]

3.3.1.5.1.3 Discussion

It must be emphasised that the Mastercard and the Cartes Bancaires procedures concern different types of interbank fees. The substantive assessment of the two types of fees under Article 101(1) and (3) TFEU may therefore in principle diverge.[404] For the present purposes of analysing the Commission's and the Court's approach regarding the remedies, a comparison of the two cases shall nevertheless be dared. It will be shown that the two judgments do not offer a uniform answer regarding the question whether the Commission can prohibit practices for which it has not yet been clarified whether they meet the requirements of Article 101 (3) TFEU. An answer to this question shall hence be attempted in a further step.

3.3.1.5.1.3.1 Comparison of the Mastercard and the Cartes Bancaires Judgments

In Mastercard, the object of the dispute was not an abstract like effects order, but the precise prescription to repeal all concerned MIFs.[405] Hence, there was no controversy whether the order was sufficiently precise. The parties and the General Court seem to have understood the order unanimously as enjoining Mastercard completely from applying the concerned MIFs, irrespective of their level.[406] The Court's finding

[400]GC, T-491/07 (Cartes bancaires, 2012), 439, 440.

[401]GC, T-491/07 (Cartes bancaires, 2012), 440.

[402]See GC, T-491/07 (Cartes bancaires, 2012), 445 and 448.

[403]GC, T-491/07 (Cartes bancaires, 2012), 449.

[404]See the opinion of AG Wahl in C-67/13 P (Cartes Bancaires, 2014), fn 5.

[405]See Article 3 of the Commission's decision and GC, T-111/08 (Mastercard, 2012), 303ff.

[406]But see also Hellström/Maier-Rigaud/Bulst (2009), 51f, according to whom the order in Mastercard required Mastercard only to stop applying its current MIF and to abstain from measures having a similar effect.

that such a complete prohibition was not disproportionate is at odds with the Commission's earlier and later decisions regarding MIFs as well as with the Commission's proposal for regulatory caps: These measures all indicate that MIFs can be justified up to a certain level and cannot therefore be completely prohibited. Nevertheless, the Court justified the complete prohibition with the fact that the burden of proof regarding Article 101(3) TFEU lied with Mastercard and that it was therefore not for the Commission to put forward a correct method for setting the MIF.

In Cartes Bancaires, the General Court took a fundamentally different approach. The object of the dispute consisted merely of an abstract like effects order. The Groupement had disputed the sufficient degree of precision of the order. By means of restrictive interpretation, the Court limited the scope of the order to the concrete level of the fees investigated by the Commission. The Court made it clear that the order did not enjoin the Groupement from applying lower fees that were justified by virtue of Article 101(3) TFEU. The latter approach appears not only to stand in a certain contrast with the Commission's refusal during the negotiations of the commitments to accept the reservation proposed by the Groupement. Moreover, it also seems at odds with the approach followed by the General Court in Mastercard. The tensions between the two judgments cannot be fully resolved, even if one takes into account that Mastercard concerned a more precisely formulated order, while Cartes Bancaires concerned merely a like effects order. Why should the Commission have the power to enjoin an undertaking from practices that can potentially be justified under Article 101(3) TFEU in a precisely formulated order, while, in a like effects order, it can only prohibit the concrete practices for which the decision has found that the fulfilment of the conditions of Article 101(3) TFEU has not been proven?

3.3.1.5.1.3.2 Can the Commission Prohibit Practices for Which It Has Not Yet Been Clarified Whether They Meet the Requirements of Article 101(3) TFEU?

In particular two arguments militate against the Commission's power to prohibit future practices for which it has not yet been clarified whether they meet the requirements of Article 101(3) TFEU. First, one might argue that such a power is at odds with the Automec judgment. The latter can be interpreted as meaning that only an abstractly formulated order to put the infringement to an end may be imposed, because the parties must be left a choice whether they want to abandon their practice completely or whether they prefer modifying it so that it complies with the requirements of Article 101(3) TFEU.[407] As discussed in more detail above in the context of the admissibility of positive obligations,[408] such an argument is, however, not convincing. If the Commission prohibits a practice completely, the parties' freedom to modify the practice is sufficiently preserved by the right of the

[407]See Sect. 3.3.1.4.1.1.1.3, footnote 281 above.

[408]See Sect. 3.3.1.4.1.1.2.2.1 with footnotes 290ff above.

parties to request the revocation of the prohibition as soon as they prove that their agreement fulfils the conditions of Article 101(3) TFEU. Second, one might argue that the acceptance of the Commission's power to prohibit practices for which it has not yet been clarified whether they meet the requirements of Article 101(3) TFEU at least partially reintroduces the notification procedure that was given up with the system change brought about by the adoption of Regulation 1/03.[409] This can be illustrated with the Mastercard case: The Commission enjoined Mastercard from using any of the MIFs in question, irrespective of their level. In theory, Mastercard therefore would have had to request a partial revocation of the order, before it could implement a modified MIF that fulfilled the requirements of Article 101(3) TFEU. The need of a partial revocation before a modified MIF could be implemented can be assimilated to the requirement of an exemption under the old notification system. In reality, the matter was settled informally: As soon as Mastercard had sufficiently reduced the relevant MIFs, the Commission stated that it would not further pursue Mastercard.[410]

Nevertheless, the better arguments militate for granting the Commission the power to prohibit future practices for which it has not yet been clarified whether they meet the requirements of Article 101(3) TFEU. If the Commission were confined to prohibiting only the particular form of a practice that it investigated and for which it found that the requirements of Article 101(3) TFEU were not met, there would be a too high risk of circumvention. In the Mastercard case, already a modest reduction would have brought the concerned MIFs outside the scope of the order. Certainly, the risk of circumvention could still be avoided, if the Commission were, on the one hand, allowed to prohibit practices with similar anticompetitive effects, whilst, on the other hand, it were obliged to define positively the conditions under which similar practices were exempted from the prohibition. Such an obligation would, however, run counter to the distribution of the burden of proof provided for by Article 2 Regulation 1/03. As the General Court rightly emphasised in Mastercard, the burden of proof regarding Article 101(3) TFEU is incumbent on the undertakings claiming its benefits. This implies that a practice for which the concerned undertakings failed to prove the justification may remain prohibited even after its modification, as long as the parties do not show that the modification has led to a justification. It bears mention that the interpretation suggested here is also consistent with the case law of the Court of Justice mentioned above regarding the grant of exemptions under the system of Regulation 17/62. According to that case law, in the context of an application for exemption, it was in the first place for the concerned undertakings to submit alternatives, if the Commission raised concerns regarding the initial notification. In the view of the Court, the Commission was allowed to give the undertakings indications as regards any possible solutions, but the Commission was not legally required to do so.[411]

---

[409]For references on the "system change" see Sect. 3.3.1.4.1.1.1 with footnote 259 above.

[410]See Sect. 3.3.1.5.1.1.1 with footnotes 377ff above.

[411]See Sect. 2.3.1.2, footnote 177 above.

3.3.1.5.2 In the Context of Article 9 Regulation 1/03

3.3.1.5.2.1 General Observations

The Article 9 procedure constitutes a way to avoid problems regarding the scope of a unilateral prohibition like the ones that arose in Mastercard and Cartes Bancaires. It has been argued convincingly that there are cases in which there is "a real need, perceived both by the Commission and the undertakings concerned, to negotiate conditions and obligations fine-tuned to the requirements of Article 101 (3) TFEU".[412] In these cases, recourse to Article 9 enables a tailor-made solution which ensures that the conditions of Article 101(3) TFEU are met. Not least from the perspective of proportionality, such a tailor-made solution is preferable to a complete prohibition of the practice in question under Article 7. The commitments that have been accepted in the wake of the Mastercard and Cartes Bancaires article 7 decisions to address concerns raised by MIFs constitute a good illustration.[413] If one follows the approach defended here that the Commission could have completely prohibited the concerned MIFs, irrespective of their level, on the basis of Article 7, then the acceptance of commitments that capped the MIFs at a certain level cannot be considered as going beyond what the Commission could have unilaterally imposed. Further examples in which the Article 9 procedure was used to satisfy needs to fine-tune agreements to the requirements of Article 101(3) TFEU are the commitments accepted to address concerns resulting from airline alliance agreements[414] or from the joint marketing of media rights by football associations.[415] As far as the latter are concerned, the Premier League decision deserves a closer look.

3.3.1.5.2.2 The Premier League Commitment and the "No-Single Buyer" Rule

The Premier League decision has been invoked as evidence that the Commission uses the Article 9 procedure to extract overbroad remedies. This criticism shall briefly be addressed here.

3.3.1.5.2.2.1 The Case

The Commission was concerned that the horizontal agreements by which the football clubs in the Premier League established a system of joint selling of media rights violated Article 101 TFEU. According to the Commission's theory of harm, the joint selling entailed the effect that a single sales organisation with significant market share replaced the individual clubs, each having a relatively small market

---

[412] Schweitzer (2010), 553f; see also von Kalben (2018), 121: "nützliches Instrument in den Händen der Kommission, um in Kooperation mit den betroffenen Unternehmen auf die Einhaltung der Voraussetzungen des Art. 101 Abs. 3 AEUV hinzuwirken".

[413] See Sect. 3.3.1.5.1.1.1 above.

[414] Section 3.3.1.4.2, footnote 356 above; Schweitzer (2010), 553.

[415] Section 3.3.1.4.2, footnote 354 above; Schweitzer (2010), 553.

share and each pursuing its own media rights strategy. As a consequence, the joint sales organisation could, depending on how and to whom the rights were sold, restrict output and create foreclosure problems on downstream markets. The Commission considered the exclusive sale of large packages of media rights to be one example of such foreclosure problems. The sale of all rights to a single buyer was mentioned as another example.[416] The commitments accepted by the Commission consisted in particular of an obligation to auction off the rights in a number of balanced packages in a transparent and non-discriminatory procedure. Moreover, the commitments contained a "no-single buyer" rule. Out of a total of six packages, a single buyer was allowed to purchase a maximum amount of five.[417] Two previous decisions of the Commission which had also concerned the joint sale of media rights by football associations had not contained a comparable "no-single buyer" rule.[418]

3.3.1.5.2.2.2 Discussion of Criticism

Ibanez Colomo portrays the inclusion of the "no-single buyer" rule in the Premier League decision as an instance in which the Commission "went beyond preserving the existing market structure and sought to alter the competitive process".[419] He also characterises the decision as an example for a case in which the Commission relied on Article 9 in order "to require stricter remedies than in similar cases decided by means of an exemption or a prohibition decision".[420] In a similar vein, Gerard invokes the decision as an example of Article 9 cases that "display a tendency to go beyond established antitrust standards and an ambition to recast market equilibriums in accordance with certain policy objectives".[421]

Such criticism calls for some moderating remarks. Only the theory of harm of the Premier League decision mentions the sale of all rights to a single buyer as a cause for anticompetitive foreclosure.[422] On the contrary, the two previous decisions explicitly left the question open whether the cumulative acquisition of several centrally marketed packages by a single exploiter would raise concerns.[423] The fact that the "no-single buyer" rule was only included in the Premier League commitments can thus be explained with the difference of the underlying theory of harm.

Certainly, the question nevertheless remains why only the theory of harm of the Premier League decision mentions the sale of all rights to a single buyer as a matter

[416]COMP/38.173 (Premier League, 2006), 25ff.

[417]COMP/38.173 (Premier League, 2006), 32f and 36.

[418]COMP/37.398 (UEFA, 2003); COMP/37.214 (Bundesliga, 2005); Kienapfel/Stein (2007), 12f; Van Rompuy (2009), fn 15; Ibanez Colomo (2010), 290.

[419]Ibanez Colomo (2010), 302.

[420]Ibanez Colomo (2010), 306.

[421]Gerard (2013), 20 together with fn 104.

[422]COMP/38.173 (Premier League, 2006), 28.

[423]COMP/37.398 (UEFA, 2003), 117; COMP/37.214 (Bundesliga, 2005), 35.

that gives rise to concerns. The reasons stated in all three decisions do not allow for a clear answer. The Premier League decision can therefore be criticised for not explaining the deviation to a sufficient extent.[424] In particular for the following two reasons, this lack of explanation does, however, not permit the conclusion that the Commission used the Article 9 procedure to extract a remedy that went beyond "established antitrust standards". First, it must be recalled that the Commission explicitly abstained in the two earlier decisions from taking a position on the lawfulness of a cumulative acquisition of several packages by a single exploiter. This abstention cannot be construed as establishing an antitrust standard according to which the acquisition of all packages by a single exploiter would be lawful.[425] Second, albeit the Premier League decision does unfortunately not contain such an elucidation, the differences between the two earlier decisions and the Premier League decision may also be explained with particularities of the concerned market. Kuik and Dawes state that the Commission may require a "no-single buyer" commitment "in circumstances where all the most valuable rights have previously been acquired by a single broadcaster".[426] Kienapfel and Stein report that the inclusion of the "no-single buyer" rule in the Premier League decision aimed at preventing the incumbent pay-TV operator in the United Kingdom, BSkyB, which had held the live rights since 1992, from acquiring all packages of valuable live rights. They also state that the issue did not arise in the two previous decisions.[427]

3.3.1.6 Remedies with Respect to Prices

The practical importance of remedies that contain specific prescriptions regarding the concerned undertakings' pricing policies is mostly limited to violations of Article 102 TFEU. This can be explained with the fact that Article 101 TFEU contains an outright prohibition for the overwhelming majority of coordinated pricing practices.[428] Some of the rare cases in which coordinated pricing may exceptionally be justified under Article 101(3) TFEU have been discussed above.[429] With the

---

[424]See Ibanez Colomo (2010), 306 and Gerard (2013), fn 104: "The Commission did not explain why the single buyer rule was necessary to bring the joint selling of football rights in line with Article 101 TFUE and why the case was different from similar joint selling cases decided in previous years and in which the remedy was not required".

[425]See also Van Rompuy (2009), 120, who reports that following the Commission's Premier League decision, Ofcom even suggested replacing the "no single buyer" obligation by a more aggressive rule that would prevent the Premier League from selling more than two of its six packages of live rights to one wholesale channel provider; later, Ofcom abandoned that suggestion.

[426]Kuik/Dawes (2014), 14.95.

[427]Kienapfel/Stein (2007), 12f together with fn 45: "In *UEFA CL* there was no need to examine the individual national market situations. In *German Bundesliga* no such issue arose considering the value of the different packages and the distribution of market players (also taking into account the bankruptcy of Kirch which had previously acquired the Bundesliga rights)".

[428]See Article 101(1)(a) TFEU and Jones/Sufrin (2011), 209f; Whish/Bailey (2012), 122 and 124.

[429]See Sect. 3.3.1.5.1 with footnotes 368ff above.

exception of such cases, coordinated pricing typically does not need to be adjusted to the requirements of Article 101 TFEU, but can be unconditionally prohibited. The following analysis will therefore limit itself to remedies for infringements of Article 102 TFEU. A distinction will be made between exclusionary and exploitative pricing.

It must be emphasised from the outset that, also for dominant operators, there is a certain area within which prices can be set freely. As pointed out above, the prohibitions enshrined in Article 102 TFEU provide merely a legal framework, by stipulating, for instance, that prices may neither be predatory nor excessively high, must be non discriminatory and not be loyalty inducing. At least in the context of Article 7, the Commission must respect this area within which prices can be set freely also when it imposes a remedy. Hence, where an undertaking infringes Article 102 TFEU by applying abusive pricing practices, the Commission can unilaterally require the undertaking to adapt these practices. For this purpose, the Commission can indicate clearly the line between legitimate and abusive pricing behaviour, for instance by setting a minimum or maximum level for the price. The Commission may, however, not take the place of the undertaking and set prices itself.[430] The logic is different under Article 9: If the concerned undertaking offers a commitment regarding its pricing policy, the undertaking continues in any case to set the price itself. The Commission only assesses whether the price alignment voluntarily proposed by the concerned undertaking is sufficient to restore compliance with the competition rules.

3.3.1.6.1 Exclusionary Pricing Practices

3.3.1.6.1.1 In the Context of Article 7 Regulation 1/03

3.3.1.6.1.1.1 Predatory Pricing

In predatory pricing cases, the Commission has up to now mostly contented itself with a cease and desist order and abstained from any more precise prescriptions as regards the dominant undertaking's future prices.[431] Only an interim order that was imposed by the Commission on Akzo contains more detailed prescriptions.[432]

The Commission prohibited Akzo from charging prices below certain static minimum amounts fixed individually for Akzo's various customers and products in an annex to the decision. The minimum amounts were calculated from the sum of Akzo's production costs, freight costs and a certain absolute gross profit. The Commission justified the inclusion of "overhead expenses" (common or joint costs) and the gross profit in the calculation of the minimum amounts with the interim nature of the order and the resulting impracticability of determining the exact level at which

[430] See Schwarze/Weitbrecht (2004), § 6, 27; Anweiler (2009), Art. 7, 53; Ritter (2012), Art. 7, 47.
[431] See eg OJ 1992 L 72, 1 (Tetra Pak II); COMP/38233 (Wanadoo).
[432] OJ 1983 L 252, 13 (Akzo interim); O'Donoghue/Padilla (2013), 927.

Akzo's prices became unlawful.[433] Akzo was allowed to set its prices below those fixed in the annex only to "meet (but not to undercut)" offers of its competitors.[434] The Commission also explicitly stated that, in case of a "proved change" of Akzo's production cost, it would alter the minimum prices set out in the annex to the order.[435] Akzo's application for interim relief before the General Court did not concern the prescriptions of the order regarding the minimum prices set by the Commission, but merely a further order to abstain from applying selective low prices.[436]

The fact that the Commission resorts mostly to abstract cease and desist orders may to some extent be due to the relatively lax standard of the EU courts regarding the necessary degree of precision of termination orders.[437] Nevertheless, it is submitted that the Commission also has the power to impose more detailed prescriptions, as long as it respects the link between infringement and remedy. Hence, after a brief overview over the test for assessing when pricing is prohibited as predatory, some basic points regarding the design of such more detailed prescriptions will be discussed below. Finally, two atypical predatory pricing remedies shall be discussed: The German case "Germania" and a condition imposed by the Commission in the context of the clearance of a cooperation agreement between Lufthansa and Austrian Airlines.

3.3.1.6.1.1.1.1 The Prohibition of Predatory Pricing

In order to determine whether a pricing practice is prohibited as predatory, the EU courts apply a three-step test[438]: Pricing below average variable costs is presumptively prohibited; pricing between average variable and total cost is prohibited if it can be proven according to the circumstances of the case at hand either that the dominant undertaking acted with anticompetitive intent or that pricing below a cost standard that is higher than average variable costs, for instance long run average incremental cost, is inappropriate[439]; pricing above average total cost does not fall under the prohibition of predatory pricing. The test is simple only at first blush. As regards the first step, the difficulties lie in particular in classifying costs as variable or fixed and in allocating common costs of multi-product firms.[440] As regards the

---

[433] OJ 1983 L 252, 13, 36 (Akzo interim).

[434] OJ 1983 L 252, 13, 38 (Akzo interim).

[435] OJ 1983 L 252, 13, 36 (Akzo interim).

[436] See CJ, 62/86 R (Akzo interim, 1986).

[437] On the relatively lax standards of EU courts as regards the necessary degree of precision of a termination order see Sect. 5.2.1 with footnotes 267ff below.

[438] See CJ 62/86 (Akzo, 1991), 71ff; C-202/07 P (France Telecom, 2009), 109; C-209/10 (Post Danmark, 2012), 27; see also Whish/Bailey (2012), 742ff; O'Donoghue/Padilla (2013), 301ff.

[439] See O'Donoghue/Padilla (2013), 307, who interpret the CJ's Post Danmark judgment, Sect. 3.3.1.6.1.1.1.2, footnote 438 above, as approval of "the use of LRAIC as a cost standard, at least in cases where high fixed costs are a strong feature of an industry".

[440] See Kellezi (2010), 245; Jones/Sufrin (2011), 393 and 397; O'Donoghue/Padilla (2013), 303f and 319ff. Already in its Akzo judgment (62/86, 1991), the CJ held "that an item of cost is not variable or fixed by nature" (95), thus requesting a classification according to the circumstances of the individual case.

second step, problems arise with respect to the proof of anticompetitive intent[441] or regarding the criteria for evaluating when a higher cost standard is appropriate and, if this is the case, the allocation of the respective costs. Finally, below cost pricing may be objectively justified, for instance in the context of promotional sales or to dispose of old stock that could otherwise no longer be sold.[442]

3.3.1.6.1.1.1.2 The Remedies Side: Fixing a Minimum Price

Looking at the remedies side, it seems doubtful whether the prohibition of prices above average variable costs due to anticompetitive intent can at all be depicted in a detailed order regarding future pricing: Should the order allow for pricing between average variable and total costs and only enjoin the dominant undertaking from acting with anticompetitive intent? Certainly, the Commission can limit itself to a conservative order that neglects the intent component of the prohibition. In this respect, it is clear that, in order to prevent circumvention, the Commission should not only prohibit the price actually practiced by the dominant undertaking, but rather impose a minimum price to prohibit all prices below the level that has been identified by the Commission as constituting the boundary between abusive and non abusive behaviour.[443] Such a minimum price can either be fixed in a static or in a dynamic manner. A static minimum price is expressed in an absolute value; the Akzo interim order mentioned above can serve as an example. The imposition of an absolute minimum price has the benefit of being easy to monitor. The sales price of the dominant undertaking, which can easily be observed on the market, only needs to be compared to the absolute value defined as minimum price. However, an absolute minimum price is inconvenient in so far as it must be adapted whenever the costs of the concerned undertaking change.[444] A dynamic manner of fixing the minimum price is to prescribe the cost factors that must be taken into account for its calculation in an abstract manner. The abstract prescription of the method to calculate the minimum price dispenses with the need for constant adaptation in case of a cost change. It is, however, more complex to monitor, since it requires data regarding all the various cost factors that need to be taken into account for the calculation of the minimum price. Finally, independently of whether the order fixes the minimum price in a static or a dynamic manner, it must allow pricing below the imposed minimum price where this would be objectively justified.

[441]See for those difficulties Jones/Sufrin (2011), 398; Whish/Bailey (2012), 741; O'Donoghue/Padilla (2013), 307ff; Bulst (2014), Art. 102, 311.

[442]See Whish/Bailey (2012), 742. Generally on potential objective justifications for predatory pricing see O'Donoghue/Padilla (2013), 343ff.

[443]See Möschel (1986), 1790ff.

[444]See Möschel (1986), 1790 and 1792.

3.3.1.6.1.1.1.3 "Germania" As an Atypical Example

A pricing practice is prohibited as predatory, if the dominant undertaking sells below a certain fraction of its own costs. If a static or dynamic minimum price is imposed as a remedy, it is thus calculated typically by reference to the own costs of the dominant undertaking. The reason why the reference point for both the finding of an infringement and the remedy is the costs of the dominant undertaking—as opposed to the costs of its competitor—is that undercutting a less efficient competitor's price through own costs savings constitutes—at least as a general rule—a desirable means of competition on the merits that is lawful also for dominant undertakings. Against this background, at least at first sight, it is astonishing to see that in Germania, the Bundeskartellamt issued an order that established the prescribed minimum price for the dominant undertaking by reference to the price applied by a competitor.

Simply speaking, the case can be summed up as follows.[445] Lufthansa initially charged 200 Euro for a one-way flight between Frankfurt and Berlin. When the low cost airline Germania entered the market and offered tickets for the same route for only 100 Euro, Lufthansa aligned its nominal price and went also down to 100 Euro. Different from Germania's offer, Lufthansa's offer also included several special features, such as higher flight frequency, better on board service and a frequent flyer program. These special features amounted to an additional value of 30 Euro. The Bundeskartellamt therefore considered that the actual price charged by Lufthansa accounted only for 70 Euro. The Bundeskartellamt found that the relevant costs of both Lufthansa and Germania amounted to 100 Euro. According to the Bundeskartellamt, Lufthansa had therefore engaged in pricing below its own cost. As a remedy, the authority required Lufthansa to charge a price that was 30 Euros above the price charged by Germania. At the same time, the order also provided that, if Germania was to raise its price above 100 Euro, Lufthansa nevertheless was only required to charge no more than 130 Euro; if Germania was to raise its price above 130 Euro, Lufthansa was no longer obliged to charge a higher price than Germania. The duration of the order was limited to 2 years.

The remedy calls for some comments. A standard static minimum price remedy might simply have required Lufthansa to raise its nominal price to at least 130 Euro, which would have corresponded to an actual price of 100 Euro and just allowed Lufthansa to cover its cost. A standard dynamic remedy might have required Lufthansa to include the value of the special features in its cost calculation and to set its prices above the so calculated cost. The remedy chosen by the Bundeskartellamt is, however, more complex. Its central feature is a dynamic element, namely the imposition of a price differential of 30 Euro to the price of Germania. The dynamic element thus does not refer to Lufthansa's own costs, but to the price charged by Germania. It is flanked by a static element that limits

[445] A summary as well as a full version of the decision in English can be found in OECD (2004), 132ff. The decision was, in its essential parts, confirmed in a procedure regarding interim relief, see OLG Düsseldorf, Kart 7/02 (2002). See also Kellezi (2010), 245ff.

Lufthansa's obligation to maintain a price difference of 30 Euro to a maximum price of 130 Euro. The static element can be considered as a reference to Lufthansa's own cost, because the nominal price of 130 Euro, which corresponds to an actual price of 100 Euro, is precisely the minimum price that allows Lufthansa to cover its current cost. As long as Lufthansa prices above this level, it is no longer guilty of predatory pricing and cannot be enjoined from charging a lower price than Germania. Both the static and the dynamic element of the order allow Lufthansa to exercise some competitive pressure on Germania. If Germania raises its price above 100 Euro, the static element prevents a price umbrella in Germania's favour by allowing Lufthansa to set the price less than 30 Euros above Germania's price, and, if Germania exceeds 130 Euro, even below Germania's price.[446] If Germania reduces its price below 100 Euro, the dynamic reference to Germania's price allows Lufthansa to follow and set its price below 130 Euro.

Nevertheless, at least at first blush, the remedy is tilted in favour of Germania. If Lufthansa reduces its costs and Germania keeps its price stable at 100 Euro, Lufthansa cannot pass on the achieved cost savings to its customers and reduce its nominal price below 130 Euro. Germania is hence shielded from price attacks on behalf of Lufthansa that are justified through cost savings. In this latter regard, the dynamic reference to Germania's price instead of Lufthansa's own cost goes at first sight beyond the Bundeskartellamt's theory of harm. If the theory of harm is based on pricing below cost, then the remedy cannot enjoin the dominant undertaking from above cost pricing simply because the price of the dominant undertaking is still below the price of its competitor. For three reasons, this should, however, not lead to the conclusion that such a remedy could not be imposed on the basis of Article 7 Regulation 1/03. First, it must be taken into account that the remedy goes beyond the theory of harm only from a dynamic perspective that takes a potential change in Lufthansa's costs into account. From a static view on Lufthansa's costs, the remedy stays within the theory of harm. As long as Lufthansa maintains costs of 100 Euro, the remedy merely has the effect of requiring Lufthansa not to set its actual price below that amount. Strictly speaking, as long as Lufthansa maintains costs of 100 Euro, the remedy even stays behind the theory of harm. If Germania reduces its price, Lufthansa is allowed to follow, irrespective of the development of its own costs. At least as long as Lufthansa's costs stay at the level of 100 Euro, the remedy thus cannot be considered as going beyond what is necessary to put the predatory pricing abuse to an end. Second, it must be underlined that the duration of the order is from the outset limited to 2 years. A reduction of Lufthansa's cost during such a rather short period is less likely to happen than during a longer period. Third, the mere fact that the dynamic mechanism of the remedy, namely the reference to Germania's price, does not allow to take account of a lowering of Lufthansa's costs, does not mean that a lowering of Lufthansa's costs cannot be taken into account at all. In this respect, it is submitted, that a lowering of Lufthansa's cost

[446] See the decision of the Bundeskartellamt, OECD (2004), 150.

during the validity of the order would constitute a change of circumstances that would oblige the authority to revoke or at least amend the decision.[447]

Overall, the remedy thus does not violate the required link between harm and remedy. Compared to a prescription of a static nominal minimum price of 130 Euro, it has the advantage to allow Lufthansa to follow eventual price reductions by Germania. Compared to a dynamic reference to Lufthansa's cost, it has the advantage of being easier to implement and monitor. Certainly, the dynamic reference to Germania's price runs the risk of going beyond the theory of harm of a predatory pricing abuse: If Germania keeps its price at 100 Euro and Lufthansa reduces its cost, Lufthansa is precluded from passing its cost savings on to its customers, although this would not amount to pricing below cost. However, since the remedy does not go beyond the theory of harm of a predatory pricing abuse from the outset, but only if Germania keeps its price at 100 Euro and Lufthansa reduces its cost, this risk is sufficiently prevented by the short duration of the remedy and the possibility of its amendment or revocation.

3.3.1.6.1.1.1.4 The Lufthansa/Austrian Airlines Cooperation Agreement

Some commentators mention a condition to which the Commission subjected the exemption of a horizontal cooperation agreement between Lufthansa and Austrian Airlines pursuant to Article 101(3) TFEU as an example of a predatory pricing remedy that could not lawfully have been imposed by the Commission under Article 7.[448]

In the Commission's view, on some of the Austrian-German flight routes concerned by the agreement, new market entry by competitors was not likely to happen, because these routes were of limited attraction to potential competitors due to reduced passenger capacities. The Commission considered that the interests of consumers using those routes nevertheless had to be taken into account. Under one of the conditions to which the agreement was subjected, the parties were therefore "required to apply any price cuts that they introduce[d] on routes subject to competition to three other Austrian-German routes on which they [did] not face competition".[449] The condition did not apply where the parties demonstrated that the price cut introduced by them was attributable to a reduction in costs.[450] The Commission argued that, by making the costs of price dumping significantly higher for the parties, the "condition afford[ed] new entrants some protection from predatory pricing by the [p]arties".[451] The condition hence served a double purpose: On the one hand, it aimed at lowering the prices on the unattractive routes, on which no competition

[447]The actual decision provided for an express revocation clause and a revocation is in any event possible under German administrative law in case of a change of circumstances.

[448]See Kellezi (2010), 252f; O'Donoghue/Padilla (2013), 928.

[449]OJ 2002 L 242/25, 110.

[450]OJ 2002 L 242/25, 110.

[451]OJ 2002 L 242/25, p. 41.

took place anyway.[452] On the other hand, it aimed at protecting competitors against predatory practices of the parties by making any price reductions more costly.

It is easy to see that and why the Commission could not impose the content of the condition as a remedy for a predatory pricing abuse under Article 7 Regulation 1/03. Instead of putting the predatory pricing on one route to an end, the remedy would allow for a—certainly expensive—compensation of the abusive conduct by requiring price reductions on routes that are not affected by the infringement. Such compensatory measures are incompatible with the requirement of a link between infringement and remedy.[453]

3.3.1.6.1.1.2 Rebates

3.3.1.6.1.1.2.1 Tetra Pak II

In Tetra Pak II, the Commission found that Tetra Pak had infringed Article 102 TFEU by applying discriminatory, predatory and loyalty inducing prices for aseptic machines and cartons for the packaging of liquid foods.[454] The Commission imposed inter alia the following order:

> Tetra Pak shall not practice predatory or discriminatory prices and shall not grant to any customer any form of discount on its products or more favourable payment terms not justified by an objective consideration. Thus, discounts on cartons should be granted solely according to the quantity of each order [. . .].[455]

On appeal, Tetra Pak argued that this order provided no guidance what was meant by an objective consideration with respect to machines. As for cartons, Tetra Pak considered that the prohibition of discounts other than for quantity precluded competitive responses by prices, based on merit, to price initiatives by a competitor.[456] The General Court upheld the order. Its reasoning is obscure and little persuasive. On the one hand, the Court argues that the prohibition of discounts for which there is no objective justification aims "to put an end to all the practices found unlawful in the Decision and to preclude any similar practice".[457] On the other hand, the Court argues that the prohibition of loyalty discounts enshrined in Article 102 TFEU justifies an order "prohibiting discounts other than according to the

[452]O'Donoghue/Padilla (2013), 928, point out that a remedy like the condition imposed by the Commission "might have the perverse effect of making life even tougher for rivals in the other markets". This concern appears less worrying if one takes into account that, under the condition imposed by the Commission, the parties had to reduce prices on routes for which there was no competition.

[453]See the also the discussion of the compatibility of compensatory measures with the principle of proportionality above (Sect. 3.2.1.4 with footnotes 112ff).

[454]See GC, T-83/91 (1994), 20 and 220.

[455]GC, T-83/91 (1994), 215.

[456]GC, T-83/91 (1994), 216.

[457]GC, T-83/91 (1994), 220.

quantity of each order".[458] According to the Court, "that prohibition does not preclude an undertaking in a dominant position from competing in particular by price where such competition is based on objective considerations such as, for example, the solvency of the customer and accordingly is not discriminatory or predatory".[459]

The statement that the prohibition of discounts for which there is no objective justification aims "to put an end to all the practices found unlawful in the Decision and to preclude any similar practice" could imply that the Court interpreted the first part of the order restrictively, similarly to a like effects order, as merely mirroring the infringement.[460] If this were the case, it would explain why the Court did not find it necessary to give any further answer to Tetra Pak's argument that, with respect to machines, the order did not give any guidance what was meant by an objective consideration, ie that the order was not sufficiently precise. However, such an understanding of the judgment does not explain why the Court also upheld the second part of the order by finding that the prohibition of loyalty discounts enshrined in Article 102 TFEU justified an order "prohibiting discounts other than according to the quantity of each order". By upholding the second part of the order, the Court confirmed an injunction that went beyond mirroring the infringement. Indeed, according to the case law, the mere fact that a discount does not solely scale with volume does not suffice as such to qualify it as an illegal loyalty discount. Rather, as long as the discount is not granted in exchange for exclusivity, a case-by-case analysis is necessary to establish whether the discount has a loyalty inducing effect.[461] Hence, the Commission's finding that Tetra Pak's past discounts for cartons had had a loyalty inducing effect cannot justify the order to grant discounts solely according to the quantity in the future. This prevented Tetra Pak without reason from applying discounts that did not scale with volume, but for which the necessary case-by-case analysis might have shown that they did not have a loyalty inducing effect.

---

[458]GC, T-83/91 (1994), 221: "[A] prohibition on loyalty rebates or equivalent practices is neither disproportionate nor discriminatory and is in accordance with settled case-law [. . .] That prohibition provides justification [. . .] for prohibiting discounts other than according to the quantity of each order [. . .]".

[459]GC, T-83/91 (1994), 221.

[460]See the discussion of like effects orders below (Sect. 5.2.1.1.2.1 with footnotes 302ff). Along the lines of GC, T-305/94 (PVC II, 1999), 1249, De Bronnet (2012), Art. 7, 10 fn 42 interprets the Tetra Pak II order as a like effects order. See also Hjelmeng (2013), 1008, fn 3, where he relies on the Tetra Pak II judgment to state that "the Commission may impose obligations in order to avoid future infringements, provided that these would represent a continuation of the infringement established".

[461]See CJ, 322/81 (Michelin I, 1983), 72f; C-95/04 P (British Airways, 2007), 65ff; GC, T-286/09 (Intel, 2014), 74ff.

3.3.1.6.1.1.2.2 Irish Sugar

In Irish Sugar, the infringement of Article 102 TFEU consisted, inter alia, of (i) the granting of sugar export rebates which discriminated against customers of industrial sugar supplying the domestic market, (ii) price discrimination against competing sugar packers, (iii) the granting of target rebates to purchasers of retail sugar, which tied the latter to Irish Sugar and (iv) the selective grant of target rebates to customers of competing sugar packers.[462] The Commission imposed a general cease and desist order, combined with a like effects order. The like effects order comprised a non-exhaustive list of prohibited practices. Inter alia, Irish Sugar was required to "refrain from applying dissimilar conditions to equivalent transactions with [...] industrial sugar clients, such as export rebates and other rebates that, because they bear no relation to the quantity of sugar supplied and the costs of the transaction, discriminate against competing sugar packers". Irish Sugar also had to "refrain from a policy of pricing of retail sugar that adversely affects the competitive position of other sugar packers, including selective pricing to customers of competing packers and the granting of target rebates to retail sugar customers".

On appeal, Irish Sugar complained that the remedy went beyond what was prohibited by the Treaty. In essence, Irish Sugar claimed, first, that the Commission had only found target rebates with a loyalty inducing effect to be abusive and hence could not generally prohibit target rebates. Second, Irish Sugar submitted that the Commission could not prohibit all rebates that are not dependent on the quantity of sugar or the cost of the transaction.[463] The General Court confirmed the remedy, albeit with a rather formalistic argument. It held that the cease and desist and the like effects order merely prohibited "conduct that [was] incompatible with the Treaty". According to the Court, the legality of the abstractly phrased cease and desist and like effects order "logically extend[ed]" to the more specifically formulated other orders, "inasmuch as the latter merely elaborate that general order".[464]

3.3.1.6.1.1.2.3 Comment

The Tetra Pak II and Irish Sugar cases illustrate the difficulties of designing precise prescriptions how to put an abusive rebate scheme to an end.[465] The problem lies in the fact that there are many different types of rebate schemes and that the assessment of the lawfulness of most of them requires an analysis of the circumstances of the case at hand. According to the case law, while quantity rebates are presumed lawful, the opposite is true only for exclusivity rebates. For all rebate schemes that do not fall into either of the said categories, an analysis of the circumstances of the case at hand is necessary to assess whether they have a loyalty inducing effect.[466] This means

---

[462] 1997 OJ L 258/1 (Irish Sugar, 1997).

[463] See GC, T-228/97 (Irish Sugar, 1999), 296f.

[464] See GC, T-228/97 (Irish Sugar, 1999), 304.

[465] For the difficulties of designing appropriate remedies to stop abusive rebate practices see also Temple Lang (2006), 291.

[466] See Sect. 3.3.1.6.1.1.2.1, footnote 461 above.

that, while the Commission can generally prohibit exclusivity rebates, it cannot generally prohibit all rebates that do not solely scale with volume. A general prohibition of all rebates that are not merely related to quantity neglects the requirement of the link between infringement and remedy. The General Court's ruling in Tetra Pak II according to which the prohibition of loyalty rebates enshrined in the competition rules justifies prohibiting all but quantity discounts[467] must hence be rejected. In Irish Sugar, the order of the Commission comprised a similar flaw like its order in Tetra Pak II: Irish Sugar was required to stop using "target rebates" and rebates that "discriminate because they bear no relation to quantity". This time, the General Court did not explicitly state that the order was justified by the prohibitions enshrined in the competition rules. Rather, it interpreted the order restrictively, in the light of the abstract cease and desist order that mirrors the infringement. Certainly, such a reinterpretation constitutes a way to save the Commission's order, if the Court does not want to annul it. The approach is consistent with the restrictive interpretation that the Court applies also to abstract like effects orders.[468] Nevertheless, it cannot belie the fact that the wording of the Commission's order neglects the requirement of the link between harm and remedy.

3.3.1.6.1.1.3 Margin Squeeze

3.3.1.6.1.1.3.1 The Prohibition

A margin squeeze can be described as the practice of a vertically integrated undertaking that is dominant on the upstream market to prevent its downstream competitors from achieving a viable price cost margin.[469] According to the definition introduced by the Commission and endorsed by the Courts, a margin squeeze occurs if "the difference between the retail prices charged by a dominant undertaking and the wholesale prices it charges its competitors is negative, or insufficient to cover the product specific costs to the dominant operator of providing its own retail services on the downstream market".[470] Simply speaking, the dominant undertaking can reach this result by making the input for its competitors too expensive, by selling its own products on the downstream market too cheap or by engaging into both practices at the same time. Margin squeeze cases overlap with other abuse categories, in particular with excessive, predatory and discriminatory pricing and with constructive refusal to deal.[471] In the literature, it is sometimes disputed that margin squeeze constitutes an independent category of abuse

[467]See Sect. 3.3.1.6.1.1.2.1, footnote 458 above.

[468]See Sect. 5.2.1.1.2.1 with footnotes 302ff below.

[469]See O'Donoghue/Padilla (2013), 366.

[470]OJ 2003 L 263/9, 107 (Deutsche Telekom); similarly CJ, C-52/09 P (Telia Sonera, 2011), 32; see also GC, T-336/07 (Telefonica, 2012), 213: "the margin squeeze test is designed [...] to establish whether a competitor having the same cost structure as that of the downstream activity of the vertically integrated undertaking is able to be profitable on the downstream market given the wholesale and retail prices charged by that undertaking".

[471]On the relationship between margin squeeze and other types of abuse see Petzold (2012), 117ff; Whish/Bailey (2012), 756; O'Donoghue/Padilla (2013), 395ff.

at all.[472] The EU Courts consider that this is the case: In Telia Sonera, the Court of Justice underlined that, in order to establish a margin squeeze, it is not necessary to demonstrate the excessive or predatory nature of the prices on the upstream or the downstream markets,[473] nor that a duty to supply exists.[474]

3.3.1.6.1.1.3.2 The Remedies Side

This decoupling of margin squeeze cases from other abuse categories entails some difficulties regarding the question of the appropriate remedy. If the finding of an infringement is limited to an isolated finding of a margin squeeze, the infringing undertaking has three options to restore compliance with the competition rules and allow for a viable profit margin of its competitors. It can decrease the price it charges its competitors on the upstream market, increase the price at which it offers its own products on the downstream market or adjust both prices.[475] Moreover, if there is no obligation to supply, the dominant undertaking also has the possibility to abandon supply completely.[476] It could thus be argued that, in such a case, the Commission must always confine itself to an abstract cease and desist order in order to preserve the infringer's freedom of choice how to comply with the competition rules.

However, in line with what has been argued above, it is submitted that the Commission can also make more precise orders, which are themselves conditional of the circumstances that justify them.[477] For instance, an order to increase the price

---

[472] See in particular Petzold (2012), 117ff, who suggests to treat margin squeeze cases as predatory pricing cases.

[473] CJ, C-52/09 P (Telia Sonera, 2011), 34; see also GC, T-336/07 (Telefonica, 2012), 187.

[474] CJ, C-52/09 P (Telia Sonera, 2011), 56; see also GC, T-336/07 (Telefonica, 2012), 177ff; CJ, C-295/12 P (Telefonica, 2014), 96. Critically in this respect Petzold (2012), 178ff; O'Donoghue/Padilla (2013), 402.

[475] See O'Donoghue/Padilla (2013), 398 and 928.

[476] This will, however, only rarely be the case, since most margin squeeze cases de facto fulfill the requirements of a refusal to deal case. See Petzold (2012), 180 with further references.

[477] The Commission's practice is so far not very instructive:

In British Sugar (OJ 1988 L 284/41, 82), the Commission abstained from imposing any order to bring the infringement to an end. British Sugar had already stopped the abusive practice before the final decision was issued. The same happened in Telefonica (COMP/38.784, 2008).

In Deutsche Telekom (OJ 2003 L 263/9), the Commission stated in the operative part of the decision that the infringement consisted of charging unfair prices to competitors and to end users. Deutsche Telekom was required in abstract terms to "bring to an end the infringement" and to refrain from repeating it. No like effects order was imposed. Hence, neither the finding of the infringement, nor the order to put the infringement to an end contain any prescriptions regarding the question whether Deutsche Telekom should reduce the price it charges its competitors or increase the price at which it offers its services to end users.

National Carbonising concerned an alleged margin squeeze by a vertically integrated producer of coal and coke. The Commission refused to intervene upon a complaint of a competing producer of coke. The latter applied to the CJ for interim relief. It claimed that the Commission should require the dominant undertaking either to lower its price for coking coal, or to raise its coke price, or both. Without making any precise prescriptions, the Court ordered the Commission to take the necessary

on the downstream market up to a certain minimum level would be conditional on a continuation of supply in general and on maintenance of the price on the upstream market above a certain maximum level. It remains nevertheless that, if the finding of an infringement rests solely on the theory of harm of a margin squeeze, the Commission cannot impose its preference regarding the question whether the downstream price should be increased or the upstream price lowered against the will of the dominant undertaking. Diverging interests can in this respect not be excluded. For instance, the Commission may favour reducing the price on the upstream market because this may lead to a lower consumer price. On the contrary, the dominant undertaking may prefer raising the price on the downstream market, because this allows it to continue extracting monopoly rents on the upstream market. In such a case, the mere finding of a margin squeeze would not suffice to require the dominant undertaking to reduce the prices on the upstream market. If the Commission wants to decide whether the downstream price should be increased or the upstream price lowered, it must take a clear stance in its theory of harm whether the margin squeeze is a result of too high upstream prices or too low downstream prices.

Moreover, if the Commission decides to make precise prescriptions how to put a margin squeeze to an end, it must prevent circumvention. For example, providing for a maximum level of the price that competitors are charged on the upstream market is not sufficient. The dominant undertaking must also be enjoined from squeezing the margin of its competitors anew by lowering the price at which it offers its own product on the downstream market. These difficulties can be avoided by the imposition of a price differential between the prices on the upstream and the downstream market.[478] Moreover, a price differential also has the benefit that it dispenses of the need to adapt a static minimum downstream price or a static maximum upstream price, if the dominant undertaking decreases the upstream price or increases the downstream price. Overall, if precise prescriptions how to put a margin squeeze to an end shall at all be made, price differentials appear thus preferable to fixing a static maximum amount for the upstream price or a static minimum amount for the downstream price.[479] The height of the required price difference between the upstream and downstream price depends on the findings regarding the infringement.

interim measures (109/75 R, 1975). After consultation with the parties, the Commission imposed an interim order in which in required the dominant undertaking to reduce the price for coking coal by £ 2.79 per ton (OJ 1976 L 35/6).

[478]The UK case Genzyme Ltd v OFT, [2005] CAT 32, can serve as an example for the imposition of a price differential as a remedy in a margin squeeze case: Genzyme was a vertically integrated undertaking active in the production of a certain drug and in related home delivery services. It was found guilty of squeezing the margin of a competitor active on the downstream market for home delivery services. As a remedy, the CAT required Genzyme to supply the drug on the upstream market at a discount of 20 pence from the price on the downstream market.

[479]For the use of price differential commitments to offset margin squeeze concerns in the context of Article 9 also Temple Lang (2006), 292: "A commitment decision could provide a solution, by which the dominant undertaking would promise to keep the price of the raw material below a stated percentage of its price for the end product".

In line with the definition given above,[480] it can generally be stated that the height of the price differential depends on the costs of the dominant operator of providing its own retail services on the downstream market.

3.3.1.6.1.2 In the Context of Article 9

Commitments that address an exclusionary pricing practice by acting directly on the investigated company's pricing policy appear to be relatively rare. To date, the Commission has not made binding commitments in a predatory pricing case. As regards rebates, the Coca-Cola decision contains a commitment not to offer target or growth rebates.[481] This commitment directly mirrors the Commission's theory of harm according to which TCCC had granted unlawful target or growth rebates.[482] The link between harm and remedy is, in this respect, not problematic.[483] In Deutsche Bahn, the Commission made binding a commitment package that included a prohibition to grant volume or duration based discounts in order to offset concerns relating to a margin squeeze. Due to its particularities, the Deutsche Bahn commitment package will be discussed further below.[484] In RWE, the Commission resolved concerns that related to a margin squeeze by accepting RWE's commitment to divest its German gas transmission network. Also this case will be discussed further below.[485]

3.3.1.6.2 Exploitative Pricing Practices

3.3.1.6.2.1 In the Context of Article 7

Different from the US system, EU competition law prohibits excessive pricing. The pros and cons of this prohibition and the difficulties of defining the right test shall not be repeated here.[486] Instead, some remarks related to the design of an appropriate remedy are called for.[487] As a preliminary caveat, it must be pointed out that the general "dearth of decisional practice" that results from the Commission's "reluctance to bring abusive pricing cases"[488] is aggravated when it comes to remedies: In

[480] See Sect. 3.3.1.6.1.1.3.1 with footnote 470 above.

[481] COMP/39.116 (Coca-Cola, 2005), 42.

[482] COMP/39.116 (Coca-Cola, 2005), 32.

[483] See for other aspects of the case Sect. 3.2.2.2 with footnotes 119ff above.

[484] See Sect. 3.4.2.3.1 with footnotes 1139ff below.

[485] See Sect. 3.4.2.1.1.1.2.1 with footnotes 969ff below.

[486] See only OECD (2011a); Jones/Sufrin (2011), 531ff; Whish/Bailey (2012), 718ff; Fuchs/Möschel (2012), 168ff; Ackermann (2012), O'Donoghue/Padilla (2013), 732ff, all with further references. For a focus on the remedies see Kellezi (2010), 212ff and O'Donoghue/Padilla (2013), 928ff.

[487] According to OECD (2011a), 12 and 75, the difficulty of crafting adequate remedies is a standard argument advanced in the discussion about whether there should be any control for excessive prices at all; similarly Whish/Bailey (2012), 719.

[488] Jones/Sufrin (2011), 535.

most of the few excessive pricing procedures that were closed with an Article 7 decision, the Commission abstained from making precise prescriptions and confined itself to a general order to put the infringement to an end.[489] The only excessive pricing case involving a more specific remedy is an atypical one, namely Duales System Deutschland (DSD). In that case, DSD was found to have charged excessive prices by requiring its customers to pay a fee for all packaging bearing the Green Dot logo relating to DSD's system for the recovery of packaging, even if customers showed that some of the packaging bearing the logo was not actually recovered in DSD's system.[490] The remedy imposed consisted of the prohibition to charge any fees for packaging that was not recovered in DSD's system.[491] The Court of Justice confirmed the remedy, repeating the General Court's statement that the remedy was "nothing other than the consequence of the finding of an abuse of a dominant position and of the exercise by the Commission of its power to oblige DSD to put an end to the infringement".[492] The case is atypical because the excessive character of DSD's pricing behaviour did not stem from the amount of the fee, but from the fact that DSD charged a fee at all. Hence, neither the finding of the infringement nor the crafting of the remedy was exposed to the typical difficulty of how to distinguish the "just" from the "excessive" price.[493]

A typical excessive pricing remedy, however, will have to draw a line between the just and the excessive price. The simple prohibition of the precise price that has been found excessive is not sufficient. The concerned undertaking can easily circumvent

---

[489]In Chiquita (1976), the Commission imposed a general order to put the infringement to an end and required United Brands to inform it twice a year about the prices charged during the previous six months. Only in the reasons of the decision, the Commission stated that it would suffice to reduce prices by 15% (see OJ 1976 L 95/1 at 16 and Anweiler [2009], Art. 7, 53; Ritter [2012], Art. 7, 47). In British Leyland (1984 OJ L 207/11, 1984), the Commission imposed a general order to put the infringement to an end and to inform it of the measures taken to this effect. In Deutsche Post (COMP/36.915, 2001), the Commission imposed a general order to put the infringement to an end, accompanied by a like effects order.

[490]See CJ, C-385/07 P (Duales System Deutschland, 2009), 30f and 143f; Jones/Sufrin (2011), 537; Kellezi (2010), 220.

[491]See CJ, C-385/07 P (Duales System Deutschland, 2009), 37ff and 145.

[492]CJ, C-385/07 P (Duales System Deutschland, 2009), 145. On a sidenote, it is worth mentioning that also in DSD, the wording of the remedy went beyond what was necessary to put the infringement to an end. According to the order, DSD was prevented from charging any fees at all for packaging that was not recovered in its system. This means that DSD was also prevented from charging fees for the mere use of the trademark protecting the Green Dot logo. However, the General Court found, in essence, that the finding of infringement contained in the Decision related only to the charge of fees for the service of the recovery of packaging, to the extent that this service was not actually provided by DSD. Since the Court could not exclude that the trademark had its own economic value, it held that the order had to be interpreted "as not precluding the possibility for DSD to levy an adequate fee for merely using the mark"; cf. GC, T-151/01, (Duales System Deutschland, 2007), 191ff.

[493]See Kellezi (2010), 220: "Les mesures correctives dans ce cas sont déterminées avec plus de facilité, dès lors qu'il s'agit de prendre en compte uniquement les services effectivement rendus, et non pas le niveau de la redevance".

such a prohibition by slightly adapting its price. Competition authorities must hence have the power to prohibit the entire price range above the line they find for demarcating the abusive from non-abusive behaviour.[494] However, it is not convincing to deduce an additional difficulty of designing excessive pricing remedies from the fact that "it is harder to determine precisely what the right price level ought to be" than to determine "above what price level a price becomes excessive".[495] When imposing an excessive pricing remedy, competition authorities do not have the power to determine "the right price level" precisely. Since they can only prohibit abusive behaviour, they cannot impose prices below the line that has been established on the infringement side to demarcate abusive and non-abusive behaviour.[496]

As regards the infringement side, there are at least two tests under EU competition law that allow to establish whether a price is excessive: This is either the case, when the profit margin of the dominant undertaking, i.e. the difference between the price and the costs of the product, is found to be excessive. Or, when the price charged is found to be excessive in comparison to prices of products in comparable markets.[497] These two competition law tests for excessive pricing are similar to the regulatory

[494]Under German law, the Bundesgerichtshof has expressly acknowledged this. See BGH, KVR 4/75 (Vitamin B12, 1976), 30: "Liegt jedoch [. . .] das beanstandete mißbräuchliche Verhalten allein in der Höhe des verlangten Herstellerabgabepreises und erfordert die Feststellung der Mißbräuchlichkeit dieses Preises ohnehin eine Klärung der Mißbrauchsgrenze, so unterliegt es keinen rechtlichen Bedenken, das Verbot auf den gesamten Preisbereich oberhalb der Mißbrauchsgrenze zu erstrecken"; Jaeger (2010), § 32 ARC, 30.

[495]But see Maier-Rigaud (2011), 76.

[496]Certainly, where a price is "manifestly excessive", the finding of an infringement will not require a precise demarcation of the line between abusive and non-abusive pricing. However, where a competition authority leaves the precise demarcation open on the infringement side, the remedy must also be limited to prohibiting "manifestly excessive" prices. In such a case, prices below the "manifestly excessive" line have not been qualified as an infringement and therefore cannot be prohibited.

[497]See Mestmäcker/Schweitzer (2004), § 17, 4ff; Eilmansberger (2008), 2-15-198ff; Deselaers (2011), Art. 102, 397ff; Fuchs/Möschel (2012), Art. 102, 174ff. In United Brands, 27/76 (1978), 252, the Court of Justice stated that the relevant question was "whether the difference between the costs actually incurred and the price actually charged is excessive, and, if the answer to this question is in the affirmative, to consider whether a price has been charged which is either unfair in itself or when compared to other competing products". This formula is ambiguous. As regards the first possible test, the Commission (COMP/36568, [Port of Helsingborg, 2006], 145ff and 228) and some commentators (eg Jones/Sufrin [2011], 533; Akman/Garrod [2011], 404; O'Donoghue/Padilla [2013], 744) infer from this passage that it is not sufficient to evaluate the excessiveness of the profit margin, but that, in a second step, also the "fairness" of the price needs to be examined. It is submitted here that there is no such second step. In para 251 of the United Brands judgment, the Court of Justice made it clear that the excessiveness of a price "could, inter alia, be determined objectively [. . .] by making a comparison between the selling price of the product in question and its cost of production, which would disclose the amount of the profit margin", cf. Eilmansberger (2008), 2-15-199. In any event, as regards the second possible test, the Court of Justice confirmed in later cases, such as 30/87 (Pompes Funèbres, 1988), 31, and 395/87 (Sacem, 1991), 38, that a comparison with products in comparable markets could serve to establish the abusiveness of a price.

concepts of "cost plus regulation" and "yardstick regulation".[498] The similarity extends also to the remedies side. On the one hand, if the finding of abuse is based on an excessive profit margin, a "cost plus remedy" could be imposed. Such a remedy prohibits the dominant undertaking to extend its profit into the zone that has been identified as abusive on the infringement side. A cost plus remedy is dynamic, because the prohibition to exceed a certain profit margin leaves the concerned undertaking the possibility to increase price when costs increase and obliges it to decrease price when costs decrease.[499] The major problem of a cost plus remedy is, however, that it does not provide incentives for the dominant undertaking to increase profits by saving costs.[500] Moreover, a cost plus remedy entails high monitoring costs, because it requires data regarding all the various cost factors. On the other hand, the Commission can impose a "yardstick remedy", if the finding of an infringement predicates on a comparison of the investigated price with prices of products in comparable markets. Under such a remedy, the dominant undertaking is prohibited from setting its price above the price of the product in the comparable market in relation to which the abuse has been established. There are at least two German cases, in which yardstick remedies have been employed.[501] The Bundesgerichtshof has emphasized in this respect that dynamic references to the prices charged by other companies are only reconcilable with the principle of legal certainty, when reference prices are either known or at least easily detectable by the undertaking concerned by the remedy.[502] Yardstick remedies cause only limited monitoring costs, because the price charged by the dominant undertaking can simply be compared to the price in the comparable market.

The Commission's method for finding the infringement determines also the remedy. A cost plus remedy cannot be inflicted, if the finding of the infringement rests solely on a comparison of the investigated price with prices of products in comparable markets. In such a case, the profit margin of the dominant undertaking has not been qualified as excessive and the competition authority can hence not make any prescriptions with respect to the profit margin. The same applies vice-versa: If the finding of the infringement is based only on the excessiveness of the profit

[498]See Ackermann (2012), 353f and 360f, who associates the two tests with "rate of return regulation" and "yardstick regulation". "Rate of return regulation" is a more specific form of "cost plus regulation", where the allowed profit margin is defined by reference to a certain rate of return on capital or investment; see Leschke (2010), § 6, 114. For the sake of simplicity, I refer to the more general concept of "cost plus regulation"; similarly Deselaers (2011), 398. See also Whish/Bailey (2012), 723, who treat the second test as "yardstick competition". For a discussion of different regulatory concepts see Viscusi/Harrington/Vernon (2005), 429ff; Leschke (2010), § 6, 108ff.

[499]See Maier-Rigaud (2011), 76f.

[500]See Viscusi/Harrington/Vernon (2005), 429ff; Leschke (2010), § 6, 109; Maier-Rigaud (2011), 77; Ackermann (2012), 354 and 360.

[501]BGH, KVR 4/94 (Weiterverteiler, 1995); KVR 25/94 (Stadtgas, 1995).

[502]See BGH, KVR 4/94 (Weiterverteiler, 1995), 12; KVR 25/94 (Stadtgas, 1995), 28; Jaeger (2010), § 32 ARC, 30; Bornkamm (2014), § 32 ARC, 43.

margin, the Commission cannot impose a yardstick remedy. However, both tests for finding the infringement give the Commission the possibility to resort to a third type of remedy, which also bears a resemblance with a concept known from regulatory theory. Irrespective of the test it uses to establish the infringement, the Commission can impose a static price cap.[503] A static price cap prohibits the dominant undertaking from increasing its price above the fixed level that has been identified as abusive either by means of an analysis of the undertaking's profit margin or by means of a comparison of its price with those of other products in comparable markets. Like yardstick remedies, static price caps have the benefit of providing an incentive for the dominant undertaking to increase its profits by enhancing efficiency.[504] They also entail only limited monitoring costs, since it is relatively simple to control whether the price charged by the dominant undertaking exceeds the static price cap. However, static price caps are inconvenient in so far as they require constant adaptation if the costs of the dominant undertaking change.

3.3.1.6.2.2 In the Context of Article 9

In Rambus, Standard & Poor's and Gazprom, the Commission accepted commitments to offset concerns relating to excessive pricing practices. Gerard invokes the first two decisions as examples for cases in which "the Commission has relied on commitments to stretch the boundaries of prevailing antitrust legal standards and, in effect, to tackle practices that could not be comfortably addressed under these standards". In support of his argument, he relies on the fact that the question of excessive prices is "notoriously complex" under EU competition law.[505] Such criticism is from the outset not persuasive. It has been argued above that the Commission has the power under Article 7 to impose remedies regarding excessive prices. The sole "complexity" of excessive pricing cases does not permit the conclusion that an excessive pricing commitment goes beyond what the Commission could have imposed under Article 7. The following section shall analyse in more detail whether there are concrete indicia that the Commission could not have imposed the commitments in Rambus and Standard & Poors under Article 7. It will also throw a quick glance at the excessive pricing remedy adopted in Gazprom.

---

[503] See Maier-Rigaud (2011), 76, for a discussion of static price caps as excessive pricing remedies. For a discussion of the related concept of "price cap regulation", see Viscusi/Harrington/Vernon (2005), 439ff; Leschke (2010), § 6, 117ff.

[504] See Viscusi/Harrington/Vernon (2005), 439; Leschke (2010), § 6, 117f.

[505] Gerard (2013), 20 together with fn 100; more carefully Dunne (2014b): "problematic, [. . .] when the Commission purports to rely on controversial theories of harm like excessive pricing" (415); "[. . .] reliance upon a more controversial competition theory, also with regulatory overtones, in the context of the Article 9 procedure" (422f).

3.3.1.6.2.2.1 Rambus

3.3.1.6.2.2.1.1 The Case

JEDEC, an industry-wide US-based standard setting organisation, developed a standard for "Dynamic Random Access Memory" (DRAM) chips. The Commission accused Rambus of having distorted the standard setting process by means of a so-called "patent ambush" during the time when Rambus was a member of JEDEC. According to the theory of harm, four conditions that were required to establish an infringement of Article 102 TFEU were met[506]: First, Rambus deliberately used its participation in JEDEC to revise and tailor its pending patent applications in an effort to gain control over JEDEC standard-compliant DRAM chips. Moreover, in spite of an obligation to do so, Rambus intentionally did not disclose any patents or patent applications which related to the relevant JEDEC standards to JEDEC.[507] Second, save for Rambus' deceit, JEDEC members were likely to have designed a "patent-free" standard around Rambus' patents.[508] Third, initial costs relating to the development of the standard and later costs associated with switching from it were significant. There were hence substantial barriers to entry on the market and the industry was locked into the JEDEC DRAM standards.[509] Fourth, as a result of its deceptive conduct, Rambus had acquired a dominant position and subsequently exploited it by claiming royalties for the use of its patents at a level which, absent its intentional deceptive conduct, it would not have been able to charge.[510]

The Commission also considered that due to the lock in of the industry into the JEDEC DRAM standards, not only the standards that were adopted during the time when Rambus was a member of JEDEC, but also subsequent standards were affected by Rambus' anticompetitive conduct.[511]

In order to offset the Commission's concerns Rambus undertook to offer a bundled licence for future DRAM products for all of its patents regarding the standards that were affected by Rambus' anticompetitive conduct. Rambus committed to charge zero royalties for patents that concerned standards adopted when it had been a JEDEC member and to cap royalties for subsequent affected standards at rates between 1.5% and 2.65% per unit of selling price.[512] In the decision, the Commission rejected submissions received in the market test that the rates were still too high. The Commission argued that Rambus had committed to charge zero royalties for patents that concerned standards adopted when it had been a JEDEC member and that the rates for subsequent affected standards were substantially lower than the 3.5% per unit price royalty that Rambus was charging prior to the adoption of the

[506] I follow the presentation of the case by de la Mano/Nazzini/Zenger (2014), 4.757ff.

[507] COMP/38.636 (Rambus, 2009), 40ff.

[508] COMP/38.636 (Rambus, 2009), 43ff.

[509] COMP/38.636 (Rambus, 2009), 22ff and 47.

[510] COMP/38.636 (Rambus, 2009), 26 and 28.

[511] COMP/38.636 (Rambus, 2009), 47.

[512] COMP/38.636 (Rambus, 2009), 49.

decision. Moreover, the Commission maintained that the commitments extended the rates to all market participants. According to the Commission, the commitments hence provided potential new entrants with a clear perspective of future royalty costs, facilitating a decision to enter the market.[513]

3.3.1.6.2.2.1.2 Discussion of Criticism

According to Dunne, the Rambus commitment illustrates that the Commission uses the Article 9 procedure to "to settle weak competition cases that would not survive the more exacting standards" of Article 7. To support her argument, Dunne relies, on the one hand, on the fact that the DC Circuit Court rejected the FTC's case against Rambus in the US.[514] On the other hand, Dunne expresses concerns regarding the fact that the Commission rejected the submissions that rates were too high.[515] The criticism is, however, not convincing.

The difficulty of the Commission's case against Rambus was that Article 102 TFEU prohibits abusive conduct only if it is engaged in by an undertaking that is already dominant. Unlike section 2 of the US Sherman Act, Article 102 TFEU does not contain a prohibition of monopolisation.[516] When Rambus engaged into its deceptive behaviour during the standard setting process, the company was not yet dominant. It acquired its dominant position only as a result of the adoption of its technology as standard. Article 102 TFEU did hence not capture Rambus' deceptive behaviour during the standard setting process as such. The Commission had to base its theory of harm on the abusive level of the royalties that Rambus was claiming once it had acquired its dominant position.[517] The Commission did not establish the excessiveness of Rambus' royalties by reference to a cost-price analysis, nor by comparison of the prices charged by Rambus with other prices charged in the market.[518] Rather, the Commission based its conclusion regarding the abusive

---

513 COMP/38.636 (Rambus, 2009), 55 and 74.

514 Dunne (2014b), 437: "The Commission's settlement with Rambus followed unsuccessful efforts by the United States' FTC to prosecute the firm for the same conduct, and it is difficult to avoid the fear that the commitment decision embodies a last ditch attempt to salvage even minor concessions from a case that was questionable in terms of both theory and evidence".

515 Dunne (2014b), 437: "the Commission pointed to the "complex and difficult nature" of the underlying competition case as justification for accepting commitments regarding royalty rates that all the respondents to the market testing process had deemed to be too high". See also Rato/Petit (2013), 31 and Gautier/Petit (2014), 24: "It is commonly accepted that the level at which Rambus agreed to cap its royalties [. . .] was higher than that it could realistically have expected to obtain in the market, in other words that the commitments decision under-remedied the issue".

516 Drexl (2009), 144.

517 See De Meese (2010), 216; Killick/Berghe (2010), 9f; Rato/Petit (2013), 30; de la Mano/Nazzini/ Zenger (2014), 4.762; for an exhaustive discussion of the question see also Picht (2013), 452ff.

518 Killick/Berghe (2010), 9, who represented Rambus before the Commission, report that Rambus argued during the administrative procedure that "a cost performance comparison of its technology with rival technologies and a benchmarking according to standard techniques for assessing royalties showed that the royalties were reasonable".

character of Rambus' royalties on the allegation that save for Rambus' deceit, JEDEC members were likely to have designed a "patent-free" standard around Rambus' patents.[519] However, in the parallel US case, the rejection of the FTC's case was based inter alia on the insufficiency of the evidence that JEDEC members were likely to have designed a "patent-free" standard.[520]

Nevertheless, in particular the following two arguments caution against projecting this outcome of the US case into a hypothetical prohibition procedure under Article 7 in the EU. First, it is controversial whether the DC Circuit Court did not apply an overly stringent causation test.[521] Critics of the US judgment argue in particular that, in view of Rambus' deceptive conduct, the causality between the conduct and the adoption of the standard should have been presumed.[522] Second, the Commission's commitment decision, which was adopted around 20 months after the judgment of the DC Circuit Court, stated concrete indicia to demonstrate the causality. On the one hand, evidence showed a general disposition in the DRAM industry against including patents in standards. On the other hand, evidence also showed that a broad range of alternative technologies had been available that were technically and commercially feasible and not exposed to any patent claims.[523] Against this backdrop, it is at least not obvious that the EU Courts would not have embraced the Commission's theory as regards the causality between Rambus' deceptive conduct and the adoption of its technology as standard.[524]

Certainly, one might also question the robustness of the Commission's accusation that Rambus engaged at all in deceptive conduct. According to the Commission's theory of harm, the royalties charged by Rambus were abusive because Rambus would not have been able to charge them absent its deceptive conduct.[525] The Commission's allegation regarding the deceptive conduct was therefore an indispensable condition of the Commission's conclusion that Rambus had committed an abuse by charging excessive royalties. It is, however, submitted that the Commission's

---

[519]Section 3.3.1.6.2.2.1.1, footnote 508 above; see also De Meese (2010), 216, who describes this as a "key element" of the Commission's analysis.

[520]522 F.3d 456 (D.C. Cir. 2008), *cert. denied*, No. 08-694, 2009 WL 425102, at 1 (2009); De Meese (2010), 217.

[521]In defence of the approach of the judgment see Wright (2009); against the approach of the judgment Wallace (2009), 683ff. See also Picht (2013), 477ff: He is of the opinion that proof of the causal link between the non-disclosure of the standard essential patents and the adoption of the standard should not at all be required.

[522]Wallace (2009), 684; see also de Meese (2010), 217: "A practical approach could also be to consider that any royalty rates charged following a patent ambush will be presumed unreasonable. This would put the burden of proof of the reasonableness of the royalty rates on Rambus".

[523]COMP/38.636 (Rambus, 2009), 44 and 46; see also Schellingerhout/Cavicchi (2010), 35.

[524]But see Rato/Petit (2013), 31, who speak of the "ill-founded" approach of the Commission. In their view, "to use the excessive pricing prohibition to sanction behaviour that occurs *ex ante* the acquisition of a dominant position is not only a *contra legem* application of Article 102, but is also fraught with practical difficulties, including the need to create entirely new legal standards to determine the types of conduct that should be deemed anticompetitive".

[525]See Sect. 3.3.1.6.2.2.1.1, footnote 510 above.

theory does not contain any obvious flaws as regards Rambus' deceptive conduct. It is true that, in the US, the DC Circuit Court expressed doubts as regards the FTC's finding that Rambus had breached JEDEC's IP disclosure rules.[526] However, also in the US, it is controversial whether a violation of a standard setting organisation's formal rules is necessary to establish anticompetitive conduct.[527] In the commitments decision, the Commission did not solely base its theory of harm on the conclusion that Rambus had violated the JEDEC patent policy. It also argued that the distortion of the decision making process within a standard-setting organisation through the withholding of relevant information was in any event abusive, regardless of whether the organisation's precise disclosure rules had been violated or not.[528] Such an approach seems in principle correct[529] and, in any event nothing suggests that the EU Courts would not have endorsed it. Certainly, Killick and Berghe report that, during the administrative procedure, Rambus defended itself in particular with the argument that Rambus could not know at the time when it committed the investigated conduct that EU competition law would impose disclosure obligations on standard setting organisation members that go beyond the rules of the organisation.[530] Nevertheless, this argument does not seriously call into question the Commission's theory of harm. The EU Courts have consistently held that Article 102 TFEU lays down an objective concept of abuse.[531] Even if Rambus really could not have known that EU competition law imposed disclosure obligations on it that went beyond the disclosure obligations of JEDEC, this would therefore not exclude the finding of an abuse. It would merely imply that Rambus did not act negligently. Pursuant to Article 23(2) Regulation 1/03, the absence of negligence would exclude the imposition of a fine. It would, however, exclude neither the finding of an infringement, nor the imposition of a remedy pursuant to Article 7.

Once one accepts the Commission's theory of harm, there are no concerns that the Commission's remedy went beyond what was necessary to put the alleged infringement to an end. Absent its deceptive conduct Rambus could not have charged royalties for the standards adopted when it was a JEDEC member. The Commission could therefore require Rambus not to charge any royalties for these standards. The remedy is in this respect comparable to the one that was endorsed by the EU Courts in DSD.[532] Rambus' obligation to reduce also the royalties for subsequent standards can plausibly be justified with the fact that these standards were still affected by Rambus anticompetitive conduct.

---

[526] 522 F.3d 456 (D.C. Cir. 2008); Killick/Berghe (2010), 9f; De Meese (2010), 217.

[527] Critically of the DC Circuit Court judgment in that regard Wallace (2009), 686f.

[528] COMP/38.636 (Rambus, 2009), 39.

[529] See Picht (2013), 471 and 475f, who considers that any non-disclosure of standard essential patents that causes increased royalties should be qualified as abusive, regardless of whether it violates the disclosure rules of the standard setting organisation.

[530] Killick/Berghe (2010), 10.

[531] Eg CJ, C-85/76 (Hoffmann-La Roche, 1979), 91; C-457/10 P (Astra Zeneca, 2012), 74.

[532] See Sect. 3.3.1.6.2.1 with footnotes 491f above.

Finally, as regards Dunne's concerns regarding the Commission's rejection of third party submissions, it is true that the Commission stated the following:

> [...] even if the possible, minor shortcomings of certain aspects of the remedies were to be considered to be substantiated, the whole package of Commitments substantially addresses the concerns expressed by the Commission in the present case. In this context, in the light of all relevant circumstances and in particular of the complex and difficult nature of the case, the Commission considers that the Community interest does not warrant continuing the investigation any further and that there are thus no longer any grounds for action by the Commission.[533]

However, it must be emphasised that in the subsequent paragraphs of the decision, the Commission set out the reasons why it considered that the commitment substantially addressed its concerns.[534] These reasons do not seem manifestly flawed. The General Court did not have to decide on 'Hynix' appeal against the commitment.[535] In any event, it is submitted that a potential insufficiency of the Rambus commitment cannot be assigned to the use of the Article 9 instead of the Article 7 procedure. Also in the context of Article 7, the Commission could have rejected requests for a further reaching remedy with the argument that the Union interest did not warrant continuing the investigation any further.[536]

3.3.1.6.2.2.2 Standard and Poor's

3.3.1.6.2.2.2.1 The Case

Banks and other financial institutions use US International Securities Identification Numbers (ISINs) in order to identify financial instruments issued in the US. The International Organization for Standardization (ISO) developed the ISIN system as ISO standard. According to the ISO rules, designated national numbering agencies (NNAs) have the responsibility of allocating ISINs for their respective territories. Standard and Poor's (S&P) is the designated NNA for the US.

The Commission was concerned that S&P infringed Article 102 TFEU by setting unfairly high licensing fees for the supply of ISINs. According to the Commission's theory of harm, S&P held a dominant position for first-hand electronic distribution and licensing of ISINs. In order to establish the excessive character of S&P's fees, the Commission relied on the rules of ISO. These rules provided for a cost recovery principle that prohibited NNAs from charging indirect users any fees and direct users more than necessary to recover the distribution costs.[537] The Commission concluded that S&P contravened the ISO cost recovery principle because it charged indirect users a fee and imposed a fee on direct users that exceeded the costs.[538]

---

[533]COMP/38.636 (Rambus, 2009), 54.

[534]See Sect. 3.3.1.6.2.2.1.1 with footnote 513 above.

[535]See Sect. 2.3.1.1.2 with footnotes 158f above.

[536]See Sect. 3.1.3.1.1.1 with footnotes 51ff above.

[537]COMP/39.592 (Standard & Poor's, 2011), 29; for descriptions of the case see also Franchoo/Pollard (2012), 377; Bansevic/Ryan/Wezenbeek (2014), 11.133ff.

[538]COMP/39.592 (Standard & Poor's, 2011), 31ff.

In order to offset the Commission's concerns, S&P committed to remove all charges for indirect users and to limit the fees imposed on direct users to its costs.[539]

3.3.1.6.2.2.2.2 Discussion of Criticism

As far as can be ascertained, the major thrust of the criticism that is levied at the S&P commitment is that the Commission relied on the theory of harm of excessive pricing, which is said to be "controversial" or "complex" or to have "regulatory overtones".[540] As mentioned above, such criticism does not prove that the Commission could not have imposed the remedy under Article 7.

Certainly, Dunne deplores also that the Commission merely sets out the legal test for excessive prices and concludes that the requirements are met, but "patently neglects [to demonstrate that this exacting standard for liability is satisfied on the facts]".[541] However, the Commission based its decision not only on the "classical United Brands jurisprudence".[542] The Commission also expressly took the view that it was possible to infer interpretative criteria for determining whether a price was excessive from sector-specific rules and regulations. As a consequence, the Commission decided to rely on the ISO cost recovery principle in order to assess whether the prices charged by S&P were unfair within the meaning of Article 102 TFEU.[543] Nothing suggests that the EU Courts would not have endorsed this approach. However, if one accepts that the Commission could rely on the ISO rules to establish the excessiveness of S&P's prices, then the Commission cannot be criticised for not having carried out a comprehensive price cost analysis.

3.3.1.6.2.2.3 Gazprom

The Commission was concerned that Gazprom infringed article 102 TFUE by engaging in an overall strategy of fragmenting and isolating the Central and Eastern European (CEE) gas markets and restricting the free flow of gas across CEE with a view to be able to maintain higher prices in some CEE countries. One of the concerns raised by the Commission was that Gazprom charged wholesalers excessive prices. In order to demonstrate the excessiveness of the prices, the Commission relied, on the one hand, on the fact that the prices charged exceeded the costs by an average of 170%. On the other hand, a comparison with prices charged in Germany and the Netherlands showed that the prices charged across the CEE exceeded prices charged in Germany and the Netherland by 9–40%. The Commission considered that the indexation of the gas price to the oil price, which was contained in Gazprom's

[539]COMP/39.592 (Standard & Poor's, 2011), 45ff.

[540]See the references in Sect. 3.3.1.6.2.2, footnote 505 above.

[541]Dunne (2014b), 424.

[542]Bansevic/Ryan/Wezenbeek (2014), 11.137; COMP/39.592 (Standard & Poor's, 2011), 27; see also Dunne (2014b), 422.

[543]COMP/39.592 (Standard & Poor's, 2011), 27f.

contracts, may not have appropriately captured the economic value of the gas sold in the CEE and therefore may have contributed to the excessiveness of the prices charged by Gazprom.[544]

As remedy, Gazprom committed to the use of price revision clauses that allow its customers, in predefined intervals, to request to align the price with the development of certain benchmark prices in Germany, France and Italy and to refer the matter to arbitration, if the parties do not agree on the price revision.[545]

The part of the Gazprom decision that deals with excessive pricing seems to contain at least no obvious indicia that the Commission went beyond what it could have imposed under article 7. As regards the infringement side, the decision seems consistent with the jurisprudence of the Court of Justice, which held in AKKA/LAA that a method to establish excessive pricing based on a comparison of prices applied in the Member State concerned with those applied in other Member States must be considered valid and that there is no minimum threshold above which a price must be regarded as excessive, given that the circumstances specific to each case are decisive.[546] Also the fact that the Commission took account of the indexation of the gas price to the oil price does not appear objectionable. In this regard, the Commission underlined the liberty of contracting parties to index gas contract prices to the prices of other products, which it did not consider in itself abusive. However, oil indexation was considered to have artificially increased the price of gas, because demand and supply for oil and gas had become largely independent over the years with oil prices reaching higher levels.[547]

As regards the remedy side, the obligation to grant the contractual partners a right to align the price with the benchmarks specified in the Commission does also not appear manifestly disproportionate. More importantly, in so far as the revision clauses put Gazprom's customers in a position where they can themselves react when the price of gas starts diverging from the competitive benchmarks, the remedy constitutes a market based mechanism to eliminate the Commission's concerns, without the need for the Commission to start prescribing specific gas prices for individual gas contracts.[548] In that regard, it has rightly been underlined that the Gazprom commitments constitute an "innovative" example of an excessive pricing remedy which allows to avoid that the Commission has to act as a regulator.[549]

[544]COMP/39.816 (Gazprom, 2018), 69ff.

[545]COMP/39.816 (Gazprom, 2018), 102f and 152ff.

[546]CJ, C-177/16 (AKKA/LAA, 2017), 38, 42 and 55; Lübking (2019), 435.

[547]COMP/39.816 (Gazprom, 2018), 75-77.

[548]COMP/39.816 (Gazprom, 2018), 164 and 176.

[549]Lübking (2019), 436.

3.3.1.7 Microsoft Tying: An Unbundling Remedy Under Article 7 vs a Must Carry Remedy Under Article 9

The different remedies adopted in the two abuse procedures against Microsoft for tying the Media Player and the Internet Explorer to the Windows operating system constitute a further opportunity to discuss whether the Commission uses the Article 9 procedure to extract remedies that it could not have imposed under Article 7. In both procedures, the Commission relied essentially on the same theory of harm.[550] In order to show that the tying requirements of coercion and foreclosure were met,[551] the Commission argued that Microsoft did not offer Windows without the Media Player and the Internet Explorer and that it was technically impossible to switch the two programs off; other media players and browsers could hence only be installed in addition to the two Microsoft programs.[552] The Commission found that, through tying the Media Player and the Internet Explorer to Windows, Microsoft created an "artificial distribution advantage", which allowed the two programs to profit from the "ubiquity" of the operating system.[553] According to the Commission's theory of harm, the artificial distribution advantage created network effects—in the Commission's words: "a positive feedback loop"[554]—because the ubiquity of the Media Player or the Internet Explorer gave content providers and software developers an incentive to code their products according to the standards employed by Microsoft.[555] According to the Commission, the artificial distribution advantage was in particular not offset by the possibility to download competing browsers and media players, because, in view of the preinstalled Microsoft programs, OEMs and consumers lacked incentives to do so.[556]

---

[550]See Buhr/Bulst/Foucault/Kramler (2010), 37, who mention that "[t]he reasoning in the statement of objections [of the Internet Explorer decision] followed to a large extent the [reasoning of the Media Player decision] as upheld by the General Court". See also Petit/Neyrinck (2011), who treat the two decisions without making a significant distinction as regards the theory of harm.

[551]In order to establish the tying abuse, the Commission examined whether the following requirements were fulfilled: (i) the tying and the tied goods are two separate products; (ii) the undertaking concerned is dominant in the tying product market; (iii) the undertaking concerned does not give customers a choice to obtain the tying product without the tied product (coercion); (iv) tying forecloses competition (foreclosure); see GC, T-201/04 (Microsoft I, 2007), 842 and 850ff; generally on the requirements for finding a tying abuse under Article 102 TFEU see Jones/Sufrin (2011), 458ff; Whish/Bailey (2012), 691ff; H. Schmidt (2009), 59ff.

[552]See COMP/37.792 (Microsoft, 2004), 827 and 829; GC, T-201/04 (Microsoft I, 2007), 945ff; COMP/39.530 (Microsoft – tying, 2009), 36, 42, 43.

[553]See COMP/37.792 (Microsoft, 2004), 833, 844; GC, T-201/04 (Microsoft I, 2007), 1036ff; COMP/39.530 (Microsoft – tying, 2009), 39f.

[554]COMP/37.792 (Microsoft, 2004), 882.

[555]See COMP/37.792 (Microsoft, 2004), 879ff; COMP/39.530 (Microsoft – tying, 2009), 55f; Petit/Neyrinck (2011), 119, contest that the "positive feedback loop" really existed as regards the Internet Explorer.

[556]See COMP/37.792 (Microsoft, 2004), 845, 858ff; GC, T-201/04 (Microsoft I, 2007), 1041f and 1050ff; COMP/39.530 (Microsoft – tying, 2009), 44 and 46.

Despite the identical theories of harm, the Commission employed different remedies in the two procedures. In the Article 7 decision regarding the Media Player, the Commission ordered Microsoft to offer a full-functioning version of the Windows operating system without the Media Player. However, Microsoft retained the right to offer a bundle of the two products.[557] On the contrary, in the commitments made binding by the Commission in the Article 9 decision regarding the Internet explorer, Microsoft undertook not only to enable OEMs and users to turn the Internet Explorer off and on, and to allow OEMs to preinstall the web browser of their choice and set it as a default web browser. Moreover, Microsoft also engaged itself to distribute a choice screen software update giving users an opportunity to choose whether to install a competing web browser and, if so, which one.[558]

Many commentators have rightly taken a critical stance towards the remedy imposed in the Article 7 decision regarding the Media Player due to its lack of effect on the market.[559] Since the Commission did not provide for a price differential,[560] Microsoft subsequently offered the version of Windows without the Media Player and the bundled version at the same price. Consequently, there was no demand for the version without the Media Player. Ahlborn and Evans point out that, according to Microsoft's uncontested submissions before the General Court, until the hearing of the case, OEMs worldwide bought no copy of the unbundled version at all and computer retailers bought only 1787 copies of it, which corresponded to less than 0.005% of all copies of Windows XP sold at retail in Europe.[561] On the contrary, at least in the Commission's view, the choice screen commitment regarding the Internet Explorer was more successful. The Commission reported that, within the 9 months following the commitment's first implementation, 84 million browsers were downloaded through the choice screen.[562] Nevertheless, classified as a "must

[557]See GC, T-201/04 (Microsoft I, 2007), 1194.

[558]See COMP/39.530 (Microsoft – tying, 2009), 60.

[559]Heinemann (2005), 79; Idot (2005), 49; Ahlborn/Evans (2009), 920, 922; Larouche (2009), 955f; First (2008), 13; H. Schmidt (2009), 90, 104ff; Kellezi (2010), 305f; Economides/Lianos (2010), 382ff; Jones/Sufrin (2011), 475; O'Donoghue/Padilla (2013), 887 and 900f; Voell (2014), 171.

[560]See COMP/37.792 (Microsoft, 2004), 1013(iii): In the like effects order, the Commission merely enjoined Microsoft from offering OEMs or consumers a discount for obtaining Windows together with the Media Player. It did, however, not prohibit the sale of the bundled version at the same price; cf. Ahlborn/Evans (2009), 893: "[The Commission] prohibited Microsoft from charging more for the unbundled version of Windows than for the bundled version but did not require Microsoft to charge less for the unbundled than for the bundled version"; similarly Heinemann (2005), 79.

[561]See Ahlborn/Evans (2009), 922. Similarly: First (2008), 13; Jones/Sufrin (2011), 475 fn 477; Economides/Lianos (2010), fn 125, who refer to a Microsoft press release from April 2006 containing the same figures. Petit/Neyrinck (2011), 117f, refer to an ironic comment in a blog according to which the 1787 sold copies of the unbundled version "may have been bought by IT geeks willing to have a copy of the first software ever designed by DG COMP".

[562]IP 13/196 of 6 March 2013. But see also Petit/Neyrinck (2011), 118, who refer to controversial positions as regards the question whether the choice screen remedy has affected Microsoft's market share on the browser market; Brenner (2014), 678, according to whom the choice screen remedy has produced as little effects as the remedy used in the Media Player case.

carry remedy",[563] the choice screen commitment has been criticised for not fitting the Commission's theory of harm.[564] According to Economides and Lianos, a must carry remedy cannot be imposed for a tying infringement, but only where the allegedly stricter conditions of a refusal to grant access abuse, in particular the requirement regarding the indispensability of the access, are met.[565]

It is tempting to associate a potential mismatch between the tying concern and the choice screen remedy with the fact that the decision regarding the Internet Explorer

[563]See eg Heinemann (2005), 81; Economides/Lianos (2010), 387ff; Lianos (2012), 193; Petit/ Neyrinck (2011), 120, fn 32.

[564]Economides/Lianos (2010), 419: "mismatch between the consumer harm story and the remedy sought"; similarly also Ibanez Colomo (2010), 294, and Lianos (2012), 193f. Petit/Neyrinck (2011), 120, fn 32, formulate more carefully. They only suggest that the imposition of a must carry remedy "possibly went beyond conventional remedies in tying cases". Even more carefully Gerard (2013), 20 fn 104: "it is a fact that the corrective measures obtained in 2009 went further than the ones imposed in the 2004 prohibition decision, while the context appeared less serious"; Brenner (2014), 677f: "Ob der [. . .] Auswahlbildschirm [. . .] nach Art. 7 VO 1/2003 rechtmäßig hätte angeordnet werden können, erscheint fraglich".

[565]Economides/Lianos (2010), 387ff, in particular 389: "[. . .] if the competition authority decides to impose a "must carry" remedy, it should bring a proper essential facilities case [. . .]"; similarly at 419: "The choice screen remedy [. . .] fits more with an essential facilities case, where Windows would have been considered indispensable for the distribution of an Internet browser. We do not criticize the remedy per se, since it could prove to be effective in terms of reinvigorating competition in the Internet browser market, but rather the apparent conceptual mismatch between the consumer harm story and the remedy". Similarly also Ibanez Colomo (2010), 294.

The idea of Economides/Lianos can be traced back to Art/McCurdy (2004). They argued with respect to the Media Player decision that the Commission's theory of harm relied essentially on the distribution advantage created by the automatic supply of Windows with the Media Player and that the Commission therefore wrongly based its finding of an infringement on the allegedly less strict standards of tying instead of the standards for refusal to supply. According to Art/McCurdy, the facts at the basis of the Media Player decision would not have met the stricter standards for a refusal to supply abuse, in particular because the distribution via Windows was allegedly not indispensable for competing media players. At least implicitly Art/McCurdy indicate that the Commission was seeking a must carry remedy, but could not impose it, because the refusal to supply standards were not met, see 700: "Prior to its final decision, the Commission gave extensive consideration to an alternative "must carry" remedy, under which it would order Microsoft to include competitors' media players with Windows in order to equalise access to the OEM distribution channel. This alternative remedy underscores the fact that the core competitive harm perceived by the Commission stemmed from Microsoft's "privileged" access to the OEM distribution channel, and could be remedied adequately by ordering Microsoft to supply such access to its competitors. But as Commissioner Monti recognised in relation to the interface information remedy, a refusal to supply a competitor may be held to be an abuse only in exceptional circumstances [. . .]".

Petit/Neyrinck (2011), 120f, follow Art/McCurdy (2004): They claim that both Microsoft tying cases are "disguised refusal to supply cases" and that the Commission only chose to "build tying cases", because it could not show that the stricter standards of a refusal to supply infringement were met. Economides/Lianos (2009), 540f, take a critical stance towards the proposition that the facts at the base of the Media Player decision would not have met the stricter standards for a refusal to supply abuse.

was taken on the basis of Article 9.[566] However, as is apparent from the latter decision, the Commission considered that the choice screen remedy was proportionate both under Article 7 and under Article 9.[567] At least the Commission hence seems to have been of the opinion that it could have imposed the must carry remedy unilaterally on the basis of Article 7.

The following analysis will show that this is in principle correct and that Economides' and Lianos' theory of a mismatch between the theory of harm of a tying infringement and a must carry remedy must be rejected. During the discussion of the Commission's theory of harm and the available remedies, the following terminology will be used: "Pure bundling" means the making available of only the bundle, i.e. the supply of Windows only together with the Media Player and the Internet Explorer. "Mixed bundling" describes the making available of the bundle and of its constituent parts, i.e. the supply of Windows with the two programs and without them. "Unbundling" designates the making available of the constituent parts only separately, i.e. the supply of the Media Player and the Internet Explorer not with Windows, but only separately from it.[568]

3.3.1.7.1 The Theory of Harm

First, it must be pointed out that, in both the Media Player and the Internet Explorer decision, the creation of an artificial distribution advantage was paramount for the Commission's theory of harm.[569] It is beyond the scope of the present work to

---

[566]See Lianos (2013), 448f fn 321, who cites the decision regarding the Internet Explorer commitments in support of his allegation that "the remedial discretion of the Commission remains important in the area of commitment decisions and that there is a risk of misfit between the remedies and the competition wrong they aim to address, possibly leading to broad prophylactic remedies of regulatory nature". Similarly Ibanez Colomo (2010), 294; Brenner (2014), 678: "Insofern bot also die Entscheidung nach Art. 9 wohl die Möglichkeit eines besonderen, marktgestaltenden Ansatzes zur Wiederherstellung des Wettbewerbs".

[567]See Comp/39.530 (Microsoft – tying, 2009), fn 48: "Even if one accepts that the assessment of proportionality under Article 9 is exactly the same as that under Article 7 [. . .], the Commission considers that the Commitments are proportionate in this case." Before the adoption of the 2004 decision, the Commission published a press release (IP/03/1150), stating that it had sent Microsoft a statement of objections containing the remedies it "intended to impose". As regards the tying of the Media Player, the statement of objections set out the untying remedy and the choice screen remedy as two "proposed alternative remedies". See also Hellström/Maier-Rigaud/Bulst (2009), 50 fn 32.

[568]The "bundling" terminology is widely used in the discussion of the Microsoft "tying" remedies. See eg Ahlborn/Evans (2009), 893, H. Schmidt (2009), 103, and Kellezi (2010), 303.

[569]See Sect. 3.3.1.7, footnote 553 above and in particular the following two passages from the two decisions: COMP/37.792 (Microsoft, 2004), 844: "Through tying WMP with Windows, Microsoft ensures that WMP is as ubiquitous on PCs worldwide as Windows is. [. . .] Microsoft obviously controls this mode of distribution and (no longer) affords competing media player vendors access to it." Comp/39.530 (Microsoft – tying, 2009), 40: "Microsoft controls the distribution of Internet Explorer with Windows and does not afford competing web browser vendors access to that mode of distribution". Petit/Neyrinck (2011), 120, rely on the latter passage in support of their theory (Sect. 3.3.1.7, footnote 565 above) that the Microsoft tying cases are "disguised refusal to deal cases".

evaluate thoroughly whether it is correct to base a finding of a tying infringement on the latter complaint. However, at least prima vista, the better reasons seem to militate for an affirmative answer. The counter-argument that the Commission can only address the complaint stemming from the artificial distribution advantage under the allegedly stricter standards of a refusal to deal infringement[570] is not convincing. In fact, one might already put the significance of the distinction between refusal to deal and tying cases into doubt by questioning whether the standards for the former are really stricter than those for the latter.[571] More important is, however, that according to the Commission's theory, precisely the tying of the Media Player and the Internet Explorer to the Windows operating system caused the artificial distri-

[570]See Sect. 3.3.1.7, footnote 565 above.

[571]Rousseva (2010), 228ff and 256 points out that "the difference between refusals to deal and tying consists of the condition for indispensability in the case of refusals to deal, and the separate product test and coercion in the case of tying". She argues, however, that "these elements of the tests do not really contribute to the establishment of the abuse[, that] they repeat arguments pertaining to other aspects of the analysis and burden the tests unnecessarily [and that] if the focus of the analysis is on the effect of the practice, these elements of the tests can be dispensed with".

See also the last sentence of Economides/Lianos (2010), 419f: "The classification of abuses under Article 102 is not a clear-cut exercise, and there is always a fine conceptual line that distinguishes different categories of abuses if one takes an effects-based approach". Moreover, as has been pointed out in Sect. 3.3.1.7, footnote 565 above, Economides/Lianos (2009), 540, are sceptic whether the Media Player decision would really not meet the refusal to deal standards. In this respect, they argue that the refusal to deal requirement of the "[i]ndispensability of access is measured with reference to the possibility of creating an economically viable distribution channel [and that it] remains to be seen if Internet downloading is an economically viable alternative to access to the OEMs to bring the product to the attention of the final consumer". It must be pointed out, however, that the Commission analysed a criterion that was at least very similar when it considered that the distribution advantage created by the tying of the Internet Explorer and the Media Player to Windows was not offset by the possibility to download those two programs, see Sect. 3.3.1.7, footnote 556 above.

Certainly, one might follow Art/McCurdy (2004), 700ff, and Petit/Neyrinck (2011), 120, and object that the indispensability requirement of a refusal to deal infringement is not met by the mere finding that alternatives to the requested supply are less advantageous, which is all that the Commission found with respect to downloads as alternative to the distribution via Windows. However, while Art/McCurdy and Petit/Neyrinck rightly underline that the Bronner case, CJ, C-7/97 (1998), 40ff, points in that direction, it must be emphasised that, in Microsoft, the GC applied a softer interpretation of the indispensability criterion when it examined the interoperability infringement. The GC rejected Microsoft's argument that other methods of interoperability would have constituted sufficient alternatives to the disclosure of the desired communication protocols. In essence, the Court argued that these alternatives would allow competitors only a de minimis market penetration and that the alternatives would not have permitted interoperability on an equal footing; see GC, T-201/04 (Microsoft I, 2007), 114, 229f, 355, 374 and Rousseva (2010), 104f. Ridyard (2004), 670, has called the lenient indispensability standard applied in Microsoft "the convenient facilities doctrine". Jones/Sufrin (2011), 518, follow Ridyard (2004) and point out the following: "The interface information might have been greatly more convenient for the competitors, but they were functioning without it. Indispensability in Microsoft did not mean exclusion from the market".

bution advantage.[572] If one requests that tying should not be classified as abusive per se, but instead be submitted to an analysis of the existence of potential foreclosure effects,[573] it is hard to see why the creation of an artificial distribution advantage through tying practices should not be taken into account. Be that as it may, in Microsoft I, the General Court fully embraced the Commission's approach of looking at the foreclosure effect generated by the artificial distribution advantage through the lens of a test for a tying infringement.

Second, although both the decision regarding the Media Player and the decision regarding the Internet Explorer are silent on this point, it needs to be stressed that not only pure bundling causes the artificial distribution advantage lying at the heart of the Commission's theory of harm. Rather, as long as there is no difference in price between the bundled and the unbundled version of Windows, the artificial distribution advantage is also generated by mixed bundling.[574] In fact, in the absence of a difference in price between the bundled and the unbundled version, there is no demand for the unbundled version, so that the distribution advantage continues to exist.[575] Certainly, it is controversial whether Microsoft's strategy to offer the unbundled and the bundled version of Windows at the same price amounts to an

---

[572]See COMP/37.792 (Microsoft, 2004), 844: "Through tying WMP with Windows, Microsoft ensures that WMP is as ubiquitous on PCs worldwide as Windows is." Comp/39.530 (Microsoft – tying, 2009), 39f: "the tying gave Internet Explorer an artificial distribution advantage [;] by tying Internet Explorer to Windows, Microsoft ensured that Internet Explorer was as ubiquitous on PCs world-wide [. . .] as was Windows".

[573]See eg Whish/Bailey (2012), 690: "The insights of the Chicago School were persuasive, and there is now general recognition that per se illegality is inappropriate for tying [. . .] it would be perverse to suggest that, when engaged in by a dominant firm, such behaviour should be stigmatised as presumptively unlawful".

[574]As is apparent from the judgment regarding the tying of the Media Player, the Commission and the General Court merely rejected Microsoft's plea that the supply of the Media Player at no extra cost would exempt it from liability, see GC, T-201/04 (Microsoft I, 2007), 968ff. This is not equivalent to basing the finding of abuse on the said circumstance. The fact that the Commission did not base its finding of abuse on the fact that there was no extra cost for the Media Player is also confirmed by the fact that the Commission pleaded before the General Court that, if Microsoft were to offer the unbundled and the bundled versions at the same price, it would have to examine in a new procedure whether this constituted an abuse; cf. GC-T-201/04 (Microsoft I, 2007), 908.

Ahlborn/Evans (2009), 893 (similarly at 921), infer from the absence of a price differential in the remedy imposed in the Media Player decision that the "Commission objected to pure bundling [. . .] but did not object to mixed bundling". While the latter statement is formally correct, it calls for two observations that paint a more nuanced picture: On the one hand, it is not possible to deduce the scope of the infringement from the scope of the remedy. In theory, the Commission could have found that a uniform pricing of the bundled and the unbundled version was abusive and nevertheless have abstained from addressing this concern on the remedies side. On the other hand, the fact that the decision's theory of harm is not based on the fact that there was no extra cost for the Media Player (see above), does not mean that the Commission found that uniform pricing of the two versions would be legal. The Commission simply did not take a decision in this respect.

[575]See Ahlborn/Evans (2009), 921, who underline that the distribution advantage disappears under a complete prohibition of any bundled sales, but continues to exist under an obligation to offer a mixed bundle, as long as there is no demand for the unbundled version: "[If Microsoft made] the naked version of Windows and WMP available separately [, . . .] WMP would lose its distribution advantage [. . .] and WMP would compete on the intrinsic merits of the two products. [. . .] In a

abuse.[576] However, in view of the previously mentioned subsistence of the artificial distribution advantage, there seems to be good reason to assume that this is the case. Mixed bundling typically constitutes an abuse where the dominant operator provides customers with an unwarranted incentive to purchase the bundle instead of purchasing its constituent parts.[577] The sale of the bundled and the unbundled version of Windows at the same price provides precisely for such an abusive incentive. The fact that media players and browsers are generally available at no charge, because they can be downloaded for free, does not preclude this conclusion. In this case, the incentive for customers to purchase the bundle simply does not stem from the fact that the price of the components of the bundle is more attractive when the components are sold in a bundle than when they are supplied separately. Rather, the incentive stems from the saving of transaction costs that customers enjoy if they obtain the Media Player or the Internet Explorer automatically with Windows. The fact that this saving of transaction costs constitutes an efficiency does not per se preclude its classification as abusive. The said saving of transaction costs also constitutes a restraint of competition, because it provides an incentive for customers to purchase the bundle and thereby forecloses competing producers of media players or browsers who do not dispose of the possibility to provide a comparable incentive to consumers. Unless the generated efficiencies outbalance the foreclosure effects, a uniform pricing of the unbundled and the bundled version of Windows must therefore be regarded as abusive.

3.3.1.7.2 The Remedies

If one accepts that the tying of the Media Player or the Internet Explorer to Windows creates an artificial distribution advantage and that the latter subsists also where a bundled version of Windows and an unbundled one are offered at the same price, it becomes clear that the remedy imposed by the Commission in the decision regarding the Media Player did not go far enough. Since the Commission had abstained from imposing a price differential, there was no demand for the version of Windows without the Media Player and the artificial distribution advantage consequently subsisted. Three other remedies could, however, have eliminated the artificial distribution advantage: An obligation to unbundle Windows and the two programs,

world in which Microsoft offered both a Windows with WMP and Windows without WMP but in which there was no demand for the unbundled version, WMP [. . .] continued to enjoy ubiquity".

[576] See, on the one hand, Dolmans/Graf (2004), 243, who argue that uniform pricing would amount to a discount on the bundled version and therefore to an unlawful price tie. On the other hand, Ahlborn/Evans (2009), 919, fn 140 argue that "the Commission was correct in not imposing a price difference for the two versions of Windows", because "WMP and other media players had been generally made available for free".

[577] The most obvious example is the grant of an unjustified rebate. See Jones/Sufrin (2011), 462; Whish/Bailey (2012), 738; Fuchs/Möschel (2012), 285 and 294f.

i.e. a prohibition of any bundled sales; the imposition of a price differential in addition to the obligation to offer a mixed bundle; or the must carry remedy.

An obligation to unbundle Windows has the major drawback that it removes the efficiencies generated by a bundled sale.[578] In this respect, one might even argue that those efficiencies were the reason why, in the decisions regarding both the Media Player and the Internet Explorer, the Commission did not enjoin Microsoft from all bundled sales, but opted merely for a mixed bundling remedy[579] and, in the second case, for a must carry obligation. Contrary to an unbundling obligation, both the imposition of a price differential in addition to the obligation to offer a mixed bundle and the must carry remedy allow at the same time to remove the artificial distribution advantage completely and to preserve the efficiencies of a bundled sale. On the one hand, making the bundled version more expensive than the unbundled one increases demand for the unbundled version, thus limiting the artificial distribution advantage brought about by the nevertheless possible sale of the bundled version. This may explain why some commentators of the Media Player decision found it "astonishing

[578]See Kellezi (2010), 303f: "[L]'intégration des deux produits peut comporter des gains d'efficience tant à l'échelle de la production qu'à celle de la distribution. Ladite intégration peut être appréciée également par les consommateurs: ils auront, à l'achat d'un ordinateur, un produit intégré avec plusieurs fonctionnalités. [...] l'obligation de la commercialisation du système d'exploitation Windows sans Windows Media Player ainsi que la faculté donnée à Microsoft d'offrir une version couplée des deux produits, visent à éliminer l'effet concurrentiel tout en sauvegardant les gains d'efficience pour le producteur et les consommateurs"; Heinemann (2005), 79: "It is questionable, if the unbundling remedy of the European Commission is correct. [...] Apparently, the Commission stopped half-way: the most logical remedy would have been to prohibit bundling entirely. However, such a radical "no-WMP" remedy would have contradicted the expectations of many end-users who prefer at least one media player to be delivered with the operating system"; Jones/Sufrin (2011), 475: "The Commission's remedy in Microsoft, the supply of an alternative naked version of Windows without WMP installed, was not a success. OEMs had no interest in such a product. It would have been different had the Commission ordered Microsoft not to supply Windows with WMP. However, that would have been prejudicial to consumers [...]".

[579]In the procedure regarding the Media Player, Microsoft argued that its tying practices were objectively justified because integrating the Media Player into Windows caused various benefits. The GC rejected the argument, in particular because the Commission had not enjoined Microsoft from offering a bundled version, but merely required it to offer also an unbundled one; cf. GC, T-201/04 (Microsoft I, 2007), 1144ff, in particular 1149f, 1155. Although this line of reasoning is not identical to the explanation given above why the Commission abstained from requiring Microsoft to fully unbundle the programs in question, it nevertheless supports it: Microsoft had argued that its practice of pure bundling was objectively justified. The GC rejected the argument because the Commission had only required Microsoft to offer a mixed bundle, which sufficiently allowed preserving the benefits. The GC thus seems to acknowledge that there were benefits linked to the bundled sale of Microsoft that needed to be taken into account for the examination whether there was an objective justification. The GC merely did not take a decision on the question whether those benefits were strong enough to preclude a prohibition of mixed bundling. Since the Commission had not prohibited mixed bundling, there was no need for the GC to decide whether the Commission could even have required Microsoft to fully unbundle the programs. See also Larouche (2009), 957, according to whom the GC rejected Microsoft's arguments regarding the objective justification, "mostly because the Commission remedy does not forbid the bundled Windows and therefore does not take away the efficiencies arising from the integration of WMP into Windows".

that the Commission did not give more precise orders concerning pricing policy".[580] On the other hand, also the must carry remedy eliminates the distribution advantage and allows at the same time to preserve the efficiencies of a bundled sale. The latter remedy does not enjoin Microsoft from selling its products as a bundle, but instead opens up the possibility for competing products to be included in the bundle offered by Microsoft.[581]

It is easy to recognise an obligation to unbundle or an obligation to offer a mixed bundle paired with a price differential as matches of a tying infringement. This is less the case for a must carry remedy. In alignment with Lianos' and Economides' theory of a "mismatch" between the theory of harm of a tying infringement and a must carry remedy,[582] one might argue that, although a must carry remedy eliminates the artificial distribution advantage created by a tying infringement, it nevertheless does not fit the theory of harm, because the reproach of a tying or a bundling infringement does not predicate on the refusal to include a competing product into the bundle, but on the joining of two of the dominant operator's own products for sale. However, it is submitted here that such reasoning falls short of the mark. At least as long as the theory of harm rests essentially on the creation of a distribution advantage, it is artificial to construe the bundling of Windows with the Media Player or the Internet Explorer and the refusal to include competing media players or browsers into the bundle as two different infringements that entail different remedies. The bundling creates the artificial distribution advantage only as long as the competing products are excluded from the bundle and an exclusion of the competing products from the bundle only generates the artificial distribution advantage as long as the bundling takes place at all. Hence, on the infringement side, the exclusion of competing media players and browsers from the bundle is a condition for the finding that the bundling of Windows with the Media Player and the Internet Explorer constitutes an infringement. Analogously, the continuation of the bundling of Windows with the Media Player or the Internet Explorer is an inherent condition for the finding that the exclusion of competing media players and browsers from the bundle constitutes an infringement. Hence, as long as the theory of harm rests essentially on the creation of an artificial distribution advantage, the bundling of

[580] Heinemann (2005), 79. Similarly H. Schmidt (2009), 104: "It is rather surprising that the Commission omitted to make any comments in respect of future Windows versions and the price of the unbundled Windows". See also Kellezi (2010), 306: "Des mesures relatives aux prix du paquet et du prix de chaque composante constiutent des éléments nécessaires".

[581] See Economides/Lianos (2010), 386f, who argue with respect to the Media Player decision that a choice screen remedy "would have guaranteed as wide a distribution of RealAudio and other players as Windows Media Player, would have erased any distributional advantage of Windows Media Player, would have dispelled any tying concerns, and would have given full decision power to consumers". They are of the opinion that the choice screen remedy "provides consumers the best of both worlds – the benefits of standalone media players and the benefits of an integrated solution." See also Heinemann (2005), 80f, who prefers the must carry remedy because it lowers competitors' entry barriers; Picker (2005), 205, who also prefers the must carry remedy, which would "directly mitigate the ubiquity advantage".

[582] See Sect. 3.3.1.7, footnotes 564 and 565 above.

Windows and the two programs, on the one hand, and, on the other hand, the refusal to include competing programs into the bundle, are not two separate infringements, but two conditions of one and the same infringement. As regards the remedies side, this entails the consequence that there are two ways of stopping the incriminated conduct: Either discontinuing the bundled supply of Windows with the Media Player and the Internet Explorer or including competing media players and browsers into the bundle. Economides' and Lianos' theory of a "mismatch" between the theory of harm of a tying infringement and a must carry remedy must hence be rejected.[583]

It follows from the above that, out of the three remedies that fully eliminate the artificial distribution advantage, not only an obligation to unbundle Windows and an obligation to offer a mixed bundle paired with a price differential, but also a must carry remedy stay within the boundaries of the theory of harm of a tying infringement. In principle, one might consider this as a situation where there are several ways to put an infringement to an end, so that the choice must be left to the infringing undertaking.[584] However, as long as it is apparent for the Commission that Microsoft wants to continue to supply the Media Player and the Internet Explorer together with Windows without charging an extra price for either of the two programs and as long as the bundled supply generates efficiencies that need to be taken into account, the imposition of a must carry remedy by virtue of Article 7 constitutes in principle a lawful solution.[585] The same conclusion applies all the more if the choice screen remedy is adopted subsequent to a voluntary commitment offer pursuant to Article 9.

There is, however, one detail of the commitment accepted by the Commission in the procedure regarding the tying of the Internet Explorer which goes beyond a mere mirroring of the Commission's theory of harm. According to the commitment, the choice screen must only appear on versions of Windows where the Internet Explorer is set as the default browser.[586] Economides and Lianos correctly point out that this tilts the remedy against Microsoft and in favour of its competitors. Contrary to

[583]See also O'Donoghue/Padilla (2013), 901, who are of the opinion that the choice screen remedy "targeted what was arguably the underlying issue – the distributional advantage that distributing Windows offered to other products".

[584]See Sect. 3.3.1.4.1.2.1 with footnotes 318ff above; see also Hellström/Maier-Rigaud/Bulst (2009), 50 fn 32.

[585]It is a different question whether the Commission could still impose the must carry remedy under Article 7, if Microsoft expressed a preference for unbundling Windows or for a price differential. In the procedure regarding the Internet Explorer, Microsoft had initially planned to distribute only an unbundled version of Windows comprising a link for downloading the Internet Explorer. The Commission criticised this plan, suggesting "that consumers should be offered a choice of browser, not that Windows should be supplied without a browser at all" (see IP/09/272 and Economides/Lianos [2010], 392). It is submitted here that in so far as the provision of a link only to the download of the Internet Explorer still provides for a distribution advantage, the Commission was right in rejecting Microsoft's plan. However, had Microsoft decided to distribute only a completely unbundled version of Windows, i.e. a version without such a link, and to leave it to OEMs and consumers to download the Internet Explorer for free, the Commission would have had to accept this remedy and could not have imposed a must carry remedy instead.

[586]See Comp/39.530 (Microsoft – tying, 2009), 60, 87 and 103.

Microsoft, the competitors can pay OEMs for setting their browsers as the default without having this distribution advantage removed by a choice screen.[587] The Commission explains in this respect that "[e]xtending the distribution of the choice screen to users who have competing web browsers set as the default browser would not address the competition problem provisionally identified [as] there is no evidence that any of the vendors of those other web browsers are in a dominant position or are engaged in any anti-competitive tying practices".[588] This explanation misses the point. That the vendors of competing browsers are not dominant and thus have no special responsibility incumbent on them is not decisive. Rather, the decisive issue is that, if the Commission's theory of harm rests on the existence of an artificial distribution advantage, the remedy may not go beyond the restoration of competition on an equal footing through the elimination of the artificial distribution advantage. Limiting the choice screen only to versions of Windows where the Internet Explorer is set as the default browser does this, because instead of creating the conditions for competition on an equal footing, it generates an advantage for producers of competing browsers. It is therefore submitted that the limitation of the choice screen remedy to versions of Windows that do not have the Internet Explorer set as the default browser goes beyond mirroring the theory of harm underlying the decision. Without further reasoning, the Commission could not have imposed such a remedy under Article 7. However, one potential justification of granting competing browser vendors an advantage is the necessity to eliminate the subsisting effects of an identified past infringement. Whether and under what conditions such a justification allows for the imposition of remedy that goes beyond a mere mirroring of the infringement will be discussed below.[589]

3.3.2 Addressing Imminent Anticompetitive Conduct

It is sometimes contended that the Commission cannot impose remedies under Article 7 Regulation 1/03 to prevent imminent anticompetitive conduct before it is committed.[590] Supporters of such a view rely in particular upon the opinion of Judge Vesterdorf acting as Advocate General in Polypropylene, who argued, in the context of fines, that there was "no place within the ambit of Article [101 TFEU] for the introduction of a separate concept of attempt".[591] However, the question whether mere attempts of infringements of Articles 101 and 102 TFEU should be punishable with fines is different from the question whether the Commission should have the

[587]Economides/Lianos (2010), 396f.

[588]Comp/39.530 (Microsoft – tying, 2009), 87 with fn 45.

[589]See Sect. 3.3.4.1.1.3.1 with footnotes 629ff and Sect. 3.3.4.1.1.3.2 with footnotes 641ff below.

[590]See Kerse/Khan (2012), 6-044; Hjelmeng (2013), 1016.

[591]Opinion of Judge Vesterdorf acting as AG in T-1/89 (Polypropylene, 1991), p. 946; similarly, also in the context of fines, Dannecker/Biermann (2012), Vor Art. 23, 142.

power to issue orders in order to prevent anticompetitive conduct which is imminent, but has not yet been committed. Under German law, the Bundesgerichtshof has consistently interpreted § 32 ARC to mean that a competition authority may issue a termination order as soon as there is a serious danger of an imminent infringement.[592] The EU Courts have not yet decided the question.[593]

It is submitted here that Article 7 can and should be construed in the same way as § 32 ARC. It is not persuasive to argue that the wording of Article 7 precludes termination orders as long as an infringement has not been committed.[594] The terms "[w]here the Commission [...] finds that there is an infringement" can readily be read as encompassing imminent infringements. It is also not convincing to deny the Commission the power to prevent imminent infringements under Article 7 by stating that, "[i]f there are clear signs that an infringement is about to be committed, the Commission may [...] intervene under Art. 8 in the form of an interim measure".[595] Interim measures are by nature preliminary. According to Article 8(2) Regulation 1/03, they may only be imposed for a limited period in time and then be renewed in so far as this is necessary and appropriate. Confining the Commission's power to address imminent infringements to interim orders would hence preclude permanent solutions and require the Commission to continuously renew an expired interim order where the parties do not give up their plan to engage in conduct which is considered anticompetitive by the Commission. Finally, it would be contradictory if the Commission did not have the power to prevent imminent infringements before they are committed, but could enjoin an infringer for the future from repeating conduct that is identical or alike to a found past infringement. In both constellations, the decisive question is whether there is a sufficiently precise risk that an infringement will be committed. Certainly, such a risk can be more readily assumed, if the concerned undertaking has already committed an identical or similar infringement in the past. Nevertheless, it cannot be categorically ruled out that the Commission succeeds in demonstrating a precise risk that an infringement will be committed in the future for the first time.

The question whether the Commission can issue Article 7 orders to prevent imminent infringements is not purely hypothetical. Kerse and Khan point out the following example which illustrates its practical significance[596]: In BA/AA/

---

[592] BGH, KVR 12/99 (Ost-Fleisch, 2001), 40 with further references. German doctrine broadly agrees with this line of case law, see Emmerich (2014), § 32 ARC, 9f; Jaeger (2010), § 32 ARC, 9; Bornkamm (2014), § 32 ARC, 15.

[593] Hjelmeng (2013), 1016 fn 42 relies on GC, T-34/92 (Fiatagri, 1994), 39, in support of his allegation that "[t]he Commission does not have power under Article 7 to intervene against potential or threatened infringements". It is submitted here that the latter conclusion does not follow from that judgment. The GC merely stated that an order to refrain from conduct having an identical or similar object like the one identified as anticompetitive was of a purely declaratory nature.

[594] But see Kerse/Khan (2012), 6-044: "Article 7 of Regulation 1/2003 is, by its terms, limited to cases where the Commission "finds that there is an infringement" (or finds that "an infringement has been committed in the past")."

[595] Hjelmeng (2013), 1016 fn 43.

[596] Kerse/Khan (2012), 6-045.

IB,[597] the Commission examined a "proposed"[598] agreement for a joint venture covering passenger air transport services on transatlantic routes. According to Kerse and Khan, the terms of the joint venture agreement provided "that it was not to take effect until clearance from the Commission had been obtained".[599] The Commission closed the procedure by accepting commitments under Article 9. However, in a hypothetical scenario, the Commission might also have refused an Article 9 decision, for instance because the commitments offered did not adequately meet its concerns or because the Commission wanted to set a precedent. According to the approach suggested here, the Commission could in this case have issued a prohibition decision under Article 7 Regulation 1/03, despite the fact that the agreement was merely a "proposed" one.

3.3.3 Eliminating the Causes of Future Anticompetitive Conduct

A remedy may also pursue the objective to deprive an infringing undertaking of the basis for future anticompetitive conduct. The questions whether and under what conditions such measures are admissible under Article 7 and whether Article 9 decisions that pursue such an objective go beyond what the Commission could have imposed under Article 7 concern mostly the so-called "structural" remedies. It will therefore be treated below in the context of the section that deals with "structural" remedies.

3.3.4 Eliminating the Subsisting Effects of Past Anticompetitive Conduct

As explained above,[600] there remain to date doubts as to whether Article 7 empowers the Commission to adopt remedies that address the subsisting effects of past anticompetitive conduct. The following section shall, in a first step, show that Article 7 provides for such powers. It will be argued that the power to eliminate the

---

[597] COMP/39.596 (BA/AA/IB, 2010).

[598] See the decision regarding the opening of proceedings of 17 April 2009: "The proceedings relate to two sets of proposed agreements [. . .] The joint practices are, or are planned to be, engaged in by the above mentioned airlines [. . .]". See also the Memo/09/430 of 2 October 2009 regarding the statement of objections: "The [Commission] can confirm that it has sent a Statement of Objections to [BA, AA, IB] in relation to their proposed cooperation on passenger air transport services on transatlantic routes [. . .]".

[599] Kerse/Khan (2012), 6-045.

[600] Section 3.1.3.2.1 with footnote 67 above.

subsisting effects of past anticompetitive conduct encompasses or at least should encompass orders to terminate follow on contracts and also orders relating to the restitution and disgorgement of illicit profits. In a second step, the Commission's practice under Article 9 will be discussed.

3.3.4.1 In the Context of Article 7

3.3.4.1.1 General Remarks

3.3.4.1.1.1 Akzo

In Akzo, the Commission found that Akzo had committed an abuse not only by offering predatory, but also selective low prices to customers of its competitor ECS.[601] With respect to the selective pricing abuse, the Commission ordered Akzo, first, to "refrain [. . .] from offering or applying prices [. . .] which would result in customers in respect of whose business it competes with ECS paying to Akzo [. . .] prices which are dissimilar from those being offered by Akzo [. . .] to comparable customers". The Commission clarified that "this provision [should] not prevent Akzo [. . .] from applying price differentials [. . .] as between different categories of customers which reasonably and objectively reflect differences in production and delivery costs attributable to the annual requirement of the customer, order size and other commercial factors". Second, the operative part of the decision stated that offers by Akzo to a more precisely defined group of customers should not be made on terms substantially more favourable than those offered to another more precisely defined group of customers.

On appeal, Akzo argued, in essence, that the order was unfair, because it precluded Akzo also from making defensive selective price offers in case ECS approached one of its customers.[602] The Court of Justice upheld the first part of the order. It stated that the order needed to be considered in "the light" of its intention "to prevent repetition of the infringement and to eliminate its consequences". Hence, according to the Court of Justice, the order prohibited "Akzo from approaching ECS's customers again by quoting to them advantageous prices without extending those prices to its own customers". It also prevented "Akzo from aligning itself on ECS's prices without giving its customers the benefits of this adjustment", if "ECS endeavour[ed] to win back the customers whom [Akzo] had taken from ECS unlawfully".[603] Nevertheless, the Court found that the order did "not prohibit [Akzo] from making defensive adjustments, even aligning itself on ECS's prices, in order to keep the customers which were originally its own".[604] The Court of

[601] OJ 1985 L 374/1 (Akzo, 1985); for a discussion of the remedy see Levy (1992), 423; Müller-Tautphaeus (2003), 244ff; O'Donoghue/Padilla (2013), 882f; Hjelmeng (2013), 1022f.

[602] CJ, C-62/86 (Akzo, 1991), 154.

[603] CJ, C-62/86 (Akzo, 1991), 155.

[604] CJ, C-62/86 (Akzo, 1991), 156.

Justice quashed the second part of the order, because it had found that the two groups of customers concerned were not comparable, so that the price discrimination between these two groups did not amount to an abuse.[605]

The remedy in Akzo merits some reflections. The annulment of the second part of the order is an unspectacular illustration of the link between harm and remedy. The Court of Justice quashed this part of the order, because it held that the Commission's corresponding finding of abuse was erroneous.[606] The first part of the order is more exciting. If one supposes that EU competition law does not prohibit the selective alignment of prices in reaction to an attack of a competitor,[607] an order to put a selective pricing abuse to an end may not prohibit such behaviour. For this reason, the Court of Justice held that the order in question did not prevent Akzo from making defensive adjustments or aligning its prices on ECS's. However, the Court did not stop by such a simple mirroring of the abuse. It further enjoined Akzo from the—otherwise allowed—alignment of prices where ECS's low price offer aimed at winning "back the customers whom [Akzo] had taken from ECS unlawfully". This additional restriction of Akzo's freedom to act went beyond a mere prevention of the continuance or repetition of the abusive conduct and aimed at the elimination of its consequences.[608] The Akzo judgment can thus be considered as a statement of the Court of Justice that a remedy may go beyond mirroring the anticompetitive conduct and provide conditions for the elimination of the lingering effects of an anticompetitive practice.[609] Finally, it must be pointed out that the wording of Commission's

---

[605]Cf. CJ, C-62/86 (Akzo, 1991), 159f in conjunction with 116ff.

[606]See Müller-Tautphaeus (2003), 246. For an identical constellation see also eg CJ, 40/73 (Suiker Unie, 1975), 607.

[607]While such a hypothesis seems to underlie the CJ's reasoning in Akzo, the precise rules on price alignment do not result clearly from the case law: cf. GC, T-340/03 (France Télécom, 2007), 176ff, where the GC found that an alignment of prices below cost could be abusive. More generally, the GC stated: "Even if alignment of prices by a dominant undertaking on those of its competitors is not in itself abusive or objectionable, it might become so where it is aimed not only at protecting its interests but also at strengthening and abusing its dominant position" (187). The judgment was confirmed by CJ, C-202/07 P (France Télécom, 2009), 43ff; see also the conclusions of AG Mazák in the latter case, 38ff.

[608]See Hjelmeng (2013), 1022f, who qualifies the Akzo remedy as a "restorative" one, "making it possible for a competitor to recover".

[609]See for a different interpretation of the Akzo judgment Müller-Tautphaeus (2003), 246: According to him, it can only be inferred from the judgment that an order, which prevents an undertaking from future abusive behaviour, opens the possibility for the competitor to gain back its former market position. According to Müller-Tautphaeus, the judgment contains no further statement regarding the question whether the Commission can order the elimination of lingering anticompetitive effects. It is submitted here that this view fails to recognise that the remedy in Akzo, such as interpreted by the CJ, went beyond a mere mirroring of the abusive conduct. Nevertheless, Müller-Tautphaeus correctly emphasises that the remedy provided only the "conditions" for an elimination of lingering anticompetitive effects. Even if the reacquisition of customers, which Akzo had unlawfully acquired, was facilitated for ECS by preventing Akzo from – otherwise allowed – alignment of prices, it was left to ECS to approach those customers again by offering them lower prices.

order was broad and—taken literally—would have prevented Akzo also from aligning itself on ECS's prices in order to keep customers which were originally its own. Nevertheless, Court of Justice did not annul the decision, but was willing to interpret it restrictively in the light of the identified abuse and the goal of the remedy "to prevent repetition of the infringement and to eliminate its consequences".

3.3.4.1.1.2 *Ufex*

A further case relating to the question whether a remedy may address the subsisting effects of anticompetitive conduct is Ufex.[610] Several companies active in the delivery of international express mail complained to the Commission that the French incumbent "La Poste" had abused its dominant position by allowing its subsidiary "SFMI" to make use of its infrastructure on unusually favourable terms.[611] The Commission rejected the complaint. It found that the alleged abusive behaviour had ceased following a merger decision, which approved a joint venture including La Poste. The merger decision was subject to the commitment of La Poste to provide non-discriminatory access to its infrastructure services.[612] The General Court did initially not object to the Commission's finding that it was not appropriate to pursue a complaint regarding practices which had ceased.[613] It argued in particular:

> In such a case, investigating the matter and establishing that infringements have taken place in the past would no longer help to ensure undistorted competition in the common market and would thus not represent fulfilment of the functions conferred on the Commission by the Treaty. The essential object of pursuing the case would be to make it easier for the complainants to prove fault in an action for damages in the national courts.[614]

However, in line with the opinion delivered by Advocate General Colomer,[615] the Court of Justice found this view on the Commission's task in the field of competition law to be incorrect.[616] According to the Court of Justice:

> [W]hen deciding the order of priority for dealing with the complaints brought before it, [. . .] the Commission is required to assess in each case how serious the alleged interferences with competition are and how persistent their consequences are. That obligation means in particular that it must take into account the duration and extent of the infringements complained of and their effect on the competition situation in the Community. If anti-competitive effects continue after the practices, which caused them, have ceased, the Commission thus remains competent [. . .] to act with a view to eliminating or neutralising them [. . .]. In deciding to discontinue consideration of a complaint against those practices on

[610]CJ, C-119/97 P (Ufex, 1999) and the subsequent judgment GC, T-60/05 (Ufex II, 2007); see for remedy related discussions of the case eg Koch (2008a), 55f and 79; Hellström/Maier-Rigaud/Bulst (2009), 45f; Krings (2012), 73ff and 120f; Hjelmeng (2013), 1022.

[611]CJ, C-119/97 P (Ufex, 1999), 3.

[612]See GC, T-60/05 (Ufex III, 2007), 81f.

[613]GC, T-77/95 (Ufex I, 1997), 57.

[614]GC, T-77/95 (Ufex I, 1997), 58.

[615]60ff.

[616]CJ, C-119/97 P (Ufex, 1999), 96.

> the ground of lack of Community interest, the Commission therefore cannot rely solely on the fact that practices alleged to be contrary to the Treaty have ceased, without having ascertained that anti-competitive effects no longer continue and, if appropriate, that the seriousness of the alleged interferences with competition or the persistence of their consequences has not been such as to give the complaint a Community interest.[617]

The Court of Justice therefore set aside the judgment of the General Court and referred the case back to the latter, where the rejection decision was annulled.[618] The Commission rejected the complaint anew. This time, the Commission established not only that the alleged abusive conduct had ceased, but also that it did not have continuing effects.[619] The General Court rejected the second appeal[620] and the complainants refrained from appealing further to the Court of Justice. This last judgment of the General Court illustrates particularly well, how difficult it is to establish a causal link between anticompetitive behaviour and continuing effects.[621] One of the applicants' arguments was that the Commission had failed to take into account the "main effect" of the abusive conduct, "namely placing SFMI in a position of market leader and maintaining it".[622] In this respect, the complainants relied on the fact that SFMI's market share increased from 4% to around 28% during the period of the abuse from 1986 to 1990 and remained above 20% thereafter.[623] The General Court rejected this argument. It held that, "on the supposition that the rapid growth of [SFMI during the period of the abuse] was connected with the alleged infringement, that does not necessarily mean that [SFMI's] market share at the date of adoption of the contested decision [2004] is connected with this development occurring during the start-up period". The Court went on:

> In the circumstances of the case, where the Commission has established that customers were very price sensitive, there were no obstacles to changing supplier, only two very small operators had left the market and no causal link was shown to exist between the exits and the alleged abuse, the Commission was entitled to form the view, without committing any manifest error of assessment, that [SFMI's] market share at the time of adoption of the contested decision did not constitute a continuing consequence of the alleged infringement. Having established these market characteristics, the Commission was justified in considering that the market structure at the time of the adoption of the contested decision was the result of the competitive conditions prevailing at that time and not of possible cross subsidies granted many years before.[624]

---

[617] CJ, C-119/97 P (Ufex, 1999), 92 to 95.

[618] GC, T-77/95 (Ufex II, 2000).

[619] See GC, T-60/05 (Ufex III, 2007), 18.

[620] GC, T-60/05 (Ufex III, 2007).

[621] See generally GC, T-60/05 (Ufex III, 2007), 123ff. For instance, the complainants argued that market exit of a competitor was a subsistent effect of the abuse. However, the Court found that this had not been proven since, in a reply to a request for information, that competitor had cited other reasons to explain it's departure from the market (125).

[622] GC, T-60/05 (Ufex III, 2007), 99.

[623] See the table of market shares in GC, T-60/05 (Ufex III, 2007), 85.

[624] GC, T-60/05 (Ufex III, 2007), 133.

3.3.4.1.1.3 Generalisation of Akzo and Ufex

It follows unequivocally from the Akzo and the Ufex case law that the Commission has in principle the power to impose remedies that aim at the elimination of subsisting effects of a past anticompetitive practice.[625] However, the precise scope of this power remains up to now still largely unclear.

3.3.4.1.1.3.1 Further Examples of Remedies That Aim at the Elimination of Subsisting Effects

For the US, Salop and Romaine come up with the following example of a pricing remedy that aims at eliminating the consequences of an anticompetitive conspiracy of a monopolist with suppliers of an essential input.[626] They assume that the conspiracy has "destroyed" the most likely potential entrant and that there are other entrants available, who are, however, less efficient than the destroyed entrant. In order to reestablish the competitive structure that would have developed absent the conspiracy, Salop and Romaine suggest requiring the monopolist to grant access to the refused input to one or more of the less efficient entrants at rates below the market price. In their view, such a remedy would allow the entrants to achieve costs as low as the excluded entrant, thus providing them with the ability to restore the market to the "pre-monopolization competitive outcome".

For the EU, Hellström et al. have pointed out a set of hypothetical behavioural remedies to address the foreclosure effects of an abusive tying practice.[627] Starting from the premise that "a mere untying [is not] sufficient to achieve a restoration of the competitive process" and that it is therefore "necessary to give the infringer's competitors an advantage over the infringer", they suggest the imposition of "a price differential between the unbundled and any bundled version that remains on sale", "a must carry remedy", "an advertising ban on the previously tied product for a specific period" or an obligation for the infringer "to contribute to an effective marketing of the competing product". They even go as far as to propose the imposition of an obligation for the infringer "to pay money to provide active product development support to competitors negatively affected by its illegal practices". Hellström et al. abstain from citing examples for their suggestions that would show that such remedies are actually used by competition authorities. However, one cannot avoid the impression that the procedures against Microsoft for the tying of the Media Player and the Internet Explorer to the Windows operating system served as a source of inspiration for their proposals. In this respect, I submitted above that both a price differential and a must carry remedy could in principle have been imposed under

---

[625] But see Krings (2012), 75ff, who is of the opinion that such a power cannot be inferred from the Ufex judgment of the CJ. Neglecting the Akzo and Ufex case law, also Baumgart/Rasbach/Rudolph (2009), 41f, interpret Article 7 as not permitting the Commission to impose remedies that address the subsisting effects of past anticompetitive conduct.

[626] See, also for the following quotations, Salop/Romaine (1998), 667f.

[627] See, also for the following quotations, Hellström/Maier-Rigaud/Bulst (2009), 59.

Article 7 simply as mirrors of the tying infringements that Microsoft was charged with.[628] The explanation of Hellström et al. according to which such remedies do "not necessarily [have the aim] to allow competition on an equal footing, but to redress harm to competition",[629] can, however, theoretically serve as an alternative justification.[630] In a similar vein, it has been suggested, with a view to the Google Search case, that, in order to neutralise the consequences of Google's conduct, the Commission could have obliged Google to make available any relevant data which the undertaking acquired as a result of the anticompetitive promotion of its own comparison shopping service in its general search results.[631]

3.3.4.1.1.3.2 The Boundaries of the Commission's Power: Required Proof of Causality Between Infringement, Actual Harm and Remedy

Nevertheless, it is submitted that any remedy may only be justified with the need to redress the subsisting effects of an infringement, if the Commission proves the causal link between infringement, actual harm and remedy to the requisite legal standard. In order to do this, the Commission must show that an infringement has had an actual impact on the market and that the remedy removes this impact, but does not go any further. Most findings of an infringement require only proof of a "potential anticompetitive effect" of the incriminated conduct, i.e. that the latter is "likely", "liable" or "has the capacity" to produce anticompetitive effects.[632] However, if the Commission wants to justify the imposition of a remedy with the need to remove subsisting anticompetitive harm, it must prove more and also show the existence of an actual anticompetitive effect.[633] A detailed elaboration of the precise standard with which the Commission must prove the causality between infringing conduct, actual harm and remedy is beyond the scope of this work. A few points shall nevertheless be made.

First, the standard of proof required to show the existence of a causal damage should be stricter than the standard of proof required to show the elimination of the

[628]See Sect. 3.3.1.7.2 with footnotes 578ff above.

[629]Hellström/Maier-Rigaud/Bulst (2009), 59.

[630]See also Salop/Romaine (1998), 669 fn 141: They argue that the potential must carry remedy discussed in the US Microsoft case did not require a finding that Windows was an essential facility, because the must carry remedy could be justified by the need to eliminate the consequences of other exclusionary conduct.

[631]Höppner (2017), 18.

[632]See eg CJ, C-8/08 (T-Mobile Netherlands, 2009), 29ff; GC, T-286/09 (Intel, 2014), 102ff; Jones/Sufrin (2011), 212 and 215; Whish/Bailey (2012), 118. CJ, C-413/14 P (Intel, 2017) has not changed this, the Court having relied on the "capacity" of the conduct to foreclose competition, but not on the conduct's actual effects (140, 142, 143, 147, 149). See also Dittert (2017), 588.

[633]Similarly Voell (2014), 56. The statement of the CJ in C-8/08 (T-Mobile Netherlands, 2009), 31, according to which the existence of anti-competitive effects "can only be of relevance for determining the amount of any fine and assessing any claim for damages" falls short of the mark. As is apparent from the Akzo and the Ufex cases, the existence of anti-competitive effects can also be of relevance for the admissible scope of a remedy.

damage through the remedy. In fact, while the former can be evaluated from an ex post perspective, the latter necessarily depends on prognostic elements, which allow for a softening of the standard of proof.

Second, as regards the taking into account of the actual effects of an infringement for the setting of a fine, the EU Courts highlight that the Commission "cannot just put forward a mere presumption but [...] must provide specific, credible and adequate evidence with which to assess what actual influence the infringement may have had on competition".[634] It is submitted that the same or at least a similarly strict approach should also be applied when it comes to remedies that aim at the elimination of harm caused by anticompetitive conduct. Certainly, one might argue that the absence of a punitive character of remedies warrants a lowering of the standard of proof. However, lowering the standard of proof nevertheless increases the risk of an unjustified interference of the Commission with the competitive process and the rights of the infringing undertakings. In this respect, it must also be stressed that the taking into account of the actual impact of anticompetitive conduct for the setting of a fine does not require a precise determination or quantification of the occurred harm. As long as the Commission adduces sufficient evidence, it can rely on rather general qualitative statements, for example that the impact was "significant".[635] It is submitted that the imposition of a remedy that aims at the lingering effects of anticompetitive conduct presupposes a more precise identification of the anticompetitive harm. If the Commission wants to intervene directly on a market by means of a remedy in order to eliminate such harm, it must know precisely what the latter consists of.

Third, the precise impact of an anticompetitive practice on the market must be established by means of a so-called "but for" approach.[636] This means that the impact cannot simply be evaluated by reference to the situation as it existed before the infringement took place. Rather, it must be assessed by reference to the situation that would have evolved in case the infringement had not taken place. Such an assessment causes difficulties and necessarily implies the use of estimates or proxies, because it is impossible to know with certainty how a market would have evolved in the absence of the infringement.[637] It is submitted here that, in view of the risk that the Commission interferes in an unwarranted manner with the competitive process

---

[634] CJ, C-534/07 P (Prym, 2009), 82; GC, T-336/07 (Telefonica, 2012), 390; T-286/09, (Intel, 2014), 1623 and 1625.

[635] See GC, T-201/04 (Microsoft I, 2007), 1357; T-336/07 (Telefonica, 2012), 391.

[636] See for the "but for" approach in the context of remedies eg Hellström/Maier-Rigaud/Bulst (2009), 58; Shapiro (2009), 748 and 751; Hjelmeng (2013), 1022; Lianos (2013), 406.

[637] See the Commission's reasoning in the Communication on quantifying harm in actions for damages (2013), 9, which applies mutatis mutandis: "The quantification of such harm requires comparing the actual position of the injured party with the position this party would have been in without the infringement. This is something that cannot be observed in reality; it is impossible to know with certainty how market conditions and the interactions between market participants would have evolved in the absence of the infringement. All that is possible is an estimate of the scenario likely to have existed without the infringement." See also Ackermann (2014a), 64.

and the rights of the infringing undertakings, such estimates and proxies should only be allowed for restrictively.[638]

Fourth, as pointed out above, the Ufex case illustrates the difficulties that exist when it comes to proving the subsistence of the impact of an anticompetitive practice on the market. It is submitted here that uniform standards must in this regard be applied for the rejection of a complaint and the imposition of a remedy. The Commission cannot apply a strict standard of proof when it wants to reject a complaint for lack of any subsisting effects on the market and at the same time enjoy the benefit of a softer standard when it imposes a remedy aiming at the consequences of an infringement.

It follows from the above that, albeit theoretically not excluded, remedies that aim at the consequences of an infringement are subject to strict requirements regarding the standard of proof. In the two Microsoft decisions regarding the Media Player and the Internet Explorer, the Commission found that Microsoft's unlawful tying practices had had an actual impact on the market.[639] However, it is submitted that neither of the decisions establishes that impact to the requisite level of precision to allow for a remedy that aims at its elimination.[640] It is hence logical that, in the Media Player decision, the Commission did not even impose a remedy that could be suspected of aiming at the elimination of lingering anticompetitive harm. As regards the Internet Explorer decision, it has been observed above that the limiting of the choice screen only to versions of Windows where the Internet Explorer is set as the default browser creates an advantage for competitors that goes beyond eliminating the artificial distribution advantage underlying the Commission's theory of harm.[641] Certainly, in alignment with the proposals of Hellström et al., one might argue that the creation of this competitive advantage was justified by the need to remove the lingering effects of Microsoft's past unlawful tying. However, nothing in the reasoning of the decision permits the conclusion that the choice screen remedy was imposed for this purpose.[642] In any event, at least under the standards for an Article

[638] See also Maier-Rigaud (2014), 9, who cautions against the "major difficulty of establishing the *status quo ante*, a process that may (positively and negatively) affect a range of economic actors and consumers that were neither part of the infringement nor aware of its existence".

[639] See COMP/37.792 (Microsoft, 2004), 1071f: "[...] the abuse has already contributed to Microsoft achieving a leading position in that market. Evidence described in this Decision suggests that the market may already be tipping in favour of WMP"; Comp/39.530 (Microsoft – tying, 2009), 54: "the Commission preliminarily concluded that as a result of the tying, Internet Explorer's market share remains much higher than that of its competitors".

[640] This would, for example, have been different, if the Commission had shown how much of the Media Player's or the Internet Explorer's market share was caused by the unlawful tying practices.

[641] See Sect. 3.3.1.7.2 with footnotes 586ff above.

[642] It results from the decision that the remedy merely aimed at eliminating the potential effects of Microsoft's tying practices, but not the actual effects; see Comp/39.530 (Microsoft – tying, 2009), 98ff: "The Commitments are appropriate as they address the Commission's competition concerns regarding potential foreclosure effects, the limitation of innovation in web development through the tying of Internet Explorer to Windows, and the potential reinforcement of Microsoft's position on the client PC operating system market."

7 remedy,[643] the need to address the lingering effects of Microsoft's conduct cannot justify the creation of the competitive advantage in the absence of more precise findings regarding the causality between Microsoft's anticompetitive conduct, the harm and the remedy.

As is the case for all remedies, the principle of proportionality subjects also the ones aiming at the elimination of lingering effects of an anticompetitive practice to the requirement of their necessity. In this respect, entrusting the elimination of anticompetitive effects to a market on which the conditions for competition on an equal footing have been restored may turn out to be a less intrusive means that can render the infliction of a remedy superfluous. However, it would not be persuasive to argue that a remedy which aims at the consequences of an infringement may never be imposed, if it is foreseeable that the self-healing powers of the market will ultimately lead to the same result. Rather, an eventual increased effectiveness of a remedy in eliminating anticompetitive effects must be taken into account and can justify the imposition of a remedy. The Akzo case can serve as an illustration: The granting of a competitive advantage to ECS by enjoining Akzo from price alignments with respect to customers that had been wooed away from ECS by Akzo's unlawful selective pricing practices[644] was not the only means to enable ECS to reacquire its customers. The restoration of competition on an equal footing through enjoining Akzo from selective pricing, subject to a general exception for price alignments, may in the long term have enabled the same result. Nevertheless, since granting the competitive advantage to ECS allowed for a more efficient reacquisition of the customers lost as result of Akzo's anticompetitive conduct, the remedy could be imposed.

As a preliminary conclusion, it can be retained that the infliction of remedies that aim at the elimination of the actual impact of anticompetitive conduct on a market is in theory not excluded. However, the imposition of such remedies must be subjected to a standard of proof regarding the causal link between conduct, harm and remedy, which is hard to meet. In view of this difficulty and the associated risk of enforcement errors, "the better solution might be to bring an end to the infringement and to let the market cure itself".[645]

3.3.4.1.2 Follow-On Contracts

Follow-on contracts can perpetuate the effects of a ceased anticompetitive practice.[646] Examples are customer contracts concluded by the parties of an

[643]For the Commission's opinion that the commitment decision regarding the Internet Explorer is consistent with the standard for Article 7 remedies, see Sect. 3.3.1.7, footnote 567 above.

[644]See Sect. 3.3.4.1.1.1 with footnotes 603f and footnotes 607ff above.

[645]Hjelmeng (2013), 1024.

[646]See Bauer (2008), 4-7-037ff; Kerse/Khan (2012), 6-047; Hjelmeng (2013), 1024; Lianos (2013), 408f.

anticompetitive joint venture,[647] a long-lasting supply contract concluded in the context of a bidding cartel[648] or, more generally, "long-term delivery contracts [. . .], the terms of which have initially been influenced by infringements of Articles 101 or 102 [TFEU]".[649] Article 101(2) TFEU does not capture such contracts and Article 102 TFEU does not stipulate civil law consequences at all. Hence, even if they perpetuate the effects of an anticompetitive practice, follow-on contracts are not automatically void or unenforceable.[650] The civil law consequences of such contracts are determined by national law, which does not necessarily provide for their voidness or unenforceability either.[651] This begs the question, whether and to what extent the Commission can issue orders regarding follow-on contracts under Article 7.

In Astra,[652] the Commission did not only prohibit a joint venture, which was contrary to Article 101 TFEU. It also ordered the parties to inform customers of this prohibition and to offer them the possibility to either renegotiate or terminate contracts, the terms of which had been determined "in the context of the joint venture agreements" and hence "under conditions of disturbed competition".[653] In the same vein, in Atlantic Container Line, the Commission did not only prohibit an agreement between shipping companies to fix prices and capacity. Again, it also ordered the infringing parties to offer customers the possibility to either renegotiate or terminate contracts, which had been concluded "in the context" of the prohibited agreement.[654] However, in the latter case, the General Court quashed the Commission's order for two independent reasons.[655] On the one hand, the General Court argued that the Commission had breached its obligation to state reasons.[656] In essence, the General Court argued that the Commission had not sufficiently explained why the order was necessary to put the infringement to an end. According to the Court, this was not "obviously" the case: Although the effects of anticompetitive horizontal agreements were usually perpetuated in follow-on contracts, the Commission had imposed a comparable order only once, namely in the Astra decision; the follow-on contracts in question were concluded for only a year, which the Court considered as being not a particularly long-term; apart from the

[647]See 1993 OJ L 20/23 (Astra, 1992); for a discussion of the remedy see Müller-Tautphaeus (2003), 266f; Mestmäcker/Schweitzer (2004), § 20, 37.

[648]Bauer (2008), 4-7-037.

[649]Hjelmeng (2013), 1024.

[650]See eg GC, T-395/94 (Transatlantic Container Line, 2002), 412; Mestmäcker/Schweitzer (2004), § 6, 41; Bauer (2008), 4-7-038; Hjelmeng (2013), 1025 with further references.

[651]Hjelmeng (2013), 1025 with further references. For the German discussion see K. Schmidt (2011), 559ff.

[652]1993 OJ L 20/23 (Astra, 1992).

[653]1993 OJ L 20/23 (Astra, 1992), 33.

[654]See GC, T-395/94 (Transatlantic Container Line, 2002), 35.

[655]GC, T-395/94 (Transatlantic Container Line, 2002), 410ff.

[656]GC, T-395/94 (Transatlantic Container Line, 2002), 416.

nullity provided for in Article 101(2) TFEU, the civil law consequences of an infringement of Article 101 TFEU were determined under national law.[657] On the other hand, the General Court found that, in any event, the Commission had breached the applicant's rights of defence because it had not mentioned the order concerning the follow-on contracts in the statement of objections.[658] The General Court expressly pointed out that it did not examine the question whether the order was appropriate and necessary to re-establish compliance with the competition rules.[659]

Many commentators take a critical stance towards an interpretation of Article 7 that would allow the Commission to issue orders concerning the renegotiation or termination of follow-on contracts.[660] Partially, such views predicate on a simple misreading of the Atlantic Container Line judgment. Contrary to what is contended, the General Court neither held that such orders go "beyond what is required to terminate the infringement"[661] nor "that the likelihood of private actions for damages should be a sufficient disincentive for the [infringing undertakings] to continue behaviour that would have maintained or facilitated the effects of the core infringement to Article 101 TFEU".[662] However, also where the criticism does not rest on such a misreading, the arguments supporting it are weak. Kerse and Khan only state that, in Astra, the Commission "arguably went beyond measures necessary to put the infringement effectively to an end".[663] Bauer argues that orders regarding follow-on contracts "would interfere with the competences of the Member States", since national law determines the civil law validity of such contracts.[664]

---

[657]GC, T-395/94 (Transatlantic Container Line, 2002), 413 to 415.

[658]GC, T-395/94 (Transatlantic Container Line, 2002), 417 to 419.

[659]GC, T-395/94 (Transatlantic Container Line, 2002), 420.

[660]See Bauer (2008), 4-7-038f; Jones/Sufrin (2011), 1083; Kerse/Khan (2012), 6-047; Lianos (2013), 408f. On the contrary, K. Schmidt (2011), 576f sees the powers of competition authorities to "promote the modification of [follow on] contracts through remedies" ("durch Abstellungsverfügungen auf Vertragsänderungen hinwirken") as one reason why a civil law voidness of such contracts is not necessary to protect customers. As regards German law, Jaeger (2010), § 32 ARC, 32, articulates also a favourable position. He expressly agrees with the decision of the Bundeskartellamt, B4-31/05 (Wirtschaftsprüferhaftpflicht, 2007), in which the latter ordered the parties of an anticompetitive joint venture of insurance companies to terminate the insurance contracts that had been concluded in the context of the joint venture. The decision was quashed for different reasons on appeal, see OLG Düsseldorf, VI-Kart 11/07 (V) (2008), and BGH, KVR 57/08 (2009).

[661]But see Jones/Sufrin (2011), 1083, who write that "the General Court annulled that part of the decision as it went beyond what was required to terminate the infringement". Similarly, Sauer (2013), 11.07, fn 33, writes that the order concerning the follow on contracts "was considered as unnecessary" by the General Court. Sorinas/Moretti (2012), 4.10: "The Court annulled [that part of the decision], since this went beyond what was necessary to bring the infringement in question to an end".

[662]But see Lianos (2013), 409.

[663]Kerse/Khan (2012), 6-047.

[664]Bauer (2008), 4-7-038; in 4-7-039, he further argues that in Atlantic Container Line, the General Court did not approve the Commission's practice.

The more convincing arguments militate for a power of the Commission to issue orders regarding follow on contracts, according to the individual circumstances of the case. First, follow-on contracts perpetuate the anticompetitive effects of an anticompetitive practice and according to the Court of Justice's rulings in Akzo and Ufex, the Commission has the power to address not only the illegal practice itself, but also its effects.[665] Second, it is not convincing to argue that private enforcement suffices to remedy the perpetuity of anticompetitive effects in follow-on contracts.[666] On the one hand, such a view misconceives that orders regarding follow-on contracts may precisely be necessary, because national law does not provide for adequate civil law consequences. On the other hand, despite all efforts to strengthen the private enforcement of competition law, there remain to date many obstacles that make private enforcement in the EU still difficult.[667] Third, the fact that EU competition law leaves the civil law validity of follow-on contracts to national law,[668] does not categorically exclude all remedies that address follow-on contracts. It is submitted here that, on the one hand, the Commission's orders concerning follow-on contracts must respect national civil law. Given that neither Article 101(2) nor 102 TFEU provide for a nullity of follow-on contracts, the Commission cannot "order" such a nullity pursuant to Article 7, where national law provides for a validity. On the other hand, the Commission does not encroach upon national law, when it determines how an infringing undertaking must use the margins of manoeuvre, which the latter has under national civil law. The Commission can hence require an infringing undertaking to exercise contractual or statutory termination or modification rights or to offer its customers the possibility to renegotiate or terminate such contracts.

Overall, it is hence submitted here that the Commission's powers under Article 7 extend also to follow-on contracts. This applies without prejudice to the Commission's obligation to state sufficient reasons why such an order is necessary in the individual case. Moreover, it must be pointed out that orders regarding follow-on contracts have to take account of the interests of the concerned customers.[669] This seems unproblematic, where the Commission confines itself to requiring the

[665]See Hjelmeng (2013), 1026, according to whom "the Commission is most likely competent under Article 7 to impose such obligations", because of the "unconditional statements of the ECJ in Ufex" and the fact that "cartel prices residing in long-term agreements are among the clear examples of lingering effect harming customers".

[666]This seems to be the thrust of Lianos' interpretation of the Transatlantic Container Line judgment, Sect. 3.3.4.1.2, footnote 662 above.

[667]For an overview, see eg Jones/Sufrin (2014), 1086; Ezrachi/Ioannidou (2011), 202ff. For an earlier discussion of the availability of relief in national courts see the opinion of judge Edwards acting as AG in T-24/90 (Automec II, 1992), 109ff.

[668]In view of the Court of Justice's Courage and Crehan doctrine, some commentators challenge whether this is actually the case. Cf. K. Schmidt (2012), Art. 101 Abs. 2, 36 with further references.

[669]The protection of customers, who may want to stick to a follow on contract, is the strongest argument against an automatic voidness of such contracts under national civil law; cf. K. Schmidt (2011), 575f.

infringing undertaking to offer its customers the possibility to renegotiate or terminate a follow on contract, as was the case in Astra and Atlantic Container Line. Under such orders, the interests of customers are sufficiently protected, because they may maintain the follow on contract, if they wish to do so. The question, whether and to what extent the Commission can also act against the will of a customer is more difficult to answer. As has been pointed out above, it is submitted here that the Commission cannot order the voidness of a follow-on contract, where national law provides for its validity. However, orders to use unilateral statutory or contractual termination or modification rights enable the Commission to act also against a customer's will. Such orders will, however, require a preponderant public interest, for example because follow-on contracts have a foreclosure effect the costs of which outweigh the interest of the customers in the maintenance of the contracts.

3.3.4.1.3 Disgorgement, Restitution and Compensation

If one accepts that, under Article 7, the Commission may impose remedies that address the consequences of an infringement, it becomes necessary to tackle also the question whether and to what extent this power encompasses ordering the disgorgement or restitution of illicit profits or the compensation of customers and consumers for their damage. Terminologically, it is in this respect useful to make the following distinction: "Disgorgement" means that one or several infringing undertakings are required to pay out the anticompetitive profits to a public institution, either to the general treasury or to the competition authority.[670] "Restitution" describes illicit profits being paid out to individual customers or consumers. Finally, "compensation" signifies the indemnification of customers or consumers for incurred damage.[671] Restitution and compensation overlap where the prejudice of customers or consumers corresponds to the illicit profits of the infringing undertakings. However, compensation may reach further than restitution, because the prejudice of a customer can consist not only of the payment of too high prices, but also of lost profits due to reduced demand.[672]

It appears that the question of the admissibility of disgorgement, restitution or compensation orders has so far not gained practical importance on the European

[670]For this distinction see Elhauge (2009), 94, who points out that, in order to prevent an agency bias to create income, US law provides that disgorgement proceeds go to the general treasury and do not affect the budget of the agencies.

[671]See Al-Ameen (2009), 328: "Restitutionary awards are those granted to a claimant in order to deprive the defendant of a gain rather than compensate the claimant for loss suffered".

[672]See Commission, Guide on quantifying harm (2013), 175ff; Rehbinder (2009), § 33 ARC, 37. According to the Court of Justice, C-295/04 (Manfredi, 2006), 95, "injured persons must be able to seek compensation not only for actual loss (*damnum emergens*) but also for loss of profit (*lucrum cessans*) plus interest"; see also Article 3(2) of the new Directive on damages actions (N° 2014/104/EU), according to which full compensation covers the right to compensation for actual loss and for loss of profit, plus the payment of interest.

level. The Commission has neither ordered the disgorgement or restitution of illicit profits nor required an undertaking to compensate victims.[673] However, Hellström et al. have suggested—albeit rather carefully—that the Commission may have the power under Article 7 to "oblige an infringer to compensate its (final) customers for the losses sustained due to [a] violation".[674] They acknowledge that compensatory measures are traditionally left to the national courts and point out that "[t]here are [...] a number of practical and policy reasons for having the distributive consequences of competition law infringements remedied via private damage claims".[675] Nevertheless, they argue that, "if the enforcement of competition law is all about protecting consumer welfare and Article 7 is about remedying the effects of an infringement, it is not obvious that Article 7 should preclude direct measures to restore consumer welfare, and, thereby, to remedy the distributive effects of an infringement".[676] Elhauge has suggested that "the Commission's authority to enter orders ending any infringement could be interpreted to include orders undoing [...] excessive prices by ordering disgorgement of the price excesses".[677] The countervailing opinion categorically excludes disgorgement, restitution or compensation orders from the ambit of Article 7.[678]

Under German law, § 34 ARC provides the Bundeskartellamt with a possibility to disgorge illicit profits in case of negligence or intent on behalf of the infringing undertaking. As regards restitutionary orders, the Bundesgerichtshof stated for the first time in an obiter dictum in the excessive pricing case Stadtwerke Uelzen that § 32 ARC gives a competition authority also the power to require the removal of an adverse effect which had occurred in the past but which was still present. The Bundesgerichtshof explicitly stated that this power encompassed orders to reimburse benefits that were acquired by means of the abusive conduct.[679] Despite the criticism

[673] Cf. Fuchs (2009), 179; Keßler (2011), 779.

[674] Hellström/Maier-Rigaud/Bulst (2009), 61.

[675] Hellström/Maier-Rigaud/Bulst (2009), 61.

[676] Hellström/Maier-Rigaud/Bulst (2009), 61; similarly with respect to § 32 ARC already Keßler (2008), § 32 ARC, 45; idem (2011), 772; also Ezrachi/Ioannidou (2011), 213 appear to be in favour of a power to impose "compensatory" measures unilaterally: "Public compensation should [...] not be dependent on the violators' willingness to compensate but remain part of the competition authority's decision making".

[677] Elhauge (2009), 92.

[678] Schütz (2013), 21: "Zur Abstellung gehört auch nicht die Wiedergutmachung"; see also Fuchs (2009), 205; Reher/Haellmigk (2010), 517; Johanns (2011), § 12, 39; Baumgart/Rasbach/Rudolph (2009), 42; Voell (2014), 54. Critically also Podszun (2012), 66, who fears that the admission of such orders would put to much emphasis on the consumer harm standard. Jones/Sufrin (2011), 1168: "The Commission does not have power to award damages or other compensation to those who have suffered"; Lianos (2013), 377: "The remedy of disgorging illegal profits is not available, as such, in EU competition law, although it remains possible under some national competition law systems".

[679] BGH, KVR 2/08 (Stadtwerke Uelzen, 2008), 16: "[D]er Senat [weist] darauf hin, dass nach § 32 Abs. 2 GWB keine grundsätzlichen Bedenken dagegen bestehen, im Rahmen einer Abstellungsverfügung auch Maßnahmen anzuordnen, die der Beseitigung einer geschehenen, aber noch gegenwärtigen Beeinträchtigung dienen. Dazu gehört die Anordnung, durch das missbräuchliche Verhalten erwirtschaftete Vorteile zurückzuerstatten."

that was raised against the described obiter dictum,[680] the Bundesgerichtshof confirmed it in the following excessive pricing case Wasserpreise Calw.[681] Subsequently, the German legislator amended Article 32 ARC. Article 32(2)(a) ARC now stipulates explicitly that a competition authority may order an infringing undertaking to reimburse the profits that have been acquired by means of an anticompetitive practice.[682]

Unlike the German ARC, Regulation 1/03 does not contain any explicit provisions enabling the Commission to issue restitutionary or disgorgement orders. However, it is submitted here that the better reasons militate for a broad interpretation of Article 7 which grants the Commission such powers. The open textured nature of Article 7 and its general clause character permit such an interpretation. The strongest counter argument is that the provision aims merely at the reestablishment of conditions which do no longer produce any anticompetitive effects; consequences of an infringement that do not themselves produce such effects can therefore not be remedied under the provision, but must be left to other mechanisms, in particular private enforcement.[683] This argument is, however, not persuasive. In certain constellations, private enforcement will not suffice to deprive the infringing undertakings of the illicit profits resulting from their violation of the competition rules. This can in particular be the case due to difficulties in proving damage[684] or because the individual interests of the harmed parties at stake are not important enough and class actions are not sufficiently readily available.[685] It has rightly been pointed out that, in any event and independently of the underlying reasons, experience shows that many victims refrain from claiming damages.[686] There is no reason why this statement should not also apply for private restitutionary claims.

However, if one accepts that private enforcement does not suffice to deprive the infringing undertakings of their illicit profits, deterrence reasons militate for empowering a competition authority to do so. Leaving the infringing undertakings the fruits of their illicit conduct would create an undesirable incentive for them and

[680]See in particular Fuchs (2009); Baumgart/Rasbach/Rudolph (2009); Reher/Haellmigk (2010); against the criticism see Nothdurft (2014), 252ff.

[681]BGH, KVR 51/11 (Wasserpreise Calw, 2012), 21f.

[682]See BR-Drs 176/12, 34 and Bosch/Fritzsche (2013), 2228. Podszun (2012), 69, criticises the fact that the legislator codified a practice that Podszun deems appropriate only in exceptional cases ("Lösungen gesetzgeberisch geadelt, die häufig nur in einzelnen Fällen legitimiert sind und eben nicht normatives Programm werden sollten").

[683]See, with respect to § 32 ARC, Fuchs (2009), 197f: "Es geht nicht um die Herstellung eines Zustandes wie er ohne den Verstoß bestünde, sondern um die vollständige Beendigung der Zuwiderhandlung, um die Herstellung eines nunmehr kartellrechtskonformen Zustands, von dem keine weiteren wettebwerbswidrigen Wirkungen mehr ausgehen. [...] Unerheblich ist dagegen, ob noch andere Folgen des Verstoßes existieren [...], die ggf. mit anderen Instrumenten beseitigt werden können".

[684]See Al-Ameen (2009), 339; Ezrachi/Ioannidou (2011), 210f.

[685]See Elhauge (2009), 83; Ezrachi/Ioannidou (2011), 210f.

[686]See Jaeger (2010), § 32 ARC, 35; Bornkamm (2014), § 32 ARC, 34 and 39; Keßler (2011), 776f; Ezrachi/Ioannidou (2011), 202ff.

others to commit further violations of competition law in the future.[687] Nor is the infliction of a fine pursuant to Article 23(2) of Regulation 1/03 necessarily sufficient to deprive infringing undertakings of illicitly obtained profits. Certainly, when setting a fine, "[t]he Commission [. . .] take[s] into account the need to increase the fine in order to exceed the amount of gains improperly made as a result of the infringement where it is possible to estimate that amount".[688] Nevertheless, on the one hand, according Article 23(2) Regulation 1/2003, the infliction of a fine requires negligence or intent and even where an undertaking acts at least negligently, the Commission may still refrain from imposing a fine for opportunity reasons.[689] On the other hand, Article 23(2) Regulation 1/2003 limits the amount of a fine imposed on one undertaking to 10% of its total turnover in the preceding business year. Thus, where the illicit conduct was not committed at least negligently or where the illicit profits exceed the 10% threshold, a disgorgement or restitution order under Article 7 may be the only means to deprive the infringing undertakings of illicit profits. There can hence be a public interest in depriving the infringing undertakings of illicit profits which justifies disgorgement and restitution orders. The same does, however, not apply to compensatory measures that require the infringing undertakings to indemnify victims for incurred damages. Although compensation may have a deterrence element to it, it aims mostly at the protection of the subjective interest of the individual victim. It is therefore submitted that the Commission should not be empowered under Article 7 to issue compensatory orders.[690]

A further counter-argument against disgorgement and restitution orders is also not persuasive: It has been argued that the reimbursement of illicit profits would promote the customer's fidelity toward the undertaking having infringed the competition rules, thereby hampering the keeping open of the market.[691] However, the reimbursement has no formal effect on the customer's possibility to switch his supplier. As regards any de facto effects, in the absence of any evidence to the contrary, it remains doubtful whether the reimbursement of an illicit profit will constitute a powerful incentive for a customer not to switch supplier.

The basic acceptance that the Commission has the power under Article 7 to order the disgorgement or restitution of illicit profits entails a variety of follow on problems that shall not be discussed here in all detail.[692] Some preliminary reflections must suffice. First, it goes without saying that the Commission can only order the disgorgement or restitution of illicit profits to the extent that it demonstrates that

[687]See Jaeger (2010), § 32 ARC, 35.

[688]Commission Fining Guidelines (2006), 31.

[689]For references regarding decisions in which the Commission abstained from imposing a fine see Sect. 5.1.4.1.1, footnotes 110f below; see also Jones/Sufrin (2014), 997ff.

[690]In favour of compensatory orders see Ezrachi/Ioannidou (2011). They do, however, not distinguish between compensation, restitution and disgorgement.

[691]See Podszun (2012), 66 and 69.

[692]See for more a more detailed discussion Bourgeois/Strievi (2010); Ezrachi/Ioannidou (2011), 212ff. For the analogous discussion under German law see Nothdurft (2014), 260ff.

the latter exist. This begs questions about the appropriate method to determine the illicit profits[693] and to what extent the Commission can rely upon estimates.[694] Second, one may ask whether there should be a time bar for orders requiring restitution or disgorgement.[695] The 5 year limitation period of Article 25(1)(b) Regulation 1/03 applies directly only to fines and penalties. The General Court has ruled that its expiration does not bar the Commission from finding that an infringement has been committed in the past pursuant to Article 7(1), 4th sentence, Regulation 1/03.[696] However, since a disgorgement or restitution order is more burdensome for the infringing undertakings than the mere finding of an infringement, some sort of limitation period seems appropriate, not least in order to meet the requirements of proportionality and legal certainty. In the absence of other statutory provisions, an analogous application of Article 25(1)(b) Regulation 1/03 could be envisaged. Third, the complex interplay of disgorgement and restitution orders, private enforcement and criminal fines needs to be considered. In the first place, as far as the relationship between disgorgement and restitution is concerned, one might contemplate a preference for restitutionary orders where it is possible to assign an illicit profit of the infringers to an individual prejudice of a customer or consumer.[697] Such a preference would, on the one hand, foster corrective justice and, on the other hand, reduce the risk of a bias of the competition authority to generate income for itself or the general treasury.[698] However, Elhauge has rightly pointed out that "it may [. . .] be easier to calculate the [total] amount of illicit profits than it is to calculate the amount of harm to each victim".[699] Where it is impossible to assign the illicit profits to individual victims, a disgorgement order may be the only

[693]The Commission's Guide on quantifying harm (2013), 136ff, contains suggestions how the "overcharge" caused by a cartel or an excessive pricing abuse can be determined. See also OECD (2011b).

[694]Under German law, § 34(4) ARC provides explicitly that the competition authority can estimate the illicit profit in the context of a disgorgement order. However, as far as restitutionary orders are concerned, § 32(2)(a) ARC only provides that the amount of interest contained in the illicit profits to be restituted may be estimated.

[695]Under German law, § 34(5) ARC provides a double time bar for disgorgement orders: "The skimming off of benefits may be ordered only within a time limit of up to five years from termination of the infringement, and only for a time period not exceeding five years." No time bar is provided for with respect to restitution orders according to § 32(2)(a) ARC. However, Bosch/Fritzsche (2013), 2228, want to interpret the latter provision restrictively, so that restitution can only be ordered while the actual infringement is still ongoing. In view of the facts that, in Stadtwerke Uelzen, Sect. 3.3.4.1.3, footnote 679 above, the Bundesgerichtshof extended the scope of restitution orders to past infringements and that the legislator wanted to codify the jurisprudence of the Bundesgerichtshof when he introduced § 32(2)(a) ARC (see BR-Drs 176/12, 34), their suggestion is hardly defendable.

[696]GC, T-22/02 (Sumitomo Chemical, 2005), 34ff; T-372/10 (Bolloré, 2012), 81.

[697]Under German law, § 34(2) ARC provides that a competition authority may only order disgorgement where the illicit profits have not already been taken into account for the setting of the amount of the fine or been reimbursed in the context of a restitution order or a damages claim.

[698]See Elhauge, Sect. 3.3.4.1.3, footnote 670 above.

[699]Elhauge (2009), 81.

solution. In the second place, it seems adequate to limit disgorgement and restitution orders to cases in which private claims have a limited chance of success[700] and to provide for the reimbursement of disgorged profits in case the infringing undertaking is exposed to a successful private claim subsequently to a disgorgement order.[701] In the third place, as regards the relationship between disgorgement and restitution orders, on the one hand, and criminal fines, on the other, it is submitted here that the Commission cannot simultaneously take illicit profits into account as an aggravating circumstance for the setting of the amount of the fine and order their restitution or disgorgement.[702] At the same time, there is no reason why non-voluntary disgorgement or restitution payments in the wake of an order of the Commission should be taken into account as a mitigating factor for the setting of a fine.[703] Fourth, pursuant to Article 278, 1st sentence, TFEU, actions against restitution and disgorgement orders do not have suspensory effect. However, it has rightly been pointed out that an undertaking may face serious difficulties in claiming restitutionary payments back from beneficiaries after a later annulment of the restitution order.[704] These difficulties should normally suffice to establish the urgency required for interim relief pursuant to Article 278, 2nd sentence, TFEU.[705] On the contrary, there will typically be no problems in claiming disgorged profits back from the Commission after the annulment of a disgorgement order.

[700]See Bornkamm (2014), § 32 ARC, 36: "[Die Kartellbehörde] wird [die Anordnung einer Rückerstattung] in aller Regel auf die Fälle beschränken, in denen die zivilrechtliche Durchsetzung des Beseitigungs- oder Schadensersatzanspruchs erkennbar Schwierigkeiten bereiten würde [. . .]".

[701]Under German law, § 34(2) ARC provides for such reimbursement.

[702]See for the similar problem of the interaction of fines and private damages claims from a ne bis in idem viewpoint Dannecker/Biermann (2012), 263; from the perspective of optimal deterrence Ackermann (2014b), 75f.

[703]The Commission has taken voluntary compensatory payments into account as a mitigating factor in two decisions: 1999 OJ L 24/1 (Preinsulated Pipes, 1998), 172; COMP/36.321 (Nintendo, 2002), 440f. Nevertheless, the General Court has confirmed that the Commission is under no obligation to do so: T-59/02 (Archer Daniels Midland, 2006), 349ff. See Wils (2009), 24, and Frese (2011), 21 fn 100; Ezrachi/Ioannidou (2011), 207.

[704]Reher/Haellmigk (2010), 522f; BR-Drs 176/12, 44. Under German law, actions against disgorgement and restitution orders have, as a rule, a suspensory effect, pursuant to Article 64 (1) ARC. Competition authorities can, however, order the immediate enforceability where there is a prevailing public interest in an immediate enforcement.

[705]On the urgency requirement as a condition for the suspension of a contested act pursuant to Article 278, 2nd sentence, TFEU, see eg Wegener (2014), § 19, 24ff; Lenaerts/Maselis/Gutman (2014), 13.35ff.

3.3.4.2 In the Context of Article 9 Regulation 1/03

3.3.4.2.1 The "Competitive Reset" in E-Books

3.3.4.2.1.1 The Case

In the E-books case,[706] the Commission accused five publishers and Apple as a retailer to have colluded to raise the retail prices of e-books. The gist of the Commission's theory of harm was that the publishers entered into agency agreements with Apple. Those agreements all contained the same key terms, allowing publishers to determine the retail prices. Previously, e-books had been sold mainly under a wholesale model whereby retailers freely determined the retail prices. The agency agreements concluded with Apple contained in particular a "most favoured nation" (MFN) clause that obliged the publishers to match lower retail prices of other retailers. Combined with other terms in the agreements, the MFN clause would have resulted in substantially lower revenues for publishers if other retailers, in particular Amazon, had continued to offer e-books at the prices then prevalent on the market. Therefore, the retail price MFN clause acted as a joint "commitment device" which ensured that the publishers had the same financial incentives to make other retailers than Apple, in particular Amazon, switch to the agency model.[707]

In order to offset the Commission's concerns, the investigated companies committed not only to terminate the agency contracts concluded with Apple. The publishers also undertook to offer retailers other than Apple the possibility to terminate agency agreements that restricted the retailer's ability to set the retail price or contained a MFN clause. Moreover, the publishers committed not to restrict the ability of retailers to set retail prices for a period of 2 years. For a period of 5 years the publishers and Apple undertook not to enter into any agreement for e-books containing a MFN clause.[708]

3.3.4.2.1.2 Discussion

The Commission's complex theory of harm shall not be discussed here. As regards the link between harm and remedy, it has been emphasised in the literature that Apple's commitment extended beyond the investigated publishers and that the publishers' commitments extended to other retailers besides Apple.[709] It also bears

[706]COMP/39.847 (Apple et al., 2012) and (Penguin, 2013). For a detailed description of the case see Kuik/Dawes (2014), 14.41ff; Smith/McComb (2013).

[707]This description of the Commission's theory of harm is mainly taken from the Commission's explanatory memorandum (MEMO/12/983) published together with the 2012 commitments.

[708]Also the description of the commitments is mainly taken from the Commission's explanatory MEMO/12/983 published together with the 2012 commitment.

[709]Dunne (2014b), 410, who does, however, not explicitly claim that the commitments went beyond what the Commission could have imposed under Article 7: "The commitments [. . .] were notable insofar as they purported to extend beyond the publishers concerned, as well as to other e-book retailers besides Apple".

mention that the commitments prohibited the use of restrictions to set retail prices and MFN clauses for certain periods, although the Commission did not take issue as such with agency agreements restraining the retailer's ability to set prices and containing MFN clauses.[710]

It is, however, submitted that these aspects do not go beyond what the Commission could have imposed under Article 7. According to the Commission's theory of harm, the collusive behaviour of the investigated companies had created joint incentives for the investigated companies to make other retailers than Apple switch to the agency model. Consequently, Amazon and other retailers actually switched to this model.[711] The commitments aimed at eliminating these effects by means of a "competitive reset", restoring the conditions that existed before the infringement was committed.[712] A commitment that would only have covered the relations between the investigated companies would not have sufficed to attain this goal. Rather, it was necessary to extend the scope of the agreement also to other retailers than Apple and to publishers that were not themselves the addressees of the decision. Moreover, the temporary prohibition of restrictions on the setting of retail prices and of MFN clauses appears justified in view of the need to re-establish a sufficient degree of uncertainty with respect to the preferred distribution model of publishers and retailers.[713]

Gerard invokes the E-books commitments as an example for a case in which "the Commission has relied on commitments to stretch the boundaries of prevailing antitrust legal standards and, in effect, to tackle practices that could not be comfortably addressed under these standards". He portrays the commitments in the following words: "[...] by challenging agency agreements and MFN clauses, which had historically been considered positively under antitrust standards, the Commission sought a "competitive reset" of the launch of e-books retail sales in the European Union".[714] This criticism is not persuasive. It predicates on a truncated and misleading presentation of the Commission's case. As stated above, the Commission's theory of harm did not challenge agency agreements and MFN clauses as such. It merely condemned them in so far as they were the consequence of the concrete anticompetitive collusion that was the subject of the procedure. Similarly, also the

[710]MEMO/12/983: "The decision does not take a position on the compatibility of the parties' agency agreements with [Article 101 TFEU] as such".

[711]See COMP/39.847 (Apple et al., 2012), 49ff and (Penguin, 2013), 42f.

[712]COMP/39.847 (Apple et al., 2012), 129: "[...] the Commission considers that the conditions of competition that existed [...] prior to the possible concerted practice should be substantially re-established ("competitive reset")"; similarly (Penguin, 2013), 107ff: "Penguin's Commitments will add to the competitive reset brought about by the Decision of 12 December 2012" (113); see also Smith/McComb (2013): "the problem within the ebooks market was that this particular set of agency agreements was the *product of collusive behaviour*".

[713]COMP/39.847 (Apple et al., 2012), 134: "[The commitments] would result in sufficient uncertainty regarding the future intentions of publishers and retailers regarding the choice of business models (that is to say, wholesale, agency or a novel model) and the pricing terms used therein".

[714]Gerard (2013), 20 together with fn 101.

"competitive reset" sought by the Commission merely addressed the effects of the said collusion.

Brenner criticises the use of the Article 9 procedure in the E-books case for reasons of legal certainty. In his view, the Commission missed an opportunity to clarify its position on MFN clauses.[715] Also this criticism must, however, be rejected. The Commission made it clear that it did not challenge MFN clauses as such, but only because they acted as a joint "commitment device" for the publishers to make other retailers than Apple switch to the agency model. The temporary obligation to abstain from using MFN clauses contained in the commitments served the goal to eliminate the subsisting effects of the concerned undertakings past anticompetitive conduct. Against this backdrop, it seems unlikely that the adoption of an Article 7 decision instead of an Article 9 decision would have brought about significantly more clarity as regards the Commission's general position on MFN clauses.

3.3.4.2.2 Disgorgement, Restitution and Compensation in the Context of Article 9

Prior to the enactment of Regulation 1/03, the Commission informally closed its investigation in the Philips/Sony CD Licensing case following an amendment of the investigated license agreements and an announcement by Philips to grant to each EEA licensee a one-time credit of US$10,000 on royalties due.[716] In the literature, this credit is sometimes referred to as an example that the Commission settled a case after the investigated companies offered compensatory payments.[717] Since the entry into force of Regulation 1/03, the Commission has not made binding any commitments under Article 9 involving disgorgement, restitution or compensation. In the Deutsche Bahn case, the Commission expressly stated that Article 9 decisions did not aim at directly compensating harm suffered from a violation of the EU antitrust rules. The importance of this statement should, however, not be overestimated. It must be read in its context: The Commission rejected submissions received during the market test according to which the level of a payment that was intended to put a margin squeeze to an end was too low.[718] If one follows the approach that was suggested above in the context of Article 7, the Commission should have the power to accept commitments involving disgorgement and restitution. It should, however, not have the power to accept commitments aiming at compensation. Under the suggested approach, commitments involving disgorgement and restitution would not go beyond what the Commission could have imposed under Article 7.

---

[715]Brenner (2014), 680f.

[716]See Peña Castellot (2003), 59.

[717]See Bourgeois/Strievi (2010), 248; Ezrachi/Ioannidou (2011), 208.

[718]COMP/39.678 (Deutsche Bahn I and II, 2013), 93; for a more thorough discussion of the case see Sect. 3.4.2.3.1 with footnotes 1139ff below.

In Germany, the Bundeskartellamt made binding commitments offered by 30 gas suppliers involving a restitution of illicit profits. The Bundeskartellamt was concerned that the gas suppliers had charged excessive prices. In order to offset the concerns, the investigated companies committed to restitute 127 million Euro to consumers through price reductions and credits. It bears mention that the commitments contained a so-called "no-repeated game" clause that prohibited the investigated companies from later recouping the restituted amounts.[719]

3.4 In Particular: So Called Structural Remedies

Critics of the Article 9 procedure point in particular to the adoption of so-called "structural" commitments in order to demonstrate that the Commission uses the Article 9 procedure to extract remedies that it could not have imposed on the basis of Article 7. The following section attempts to refute that criticism.[720] For this purpose, I will, in a first step, address the Commission's powers to impose structural remedies under Article 7. In that connection I will call into question the approach that assesses the admissibility of a given remedy by allocating the remedy either to the structural or the behavioural category and posits a subsidiarity of structural remedies. In my view, the admissibility of a remedy under Article 7 should be assessed on a case-by-case basis, regardless of the classification of the remedy as structural or behavioural. In a second step, I will evaluate the criticism that is levied at the so-called structural remedies that have been adopted on the basis of Article 9. I will argue that the Commission could have imposed the remedies in question also on the basis of Article 7.

3.4.1 The Irrelevance of the Distinction in the Context of Article 7

Merger related doctrine has developed many different classifications for remedies,[721] the "most prevalent" being the dichotomy between structural and

---

[719]Bundeskartellamt, B10-16/08 (Gaspreisverfahren, 2008); Ackermann (2012), 362f; Bornkamm (2014), § 32 ARC, 37; Nothdurft (2014), 249.

[720]See also Schütz (2013), Art. 9, 6, who states that in view of the voluntary nature of commitments, concerns regarding the use of structural remedies in the context of Article 7 do not apply to Article 9. The legitimisation of structural remedies through recourse to the voluntary nature of commitments is, however, different from the approach that is suggested here.

[721]For more recent proposals of categories see eg Wang/Rudanko (2012), 563; for a general overview of ways of categorising see eg Heithecker (2002), 220ff; Davies/Lyons (2007), 13f; Prümmer (2007), 148ff. The distinction between structural and behavioural remedies is also known in most other legal systems: see only OECD (2006, 2011c).

behavioural ones.[722] The same dichotomy underlies also the language of Article 7 (1) of Regulation 1/03 and of Article 10(1) Regulation 2019/1. However, even if recital 37 of Regulation 2019/1 now refers to structural remedies as being the ones that "affect the assets of an undertaking" and mentions "obligations to dispose of a shareholding in a competitor or to divest a business unit" as examples, neither the primary nor the derived sources of EU law seem to provide for an exhaustive definition of what constitutes a structural or behavioural remedy.[723]

Commentators have criticised the dichotomy as "artificial",[724] "oversimplifying", "confusing", "irrelevant"[725] and "useless".[726] Even among those who do not express such strong opinions, it is universally acknowledged that the distinction between the two categories causes problems.[727]

In the context of merger control, the importance of the dichotomy appears to be fading.[728] The EU Courts have expressed their scepticism vis-à-vis too much "categorical thinking"[729] and insist on a case-by-case examination of the legal admissibility of remedies.[730] The Commission has generally accepted this,[731] even if it continues to express a clear preference for "divestiture remedies".[732] It has been

[722]Hoeg (2014), 43.

[723]For merger control see Went (2006), 455; Papon (2009), 37. For Regulation 1/03 see Koch (2008a), 28; Hauser (2009), 7; Maier-Rigaud (2014), 3; generally Sofianatos (2009), 256; von Rosenberg (2009), 238.

[724]Jalabert-Doury/Nouvel (2007), 29.

[725]Levêque (2000).

[726]Heithecker (2002), 84ff; see also Prümmer (2007), 260: "unscharf [. . .] problematisch und schon wegen Ungenauigkeiten zu verwerfen".

[727]Eg Commission, in OECD (2006), 185; O'Donoghue/Padilla (2006), 718; Bauer (2008), 4-7-031; Dreher/Thomas (2008), 1558; Jaeger (2008), Art. 7, 14; Kellezi (2010), 76; Polster/Petschko (2010), 110; De Bronnet (2012), Art. 7, 13; Ritter (2012), Art. 7, 43; Lianos (2013), 418f; Voell (2014), 25ff. But see Krings (2012), 229 and 241, who is of the opinion that it is possible to draw a clearcut distinction between structural and behavioural remedies.

[728]See eg Papon (2009), 37ff: "Irrelevance of a theoretical preference"; Kellezi (2010), 76, who is of the opinion that for EU merger control, the distinction between structural and behavioural remedies does "not entail any legal consequences" ("n'entraîne [pas] de consequences juridiques [. . .] en droit communautaire"); similarly Wang/Rudanko (2012), 563, who consider that "there is no necessity to clarify whether a remedy is structural or behavioural when assessing its appropriateness and effectiveness".

[729]I borrow this term from the title of Lianos' (2009) paper: "Categorical Thinking in Competition Law and the "Effects-Based" Approach in Article 82 EC".

[730]See eg CJ, C-12/03 P (Tetra Laval, 2005), 86; GC, T-102/96 (Gencor, 1999), 319; T-158/00 (ARD, 2003), 193; T-114/02 (Babyliss, 2003), 170 and 191; T-177/04 (Easyjet, 2006), 182; T-87/05 (EDP, 2005), 100.

[731]Remedies Notice (2008), 16.

[732]See eg Remedies Notice (2008), 17: "Divestiture commitments are the best way to eliminate competition concerns resulting from horizontal overlaps, and may also be the best means of resolving problems resulting from vertical or conglomerate concerns [. . .] Other structural commitments may be suitable to resolve all types of concerns if those remedies are equivalent to divestitures in their effects"; ibid, 61: "divestitures are the benchmark for other remedies in terms of

pointed out that "the Commission has been reluctant to use the structural/behavioural dichotomy in official documents in recent years"[733] and that "the classifications employed in the Remedies Notice [2008] signal a less formal or rigid way of labelling remedies with emphasis on the importance of examining the remedial solutions at hand on a case by case basis".[734] In a similar vein, the 2011 OECD report on remedies in merger cases found a "discernible move away from focusing on the type of remedy applied" on a worldwide scale and that "[c]ompetition agencies are increasingly looking at what makes a remedy successful in dealing with the relevant competition risk, rather than at whether the remedy can be characterized as structural or behavioural".[735]

These developments in the field of merger control have so far had at best a limited impact on the thinking about remedies under Regulation 1/03. Here, the opinion still prevails that a distinction between structural and behavioural remedies is indispensable.[736] This opinion predicates on the assumption that there is a general "subsidiarity" of structural vis-à-vis behavioural remedies.[737] The distinction between the two types of remedies was also upheld by the legislator in recital 37 and article 10 (1) of Directive 2019/1; recital 37 postulates also the general subsidiarity of structural remedies, albeit in a slightly attenuated form which underlines the necessity to analyse the concrete circumstances of the case at hand.

However, in particular members of the Commission's services dispute that such a subsidiarity really exists.[738] Inspired by this controversy and by the developments regarding merger control, it will be argued in the following section that, also where remedies under Regulation 1/03 are concerned, the more convincing arguments militate for a case-by-case analysis. Two major reasons support this argument: On

effectiveness and efficiency"; Commission, in OECD (2011c), 234; Italianer (2012), 4: "The benchmark for the acceptance of any other remedies in mergers is that they should be as effective as divestitures".

[733]Hoeg (2014), 44; see also, with respect to the 2006 merger remedies study Papandropoulos/Tajana (2006), 444: "A farewell to the structural/behavioural distinction?".

[734]Hoeg (2014), 45.

[735]OECD (2011c), 12.

[736]Eg Bauer (2008), 4-7-031; Hauser (2009), 8 and 155; Kellezi (2010), 76; Polster/Petschko (2010), 110; De Bronnet (2012), Art. 7, 13; Emmerich (2014), § 32 ARC, 37. See also O'Donoghue/Padilla (2006), 719: "useful and valid as a general matter".

[737]See the references in Sect. 3.4.1, footnote 736 and moreover Jung (2011), Art. 102, 377; Immenga (2011), 296; O'Donoghue/Padilla (2006), 676: "express preference for behavioural remedies"; Petit/Neyrinck (2011), 120, fn 32: "prevalence of behavioural over structural remedies"; Wolter (2011), 116: "klare Präferenz für verhaltensorientierte Maßnahmen"; Lianos (2013), 370f: "Structural remedies are subject to a stricter proportionality test"; Kellezi (2010), 141: "les mesures structurelles présentant un caractère subsidiaire"; Krings (2012), 185f: "Art. 7 VO 1/2003 bestimmt ausdrücklich die Subsidiarität einer strukturellen Maßnahme gegenüber einer Maßnahme verhaltensorientierter Art"; Wagner-Von Papp (2012), 960 and 963: "statutory preference for behavioural remedies"; Alexiadis/Sependa (2013), 15: "acting under Article 7(1) [the Commission] is required to prioritise behavioural over structural remedies".

[738]See Hellström/Maier-Rigaud/Bulst (2009), 46; Maier-Rigaud (2012, 2014).

the one hand, it is impossible or at least very difficult to clearly delineate the categories of structural and behavioural remedies; on the other hand, the distinction is also irrelevant in view of the fact that the claims regarding a general subsidiarity of structural vis-à-vis behavioural remedies must be rejected.

3.4.1.1 The Impossibility to Distinguish Between Structural and Behavioural Remedies

3.4.1.1.1 Doctrine

It is universally conceded that the distinction between structural and behavioural remedies is problematic.[739] In view of the difficulties to find a positive definition for the innumerable manifestations of behavioural remedies,[740] the distinction depends to a large extent on the positive determination of what constitutes a structural remedy.[741] Behavioural remedies can then be negatively defined as everything that is not structural. Even if one takes this insight as a starting point, clarity exists at best with respect to the extreme: There is a general agreement that the "divestiture", i.e. a change in the property, of an entire business, parts of it or of certain assets constitutes a structural remedy.[742] Beyond that, the boundaries blur. There are numerous examples of controversial borderline cases, in which the only way of dealing with problems of classification seems to be to refer to "quasi-structural remedies"[743] or "remedies of behavioural nature but of structural effect".[744] On a very rough scale, these borderline cases of non-divestiture remedies can be grouped into two categories[745]: On the one hand, there are the remedies that aim at barriers to entry. They are attributed a "structural effect" because, by lowering or eliminating such barriers, they encourage market access and thus pave the way for a change in the structure of the

[739] See the references in Sect. 3.4.1, footnote 727 for Regulation 1/03; for merger control see eg Drauz (1997), 225; Prümmer (2007), 156ff; Sofianatos (2009), 258.

[740] Cf. Sofianatos (2009), 233; Kellezi (2010), 80.

[741] Cf. Hauser (2009), 8, according to whom the inverse way of a merely negative distinction of structural remedies from positively defined behavioural remedies is exposed to serious problems.

[742] See eg Motta/Polo/Vasconcelos (2007), 606; Motta (2004), 265; Paas (2006), 209; Papon (2009), 37; ICN (2005), 3.8: "Divestitures are the most common form of structural remedy"; Prümmer (2007), 157: "Veräußerungszusagen als Prototyp"; Sofianatos (2009), 256: "La cession d'une activité, la mesure phare structurelle"; Hoeg (2014), 44: "The principle structural remedy is a divestiture [. . .] entailing a change in property rights".

[743] Eg Motta/Polo/Vasconcelos (2007), 621; Went (2006), 456; Sofianatos (2009), 258; Hoeg (2014), 44; Alexiadis/Sependa (2013), 11f.

[744] Idot/Momège (2001), 37: "engagements comportementaux à effet structurel"; Sofianatos (2009), 259 and 265.

[745] For an overview of borderline cases see the references in Sect. 3.4.1.1.1, footnote 743 above; moreover Prümmer (2007), 158f. The grouping into the two categories is my own and only meant to facilitate the presentation.

market.[746] This first group includes the granting of access to networks, slot releases or the mandatory license of IP.[747] Besides such classic "access remedies", it also encompasses the termination of existing contracts, for example long term exclusive supply or license agreements.[748] On the other hand, there are the non-divestiture remedies that aim at increasing the independence of separate undertakings or of parts of an integrated undertaking. Their structural effect consists in removing existing links between undertakings or within an undertaking. This second group includes the waiving of rights linked to minority stakes in a competitor,[749] the termination of distribution agreements with competitors,[750] the erection of firewalls[751] and the various ways to unbundle vertically integrated companies below the divestiture level.[752]

The problem of whether to assign the described borderline cases to the structural or the behavioural category is reflected in the way commentators deal with them with respect to remedies under Article 7 of Regulation 1/03. In a very simplified manner, the positions can be summed up as follows: Many authors abstain from clear statements.[753] Some follow a broad approach and count "access remedies" as structural.[754] Such an approach predicates on an understanding of the term "structural" that captures not only changes to existing links between undertakings or to the internal organisation of one undertaking, but also changes to the general structure of the market brought about by the entry of new competitors. Consequently pursued, such an approach therefore means that both described groups of borderline cases fall within the "structural" category. A narrower definition excludes the first group of the

[746] Cf. Prümmer (2007), 158: "Mit der Bezeichnung "quasi-strukturell" wird zum Ausdruck gebracht, dass solche Zusagen das Entstehen von Wettbewerbern ermöglichen sollen und somit einen strukturellen Effekt haben können".

[747] Cf. Merger Remedies Notice (2008), 62ff.

[748] Cf. Merger Remedies Notice (2008), 67.

[749] Cf. Merger Remedies Notice (2008), 59.

[750] Cf. Merger Remedies Notice (2008), 60.

[751] Cf. Motta/Polo/Vasconcelos (2007), 622f; Sofianatos (2009), 259; Kellezi (2010), 101ff.

[752] Cf. Hauser (2009), 10f, who points out that not only full ownership unbundling, but also functional or legal unbundling interferes with the structure of an undertaking; see also ibid., 229; similarly for the corresponding situation regarding § 32 ARC: Wilhelmi (2013), 760f; for different types of unbundling see eg Krings (2012), 142f with further references. He distinguishes between unbundling of accounts; department unbundling; legal unbundling; management unbundling; ownership unbundling. Krings also considers all types of unbundling as "structural" remedies (142f and 228).

[753] See eg Kerse/Khan (2012), 6-046 and Sorinas/Moretti (2012), 4.11, who do not define structural remedies at all; Sauer (2013), 11.08, who mentions only the sale of assets as an example.

[754] Eg Willis/Hughes (2008), 153ff; Polster/Petschko (2010), 110; Ritter (2012), Art. 7, 48; De Bronnet (2012), Art. 7, 13; similarly for the corresponding discussion regarding § 32 ARC: Dreher/Thomas (2008), 1559; Wilhelmi (2013), 360f, 373f; Emmerich (2014), § 32 ARC, 39; Bornkamm (2014), § 32 ARC, 32. See also OECD (2006), 37, where mandatory licensing of IP is classified as "structural", "because it has the capability to alter market structure by introducing new competitors". See also Bechtold/Bosch/Brinker (2014), Art. 9, 11, who classify the browser choice screen adopted in COMP/39.530 (Microsoft – tying, 2009), as a "structural" remedy.

described borderline cases, but includes the second one. Relying on Recital 12 of Regulation 1/03, this definition limits "structural" remedies to those that change the structure of undertakings. It thereby excludes remedies that merely change the general structure of the market by lowering or eliminating barriers to access.[755] Finally, the narrowest position consists of excluding all borderline cases from the structural category by requesting a change in the allocation of property rights.[756] According to this position, nothing but "divestiture", i.e. a change in the property, of an entire business, parts of it or of certain assets constitutes a structural remedy.[757]

This simplified presentation of the controversial approaches how to distinguish structural and behavioural remedies requires two complementary observations. First, it should be noted that Davies and Lyons have proposed the "clean break principle" as a criterion to evaluate merger remedies. According to them, "[a] clean break remedy should not create relationships between the merged firm and other market players [...] or the regulator".[758] In particular remedies that require a lot of monitoring fail the test. Although the authors state that "[c]lean break remedies are naturally associated with structural remedies", they underline that "the clean break principle will not always correspond to the structural/behavioural dichotomy".[759] Their "clean break principle" is not meant to be a criterion to distinguish structural from behavioural remedies. It is only a means to evaluate the effectiveness of a given remedy, independently of its classification.[760] Nevertheless, other authors rely on

[755]See Hauser (2009), 8ff, 15f, who expressly excludes access remedies, but includes unbundling measures below the divestiture threshold. See also Hjelmeng (2013), 1018, who classifies the erection of "organizational barriers between business areas" as a structural remedy. Also O'Donoghue/Padilla (2013) define structural remedies by reference to the "structure of the dominant undertaking" (880 and 944), consider compulsory dealing as a behavioural remedy (931ff) and classify accounting separation as structural (944); similarly also Voell (2014), 32.

[756]Koch (2008a), 29f: (endgültige) "Veränderung der dinglichen Zuordnung von Unternehmensbestandteilen unter Wahrung der mit ihr einhergehenden Ausschließlichkeitswirkung"; Alexiadis/Sependa (2013), 10: "discontinuation of a part of the infringing undertaking's business or its sale to a third party".

[757]See also Dalheimer (2005), Art. 7, 11, who qualifies the "unbundling of accounts" as "behavioural" remedy; Lowe/Maier-Rigaud (2008), 604, who qualify "Chinese wall remedies" (i.e. firewalls) as "behavioural"; Hellström/Maier-Rigaud/Bulst (2009), 53, who qualify "legal unbundling" as a "behavioural" remedy.

[758]Davies/Lyons (2007), 42.

[759]Davies/Lyons (2007), 43. The authors mention "a divestiture with full transfer of property rights for an indefinite duration [where] the buyer of the divested assets is still dependent on the merging parties for key supplies in the future" as an example for a remedy that "will not imply a clean break".

[760]This becomes evident if one reads the following conclusion by Davies/Lyons (2007), 43: "We accept the standard structural/behavioural dichotomy as a helpful starting point for categorizing remedies. However, we do not agree that a structural remedy is necessarily better than a behavioural remedy, though it often will be. We argue that the central issue is to form a view of how the remedy is expected to affect the competitive process, once it is imposed. Because of this, remedies – however they are labelled – should always be examined on a case-by-case basis, in the context of the particular market and merger in which they are agreed. The importance of the clean break principle is that it focuses attention on an important aspect of a remedy that simple classification would fail to pick up."

concepts that are similar to the "clean break principle" in order to distinguish behavioural and structural remedies.[761] Second, it should be pointed out that structural and behavioural remedies are sometimes contrasted by stating that the former "are aimed at changing the incentives of the firm(s) in the market" while the latter "try to redress specific conduct in a context where incentives remain essentially unchanged".[762]

3.4.1.1.2 Position of Commission

The Commission's position on the distinction between the categories of structural and behavioural remedies is not clear. The Remedies Notice (2008) classifies "divestiture" and "access remedies" as structural, avoids an assignment to either of the categories for the "removal of links with competitors" and the "change of long-term exclusive contracts" and qualifies "promises by the parties to abstain from certain commercial behaviour (e.g. bundling products)" as "non-structural".[763] The Best Practices (2011) refer to the terms "structural" and "behavioural" remedy, but abstain from any further definitions.[764] The Antitrust Manual of Procedures mentions a "supply obligation" as an example for a behavioural and the "divestiture of a

[761] See von Rosenberg (2009), 238: "Structural remedies are [...] remedies which do not need any further monitoring measures once implemented. Behavioural remedies are remedies which do require medium or long-term monitoring"; O'Donoghue/Padilla (2013), 927, who consider that – despite admitted problems of definition – the distinction between structural and behavioural remedies is "useful and valid as a general matter [because] it distinguishes continuing behaviour (behavioural remedies) and one-off acts (structural remedies)".

[762] Lowe/Maier-Rigaud (2008), 604; Hellström/Maier-Rigaud/Bulst (2009), 46. Similarly Bougette/Marty (2012), 7; Maier-Rigaud (2014), 6; see also Klees/Hauser (2007), 603 and Hauser (2009), 224: structural and behavioural remedies have different effects; Krings (2012), 231: "eine strukturelle Maßnahme [muss] dazu führen, dass ein bestimmtes [...] Verhalten nach Befolgung der Anordnung nicht mehr möglich ist".

[763] On the one hand, the Remedies Notice 2008 makes a general distinction "between divestitures, other structural remedies, such as granting access to key infrastructure or inputs on non-discriminatory terms, and commitments relating to the future behaviour of the merged entity" (17). On the other hand, the Commission relies on the categories of "divestiture", "removal of links with competitors" and "other remedies" (22ff). The latter category is subdivided into "access remedies" (62ff), "change of long term exclusive contracts" (67ff) and "other non divestiture remedies" (69). Only "other non divestiture remedies", "such as promises by the parties to abstain from certain commercial behaviour (e.g. bundling products)" are expressly referred to as "non structural remedies" (69). While "access remedies" are therefore classified as structural remedies, the Commission avoids a statement whether this is also the case for the "removal of links with competitors" and the "change of long term exclusive contracts".

[764] 83: "If structural remedies are envisaged, in accordance with Article 7(1) of Regulation (EC) No 1/2003, the Statement of Objections will spell out why there is no equally effective behavioural remedy or why the Commission considers any equally effective behavioural remedy would be more burdensome for the undertaking concerned than the structural remedy"; 127: "The parties can offer commitments of a behavioural or structural nature that address adequately the competition concerns identified".

part of a company" as an example for a structural remedy.[765] For the rest, the Manual limits itself to refer to the Remedies Notice (2008) in order to point out that the "boundaries between both commitment types are not always entirely clear".[766]

A 2006 OECD report on "remedies and sanctions in abuse of dominance cases" is slightly more instructive. The Commission states that Recital 12 of Regulation 1/03 defines structural remedies as "changes to the structure of an undertaking" and that "the most obvious one is the divestiture of an existing business".[767] With respect to behavioural remedies, the Commission distinguishes between performance and conduct remedies. The former are qualified as belonging to the "toolkit of a regulator" and said generally not to be used by the Commission.[768] With respect to the latter, the report provides for a "non exhaustive list of examples": "the obligation to supply third parties with certain goods, services or technology licenses, or to provide third parties with access to certain facilities or networks on a non-discriminatory basis; the obligation to provide certain information to third parties, which is essential for their ability to develop certain products or provide certain services; the obligation to unbundle two or more goods previously offered jointly; the obligation not to tie certain services to the sale of a good; the obligation to discontinue the offer of certain rebate schemes; the obligation not to price discriminate between customers; the obligation not to share certain information between several firms or between business units within a single firm (information firewalls)".[769] The Commission even comes up with "tentative" definitions for structural and behavioural remedies: "A structural remedy is a measure that effectively changes the structure of the market by a transfer of property rights regarding tangible or intangible assets, including the transfer of an entire business unit, and that does not lead to any on-going relationships between the former and the future owner. After its completion, a structural remedy does not require any further monitoring. [. . .] A behavioural remedy is a measure that obliges the concerned undertaking(s) to act in a specific way or to omit specific anti-competitive conduct. Compliance with behavioural remedies has to be monitored and enforced."[770] Despite these efforts to distinguish structural from behavioural remedies, the Commission nevertheless points out that "the line between behavioural and structural remedies is not always

[765]45.

[766]45 fn 12.

[767]OECD (2006), 185.

[768]OECD (2006), 186. The report mentions "production level maintenance, price control, production increases, export increases, investments, marketing expenditure increases, quality improvement, sales increases, price decreases, enlargement of the distribution network, maintenance of brands, and maintenance of obsolete goods in the market" as examples for performance remedies.

[769]OECD (2006), 186f.

[770]OECD (2006), 185f; Maier-Rigaud (2014), 4, seems to follow that definition: "A structural remedy is defined as a measure that effectively changes the structure of the firm by a transfer of property rights regarding tangible or intangible assets, including the transfer of an entire business unit, that does not lead to any on-going relationships between the former and the future owner. After its implementation, a structural remedy does not require any further monitoring".

easy to draw".[771] The "removal of cross placement of directors on the board of directors (interlocking directorates)", "remedies creating information firewalls within an undertaking" and "the mandatory granting of an exclusive, non-limited and irrevocable licence that is paid upfront" are mentioned as borderline cases. According to the Commission, the former two "may change the organisation of the undertaking, [but] do not as such have an impact on its structural presence on the market". The latter is said not to "change the organisation of an undertaking but [to be capable of having] the same effect on the market as the divestiture of a business branch".[772]

3.4.1.1.3 Position of EU Courts

The EU Courts have so far not developed a clear stance on the distinction between structural and behavioural remedies either.[773] As regards merger control, the Gencor judgment of the General Court contains nevertheless important statements in this respect. The Court held that a concentration, which has been found to create or strengthen a dominant position, must be prohibited even if the merging parties commit not to abuse that position.[774] The Court emphasised that "[t]he categorisation of a proposed commitment as structural or behavioural [was] immaterial" for the finding of whether the concentration, such as modified by the commitments, would create or strengthen a dominant position.[775] The Court went on as follows:

> It is true that commitments which are structural in nature, such as a commitment to reduce the market share of the entity arising from a concentration by the sale of a subsidiary, are, as a rule, preferable from the point of view of the Regulation's objective, inasmuch as they prevent once and for all, or at least for some time, the emergence or strengthening of the dominant position previously identified by the Commission and do not, moreover, require medium or long-term monitoring measures. Nevertheless, the possibility cannot automatically be ruled out that commitments which prima facie are behavioural, for instance not to use a trademark for a certain period, or to make part of the production capacity of the entity arising from the concentration available to third-party competitors, or, more generally, to grant access to essential facilities on non-discriminatory terms, may themselves also be capable of preventing the emergence or strengthening of a dominant position. It is thus necessary to examine on a case-by-case basis the commitments offered by the undertakings concerned.[776]

This line of argumentation was confirmed in several later cases. In ARD, the General Court restated the cited passage as follows: "The Court recalls that commitments as to conduct may be accepted if they have a structural effect, that is to say, if they are capable of preventing the emergence or strengthening of a dominant

[771] OECD (2006), 185.

[772] OECD (2006), 185.

[773] See for the EU Courts' approach for categorising merger remedies also Prümmer (2007), 186ff.

[774] T-102/96 (Gencor, 1999), 316f.

[775] T-102/96 (Gencor, 1999), 319.

[776] T-102/96 (Gencor, 1999), 319f.

position (Gencor v Commission)."[777] Moreover, it confirmed that access commitments had such a "structural effect"[778] because they would "open the market structurally to suppliers of competing [products]".[779] In Babyliss, the General Court relied on its case-by-case approach to avoid a statement whether a commitment, which consisted of a grant of exclusive licenses to third parties for a certain period, was structural or behavioural.[780] In Easyjet, the merging parties Airfrance and KLM had committed to release take-off and landing slots for an unlimited period in time and without possibility to recover the released slots.[781] The slot commitment was accompanied by several auxiliary measures, in particular by the obligation for KLM and Airfrance to refrain from increasing their offer of flights on the affected routes. In reply to Easyjet's argument that the commitments were weak because they were behavioural, the General Court again recalled "that behavioural commitments are not by their nature insufficient to prevent the creation or strengthening of a dominant position, and that they must be assessed on a case-by-case basis in the same way as structural commitments".[782] Moreover, the Court classified the commitment regarding the "divestiture" of slots expressly as "structural".[783]

3.4.1.1.4 Comment

The different positions regarding the distinction between structural and behavioural remedies attest a lack of a universally accepted theory. This applies in particular if one takes an overarching perspective that looks both at merger control and Regulation 1/03. From such a perspective, the Commission's own position seems contradictory: The Merger Remedies Notice (2008) classifies "access remedies" as structural whilst the Antitrust Manual of Procedures categorises "supply obligations", which are also a sort of access remedy, as behavioural.[784] The existing

[777] T-158/00 (ARD, 2003), 250. This paragraph should be read in conjunction with paragraph 193.

[778] T-158/00 (ARD, 2003), 221 and 251f.

[779] T-158/00 (ARD, 2003), 252; similarly already at 199: "although the [access] commitments appear to be rather behavioural in nature, they are nevertheless structural because they are aimed at resolving a structural problem, namely market access by third parties".

[780] T-114/02 (Babyliss, 2003), 170, 191. The court used a slightly modified version of the Gencor formula which substituted the term "sale of assets" for the previously employed term "commitments which are structural in nature".

[781] See IP/04/194; T-177/04 (Easyjet, 2006), 183 in conjunction with 16. That the English version of 183 mentions a "limited period" is a translation error, see the French version of the judgment.

[782] T-177/04 (Easyjet, 2006), 182.

[783] T-177/04 (Easyjet, 2006), 183.

[784] See also OECD (2006), 186, where "the obligation to supply third parties with certain goods, services or technology licenses, or to provide third parties with access to certain facilities or networks on a non-discriminatory basis" are all classified as behavioural remedies. Italianer (2012) treats "access remedies" as an independent category besides "structural" and "behavioural" ones.

jurisprudence on merger remedies does not offer guidance either. The Courts resort to a case-by-case analysis which takes away most of the distinction's significance.

Albeit desirable to ensure the coherence of the legal system, a uniform use of the structural-behavioural-dichotomy in the fields of merger control and Regulation 1/03 is of course not indispensable. However, even if one limits the question to Article 7 of Regulation 1/03, a normative position on how the two categories should be distinguished is hard to take. The legislative history of the provision is not conclusive.[785] The explanatory memorandum for the proposal for Regulation 1/03 mentions only the uncontroversial "divestiture of certain assets" as an example for a structural remedy.[786] A broad understanding of the structural category, according to which every remedy that somehow brings about a change in the general "structure of the market" is considered to be "structural", faces the universally accepted objection that the categories of "market structure" and "market behaviour" cannot be distinguished with a sufficient amount of clarity.[787]

At the same time, the arguments supporting the exclusion of remedies that aim at barriers to entry and in particular access remedies[788] from the structural category are weak. Certainly, one can for the latter purpose try to distinguish between remedies that change the "structure of an undertaking" and remedies that merely change the "general market structure". The wording of Recital 12, which provides that "[c] hanges to the structure of an undertaking as it existed before the infringement was committed would only be proportionate where there is a substantial risk of a lasting or repeated infringement that derives from the very structure of the undertaking", can serve as a basis for such a distinction.[789] However, on the one hand, the wording of Recital 12 does not exclude that a "behavioural remedy" brings about a "change" to the "structure of an undertaking". On the other hand, the wording of Article 7(1), 2nd and 3rd sentence, and of recital 12, 2nd sentence, refers only generally to "structural remedies". Overall, the wording of Recital 12 and Article 7 of Regulation 1/03 thus does not exclude that a change to "the structure of an undertaking", which is mentioned only in the 3rd sentence of Recital 12, is only a subcategory of the broader category of structural measures in general.[790] What is more important is that the

785 See Hauser (2009), 8 and more extensively on the legislative history ibid, 49ff, 53ff.

786 Com(2000) 582 final, 17: "Secondly, the Commission is empowered to impose all remedies necessary to bring the infringement to an end, including structural remedies. Structural remedies can be necessary in order to bring an infringement effectively to an end. This may in particular be the case with regard to cooperation agreements and abuses of a dominant position, where divestiture of certain assets may be necessary."

787 Cf. Heithecker (2002), 87f; Prümmer (2007), 159; Koch (2008a), 29.

788 See Koch (2008a), 28ff; Hauser (2009), 7ff, 15f; Krings (2012), 227f, who all exclude access remedies.

789 See Commission, in OECD (2006), 185; Hauser (2009), 8f, who rely on recital 12.

790 But see Hauser (2009), 8 fn 40, whose interpretation that only changes to the structure of an undertaking "as it existed before the infringement was committed" constitute the particular case addressed by recital 12 is possible, but not compelling.

notion "structure of an undertaking" is not a precisely defined term either.[791] There is no reason why the distinction between the structure and behaviour of an undertaking should be easier to make than that between market structure and behaviour. EU competition law provides only for a concept of "undertaking". Article 102 TFEU relies on concepts of dominance and abuse, not on a concept of "structure of an undertaking".[792] If one were to assimilate the concept "structure of an undertaking" with the economic concept of "characteristics of market structure that relate to undertakings",[793] the "structure of an undertaking" would also include an undertaking's contractual relations to competitors, customers and suppliers[794] and the prohibition of such contractual relations could be categorized as a "structural remedy". Overall, the use of the concept "structure of an undertaking" does therefore not offer a sufficiently precise criterion of distinction.

Another way to exclude remedies that aim at barriers to entry from the structural category is the distinction between a direct and an indirect effect on the structure of the market or, in different words, between remedies of truly "structural nature" and those of "behavioural nature, but of structural effect".[795] This distinction rests on the assumption that remedies which aim at entry barriers entail only an indirect change in the structure of the market.[796] However, this distinction only looks at a remedy's

---

[791]In Germany, during the 7th amendment of the ARC, the legislator abstained from employing the term "structural" in § 32 ARC, because, under German law, this was not a precise legal concept, cf. BT-Drs 15/3640, 33, but also 51. During the 8th amendment of the ARC, such concerns were no longer upheld and § 32 ARC was changed to mirror Article 7 of Regulation 1/03, cf. BR-Drs 176/12, 33f. Heithecker (2002), 84f, expresses similar concerns with respect to the lack of a legal concept of "market structure". Hauser (2009), 10, states that the "structure of an undertaking" encompasses not only its "property law structure" (eigentumsrechtliche Struktur), but also its "company law structure" (gesellschaftsrechtliche Struktur), financial links (finanzielle Verflechtungen) and capital participations (Kapitalbeteiligungen). Similarly Krings (2012), 142f and 228 for "structural measure".

[792]The notion "structure of an undertaking" appeared in Recital 23 of Regulation 4064/89, which read: "Whereas it is appropriate to define the concept of concentration in such a manner as to cover only operations bringing about a lasting change in the structure of the undertakings concerned", cf. Heithecker (2002), 85. However, it no longer appears in Recital 20 of Regulation 139/2004, which now reads: "It is expedient to define the concept of concentration in such a manner as to cover operations bringing about a lasting change in the control of the undertakings concerned and therefore in the structure of the market."

[793]"Unternehmensbezogene Marktstrukturmerkmale". This seems to be the approach of Hauser (2009), 9: "Jede Änderung der Unternehmensstruktur ist zugleich eine Änderung der Marktstruktur, denn als übergeordneter Parameter umfasst die Marktstruktur unter anderem die interne Unternehmensstruktur, die Unternehmensgröße sowie auch personelle und finanzielle Verflechtungen als unternehmensbezogene Marktstrukturmerkmale".

[794]Cf. Pohlmann (1999), 82.

[795]Cf. Koch (2008a), 29; Hauser (2009), 10.

[796]Cf. Koch (2008a), 29; Hauser (2009), 10; see also Prümmer (2007), 158, who points out that remedies which aim at barriers to entry create only the possibility for entry; it is not sure whether entry will actually take place. Prümmer, ibid, also correctly underlines that the actual entry may be irrelevant from the point of view of contestable markets theory, because already the possibility of entry may change the behaviour of market participants.

"indirect" impact on the general structure of the market. It blinds out that a remedy which aims at barriers to entry may also affect the "structure of the undertaking" which implements the remedy. For example, the implementation of an access obligation can require a change in the internal organization of an undertaking because new staff is needed.[797] Where this interference of access remedies with the structure of an undertaking is recognized, it is sometimes qualified as a mere "affection" of the structure of an undertaking in order to exclude the respective remedy from the structural category.[798] However, this suggestion does not develop criteria how to distinguish a mere "affection" from a "change" of the structure of an undertaking. The criterion "durability"[799] is not of much help in this respect, because it does not solve the difficulties which occur, when access obligations or the prohibition of exclusive contracts are imposed for an indefinite period or when a divestiture is only accompanied by a short non-reacquisition period.

If therefore neither the notion "structure of an undertaking" nor the "directness" of a remedy's impact on the general market structure can overcome problems of definition in a satisfactory manner, the possibility remains to confine the category of "structural remedies" to a reallocation of property rights. This may be a practicable way, if one construes the term "reallocation" narrowly as "expropriation" and excludes the mere imposition of constraints of a property rights use.[800] However, also the line between expropriation and a mere constraint of a property right is not easy to draw.[801] In any event, many authors who rely on property rights do not go that far, but define already a "bearing on"[802] or an "interference with"[803] property

[797]The contention of the Commission in OECD (2006), 185, according to which "the mandatory granting of an exclusive, non-limited and irrevocable licence that is paid upfront does not change the organisation of an undertaking", is in this respect not convincing. Such a license has the effect that the granting undertaking is no longer allowed to use the licensed IP itself. The undertaking may therefore have to reorganise its branches that dealt originally with that use.

[798]Krings (2012), 228: "Eine bloße Betroffenheit der Unternehmensstruktur insofern, als dass ein Unternehmen zur Gewährung eines Zugangs zu einer bestimmten, in die Struktur des Unternehmens integrierten wesentlichen Einrichtung verpflichtet wird, kann demnach nicht als strukturelle Maßnahme i.S.d. Art 7 VO 1/2003 verstanden werden".

[799]Krings (2012), 228: "[Eine strukturelle Maßnahme dient] der dauerhaften Veränderung der Unternehmensstruktur"; ibid, 233: "Da eine strukturelle Maßnahme einen dauerhaften Eingriff in die Unternehmensstruktur bedeutet und damit eine dauerhafte Veränderung dieser Struktur bewirkt, handelt es sich bei der strukturellen Maßnahme regelmäßig um das stärkere belastende Mittel".

[800]For such a strict approach see Sect. 3.4.1.1.1, footnote 756 above.

[801]For the difficulties to distinguish an expropriation from a mere restriction of the use of property see eg Kaiser/Wischmeyer (2010), 51ff; Calliess (2011), Art. 17, 14ff; Jarass (2013), Art. 17, 18ff. See also Waller (2009), 26f, who suggests that the obligation to disclose interoperability, which was imposed on Microsoft (cf. T-201/04, 2007) and which is typically considered as a behavioural remedy, amounted in fact to a "divestiture", because "disclosure is divestiture when it comes to our high-tech, information-based, intellectual property-driven economy".

[802]Hellström/Maier-Rigaud/Bulst (2009), 47: "while structural remedies may have a bearing on property rights if, for instance, a sale of assets is required, behavioral remedies bear upon the freedom to conduct a business, including the freedom to contract."

[803]Dalheimer (2005), Art. 7, 11: "Der Begriff der strukturellen Abhilfemaßnahme (structural remedy) ist weit gefasst. Er beinhaltet alle Abhilfemaßnahmen durch die in Eigentumsrechte der

rights as a structural measure. Such a definition is not very telling, because too many remedies will put some constraint on the use of property rights. These reservations apply also in regard of recital 37 of directive 2019/1, which seems to suggest that the notion "structural remedy" comprises not only the obligation to dispose of a shareholding in a competitor or to divest a business unit, but also any obligation that "affects" the assets of an undertaking.

The "clean break principle" and the "incentives theory" fail as well to offer reliable criteria to distinguish behavioural from structural remedies. First, as regards the "clean break principle", it needs to be recalled that Davies and Lyons do not understand this principle as a relevant criterion of distinction between the two categories.[804] Moreover, they point out that the question whether a remedy implies a "clean break" cannot always be answered with a schematic yes or no, but that "a grey area"[805] exists. The Commission seems to accept this, given that in the definitions contained in its 2006 OECD report, it does not rely exclusively on the "clean break principle" to distinguish structural from behavioural remedies, but includes in particular the "transfer of property rights regarding tangible or intangible assets" as a condition for the classification of a remedy as structural.[806] Second, as regards the "incentive theory", it must be noted that the proponents of this theory[807] do not claim it to be a criterion of distinction between structural and behavioural remedies. In any event, it is submitted that the concept "incentive" is so vague that it cannot serve as a basis for a meaningful legal distinction. Finally, in the context of Article 7, the recourse to the intermediate category of "quasi-structural" remedies[808] does not answer the question whether the alleged subsidiarity of structural remedies applies also to quasi-structural ones or not.

Summing up it can be stated that a sufficiently clear line between structural and behavioural remedies does not exist. Even if it were possible to draw this line, a further problem would nevertheless remain. Remedies are often of a "hybrid" nature, which means that they encompass both "structural" and "behavioural" components at the same time.[809] Such hybrid remedies do not withstand a classification when one element is clearly dominant.[810] This applies for example for the "structural" element

Unternehmen eingegriffen wird"; Jaeger (2008), Art. 7, 18: "Der weit gefasste Begriff der Abhilfemaßnahmen struktureller Art umfasst alle (Abhilfe-) Maßnahmen, durch die in Eigentumsrechte, eigentumsgleiche Rechte (z.B. Patente, Markenrechte) und gesellschaftsrechtliche Beteiligungen der betroffenen Unternehmen eingegriffen wird".

[804]See Sect. 3.4.1.1.1, footnote 760 above.

[805]Davies/Lyons (2007), 43. They discuss the example of a license, which is paid up front. When the license is granted for an indefinite period, it is considered to bring about a clean break. This is, however, not the case, when the license is only granted for a short period. Intermediate periods are considered as a "grey area".

[806]See Sect. 3.4.1.1.2, footnote 770 above.

[807]See Sect. 3.4.1.1.1, footnote 762 above.

[808]Eg Alexiadis/Sependa (2013), 12, 15 and 24ff.

[809]See for merger remedies: eg Drauz (1997), 224f; Hauser (2009), 217f, fn 1290; Hoeg (2014), 44.

[810]Cf. Krings (2012), 229: "Zu fragen ist immer nach dem Schwerpunkt der Maßnahme [. . .]".

of a divestiture, which is usually accompanied by a multitude of auxiliary "behavioural" measures such as the obligations of the parties in the interim period, the appointment of trustees or non-reacquisition obligations.[811] However, it is not always possible to make out the dominant element of a hybrid remedy. A more recent example from merger control is the interoperability remedy accepted in the Cisco/Tandberg merger.[812] On the one hand, the remedy consisted of a divestment of IP to an independent industry body and the open sourcing of an IT protocol. On the other hand, Cisco committed to continue to implement this protocol as licensed by the independent body.[813] Italianer, then Director-General of DG COMP, described the former part of the remedy as "structural" and the latter as "behavioural".[814] The behavioural element is not a mere annex to the structural one since "the availability of the protocol would not be of use if Cisco did not itself continue using it".[815] Another example are the remedies accepted in Article 102 TFEU procedures against GDF[816] and E.On[817] for foreclosure of gas imports through long term booking of transmission capacities. The remedies consisted, on the one hand, of an "immediate divestiture of significant capacity"[818] and, on the other hand, of a commitment to limit capacity reservations for a period of 10 years to under 50% of the long term bookable capacity. Again, the former element of the commitments could be considered a "structural"[819] and the latter a "behavioural" one.[820] Moreover, it is not apparent that either the "structural" or the "behavioural" part of the commitments is more important.

Whether a satisfactory theory to distinguish structural and behavioural remedies can at all be developed and what such a theory might look like is beyond the scope of the present work. What can be said here is that its development would have to take a functional approach, which would start by identifying the purpose of the distinction.

---

[811] See the Merger Remedies Notice (2008), 107ff (interim period), 43 (non-reacquisition clause), 117ff (trustees).

[812] M.5669.

[813] See IP/10/377 and in particular the description by Italianer (2012), 8.

[814] Italianer (2012), 8.

[815] Italianer (2012), 8.

[816] COMP/39.316.

[817] COMP/39.317 (Gas).

[818] Italianer (2012), 8.

[819] But see von Rosenberg (2009), 239, who classifies the auctioning of capacity as a behavioural remedy.

[820] However, the "behavioural" part of the E.On commitments illustrates once more the difficulties to categorise remedies: The commitments left a choice to GDF and E.On how to limit the capacity reservations to under 50%. The undertakings could either return capacities to the transmission system operator or increase the capacity in the grid, cf. Summary Decision, 4. While prima facie the obligation to reduce capacity reservations seems to be "behavioural", the means to implement that obligation, ie the return of capacities to the system operator or the increase of capacity in the grid could also be considered as "structural". See also Sect. 3.4.2.1.2.2.1 with footnote 1055 and Sect. 3.4.2.1.2.2.2 with footnote 1071ff below.

Several purposes are imaginable, the most obvious being to express preferences for certain types of remedies over others in terms of certain characteristics.[821] Relevant characteristics are in particular the compatibility of a remedy with the underlying principles of Articles 101 and 102 TFEU and the principle of proportionality. However, the division of remedies in structural and behavioural ones is devoid of meaning if statements about these characteristics cannot be generalised for the two categories.[822] The following section will demonstrate that there are strong reasons for the latter assumption.

3.4.1.2 The Lack of Necessity of a Distinction: No General Subsidiarity of Structural Measures

From a legal point of view, a categorisation of remedies along the line of the structure—behaviour dichotomy is only necessary if there is some sort of legal preference of one category over the other. With respect to merger control, it is certainly true that in Gencor, the General Court stated that "commitments which are structural in nature [were], as a rule, preferable from the point of view of the Regulation's objective".[823] Nevertheless, the EU Courts have made it clear that this passage does not entail any formal legal consequences and that a case-by-case analysis is decisive.[824] This corresponds to the submissions of many commentators who take a critical stance on generalised preferences for structural remedies.[825] Hence, for merger control, it is broadly accepted that the distinction between structural and behavioural remedies is superfluous.[826]

[821]Cf. Prümmer (2007), 159: "Im Ergebnis ist somit festzuhalten, dass Marktstruktur und Marktverhalten zu sehr ineinander verflochten sind, als dass daraus ein rechtlich genügendes Abgrenzungskriterium entwickelt werden könnte, um die Wirksamkeit beziehungsweise Zulässigkeit von Zusagen von vornherein zu kategorisieren oder auf solcher Grundlage Präferenzen zu formulieren".

[822]See Maier-Rigaud (2012), 493: "Eine [. . .] Unterscheidung [struktureller und verhaltensorientierter Maßnahmen] wäre auch nur dann sinnvoll, wenn aus dieser Unterscheidung auch eine unterschiedliche Behandlung folgen würde. Dies ist aber [. . .] auch in Artikel 7 Abs. 1 nicht oder nur sehr begrenzt der Fall".

[823]See Sect. 3.4.1.1.3, footnote 776 above.

[824]See Sect. 3.4.1, footnote 730 and Sect. 3.4.1.1.3, footnotes 775 to 783 above. It is interesting to note that most judgments do not absorb the part of the Gencor formula according to which there is, as a rule, a preference for structural remedies. Most judgments only point out the importance of a case-by-case analysis: CJ, C-12/03 P (Tetra Laval, 2005), 86; GC, T-177/04 (Easyjet, 2006), 182; T-87/05 (EDP, 2005), 100; also in T-114/02 (Babyliss, 2003), 170, the General Court did not express a preference for structural remedies: It stated merely that "a sale of assets [was] often the most suitable corrective measure for easily remedying a competition problem, particularly in the case of horizontal overlap" and went on to underline the importance of a case by case analysis.

[825]Eg Prete/Nucara (2005), 703; Papandropoulos/Tajana (2006), 449f; Ezrachi (2006), 463; Prümmer (2007), 200 and 210; Papon (2009).

[826]See Sect. 3.4.1, footnotes 728 and 733 to 735 above.

However, as far as the enforcement of Articles 101 and 102 TFEU through Regulation 1/03 is concerned, the overwhelming majority of commentators advocates some sort of formal subsidiarity of structural to behavioural remedies, which would make a distinction necessary.[827] Also recital 37 of directive 2019/1 postulates such a subsidiarity, albeit in a slightly attenuated form which underlines the necessity to analyse the concrete circumstances of the case at hand.

Simplified, the two different lines of argumentation upon which such subsidiarity hypotheses rest can be summarised as follows: On the one hand, commentators derive limitations for the admissibility of structural remedies from the underlying principles of Articles 101 and 102 TFEU.[828] From this point of view, structural remedies are considered an element that is alien to the system of behavioural control set up by the prohibition of anticompetitive collusion and of abuse of a dominant position.[829] On the other hand, a priority of behavioural remedies is derived from the principle of proportionality. In the following sections, it will be submitted that neither of the two lines of argumentation can justify the generalised assumption of a subsidiarity of structural remedies to behavioural ones. This demonstration presupposes the existence of a definition for a structural remedy. Despite the already mentioned difficulties to draw a clear line, it will therefore be assumed that it is possible to distinguish structural from behavioural remedies. For the present purposes, a structural remedy shall be defined as one that changes the structure of an undertaking—regardless of how that latter concept is defined.

3.4.1.2.1 Subsidiarity of Structural Remedies and the Principles of Articles 101 and 102 TFEU

Standard arguments against structural remedies in Article 102 TFEU cases are that "abuse provisions aim at monitoring conduct whereas merger control aims at monitoring structures"[830] or that Article 102 TFEU does not prohibit dominance

---

[827] See Sect. 3.4.1, footnotes 736 and 737 above; see also BGH, KVZ 55/07 (Nord KS, 2008), 18: The Bundesgerichtshof held in essence that an interpretation of § 32 ARC according to which structural measures are subsidiary to behavioural ones due to the significant burden entailed by the former corresponds to Article 7(1) of Regulation 1/03.

[828] Articles 101 and 102 TFEU do not contain any direct statements, how far a remedy that is imposed for their infringement may go. The dogmatic construction of limitations must therefore rely on Article 103 TFEU. According to this provision, implementing legislation must be "appropriate [. . .] to give effect to the principles set out in Articles 101 and 102". It is controversial whether this prevents all modifications of the scope and substance of the primary law, cf. Rapp/Jung (2008), 2-16-004; Hauser (2009), 114f. In any event, the limitations under Article 103 TFEU are without prejudice to legislation based on different provisions such as Article 352 TFEU, cf. Rapp/Jung (2008), 2-16-004; Krings (2012), 131.

[829] See Immenga (2011), 296, according to whom the subsidiarity of structural remedies follows from the fact that Articles 101 and 102 TFEU concern the "conduct" of undertakings. Similarly Krings (2012), 229 fn 1087.

[830] BKartA, in OECD (2006), 121; see also eg Bauer (2008), 4-7-033: "[C]ontrol of a market structure is carried out only through merger control".

as such, but only its abuse.[831] Similar arguments can also be made with respect to Article 101 TFEU.[832] Such arguments face the conceptual difficulty that the "structure vs behaviour" dichotomy upon which they rely has at least three dimensions. Anticompetitive conduct, which is generally considered a legitimate object of a remedy, can be contrasted with three different allegedly illegitimate "structural" objects of a remedy, namely either the "general market structure" or the "structure of an undertaking", i.e. the undertaking's internal organisation, or, where Article 102 TFEU is concerned, the "dominant position" of the concerned undertaking. The concepts overlap to a large extent, but they are not necessarily identical.[833] For the present purpose, a further discussion of the three dimensions of the "structure vs behaviour" dichotomy is not necessary, because a structural remedy has been defined as one that changes the structure of an undertaking.

According to the view defended here, the fact that structural elements—regardless of whether they consist of the general market structure, the structure of the concerned undertakings or the existence of dominance—do not as such violate Articles 101 or 102 TFEU, but that a finding of anticompetitive conduct is always necessary, does not mean that structural remedies are generally incompatible with the principles of Articles 101 or 102 TFEU.[834] The said fact merely means that a structural remedy can only be imposed if it is prompted by anticompetitive conduct and if there is a sufficiently close link between the identified anticompetitive conduct and the object of the structural remedy. Three constellations where this can potentially be the case must be distinguished: First, the anticompetitive conduct itself can consist of a change in the structure of an undertaking. Second, the structure of an undertaking may be a precondition for anticompetitive conduct, in particular for

[831] See generally eg CJ, 322/81 (Michelin I, 1983), 57; C-209/10 (Post Danmark, 2012), 21, 22; AG Kirschner, T-51/89 (Tetra Pak I, 1990), 63; Commission Guidance Article 82, 1; Jones/Sufrin (2014), 272; Mestmäcker (1995), 445; Mestmäcker/Schweitzer (2004), § 15, 7 and § 20, 38; Wurmnest (2010), 107, 110; Roth (2011), 511; Fuchs/Möschel (2012), Art. 102, 2. With respect to the remedies discussion: eg Klees (2005), § 6, 78; Bauer (2008), 4-7-033; Kellezi (2010), 141; Hjelmeng (2013), 1014; Schütz (2013), Art. 7, 24; Voell (2014), 33ff.

[832] See Immenga (2011), 294: "Ausgangspunkt müssen die von der Kommission zu beurteilenden Formen des Wettbewerbsschutzes sein. [. . .] In der Fusionskontrolle [. . .] steht die Frage nach den Marktstrukturen [im Vordergrund]. Wettbewerbsbeschränkende Vereinbarungen [. . .] sowie der Missbrauch marktbeherrschender Stellungen betreffen unternehmerisches Verhalten. [. . .] Diese Skizze zeigt, dass Auflagen und Bedingungen [author's note: this is meant to include Article 9 decisions] jeweils unterschiedlicher Ansatzpunkte bedürfen". On the limits of such an approach see also Lübking (2011), 1227ff.

[833] For example, where the dominance of an undertaking is not the result of vertical integration, the disintegration of the undertaking through divestiture will interfere with the "structure of the undertaking", but leave the dominant position intact. This could be the case where a divestiture remedy splits up a two-product undertaking in order to prevent abusive tying, but leaves intact the dominant position(s) on the respective product market(s).

[834] See also Voell (2014), 47: "Der üblicherweise konstatierte Gegensatz von Marktverhalten und Marktstruktur lässt sich [. . .] auf Rechtsfolgenseite nicht aufrechterhalten. Somit stellt sich nicht die Frage, ob Struktureingriffe in die Verhaltensaufsicht systemkonform sind. Entscheidend ist vielmehr, welche rechtlichen und tatsächlichen Voraussetzungen erfüllt sein müssen".

abusive behaviour. Third, the structure of an undertaking can be the consequence of abusive conduct.

3.4.1.2.1.1 Anticompetitive Conduct Consists of a Change to the Structure of the Undertaking

There are several constellations in which changes to the structure of an undertaking can amount to an infringement of Articles 101 and 102 TFEU. A first example is the Continental Can case,[835] in which the Court of Justice confirmed that the acquisition of a competitor by an undertaking in a dominant position could constitute an abuse. Similarly, in BAT and Reynolds,[836] the Court of Justice ruled that Article 101 TFEU was under certain circumstances applicable to the acquisition of minority shareholdings. Certainly, Continental Can and BAT were decided at a time when the EU competition rules did not yet provide for specific rules on concentrations between undertakings. Today, the Merger Regulation precludes the enforcement of Articles 101 and 102 TFEU by the Commission within its scope of application.[837] Nevertheless, changes to the structure of an undertaking that fall outside the scope of the merger regulation may still be treated under Articles 101 and 102 TFEU.[838] For example, in the Gillette decision, the Commission found that the acquisition of a minority participation, which did not constitute a concentration within the meaning of Article 3 Merger Regulation, could amount to an infringement of Articles 101 and 102 TFEU.[839] Another example are partial-function joint ventures[840] or cooperative full-function joint ventures without a community dimension.[841] Since the Merger Regulation does not capture these, they must be assessed under Article 101 TFEU.[842] Finally, in Tetra Pak I,[843] the General Court held that the acquisition

[835]CJ, 6/72 (1973).

[836]CJ, 142/84 (1988), 37ff.

[837]See Article 21(1) MR and Schild (2008), 5-23-005ff; Hauser (2009), 193ff; Jones/Sufrin (2011), 896f; Whish/Bailey (2012), 845.

[838]Theoretically, this is the case for concentrations that do not meet the thresholds of Community dimension provided for in Article 1 MR and for acquisitions that do not constitute a concentration within the meaning of Article 3 MR. Practically, only the latter cases are of importance, see Koch (2008b), 5-1-116 and 5-1-119; Jones/Sufrin (2011), 863; Whish/Bailey (2012), 835, fn 41; Krings (2012), 208f.

[839]1993 OJ L 116/21 (Gillette, 1992); cf. Müller-Tautphaeus (2003), 271; Hauser (2009), 148; Krings (2012), 208.

[840]See Pohlmann (2008), 2-4-121; Hauser (2009), 197f; Jones/Sufrin (2011), 863; Whish/Bailey (2012), 837.

[841]See Article 21(1) MR and Pohlmann (2008), 2-4-084ff; Schild (2008), 5-23-014ff; Hauser (2009), 198.

[842]Dalheimer (2005), Art. 7, 11, and Bauer (2008), 4-7-032 and 034, mention joint ventures that are not captured by the MR as an example for the application of structural remedies under Article 7 of Regulation 1/03; similarly Emmerich (2014), § 32 ARC, 40; Jaeger (2010), § 32 ARC, 36; Wilhelmi (2013), 361; Bornkamm (2014), § 32 ARC, 32.

[843]T-51/89 (1990).

of an exclusive patent license could under certain circumstances be abusive.[844] All these cases share the common feature that the incriminated conduct consists precisely of a change in the structure of the undertakings concerned. Where this is the case, there can be little doubt that the Commission can order the undertakings to reverse the anticompetitive change in their structure.[845]

3.4.1.2.1.2 Structure of Undertaking Is a Cause for Anticompetitive Conduct

Cases in which the structure of an undertaking is the cause for anticompetitive conduct are relevant in particular with respect to Article 102 TFEU.[846] In this respect, most commentators agree that a structural remedy can, under certain conditions, also be compatible with the underlying principles of Article 102 TFEU if it addresses the causes of abusive conduct.[847]

3.4.1.2.1.2.1 The Conditions for the Compatibility of a Structural Remedy That Aims at the Causes of Abusive Conduct with the Underlying Principles of Article 102 TFEU

There is a variety of constellations in which the structure of an undertaking can potentially cause abusive behaviour and where the structure of an undertaking may for this reason—and without prejudice to further requirements, in particular the observation of the principle of proportionality—constitute the object of a remedy.[848] A broad set of constellations has been presented by Krings.[849] He shows that most

---

[844]The Tetra-Pak I case can be considered as an example of a "structural abuse"; cf. Mestmäcker/Schweitzer (2004), § 15, 14 and 30, who highlight the case's relation to the Continental Can doctrine; cf. also Kellezi (2010), 141f.

[845]See Ngoc (2007), 99f; Hauser (2009), 133ff; Krings (2012), 117f, 124, 207ff; Petzold (2012), 201 fn 784; see also Hjelmeng (2013), 1023, who discusses these cases under the headline "terminating harmful effects": "[. . .] structural measures would be appropriate where the competitive structure has been harmed on a lasting basis because of a single reversible legal transaction. For example where the acquisition of a minority shareholding constitutes an infringement under the Continental Can and Philip Morris doctrines, the Commission may order divestiture in order to terminate the restrictive effects".

[846]See Krings (2012), 159ff for theoretically imagineable Article 101 TFEU cases.

[847]See Ngoc (2007), 102f, 122; Koch (2008a), 78f and 152; Hauser (2009), 156ff; Kellezi (2010), 139ff; Krings (2012), 124, 145, 185ff. Implicitly also Dalheimer (2005), Art. 7, 14.

[848]The German Monopolkommission pointed out that it was not possible to come up with abstract classifications of constellations in which the structure of an undertaking causes abusive behaviour with a sufficient degree of likeliness to justify structural remedies. However, it indicated that this might in particular be the case where exploitative abusive practices occurred and where highly concentrated market shares existed; cf. MK (1980), 733. See also Koch (2008a), 115ff, who discusses refusals to grant access by vertically integrated companies and abusive cross subsidies as examples; Hauser (2009), 157ff, who discusses abusive cross subsidies and oligopolistic markets as examples; Kellezi (2010), 139, who mentions discriminatory practices by a vertically integrated undertaking and tying practices by multi-product companies as examples.

[849]Krings (2012), 185ff; for a similar overview also Voell (2014), 139ff.

types of abusive behaviour can somehow be linked back to the structure of the infringing undertaking. For example, Krings is of the opinion that a potential causal link between the structure of the undertaking and the abusive conduct can be assumed "without problems" for exploitative abuses[850] and margin squeeze[851] and essential facilities[852] cases. For other types of exclusionary conduct, such as predatory pricing, exclusivity relations, rebates and tying, he requests an analysis of the individual case.[853] As relevant criteria for this analysis he suggests for example the questions whether the resources for predatory pricing practices or rebates come from cross subsidies[854] or whether exclusivity relations or tying practices are only made possible vis-à-vis the dominant undertaking's customers due to the former's status as an unavoidable trading partner.[855]

However, it must be emphasised that the existence of an abstract, potential causal relation between the structure of the undertaking and the risk for a future infringement is not sufficient. The Commission must rather demonstrate the existence of the causal link according to the circumstances of the concrete case. Moreover, according to Recital 12 Regulation 1/03, the infringement caused by the structure of the undertaking must be "lasting or repeated". Overall, the Commission must therefore show that it is not sufficient to address the infringing conduct itself, because there is a substantial risk that the structure of the undertaking would cause the subsistence or recurrence of the infringing conduct.[856] In this latter regard, an analogy to the Tetra-Laval merger jurisprudence can be drawn.[857] The Commission prohibited the purchase of Sidel by Tetra-Laval, because it was concerned that Tetra-Laval would leverage its dominant position on the market for aseptic cartons onto the market for PET packaging, on which Sidel was active. The General Court annulled

[850] Krings (2012), 188: "[...] unproblematisch bejaht werden. Nur aufgrund der besonderen Unternehmensstruktur – in diesem Fall der marktbeherrschenden Stellung – und der damit verbundenen Tatsache, dass das Unternehmen keinem wesentlichen Wettbewerb ausgesetzt ist, wird das Fordern unangemessener Preise oder Konditionen ermöglicht". See also O'Donoghue/ Padilla (2013), 929, who consider that, in spite of the risks of structural remedies, "excessive pricing cases [...] might be a good candidate for considering structural remedies, but only where there is strong evidence that the market will not correct itself over time".

[851] Krings (2012), 195: "[...] unproblematisch zu bejahen. [...] Das zu beanstandende Verhalten wird gerade erst aufgrund der mehrstufigen Integration anderer Unternehmen auf vertikaler Ebene ermöglicht und ist damit als strukturbedingt zu bezeichnen."

[852] Krings (2012), 201: "[...] unproblematisch auszugehen. Eine besondere Struktur des Unternehmens – nämlich das Vorhandensein einer für den Markteintritt unerlässlichen Einrichtung – führt erst dazu, dass ein Verstoß gegen Art. 102 [AEUV] in dieser Form möglich wird."

[853] Krings (2012), 193 (predatory pricing); 196f (exclusivity relations); 199 (rebates); 199 (tying).

[854] Krings (2012), 193 (predatory pricing); 199 (rebates).

[855] Krings (2012), 197 (exclusivity relations); 205 (tying). Generally on the concept of an unavoidable trading partner see eg GC, T-336/07 (Telefonica, 2011), 149 and Commission, Guidance Article 82, 36.

[856] See Voell (2014), 73: "strukturinhärente Wiederholungsgefahr".

[857] See Koch (2008a), 112f; Hauser (2009), 209; Voell (2014), 73; similarly also Gyselen (2014), 256f, who refers to the General Electric case instead of Tetra Laval.

the decision, in essence because it found that the emergence of a structural incentive to engage in leveraging practices was not as such sufficient for a prohibition. According to the General Court, the Commission had failed to examine to the requisite legal standard whether, on the one hand, commitments offered by Tetra-Laval regarding its future conduct and, on the other hand, the eventual unlawfulness of the leveraging practices and the threat of enforcement action were capable of reducing or even eliminating the incentive to engage in the latter.[858] Applied to Article 7 Regulation 1/03, the Tetra-Laval jurisprudence thus confirms that a remedy which addresses the structure of an undertaking as it existed before the infringement was committed cannot simply be justified by the fact that the structure of the undertaking provides for an incentive to engage in anticompetitive conduct.[859] Rather, it is necessary to show that measures addressing the anticompetitive conduct directly will not be sufficient to prevent the infringements' recurrence or subsistence. In this respect, it is broadly accepted that the past behaviour of the undertaking can serve as a factual basis to examine whether measures addressing the anticompetitive conduct directly are sufficient to prevent its recurrence or subsistence.[860] The fact that an undertaking has repeatedly committed infringements of a similar type,[861] that it disregarded past remedies that addressed those infringements, or that an infringement occurred despite regulatory obligations,[862] constitutes strong evidence for the justification of a remedy addressing the structure of the undertaking as the cause of repeated or lasting infringements.

Recital 12 of Regulation 1/03 does, however, not necessarily require that several separate findings of comparable infringements in the past exist.[863] In that connection, it bears also mention that the above-mentioned analogy to the Tetra-Laval merger jurisprudence has limits. A merger control procedure is mostly of a

---

[858]See GC, T-5/02 (Tetra-Laval, 2003), 159ff. In C-12/03 P (Tetra-Laval, 2005), 74ff, the CJ confirmed the essential points of the judgment of the GC. Only in so far as the GC had postulated an obligation for the Commission to examine also to what extent enforcement on the national level was likely to deter future anticompetitive conduct, the CJ found that the GC had erred in law, because such an obligation "would run counter to the [Merger Regulation's] purpose of prevention" and "would be too speculative" (see paras 159 of the judgement of the GC and 75ff of the judgment of the CJ).

[859]See, with respect to § 32 ARC, also Wilhelmi (2013), 363: "Der Ansicht, dass die praktische Unvermeidbarkeit missbräuchlichen Verhaltens genüge, ist [. . .] nicht zu folgen".

[860]See eg Sullivan (2003), 410; Dalheimer (2005), Art. 7, 14; Koch (2008a), 114; Kellezi (2010), 142.

[861]Krings (2012), 236, rightly emphasises that it is not sufficient to show that an undertaking has repeatedly infringed Articles 101 or 102 TFEU, but that the infringements must constitute the repetition or continuation of a previously committed type of infringement. Similarly Koch (2008a), 79: "Der Schluss auf eine derartige Wiederholungsgefahr wird nur dann gerechtfertigt sein, wenn mehrere gleichartige Beschränkungshandlungen in der Vergangenheit festgestellt wurden".

[862]Lowe/Maier-Rigaud (2008), 607.

[863]Wilhelmi (2013), 364: "[. . .] ergibt sich aus Erwägungsgrund 12 S. 3 der VO 1/2003, der ja ein erhebliches Risko wiederholter Zuwiderhandlungen verlangt, noch kein Erfordernis wiederholt begangener Zuwiderhandlungen".

prospective nature. Typically, it will therefore not imply any findings regarding past infringements of the competition rules. On the contrary, proceedings for violation of Articles 101 or 102 TFEU are mostly retrospective. They normally imply a finding that the investigated company has committed an infringement in the past. It is submitted that it depends on the circumstances of the individual case whether past anticompetitive conduct that constitutes the subject of a current procedure can in itself suffice to justify the imposition of a remedy that addresses the structure of the investigated company.

Generally speaking, in particular the following two aspects need to be taken into account[864]: The strength of the indicia that the structure of the undertaking provides an incentive to continue the anticompetitive practices; and the effort necessary to suppress that incentive successfully through supervision. With a view to the former, factors that may play a role are in particular the duration, systemic nature and gravity of past infringements, regardless of whether they have led to separate infringement decisions or not. As far as the latter are concerned, important aspects are whether supervisory instruments have in the past prevented an occurrence of anticompetitive conduct and how high the costs of such supervisory instruments are. In that regard, it is submitted that the requirement of a "substantial risk of a lasting or repeated infringement that derives from the very structure of the undertaking" is still met, if the incentive to engage in future anticompetitive conduct can only be suppressed through unreasonable monitoring costs.

Summing up, the Commission may therefore impose a remedy that addresses not the infringing conduct, but its causes, if it proves to the requisite standard that there is a causal link between the object of the remedy and the infringing conduct and that directly addressing the latter would not prevent its recurrence or subsistence. The Commission's ARA decision[865] may serve as an illustration. The Commission found that ARA, the dominant Austrian provider of recycling services related to household packaging waste, had infringed article 102 TFEU by refusing to grant access to the nationwide collection infrastructure, which was partly controlled and partly owned by ARA and which could not be duplicated. As a remedy, the Commission ordered ARA in particular to divest the part of the household collection infrastructure which it owned. The Commission considered that this "structural" remedy was necessary to prevent the future recurrence of the infringement. In that regard, the Commission differentiated between the infrastructure which was owned by ARA and the infrastructure which this undertaking merely controlled. With regard to the latter, the Austrian Abfallwirtschaftsgesetz (AWG) had, after the end of the infringement, introduced a legal obligation which made it clear that ARA had to allow for the shared use of the infrastructure. However, as far as the part of the infrastructure which ARA owned was concerned, the AWG did not explicitly contain such an obligation and hence did not bring about the required degree of clarity, so that there

[864]For a more detailed discussion of the factors that may be relevant for the assessment whether there is a risk of a lasting or repeated infringement see Voell (2014), 77ff.

[865]COMP/39.759 (ARA, 2016).

remained a risk that ARA would in the future repeat the infringement by refusing to grant access to these parts of the infrastructure.[866] The reality of that risk and the insufficiency of a "behavioural" order to grant access were established by taking account of ARA's historic behaviour[867]: The undertaking had in the past repeatedly exploited legal uncertainties in order to refuse access to its infrastructure, despite the existence of an earlier exemption decision adopted by the Commission under article 101(3) TFEU and despite negotiations about the implementation of this decision that had lead to the modification of ARA's contracts in order to provide a clear framework to all relevant parties for a shared use of the infrastructure.

Although the ARA remedy was adopted on the basis of article 7, it is certainly no typical example of a unilaterally imposed divestiture.[868] In fact, ARA had itself proposed the remedy and admitted its necessity and proportionality in the context of a cooperative strategy adopted during the administrative procedure, for which the Commission granted the undertaking a 30% reduction of the fine.[869] While this exposes the remedy at first blush to concerns similar to the ones levelled at structural remedies adopted under article 9, a closer look appears to show that the necessity and proportionality of the remedy are plausibly motivated in the decision and that the remedy meets the standard of an article 7 decision.

3.4.1.2.1.2.2 Consequences for the Subsidiarity Hypotheses

The dependency of a remedy aiming at the structure of an undertaking as the cause of anticompetitive conduct of a prove that directly addressing the infringing conduct would not prevent the latter's recurrence or subsistence could, in principle, be understood as implying a subsidiarity of structural to behavioural remedies. For instance, in order to inflict the "structural" break up of a vertically integrated company that has engaged in a margin squeeze, the Commission must demonstrate the existence of a substantial risk that a "behavioural" remedy such as a cease and desist order or a price differential would not prevent the recurrence of the margin squeeze.

However, while the substance of this subsidiarity relation must be approved of, it is not necessary to express the subsidiarity in the terms of the dichotomy between structural and behavioural remedies. The prove that directly addressing the infringing conduct would not prevent its recurrence or subsistence is required for any remedy that addresses not the infringing conduct itself, but merely its causes—irrespective of whether the remedy is labelled as "structural" or "behavioural". In view of the difficulties to define structural remedies, it seems preferable to rely only

---

[866]The Commission found that, due to the requirement of nationwide coverage, the refusal of access to ARA's own infrastructure was enough to foreclose competitors from the entire market [COMP/39.759 (ARA, 2016), 143].

[867]COMP/39.759 (ARA, 2016), 144 and 147.

[868]See Wollmann (2017), 167, who considers the decision as "a step towards consent decrees in EU Antitrust proceedings".

[869]COMP/39.759 (ARA, 2016), 148 and 161f.

on the distinction whether a remedy directly addresses the infringing conduct or whether it merely eliminates its causes. This shall be illustrated with the following two examples. Both involve remedies that are difficult to classify as structural or behavioural.

3.4.1.2.1.2.2.1 Separate Accounts As a Remedy for a Margin Squeeze

If the infringement consists of a margin squeeze committed by a vertically integrated undertaking and the Commission wants to impose the keeping of separate accounts for the upstream and downstream businesses as remedy, it is immaterial whether the keeping of separate accounts is classified as a structural or behavioural remedy.[870] Since the keeping of separate accounts does not address the infringing conduct, namely the margin squeeze, as such, but merely one of its causes, the Commission can only impose the remedy, if it shows that unified accounts contribute to the occurrence of the margin squeeze and that merely addressing the latter directly, for instance by a cease and desist order, would not suffice to prevent its subsistence or recurrence.

3.4.1.2.1.2.2.2 IP Licenses As a Remedy for Excessive Pricing

In Volvo, the Court of Justice ruled that a car manufacturer's refusal to license a design right to a manufacturer of spare parts, even in return for a reasonable royalty, was not in itself abusive. However, the Court also found that such a refusal to license could amount to an infringement of Article 102 TFEU, if it involved "certain abusive conduct" such as the refusal to supply spare parts to independent repairers, the fixing of prices for spare parts at an unfair level or a decision no longer to produce spare parts for a particular model even though many cars of that model were still in circulation.[871] The judgment is sometimes interpreted as meaning that a duty to deal may be imposed as a remedy for other abuse categories than a refusal to deal, in particular for excessive pricing abuses.[872] From this perspective, the judgment fits the context of the present discussion. The imposition of a compulsory license as a remedy for excessive pricing can be perceived as a remedy that aims at eliminating the causes of the abusive conduct—namely the monopoly position secured by the IP right that enables the dominant undertaking to charge excessive prices—by introducing competition through the grant of licenses. O'Donoghue and Padilla rightly emphasise that, in principle, the correct remedy for an excessive pricing abuse is a reduction of the price by the excessive amount and that only where the latter remedy

---

[870]See Sect. 3.4.1.1.1 with footnotes 752 and 755 to 757 above for references regarding the controversial question whether unbundling remedies below the divestiture threshold, in particular the separation of accounts, should be classified as structural or behavioural.

[871]CJ, 238/87 (Volvo, 1988), 9.

[872]See Temple Lang (2003), 300f; O'Donoghue/Padilla (2013), 536 and 929; Jones/Sufrin (2014), 527.

is ineffective, a compulsory license may exceptionally be imposed.[873] However, in order to arrive at the conclusion that, in an excessive pricing case, a compulsory license remedy is subsidiary to a remedy that directly reduces the excessive price, it is not necessary to decide whether the imposition of a compulsory license must be classified as a structural or a behavioural remedy.[874] The said result follows already from the fact, that, in the present case, the license does not directly address the infringement, but merely its cause.

3.4.1.2.1.3 Structure of Undertaking Constitutes the Consequence of Anticompetitive Conduct

It is controversial, whether the compatibility of a structural remedy with the principles of Articles 101 and 102 TFEU can be justified by the fact that the remedy aims at the subsisting effects of an infringement. An extreme position wants to exclude this justification completely.[875] However, many commentators take a more nuanced approach according to which the principles of Articles 101 and 102 TFEU do not categorically exclude a structural remedy that merely aims at the consequences of the infringement.[876] It was shown above that, according to the Akzo and Ufex case law,

[873]O'Donoghue/Padilla (2013), 536 and 929.

[874]See Sect. 3.4.1.1.1 with footnotes 746, 747, 754ff and Sect. 3.4.1.1.4 with footnotes 784 and 788 for references regarding the controversial question whether an IP license constitutes a structural or a behavioural remedy.

[875]Krings (2012), 122ff, in particular 132: "Deutlich ist bisher [...] geworden, dass eine [eigentumsrechtliche Entflechtung] nicht mit der Begründung erlassen werden kann, eine Abhilfemaßnahme müsse den vor dem Wettbewerbsverstoß bestehenden Zustand der Marktstruktur wiederherstellen"; Voell (2014), 95: "Der Einsatz einer Entflechtung zur Folgenbeseitigung durch die Behörde ist [...] abzulehnen".

[876]Ngoc (2007), 96f, in particular 99: "[S]trukturelle Abhilfen [können] erforderlich sein, um den geschützten Wettbewerb wiederherzustellen, also den, der bestünde, wäre er nicht beschränkt worden"; Koch (2008a), 78: "Raum für eine Entflechtung im Sinne einer Folgenbeseitigung bleibt [...] allenfalls dann, wenn die wesentliche Kausalität des Missbrauchs für einen strukturellen Erfolg messbar ist"; idem, 136f: "Zielsetzung des Artikels 82 EG [...], die durchaus eine Folgenbeseitigung zulässt"; idem, 139: "Maßnahmen struktureller Art zur Beseitigung der durch einen Behinderungsmissbrauch verursachten Folgen [...] sind systemkonform"; Maier-Rigaud (2012, 496): "Der Rechtsprechung in der Sache Ufex folgend sind unter "wirksamer Abstellung" zusätzlich auch nachwirkende Effekte gemeint, die vom ursprünglichen Verhalten völlig entkoppelt sein können, aber eben dennoch durch dieses Verhalten erzeugt wurden. Dies schließt strukturelle Maßnahmen grundsätzlich ein"; Kellezi (2010), 143ff, in particular 146: "Si les mesures comportementales sont capables de réduire les barrières à l'entrée érigées par le[s] comportement [s] [abusifs] de l'entreprise en position dominante, la suppression desdits comportements n'agit pas sur d'autres barrières à l'entrée, pourtant occasionnées par ces comportements: les économies d'échelle et de gamme ou les effets de réseaux qui bénéficient désormais à l'entreprise en position seront difficilement partagés par les autres concurrents. Cette réflexion nous permet d'être prudents quant à la possibilité des mesures comportementales de restaurer totalement le degré de concurrence qui prévalait avant les comportements abusifs et de considérer l'adoption de mesures structurelles comme proportionnée". For the US, Salop/Romaine (1998), 666ff, plead in favour of structural remedies to eliminate the consequences of anticompetitive conduct.

the Commission can, in principle, impose remedies that address the consequences of an infringement. There is no reason why this power should not extend to structural remedies. Certainly, one might object that, where the infringing undertaking has strengthened its position at the cost of a competitor, "directly limiting [its] market share would seem anticompetitive" while "promoting new competition is the sole means of reversing the lingering effects".[877] However, requiring the offender to divest the part of its business that was acquired unlawfully and promoting new competition do not necessarily exclude each other. On the contrary, the Commission's practice regarding merger remedies shows that divestiture remedies typically serve the creation of a new competitive entity or the strengthening of existing competitors.[878] Moreover, in particular where anticompetitive conduct has benefited the infringer by leading to important network effects, economies of scale or scope or to the tipping of a market in favour of a certain technology, a structural remedy may, according to the circumstances of the case, be an appropriate way to bring competition back to the market.[879] Overall, it is hence submitted here that a structural remedy can also be justified with the goal to eliminate the lingering effects of anticompetitive conduct. However, as far as the precise requirements for such a remedy are concerned, it was already pointed out above[880] that the Commission faces a difficult burden as regards the proof of the causality between infringement, damage and remedy.

Finally, the importance of Recital 12, 3rd sentence, Regulation 1/03 for remedies that address the structure of an undertaking as a consequence of past anticompetitive conduct must be clarified. The latter provision applies only to "[c]hanges to the structure of an undertaking as it existed before the infringement was committed". It does hence not capture remedies that address a subsisting change in the structure of an undertaking that is the result of past anticompetitive conduct. For example, to the extent that an increase in market share of an undertaking on the downstream market is the result of an abusive margin squeeze, the Commission could—at least in theory—impose a horizontal divestiture remedy that aims at the corresponding lowering of the market share without having to meet the conditions of Recital 12, 3rd sentence, Regulation 1/03. However, the Commission might also address the lingering effects of the margin squeeze on the downstream market indirectly by ordering a vertical break

[877] Hjelmeng (2013), 1023.

[878] See the Merger Remedies Notice (2008), 22f: "Where a proposed concentration threatens to significantly impede effective competition the most effective way to maintain effective competition, apart from prohibition, is to create the conditions for the emergence of a new competitive entity or for the strengthening of existing competitors via divestiture by the merging parties. [...] The divested activities must consist of a viable business that, if operated by a suitable purchaser, can compete effectively with the merged entity on a lasting basis".

[879] See Kellezi, Sect. 3.4.1.2.1.3, footnote 876 above. See also Salop/Romaine (1998), 666; O'Donoghue/Padilla (2013), 945: "Since abusive conduct may have irreversible market consequences, behavioural remedies may be insufficient to restore the market to the competitive structure that existed before the anticompetitive conduct occurred"; also Voell (2014), 54.

[880] See Sect. 3.3.4.1.1.3.2 with footnotes 632ff above.

up of the company in order to strengthen competition on the downstream market. In the latter case, the remedy would address the structure of the undertaking as it existed before the infringement was committed. The primary goal of the remedy would be to eliminate the structure of the undertaking as a cause for future anticompetitive conduct. The reduction of the infringing undertaking's anticompetitively attained market share on the downstream market through increased competition would only be a side effect of the remedy. The Commission would therefore have to meet the requirements of Article 12, 3rd sentence, Regulation 1/03.

There is a third constellation in which it is questionable whether the requirements of Recital 12, 3rd sentence, Regulation 1/03 apply. The following simplified example shall serve as an illustration.[881] Suppose a dominant multiproduct company has ten facilities for the production of a widget. The company learns about of a potential competitor who wants to enter the market for widgets with two new production facilities. The dominant manufacturer engages into a predatory pricing strategy. That strategy is made possible by cross-subsidies from a different branch of its product portfolio. The predatory pricing is successful and prevents the entry. In order to remedy the subsisting effect on competition, the Commission could theoretically require the infringer to divest two of its production facilities. Such a remedy would not aim at the elimination of the cause of the predatory pricing strategy to prevent its recurrence.[882] Rather, it would pursue the goal of redressing the subsisting anticompetitive effects. Nonetheless, such a remedy would affect the structure of the infringer "as it existed before the infringement was committed". If taken literally, Recital 12, 3rd sentence, Regulation 1/03 would therefore apply. Since the dominant company's amount of production facilities for the widget is not creating a "substantial risk of a lasting or repeated infringement", Recital 12, 3rd sentence, Regulation 1/03 would oppose the imposition of the remedy.

It is, however, submitted that the wording of Recital 12, 3rd sentence, Regulation 1/03 is overbroad. The requirement that the structure of an undertaking that is addressed by a remedy must create a "substantial risk of a lasting or repeated infringement" only makes sense for remedies that aim at the prevention of the recurrence of an infringement through the elimination of its causes. The requirement does not make sense for remedies that aim at the elimination of the lingering effects of past anticompetitive conduct. Nor can Recital 12, 3rd sentence, Regulation 1/03 be interpreted as a general decision of the legislator against remedies that address the structure of an undertaking in order to remove such lingering effects. As explained above, Article 12, 3rd sentence, Regulation 1/03 protects only the structure of an undertaking "as it existed before the infringement was committed". This should be interpreted restrictively as not extending to the structure of an undertaking that is the consequence of anticompetitive conduct. A structure that existed already before the

[881] A concrete example from the Commission's practice will be discussed in the context of the CEZ Article 9 decision; see Sect. 3.4.2.1.2.3.1 with footnotes 1074ff below.

[882] To eliminate the causes of the predatory pricing strategy, the remedy would have to prevent the cross subsidies by breaking up the company along the lines of the different products.

infringement was committed, but that could only be maintained due to anticompetitive conduct should not be covered. In the described example, absent the predatory pricing, the entry of the competitor would have had a negative impact on the structure of the dominant undertaking in terms of market-shares. Either the dominant undertaking would have had to close two of its production sites for lack of profitability. Or there would have been an increase in the overall quantity of widgets produced. The maintenance of the dominant undertaking's market share is the result of the predatory pricing strategy. In the view defended here, the Commission can address it without having to prove that its remedy removes a "substantial risk of a lasting or repeated infringement".[883]

3.4.1.2.1.4 Conclusion

The preceding overview illustrates that structural remedies cannot generally be considered incompatible with the underlying principles of Articles 101 and 102 TFEU. The compatibility is beyond doubt for the cases, in which the incriminated anticompetitive conduct consists precisely in a change of the structure of the concerned undertaking. To claim a subsidiarity of structural remedies for these cases would be mistaken.[884] Whether structural remedies are also compatible with the principles of Articles 101 and 102 TFEU where they merely address a cause of anticompetitive behaviour or its consequence is less evident. It is submitted here that—if a distinction between structural and behavioural remedies were necessary—this should be accepted in both case. The requirement of a causal link between a concrete anticompetitive conduct and the structure of the undertaking makes the interference with the structure of the undertaking compatible with the principles established by Articles 101 and 102 TFEU, according to which public intervention in the market is only legitimate to address concrete anticompetitive conduct.

More importantly, however, the preceding overview demonstrates that it is not necessary to distinguish between structural and behavioural remedies in order to examine their compatibility with the principles of Articles 101 and 102 TFEU. In fact, in order to decide about a remedy's compatibility with the principles of Articles 101 and 102 TFEU, it is only necessary to distinguish between remedies that "mirror" the anticompetitive conduct and such that go "beyond",[885] because they address its causes or its consequences.[886] Remedies that merely mirror, i.e. stop or reverse, the anticompetitive conduct are without further conditions compatible with the principles of Article 101 and 102 TFEU, irrespective of their classification as structural or behavioural. For example, it is immaterial whether the dissolution of a joint venture that violates Article 101 TFEU, the divestiture of an abusively acquired

[883] See for a similar result, albeit with a slightly differing reasoning, Gauer/Kjølbye (2014), 12.178.

[884] It must, however, be admitted that the practical significance of such cases is limited.

[885] The distinction between remedies that "mirror the abuse" and those that go "beyond mirroring the abuse" is, in a different context, also made by Hellström/Maier-Rigaud/Bulst (2009), 58ff.

[886] See Krings (2012), 227, who defines behavioural remedies as such that mirror the abuse.

minority participation or patent license, the termination of abusively concluded exclusivity contracts or the grant of an abusively withheld access are classified as structural or behavioural remedies. All are without doubt compatible with the principles of Articles 101 and 102 TFEU, because they merely mirror the anticompetitive conduct.[887] In the same vein, it is superfluous to classify unbundling obligations below the divestiture threshold aimed at preventing a margin squeeze or an order to disgorge the illicit profits of a cartel as structural or behavioural. Their compatibility with the principles of Articles 101 and 102 TFEU is more problematic, because they go "beyond" the anticompetitive conduct and only address its cause or its consequence. They are only compatible with the underlying principles of Articles 101 and 102 TFEU, if a strict standard regarding the causality between the object of the remedy and the anticompetitive conduct is met.

Besides the preceding analysis, the argument that structural remedies cannot generally be considered incompatible with the underlying principles of Articles 101 and 102 TFEU is also supported by the developments regarding merger remedies.[888] If behavioural remedies are considered compatible with the "structural approach" of the merger regulation, there is little reason why structural remedies should be incompatible with the "behavioural approach" of Articles 101 and 102 TFEU.

3.4.1.2.2 Subsidiarity of Structural Remedies and Proportionality

This leads to the question whether the dichotomy between structural and behavioural remedies is necessary, because the principle of proportionality establishes a priority of behavioural remedies.[889] Klees has probably put forward the most elaborate argumentation that this is the case.[890] His theory rests on the generalised assumption that structural remedies are not only more effective to put an infringement to an end, but also more burdensome for the concerned undertakings. In its core, the theory postulates that the principle of proportionality, such as it constitutes a general principle of EU law and is codified in Article 7(1), 2nd sentence, forbids the imposition of a more effective, but also more burdensome structural remedy,

[887]The complicated question is of course, whether the respective conduct should be qualified as abusive at all. This question is, however, beyond the scope of this work. Cf. Möschel (1979), 32, who states with respect to the Continental Can judgement: "Problematisch ist dabei weniger die grundsätzliche Möglichkeit einer solchen Rechtsfolgenanordnung als auf der Seite der Tatbestandsvoraussetzungen die Frage, auf welche Sachverhalte von Zuwiderhandlungen sich ein Entflechtungsausspruch erstrecken kann".

[888]See Sect. 3.4.1 with footnotes 728ff above.

[889]See Krings (2012), 186 fn 878, according to whom the subsidiarity of structural measures follows from the principle of proportionality.

[890]Klees (2005), § 6, 75ff; Klees/Hauser (2007), 603; Klees (2010), 691 fn 35.The following authors all follow Klees suggestion: Jaeger (2008), Art. 7, 19f; Hauser (2009), 221ff; Krings (2012), 230ff.

where a less burdensome behavioural remedy suffices to put an infringement to an end. This means that, as soon as there is a "sufficiently effective" behavioural remedy, the Commission is barred from imposing a structural one, even if the latter would be more effective.[891] Klees concludes that if the Commission wants to impose a structural remedy, it is obliged to examine first whether behavioural remedies exist, that could also put the infringement in a sufficiently effective manner to an end.[892] Klees' student Hauser has proposed to apply this subsidiarity theory also to quasi-structural measures.[893]

Klees' subsidiarity theory has been fiercely criticised by Maier-Rigaud.[894] In essence, Maier-Rigaud's criticism rests on two pillars. On the one hand, Maier-Rigaud underlines that the questions, how effective and burdensome a certain remedy is, cannot be generalised and that these questions need to be analysed on a case-by-case basis.[895] On the other hand, he rejects the proposition that the principle of proportionality forbids the imposition of a more effective, but also more burdensome remedy where a less burdensome, but sufficiently effective remedy is available. Maier-Rigaud emphasises that the Commission must always choose the most effective remedy[896] and that the question, how burdensome a remedy is, arises only where two remedies are equally effective.[897] According to Maier-Rigaud, neither the wording nor the logic structure of Article 7(1) imply a subsidiarity of structural vis-à-vis behavioural remedies.[898] In order to show this he suggests the following paraphrasing of Article 7(1), 3rd sentence, which he considers "logically equivalent"[899]: "Behavioural remedies can only be imposed either where there is no more effective structural remedy or where any equally

[891] O'Donoghue/Padilla (2006), 735, put forward the identical argument: "If a behavioural remedy is sufficient to bring the identified infringement to an end, [. . .] it would have to be regarded as effective, in which case no structural remedy could be imposed"; K. Schmidt (2003), 1242, had also already insisted that the wording of Article 7(1) was incorrect and that it should read "sufficiently effective" instead of "equally effective".

[892] Klees (2005), § 6, 82; Hauser (2009), 226.

[893] Hauser (2009), 226: "Um eine praktische Relativierung der Subsidiarität struktureller Maßnahmen auszuschließen, muss die Verhängung verhaltensorientierter Maßnahmen mit strukturorientiertem Charakter den gleichen Anforderungen unterliegen wie die Verhängung einer eindeutig als strukturell zu qualifizierenden Maßnahme"; see also ibid, 155f.

[894] Maier-Rigaud (2012) and (2014); similarly already Lowe/Maier-Rigaud (2008), 606f. Also Voell (2014), 110ff expressly rejects the idea of a subsidiarity of structural measures.

[895] Maier-Rigaud (2012), 500: "allein empirisch zu beantwortende Frage der Wirksamkeit (Effektivität sowie Effizienz) und Eingriffsintensität von strukturellen und verhaltensorientierten Maßnahmen"; ibid., 498: "Diese Kriterien gilt es in jedem einzelnen Fall empirisch auszuloten."

[896] Maier-Rigaud (2012), 496: "Das oberste Ziel wettbewerbspolitischen Handelns ist nicht irgendeine, sondern eine ökonomisch möglichst effiziente Abstellung der Zuwiderhandlung. [. . .] Das substantielle Kriterium von Artikel 7 bleibt [. . .] Wirksamkeit, d. h. es gilt die wirksamste aller erforderlichen und verhältnismäßigen Maßnahmen zu wählen"; ibid., 493: "Unabhängig von Kategorisierungen geht es in VO 1/2003 natürlich um die wirksamste, noch verhältnismäßige und erforderliche Abstellung der Zuwiderhandlung".

[897] Maier-Rigaud (2012), 498: "lediglich wenn mehrere gleich wirksame Maßnahmen existieren, kommt die Maßnahme mit der geringsten Belastung für die Unternehmen zum Zuge".

[898] Maier-Rigaud (2012), 496 and (2014), 15.

[899] Maier-Rigaud (2012), 500, and (2014), 16.

effective structural remedy would be equally or more burdensome for the undertaking concerned than the behavioural remedy".[900]

Between the extreme positions of Klees and Maier-Rigaud lies for instance the more nuanced approach of Dalheimer.[901] On the one hand, it coincides with Maier-Rigaud's proposition under two aspects. First, Dalheimer abstains from making any generalised assumptions about the respective effectiveness of behavioural and structural remedies. Second, she underlines that the Commission is not obliged to rely on a less effective behavioural remedy, where a more effective structural one is available. On the other hand, Dalheimer states that Article 7(1), 3rd sentence, relies on the assumption that a behavioural remedy is less burdensome for the concerned undertakings. She claims that the Commission is therefore exposed to a particular obligation to state reasons where it considers that a structural remedy is less burdensome.

The legislator of directive 2019/1 also opted for a nuanced approach. On the one hand, recital 37, fourth sentence, states that structural remedies "can be presumed to be more burdensome for the undertaking than behavioural remedies". On the other hand, the fifth sentence of the same recital underlines that "this should not preclude NCAs from finding that the circumstances of a particular infringement justify the imposition of a structural remedy because it would be more effective in bringing the infringement to an end than a behavioural remedy."

The controversy whether the principle of proportionality imposes a priority of behavioural remedies thus depends on the one hand on whether one makes generalised assumptions about how effective and burdensome the respective types of remedies are. On the other hand, the controversy is based on different views on whether advantages, which one type of remedy has over the other in terms of effectiveness, can justify the imposition of a more burdensome remedy, where a less burdensome, but sufficiently effective one is available. In order to demonstrate that, from a proportionality perspective, there is no preference for either structural or behavioural remedies and that the dichotomy is hence superfluous, it is in principle enough to deal with the first aspect and to show that no generalised assumptions how effective and burdensome the respective remedies are can be made. Nonetheless, for the sake of completeness, also the second aspect shall briefly be touched upon below.

3.4.1.2.2.1 Are Generalised Assumptions About the Intrusiveness and Effectiveness of Structural and Behavioural Remedies Possible?

3.4.1.2.2.1.1 Can Structural Remedies Be Considered As Generally More Burdensome?

Many commentators assume that structural remedies are—at least as a rule—more burdensome than behavioural ones.[902] This appears correct if one contrasts the

[900] Maier-Rigaud (2012), 500 and (2014), 16.

[901] Dalheimer (2005), Art. 7, 12.

[902] Eg Klees (2005), 81; O'Donoghue/Padilla (2006), 682; Hauser (2009), 222; Krings (2012), 230, 233.

divestiture of parts of a company with a simple cease and desist order as remedies in a predatory pricing case.[903] However, when generalised, such assumptions often lack a satisfactory justification.[904] The contrary opinion, according to which the burden brought about by a remedy must be assessed on a case-by-case basis, is preferable.[905] In order to demonstrate this, it will be assumed that not only all sorts of divestitures, but also unbundling obligations below the divestiture level, constitute structural remedies and that obligations to grant access constitute behavioural remedies.[906]

If one takes this classification as a starting point, it is obvious, first, that neither structural nor behavioural remedies do necessarily require a formal transfer of a

---

[903]In the economic literature, it has, however, been argued that ownership unbundling may have a positive impact on shareholder's return where the company to be divested is a medium sized or large firm and that therefore the opposition to ownership unbundling may be irrational; see Rammerstorfer (2010); see also Lowe/Maier-Rigaud (2008), 604: "behavioural remedies may be more burdensome than structural remedies in particular in cases where a rather competitive takeover market for the business to be severed exists. In that case, the price obtained for the business is likely to be at least close to the expected discounted future revenue stream that the business will generate as a stand alone unit". Also Maier-Rigaud (2014), 5f, seems to suggest that structural remedies may be advantageous from the perspective of the concerned undertaking.

[904]For example, Hauser (2009), 222, simply suggests that it follows from Article 7(1), 3rd sentence, that structural remedies are more burdensome: "Dass strukturelle Maßnahmen allerdings regelmäßig eingriffsintensiver und damit belastender für die betroffenen Unternehmen sein werden, während das Gegenteil nur ausnahmsweise der Fall ist, folgt aus Artikel 7(1) Satz 3 Halbsatz 1 VO 1/2003 [. . .]". This is little convincing, because the intensity of an intervention is a question of fact, which cannot be derived from a legal text. Krings (2012), 233, infers the higher burden of a structural remedy from its increased durability: "Da eine strukturelle Maßnahme einen dauerhaften Eingriff in die Unternehmensstruktur bedeutet und damit eine dauerhafte Veränderung dieser Struktur bewirkt, handelt es sich bei der strukturellen Maßnahme regelmäßig um das stärker belastende Mittel". This is also little convincing: According to Krings' own classification, access remedies are behavioural (cf. 227) and unbundling remedies below the divestiture level are structural (cf. 142f and 228). However, if an access remedy is imposed for an indefinite period, it is – from a durability point of view – as burdensome as a divestiture. Similarly, an obligation to unbundle managements can be imposed only temporarily and therefore – from a durability point of view – be less burdensome than an obligation to grant access for an indefinite period.

[905]See Commission, in OECD (2006), 181: "[I]t will also depend on the individual circumstances of the case and of the envisaged remedies, whether a structural measure is more burdensome than a behavioural obligation. [A] behavioural remedy in the form of price control, with accompanying accounting requirements and monitoring for an extended duration, may be significantly more burdensome than a structural remedy in the form of an obligation to sell a shareholding"; Maier-Rigaud (2011), Sect. 3.4.1.2.2, footnote 895 above; Bougette/Marty (2012), 23: "[C]omparer les contraintes posées par les deux types de remèdes n'est pas une sinécure même si on pourrait être tenté de conclure qu'un remède comportemental est moins contraignant puisqu'il ne touche pas aux fondamentaux sur les droits de propriété. Malgré tout, des remèdes comportementaux qui réduisent la liberté de contracter ou forcent l'accès des tiers à des actifs précieux peuvent également être de nature contraignante bien plus forte qu'un transfert d'actifs déjà autonomes. Tout dépendra bien évidemment du périmètre de l'engagement imposé".

[906]Such classifications are used eg by Hauser (2009), 8ff, and Krings (2012), 142f and 227f, who are both of the opinion that structural remedies are generally more burdensome than behavioural ones.

property right. However, this makes it difficult to say that, appreciated from the perspective of a remedy's degree of interference with property rights, one category is more burdensome than the other. There is little reason to suggest that unbundling obligations below the divestiture level, such as the obligation to separate accounts or managements, interfere more heavily with property rights than an obligation to grant access. Second, in particular if one looks at implementation costs for the concerned undertaking, there are good reasons to assume that behavioural remedies are not generally the gentler ones.[907] Albeit certainly an extreme example, the E.On commitments decision[908] illustrates this well: Since the concerned balancing market was organised on a quarter of an hour basis, the Commission found that a behavioural remedy controlling E.On's purchasing behaviour would have been more burdensome for E.On than the divestiture of its electricity network.[909] But also in less extreme cases, it is not obvious that the implementation of an access remedy should be less burdensome for the concerned undertaking than the implementation of the divestiture of the respective part of its business or of an asset.[910] Third, generalised statements about whether structural remedies are more burdensome than behavioural ones are hindered by the fact that for both structural and behavioural remedies, the respectively entailed degree of burden depends to a large extent on the concrete design of the remedy. In this respect, the compensation granted for the remedy and the latter's duration play an important role. Somewhat exaggerated, it is hard to see why the divestiture of a patent at a "fair" price and with a short non-reacquisition period should be more burdensome than the royalty free grant of an exclusive license for an indefinite period.

3.4.1.2.2.1.2 Can Structural Remedies Be considered to Be Generally More Effective?

In order to refute the hypothesis that the principle of proportionality imposes a general subsidiarity of structural remedies, it is sufficient to show that structural remedies are not generally more burdensome than behavioural ones. Nevertheless, for the sake of completeness, it must be pointed out that a preference for either type of remedy can also not be inferred from generalised assumptions about effectiveness. For this purpose, the intense debate about the effectiveness of remedies in general shall

---

[907]Hauser (2009), 228, and Krings (2012), 234, are of the opinion that cases in which a behavioural remedy is more burdensome due to its increased duration and implementation costs are merely hypothetical.

[908]COMP/39.389, 86; the example is taken from Maier-Rigaud (2012), fn 10.

[909]Critically Klees (2009), 381f and (2011), 18. In the latter contribution (fn 38), he refers to an obligation to carry out a transparent, non-discriminatory procurement procedure as a less onerous "behavioural" alternative. Klees does, however, not take the frequency of the transactions into account.

[910]See GC, T-69/89 (RTE, 1995), 105: RTE argued that the monitoring of the licenses it was obliged to grant "would entail a disproportionate burden in terms of cost and personnel". Admittedly, this argument was not made in comparison to a divestiture of the concerned IP.

not be repeated here in all its facets.[911] It suffices to highlight some major points. First, while it may be easier to appreciate whether a remedy has put an identified anticompetitive conduct to an end, an evaluation of its effectiveness in terms of its overall impact on the market is from the outset exposed to serious methodological problems.[912] This applies independently of whether a remedy is structural or behavioural. On the one hand, market entry of competitors, their persistence on the market[913] or the development of market shares[914] are but approximate indicators of the competition restored or enabled by a remedy. On the other hand, the existence of exogenous factors[915] and the lack of counter-factual scenarios[916] make statements about a remedy's effectiveness particularly prone to errors. Any statements about a type of remedy's effectiveness in terms of its overall impact on the market must hence from the outset be met with caution.[917] While this applies also to the ex post analysis of remedies, it is even more true for the prognostic perspective which competition authorities necessarily have to take when they impose a remedy.[918]

Second, still with a focus on a remedy's overall impact on a market, the general trend in the US seems to favour behavioural remedies. Hovenkamp points out that "[u]nsatisfactory experiences with structural remedies have led to the current trend

[911] See for more detailed discussions in particular of structural remedies see eg Oehler (1976), 210ff; Möschel (1979), 61ff; Posner (2001), 104ff; Hauser (2009), 68ff; Epstein (2009); Bougette/Marty (2012). For an overview of various merger remedies studies conducted by the Commission, the US FTC, the OECD and the ICN see eg Hauser (2009), 75f; Hoeg (2014), 21ff.

[912] Cf. Hauser (2009), 76f; Commission Merger Remedies Study (2005), 17ff. For an attempt to evaluate the effectiveness of several decisions in which the Bundeskartellamt had addressed long-term gas supply contracts see Zapfe/Mecke (2011).

[913] See Bougette/Marty (2012), 10.

[914] See Commission Merger Remedies Study (2005), 128.

[915] In the Commission Merger Remedies Study (2005), 17f, the liberalisation of an industry or the entry of a rival independently of a divestiture remedy are mentioned as exogenous factors that make assessments difficult.

[916] In the Commission Merger Remedies Study (2005), interviews with industry participants were used to provide for views on counterfactual scenarios. It was admitted that all counterfactual scenarios remained nevertheless speculative (28). For the difficulties of counterfactual scenarios see also Bougette/Marty (2012), 36 and 54.

[917] Again, the Commission Merger Remedies Study (2005) illustrates this well: The study concludes that "overall, [joint venture] remedies were the most effective type of remedy, while the effectiveness of access remedies was weak" (171). However, it is admitted that "the assessment of the effectiveness of the [...] access remedies [...] was frequently limited to a verification of whether implementation had actually occurred, with supplemental market information being considered, where it existed", that "neither was there an opportunity to systematically interview the companies which had complained of possible foreclosure risks during the initial investigation, nor to interview companies which could, but did not, seek to benefit from the access commitment" and that such "limitations and difficulties encountered in collecting all the necessary information naturally circumscribe the robustness of the statistical results presented in [the] Study, which should therefore be treated as mainly indicative" (18).

[918] Cf. Dalheimer (2005), Art. 7, 14, who points out that all remedies are future oriented and that therefore a prognosis is decisive.

toward "regulatory", or conduct-oriented decrees".[919] However, such a preference for behavioural remedies is often not owed to a belief in their higher effectiveness, but due to their appraisal as the lesser evil.[920]

Third, as far as the European debate about remedies under Article 7 of Regulation 1/03 is concerned, two advantages of structural remedies vis-à-vis behavioural ones are advanced in order to justify the former's alleged increased effectiveness: On the one hand, structural remedies are considered more durable[921] than behavioural ones, because they deprive the dominant operator of the possibility[922] or at least the incentive[923] to engage in abusive conduct. On the other hand, structural remedies are said not to require medium or long-term monitoring.[924] However, in line with many commentators,[925] it is submitted that these two potential advantages of structural remedies cannot be turned into a generalised assumption that structural remedies are more effective than behavioural ones.[926] In the first place, the two

[919]Hovenkamp (2008), 301; see also Waller (2012); for an more positive view on structural remedies see Carstensen (2012), 825: "can on balance have positive effects [;] little hard evidence on any significant adverse effects on efficiency [;] failure of regulatory type decrees".

[920]See Epstein (2009), 206: "There is something to be said for modest "behavioral" remedies limiting certain kinds of contractual provisions. The best evaluation of these is that they do little good, but, by the same token, do little harm as well. The same cannot be said of the more ambitious effort to impose "structural" remedies intended to break up the unitary corporate structure of firm"; Hovenkamp (2008), 302: "But our experience with conduct remedies has also not been satisfying"; Bougette/Marty (2012), 10ff, who point out that US literature generally takes a rather sceptic stance on the effectiveness of both structural and behavioural remedies in terms of their overall impact on a market.

[921]Cf. Merger Remedies Notice (2008), 15: "commitments with are structural in nature [...] prevent, durably, the competition concerns"; Klees (2005), 81, who relies on the Merger Remedies Notice (2001), 9, to assume that structural remedies put an infringement to an end in a "more durable, more comprehensive and hence also more effective manner" (my translation); see also Italianer (2012), 5: "Once the mandated divestiture has taken place, the change in the market structure will solve the antitrust concerns if behavioural commitments cannot do the job. There will be virtually no way to circumvent the remedy or alter its effectiveness. [...] The divestiture remedies in the RWE and ENI cases] ensured that the abuse could never be repeated and created the conditions for undistorted competition downstream."

[922]Krings (2012), 231.

[923]See the references in Sect. 3.4.1.1.1, footnote 762 above.

[924]Cf. Merger Remedies Notice (2008), 15; Bougette/Marty (2012), 24; Maier-Rigaud (2014), 4ff. But see also Bougette/Marty (2012), 43, where they infer from the US experience in the AT&T case that structural remedies can have high implementation costs and require close monitoring.

[925]See eg Maier-Rigaud (2012), Sect. 3.4.1.2.2, footnote 895 above. Also Hauser (2009), 224, correctly takes a critical stance towards a generalised assumption of a superiority of structural measures. Similarly for merger remedies eg Ezrachi (2006), 463; Papandropoulos/Tajana (2006), 449f; Papon (2009).

[926]But see Klees (2005), 81: "Geht man davon aus, dass strukturelle Maßnahmen Zuwiderhandlungen dauerhafter, umfassender und damit im Ergebnis auch wirkungsvoller abzustellen vermögen, wird es regelmäßig an einer gleich wirksamen verhaltensorientierten Maßnahme fehlen"; Wolter (2011), 114: "strukturelle Maßnahmen [können] langfristig etwaige Wettbewerbsverstöße sicherlich am effektivsten verhindern"; Krings (2012), 231f: "[E]ine strukturelle Maßnahme [vermag] eine Zuwiderhandlung wesentlich dauerhafter und auch wirkungsvoller abzustellen als eine [verhaltensorientierte] Maßnahme [...] An verhaltensorientierten Maßnahmen gleicher Wirksamkeit [...] dürfte es daher regelmäßig fehlen".

described advantages are not, or not to the same extent, inherent to all types of "structural" remedies. For example, unbundling obligations below the divestiture level or information firewalls may be imposed temporarily and require monitoring. A one time "divestiture", or "release", of transport capacity will not durably put an end to an infringement that results from long term capacity reservations—the dominant undertaking must be enjoined from making such reservations for the future.[927] Horizontal unbundling that aims at the elimination of the consequences of past anticompetitive behaviour does not address the incentives for future anticompetitive conduct that are caused by vertical integration. More generally, where multiproduct or vertically integrated undertakings are concerned, a break up does not necessarily disperse monopoly power.[928] In the second place, the focus on the two described advantages seems myopic, because it merely takes into account the effectiveness of a remedy for putting the abusive conduct to an end. However, such a focus fails to see that there may be important disadvantages of a structural remedy in terms of overall efficiency. A structural remedy may have a negative impact on efficiencies created for example by network effects,[929] economies of scale[930] or vertical integration.[931] A behavioural remedy may allow preserving such efficiencies.[932] In the third place, in particular in fast moving markets, a flexible behavioural remedy may be preferable to an irreversible structural one.[933] In the fourth place, according to the circumstances of the individual case and just like behavioural remedies, structural ones may prove complicated to implement. Difficulties may result in particular from the need to identify a viable object for a divestiture[934] and a suitable purchaser.[935]

[927]See Sect. 3.4.1.1.4 with footnotes 816 to 820 above.

[928]Cf. Hovenkamp (2008), 301; Krings (2012), 205.

[929]See Koch (2008a), 316f; Epstein (2009), 225f.

[930]See eg Posner (2001), 112ff; Koch (2008a), Hovenkamp (2008), 156; Hauser (2009), 78f.

[931]See Koch (2008a), 313. With respect to mergers Ezrachi (2006), 463.

[932]With respect to mergers Ezrachi (2006), 463; OECD (2011c), 20.

[933]With respect to mergers Ezrachi (2006), 463; OECD (2011c), 20; see also Waller (2012).

[934]See Hauser (2009), 234ff; Bougette/Marty (2012), 44. With respect to mergers Merger Remedies Notice (2008), 23ff; Commission Merger Remedies Study (2005), 142ff; Hoeg (2014), 79.

[935]See Hauser (2009), 238f; Bougette/Marty (2012), 44. With respect to mergers OECD (2011c), 20: "The success of a structural divestiture depends largely (if not exclusively) on the existence of suitable purchasers interested in acquiring the assets to be divested. The recent financial and economic turmoil has emphasised the fact that there may be circumstances when there are simply no purchasers interested in these assets." See also Merger Remedies Notice (2008), 47ff; Commission Merger Remedies Study (2005), 160ff; Hoeg (2014), 101ff.

3.4.1.2.2.2 *Can the Advantages of a More Burdensome Structural Remedy in Terms of Effectiveness Justify Its Imposition Despite the Existence of a Less Burdensome and Sufficiently Effective Behavioural Alternative?*

The question has already been answered above[936] in the context of the general discussion of the principle of proportionality. It was submitted that the Commission could not be compelled to pursue its goal of putting an infringement to an end with a less effective alternative, as long as the more effective and more burdensome remedy meets the third step of the proportionality test. This conclusion applies also to the comparison of a structural and a behavioural remedy. Hence, where a structural remedy proves to be more effective to put an infringement to an end, for example because vertical unbundling removes the incentives of the infringing undertaking to continue its anticompetitive practices in a durable manner and entails less monitoring costs, such a remedy meets the second step of the proportionality test. It must be considered as necessary. Contrary to what is defended by some of the proponents of the subsidiarity hypothesis,[937] the Commission does not have to rely on a less burdensome, but still "sufficiently" effective behavioural alternative. Recital 37 of directive 2019/1 seems to confirm this conclusion. It states explicitly that the more burdensome nature of a structural remedy should not preclude NCA's from imposing such a remedy, if the latter is more effective than the behavioural remedy.

However, this does not mean that the burden entailed by the structural remedy does not have to be taken into account. The Commission can only impose the structural remedy, if it satisfies the overall balancing of costs and benefits that takes place in the third step of the proportionality test.[938] The outcome of the balancing test depends again on the circumstances of the individual case. Overall, the principle of proportionality does hence not impose a general subsidiarity of structural remedies.

---

[936] See Sect. 3.2.1.2 with footnotes 102ff above.

[937] See Sect. 3.4.1.2.2 with footnotes 890ff above.

[938] At least to some extent, this seems to be admitted also be Maier-Rigaud (2012), 496 and (2014), 12, who emphasises that all remedies must meet the requirement of proportionality. It must, however, be pointed out that Maier-Rigaud suggests a more complex proportionality test that deviates from the classic "German" three step model that was followed here and that also seems to be followed by the EU Courts (see Sect. 3.2.1.1, footnote 94 above). It cannot therefore be said with sufficient clarity whether Maier-Rigaud's approach corresponds to the one that was suggested here.

See in that connection Maier-Rigaud (2014), 10: "Proportionality is typically not an ultimate selection criterion for remedies and the same applies to necessity. Necessity is a general filter that determines whether the remedy is *generally capable of bringing the infringement to an end, does not go beyond this goal* and *does not concern aspects that are not part of the procedure.* In contrast to German law, the European concept of proportionality says nothing about effectiveness just as effectiveness says nothing about proportionality. A more effective remedy is therefore not automatically a less proportionate one in the sense of a milder means".

3.4.1.2.3 Concluding Example: Nord KS/Xella

Summing up, the distinction between structural and behavioural remedies is not necessary, because neither the underlying principles of Articles 101 and 102 TFEU nor the principle of proportionality impose a formal preference of behavioural remedies. In view of the difficulties to draw a line, the distinction should be given up and a case-by-case analysis should be applied that is independent of the type of remedy. This would also correspond to the developments in merger control. A last example shall illustrate the arbitrariness of the application of the dichotomy between structural and behavioural remedies and of the hypothesis of a subsidiarity of structural remedies: The German case Nord KS.[939]

Having found that a joint venture active in the production of and trade with sand-lime bricks infringed § 1 ARC,[940] the Bundeskartellamt ordered one of the mother companies to withdraw from the joint venture. The court of appeal interpreted § 32 ARC, upon which the remedy was based, expressly in the light of Article 7 of Regulation 1/03, into which it read a subsidiarity of structural measures.[941] It quashed the order of the Bundeskartellamt, because it found that a less burdensome "behavioural" remedy was available, namely the order to "abstain from a further implementation of the articles of association"[942] of the joint venture. The court argued that the latter order would interfere less with the mother company's entrepreneurial freedom, because it left the choice between several options: The mother company could either withdraw from the joint venture; it could change the joint venture into a "concentrative" one by transferring its own sand-lime brick activities to the joint venture or by giving up its own sand-lime brick activities; it could change its participation in the joint venture to a merely financial one.[943] The result of the judgment is not necessarily wrong. The solution of the court of appeal leaves more entrepreneurial freedom to the mother company and can therefore be considered as less burdensome. Little convincing, however, is that the court of appeal qualified its own solution as "behavioural".[944] The three options for the mother company which the court of appeal

---

[939]OLG Düsseldorf, VI-Kart 14/06 (V) (2007); confirmed by BGH, KVZ 55/07 (Nord KS, 2008). For a discussion of the remedy see Ulshöfer (2011), 830f; Lohse (2011), 832.

[940]The provision is the equivalent of Article 101 TFEU. In the present case, the court of appeal found that Article 101 TFEU could not be applied, because the Bundeskartellamt had not proved that there was an appreciable effect upon trade between member states (31).

[941]OLG Düsseldorf, Sect. 3.4.1.2.3, footnote 939 above, 34: "§ 32 Abs. 2 GWB ist Art. 7 Abs. 1 VO 1/2003 nachgebildet, so dass die dort vorgesehenen Regelungen eine Orientierungshilfe bieten. [...] Strukturelle Maßnahmen sind also wegen ihrer erheblichen Eingriffsintensität stets gegenüber den verhaltenbezogenen Maßnahmen subsidiär."

[942]OLG Düsseldorf, Sect. 3.4.1.2.3, footnote 939 above, 36: "erforderlich, aber auch ausreichend, [...] eine weitere Durchführung des (nach § 1 GWB nichtigen) Kommanditgesellschaftsvertrages zu untersagen."

[943]OLG Düsseldorf, Sect. 3.4.1.2.3, footnote 939 above, 36. The court left it open, whether the last option would be compatible with § 1 ARC.

[944]But see K. Schmidt (2011), 958, who explicitly agrees with the reasoning of the OLG Düsseldorf and its confirmation by the Bundesgerichtshof.

pointed out all imply changes in the "structures" of the joint venture and the mother company. But can the mere fact that a remedy leaves a choice between several "structural" measures make it a "behavioural" one[945]? The case shows once more that the distinction between structural and behavioural remedies is not necessary: The court of appeal could simply have argued that its own solution was less burdensome.

3.4.2 *Evaluation of the Criticism Regarding Structural Remedies Under Article 9*

3.4.2.1 Energy Sector

In the energy sector, the Commission has made several "structural" commitments binding. As explained above,[946] critics of the Article 9 procedure invoke these commitments in support of the allegation that the Commission instrumentalises the procedure for regulatory purposes. For instance, the German Monopolkommission expressed its "strongest possible reservations" against the Commission's approach. The latter was conceived by the Monopolkommission as improper recourse to Article 102 TFEU procedures in pursuit of the political goal to design the structure of the energy markets.[947] In order to assess whether such criticism is justified, it is useful to distinguish between two types of commitments: Those that entail a vertical unbundling through a divestiture of transmission grids; and those that entail a horizontal unbundling through a divestiture of production capacities. Moreover, the Swedish Interconnectors decision will be analysed.

3.4.2.1.1 Vertical Unbundling Through Divestiture of Transmission Grids

The vertical separation of the transmission networks from other parts of the supply chain has for a long time formed part of the EU's strategy to liberalise the energy sector. Starting off from comparatively weak obligations to keep separate accounts, the provisions on vertical unbundling contained in the various liberalisation directives were gradually reinforced.[948] In its 2007 sector inquiry, the Commission

[945]See also the example in Sect. 3.4.1.1.4, footnote 820 above. Bornkamm (2014), § 32 ARC, 32, rightly mentions the Nord KS case as a clear example for the admissibility of a structural remedy, because he considers that also the underlying infringement, i.e. the conclusion of the anticompetitive joint venture agreement, has a structural nature.

[946]See the references in Sect. 3.1.2.3, footnote 41 above.

[947]MK (2009), 495: "[...] in den vorliegenden Fällen [wird] das politische Ziel einer adäquaten Gestaltung der Marktstruktur in sachwidriger Weise mit Missbrauchsverfahren gegen marktbeherrschende Verbundunternehmen verknüpft. Die Vorgehensweise der Europäischen Kommission trifft daher auf die größten Bedenken der Monopolkommission."

[948]Pursuant to Article 14(3) Directive 96/92/EC and to Article 13(3) Directive 98/30/EC, integrated electricity and gas companies had to keep separate accounts for their generation, transmission and

concluded that the current level of unbundling was inadequate and recommended full ownership unbundling.[949] However, several Member States, in particular France and Germany, fiercely opposed the introduction of full ownership unbundling during the legislative procedure for the Third Energy Liberalisation package.[950] A compromise was reached only in 2009. In the directives that were finally adopted, the Member States were provided with the possibility to choose between full ownership unbundling or two weaker unbundling models.[951] Against the background of the political opposition against the Commission's push for full ownership unbundling, it came as a surprise when E.On committed in 2008 to divest its extra-high voltage network.[952] In 2009 and 2010, the Commission made two further commitments by RWE[953] and ENI[954] binding. The two companies engaged themselves to sell their gas transmission networks.

3.4.2.1.1.1 The Three Commitments[955] and Their Criticism

3.4.2.1.1.1.1 E.On

3.4.2.1.1.1.1.1 The Case

E.On's commitment to divest its extra-high voltage network addressed the concern that E.On was infringing Article 102 TFEU by favouring its own affiliate on the market for balancing energy through two practices.[956] On the one hand, the Commission accused E.On of having systematically bought balancing energy from its own affiliate at an inflated price instead of from a more competitive environment. The Commission took the preliminary view that E.On had thus increased its own costs, while being able to pass the inflated price on to the final consumers. On the other hand, the Commission was concerned that E.On had prevented the import of balancing energy by power producers from other Member States into the E.On

---

distribution activities. By virtue of Article 10 Directive 2003/54/EC and of Article 9 Directive 2003/55/EC, transmission system operators had to be independent from other activities in terms of their legal form, organisation and decision making.

[949] COM(2006) 851 final, 54ff.

[950] See Von Rosenberg (2009), 237; Hancher/de Hauteclocque (2010), 323; Sadowska (2011), fn 4 and 5; Dunne (2014b), 431; Kreße (2014), 16; Kipiani (2014), 430.

[951] See Article 9 Directive 2009/72/EC; Article 9 Directive 2009/73/EC. For a more detailed discussion of the EU's unbundling policy in the energy sector see eg Boscheck (2009); Manoussakis (2009); Johnsten/Block (2012), Chapter 3; Sadowska (2014), 19ff.

[952] COMP/39.388 (German electricity wholesale and balancing market, 2008).

[953] COMP/39.402 (RWE Gas Foreclosure, 2009).

[954] COMP/39.315 (ENI, 2010).

[955] For an overview over the three decisions see eg Marty (2011), 101f; Bougette/Marty (2012), 27ff; Botteman/Patsa (2013), 353f.

[956] COMP/39.388 (German electricity wholesale and balancing market, 2008), 50ff. For a discussion of the case from the perspective of members of the Commission's services see Chauve/Godfried/Kovács/Langus/Nagy/Siebert (2009); Hellström/Maier-Rigaud/Bulst (2009), 56f.

balancing area. According to the Commission's preliminary assessment, the latter practice amounted to an abusive discrimination.

With a view to the necessity of the commitment, the Commission argued, on the one hand, that the balancing market was organised on a quarter of an hour basis. A behavioural remedy controlling E.On's purchasing behaviour would therefore have been difficult to administer for the Commission and also more burdensome for E.On. On the other hand, the Commission relied on the fact that there was a substantial risk of a lasting or repeated infringement that derived from the very structure of the undertaking. According to the Commission, E.On's practices permitted the conclusion that the company was exposed to an inherent conflict of interests as a vertically integrated undertaking.[957]

3.4.2.1.1.1.1.2 Discussion of Criticism

Several commentators have criticised E.On's commitment to divest its transmission grid as excessive, because it allegedly went beyond what was necessary to address the Commission's concerns.[958] However, opponents of the commitment hardly ever put forward any detailed reasoning why the Commission would not have been able to impose a comparable remedy unilaterally under Article 7. The criticism remains essentially confined to abstract statements like the following: It is claimed that under Article 7 "any attempt by the [Commission] to impose ownership unbundling [...] would have been extensively disputed"[959] or that "the statutory preference for behavioural remedies over structural remedies would [have made] a successful appeal not unlikely".[960] More substantiated arguments against the decision are hard to find. Where they exist, they are not convincing. The more detailed discussion of the E.On commitment by the Monopolkommission[961] may in this regard serve as an illustration.

The Monpolkommission expressed doubts in respect of the suitability and the necessity of the commitment to resolve the Commission's concerns. The doubts regarding the suitability predicate on the assumption that prices for balancing energy would continue to be artificially high after the divestiture of the transmission grid. In the view of the Monopolkommission, the real competition problem was not E.On's vertical integration, but the high concentration on the market for balancing energy. The Monopolkommission therefore concluded that a sale of production power plants to different owners would have constituted a more expedient measure. With a view to the necessity, the Monopolkommission criticised that the Commission's preliminary assessment was based on an out-dated factual basis, because it neglected regulatory reforms that had taken place in Germany, in particular the entrustment of the

[957] COMP/39.388 (German electricity wholesale and balancing market, 2008), 86ff.

[958] Eg Klees (2009), 381 and (2011), 18; Polster/Petschko ÖZK 2010, 112; Immenga (2011), 296; Hennig (2010), 181; Podszun (2012), 60.

[959] Botteman/Patsa (2013), 354.

[960] Wagner-Von Papp (2012), 960.

[961] See, also for the following observations, MK (2009), 497f.

Bundesnetzagentur with an ex ante regulation of the network charges. Against this backdrop, the Monopolkommission indicated that it considered the imposition of a fine, followed by a subsequent "more restrictive" supervision and regulation a less onerous alternative solution.

The arguments of the Monopolkommission are not convincing. First, the Monopolkommission relies on an erroneous, overbroad goal in support of its criticism of the suitability of the commitment. The divestiture of the transmission grid aims primarily at preventing the subsistence or recurrence of the concretely circumscribed anticompetitive conduct that gave rise to the Commission's concerns. The broader goal of lower prices for balancing energy upon which the Monopolkommission bases its criticism is at best an indirect, secondary objective. The Monopolkommission acknowledges itself that the divestiture of the network prevents E.On from purchasing balancing energy from its own affiliate at an inflated price. The Monopolkommission derives the remedy's alleged lack of suitability only from the fact that the commitment does not resolve the high concentration on the market for balancing energy.[962] However, the high concentration on the market for balancing energy does not correspond to the anticompetitive conduct that the Commission wanted to address. On the basis of the theory of harm employed in the decision, the Commission could not legitimately have pursued the goal of deconcentrating the market for balancing energy. The Monopolkommission hence substitutes an illegitimate goal for the legitimate one pursued by the Commission when it assesses the suitability of the Commission's remedy.

Second, even if one wanted to accept the goal of lower prices for balancing energy as the legitimate primary objective of the Commission's remedy, the criticism of the Monopolkommission regarding the suitability would remain unfounded. The Monopolkommission relies on an incorrect, too ambitious standard for the suitability stage of the proportionality test. A remedy passes the suitability threshold, if it contributes with a sufficient likeliness to the attainment of the pursued objective. It is not necessary that the remedy fully accomplishes the objective pursued.[963] Even

---

[962] MK (2009), 497: "Auch die Veräußerung des E.ON Höchstspannungsnetzes kann als Abhilfemaßnahme nicht überzeugen. Zwar wird hierdurch zutreffend verhindert, dass der E.ON-Netzbetreiber bei der E.ON-Erzeugungstochter Regelenergie zu überhöhten Konditionen einkauft. Kritisch bleibt im Strommarkt jedoch, dass auch bei einer vertikalen Entflechtung von Erzeugung und Transport das eigentliche Problem der hohen Anbieterkonzentration in der Erzeugung nicht ausgeräumt wird. Durch die vertikale Entflechtung wird entsprechend unmittelbar missbräuchliches Verhalten durch Verbundunternehmen unterbunden, die maßgeblichen marktstrukturellen Gründe auf dem Erzeugermarkt für überhöhte Strompreise können jedoch nicht beseitigt werden. Zielführender wäre ein Verkauf der Regelenergiekraftwerke an unterschiedliche Eigentümer gewesen."

[963] See, with respect to German constitutional law, Grzeszick (2006), Art. 20, 112, with references to the consistent case law of the Bundesverfassungsgericht: "Nicht notwendig ist der Nachweis, daß der angegebene Zweck durch das eingesetzte Mittel vollständig erreicht wird; es genügt, daß das Mittel die Wahrscheinlichkeit erhöht, daß der angestrebte Erfolg zumindest teilweise eintritt". The same idea applies mutatis mutandis also under EU law: See eg CJ, C-283/11 (Sky Österreich, 2013), 53; C-293/12 (Digital Rights, 2014), 49f.

if the concentration on the market for balancing energy may constitute one cause for inflated prices, this does not exclude E.On's vertically integrated structure as a further source of artificially high prices. In its preliminary assessment, the Commission accused E.On of having unnecessarily increased its own costs by purchasing balancing energy from its own affiliate instead of from an existing more competitive environment.[964] Hence, if it is true that the divestiture of the transmission grid does not eliminate all causes for inflated prices of balancing energy, it nonetheless eliminates one of its causes, namely the one that underlies the Commission's theory of harm. The remedy therefore contributes with a sufficient probability to the attainment of the goal of lower prices for balancing energy. Even from the perspective of the Monopolkommission, the remedy must be considered as suitable. In that connection, it should be added that both practices upon which the Commission's theory of harm rests involve an exclusionary effect.[965] According to the Commission's theory of harm, E.On restricted competition on the market for balancing energy by favouring its own affiliate and preventing power producers from other Member States from selling their energy into the E.On balancing area. The divestiture of the transmission grid eliminates the conditions for the subsistence or recurrence of such restrictions. It thereby contributes with a certain likeliness to an increase in competition and to lower prices on the market for balancing energy.

Third, also the grounds on which the Monopolkommission calls into the question the necessity of the remedy are not compelling. On the one hand, one may doubt whether the imposition of a fine paired with an intensified supervision and regulation constitutes really a less burdensome alternative to the divestiture of the network. In that regard, it should be recalled that the Commission arrived at the conclusion that controlling E.On's purchasing behaviour would have been more burdensome for E. On, because the market for balancing energy was organised on a quarter of an hour basis. This conclusion does not seem implausible. Moreover, one may legitimately ask why E.On consented to the commitment, if it considered the imposition of a fine paired with an intensified supervision and regulation a less burdensome alternative.[966] On the other hand, even on the assumption that the imposition of a fine paired with an intensified supervision and regulation is less burdensome than the divestiture of the transmission grid, the former alternative would still have to be

---

[964]See COMP/39.388 (German electricity wholesale and balancing market, 2008), 51: "[. . .] E.On Netz bought systematically [. . .] secondary reserves from its own affiliate [. . .] instead of procuring other forms of balancing energy, i.e. tertiary reserves, from a more competitive environment. Thereby E.On Netz increased its own costs [. . .]".

[965]But see Hellström/Maier-Rigaud/Bulst (2009), 56, who emphasise the exploitative character of the first practice.

[966]See also Kreße (2014), 26, who states that the commitments in the E.On and the RWE procedure were not only formally, but also materially of a voluntary nature.

Certainly, Budzinski/Kuchinke (2012), 274, refer to the possibility that E.On offered the divestiture of the transmission grid only in the context of a "cross policy deal" in consideration for the closing of two further proceedings "in spite of an excellent state of evidence". However, since Budzinski/Kuchinke themselves describe that possibility as "speculation", it cannot seriously call the commitment decision into question.

equally effective as the latter. This applies also for other less burdensome alternatives, like for instance the deployment of an unbundling model below the divestiture threshold. However, alternatives to full ownership unbundling would not, or at least not to same extent, have changed the incentives for E.On to engage in anticompetitive conduct. They would therefore have required an increased amount of monitoring when compared to the divestiture of the transmission grid. The commitment decision contains two concrete indicia why such monitoring was likely to be less effective than the divestiture of the transmission grid. In the first place, the Commission considered that there was a risk of a lasting or repeated infringement. The existence of such a risk of a lasting or repeated infringement casts from the outset a shadow over the effectiveness of solutions that depend to a high degree on monitoring. The Commission did not derive the risk of a lasting or repeated infringement merely abstractly from E.On's vertically integrated structure.[967] Rather, the Commission relied on E.On's past behaviour to substantiate its concerns. In the second place, the Commission considered that monitoring E.On's purchasing behaviour on a quarter of an hour basis would be difficult. It is submitted that such additional costs for the general public render the alternative solutions less effective than the divestiture of the network and that the Commission can take this aspect into account,[968] regardless of whether it would have to bear the monitoring costs itself or whether these would be incurred by a sector specific regulator.

3.4.2.1.1.1.2 RWE

3.4.2.1.1.1.2.1 The Case

RWE's commitment to divest its German gas transmission network addressed the concern that the company violated Article 102 TFEU by way of a refusal to supply gas transmission services to third parties and by a margin squeeze aimed at RWE's downstream competitors in gas supply.[969] As far as the refusal to supply is concerned, the Commission took the preliminary view that RWE understated the transmission capacity that was technically available to third parties. Moreover, the Commission accused RWE of allocating the scarce capacities of its network in an inefficient manner. The Commission also took account of the fact that RWE had erected its gas transmission network in a period during which its market position was protected by a regional monopoly granted by the German State.[970] With a view to the

[967]On the fact that, at least under Article 7, the Commission cannot infer a substantial risk of a lasting or repeated infringement simply from the structure of the undertaking, see Sect. 3.4.1.2.1.2.1 with footnote 855 above.

[968]See on that question also Sect. 3.2.1.3 with footnotes 108ff and Sect. 3.4.1.2.1.2.1 with footnote 863 above.

[969]COMP/39.402 (RWE Gas Foreclosure, 2009), 21ff. For a discussion of the case from the perspective of members of the Commission's services see Koch/Nagy/Pucinskaite-Kubik/Tretton (2009); Hellström/Maier-Rigaud/Bulst (2009), 56f.

[970]COMP/39.402 (RWE Gas Foreclosure, 2009), fn 24.

margin squeeze, the preliminary assessment concluded that RWE intentionally set transmission tariffs at an artificially high level. As regards the necessity of the commitment, the Commission argued, on the one hand, that a behavioural remedy would have been difficult to administer for the Commission and also burdensome for RWE. On the other hand, the Commission relied on the fact that there was a substantial risk of a lasting or repeated infringement. According to the Commission, RWE's practices permitted the conclusion that the company was exposed to an inherent conflict of interests as a vertically integrated undertaking.[971]

3.4.2.1.1.1.2.2 Discussion of Criticism

Like E.On, also the RWE case is relied on by critics of the Article 9 procedure to illustrate that the Commission uses commitments to impose remedies which it could not have imposed under Article 7 and thereby instrumentalises the Article 9 procedure for regulatory purposes.[972] Again, substantiated claims why the Commission could not have imposed the remedy under Article 7 are hard to find. And again, where they exist, they are not convincing. For instance, Dunne's criticism predicates essentially on the allegedly "dubious merits"[973] of the Commission's theory of harm. In that regard, she contends that the Commission accused RWE of strategic underinvestment. According to Dunne, this accusation "goes considerably beyond the parameters of the already controversial refusal to supply doctrine, at least as recognized by the EU courts". By the refusal to supply doctrine "as recognized by the EU courts", Dunne means the "significant restrictions" that were the result of the Oscar Bronner case.[974]

Such criticism seems flawed for the following reasons. First, the Commission's theory of harm is not—or at least not only—based on strategic underinvestment.[975] Certainly, in a footnote of the commitment, the Commission stated that the mere fact that current capacities were fully used by an essential facility holder was not sufficient to exclude an abuse under Article 102 TFEU. Rather, the Commission considered the essential facilities holder to be in such a situation under the obligation to take all possible measures to remove the constraints imposed by the lack of

[971]COMP/39.402 (RWE Gas Foreclosure, 2009), 50.

[972]See eg Hennig (2010), 181; Körber (2010), 87: "Dass diese Entscheidung verhältnismäßig ist, erscheint [. . .] höchst zweifelhaft"; Gerard (2013), 19f, who quotes the RWE decision in support of the statement that "unconstrained by the limitations set forth by Article 7 of Regulation 1/2003 with respect to infringement decisions, [commitments] have enabled the Commission to impose structural remedies". At least implicitly, Gerard hence states that the RWE commitment went beyond what the Commission could have imposed under Article 7.

[973]Dunne (2014b), 431.

[974]Dunne (2014b), 421 with fn 119.

[975]See also Jones/Sufrin (2014), 522, who mention only the ENI case as raising "the question of the existence of a "duty to invest" as well as a "duty to supply"; Gauer/Kjølbye (2014), 12.151, who mention that the "most innovative type" of refusal to deal, namely strategic underinvestment, was addressed in ENI and GdF gas foreclosure.

capacity and to organise its business in a manner that makes the maximum capacities of the essential facility available.[976] In so far as the Commission accused RWE of allocating the capacities of its network in an inefficient manner, this may perhaps be considered as recourse to a theory of harm of strategic underinvestment. However, Commission's second reproach regarding RWE's alleged refusal to supply, namely the understatement of transmission capacity, is not a reproach of strategic underinvestment. Moreover, reducing the Commission's theory of harm in the RWE commitment to a theory of strategic underinvestment completely blends out the margin squeeze accusations contained in the preliminary assessment. Second, it is little persuasive to suggest that the Commission could under Article 7 not have relied on a theory of harm that doesn't meet the strict conditions of the Bronner case. In fact, several judgments caution against a too far-reaching generalisation of these conditions.[977] This applies in particular to the Bronner condition that the refusal to supply must be likely to eliminate all competition in the downstream market from the person requesting access.[978] In fact, in Microsoft the General Court relaxed that condition even with respect to refusal to supply cases. The General Court said that it was sufficient to demonstrate the elimination of all "effective" competition.[979] Moreover, in Telia Sonera and Telefonica, the Court of Justice made it clear that the strict conditions of the Bronner case were, in any event, not applicable to the independent abuse category of a margin squeeze.[980] Finally, in Post Danmark, the Court of Justice stated with a view to the special responsibility of dominant undertakings that the origins of the dominant position in a former legal monopoly was a fact to be taken into account.[981] Against the background of what was just said, Dunne's doubts that the Courts would have endorsed the Commission's theory of harm also under Article 7 do not seem to be based on solid grounds.[982]

---

[976]COMP/39.402 (RWE Gas Foreclosure, 2009), 25. Dunne (2014b), 421 fn 119 relies on that fn in support of her criticism.

[977]See for the following remarks the discussion of the Bronner criteria in Jones/Sufrin (2014), 520ff.

[978]CJ, C-7/97 (Oscar Bronner, 1998), 41; Jones/Sufrin (2014), 520.

[979]GC, T-201/04 (Microsoft I, 2007), 563; for a discussion see only Jones/Sufrin (2014), 521 and 546f. See also Sect. 3.3.1.7.1, footnote 571 above.

[980]CJ, C-52/09 P (Telia Sonera, 2011), 56; C-295/12 P (Telefonica, 2014), 75. See also Sect. 3.3.1.6.1.1.3.1, footnote 474 above.

[981]CJ, C-209/10 (Post Danmark, 2012), 23.

[982]See also Hancher/de Hautecloque (2010), 324: "[. . .] in the RWE case the Commission was tackling under the antitrust rules a fairly straightforward case of discriminatory (or inefficient) access to the network of competitors"; identically de Hautecloque (2013), 69; see also Schweitzer (2010), 549 fn 13, who mentions the RWE case as an "obvious example" of a "clear-cut infringement"; Gautier/Petit (2014), 22: "In RWE gas fore-closure, the Commission took objection to a plain vanilla refusal of access by RWE to its transport network, and to the setting of excessive prices that squeezed rivals".

3.4.2.1.1.1.3 ENI

3.4.2.1.1.1.3.1 The Case

ENI's commitment to divest its gas transmission network addressed the concern that the company violated Article 102 TFEU by way of a refusal to supply gas transmission services to third parties.[983] As a preliminary remark, it should be mentioned that, unlike the E.On and RWE cases, the ENI commitment was not based merely on a preliminary assessment, but on an in-depth investigation and the issuing of a statement of objections.[984] The statement of objections envisaged already a structural remedy of the type that was later offered by ENI.[985] According to the Commission's theory of harm, ENI's refusal to supply strategy consisted of three different practices: refusing to grant competitors access to capacity available on the transport network (capacity hoarding); granting access in an impractical manner (capacity degradation); and strategically limiting investment (strategic underinvestment) in ENI's international transmission pipelines. As regards the necessity of the commitment, the Commission stated, on the one hand, that a behavioural remedy would have required additional monitoring. However, in the Commission's view, such monitoring would not have been sufficient to alleviate its concerns. In that connection, the Commission noted that during the period of investigation, compliance programmes and monitoring already formed an integral part of the regulatory framework but did not prevent ENI from engaging in the alleged anticompetitive conduct.[986] On the other hand, the Commission relied on the fact that there was a substantial risk of a lasting or repeated infringement that derived from the very structure of the undertaking. In that regard, the Commission took the view that ENI's investigated conduct had in the past limited capacity available to third parties for a period of several years.[987] The Commission considered that this conduct was a manifestation of an inherent conflict of interests within ENI as a vertically integrated undertaking. In the view of the Commission, absent a structural remedy, ENI's incentives to further adopt the alleged anticompetitive behaviour would not have been removed.[988]

3.4.2.1.1.1.3.2 Discussion of Criticism

Like E.On and RWE, also the ENI case is relied on by critics of the Article 9 procedure to illustrate that the Commission uses commitments to impose remedies which it could not have imposed under Article 7 and thereby instrumentalises the

[983]COMP/39.315 (ENI, 2010), 43ff. For a discussion of the case from the perspective of members of the Commission's services see Maier-Rigaud/Manca/von Koppenfels (2011).

[984]See Maier-Rigaud/Manca/von Koppenfels (2011), 20.

[985]COMP/39.315 (ENI, 2010), 88.

[986]COMP/39.315 (ENI, 2010), 92.

[987]Maier-Rigaud/Manca/von Koppenfels (2011), 20, mention that ENI was accused of having engaged in the anticompetitive conduct at least from 2000 until 2008.

[988]See COMP/39.315 (ENI, 2010), 90f.

Article 9 procedure for regulatory purposes.[989] Again, the criticism is either not substantiated at all or not convincing. Certainly, to the extent that the ENI commitment predicates on an accusation of strategic underinvestment, the Commission relies on a theory of harm that has not yet been endorsed by the EU Courts.[990] However, this fact alone does not seriously call into question the assumption that the Courts would have confirmed the Commission's remedy also on the basis of Article 7. On the one hand, it must be emphasised that the allegation of strategic underinvestment is only one of three pillars of the Commission's theory of harm.[991] On the other hand, in the light of what has been explained above in the context of the RWE decision, the assumption that the Courts would even have embraced the Commission's novel theory of harm in the context of an Article 7 decision appears at least as plausible as the opposite.

Finally, as far as the proportionality of the remedy is concerned, the argument that the Commission should have required a capacity release instead of a network divestiture must also be rejected. On the one hand, Maier-Rigaud et al. have convincingly shown that the cases in which the Commission made binding commitments that involved capacity releases predicated on theories of harm that differed substantially from theory of harm underlying the ENI commitment.[992] On the other hand, even if one assumes that a capacity release could have resolved the Commission's competition concerns in the ENI case in an equally effective manner as the divestiture of the network, this does not mean that a capacity release would also have constituted a less burdensome remedy that ENI would have been willing to offer.

3.4.2.1.1.2 Overall Comment on the Divestiture of Transmission Grids

The three decisions in which E.On, RWE and ENI committed to divest their respective transmission networks do not support the conclusion that the Commission uses the Article 9 procedure to adopt remedies that go beyond what the Commission could have imposed under Article 7. Nor do they confirm that the Commission instrumentalises the commitment procedure for regulatory purposes. The fact that the Commission did not gain the necessary political support to impose sectorwide compulsory full ownership unbundling through regulation[993] does not as such make it unlawful for the Commission to adopt remedies in individual cases involving full ownership unbundling on the basis of competition law.[994] As explained above, the

[989] See eg Gerard (2013), 19f, who quotes also the ENI decision in support of the statement reproduced in Sect. 3.4.2.1.1.1.2.2, footnote 972 above; Dunne (2014b), 421 and 431.

[990] This is the major criticism of Dunne (see Sect. 3.4.2.1.1.1.2.2 with footnotes 973f above).

[991] See Scholz/Purbs (2011), 65.

[992] Maier-Rigaud/Manca/von Koppenfels (2011), 23.

[993] See Sect. 3.4.2.1.1 with footnotes 948ff above.

[994] See also Koch/Nagy/Pucinskaite-Kubik/Tretton (2009), 34, who emphasise the independence of the RWE commitment from the discussions about full ownership unbundling in the political context of the Third Liberalisation Package.

areas of competition law and regulation may overlap.[995] The decisive question is therefore only whether competition law provides a sufficient basis for the adoption of the remedies in question.[996] In that connection, a closer analysis of the E.On, RWE and ENI cases shows that the criticism that is levied at the respective commitments lacks a sufficient basis.

In that connection, one particular point shall be stressed once again. It was shown above that remedies that change the structure of an undertaking in order to eliminate the causes for future infringements are in principle admissible under Article 7 in particular on the following condition: The Commission must show that it is not sufficient to address the infringement itself because there is a substantial risk that the structure of the undertaking would cause the infringement's subsistence or recurrence.[997] Albeit only succinctly, all three decisions substantiate why the Commission considered this condition to be met. In that connection, the Commission legitimately relied, in all three decisions, on two facts. On the one hand, it found that the past infringements of the concerned undertakings indicated that there was an inherent conflict of interest that resulted from the vertical integration.[998] There were therefore concrete indicia that the very structure of the concerned undertakings provided an incentive to continue the anticompetitive conduct. On the other hand, the Commission took account of the impracticability or the high costs of the supervision that would be necessary to suppress those incentives through a behavioural remedy. It is true that, in an Article 7 decision, the Commission would probably have had to substantiate the risk of a lasting or repeated infringement still to a greater extent. However, the fact that the Commission abstained from doing so in the three commitment decisions does not permit the conclusion that it could not have done so, where necessary. At least prima facie and on the basis of the available information, there seems to be hence no compelling reason to doubt that the Commission could have imposed the three remedies also unilaterally under Article 7.

---

[995] See Sect. 3.1.3.2.2 with footnotes 75ff above.

[996] See also Kreße (2014), 28: "Dass die Kommission in den Entflechtungsfällen vielleicht auch ein – kompetenzrechtlich bedenkliches – Regulierungsziel verfolgt, ändert an der Rechtmäßigkeit einer auf die eigentumsrechtliche Entflechtung gerichteten Zusagenentscheidung nichts, solange nicht die hoheitliche Anordnung einer solchen Entflechtung kartellrechtlich schlechthin unvertretbar wäre und die Kommission damit den Boden des Kartellrechts, für dessen Durchsetzung sie zuständig ist, verließe".

Gauer/Kjølbye (2014), 12.172, who mention that the legislative development around the Third Energy package is irrelevant, "as the only requirements to be met by the Commission in imposing a remedy are the conditions set in Article 7 of Regulation 1/2003".

[997] See Sect. 3.4.1.2.1.2.1, after footnote 855 above.

[998] See in this context also the reproduction of the speech of Gauer in Gussone (2011), 42 and Wilhelmi (2013), 364. Gauer and Wilhelmi underline that the structural commitments made binding by the Commission in the energy cases predicate on repeated past infringements.

3.4.2.1.2 Horizontal Unbundling[999]

The Commission also made binding several structural commitments with a horizontal effect. These must be clearly distinguished from the three commitments that have been mentioned so far, which all entailed a vertical break up.

3.4.2.1.2.1 E.On

3.4.2.1.2.1.1 The Case

In the same decision that made binding E.On's commitment to divest its extra-high voltage network, the Commission also accepted a further commitment by E.On to address a different theory of harm.[1000] In order to meet the concern that E.On violated Article 102 TFEU by withholding capacity and deterring investment in generation by third parties on the German electricity wholesale market, E.On committed to divest around 20% of its generation capacity. According to the Commission's theory of harm, E.On, RWE and Vattenfall collectively dominated the German wholesale electricity market.[1001] The Commission accused E.On, on the one hand, to have raised electricity prices by not offering some of its available capacities on the spot market.[1002] The Commission suspected that the capacity withholding was made profitable for E.On by the size and composition of its portfolio of power plants, which included base-load and flexible plants. In the Commission's view, an increase in prices on the spot market indirectly affected also the remainder of prices on the wholesale electricity market.[1003] Therefore, E. On's loss of profit that resulted from the withholding of flexible capacities on the spot market was compensated by the increased profits that resulted from the capacities that continued to be produced, in particular E.On's large base-load

[999]The term "horizontal unbundling" was used also by MK (2009), 495: "horizontale Entflechtung durch Veräußerung von Kraftwerkskapazitäten".

[1000]Initially, the Commission had opened two procedures COMP/39.388 and COMP/39.389. For the sake of brevity, I refer to the decision as COMP/39.388.

[1001]COMP/39.388 (German Electricity Wholesale), 13ff.

[1002]COMP/39.388 (German Electricity Wholesale), 28ff; for a more detailed description of the Commission's complex theory regarding the short term capacity withdrawal see also Hellström/Maier-Rigaud/Bulst (2009), 54ff; Chauve/Godfried/Kovács/Langus/Nagy/Siebert (2009), 51ff; generally on limiting production as infringement of Article 102 TFEU see Jones/Sufrin (2014), 583f.

[1003]See COMP/39.388 (German Electricity Wholesale), 38; Chauve/Godfried/Kovács/Langus/Nagy/Siebert (2009), 51f: "Electricity consumed by end-users is procured by retail suppliers partly through the spot market and partly through forward/futures products. The price of electricity procured through the spot market is directly affected by withdrawals of capacity. The price of electricity procured through forward products is indirectly affected by withdrawals of capacity. A purchaser of electricity has the choice to cover its needs by buying forward or spot. Usually it tries to cover most of its needs in advance (thus forward) in order to avoid the volatility of spot markets. In doing so it will take spot prices into account to determine how much it is ready to pay for forward products."

capacities.[1004] On the other hand, the Commission was concerned that E.On had deterred investment in generation by third parties through long-term electricity supply contracts and through offering new competitors a participation in an E.On power plant. According to the Commission, the latter practices complemented E. On's withholding of capacity on the spot market.[1005]

In order to offset the Commission's concerns, E.On committed to divest not only power plants that generated electricity for the spot market, but also such that produced base-load capacities.[1006] To justify the necessity of the commitment, the Commission relied in particular on the following reasons. First, due to the diversity and the quantity of the electricity that was concerned by E.On's withdrawal and due to the trading frequency on the German spot market, a behavioural remedy controlling the bidding procedure would have been difficult to administer for the Commission and more burdensome for E.On. Second, it was precisely the size and composition of E.On's portfolio of power plants that made the capacity withdrawing profitable, thereby providing for an incentive to engage in anticompetitive conduct. The concerns regarding the capacity withdrawal stretched over a period from 2002 to 2007. There was hence a substantial risk of a lasting or repeated infringement that derived from the very structure of the undertaking. In order to remove the incentive to continue the anticompetitive conduct, the plants to be divested had to reflect E. On's portfolio.[1007] Third, the divestiture commitment also addressed the concerns with regard to the deterrence of investment of third parties. The acquisition of the plants to be divested would in particular allow competitors to get access to new plants and technologies and to have a more balanced portfolio and more capacity to exert competitive pressure.[1008]

3.4.2.1.2.1.2 Discussion of Criticism

Also the horizontal unbundling commitment used in E.On is invoked in the literature as prove that the Commission instrumentalises the Article 9 procedure for regulatory purposes and imposes remedies that go beyond what the Commission could have imposed under Article 7.[1009] Again, most of that criticism is not substantiated. A

[1004]COMP/39.388 (German Electricity Wholesale, 2008), 40; Chauve/Godfried/Kovács/Langus/Nagy/Siebert (2009), 51f: "In practice, capacity withdrawal requires a portfolio including (i) plants to withdraw ("ability to withdraw") and (ii) a sufficiently large capacity of cheap plants to reap the benefits ("incentive to withdraw")".

[1005]COMP/39.388 (German Electricity Wholesale, 2008), 41ff.

[1006]COMP/39.388 (German Electricity Wholesale, 2008), 57; Hellström/Maier-Rigaud/Bulst (2009), 56.

[1007]COMP/39.388 (German Electricity Wholesale, 2008), 82 and 84: "In order to be able to implement a successful strategy of withdrawing capacity [. . .] it is necessary to own and operate a portfolio of power plants which consists of plants along the entire merit curve, i.e. base-load plants as well as flexible plants".

[1008]COMP/39.388 (German Electricity Wholesale, 2008), 85.

[1009]Eg Klees (2009), 381; Podszun (2012), 60; Gerard (2013), 19f; Voell (2014), 164f.

remarkable exception is, however, the very thorough analysis by Sadowska. Together with some more detailed observations that were presented by the German Monopolkommission, this analysis shall provide the basis for the following discussion.

3.4.2.1.2.1.2.1 Sadowska's Criticism of the Commission's Theory of Harm

Sadowska criticises the Commission's theory of harm as "far-fetched".[1010] In order to show that this claim is not justified, the three major points of criticism that have been raised by Sadowska shall be addressed.

First, as regards the Commission's concerns regarding the existence of a dominant position, Sadowska highlights that the Commission left open the question whether Vattenfall belonged at all to the collectively dominant group.[1011] According to Sadowska, this calls into question the Commission's entire theory of collective dominance. In her view, "if the asymmetries between Vattenfall and the two remaining operators were indeed so apparent that it could not be part of the collectively dominant group, E.On and RWE might not have pursued any common policy at all, either because it was less attractive in the first place or the collusion was unsustainable".[1012]

This argument does not cast serious doubts on the Commission's preliminary conclusion regarding the existence of dominance. As is apparent from the decision, the Commission concluded that E.On, RWE and Vattenfall collectively dominated the German wholesale electricity market.[1013] However, in the context of the market test, the Commission received a submission that Vattenfall should not be considered part of the collectively dominant group of undertakings. The submission was based on a recent case in which the German courts had found that E.On and RWE were collectively dominant.[1014] The Commission explicitly referred to that finding by the German courts in a footnote of the decision.[1015] Even though the German case law is not binding on the Commission, the latter could use it as evidence that at least E.On

[1010]Sadowska (2011), passim. The article is reprinted in Sadowska (2014), 93ff.

[1011]See COMP/39.388 (German Electricity Wholesale, 2008), 23f. Also Dunne (2014b), 422, criticises the Commission for relying on the concept of collective dominance, because the concept is "controversial" and has "regulatory overtones".

[1012]Sadowska (2011), text after fn 27.

[1013]COMP/39.388 (German Electricity Wholesale, 2008), 13 and 22; see also Gauer/Kjølbye (2014), 12.190 fn 287.

[1014]OLG Düsseldorf, VI-2 Kart 7/04 (V) (Stadtwerke Eschwege, 2007); confirmed by Bundesgerichtshof, KVR 60/07 (E.On/Stadtwerke Eschwege, 2008). The judgment of the Bundesgerichtshof contains a detailed examination of the question whether E.On and RWE held a collective dominant position (in particular paras 35ff). Moreover, the Bundesgerichtshof expressly left the question open whether there was not only a duopoly consisting of E.On and RWE, but also an oligopoly consisting of E.On, RWE, Vattenfall and EnBW. It is therefore submitted that the judgment of the Bundesgerichtshof does not oppose the Commission's conclusion that E.On, RWE and Vattenfall collectively held a dominant position.

[1015]COMP/39.388 (German Electricity Wholesale, 2008), fn 13.

and RWE were collectively dominant. Against that background, the Commission cannot seriously be criticised for not investigating more thoroughly whether Vattenfall was part of the collectively dominant group. For the sake of completeness, it should be added that, according to the Commission's preliminary assessment, even alone, E.On may even have held a dominant position, due to the particularities of the electricity sector and in spite of its relatively low market shares between 20% and 30%.[1016] At least implicitly, Sadowska seems to acknowledge this. She criticises the Commission for having resorted to a theory of collective dominance in order to establish dominance in spite of E.On's comparatively low market shares. According to Sadowska, the Commission should have used "electricity-specific indices to measure E.ON's market power" instead.[1017]

Second, Sadowska considers that there is an inconsistency between, on the one hand, the allegation of "a common policy to raise prices" in the part of the preliminary assessment that deals with the finding of dominance and, on the other hand, the fact that the Commission relied only on a capacity withdrawal that was committed individually by E.On in the part of the preliminary assessment that deals with the finding of an abuse. In her view, it follows from the fact that E.On's capacity withdrawal is "depicted [. . .] as a unilateral profit-maximising strategy" that "the only valid argument" for the allegedly collectively dominant group to adopt a common strategy "remains the advantage [the members of the group] take from the price increase". However, Sadowska is of the opinion that this incentive "cannot constitute a standalone ground for developing a theory of coordination", because "the price increase brings a windfall profit for all the generators in the market".[1018]

Also this argument cannot convince. As is acknowledged by Sadowska,[1019] it follows from the case law of the General Court that a company may individually abuse a dominant position that it holds collectively with other undertakings, at least as long as the abuse is committed to protect the joint dominant position.[1020] It is not clear whether Sadowska's criticism is directed at the Commission's findings regarding collective dominance or regarding the abuse. Sadowska herself presents her criticism as an inconsistency regarding the Commissions finding of abuse.[1021] However, her conclusion that the individual advantage that results from the price

[1016]COMP/39.388 (German Electricity Wholesale, 2008), 13: "[. . .] specific characteristics of the electricity sector may allow each of the largest power generators within the same market to be individually dominant even with limited market presence [. . .]". See also Sadowska (2014), 99 fn 323, where she points out that the Bundeskartellamt found in its 2011 sector enquiry that the three major electricity generators on the German market, E.On, RWE and Vattenfall, held individual dominant positions.

[1017]Sadowska (2011), text accompanying fn 19ff.

[1018]Sadowska (2011), text accompanying fn 28ff.

[1019]Sadowska (2011), text accompanying fn 30.

[1020]GC, T-228/97 (Irish Sugar, 1999), 66; T-191/98 (Atlantic Container Line, 2003), 633; COMP/39.388 (German Electricity Wholesale, 2008), 27; for a discussion see eg Jones/Sufrin (2014), 591 and 725.

[1021]Sadowska (2011), text before fn 28.

increase for each of the members of the alleged collectively dominant group cannot justify a theory of coordination seems to be directed in reality against the Commission's finding regarding collective dominance. If one follows the latter assumption, Sadowska's argument does not seriously call the Commission's theory of harm into question. In fact, the Commission based its finding that E.On, RWE and Vattenfall could have adopted "a common policy to raise prices" on the following two aspects: On the one hand, the Commission relied on the structural links on production and the high degree of transparency between the three companies. On the other hand, the Commission argued that the operators had a possibility to counter a deviation by one of them, both as regards a potential increase in capacity or a decrease in price.[1022] Contrary what Sadowska seems to suggest, the Commission's theory of collective dominance did therefore not, or at least not only, predicate on the assumption that E. On, RWE and Vattenfall would actively collude to raise prices.[1023] Rather, it was based on the likeliness that RWE and Vattenfall would abstain from competing away the increase in price that was prompted by E.On's individual capacity withholding by either reducing their own prices or by increasing their own capacities.[1024] In other terms, the Commission's theory of collective dominance was not based on explicit, but merely on "tacit" collusion. That tacit collusion suffices to establish collective dominance is confirmed by the case law.[1025] Against this backdrop, there is no inconsistency between the Commission's finding of collective dominance and its finding regarding the abuse.

Third, as regards the deterrence of investment in generation by third parties, Sadowska criticises in particular that the Commission did not take into account that the long-term electricity supply agreements mitigate the effects of the capacity withdrawal on the spot market. According to Sadowska, "if a big share of E.On's capacity is tied up by contracts (excluded from the electricity pool), its incentive and

---

[1022]COMP/39.388 (German Electricity Wholesale, 2008), 20.

[1023]It must, however, be conceded that the Commission's decision contains the unfortunate formulation that "E.On, RWE and Vattenfall could have adopted a common policy to raise prices" (Sect. 3.4.2.1.2.1.2.1, footnote 1022 above). This can easily be misunderstood as implying the active collusion to raise prices that seems to underlie Sadowska's criticism.

[1024]In my view, Sadowska's assertion that "withdrawal appertained to the common policy adopted by the two (or potentially three) operators" (text following fn 31) misrepresents the Commission's theory of collective dominance. Rather, as pointed out above, the Commission's theory of collective dominance was based on the likely "collective" abstention from competition by increasing capacity or reducing price. This must, however, be distinguished from E.On's individual abusive practice to withhold capacity.

[1025]See in particular GC, T-193/02 (Laurent Piau, 2005), 111. See also CJ, C-395/96 P (Compagnie Maritime Belge, 2000), 45: "[...] the existence of an agreement or of other links in law is not indispensable to a finding of a collective dominant position; such a finding may be based on other connecting factors and would depend on an economic assessment and, in particular, on an assessment of the structure of the market in question". Jones/Sufrin (2014), 721f, interpret that passage of the CJ's judgment as confirming the GC's case law according to which "undertakings which are able to engage in a parallel manner on a market by tacitly coordinating their behaviour may be found collectively to hold a dominant position of a market".

ability to reduce output in order to manipulate the price decrease, since less volume is traded in the pool and the higher price accounts only for the uncontracted capacities".[1026]

Also this argument does not seriously call into question the commitment decision. First, as will be explained below, the accusation regarding the capacity withdrawal constitutes in principle a sufficient basis for E.On's commitment. Even if the Commission's theory of harm regarding the long-term electricity supply agreements were flawed, this would therefore not affect the justification of the remedy. Moreover, Sadowska blends out that the Commission's findings regarding the deterrence of investment in generation predicated also on the accusation that E.On was offering new competitors a participation in an E.On power plant. Second, Sadowska's assumption of a mitigating effect is from the outset only valid for long-term contracts that were concluded prior to a given capacity withholding. Long-term contracts that were concluded subsequent to a given capacity withholding were, according to the Commission's theory of harm, affected by the price increase.[1027] Such contracts therefore rather perpetuated than mitigated the anticompetitive price increase that resulted from the capacity withholding. Third, it must be conceded that long-term contracts that were concluded prior to a given capacity withholding may have mitigated E.On's future incentive to withhold capacity on the spot market. However, this mitigating effect does from the outset not affect the qualification of the capacity withholding and the conclusion of long-term contracts as abusive when looked at individually. Nor does it render the Commission's conclusion incorrect that the capacity withdrawal and the deterrence of investment in generation by third parties "complemented" each other in that they both allowed E.On to maintain a wholesale price level which would not have developed under competitive circumstances.[1028] In view of the fact that the Commission did not precisely quantify the anticompetitive effects of the incriminated practices, it could legitimately abstain from taking the mitigating effect of long-term contracts into account.

3.4.2.1.2.1.2.2 Criticism Regarding the Link Between Harm and Remedy

As far as the link between harm and remedy is concerned, one must distinguish between two different aspects. First, there is the question whether there was a behavioural alternative. Second, one may ask whether the precise shape of the structural remedy that was made binding by the Commission matched the Commission's theory of harm.

As regards the first question, Sadowska discusses several "behavioural" alternatives. She acknowledges that "controlling E.ON's bids and constant monitoring of its power plants to prevent eventual capacity withdrawal would be [...] burdensome

[1026] Sadowska (2011), text after fn 38.

[1027] See Sect. 3.4.2.1.2.1.1, footnote 1003 above. Sadowska does not seem to contest that part of the Commission's theory of harm.

[1028] COMP/39.388 (German Electricity Wholesale, 2008), 44.

both for the Commission and for the operator".[1029] However, Sadowska suggests "forward contract commitments" or "capacity divestment commitments" (Virtual Power Plants—VPPs) as viable "behavioural" alternatives to eliminate the incentives for E.On to engage in further capacity withholding.[1030] Both types of remedies imply an obligation to divest certain amounts of capacity in certain intervals at certain prices. Both would reduce the capacities that can be used by E.On to compensate the forgone profits that result from a capacity withholding. They would hence counteract against E.On's incentive to withhold capacity. Depending on how much capacity E.On would be obliged to divest, the said incentive could be completely eliminated.

Whether the said types of commitments are at all of a "behavioural" nature shall not be discussed here.[1031] In any event, they do not constitute an alternative that is evidently equally effective and less burdensome than the obligation to divest power plants that was made binding by the Commission.[1032] First, neither of the two alternatives entails a permanent effect. As long as the market circumstances do not change, both alternative remedies would therefore have to be renewed in order to prevent a revival of E.On's anticompetitive conduct after their expiration. Moreover, the longer the duration of the alternatives is, the more their effects for E.On resemble the commitment that was made binding by the Commission. In that regard, it bears mention that the non-reacquisition period that was contained in the commitment that was made binding lasted only 10 years.[1033] Second, there is a likeliness that E.On's implementation costs and the Commission's costs of monitoring compliance would be higher for the alternatives than for the commitment that was made binding.[1034] Third, Sadowska states herself that the two alternatives would have had a deterrent effect on investment in generation capacity and not eliminated the Commission's second prong of concerns, the deterrence of investment.[1035] In Sadowska's view, this indicates that the Commission deliberately included the—according to Sadowska "far fetched"—allegations regarding the deterrence of investment only

---

[1029]Sadowska (2011), text accompanying fn 46.

[1030]For a description of such types of commitments see eg Hancher/de Hauteclocque (2010), 326; de Frutos/Fabra (2012), 451; de Hauteclocque (2013), 91f; "VPP" remedies have, for instance, been used by the Commission in M.1853(EDF/EnBW) or by the French Autorité de la Concurrence in the margin squeeze case 07-D-43 (EDF, 2007).

[1031]See eg Hancher/de Hauteclocque (2010), who classify "forced divestitures or forced auctions (so-called Virtual Power Plants auctions and gas release programs)" as "quasi-regulatory, structural measures" (322) or as "hybrid remedies, between structural and behavioural" (326). See also, more generally, Sect. 3.4.1 with footnotes 721ff above.

[1032]Sadowska (2011), text before fn 48, explicitly acknowledges that "it is not clear whether a 'virtual' divestment is equally effective in terms of mitigating market power in the pool compared with a 'physical' one".

[1033]COMP/39.388 (German Electricity Wholesale, 2008), 57.

[1034]See Hancher/de Hauteclocque (2010), 327, who emphasise the high monitoring costs of VPPs.

[1035]Sadowska (2011), text accompanying fn 48. For the deterrent effect of VPPs on investment into generation capacity see also Hancher/de Hauteclocque (2010), 327.

in order to justify the extraction of a far reaching remedy.[1036] This conclusion is from the outset not persuasive, if one follows the suggestion made above that there are no reasonable doubts in respect of the Commission's allegations regarding the deterrence of investment.[1037] However, the concerns regarding the capacity withholding would also suffice alone to justify E.On's commitment when compared with the alternatives suggested by Sadowska. In fact, even if the Commission had only relied on the capacity withholding, it could have taken the deterrent effect of the alternatives on investment into account as a side effect that rendered those remedies less effective than the divestiture of the power plants.

Second, as regards the question whether the precise shape of the structural remedy that was made binding by the Commission matched the Commission's theory of harm, Sadowska criticises in essence that the commitment merely scaled down E.On's generation portfolio in terms of figures, but left the structural composition of the portfolio untouched. Relying on the economic insight that in energy markets "the ownership of marginal generation confers greater market power than the ownership of base-load plants",[1038] Sadowska argues that it would have been preferable if the Commission had required a targeted divestiture of E.On's flexible plants instead of an across the board divestiture spreading over E.On's entire portfolio.[1039] The German Monopolkommission raised the same argument against the commitment decision.[1040]

Also this criticism is not persuasive. In the first place, it must be doubted that a targeted divestiture of E.On's entire flexible capacity would at all have met the proportionality requirements under Article 7. Nothing suggests that the targeted divestiture is not at least equally burdensome for E.On as the across the board divestiture. Consequently, the targeted divestiture is only necessary if it is more effective. However, in particular two aspects put the alleged higher effectiveness of the targeted divestiture into question. On the one hand, it must be recalled that the Commission's theory of harm regarding the capacity withholding predicated on the assumption that the withholding was profitable for E.On as long as the foregone profits were compensated by the gains made with base-load capacity.[1041] It is true

[1036]See Sadowska (2011): "deliberate attempt [...] to extend the scope of concerns to include the allegations of exclusionary nature" (text before fn 37); "by extending the scope of its concerns to exclusionary abuses, the Commission precludes any potentially equally effective behavioural remedies, and justifies recourse to a structural solution" (text following fn 49).

[1037]See Sect. 3.4.2.1.2.1.2.1 with footnotes 1026ff above.

[1038]Sadowska (2011), text accompanying fn 57.

[1039]Sadowska (2011), text following fn 62 and passim.

[1040]MK (2009), 497: "Gegenüber den großen Kapazitäten, die E.ON im Bereich der Grundlast veräußert, fallen die zu veräußernden Kapazitäten im Bereich der für die missbräuchliche Preisbildung entscheidenden Mittel und Spitzenlastkraftwerke gering aus. Der Monopolkommission wäre daher im Hinblick auf die zukünftige Vermeidung missbräuchlichen Verhaltens beispielsweise eine Verpflichtungszusage dergestalt überzeugender erschienen, dass E. ON seine sämtlichen Spitzenlastkraftwerke veräußert".

[1041]See Sect. 3.4.2.1.2.1.1 with footnotes 1003f and 1007 above.

that a remedy that would have deprived E.On of all of its flexible production capacities would have removed the possibility for E.On to withhold such capacity. However, such a remedy would have left the underlying incentive for capacity withholding intact. Once E.On would have built up new flexible capacities, there would hence have been a likeliness of a revival of the anticompetitive practices. Certainly, the same argument can also be made with respect to a rebuilding of base-load capacities. Once E.On rebuilds base-load capacities, the incentive to withdraw flexible capacities in order to increase the price revives. However, rebuilding base-load capacities is more difficult than rebuilding flexible capacities, because the former involves a higher amount of fixed-costs.[1042] Therefore, taking away base-load capacity from E.On prevents the recurrence of the anticompetitive practices in a more effective manner than taking away flexible capacities.

On the other hand, it must be recalled that the Commission justified the composition of the commitment made binding also with the concerns regarding the deterrence of investment in generation by third parties. In that regard, the Commission argued that the acquisition of the plants to be divested would in particular allow competitors to get access to new plants and technologies and to have a more balanced portfolio and more capacity to exert competitive pressure.[1043] This statement must be read in the light of the Sector Inquiry. The Commission had found that investments by new entrants focused only on gas fired plants and renewable energies, in particular wind technologies.[1044] This can at least partly be explained with the high fixed costs of base-load generation plants. In any event, it means that competitors had access to flexible capacities.[1045] Conversely, E.On's practice of deterring investment through long-term contracts must mostly have affected investment in base-load capacities. The across the board remedy can therefore in any event be justified with the Commission's concerns regarding the deterrence of investment. This is in principle also acknowledged by Sadowska. However, in her view, the Commission included the concerns regarding the deterrence of investment in the preliminary assessment in order to justify the commitment that was made binding.[1046] As mentioned before, this reading of the Commission's decision is from the outset not persuasive, if one follows the suggestion made above that there are no

[1042]See MK (2009), 172; Sadowska (2011), text following fn 69; also Chauve/Godfried/Kovács/Langus/Nagy/Siebert (2009), 52 fn 11: "investment in baseload plants (which are cheaper on a per MW basis and could thus exert a downward pressure on prices) takes longer, faces more environmental and political scrutiny and is sometimes restricted (nuclear plants for legal reasons, hydro plants for availability reasons)".

[1043]See Sect. 3.4.2.1.2.1.1 with footnote 1008 above.

[1044]Commission, SEC(2006)1724, 407; also in COMP/39.388 (German Electricity Wholesale, 2008), 39, the Commission stated new entrants invested in practice only in gas fired capacity after 2001.

[1045]See Sadowska (2011), text following fn 67.

[1046]See Sadowska (2011), text following fn 70: "the concerns of exclusionary nature appear to be an excuse for the across-the-board divestiture, as only in that way the Commission is able to explain the disposal of E.ON's baseload generation".

reasonable doubts in respect of the Commission's allegations regarding the deterrence of investment.[1047] However, the concerns regarding the capacity withholding would also suffice alone to justify the across the board divestiture. In fact, even if the Commission's accusations had only consisted of the capacity withholding, the Commission could have taken the positive effect of the across the board divestiture on the investment of third parties in generation capacities into account as a beneficial side effect that increased the effectiveness of the across the board divestiture remedy when compared to a targeted divestiture of flexible capacity only. For the sake of completeness, it should also be emphasised that the remedy that was made binding by the Commission implied a divestiture of both base-load and flexible capacity. The Commission did hence not count exclusively on a complete elimination of E.On's "ability" to withdraw capacity, nor on a complete elimination of E.On's "incentive" to withdraw capacity. Rather, the effect of the remedy was spread out over both the "ability" and the "incentive". This appears justified in view of the pros and cons that the divestiture of base-load capacity and of flexible capacity respectively have.

In the second place, it must be stressed that in any event the criticism of Sadowska and the Monopolkommission decries an alleged under-enforcement. Even if the criticism were justified, it could hence from the outset not serve to substantiate the hypothesis that the Commission instrumentalises the Article 9 procedure to extract overbroad, regulatory remedies. Sadowska seems to acknowledge this. She interprets the across the board remedy as a manifestation of an alignment of the Commission with E.On's own strategic interest.[1048] In that regard, it has been pointed out above that the risk of under-enforcement errors is no peculiarity of the Article 9 procedure. Also under Article 7, the Commission may have abstained from imposing a remedy that would only have targeted E.On's flexible production capacities.[1049]

Overall, it is hence submitted that there are no concrete indicia that the Commission made binding a commitment that it could not have imposed unilaterally under Article 7. In that connection, one additional observation is still called for. In the part of the decision that deals with the market test, the Commission rejected the suggestion to increase the overall amount of capacity to be divested in order to improve the competitive structure on the German wholesale electricity market. The Commission argued that the suggestion went beyond the scope of its investigation "as the commitments [should] address specific concerns of an abuse expressed in the preliminary assessment and not the dominant position of the undertaking concerned".[1050]

[1047] See Sect. 3.4.2.1.2.1.2.1 with footnotes 1026ff above.

[1048] Sadowska (2011), text accompanying fn 66 and before fn 71. See generally on the risk of alignment of interests in the context of consensual procedures as a source for under-enforcement errors Sect. 3.1.2.1 with footnote 24 above.

[1049] See Sect. 3.1.3.1.1.2 with footnote 53ff above.

[1050] COMP/39.388 (German Electricity Wholesale, 2008), 60.

3.4.2.1.2.2 E.On Gas and GDF

3.4.2.1.2.2.1 The Cases[1051]

In E.On Gas, the Commission accused E.On of having violated Article 102 TFEU. According to the preliminary assessment, E.On had engaged in a refusal to supply by way of long-term bookings in its gas transmission system.[1052] In order to meet the Commission's concerns, E.On made two commitments: In a first step, it had to immediately release a certain amount of entry capacities into its transmission grid. In a second step, it had to reduce its overall share in the bookings of entry capacity to around 50% (H-gas) and 64% (L-gas) by 2015. E.On could reach these thresholds either by returning capacities to the transmission system operator or by increasing the entry capacity into the grid, either through investments or by entering into market area co-operation. E.ON committed not to exceed the said thresholds until 2025.[1053] According to the Commission, both the immediate capacity release and the long-term reduction of E.On's share in the bookings of entry capacity were proportionate. In that connection, the Commission stated in particular that the immediate capacity release would make around 15% of the current capacity immediately available. The Commission considered this as sufficient to stimulate competition without imposing a disproportionate burden on E.On.[1054] The long-term capacity reductions were expressly classified as a structural remedy by the Commission.[1055] They were considered proportionate in view of the choice that was left to E.On how to achieve the reduction of its booking shares and of the sufficiently long transition period to achieve the target thresholds.[1056] The difference as regards the precise amounts was justified with particularities of the L-gas market.[1057] The duration of the commitments until 2025 was considered necessary in particular with a view to the long contract duration in the gas transport and supply markets and to the time necessary to attract new customers and gain market share in the gas supply market.[1058]

The GdF decision is similar to the E.On decision. It shall only be presented here briefly. Like in E.On, the Commission was concerned that GdF had committed a refusal to supply by way of long-term bookings in its gas transmission system.[1059] The theory of harm comprised also two additional allegations of refusal to supply: On the one hand, GdF was accused of having failed to conduct an open, transparent and

[1051]For a discussion see also Scholz/Purbs (2011), 64f.

[1052]COMP/39.317 (E.ON Gas, 2010), 31ff.

[1053]COMP/39.317 (E.ON Gas, 2010), 43ff.

[1054]COMP/39.317 (E.ON Gas, 2010), 65.

[1055]COMP/39.317 (E.ON Gas, 2010), 68: "the Long-Term Release is of a structural nature, because the capacities will be handed back on a lasting basis, which guarantees that the effect of the commitment will not be dependent on E.ON's future behaviour".

[1056]COMP/39.317 (E.ON Gas, 2010), 68.

[1057]COMP/39.317 (E.ON Gas, 2010), 69.

[1058]COMP/39.317 (E.ON Gas, 2010), 70.

[1059]COMP/39.316 (GdF, 2010), 26ff.

non-discriminatory procedure to allocate capacity at a particular terminal.[1060] On the other hand, the Commission suspected that GdF had strategically limited investment in additional capacity in another terminal.[1061] In order to offset the Commission's concerns, GdF undertook to release a pre-defined amount of pre-booked capacities immediately. Moreover, GdF committed to further reduce its capacity bookings to less than 50% by 2014 and to keep them under this threshold for another 10 years.[1062]

3.4.2.1.2.2.2 Discussion of Criticism

In the literature, the E.On and GdF gas foreclosure commitments are perceived as "less far-reaching" than the earlier E.On electricity and the RWE gas decisions and as "more likely consistent with the principle of proportionality". Moreover, it was suggested to interpret these decisions as a reaction by the Commission to the criticism that was levied before at the E.On electricity and the RWE gas decisions.[1063] The latter suggestion is, however, of limited plausibility. Subsequent to the E.On and GdF gas foreclosure commitments, the Commission made binding another vertical unbundling remedy in ENI.[1064] The differences between the E.On electricity, RWE gas and ENI gas decisions, on the one hand, and, on the other hand, the E.On and GdF gas foreclosure decisions, can be explained more plausibly with the different underlying theories of harm.[1065] In that connection, it should be recalled that in none of the three cases that were resolved with a vertical unbundling remedy did the theory of harm involve allegations of long-term capacity bookings. Nor do the preliminary assessments of the E.On and GdF gas foreclosure cases contain allegations regarding the existence of a risk of a repeated or lasting infringement that results from the vertically integrated structure.

In any event, the criticism that is levied at the E.On and GdF gas foreclosure commitments is less fierce than that of other decisions. It is essentially confined to an emphasis of the novelty of the Commission's theories of harm. Commentators emphasise that the Commission extended the essential facilities doctrine in that it condemned the refusal to supply capacities that GdF and E.On were effectively using for themselves.[1066]

[1060]COMP/39.316 (GdF, 2010), 31ff.

[1061]COMP/39.316 (GdF, 2010), 37ff.

[1062]COMP/39.316 (GdF, 2010), 42ff.

[1063]Wirtz/Möller (2010), 419.

[1064]The E.On gas foreclosure decision dates from the beginning of May 2010, whilst the ENI decision dates from the end of September 2010.

[1065]See Sect. 3.4.2.1.1.1.3.2 with footnote 992 above; also Gauer/Kjølbye (2014), 12.173.

[1066]Hancher/de Hautecloque (2010), 324; de Hautecloque (2013), 69; Scholz/Purbs (2011), 65: "The alleged abuse goes beyond established Art. 102 TFEU case law. The Commission did not focus on whether GDF Suez and E.ON actually used or needed these capacities to fulfil their own (long-term) import and downstream supply contracts but rather only concentrated on the potential effects on market access by competitors"; only slightly differently Kipiani (2014), 423: "[...] au niveau des préoccupations de concurrence, aucune évaluation n'a été réalisé quant au degré effectif d'utilisation des capacités. L'acceptation d'engagements permet ainsi la Commission de contourner toutes ces questions sur le terrain de la preuve".

This criticism does not seriously call into question the Commission's theory of harm. In the E.On decision, the Commission explicitly defended the view that "the mere fact that the current capacities may have been actually used by the essential facility holder for its supply business [was] not sufficient to exclude an abuse under Article 102 TFEU". Rather, the Commission considered that in such a situation, the essential facility holder was "under the obligation to take all possible measures to remove the constraints imposed by the lack of capacity (e.g. by limiting the duration and volume of its own bookings or by expanding its capacities)".[1067] Albeit it was not explicitly stated there, the same idea underlies also the GdF decision. It is true that this aspect of the Commission's theory of harm has to date not been confirmed by the EU Courts. However, the assumption that the Courts would embrace it appears at least as plausible as the opposite.[1068] As already mentioned, in Post Danmark, the Court of Justice stated with a view to the special responsibility of dominant undertakings that the origins of the dominant position in a former legal monopoly was a fact to be taken into account.[1069] In both the GdF and E.On gas decisions, the Commission relied explicitly on the historic responsibility of the two companies.[1070]

On a final note, two brief observations are still called for. On the one hand, depending on how one defines a structural remedy, one might question the "structural" nature of the E.On and GdF gas foreclosure commitments, at least in so far as the obligation to reduce capacity reservations are concerned. The question shall not be treated here in more detail.[1071] In any event, it seems misplaced to apply the "subsidiarity hypothesis"[1072] to the present remedy. Unlike the vertical unbundling remedies that were accepted in E.On electricity, RWE and ENI, the present remedies do not address the causes of future anticompetitive conduct. Nor do they aim at redressing the lingering effects of past anticompetitive conduct. The obligation to reduce capacity reservations directly mirrors the alleged anticompetitive conduct, i.e. the abusive reservation of capacity.[1073]

[1067] COMP/39.317 (E.ON Gas, 2010), 40 together with fn 46.

[1068] See also Sect. 3.4.2.1.1.1.2.2 with footnotes 977ff above for the related discussion of Dunne's criticism of the RWE decision. Gauer/Kjølbye (2014), 12.147 fn 254 point out that the Bundeskartellamt applied a similar theory of harm in Fährhafen Puttgarden. The latter case will be analysed in more detail below (Sect. 5.2.1.2).

[1069] See Sect. 3.4.2.1.1.1.2.2 with footnote 981 above.

[1070] In COMP/39.316 (GdF, 2010), 28, the Commission stated that "capacity had generally been reserved for historical reasons and had not been assigned to GDF Suez by any transparent or non-discriminatory procedure". In COMP/39.317 (E.ON Gas, 2010), fn 46, the Commission mentioned that E.On had "erected its gas transmission networks before the liberalisation of the gas transmission markets, i.e. largely protected from competition".

[1071] As explained in Sect. 3.4.2.1.2.2.1, footnote 1055 above, the Commission explicitly classified the long-term capacity reductions as "structural". See also the discussion in Sect. 3.4.1.1.4, footnote 816 above.

[1072] See Sect. 3.4.1 with footnote 737 above.

[1073] For the conclusion that the subsidiarity hypothesis should not be applied where a remedy directly mirrors the anticompetitive conduct see Sect. 3.4.1.2.1.4 with footnote 884 above.

3.4.2.1.2.3 CEZ

3.4.2.1.2.3.1 The Case

According to the Commission's theory of harm, the state owned Czech company had violated Article 102 TFEU by making a pre-emptive capacity reservation in the Czech electricity transmission system. CEZ had made the reservation in view of two alternative projects: 1000–1500 MW of lignite-fired or 1000–1500 MW of gas-fired capacity. However, according to the preliminary assessment, the reservation did not correspond to genuine generation projects. Regarding the lignite-fired alternative, the Commission suspected that CEZ would not have been in position to procure fuel in volumes necessary to carry out the project. With a view to the gas alternative, the Commission was concerned that the reservation was not backed by a genuine underlying project: The reservation did not fit with CEZ's overall portfolio development strategy; it was made at a moment which was at odds with the company's standard practice of project development; and it had been made long before the site for the gas-fired project was eventually selected. Moreover, the preliminary assessment concluded that CEZ's pre-emptive reservation had prevented the realisation of a competing project. The competing project would have connected 1000–1500 MW of lignite-fired capacity to the transmission network through the substation at which CEZ had made its pre-emptive reservation. Moreover, the Commission presumed that the competitor would have, in the long run, developed a wider portfolio of generation units.[1074]

In order to offset the Commission's concerns, CEZ committed to sell one out of several proposed power plants. The generation capacity to be divested amounted to 800–1000 MW.[1075] With a view to the necessity of the remedy, the Commission stated that transfer of generation capacity was necessary because no other type of remedy could have addressed the effects of CEZ's conduct.[1076]

3.4.2.1.2.3.2 Discussion of Criticism

It must be stressed that the remedy that was accepted in CEZ aimed at reversing the subsisting anticompetitive effects of a past practice. It was argued above that this should in principle be considered a legitimate goal of a remedy. If the Commission wants to impose such a remedy unilaterally under Article 7, it only faces a high burden as regards the causal link between anticompetitive conduct, harm and remedy.[1077] In CEZ, the Commission did not merely rely on the allegation that the abusive pre-emptive reservation had the abstract capacity to foreclose a competitor. Rather, the Commission's theory of harm identified a concrete effect of CEZ's anticompetitive conduct: The foreclosure of a competing project with

---

[1074]COMP/39.727 (CEZ, 2013), 21ff.

[1075]COMP/39.727 (CEZ, 2013), 39. See also the Commission's press release of 10 April 2013.

[1076]COMP/39.727 (CEZ, 2013), 79.

[1077]See Sect. 3.4.1.2.1.3 with footnote 880 above.

1000–1500 MW.[1078] The remedy to divest a plant with a generation capacity of 800–1000 MW adequately addresses this effect. Certainly, one might argue that the remedy stays behind the Commission's theory of harm. However, in view of the uncertainties that are linked to the "but for approach",[1079] the conservative approach of the Commission appears justified.[1080] On the other hand, one might argue that it was not necessary to address the subsisting effects of CEZ's past practice and that a simple order to abstain from pre-emptive reservations in the future would have been sufficient. However, as explained above, the Commission could legitimately assume that the self-healing powers of the electricity market would not be sufficient to eliminate the lingering effects of CEZ's anticompetitive conduct or that they would at least not be equally effective as the remedy that was made binding.[1081] Finally, one might also take offence at the fact that the condition of a "substantial risk of a lasting or repeated infringement" enshrined in Recital 12, 3rd sentence, Regulation 1/03 was not fulfilled. However, as explained above, that requirement should not be applied where a remedy aims at the elimination of the subsisting consequences of past anticompetitive conduct and where the subsistence of the structure of the undertaking as it existed before the infringement was committed is a consequence of abusive behaviour.[1082] In CEZ's case, the competing project would have reduced CEZ's market share. Its subsistence was merely a result of CEZ's anticompetitive conduct. The Commission could hence address the consequences of CEZ's conduct without having to meet the requirements of Recital 12, 3rd sentence, Regulation 1/03.[1083] Overall, there is hence no compelling reason to assume that the Commission could not have imposed the CEZ remedy also under Article 7.[1084]

3.4.2.1.3 Swedish Interconnectors[1085]

3.4.2.1.3.1 The Case

In Sweden, there is a geographic imbalance between supply and demand of electricity. Demand is strong in the south, where Sweden is more densely populated and where electricity is exported to the continent. Supply is strong in the north, where

---

[1078] Gauer/Kjølbye (2014), 12.176: "[. . .] CEZ's conduct had prevented, or at least substantially delayed, a specific competing generation project [. . .]. The divestiture of generation assets to a competitor served to address the persisting effects of the conduct".

[1079] See Sect. 3.3.4.1.1.3.2, footnote 636 above.

[1080] See also Gauer/Kjølbye (2014), 12.177, who emphasise that the Commission has the power to restore competition "to how it would have developed but for the anticompetitive conduct".

[1081] See Sect. 3.3.4.1.1.3.2 with footnote 644 above.

[1082] See Sect. 3.4.1.2.1.3, before footnote 883 above.

[1083] See for the same result Gauer/Kjølbye (2014), 12.178.

[1084] See Gauer/Kjølbye (2014), 12.176: "[. . .] the CEZ commitments are consistent with the Court of Justice's case law and the principles enshrined in Article 7(1) of Regulation 1/2003".

[1085] For discussions of the case see eg De Hautecloque/Hancher (2011), 20; Sadowska/Willems (2013); Sadowska (2014); Gauer/Kjølbye (2014), 12.53ff; Kipiani (2014), 424; Brisimi (2014), 45f and 103.

Swedish generation facilities are located and where energy is imported from Norway. There is hence a need to transport electricity from the north to the south.[1086] Due to capacity restraints in the Swedish national power grid, the Swedish network operator Svenska Kraftnät (SvK) must take action in order to prevent the congestion of the grid. Investing in new transmission capacity is only a long-term option. In the short term, congestion can be prevented by market splitting, congestion shifting and counter-trading. Market splitting implies the creation of separate price areas, thereby giving price signals to increase production and decrease consumption in the area where electricity is more expensive. Congestion shifting means that the network operator reduces trading capacities with neighbouring countries, for instance by limiting export capacities in the area where there is an energy deficit. This practice shifts congestion from internal bottlenecks to interconnectors, i.e. cross-border transmission lines. Counter-trading means that the network operator pays generators or large consumers to change their planned production or consumption. The network operator disseminates the costs of such countertrading over the users of the network.[1087]

SvK was of the opinion that it was in the best interest of Swedish electricity consumers to maintain Sweden as a single pricing zone.[1088] According to the Commission's theory of harm, SvK hence limited electricity exports, due to internal bottlenecks, on several interconnectors during a significant number of hours between 2002 and 2008. In the view of the Commission, this amounted to an infringement of Article 102 TFEU by object, because it led de facto to discrimination between the customers in Sweden and the customers in the Member States and Contracting Parties to the EEA Agreement importing electricity from Sweden. By curtailing interconnector capacity because of internal congestion, SvK treated domestic transmission services and transmission services to an interconnector intended for exporting electricity differently.[1089] The Commission also took the view that SvK had not provided the evidence necessary to demonstrate that its conduct was objectively justified.[1090]

In order to offset the Commission's concerns, SvK committed to subdivide the Swedish transmission system into two or more bidding zones and operate the Swedish transmission system on that basis by a certain date. From the date the bidding zones were operative, SvK was obliged to manage congestion without limiting trading capacity on interconnectors. In a certain area, congestion could not be a managed in an efficient manner by bidding zones, as this area did not contain sufficient suitable generation resources to be able to set a market price by itself. With a view to that area, SvK committed to increase transmission capacity by a certain date. Moreover, during

[1086]COMP/39.351 (Swedish Interconnectors, 2010), 31ff.

[1087]COMP/39.351 (Swedish Interconnectors, 2010), 37; Sadowska/Willems (2013), 133f = Sadowska (2014), 172.

[1088]Gauer/Kjølbye (2014), 12.53.

[1089]COMP/39.351 (Swedish Interconnectors, 2010), 42ff.

[1090]COMP/39.351 (Swedish Interconnectors, 2010), 45.

the interim period until the new bidding zones were operative, SvK committed to address any anticipated congestion by using counter trade.[1091]

3.4.2.1.3.2 Discussion of Criticism

Sadowska considers the Swedish Interconnectors case to be a manifestation of the "instrumental use of commitment decisions to foster primarily regulatory objectives, liberalisation and integration of electricity markets".[1092] She relies on an Article published together with Willems, in which the two authors analyse the Swedish Interconnectors case in detail.[1093] Although Sadowska and Willems conclude overall that "the final commitment to split up the market into separate price zones provides an economically sound, long-term solution to Swedish congestion", they argue nevertheless that "the Commission's action under competition rules [was] contrived and lack[ed] economic depth".[1094] They consider that the Commission could not have imposed the remedy on the basis of Article 7.[1095] In essence, Sadowska and Willems criticise four points: As regards the theory of harm, they denounce, first, that the Commission "intertwines anticompetitive concerns [...] with an internal market interest".[1096] Second, they argue that the Commission's analysis fails to take account of potential objective justifications.[1097] As far as the link between harm and remedy is concerned, they argue, third, that the remedy was insufficient inasmuch as market splitting alone does not prevent SvK from curtailing export capacities.[1098] Fourth, they decry that the remedy aimed at market integration and not at efficiency. In the view of Sadowska and Willems, had the Commission followed a pure efficiency standard, a remedy consisting of a "combination of counter-trading and partial congestion shifting" would have been equally effective and less burdensome.[1099]

None of the four arguments is convincing. The first and the fourth argument can be addressed together. They are based on the identical idea that the Commission should not pursue the goal of market integration by means of the EU competition rules. However, as is acknowledged also by Sadowska and Willems,[1100] the Interconnectors decision is in this regard backed up by a consistent line of case law.[1101] The EU Courts have constantly confirmed that a dominant undertaking

[1091]COMP/39.351 (Swedish Interconnectors, 2010), 47ff; Gauer/Kjølbye (2014), 12.54.

[1092]Sadowska (2014), 214.

[1093]Sadowska/Willems (2013), reprinted in Sadowska (2014).

[1094]Sadowska/Willems (2013), 132 = Sadowska (2014), 170.

[1095]Sadowska/Willems (2013), 153 fn 96 = Sadowska (2014), 191 fn 609.

[1096]Sadowska/Willems (2013), 143 = Sadowska (2014), 181.

[1097]Sadowska/Willems (2013), 145ff = Sadowska (2014), 183ff.

[1098]Sadowska/Willems (2013), 153 = Sadowska (2014), 191.

[1099]Sadowska/Willems (2013), 153f = Sadowska (2014), 191.

[1100]Sadowska/Willems (2013), 144 = Sadowska (2014), 181f.

[1101]See the references in COMP/39.351 (Swedish Interconnectors, 2010), fn 39ff.

violates Article 102 TFEU if it unduly restricts the integration of the single market.[1102] Sadowska and Willems criticise that the Commission's approach of sticking to the case law of the Courts is "very formalistic [and] lacks economic foundations".[1103] For the present purposes, it is, however, unnecessary to address the question whether EU competition law should in general also pursue the objective of market integration. It is submitted that, in any event, in view of the existing line of consistent case law, there is no reason to doubt that the Commission could have relied on a theory of harm based on an undue restriction of market integration also in an infringement decision and that it could have adopted a remedy pursuing the goal of market integration also on the basis of Article 7. Against this backdrop, also under the standard of Article 7, the Commission would not have had to resort to a remedy involving partial congestion shifting as a less burdensome alternative. In fact, any remedy involving partial congestion shifting would have been less effective to stop the investigated restriction of market integration than the splitting up of the market.[1104]

Next, in so far as Sadowska and Willems argue that the Commission failed to take account of potential objective justifications, it should be recalled that the concerned undertaking has the burden to prove that its abusive conduct was objectively justified.[1105] As Sadowska and Willems acknowledge,[1106] the requirements that must be met to prove an objective justification are strict.[1107] In the Interconnectors decision, the Commission stated that SvK had not provided the evidence necessary to demonstrate that its conduct was objectively justified.[1108] It may be deplorable that the decision does not contain any more detailed explanations in that regard. However, it remains very unlikely that, in an Article 7 procedure, SvK would have succeeded in proving that its conduct was objectively justified.[1109] In fact, it is improbable that either of the two potential objective justifications relied on by SvK and subsequently by Sadowska and Willems would have convinced the EU Courts. On the

---

[1102] See Jones/Sufrin (2014), 584ff; Brisimi (2014), 42ff; more generally on the single market imperative as an objective of EU competition law, Whish/Bailey (2012), 23ff; Jones/Sufrin (2014), 38ff; Brisimi (2014).

[1103] Sadowska/Willems (2013), 145 = Sadowska (2014), 182.

[1104] This is acknowledged by Sadowska/Willems (2013), 154 = Sadowska (2014), 191: "If [the Commission pursues the objective of market integration], then market splitting is more adequate to address the Commission's concerns regarding cross-border trade than any other method which involves cross-border capacity reductions".

[1105] GC, T-201/04 (Microsoft I, 2007), 688 and 1114; T-301/04 (Clearstream, 2009), 185; see also CJ, C-209/10 (Post Danmark, 2012), 40f; GC, T-286/09 (Intel, 2014), 94; Whish/Bailey (2012), 213; Mestmäcker/Schweitzer (2014), § 16, 54. According to Jones/Sufrin (2014), 389, the question of whether the burden of proof regarding the objective justification is on the concerned undertaking "is not beyond doubt".

[1106] Sadowska/Willems (2013), 147 = Sadowska (2014), 185.

[1107] See Drexl (2010), 185; Jones/Sufrin (2014), 390f; Mestmäcker/Schweitzer (2014), § 16, 54ff.

[1108] See Sect. 3.4.2.1.3.1, footnote 1090 above.

[1109] Sadowska/Willems (2013), 147 = Sadowska (2014), 185 recognise that it "is difficult to predict whether [SvK] would have been more successful in justifying its actions under a standard infringement procedure".

one hand, SvK argued that shifting congestion from internal bottlenecks to interconnectors was necessary to protect a legitimate public interest. The company contended that market splitting instead of shifting congestion would have a negative impact on the wholesale and retail electricity markets.[1110] However, this alleged negative impact on the wholesale and retail markets was disputed by the Commission. A survey carried out by the Nordic Council of Ministers had recommended market splitting. The Commission's decision contains a detailed rejection of submissions regarding an alleged negative impact on the wholesale and retail markets made by third parties during the market test.[1111] On the other hand, SvK argued that shifting congestion from internal bottlenecks to interconnectors created an efficiency when compared to counter-trading. The argument was that the costs of counter trading had to be absorbed by the Swedish consumers and not by those who profited from the export of electricity.[1112] However, this argument does not prove that the conditions for an efficiency defence are fulfilled. The said disadvantage of counter-trading could also be avoided by the splitting of the Swedish market. In fact, as the Commission explained in the decision, most of the amount of counter-trade that existed prior to the implementation of the remedy was going to disappear following the introduction of bidding zones.[1113] The shifting of congestion from internal bottlenecks to interconnectors was hence not indispensable.

Finally, also the argument that the remedy was insufficient inasmuch as market splitting alone does not prevent SvK from curtailing export capacities is not convincing. The commitment made binding by the Commission required SvK to "manage congestion in the Swedish transmission system without limiting trading capacity on interconnectors" from the date the bidding zones were operative.[1114] This means that the Commission could have imposed fines and periodic penalty payments on SvK on the basis of the commitment decision, if SvK had again curtailed export capacities in order to manage the congestion of the network. Contrary to what seems to be suggested by Sadowska and Willems, the remedy in the decision hence passes the first step of the proportionality test: The deterrent effect of fines and penalties increases the likeliness that SvK will comply with its obligation not to limit trade capacity on interconnectors.[1115] The remedy is hence suitable to put the infringement to an end.[1116] The fact that monitoring is required to ensure

[1110]Sadowska/Willems (2013), 150 = Sadowska (2014), 187.

[1111]COMP/39.351 (Swedish Interconnectors, 2010), 53ff and 86; Sadowska/Willems (2013), 148f = Sadowska (2014), 195.

[1112]Sadowska/Willems (2013), 148f = Sadowska (2014), 186f.

[1113]COMP/39.351 (Swedish Interconnectors, 2010), 89.

[1114]COMP/39.351 (Swedish Interconnectors, 2010), 47; see also 3.1. of the final commitments.

[1115]See Gippini-Fournier (2008), 417, who argues that "the incentives to comply [with an Article 9 decision] are just too high for non-compliance to constitute a practical risk".

[1116]As explained above (Sect. 3.4.2.1.1.1.1.2 with footnote 963), a remedy passes the suitability threshold, if it contributes with a sufficient likeliness to the attainment of the pursued objective. It is not necessary that the remedy fully accomplishes the objective pursued. This means that the remedy accepted in the Interconnectors case did not have to completely remove all possibilities for SvK to limit export capacities. It was sufficient that the remedy contributed with a sufficient likeliness to preventing SvK from limiting export capacities in the future.

compliance with the remedy does not call this conclusion into question.[1117] In that regard, it should also be pointed out that the commitment contained provisions on monitoring.[1118] In any event, nothing suggests that the Commission would have imposed a stricter remedy on the basis of Article 7. In fact, in an Article 7 procedure, the Commission might even have contented itself with a simple cease and desist order.

Overall, there is therefore no reason to doubt that the Commission could have imposed the remedy adopted in the Swedish Interconnectors decision also on the basis of Article 7. The decision does not support the claim that the Commission instrumentalises the Article 9 procedure to adopt remedies that it could not have imposed on the basis of Article 7. For the sake of completeness, one additional observation is, however, still called for: Kipiani has classified the Swedish Interconnectors decision as a "quasi-structural" remedy.[1119] The pros and cons of this classification shall not further be discussed. In the view defended here, the Swedish Interconnectors decision confirms yet again the futility of a classification of remedies along the lines of the structure versus behaviour dichotomy for the assessment of a remedy's lawfulness. Even if the remedy adopted in the Interconnectors decision were to be classified as a structural remedy, would this imply some sort of formal subsidiarity vis-à-vis a behavioural remedy, for instance a simple cease and desist order?

3.4.2.1.4 Conclusion Regarding the "Structural" Remedies in the Energy Sector

Overall, there is hence no compelling reason to doubt that the Commission could have imposed the "structural" remedies discussed above unilaterally on the basis of Article 7.[1120] The criticism that has been levied in the literature against the said remedies is either not substantiated at all. Or, where it is substantiated, it is not convincing. The remedies discussed above do not support the allegation that the Commission instrumentalises the Article 9 procedure for regulatory purposes. Nor does the Commission seem to extract remedies that it could not have imposed under Article 7.

[1117] The need of monitoring seems to be the essential part of Sadowska's and Willem's criticism: see Sadowska/Willems (2013), 153 = Sadowska (2014), 191: "market splitting alone, without sufficient monitoring, is not sufficient to address the Commission's concerns".

[1118] See 5. of the final commitments and COMP/39.351 (Swedish Interconnectors, 2010), 97.

[1119] Kipiani (2014), p. 308 and 489.

[1120] See also Gauer/Kjølbye (2014), 12.169, who state with respect to the RWE, ENI, E.On gas, GdF and CEZ cases that "[a]lthough the Court of Justice clarified [. . .] that the proportionality test applicable in commitment decisions is less stringent than the proportionality test pursuant to Article 7, it seems clear that the structural remedies accepted in all five cases would have met the standards set for prohibition decisions".

This conclusion should not be understood as a definitive statement that the Commission could have lawfully imposed the commitments discussed above on the basis of Article 7. Since the Commission did not adopt the decisions in question on the basis of Article 7 and since these decisions were never put to the test before the EU Courts, any such statement would necessarily remain speculative. However, what can be said is that, at least prima facie and on the basis of the available information, the remedies in question seem to satisfy the standards of Article 7 both with regard to the Commission's theory of harm and to the required link between harm and remedy. To the extent that criticism has in this connection been levied at the three commitments, it is unfounded.

3.4.2.2 Aviation Sector

In the aviation sector, the Commission accepted commitments in which the concerned undertakings offered inter alia the release of take-off and landing slots in order to offset concerns that their airline alliance agreements would violate Article 101 TFEU.[1121] The Commission itself classifies these remedies as "structural (or at least quasi-structural)".[1122] As mentioned above, in the context of merger control, also the General Court referred to the divestiture of slots as a structural remedy.[1123]

As far as can be ascertained, in spite of their "structural nature", the slot release commitments are not invoked as evidence that the Commission abuses the Article 9 procedure to extract excessive remedies or to pursue regulatory goals.[1124] For example, Dunne only mentions them as an example "of remedies that shift the focus of enforcement from mere proscription of anticompetitive behaviour toward a more pro-active approach to market control". In that connection, she describes them as "a concession that is more typically associated with ex ante airline merger control proceedings".[1125] While such statements clearly have a critical undertone, in particular when read in the broader context of the criticism of a regulatory shift of competition law, they do not imply that the Commission uses Article 9 to adopt remedies that it could not have imposed under Article 7. Against this backdrop, the following section shall not analyse the slot release commitments in the aviation

[1121] COMP/39.596 (BA/AA/IB, 2010); COMP/39.595 (Continental/United/Lufthansa/Air Canada, 2013); COMP/39.964 (Air France-KLM/Delta/Alitalia, 2017).

[1122] Commission, Ten Years of Antitrust Enforcement under Regulation 1/2003, SWD(2014) 230/2, 188 fn 268. See also OECD (2016), 21, where slot release commitments are classified as "structural".

[1123] See Sect. 3.4.1.1.3, footnote 783 above.

[1124] But see Kipiani (2014), 435ff: Although she does not expressly state that the slot release commitments went beyond what the Commission could have imposed under Article 7, she discusses those commitments under the title "L'ouverture à la concurrence par la voie détournée des engagements [. . .]".

[1125] Dunne (2014b), 427f.

sector with the same degree of detail as the structural commitments in the energy sector. Nonetheless, two basic observations are called for.

3.4.2.2.1 Limited Value of Contrasting "Structural Control" and "Behavioural Control"

The slot release commitments used in the aviation sector confirm that there is little to be gained for the evaluation of the lawfulness of a given remedy from contrasting a "structurally" oriented control of concentrations with a "behaviourally" oriented control of agreements and abuse of dominance.[1126] The theories of harm that are applied for the assessment of airline alliances under Article 101 TFEU and for the assessment of concentrations under the Merger Regulation are similar. This similarity regarding the theories of harm explains the similarity of the remedies.[1127]

Airline "alliances"—i.e. agreements that do not entail the necessary degree of integration to fall under the Merger Regulation—must be assessed under Article 101 TFEU. However, as regards the substantive criteria, the difference between the assessment of alliances under Article 101 TFEU and the assessment of concentrations under the Merger Regulation is more of a gradual than of a principled nature.[1128] The stronger the integration that is entailed by an alliance agreement, the more its assessment under Article 101 TFEU resembles that of a concentration pursuant to Article 3 Merger Regulation. As the Commission points out in its Guidelines on horizontal cooperation agreements, "[t]here is often only a fine line between full-function joint ventures that fall under the Merger Regulation and non-full-function joint ventures that are assessed under Article 101".[1129] Certainly, one difference between an alliance and a merger is that the latter typically brings about a more durable change of the structure of the market than the former. However, also that difference is only gradual. Airline alliances are normally concluded on a long-

[1126]For such an approach see the references in Sect. 3.4.1.2.1, footnotes 830ff above.

[1127]See Whish (2006), 564: "Article 9 may be particularly useful for dealing with cases [. . .] in the aviation sector, where a transaction that in many ways is like merger nevertheless falls to be analysed under Article [101 TFEU], and where complex remedies may be necessary"; see also Schweitzer (2010), 553f fn 35.

[1128]See de Broca/Mielecka Riga/Subočs (2014), 15.75: "The Commission's assessment of the airline alliances (in particular, highly integrated alliances) and mergers is broadly similar in substance"; Soames/Goeteyn/Camesasca/Hugmark (2006), 604 ff, who discuss the competitive assessment of airline concentrations and alliances under the Merger Regulation and Article 101 TFEU and the remedies employed without making a distinction between the two areas; Papy (2014): "Il est possible de dire que l'évaluation des fusions et des alliances suit une trame cohérente" (366); "Les effets anticoncurrentiels générés par un regroupement aérien ont souvent des caractéristiques communes quel que soit le type de regroupement (partages de code, alliances globales, joint ventures, fusions)" (377); "En réalité, dans les affaires d'alliances aériennes, la Commission opère un contrôle structurel des alliances très proche de celui qu'elle réalise lors des fusions malgré une base juridique différente" (660).

[1129]OJ 2011 C 11/1, 21.

term or even an indefinite basis.[1130] In any event, a potential difference between alliances and concentrations as regards their durability does not call into question the similarity of the substantive criteria for their assessment under Article 101 TFEU and the Merger Regulation. Both standards require an evaluation whether the alliance or concentration restricts competition by effect.[1131] In the context of that evaluation, the constraints imposed upon the parties of an alliance or a concentration by actual and potential competitors must be taken into account. In the latter context, the existence of entry barriers is of paramount importance.[1132] In aviation markets, the most important entry barriers are the lack of take-off and landing slots.[1133]

In aviation markets, the assessment of alliances under Article 101 TFEU and of concentrations under the Merger Regulation hence resemble each other to the extent that, under both standards, the outcome of the respective assessment may depend on the availability of slots. It is this similarity—and not an overbroad or regulatory use of the Article 9 procedure for "structural purposes"—that explains why "structural" slot release commitments are not only used in the context of merger control, but also in the context of Article 101 TFEU.

3.4.2.2.2 No Doubts As Regards the Fundamental Possibility to Impose Slot Releases Under Article 7

Prior to the enactment of Regulation 1/03, the Commission imposed slot releases in several decisions as conditions for the exemption of alliance agreements.[1134] There are in principle no reasons why the Commission should not equally have the power to order slot releases on the basis of Article 7, where its finding that an airline alliance agreement

[1130]De Broca/Mielecka Riga/Subočs (2014), 15.71 together with fn 99.

[1131]See, also with regard to the following observations, de Broca/Mielecka Riga/Subočs (2014), 15.87ff.

[1132]Papy (2014), 422: "L'analyse des barrières à l'entrée est l'un des critères principaux d'analyse des effets anticoncurrentiels. La probabilité qu'une alliance ou une fusion entre compagnies aériennes restreigne la concurrence diminue généralement en fonction de la probabilité d'entrée d'un concurrent sur le marché".

[1133]See GC, T-177/04 (EasyJet, 2006), 166: "the main barrier to entry in the air transport sector is the lack of available slots at the large airports"; see also Papy (2014), 433: "La pénurie de crénaux horaires est souvent considérée comme un élément important empêchant l'entrée de nouveaux concurrents".

[1134]OJ 1996 L 54/28 (LH/SAS, 1996); COMP/37.730 (AuA/LH, 2002); COMP/38.284 (AF/Alitalia, 2004); Whish/Bailey (2012), 976. It must be conceded that it is unclear to what extent conditions attached to an exemption can serve as a benchmark for injunctions pursuant to Article 7. It results from the AuA/LH and the AF/Alitalia decisions that the slot release conditions predicated on commitments offered to the Commission by the concerned undertakings. It could therefore be argued that there is a risk that the Commission extracted overbroad conditions. It seems, however, to follow from the case law of the General Court that conditions imposed by the Commission could not go beyond what was indispensable for the purpose of granting an exemption, see GC, T-374/94 (ENS, 1998), 206.

violates Article 101 TFEU predicates on an insufficient availability of slots. Certainly, one might argue that Article 7 does not allow the Commission to impose positive obligations to put an infringement of Article 101 TFEU to an end. However, as explained above, such an argument is not persuasive, at least where a prognosis shows that the parties are not willing to abandon their agreement. Where this is the case, prohibiting the alliance in its entirety would be disproportionate.[1135] Also the structural nature of the slot releases does not withstand their use under Article 7. Like a concentration, also an airline alliance agreement may bring about a structural effect on the market in that it eliminates or at least weakens competition between the parties on the affected flight routes. The release of slots eliminates that effect by promoting access of competitors to the market. There is hence a direct match between the competitive harm and the remedy.[1136]

In principle, the required link between harm and remedy is only maintained as long as the slots to be divested correspond to the flight routes and the number of flights for which competition between the parties is eliminated through the parties' cooperation. However, according to the circumstances of the individual case, a slot release that only mirrors precisely the affected flight routes and number of flights may not be attractive enough for competitors to spur effective entry. It may therefore not suffice to eliminate the harm that is created. It may hence be necessary to release a larger number of slots or slots on routes that are not directly affected by the cooperation.[1137] As explained above, such remedies are not automatically disproportionate under Article 7.[1138]

3.4.2.3 Deutsche Bahn

3.4.2.3.1 The Case

Deutsche Bahn (DB) is a vertically integrated state owned undertaking. Its core activity is to provide rail freight and passenger transport services. Besides that, DB also manages the rail infrastructure and the electric network used for providing trains

[1135] See Sect. 3.3.1.4.1.1.2.2.1 with footnotes 291ff above.

[1136] See de Broca/Mielecka Riga/Subočs (2014), 15.114: "Typically, the number of slots made available corresponds to the overlap between the parties (ie the total number of flights of the party which operates the lowest frequency). Such an approach aims to replicate the competitive constraint that the parties exercised on each other pre-transaction".

[1137] See de Broca/Mielecka Riga/Subočs (2014), 15.114: "[...] a competitor may need a higher frequency than the overlap in order to be able to attract business passengers or to set up a base and achieve a critical size of operations at the airport". Another means to increase the attractiveness of slot releases are so-called "grand-fathering rights". These allow the competitor "to operate slots on any route [...] after it has operated services on the specified routes of concern for a particular number of consecutive seasons" (ibid, 15.115). See also Soames/Goeteyn/Camesasca/Hugmark (2006), 606, who discuss remedies involving a "flexibility as to where to give up slots" as a challenge for EU competition law.

[1138] See Sect. 3.2.1.4 with footnote 115 above.

with traction current. It also directly supplies electric energy and diesel to railway undertakings.[1139] Already prior to the Commission's decision, third railway companies active on the downstream transport markets had in principle two ways to source traction current. They could either purchase an "all-inclusive" offer from DB that comprised both the consumption of traction current and the use of the traction current network. Or they could secure their demand from third party energy suppliers and purchase only the transmission services from DB. The Bundesgerichtshof ruled that the German energy regulation law (EnWG) applied to the electric network used for providing trains with traction current. The grid access fees were hence regulated.[1140] In practice all railway undertakings nevertheless opted for DB's "all-inclusive" offer and sourced their traction current from DB.[1141]

The Commission was concerned that DB violated Article 102 TFEU. According to the theory of harm, DB held a dominant position on the market for the supply of traction current. For the purposes of the decision, that market was considered to comprise both the transmission and the sale of energy. Being the sole supplier, DB's market shares amounted to 100%. The Commission accused DB of having abused its dominant position on the market for the supply of traction current by creating a margin squeeze on the rail long distance passenger and freight transport markets. According to the preliminary assessment, DB had granted its own affiliates discounts on traction current that prevented other companies from competing profitably on the downstream markets for passenger and freight transport. The Commission conducted an as-efficient-competitor test that showed that DB itself would not have been able to compete profitably on the downstream market, if it had had to pay the same higher prices for traction current as its competitors.[1142]

In order to offset the Commission's concerns, DB offered a commitment package that consisted of five essential elements. First, DB was obliged to introduce a new pricing system for traction current. The new pricing system had to account separately for supply prices for electricity and for the grid access fees that were regulated by the Bundesnetzagentur. As regards the supply of electricity, DB undertook to charge the same price to all railway undertakings without volume or duration based discounts. Second, DB committed to grant access to its transmission grid. However, it was expressly stipulated that the commitment did not cover the precise rules and conditions under which access had to be granted. These were left to national regulatory law. Third, DB was required to separate accounting and information between its activities as traction current network manager and as provider of electricity. Fourth, DB committed to allow its customers to terminate their contracts for the supply of traction current and to limit future supply contracts to a maximum duration of 1 year. Fifth, DB had to pay to competing railway undertakings in Germany a one-time

[1139] COMP/39.678 (Deutsche Bahn I and II, 2013), 3ff.

[1140] Bundesgerichtshof, EnVR 1/10 (Bahnstromfernleitungen, 2010); COMP/39.678 (Deutsche Bahn I and II, 2013), 21.

[1141] COMP/39.678 (Deutsche Bahn I and II, 2013), 20.

[1142] COMP/39.678 (Deutsche Bahn I and II, 2013), 36ff.

payment of 4% of their yearly traction current invoice.[1143] The commitments had a default duration of 5 years. However, they were to come to an early end if the market share of third party electricity providers reached 25% of the market for supplying traction current to non-DB railway undertakings over one calendar year.[1144]

The Commission stated that the aim of the commitments was to introduce competition on the market for the supply of traction current by promoting entry of third party electricity providers. The Commission considered that the competition from third party electricity provider would in turn constrain the price setting ability of DB for traction current and remove the possibility of a margin squeeze.[1145] The Commission considered that it was not necessary to include a price cap for electricity in the new pricing system. In its view, DB's ability to charge a margin squeeze was sufficiently limited in the short term by the one time payment and in the long term by the introduction of competition on the market for the supply of traction current.[1146] The Commission also rejected submissions received during the market test that the one time payment of 4% was too low. In that connection, the Commission stressed that the payment granted in the commitments was not a compensation for harm suffered by competitors.[1147]

3.4.2.3.2 Discussion of Criticism

The Commission's theory of harm predicates on a straightforward margin squeeze.[1148] It shall not further be discussed here.[1149] The fit between the theory of harm and the remedy package requires a closer look. Steinvorth argues that, under Article 7, "the Commission could have requested no more than the decrease of the traction current prices to third-party customers since it had found that this adjustment would have prevented a margin squeeze". In his view, "[t]he offering of additional

[1143] COMP/39.678 (Deutsche Bahn I and II, 2013), 70.

[1144] COMP/39.678 (Deutsche Bahn I and II, 2013), 81.

[1145] COMP/39.678 (Deutsche Bahn I and II, 2013), 70, 83 and 99; see also Steinvorth (2014), 629.

[1146] COMP/39.678 (Deutsche Bahn I and II, 2013), 92.

[1147] COMP/39.678 (Deutsche Bahn I and II, 2013), 93.

[1148] See also Steinvorth (2014), 629: "The application of the margin squeeze concept to the case at hand appears to be straightforward – even under the more narrow effects-based approach of the Commission's Guidance on abusive exclusionary conduct since DB as the owner of the electrical grid is under a duty to supply traction current to its competitors".

[1149] But see Rummel (2014): He emphasises that the Commission deviated from its normal practice in that it did not apply short reference periods for the AEC test, but relied on average values for the entire investigated period instead. Rummel also points out that recourse to average values for longer periods instead of short reference periods reduces the necessary amount of calculation and is thus advantageous in terms of procedural economy. He admits that such an analysis may be appropriate in the context of Article 9. Rummel nevertheless expresses doubts whether the Commission would have relied on the less precise calculation on the basis of average values also in the context of an Article 7 decision (355: "Ob sich die Kommission hingegen auch für eine abschließende Entscheidung mit einer Durchschnittsbetrachtung begnügt hätte, darf bezweifelt werden)".

commitments could be seen as the price that DB had to pay to settle the allegations".[1150]

At first blush, the Commission's remedy is not easy to comprehend. It is at least not evident that the Commission can address the foreclosure effects that a margin squeeze entails for the downstream market by promoting competition on the upstream market. One might therefore accuse the Commission of having illegitimately pursued the regulatory goal of promoting competition on the upstream market. However, a closer analysis reveals that the remedy made binding in Deutsche Bahn can be linked back to the theory of harm of the Commission. At least in principle, the remedy does not go manifestly beyond what the Commission could have imposed pursuant to Article 7.

The Commission's allegations regarding DB's margin squeeze predicated on the accusation that DB made the input price of traction current on the upstream market too expensive for its competitors. In order to put the margin squeeze to an end, the remedy therefore had to lower the price for traction current that DB was charging its downstream competitors on the upstream market. A "normal" margin squeeze remedy would in such a case have capped the upstream price at a certain maximum level. Instead, the Commission chose to lower the upstream prices indirectly by promoting competition on the upstream market. The promotion of upstream competition provided downstream competitors with alternate sources for the supply of traction current. It thus eliminated the dependence of DB's downstream competitors from DB's upstream input and thereby removed DB's capacity to squeeze the margins of its downstream competitors. At least in principle, the remedy therefore fulfils the requirement of a link between theory of harm and remedy.

It is also clear that the Commission's remedy does not address DB's too high upstream prices directly. Rather, it removes the cause that permits DB to charge these prices. It was argued above that remedies which do not address the anticompetitive conduct itself, but merely its causes, are only consistent with the principles of Articles 101 and 102 TFEU, if a strict standard regarding the causality between the object of the remedy and the anticompetitive conduct is met. As explained above, this causality requirement should apply regardless of whether the remedy is classified as "structural" or "behavioural". For remedies that change the structure of an undertaking "as it existed before the infringement was committed", Recital 12, 3rd sentence, Regulation 1/03 expressly requests such a causality in that it requires a substantial risk of a lasting or repeated infringement that derives from the very structure of the undertaking. The DB decision does not address the question whether there was such a risk. It could, however, be argued that Recital 12, 3rd sentence, Regulation 1/03 should be applied to the decision. The remedy could be said to change DB's structure as it existed before the infringement was committed, in particular because it addresses DB's dominant position on the market for the supply

[1150]Steinvorth (2014), 629: "The decision, thus, illustrates that companies may end up offering more in terms of commitments than might have otherwise been imposed against them under Article 7 at the end of a full investigation".

of traction current and DB's supply contracts and required DB to separate accounting and information between its activities as traction current network manager and as provider of electricity. Ultimately, the question whether Recital 12, 3rd sentence, Regulation 1/03 is applicable to the DB remedy does not need to be decided here. Even if the mentioned aspects were not considered as "changes to the structure of the undertaking", the Commission would, according to the approach suggested above, have to prove a sufficient causal link between the object of the remedy and the anticompetitive conduct in question. In this regard, the DB decision can be criticised for not containing any express explanations as regards the likeliness that DB's dominant position on the market for the supply of traction current, its supply contracts and the lack of separation of accounting and information between its activities as traction current network manager and as provider of electricity would in the future again lead to a margin squeeze. On the other hand, the period for which the Commission accused DB of having committed a margin squeeze in the past stretched from 2003 until 2011.[1151] The imposition of a maximum price for traction current would only have temporarily suppressed DB's ability to squeeze the margins of its downstream competitors by charging too high input prices. This ability would have resurged with the expiry of a hypothetical price cap remedy. It can therefore be argued that there was a risk of a repeated or lasting infringement that justified addressing not only the margin squeeze as such, but also its underlying causes or—in the language of Recital 12, 3rd sentence, Regulation 1/03, "the structure of the undertaking as it existed before the infringement was committed".

So far it has been argued that the Commission could, in principle, have addressed DB's dominant position on the upstream market as a cause for likely future margin squeezes also under the standard of Article 7. This leads to the question whether also the more precise contours of the DB remedy are consistent with this standard. In that regard, one might in particular doubt that Article 7 would have empowered the Commission to enjoin DB from applying any volume or duration based discounts. The Commission's theory of harm predicated on the fact that DB had not granted the same rebates to its downstream competitors that it had granted to its own affiliates. It could therefore be argued that the Commission could only have required DB to grant its downstream competitors the same rebates that it was granting to its own affiliates. However, such an argument falls short of the mark. The DB remedy aimed at eliminating DB's capacity to squeeze the margins of its downstream competitors through the promotion of competition on the upstream market. The Commission considered that DB's renouncement to offer volume- or duration-based discounts would promote the development of competition on the upstream market both by increasing price transparency and by preventing DB to leverage its inherited economies of scale while its competitors had not yet been able to develop similar efficiencies.[1152] This is a valid line of reasoning. Next, it must be emphasised, that the remedy did not promote competition on the upstream market without limits. In

[1151]COMP/39.678 (Deutsche Bahn I and II, 2013), 54.

[1152]COMP/39.678 (Deutsche Bahn I and II, 2013), 90.

particular, the commitment was to end prematurely if the market share of third party electricity providers reached 25% of the market for supplying traction current to non-DB railway undertakings over one calendar year. As is apparent from the decision, the 25% threshold corresponded to the demand of DB's four biggest downstream competitors.[1153] Hence, as soon as the 25% threshold was reached, DB's four biggest downstream competitors were no longer dependent on DB's supply of traction current and DB was deprived of the possibility to engage into a margin squeeze.

It should also be pointed out that the remedy that was accepted by the Commission is at least not manifestly more burdensome for DB than the imposition of a maximum price for the supply of traction current. Speaking more generally, there is good reason to assume that the promotion of competition on the upstream market constituted a way to counter DB's margin squeeze that was more in line with the principles of competition law than the imposition of a maximum price for traction current would have been. Price caps are generally considered to belong more to the toolkit of regulators than of competition authorities.

One final observation is still called for. Irrespective of whether one agrees with the view that was defended here regarding the question whether the DB remedy is compatible with the standard of Article 7, the remedy confirms in any event once again that the dichotomy between "structural" and "behavioural" remedies contributes at best very little to the question whether a remedy is admissible or not. Was the DB remedy of a behavioural, structural, quasi-structural or hybrid nature[1154]? Supporters of a behavioural nature could for instance rely on the lack of a transfer of property. They might also claim that the promotion of competition on the upstream market changes merely the general structure of the market, but not the structure of the undertaking DB. On the contrary, supporters of a structural nature could argue for instance that the remedy does not address the anticompetitive conduct as such, but aims at changing the structure of the upstream market. They could also argue that the remedy aimed at durably eliminating DB's future capacity to engage into anticompetitive conduct; or that the reduction of DB's market shares on the upstream market, the provision for termination rights as regards DB's supply contracts and the obligation to separate accounting and information change the "structure" of DB as it existed before the margin squeeze was committed. Moreover, even if one could classify the remedy as either structural or behavioural, would this permit a meaningful conclusion as regards the remedy's admissibility under Article 7? If one classified the remedy as "structural", would this imply its formal subsidiarity vis-à-vis a "behavioural" capping of the price of traction current?

[1153] COMP/39.678 (Deutsche Bahn I and II, 2013), 96.

[1154] Kipiani (2014), p. 498 classifies the remedy as "quasi structural and behavioural".

3.5 Ancillary Remedies

To achieve its purpose, a remedy needs to be implemented effectively. Besides the main obligation that prescribes how to put the found infringement to an end or how to offset the competition concerns, a complete remedy package will therefore often comprise ancillary obligations for the concerned undertaking that aim at ensuring an effective implementation.[1155] Ancillary remedies play a role both in the context of Article 7 and Article 9. The following section will, first, briefly touch upon two types of ancillary remedies that are unproblematic under both provisions: The obligation to inform customers and the obligation to report to the Commission. The focus of the present section will, however, lie on a closer look at the Commission's practice under Article 9 to outsource tasks related to the implementation of a remedy to external bodies, in particular monitoring trustees and alternative dispute resolution mechanisms. It will be argued that the latter practice is, at least in principle, compatible with the standards of Article 7.

3.5.1 Information of Customers

A rather straightforward way to foster the enactment of a remedy consists of requiring the infringing undertaking to inform the market about it. The Commission has made frequent use of this possibility under Article 7.[1156] Information obligations have been imposed on associations of undertakings vis-à-vis their members,[1157] on suppliers vis-à-vis their customers, both in the context of Article 101[1158] and 102 TFEU,[1159] and even vis-à-vis the general public.[1160] A more recent example of an information obligation is the Mastercard decision. Having found that Mastercard's MIFs infringed Article 101 TFEU, the Commission did not content itself with ordering Mastercard to repeal the MIFs.[1161] It also required Mastercard to communicate the changes to its member banks and to other relevant financial institutions.[1162] Information obligations are also used in the context of Article

---

[1155]See also Hennig (2010), who distinguishes in the context of Article 9 decisions between "core commitments" and "auxiliary commitments" (Kernzusagen und Hilfszusagen); Brückner (2012), 19f, who distinguishes in the context of merger remedies between "primary" and "secondary" obligations.

[1156]For references see Müller-Tautphaeus (2003), 271ff; Kerse/Khan (2012), 6-047 fn 134; O'Donoghue/Padilla (2013), 885.

[1157]Eg OJ 1982 L 54/36 (VBBB, 1981); Müller-Tautphaeus (2003), 271f.

[1158]Eg OJ 1980 L 377/16 (Johnson, 1980); Müller-Tautphaeus (2003), 272.

[1159]Eg OJ 2001 L 166/1 (DSD, 2001); Müller-Tautphaeus (2003), 272.

[1160]Eg OJ 1982 L 161/18 (Hasselblad, 1982); Kerse/Khan (2012), 6-047 fn 134.

[1161]See Sect. 3.3.1.5.1.1.2 with footnote 385 above.

[1162]COMP/34.579 (Mastercard, 2007); Kerse/Khan (2012), 6-047.

9. For example, the Deutsche Bahn commitments obliged DB to provide competing railway undertakings with detailed information on their individual consumption pattern for traction current.[1163]

3.5.2 *Reporting to the Commission*

A further simple and frequently used ancillary measure to ensure compliance with a remedy is the imposition of an obligation to report on the implementation to the Commission.[1164] The Deutsche Post decision can serve as an illustration. The Commission found that Deutsche Post had infringed Article 102 TFEU, inter alia by using revenues from its letter-mail monopoly to cross-subsidise a predatory pricing strategy on the liberalised market for business parcel services. During the administrative procedure, the company undertook to separate the business parcel services from the rest of its business.[1165] In the final decision, the Commission required Deutsche Post to put an end to the predatory pricing strategy. In order to ensure compliance with that obligation, the company had to submit to the Commission a yearly statement of the costs and the revenue of its new affiliate operating the business parcel services and a statement of the transfer price paid by the latter for goods and services procured from Deutsche Post.[1166] A similar reporting obligation was imposed in Wanadoo, a further predatory pricing case: Wanadoo was required to forward to the Commission the revenue account for its different ADSL services, showing its accrued income, operating costs and customer acquisition costs.[1167] The Coca-Cola commitments constitute an example where an obligation to report to the Commission was included in an Article 9 decision.[1168]

3.5.3 *Delegation of the Implementation of a Remedy*

The Commission may also rely on external help to implement a remedy, in particular in more complex cases that are resource-intense or require expert knowledge. The two most important mechanisms that may be used in this context are trustees and alternative dispute resolution (ADR) bodies. The following section will analyse their

---

[1163] COMP/39.678 (Deutsche Bahn I and II, 2013), 81.

[1164] Eg OJ 1998 L 252/47 (AAMS, 1998); OJ 2001 L 166/1 (DSD, 2001); COMP/38.698 (CISAC, 2008); for further references see Müller-Tautphaeus (2003), 273; see also the Commission's Manual of Procedure (2012), Module 25, 26.

[1165] See IP/01/419.

[1166] COMP/35.141 (Deutsche Post, 2001); Kerse/Khan (2012), 6-047.

[1167] COMP/38.233 (Wanadoo, 2003).

[1168] COMP/39.116 (Coca-Cola, 2005), 51.

role in more detail. The discussion will be confined to private actors, upon which the tasks of trustees and ADR bodies are typically conferred. However, for the sake of completeness, it should be pointed out that sector specific regulators can also assume the functions of a trustee or an arbitrator.[1169] Some merger remedies and Article 9 commitments contain clauses in which the concerned undertakings subjected themselves to the monitoring[1170] or the arbitration[1171] of such an authority.

The following section will, in a first step, give an overview of the Commission's practice to rely on external actors to assist with the implementation of remedies. In this respect, a distinction will be made between trustees, on the one hand, and ADR mechanisms on the other. In a second step, the partial annulment of the monitoring mechanism in the Microsoft case and its implications for the Commission's practice shall be analysed. The latter analysis is of particular importance for the overall goal of the present chapter to assess to what extent the Commission's commitment practice goes beyond the Commission's powers under Article 7. In the literature, the Commission's frequent recourse to monitoring trustees in commitment decisions is perceived as a manifestation of the regulatory instrumentalisation of the Article 9 procedure and of the fact that the Commission makes binding commitments that it could not have imposed under Article 7.[1172]

3.5.3.1 The Practice of the Commission

3.5.3.1.1 Trustees

The origins of the Commission's deployment of trustees can be traced back at least to the mid 1990s, when the Commission started using them to assist with the implementation of merger remedies.[1173] The practice developed mostly in the context of divestiture commitments, due to the important role played by the latter under the Merger Regulation. An initial phase of experimentation[1174] has in the meantime lead to a variety of soft law that is predominantly concerned with the

[1169]See Lübking (2008), 82; Brückner/Hoehn (2010), 77; Hoehn (2012), 15f; Idot (2012), 9.

[1170]COMP/M.2947 (Verbund Allianz, 2003), 154; COMP/36246 (GDF, 2004); COMP/39386 (EDF, 2010), 98; COMP/39316 (GDF, 2010), final commitments p. 10f.

[1171]COMP/M.2876 (Newscorp, 2003), 225(l); COMP/M.3916 (T-Mobile Austria, 2006), 140.

[1172]Dunne (2014b), 427: "Commitments that are made binding also generally involve provisions regarding implementation and compliance. These include the possible appointment of a third party monitoring trustee to oversee performance, a supervisory mechanism that was held by the General Court to be unavailable in the context of Article 7 decisions in the first Microsoft case. Accordingly, under Article 9, a firm might agree to assume quasi-regulatory market obligations, as well as the establishment of a regulator-like monitoring body".

[1173]Brückner (2012), 2, mentions OJ L 354/32 (Procter & Gamble II, 1994), 186, as the first decision in which the Commission relied upon a trustee.

[1174]For a detailed description of the trustee practice under the Merger Regulation see Brückner (2012), 29ff.

appointment of trustees to ensure the divestiture of a viable business.[1175] After the General Court partially annulled the part of the Commission's 2004 Microsoft decision that had required the establishment a monitoring mechanism under Article 7 Regulation 1/03,[1176] the Commission even inserted an explicit statutory basis for the use of trustees into the implementing regulation of the Merger Regulation.[1177] The Commission also extended its recourse to trustees to remedies adopted in regard of Articles 101 and 102 TFEU.[1178] Although to date the vast majority of decisions providing for a trustee has in this respect been adopted on the basis of Article 9,[1179] the 2004 Microsoft decision demonstrates the Commission's basic readiness to impose an obligation to appoint a trustee also unilaterally on the basis of Article 7.[1180] In a speech given in 2012, DG Italianer pointed out that the Commission was considering an even more frequent appointment of trustees in order to strengthen the monitoring of its remedies.[1181]

The role of trustees that assist in the implementation of competition remedies has been described as "schizophrenic".[1182] The description is due to the fact that a trustee is formally engaged and in particular remunerated by the concerned undertaking, but acts nevertheless on behalf and under the instruction of the Commission.[1183] The following section will analyse this role in more detail. Two preliminary caveats are called for: First, it must be pointed out that the presentation that will be given rests to a large extent on the Commission's practice in the context of merger

---

[1175]See the Remedies Notice (2001), 26; Remedies Notice (2008), 117 to 13; moreover the Commission's Model Texts for Divestiture Commitments and the Trustee Mandate under the Merger Regulation and the corresponding Best Practice Guidelines. The latter documents were all updated in 2013.

[1176]GC, T-201/04 (Microsoft, 2007), 1230ff.

[1177]See Article 20a Regulation 802/2004. A member of the Commission's services described the new provision as "nothing more than a codification of the past practice" that was not considered to revisit the role of the trustee in merger control, see Rakovsky (2009), 2. For a more detailed discussion of the provision see Brückner (2012), 109ff, who raises doubts regarding its compatibility with higher-ranking law.

[1178]The Commission has in the meantime described the appointment of a trustee as in line with its "usual practice" as regards remedies in respect of mergers and the application of article 101 and 102 TFEU, see COMP/39.316 (GDF, 2009), 86, and COMP/39.317 (E.ON Gas, 2010), 71. See also the Commission's Manual of Procedure (2012), Module 16, 48 and 83.

[1179]Examples of Article 9 decisions concerning Article 101 TFEU and containing are trustee commitment are: COMP/38.173 (Premier League, 2006); COMP/38.348 (REPSOL, 2006); COMP/39.596 (BA/AA/IB, 2010); COMP/39.398 (Visa, 2010).

With respect to Article 102 TFEU one can mention the following examples: COMP/38.381 (Alrosa, 2006); COMP/39.388 (German electricity wholesale and balancing market, 2008); COMP/39.402 (RWE, 2009); COMP/39.316 (GDF, 2009); COMP/39.317 (E.ON Gas, 2010); COMP/39.315 (ENI, 2010); COMP/39.654 (Reuters, 2012); COMP/39727 (CEZ, 2013); COMP/39678 (Deutsche Bahn I, 2013).

[1180]COMP/37792 (Microsoft, 2004), 1043ff.

[1181]Italianer (2012), 9.

[1182]Turnbull/Holmes (2002), 504, 507; see also Sofianatos (2009), 561 fn 118; Brückner (2012), 3.

[1183]See Kellezi (2010), 499f; Hoeg (2014), 127.

remedies. However, as far as trustees are concerned, the Commission does not seem to distinguish between whether a remedy has been adopted on the basis of the Merger Regulation or on the basis of Article 9 Regulation 1/03.[1184] In principle, there is no reason why the same practice should not also be applied in the context of Article 7 Regulation 1/03.[1185] The boundaries that have been drawn in that latter regard by the General Court in Microsoft will be discussed further below. Second, it must be emphasised that the role of the trustee in a particular case depends always on the individual mandate.[1186] The generalised observations made below apply hence without prejudice to diverging provisions in the individual case.

3.5.3.1.1.1 Tasks and Powers of Trustees

The tasks and powers of a trustee cannot be described without further differentiation. A distinction must be made between general tasks and powers that are common to all trustees and specific ones that depend on the type of remedy.

3.5.3.1.1.1.1 General Tasks and Powers

To date, trustees are not involved with the initial design of a remedy. Their mandate remains confined to the implementation phase.[1187] Three general functions can be made out: First, trustees serve as monitors for the Commission. They can, at any time and at the Commission's request or on their own initiative, report to the Commission on the compliance of the undertaking with the remedy.[1188] Further, in regular predefined intervals, they must draw up extensive compliance reports, the confidential version of which is only communicated to the Commission.[1189] Second, trustees generally serve as advisors, both to the Commission and to the concerned undertakings. They may propose such measures as they consider necessary to ensure an undertakings' compliance with a remedy. Their closely related role as a mediator will be presented in more detail below. In the event that the undertaking does not

---

[1184] See the Commission's Manual of Procedure (2012), Module 16, 83f.

[1185] See, with respect to arbitration clauses, Blanke (2011a), 30-242.

[1186] Brückner/Hoehn (2010), 73; see also Merger Remedies Notice (2008), 119: "[...] duties and obligations will be specified in detail in the trustee mandate".

[1187] See Remedies Notice (2008), 119: "The tasks of the trustee will normally start immediately after the adoption of the Commission decision..."; but see De Valois Turk (2009), 339, who suggests that the increased amount of data the Commission requires before it accepts remedies may favour an earlier involvement of the trustee.

[1188] For divestiture remedies see the model text for the trustee mandate, 19; for other types of remedies see, for example, annex V to the final commitments in COMP/39.654 (Reuters, 2012), 6 (c); final commitments in COMP/39298 (Visa, 2010), 8.7(c).

[1189] For divestiture remedies see the model text for the trustee mandate, 16ff and the Remedies Notice (2008), 119, fifth indent; for other types of remedies see, for example, the final commitments in COMP/39.316 (GDF, 2009), 4.2; COMP/39.317 (E.ON Gas, 2010), 17.4; COMP/39.596 (BA/AA/IB, 2010), 5.2.1.d) and 5.2.6; COMP/39298 (Visa, 2010), 8.7(b).

follow the trustee's proposals, the latter may propose necessary measures to the Commission.[1190] Adaptations of remedies under a review clause can require a previous hearing of the trustee.[1191] Third, trustees serve as a contact point for potential purchasers of a business that is to be divested or beneficiaries of a non-divestiture remedy.[1192]

These general functions common to all types of trustees are accompanied by rather broad investigative powers.[1193] The undertakings have to grant the trustee full and complete access to books, records, documents, management or other personnel, facilities, sites and technical information necessary for fulfilling his duties under the mandate.[1194] The trustee may demand copies of documents of any document, has the right to occupy office space on the premises of the concerned undertakings and can request meetings with the personnel.[1195] Overall, the investigative powers do not lag much behind those provided to the Commission itself by Article 20 II of Regulation 1/2003 and Article 13 II of the Merger Regulation.[1196] However, as will be further explained below, there is one significant difference between the investigative powers of the trustee and those of the Commission: Different from the Commission, the trustee does not have any coercive means. If the undertaking refuses to grant the trustee the required access, the trustee has only the possibility to report to the Commission. The latter will then have to decide whether the trustee's request was justified and, when appropriate, take action to compel the undertaking.

3.5.3.1.1.1.2 Specific Tasks and Powers

Trustees dispose of further tasks and accompanying powers that vary according to the type of remedy. Where a divestiture remedy is concerned, the tasks and powers of the trustee are defined rather precisely in the existing soft law. The latter does not give a comparably precise outline in the context of non-divestiture remedies. The 2008 Merger Remedies Notice states that in view of the wide range of non-divestiture commitments, no general and comprehensive requirements for the implementation of non-divestiture commitments can be set out.[1197]

[1190]Model text for trustee mandate, 6; see also annex V to the final commitments in COMP/39.654 (Reuters, 2012), 6(e); final commitments in COMP/39298 (Visa, 2010), 8.7(e).

[1191]Final commitments in COMP/39.316 (GDF, 2009), 5.2.2; COMP/39.317 (E.ON Gas, 2010), 25; see also the final commitments in COMP/39.596 (BA/AA/IB, 2010), 8.4.

[1192]Remedies Notice (2008), 119, fourth indent; see also the final commitments in COMP/39.596 (BA/AA/IB, 2010), 5.2.3.

[1193]It follows from the Remedies Notice (2008), 122, that the investigative powers do, in principle, also apply to the divestiture trustee.

[1194]Model text for the trustee mandate, 21; see also Remedies Notice (2008), 120.

[1195]Model text for divestiture commitments, 32; model text for trustee mandate, 21.

[1196]See Brückner (2012), 121f.

[1197]Remedies Notice (2008), 129.

3.5.3.1.1.1.2.1 Divestiture

Trustees get involved with the implementation of a divestiture remedy either as a monitoring trustee or as a divestiture trustee.[1198] The two roles may eventually be exercised by separate entities.[1199] Both must be distinguished from another actor: The hold separate manager. A divestiture remedy will only fulfil its purpose if the divested business is viable and operated by a suitable purchaser.[1200] To prevent the divesting parties from extracting valuable resources from the business to be divested, hold-separate and ring fencing obligations are generally indispensable during the interim period between the adoption of the decision and the completion of the divestiture.[1201] The most important of those is the nomination of a hold-separate manager. The hold separate manager is responsible for the management of the business to be divested and the implementation of further hold-separate and ring fencing obligations.[1202] Ideally, he "is a senior executive from within the business to be divested who is likely to take charge of developing it [...] after disposal".[1203]

Like the hold-separate manager, also the monitoring trustee guarantees for the maintenance of the viability of the business during the interim period.[1204] Compared to the former, the role of the latter is, however, more focused on supervision than on managing. Besides the general tasks and powers pointed out above, the monitoring trustee may instruct the hold separate manager and even remove him, if the latter endangers the timely and proper implementation of the remedy. In such a case, the appointment of a new hold separate manager will be subject to approval by the monitoring trustee.[1205] The monitoring trustee can even be given the power to exercise the divesting party's rights as shareholder in the business to be divested and to replace members of its boards.[1206] It has been pointed out that these rather far reaching powers of the trustee during the interim period blur the boundaries between monitoring and managing.[1207] Apart from the supervisory tasks during the interim period, the monitoring trustee also plays a role for the actual divestiture. Most important in this respect is his task to provide the Commission with a reasoned opinion as to the suitability of a potential purchaser.[1208] Furthermore, in carve out

---

[1198] See the Remedies Notice (2008), 117ff and 121f.

[1199] Remedies Notice (2008), 123. According to the Best Practice Guidelines, the tasks of the monitoring and the divestiture trustee can be assigned to different Trustees in practice (10); the decision whether one or more trustees are appointed should be determined on a case-by-case basis by the parties (35).

[1200] Remedies Notice (2008), 23f.

[1201] Remedies Notice (2008), 36 and 107ff.

[1202] Remedies Notice (2008), 112.

[1203] Cook (2011), 45-105.

[1204] Remedies Notice (2008), 112; Best Practice Guidelines, 30.

[1205] Remedies Notice (2008), 112.

[1206] Best Practice Guidelines, 22; see also Hoeg (2014), 141, who mentions that such situations are not uncommon and cites examples from the Commission's merger practice.

[1207] Brückner/Hoehn (2010), 75ff.

[1208] Remedies Notice (2008), 119, third indent.

cases he has to monitor the splitting of assets and the allocation of personnel between the divested and the retained business.[1209]

In contrast to the monitoring trustee, the divestiture trustee only intervenes if the parties do not themselves succeed in finding a suitable purchaser within a fixed period of time. In this case, a divestiture trustee will be appointed with an irrevocable and exclusive mandate to dispose of the business at no minimum price.[1210] A divestiture trustee is allowed to include in the sale and purchase agreement such terms and conditions as he considers appropriate for an expedient sale.[1211] The parties have to grant him comprehensive powers of attorney, covering all stages of the divestiture.[1212] Although provided for in virtually all divestiture remedies, divestiture trustees are in practice hardly ever used. In view of their unattractiveness, divesting undertakings have an incentive to comply with the remedy before the lapse of the deadline that triggers the appointment of a divestiture trustee.[1213]

3.5.3.1.1.1.2.2 Non-divestiture

Given the lack of soft law on the matter, it is difficult to make generalised statements about the tasks and powers of trustees in the context of non-divestiture remedies. It seems that they are mostly confined to the general missions to report and advise.[1214] To the extent that dispute resolution may require decision-making, it is essentially reserved to arbitration tribunals and experts and not to trustees. As will be further explained below, trustees merely assume the function of a mediator in the early stages of an arbitration procedure.

There are, however, some examples in which limited decision making powers have been conferred on trustees: In Premier League, the trustee had a decisive influence on the selection of the bidders in the auction of the concerned football rights.[1215] In BA/AA/IB, the trustee had the power to verify whether adjustments and annual renegotiations of special prorate agreements complied with the commitments[1216]; he could even make adjustments to the special prorate agreements rate[1217] or exclude certain prorate agreements from application vis-à-vis third parties.[1218] In the merger remedy in SNCF, a trustee was empowered to render a binding expert

[1209]Remedies Notice (2008), 119, second indent.

[1210]Remedies Notice (2008), 121; Best Practice Guidelines, 15.

[1211]Remedies Notice (2008), 121.

[1212]Remedies Notice (2008), 122.

[1213]See Hoeg (2014), 127 and 142ff.

[1214]See, for instance, the final commitments in the following non-divestiture cases, in which the trustee's tasks and powers were confined to reporting and giving advise: COMP/38348 (Repsol, 2006), annex II, II.2; COMP/38348 (E.On Gas, 2010), 17; COMP/39398 (Visa, 2010), 8.7; COMP/39678 (Deutsche Bahn I, 2013), 2.7.

[1215]Final commitments in COMP/38173 (Premier League, 2006), 7.8.2.

[1216]Final commitments in COMP/39.596 (BA/AA/IB, 2010), 3.5.d), 3.12, 3.13.

[1217]Final commitments in COMP/39.596 (BA/AA/IB, 2010), 3.9.

[1218]Final commitments in COMP/39.596 (BA/AA/IB, 2010), 3.8.

opinion in a fast track dispute resolution procedure that was subject to review by a national regulator.[1219]

3.5.3.1.1.1.3 Overall Development of the Tasks and Powers Conferred on Trustees in the Commission's Practice

Observers have noted that the Commission has over time oriented the role of trustees away from decision-making and towards a mostly supervisory role.[1220] According to the old 2001 Remedies Notice, the mandate of a trustee could include also the right to "impose" measures.[1221] Under the 2008 Remedies Notice, this was reduced to a mere right to propose.[1222] As far as divestiture remedies are concerned, decision-making tasks are today exercised by the hold separate manager under the mere supervision of the trustee.[1223] Nevertheless, the trustee retains the right to instruct and replace the hold separate manager and to exercise shareholders rights. As regards non-divestiture remedies, decision-making powers are in principle conferred to arbitration tribunals and experts; trustees are given at best a mediatory role. However, also here, in rare cases trustees obtain the power to take decisions.

3.5.3.1.1.2 Appointment, Qualifications, Remuneration and Discharge

The trustee is proposed and appointed by the concerned undertaking on the basis of the mandate, which is concluded as a contract between the undertaking and the trustee.[1224] Both the mandate and the trustee need the Commission's approval.[1225] In order to be eligible, trustees must dispose of the necessary qualifications. The Commission considers auditing and other consulting firms as particularly well placed to fulfil the task.[1226] The concerned undertaking can also replace or discharge the trustee only after approval by the Commission. The trustee may only cease his functions in agreement with the Commission.[1227]

[1219]COMP/M.5655 (SNCF, 2010) 125, 134f and 145; see Idot (2012), 8.

[1220]Brückner (2012), 53 and 125; Hoeg (2014), 140.

[1221]Remedies Notice (2001), 52; Hoeg (2014), 140 fn 124.

[1222]Remedies Notice (2008), 118.

[1223]See Hoeg (2014), 140.

[1224]Remedies Notice (2008), 123f. In the context of Regulation 1/03 see eg the final commitments in COMP/39654 (Reuters, 2012), annex V; COMP/39678 (Deutsche Bahn I, 2013), Anlage 1.

In the Microsoft case, the Commission made an exception to this general rule: Microsoft had to submit a list with suitable candidates. The actual designation of the trustee was, however, reserved to the Commission (see COMP/37792 [Microsoft, 2004], 1048(i)).

[1225]Remedies Notice (2008), 124ff; see for more details Brückner (2012), 31ff; Hoeg (2014), 127ff.

[1226]Remedies Notice (2008), 125; see for more details Brückner (2012), 40; Hoeg (2014), 135f, who points also out that several specialised trustee firms have emerged (131 fn 57).

[1227]Remedies Notice (2008), 125f; model text for the trustee mandate, 33ff; in the context of Regulation 1/03 see eg the final commitments in COMP/39654 (Reuters, 2012), annex V; COMP/39678 (Deutsche Bahn I, 2013), Anlage 1; for more details see Brückner (2012), 69ff; Hoeg (2014), 138f.

Finally, the concerned undertaking and not the Commission remunerates the trustee.[1228] As part of the mandate, the fee structure is subject to the Commission's approval.[1229] On the condition that it does not impede the trustee's independence and effectiveness in fulfilling the mandate, the Commission leaves the choice of the remuneration structure in principle to the concerned undertaking. It has, however, expressed a certain scepticism towards fixed fees instead of hourly rates and, as regards divestiture remedies, towards success premiums that are tied to the sales price of the business to be divested. Whilst fixed fees may run counter to the need for careful action, success premiums can provide an incentive not to focus on the swiftness of the divestiture, but on the time consuming search for the purchaser offering the highest sales price.[1230]

3.5.3.1.1.3 Relations with Market Participants and the Commission

3.5.3.1.1.3.1 The Trustee's Independence from Market Participants

3.5.3.1.1.3.1.1 Independence from the Addressee of the Remedy

A trustee must be independent from the addressee of the remedy.[1231] As a general rule, the Commission will therefore not accept persons or institutions that serve at the same time as auditor or investment advisor of such an undertaking.[1232] However, not every relation with the undertaking excludes the necessary degree of independence. Rather, it must be examined according to the circumstances of the case at hand whether a relation "will not impair the Trustee's objectivity and independence in discharging its tasks".[1233] Apart from the exercise of his mandate, a trustee may neither be employed nor appointed to the management or board by the undertaking. Other business relationships, in particular investments in the stocks of the undertaking, can, however, be admissible, as long as they are "in the normal course of business" and not "material" for either side.[1234] The trustee, his team and partner firms must disclose all existing relationships with the undertaking[1235] and obtain the approval of the Commission.[1236] The independence of the trustee must cover not only the period of the mandate, but also a certain time preceding and following it.[1237] Finally, the independence from the undertaking engaged by a remedy is further

[1228] Remedies Notice (2008), 125; for more details see Brückner (2012), 66; Hoeg (2014), 137f.

[1229] Model text for the trustee mandate, 30; Brückner (2012), 66; Hoeg (2014), 137.

[1230] See the Merger Remedies Study (2005), p. 93, 21ff; Hoeg (2014), 137f.

[1231] See Remedies Notice (2008), 124f; model text for the trustee mandate, 24ff; for more details Brückner (2012), 37ff; Hoeg (2014), 130ff.

[1232] See Remedies Notice (2008), 125.

[1233] Remedies Notice (2008), 125.

[1234] Model text for the trustee mandate, 26.

[1235] Model text for the trustee mandate, 24; Hoeg (2014), 131.

[1236] Model text for the trustee mandate, 27.

[1237] See model text for the trustee mandate, 29; Hoeg (2014), 131.

strengthened by the fact that the latter may not instruct the trustee in the exercise of his mandate.[1238]

3.5.3.1.1.3.1.2 Independence from Other Market Participants and Consequences of a Lack of Independence

It is not quite clear whether and to what extent a trustee must also be independent from other market participants besides the undertaking engaged by a remedy. The 2008 Remedies Notice provides that "[t]he trustee shall be independent of the parties [...] and shall not be, or become, exposed to a conflict of interests".[1239] Hoeg suggests that competitors are not captured by the independence criterion, but by the prohibition of a conflict of interests.[1240] Other commentators do not make such a distinction and consider that the independence requirements provided for by the soft-law only cover the undertaking engaged by a remedy.[1241] The latter view appears convincing, given that the model text for the trustee mandate explicitly leaves it up to the parties to insert clauses regarding the trustee's independence from potential purchasers of the business to be divested.[1242]

The Court of Justice so far seems to take a strict stance on the independence that is required of a trustee. In the merger case Éditions Odile Jacob, it confirmed a judgment of the General Court that had annulled the Commission's approval of a buyer in the context of a divestiture commitment for lack of independence of the trustee.[1243] The case concerned Vivendi's sale of its European publishing business to Lagardère. The transaction was carried out as a so-called "warehousing" arrangement.[1244] This means that the sold business was not sold directly from Vivendi to Lagardère, but initially "parked" with an investment bank until clearance of the concentration by the Commission. The investment bank first appointed an independent trustee as a member of the board of the sold business. In order to be allowed to acquire the business from the investment bank, Lagardère later committed to the Commission to divest essential parts of it. With the Commission's approval, the same person who had initially served as trustee for the entire sold business was reappointed as trustee for the implementation of the divestiture commitment. When the Commission approved the sale of the parts of the business that were concerned

[1238]The Remedies Notice (2008), 118, only requires the Commission's approval for an instruction of the trustee; the Best Practice Guidelines, 9, and the model text for the trustee mandate, 5, fully exclude the undertaking's right to give instructions to the trustee.

[1239]Merger Remedies Notice (2008), 125.

[1240]Hoeg (2014), 130 fn 51.

[1241]Brückner (2012), 39; von Koppenfels (2013), 12.

[1242]Model text for the trustee mandate, 28.

[1243]CJ, C-553/10 (Éditions Odile Jacob, 2012). For general discussions of the case see eg Goyder (2012), 16f; von Koppenfels (2013), 12; Hoeg (2014), 132ff.

[1244]For the term and the open questions regarding the legal treatment of such transactions see Goyder (2012), 16f; Jones/Sufrin (2014), 1147f.

by the divestiture commitment to an investment firm, an unsuccessful purchaser challenged the approval decision.

The General Court took offence at the fact that the first and the second trustee mandate had been exercised by the same person.[1245] In the Court's view, under the first mandate, the trustee was necessarily implicated in the performance of the full range of statutory powers of a member of the executive board in relation to the entirety of the business that was sold from Vivendi to Lagardère.[1246] On the contrary, under the second trustee mandate, the trustee was responsible to ensure that the divestiture of only parts of these target assets was executed in compliance with the commitments.[1247] As regards the effect of the trustee's report on the content of the Commission's decision approving the sale to the investment firm, the General Court held that even though it was true that the decision was not exclusively based on that report, it was nonetheless clear that the report had had a decisive influence on that decision.[1248]

In his opinion on the case, Advocate General Mazák suggested to set aside the judgment of the General Court. In his view, the General Court had not analysed thoroughly enough whether the trustee had actually not acted in an independent manner and whether his report had really had a decisive influence on the approval decision. According to the Advocate General, only if this were the case, a potential lack of independence would have had an impact on the lawfulness of the approval decision.[1249] The Court of Justice took a different view. As regards the question of whether the trustee disposed of the necessary independence, it sided with the General Court.[1250] Moreover, the Court of Justice ruled that the lack of independence of the trustee was as such sufficient to trigger the annulment of the approval decision. The General Court was therefore under no obligation to examine whether the trustee really acted in a way that was not independent.[1251]

The Éditions Odile judgments still do not fully clarify the question whether and to what extent a trustee must generally be independent from other parties besides the undertaking engaged by a remedy. In the case, the divestiture commitment stipulated that the trustee had to be independent from Largardère and from the business that was sold to it and the Courts relied directly on the commitment as a basis for the independence requirement.[1252] It remains open, however, whether the Courts would have taken an equally strict approach, if the commitment had not expressly required the trustee's independence from the target of the acquisition. Another question has, however, been answered in an unequivocal manner[1253]: A lack of independence warrants annulment,

[1245]Cf. GC, T-452/04 (Éditions Odile Jacob, 2010), 88, 89, 94, 100.

[1246]Cf. GC, T-452/04 (Éditions Odile Jacob, 2010), 103.

[1247]Cf. GC, T-452/04 (Éditions Odile Jacob, 2010), 106.

[1248]Cf. GC, T-452/04, 110.

[1249]Opinion of AG Mazák, C-553/10 (Éditions Odile Jacob, 2012), 27ff.

[1250]CJ, C-553/10 (Éditions Odile Jacob, 2012), 44.

[1251]CJ, C-553/10 (Éditions Odile Jacob, 2012), 51f.

[1252]See CJ, C-553/10 (Éditions Odile Jacob, 2012), 44 and 50; von Koppenfels (2013), 12.

[1253]See Hoeg (2014), 134; critically Von Koppenfels (2013), 12.

irrespective of whether the trustee has actually not acted in an independent manner and whether his report had an influence on the Commission's decision.

3.5.3.1.1.3.2 The Trustee's Submission Under the Influence of the Commission

The Commission is not confined to an indirect influence on the exercise of the trustee's tasks via the approval of his mandate, appointment and discharge. Rather, the Commission also has the power to interfere with the day-to-day business of the trustee. In this regard, the undertaking's right to instruct the trustee is replaced by a corresponding right of the Commission, who may give any orders or instructions to the trustee in order to ensure compliance with the commitments.[1254]

3.5.3.1.2 ADR

The reliance on alternative dispute resolution (ADR) and in particular arbitration mechanisms for the implementation of remedies must be distinguished from the broader topic of their use to resolve competition conflicts in general,[1255] even if the related problems overlap to a certain extent. Both topics have sparked an overwhelming amount of interest,[1256] compared to the relatively modest attention that has been paid to the Commission's deployment of trustees. The present analysis is from the outset confined to the use of ADR in the context of remedies. Even in that regard, it must be limited to some selected points. For a more comprehensive discussion, reference is made to the specialised literature that exists in the field.

The Commission started already in the mid 1960s to request the use of ADR mechanisms as condition for the grant of an exemption.[1257] Later on, also the grant of block exemptions was made dependent on the use of such mechanisms.[1258] Nowadays, the Commission makes widespread use of ADR in remedies adopted in the fields of Articles 101[1259] and 102[1260] TFEU and of merger

---

[1254]Remedies Notice (2008), 118; Best Practice Guidelines, 9; model text for divestiture commitments, 27; model text for the trustee mandate, 5. See also Brückner (2012), 58, who points out that the Commission's right to instruct the trustee replaces the contractual right of the undertaking.

[1255]See for that distinction Idot (2010), 54; Blanke (2011a), 30-001 fn 4, who distinguishes between "EU-remedy-related arbitrations" and "ordinary EU antitrust arbitrations".

[1256]See DiBrozolo (2004), 23: "very trendy topic". More recent publications containing abundant references to prior literature include: Blanke/Landolt (2011); Idot (2012); Liebscher (2013); Carbone (2013); Blanke (2013); see also Sofianatos (2009), 564ff; Kellezi (2010), 504ff.

[1257]See for a comprehensive overview of the Commission's practice Blanke (2011a), 30-027 fn 77. He cites OJ L 163/10 (Transocean Marine Paint, 1967) as the first relevant decision.

[1258]See Idot (2010), 52; Blanke (2011a), 30-117.

[1259]Eg COMP/37214 (Bundesliga, 2005); COMP/39140 (DaimlerChrysler, 2007); COMP/39141 (Fiat, 2007); COMP/39416 (Ship Classification, 2009); COMP/39596 (BA/AA/IB, 2010).

[1260]Eg COMP/38044 (IMS interim, 2001); COMP/39388 (German Electricity Wholesale, 2008); COMP/39230 (Rio Tinto, 2012); COMP/39654 (Reuters, 2012).

control.[1261] Their primary field of application lies in non-divestiture, in particular access remedies.[1262] Idot suggests, however, that even where the relevant clauses have been inserted into a remedy, ADR mechanisms are hardly ever used. Besides a discrepancy between the theoretical interest and the practical importance, she offers the explanation that the sheer presence of such mechanisms may contribute to compliance with a remedy.[1263]

To the best of my knowledge there is neither a statutory provision nor any soft-law document that deals with the use of ADR in remedies, with the exception of the 2008 Remedies Notice. It seems that plans to complement the Commission's model texts regarding divestiture commitments and trustee mandates by a "model arbitration clause"[1264] never materialised. The relevant passage in the 2008 Merger Remedies Notice has remained rudimentary: In essence, it states only that the Commission may require an ADR mechanism, possibly in combination with a trustee.[1265] A look at the individual decisions reveals that the deployed mechanisms are indeed not uniform, but vary significantly.[1266] This observation applies even to closely related cases: In 2007, the Commission accepted commitments pursuant to Article 9 by four carmakers to make repair information available to independent garages.[1267] While ADR mechanisms were provided for in all four commitments, their types and concrete design differed.[1268] Against the backdrop of the large variety of ADR mechanisms that may be deployed to implement a remedy, it is difficult to make any generalised statements. Nor

---

[1261]Eg M.2830 (Telia, 2002); M.5650 (T-Mobile, 2010); M.5984 (Intel, 2010); for a comprehensive overview see Blanke (2011b).

[1262]See Merger Remedies Notice (2008), 130; Lübking (2008), 77; Kellezi (2010), 504f.

[1263]Idot (2012), 3 and 37, with respect to merger remedies.

[1264]For plans of the Commission to publish a model arbitration clause following the revision of the Merger Remedies Notice, see Lübking (2007), 9, and (2008), 86f. Mourre (2007), 158, points out that the ICC established a "Task Force on Arbitrating Competition Law Issues" that developed a draft for a model arbitration clause to be inserted in remedies, which was accompanied by draft guidelines on the burden of proof and on the Commission's role in arbitration proceedings. In that latter regard see also Nisser/Blanke (2006, 2007) and Idot (2012), 34.

[1265]Merger Remedies Notice (2008), 130: "[T]he Commission will often require the involvement of a trustee to oversee the implementation of [non-divestiture] commitments and the establishment of a fast-track arbitration procedure in order to provide for a dispute resolution mechanism and to render the commitments enforceable by the market participants themselves. In past cases, the Commission has often required both the appointment of a trustee and an arbitration clause. In those circumstances, the trustee will oversee the implementation of the commitments but will also be able to assist in arbitral proceedings to the effect that they may be finalised in a short period of time".

[1266]See the decisions cited in Sect. 3.5.3.1.2, footnotes 1259 to 1261 above; also Idot (2012), 11f.

[1267]See IP/07/1332.

[1268]The Fiat commitment (COMP/39141) merely contains a mediation clause. On the contrary, the Opel (COMP/39143), Toyota (COMP/39142) and Daimler (COMP/39140) commitments all provide for an arbitration clause. The latter clauses still differ in that the Daimler clause does not subject the arbitration to the realisation of a prior internal review process, whilst the Opel clause provides for a one instance internal review prior to arbitration and the Toyota clause even for two instances of internal review. See also Idot (2010), 83 and (2012), 11; for a detailed description of the ADR mechanisms in the four cases see Blanke (2011a), 30-179ff and 30-198.

is it in the present context possible to analyse the various details of all the individual clauses. The following section will therefore be confined to an overview of the main types of ADR mechanisms that have been used. Moreover, the particular influence of the Commission on the respective ADR mechanisms that has been provided in some remedies shall briefly be touched upon.

3.5.3.1.2.1 Main Types of ADR Mechanisms Used for the Implementation of Remedies

ADR is an umbrella term that covers various ways in which parties can settle conflicts short of litigation in courts. On a rough scale, ADR mechanisms can be divided into non-adjudicative and adjudicative ones.[1269] At least in the context of competition law remedies, the most important non-adjudicative ADR mechanism is mediation. The main adjudicative ones are arbitration and expert determination. Before these three mechanisms shall be addressed in a slightly more detailed manner below, one common particularity should still be pointed out that arises when ADR mechanisms are based on a competition remedy: Since the remedy engages only the undertaking upon which it is imposed, only the latter is obliged to resort to the respective ADR mechanism. In typical situations, the remedy does not bind the beneficiaries, so that the ADR mechanism constitutes merely an option, but no obligation for them.[1270] It is hence true that beneficiaries remain, in principle, at liberty to resort to the Commission or a national court to seek compliance with the remedy.[1271] However, it is submitted that the Commission can take the lack of realisation of a possible ADR procedure into account when it decides whether to treat a complaint with priority or not.[1272]

3.5.3.1.2.1.1 Mediation

Mediation is a structured process whereby parties to a dispute rely on the assistance of an impartial third person to attempt to reach a settlement by themselves.[1273] The paramount feature of the mediator is that he does not decide the outcome of the

[1269]For an overview about the various types of ADR see Blake/Browne/Sime (2011): They treat, on the one hand, negotiation, mediation, evaluation, conciliation, ombudsmen and recording settlement as non-adjudicative ADR, and, on the other hand, expert determination, construction industry adjudication and arbitration as adjudicative ADR. For the importance of the distinction between non-adjudicative and adjudicative ADR see also Idot (2010), 51f. From a terminological point of view, it bears mention that sometimes only the non-adjudicative mechanisms are classified as ADR: see eg the Commission's Green Paper on alternative dispute resolution in civil and commercial law (COM/2002/0196 final), 2; Blanke (2011a), 30-001f.

[1270]See Sofianatos (2009), 570; Kellezi (2010), 509; Blanke (2011a), 30-058; Idot (2012), 19f; Blanke (2013), 29.93.

[1271]See Idot (2012), 20.

[1272]On the Commission's right to prioritise cases see Sect. 5.1.3 with footnotes 75ff below.

[1273]See the definition of mediation in Article 3 Regulation 2008/52/EC on certain aspects of mediation in civil and commercial matters.

controversy for the parties.[1274] The Commission uses remedies that provide for an isolated mediation mechanism only scarcely.[1275] However, if the Commission relies on a trustee, the latter often exercises the function of a mediator in addition to his supervisory role.[1276]

3.5.3.1.2.1.2 Arbitration

Different from mediators, arbitrators decide a dispute.[1277] Moreover, arbitration can be distinguished from litigation in that it necessitates an arbitration agreement and that arbitrators are appointed by the parties whereas a judge is appointed by the state.[1278] In view of its roots in private autonomy,[1279] arbitration can take many forms. With a view to merger remedies it has been observed that institutional arbitration within the framework provided by the International Chamber of Commerce and the London Court of International Arbitration has become the most common form.[1280] Furthermore, it bears mention that the Commission makes frequent use of hybrids between mediation and arbitration, so-called "med-arb" procedures.[1281] In particular, arbitration can be made subject to a prior attempt to settle the dispute with the assistance of the monitoring trustee.[1282]

3.5.3.1.2.1.3 Expert Determination

Expert determination is another form of adjudicative ADR.[1283] In particular the following characteristics distinguish the expert from the arbiter: his specialised know-how; his power to investigate of his own motion; his greater independence as regards the procedure; and the greater scope for review of his decisions.[1284] The

---

[1274]See Blake/Browne/Sime (2011), 11.02.

[1275]Blanke (2011a), and (2011b), 46-1184ff mentions merely one example in the context of Articles 101 and 102 TFEU, namely COMP/39141 (Fiat, 2007), and two examples in the context of merger control, namely M.3696 (E.On, 2005) and M.3868 (Dong, 2006). See also Idot (2012), 11 fn 101.

[1276]Remedies Notice (2008), 119, fourth indent: "In case of disagreement between the parties and third parties [. . .], the monitoring trustee shall discuss those matters with both sides and report to the Commission"; see for the trustee's role as a mediator Brückner/Hoehn (2010), 77f; Cook (2011), 45-137; Blanke (2011b), 46-169, 46-175 and 46-184f; Idot (2012), 8.

[1277]See Blake/Browne/Sime (2011), 23.01; Idot (2010), 51f.

[1278]See Blake/Browne/Sime (2011), 23.05.

[1279]See Blake/Browne/Sime (2011), 23.59: "The second general principle in arbitration is that the parties should be free to decide how their dispute should be resolved. This flows from the entire concept of arbitration, in that it is a consensual process based on an agreement by the parties to refer their dispute to an impartial arbitral tribunal".

[1280]Idot (2012), 25; see also Blanke (2011a), 30-072 and (2011b), 46-091.

[1281]Generally on "med-arb" procedures see Blake/Browne/Sime (2011), 23.72; in the context of competition remedies see Blanke (2011b), 46.176 and Idot (2012), 27.

[1282]See, in the context of Article 101 TFEU, COMP/39596 (BA/AA/IB, 2010); in the context of merger control see Lübking (2008), 84.

[1283]For an overview see Blake/Browne/Sime (2011), 21.01ff; Kendall/Freedman/Farrell (2008).

[1284]See Sessler/Leimert (2004), 153.

distinction is often difficult to make and the boundaries between the two types of adjudicative ADR blur.[1285] Also expert determination is frequently used by the Commission in competition law remedies.[1286] Like arbitration, also expert determination can be made subject to a prior attempt to settle the dispute with the assistance of the monitoring trustee.[1287]

3.5.3.1.2.2 Role of the Commission in Arbitration Procedures

Some remedies contain arbitration clauses that provide for an unusually strong influence of the Commission on the procedure when compared with ordinary arbitration or litigation. This influence receives particular attention in the literature[1288] and shall hence briefly be sketched here. Three main topics can in this respect be distinguished: The information of the Commission about the arbitration proceedings; the possibilities for the Commission to participate in the proceedings; and the relation between the Commission's own enforcement powers and the arbitral procedure. As a preliminary caveat, it bears mention, however, that the Commission does not seem to use the clauses in question in a systematic manner.[1289]

3.5.3.1.2.2.1 Information of the Commission About Arbitration Procedures

Remedies provide frequently that the Commission must be informed about arbitration taking place. The precise scope of this obligation varies.[1290] It can, however, reach far: There are cases in which the Commission did not only have to be informed about the beginning, progress and outcome of the procedures, but in which it also had to receive copies of all related documents, in particular the written submissions and the arbitral awards.[1291] The monitoring trustee may be used as a channel to report about arbitration.[1292]

[1285] For the difficulty of distinguishing expert determination from arbitration under German law see Sessler/Leimert (2004), 156.

[1286] See COMP/38044 (IMS interim, 2001); COMP/39230 (Rio Tinto, 2012); COMP/39654 (Reuters, 2012); Blanke (2011a), 30-210ff and 30-265ff; Idot (2012), 11.

[1287] COMP/39654 (Reuters, 2012).

[1288] See eg Lübking (2008), 85f; Sofianatos (2009), 567, Kellezi (2010), 511f; Blanke (2011a), 30-037ff, and (2011b), 46-069ff; Idot (2012), 36,44 and 48.

[1289] See for instance the arbitration clause in COMP/39388 (German Electricity Wholesale, 2008), which does not provide for any influence of the Commission.

[1290] For an overview see Blanke (2011a), 30-038ff and 30-084ff and (2011b), 46-071.

[1291] Eg COMP/39596 (BA/AA/IB, 2010); M. 5984 (Intel, 2010); Idot (2012), 35 with further references.

[1292] See, albeit in the context of an expert determination clause, COMP/39654 (Reuters, 2012).

3.5.3.1.2.2.2 Possibilities for the Commission to Participate in the Arbitration Procedures

Some clauses stipulate that the Commission has a right to file amicus curiae briefs and to participate actively in a hearing, including the right to question parties, witnesses and experts.[1293] Occasionally, the arbitration procedure defined in a remedy even provides for a sort of "preliminary reference" technique: In case of disagreement between the parties about the interpretation of the remedy, the arbitral tribunal may ask the Commission for an interpretation, which is then binding.[1294] Due to its tension with the independence of the arbitral tribunal, this binding effect may cause irritations.[1295] Ultimately, it seems, however, justified: On the one hand, the independence of the arbitral tribunal appears sufficiently preserved by the design of the preliminary reference mechanism as an option instead of an obligation.[1296] On the other hand, it must be taken into account that arbitration in the context of remedies differs from ordinary competition arbitration in that it pursues a public enforcement goal, namely to implement a remedy adopted by the Commission.[1297]

3.5.3.1.2.2.3 Relation Between the Commission's Own Enforcement Powers and the Arbitral Procedure

As regards the relation between the Commission's own enforcement powers and the arbitral procedure, two questions shall be treated: First, whether compliance with an arbitral procedure and later an arbitral award bars the Commission from taking action against an undertaking for non-compliance with the underlying remedy. Second, whether non-compliance with an arbitral award is as such sufficient to establish also the non-compliance with the remedy.

The first question has two different aspects. First, one must ask whether the Commission is precluded from taking action for non-compliance against an undertaking as long as no arbitral award has been delivered and the undertaking merely asserts its rights under the arbitration clause. The General Court seems to be of the opinion that this is not the case. In Microsoft II, the Court stated that Microsoft was obliged to comply with the interoperability remedy "on its own initiative" and that the existence of an ex post arbitration mechanism was, at the very most, intended "to attenuate the consequences" should the company persist in the abuse. In the Court's view, the implementation of an arbitration mechanism was therefore not sufficient to prevent the Commission from imposing periodic penalties.[1298] This approach may at

---

[1293] Eg COMP/39596 (BA/AA/IB, 2010); M. 5984 (Intel, 2010); Idot (2012), 36 with further references.

[1294] Eg COMP/39596 (BA/AA/IB, 2010); M. 5984 (Intel, 2010); Blanke (2011b), 46-070, and Idot (2012), 44 with further references.

[1295] See Idot (2012), 44; also Mourre (2007), 18 and 20.

[1296] See Lübking (2008), 85.

[1297] See Idot (2012), 49.

[1298] GC, T-167/08 (Microsoft II, 2012), 115; for a comment on this aspect see Lawrance (2012), 9.

first blush seem very rigid. It is, however, broadly acknowledged that the reliance on arbitration leaves the Commission's statutory powers regarding the implementation of remedies unaffected.[1299] If one accepts the latter point, also the second aspect of the first question is easy to answer: Even compliance with a sentence does not preclude the Commission from acting[1300] and thus cannot offer a safe harbour for the undertaking. Unlike a court enforcing an arbitral award, the Commission is in this respect not confined to examining whether the sentence complies with ordre publique standards. Clauses that expressly stipulate that the Commission's powers remain unaffected are superfluous,[1301] since these powers are anyway neither at the Commission's nor at the parties' disposal.

The second question, whether non-compliance with an arbitral award is as such sufficient to establish also the non-compliance with a remedy, is more difficult to answer. In the literature, there are voices in favour[1302] and against[1303] such an automatism.[1304] The better arguments militate for the latter view. It is contradictory to allow the Commission to rely on the deficiency of a sentence and take independent action to ensure compliance with a remedy, but to deny the possibility to rely on the deficiency of the sentence to the concerned undertaking. However, it is submitted that non-compliance with an arbitral award establishes a rebuttable presumption for non-compliance with the underlying remedy. In order to prevent action from the Commission, the undertaking must show that the neglect of the sentence is justified because the latter is inconsistent with the remedy.

3.5.3.2 The Microsoft I Judgment and Its Implications

In Microsoft I, the General Court partially annulled the part of the Commission's 2004 decision that had required Microsoft under Article 7 to establish a mechanism to assist the Commission in monitoring compliance with the remedies.[1305] The judgment deserves a closer look, not least in view of the uncertainty it generated as regards the general admissibility of trustees and ADR mechanisms for the implementation of remedies.

[1299] See Lübking (2008), 80; Sofianatos (2009), 567; Kellezi (2010), 512; Idot (2012), 48.

[1300] See Kellezi (2010), 512.

[1301] Idot (2012), 48.

[1302] See Lübking (2008), 81: "Non-compliance with the arbitral award would be a violation of the commitments by the merging parties and the Commission could rely on the provisions of the EC Merger Regulation relating to the enforcement of commitments."

[1303] See DiBrozolo (2004), 35: "A decision of the arbitrators cannot of itself be considered evidence of a breach of the commitments, and even less can it be relied upon as a basis for the imposition of sanctions for breach of the commitments or for the repeal of the decision authorising the merger." Sofianatos (2009), 571, seems to support this view.

[1304] Unclear Blanke (2011b), 46-059, who seems to agree with both opinions.

[1305] See GC, T-201/04 (Microsoft I, 2007), 1230ff.

3.5.3.2.1 The Case

In the 2004 decision, the Commission required Microsoft to submit a proposal for the establishment of a monitoring mechanism. At the same time, the Commission reserved its right to impose such a mechanism by way of decision, should it consider that Microsoft's proposal was not suitable.[1306] The decision specified in particular that the primary responsibility of the monitoring trustee should be to issue opinions, upon application by a third party or by the Commission or on his own initiative, on Microsoft's compliance with the decision.[1307] In a footnote, the decision mentioned that the trustee "should not only be reactive, but should play a proactive role in the monitoring of Microsoft's compliance".[1308] The trustee had to be independent of Microsoft. He had to have access to the information required for carrying out his task, which included full access to the source code of the relevant products. Finally, Microsoft had to bear all related costs.[1309] The details of the trustee mandate were in 2005 specified in a further decision that was adopted after repeated consultations between the Commission and Microsoft.[1310] In 2007, the General Court partially annulled the part of the 2004 decision that dealt with the trustee. The partial annulment was essentially based on two aspects:

First, the General Court held that there was no legal basis to compel Microsoft to grant to an independent monitoring trustee powers which the Commission was not itself authorised to confer upon a third party. In the Court's view, the Commission had done this: Due to the fact that the trustee could also act on his own initiative and upon request of third parties, the Court considered him to be "independent not only of Microsoft but also of the Commission itself".[1311] Furthermore, in the Court's view, the investigative powers granted to the trustee were powers that the Commission could only exercise itself.[1312] In that regard, the Court distinguished the trustee from the Commission's own external experts, the deployment of which was considered admissible: To its own external expert, the Commission could communicate any information it had received itself under its own investigative powers, which were subject to judicial control.[1313]

Second, the Court argued that there was no legal basis for imposing the costs of the trustee on Microsoft.[1314] Although the Court had stated in an earlier passage of the judgment that an undertaking was required not only to implement a remedy, but also to assume all the costs associated with that implementation,[1315] it considered

[1306]COMP/37792 (Microsoft I, 2004), Article 7.
[1307]COMP/37792 (Microsoft I, 2004), 1045.
[1308]COMP/37792 (Microsoft I, 2004), fn 1317.
[1309]COMP/37792 (Microsoft I, 2004), 1048.
[1310]See COMP/37792 (Microsoft, decision concerning the trustees, 2005).
[1311]GC, T-201/04 (Microsoft I, 2007), 1269.
[1312]GC, T-201/04 (Microsoft I, 2007), 1271.
[1313]GC, T-201/04 (Microsoft I, 2007), 1266ff.
[1314]GC, T-201/04 (Microsoft I, 2007), 1273.
[1315]GC, T-201/04 (Microsoft I, 2007), 1256.

that there was no provision authorising the Commission to require an undertaking to bear the costs which the Commission incurred as a result of monitoring the implementation of remedies. According to the Court, to depend on or be influenced by the willingness or the capacity of an undertaking to bear such costs would be incompatible with the Commission's responsibility to pursue the implementation of infringement decisions in an independent, objective and impartial manner.[1316]

As a consequence, the General Court annulled the part of the 2004 decision that dealt with the establishment of the monitoring mechanism in so far as it required the trustee to be independent of the Commission and to have investigative powers and in so far as it provided that Microsoft had to bear the costs.[1317] Prior to the judgment, the Commission had appointed a computer expert as trustee on the basis of the mandate adopted in 2005. Following the judgment, this trustee initially continued his work.[1318] The Commission solely reimbursed Microsoft for the costs incurred in the past and, from the date of the judgment, funded the trustee through the general budget of the EU.[1319] In 2009, the Commission discharged the trustee, announcing that it would in the future rely on ad hoc technical consultants rather than full time monitoring. A decisive reason for this change was that the Financial Regulation[1320] imposed constraints on the procurement of monitoring services.[1321]

3.5.3.2.2 Discussion

The precise conclusions that must be drawn from the partial annulment of the monitoring mechanism in Microsoft for the Commission's "outsourcing"[1322] practice remain to date largely unclear. Two statements can be considered to stand on fairly solid grounds: First, the judgment has a bearing not only on the admissibility of the use of trustees, but also on that of ADR mechanisms and in particular arbitration.[1323] For the sake of simplicity, the following section will make no distinction in that regard.[1324] Second, the Court did not call into question the Commission's recourse to external mechanisms for the implementation of remedies as such, but merely censured the conferral of overbroad and autonomous powers and

[1316]GC, T-201/04 (Microsoft I, 2007), 1275.

[1317]GC, T-201/04 (Microsoft I, 2007), 1278; see also COMP/37792 (Microsoft, decision concerning the trustees, 2009), 6.

[1318]See Page/Childers (2008), 344: "the EC interpreted the CFI's decision as restricting only the trustee's remuneration and some other formal aspects of his relationship to the commission"; Waller (2012), 589.

[1319]See COMP/37792 (Microsoft, decision concerning the trustees, 2009), 10f.

[1320]N° 1605/2002.

[1321]See COMP/37792 (Microsoft, decision concerning the trustees, 2009), 14f.

[1322]Hofmann/Rowe/Türk (2012), 704.

[1323]See Gunther/Tayar (2008), 169, 174 and 175; Sofianatos (2009), 563 and 570; Idot (2010), 82; Blanke (2011a), 30-273ff and (2011b), 46-033; Najar (2011), 4-021ff.

[1324]For such a distinction in the context of the consequences of the Microsoft judgment see Najar (2011), 4-031; Blanke (2011a), 30-276 and (2011b), 46-034.

the allocation of costs.[1325] Less certainty exists with respect to the question whether the rationale of the judgment is limited to unilateral injunctions[1326] or whether it covers also consensual remedies.[1327] This uncertainty is fuelled by the fact that, both prior to[1328] and after[1329] the Microsoft judgment, the EU Courts have dealt several times with consensually established trustees and ADR mechanisms and never raised any objections similar to those relied on by the General Court in Microsoft I. However, since these judgments do not formally address the aspect of the lawfulness of the outsourcing, they can at best be considered as implicit confirmations of the practice.

The following section will discuss the implications of the Microsoft judgment on the lawfulness of the Commission's outsourcing practice in more detail. To structure the discussion, it will distinguish between the two essential lines of argument upon which the General Court relied in support of the partial annulment: The conferral of investigative powers to a body that was independent from the Commission on the one hand, and, on the other hand, the imposition of the costs on Microsoft.

3.5.3.2.2.1 The Trustee's Investigative Powers and His Independence from the Commission

In order to assess the range and persuasiveness of the argument of the General Court that the Commission acted unlawfully by conferring investigative powers to a body that was independent from it, one must ask for the justifications of the Court's approach. The wording of the judgment is in this respect silent. Nevertheless, in particular two different lines of argument qualify as implicit justifications why the Court considered the conferral of investigative powers to a body that was independent from the Commission unlawful: A conflict with the Meroni doctrine and the protection of Microsoft's individual rights.

[1325] See Gunther/Tayar (2008), 173; Rachwol (2010), 244; Blanke (2011a), 30-274f; Idot (2012), 4. But see also Frese (2014), 173 together with 181, and Dunne (2014b), 427, who seem to be of the opinion that the General Court generally prohibited the recourse to monitoring trustees under Article 7.

[1326] In that direction Kerse/Khan (2012), 6-050 fn 147; Idot (2012), 4; Blanke (2011a), 30-275, who argues that "[t]he lack of consensual element is, no doubt, key to the CFI's refusal to approve of the monitoring mechanism"; Kipiani (2014), 581: "Il apparait que les restrictions apportées par le Tribunal en la personne du mandataire [...] ne trouvent pas à s'appliquer lorsque la décision de la Commission se borne à entériner un engagement volontairement pris par une entreprise".

[1327] In that direction Gunther/Tayar (2008), 173; Rachwol (2010), 244f; Brückner (2012), 136f: "Den Ausführungen ist zu entnehmen, dass das Gericht einem vergleichbaren Treuhändereinsatz auf einvernehmlicher Grundlage kritisch gegenüberstehen würde. Die geäußerten Bedenken gegenüber der Durchführung von Befugnissen der Kommission durch Private lösen sich nicht dadurch auf, dass die beteiligten Unternehmen der Kommission die Durchführung anbieten".

[1328] GC, T-158/00 (ARD, 2003), 203, 212, 295, 297 and 352; T-87/05 (EDP, 2005), 105; T-177/04 (EasyJet, 2006), 186f.

[1329] CJ, C-553/10 (Éditions Odile Jacob, 2012); see also GC, T-108/07 (Spira, 2013), in particular 323ff, which deals with the question whether the mandate of an "ombudsman" offered by parties to dispel competition concerns and accepted by the Commission was sufficiently powerful.

3.5.3.2.2.1.1 Conflict with the Meroni Doctrine

The Court's approach according to which the Commission cannot delegate investigative powers to a body that is independent from it could be justified against the backdrop of the Meroni doctrine, which was developed by the Court of Justice already in 1958. In Meroni,[1330] the Court inferred from the concept of institutional balance, first, that a delegating authority cannot confer on another body powers different from those possessed by the delegator, and, second, that it is impossible to delegate powers involving a wide margin of discretion.[1331]

It must be pointed out that the General Court did not refer to the Meroni doctrine in Microsoft I. Nevertheless, the doctrine is sometimes seen as imposing strict limitations on the Commission's recourse to external mechanisms in the context of remedies.[1332] A detailed discussion of the Meroni case and the evolution of the doctrine are beyond the scope of the present work.[1333] Two points shall, however, be made: First, it is submitted that any potential limitations for the Commission's recourse to trustees and ADR mechanisms that follow from the Meroni doctrine apply also to consensual remedies adopted under Article 9 Regulation 1/03 or Articles 6(2) or 8(2) Merger Regulation. The institutional balance, which lies at the heart of the doctrine, is neither at the disposal of the Commission nor of an undertaking. Second, it must, however, be stressed that the Meroni doctrine has evolved over time and that, at least in its present contours, it leaves room for the delegation of discretionary powers, as long as the latter are sufficiently circumscribed.[1334] The increasing delegation of tasks to agencies[1335] and private

---

[1330] CJ, 9/56 (Meroni, 1958), p. 146ff.

[1331] See Craig (2012), 154.

[1332] See Brückner (2012), 124ff, who raises serious concerns (127) as regards the compatibility of the Commission's trustee practice with the Meroni doctrine.

[1333] For more detailed discussion of the Meroni doctrine see Craig (2012), 154f and 175; Hofmann/Rowe/Türk (2012), 241ff; Brückner (2012), 123ff.

[1334] See eg CJ, C-270/12 (Powers of intervention conferred on the European Securities and Markets Authority, 2014), 41ff: The CJ did not object to a delegation of discretionary powers that were circumscribed by various conditions and criteria. See also Hofmann/Rowe/Türk (2012), 245, who infer from GC, T-187/06 (Schräder 2008), 63, that an agency "can be entrusted with the exercise of administrative decisions which require a margin of appreciation".

[1335] See Hofmann/Rowe/Türk (2012), 285ff. Nettesheim (2010), Art. 13 EU, 50, rightly explains that the initial Meroni-doctrine has been overtaken by the factual evolution of EU law: Agencies created by secondary law can today adopt decisions involving discretion that bind individuals. Examples are the OHIM (Office for Harmonization in the Internal Market) created on the basis of Regulation 40/94 (replaced by Regulation 207/2009), the ECHA (European Chemicals Agency) established on the basis of Regulation 1907/2006, the EASA (European Aviation Safety Agency) established on the basis of Regulation 1592/2002 (replaced by Regulation 216/2008), or the EBA (European Banking Agency), established on the basis of Regulation 1093/2010. At least implicitly, the Treaty of Lisbon acknowledges that decision-making powers may be conferred upon agencies: Article 263(1) and (5) TFEU provides that actions can be brought against acts adopted by bodies, agencies and offices of the Union intended to produce legal effects in relation to individuals and that specific conditions and arrangements for such actions may be laid down in the in act creating the respective body, agency or office.

parties,[1336] for instance in the context of standardisation,[1337] supports the latter argument. Against this backdrop, it is submitted that the Meroni doctrine does not preclude the use of external mechanisms to implement a remedy as long as the remedy circumscribes these powers to a sufficient degree. Whether this is the case can only be assessed according to the respective circumstances of the given case. On a general level, it seems, however, that the powers granted to trustees and ADR mechanisms for the implementation of remedies are sufficiently circumscribed in order not to enter into conflict with the Meroni doctrine. As will be shown below, the latter conclusion applies in particular for the actual mandate of the trustee in Microsoft, the conditions of which were stipulated in the 2005 decision.

3.5.3.2.2.1.2 Conflict with Protection of Individual Rights

A different justification of the approach of the General Court besides the possible wish to preserve the institutional balance could be the endeavour to protect Microsoft's individual rights and in particular the right to effective judicial protection.[1338] The emphasis put by the Court on the fact that the exercise of the Commission's own investigative powers was subject to judicial review points in this direction.[1339] Again, two points shall be made: First, it is submitted that any potential limitations for the use of trustees and ADR mechanisms that flow from the necessity to protect the individual rights of the undertaking upon which the remedy is imposed differ from the limitations that flow from the Meroni doctrine in that the former do not apply to consensual remedies. An undertaking that proposes voluntarily to make use of a trustee or an ADR mechanism waives any withstanding individual rights.[1340]

Second, as far as unilateral injunctions are concerned, it is submitted that, in principle, the reliance on external mechanisms to assist in the implementation of remedies can indeed not be allowed to curtail individual rights, in particular the right to effective judicial protection. Again, only an analysis of the circumstances of the respective case at hand can show whether this is the case. However, one must doubt that the actual mandate of the trustee in Microsoft really caused a danger for Microsoft's individual rights or that, on a general level, the current practice of the Commission as it has been described above does so in respect of other companies. In Microsoft I, the General Court argued that the Commission exceeded its powers by requiring Microsoft to establish a mechanism that was independent of the

---

[1336]See Hofmann/Rowe/Türk (2012), 328ff and 587ff.

[1337]See Hofmann/Rowe/Türk (2012), 589ff.

[1338]See Najar (2011), 4-031, who emphasises that "Microsoft's arguments were based on the fact that by delegating its powers, the Commission deprived Microsoft of guarantees recognized to undertakings by the case law to safeguard their rights of defence".

[1339]See GC, T-201/04 (Microsoft I, 2007), 1267.

[1340]See with regard to the right to effective judicial protection Brückner (2012), 135: "Bei einem entsprechenden Zusagenangebot ist allerdings von einem Verzicht auf mögliche gerichtliche Nachprüfung auszugehen."

Commission and equipped with investigative powers that the Commission could only have exercised itself. For this purpose, the Court only looked at the rather abstract wording of the 2004 decision under appeal, but not at the more specific conditions for the actual trustee mandate laid down in the 2005 decision, predating the judgment. In this regard, it is submitted that the Court's argument is not persuasive, neither with respect to the alleged independence of the trustee from the Commission, nor with respect to the trustee's alleged investigative powers.

In the first place, as far as the trustee's independence from the Commission is concerned, the Court bases its argument essentially on the circumstance that the latter was supposed to act also on its own initiative and on request of third parties.[1341] Does this really suffice to conclude that the Commission envisaged the trustee to act with an important degree of independence of it? A look at the 2005 decision unveils that any significant proactive action of the trustee was subject to close supervision by the Commission.[1342] In the second place, as far as the trustee's investigative powers are concerned, the Court argued that the Commission delegated powers that it could only exercise itself.[1343] However, according to the 2005 decision, Microsoft was free not to comply with the trustee's investigative requests. In case of a refusal, the company merely risked that the Commission would revert to its own powers of investigation and enforcement.[1344] It should be underlined that, in Microsoft II, the General Court relied precisely on this lack of coercive power of the trustee to find that the investigative powers of the trustee as laid down in the 2005 decision were not affected by the partial annulment of the trustee mechanism in the Microsoft I judgment.[1345] According to the view expressed by the Court in Microsoft II, the partial annulment in Microsoft I did thus not preclude the Commission from basing the imposition of the periodic penalties on reports drawn up by the trustee.[1346] The non-coercive investigative powers of the trustee provided for in the 2005 decision therefore clearly differ from the coercive ones that could be exercised by the Commission. In reality, the Commission did not delegate powers that it could only exercise itself. It is submitted that, by its ruling in Microsoft II, the

[1341]See GC, T-201/04 (Microsoft I, 2007), 1269.

[1342]See COMP/37792 (Microsoft, decision concerning the trustees, 2005), clause 5.6: "The Trustee is required to be proactive in its monitoring of Microsoft's compliance with the Decision, but shall not undertake any significant work not covered by the Work Plan unless it has received express written instructions from the Commission. Where the Trustee is required to exercise its own initiative, it shall discuss the work involved with the Commission and obtain its prior approval before undertaking any significant work".

[1343]See GC, T-201/04 (Microsoft I, 2007), 1271.

[1344]See COMP/37792 (Microsoft, decision concerning the trustees, 2005), clause 4.1: "Microsoft may comply with any request made by the Trustee [. . .] in its sole discretion, subject only to the obligations entered into by Microsoft in the Trustee Mandate. Should Microsoft fail to comply voluntarily and promptly with a request made by the Trustee [. . .], the Commission may revert to its powers of investigation and enforcement provided for under [. . .]".

[1345]GC, T-167/08 (Microsoft II, 2012), 175.

[1346]See GC, T-167/08 (Microsoft II, 2012), 165ff.

General Court acknowledged that non-coercive investigative powers can lawfully be conferred on a trustee.

Certainly, it must be stated in defence of the Microsoft I judgment that the 2005 decision was not the subject of the appeal[1347] and that formally the Court was barred from taking that decision into account, because the remedy imposed in the 2004 decision had to be assessed on the basis of the matters of fact and law existing at the time of its adoption.[1348] Against this background, the Court's interpretation that the 2004 decision required a trustee that was independent of the Commission and equipped with the same investigative powers as it, can be considered as remaining within the boundaries of the abstract wording of the 2004 decision. Nevertheless, it is submitted that it would have been more convincing if the Court had refrained from an annulment by simply interpreting the 2004 decision in a more restrictive manner: Also without taking the 2005 decision into account, the Court could have stated that the proactive role of the trustee did not exclude supervision by the Commission and that the investigative powers of the trustee remained confined to non-coercive ones.[1349]

3.5.3.2.2.2 The Allocation of Costs

As regards the argument of the General Court in Microsoft I that the Commission could not impose the costs of the monitoring mechanism on Microsoft, a distinction shall again be made between two potential justifications: On the one hand, the public interest in an effective enforcement of competition law and, on the other hand, the protection of Microsoft's individual interest.

[1347] As is apparent from GC, T-167/08 (Microsoft II, 2012), 172, Microsoft never appealed the 2005 decision specifying the precise conditions of the trustee mandate.

[1348] GC, T-201/04 (Microsoft I, 2007), 1253.

[1349] Moreover, it is difficult to understand why the Court did not classify the abstract prescriptions regarding the trustee mandate that were contained in the 2004 decision as non-reviewable, preparatory act. Microsoft would then have had to challenge the more precise conditions contained in the 2005 decision. The Commission had raised a similar plea. The Court rejected it, because it found that Microsoft was exposed to a risk of being sanctioned for non-compliance with the 2004 decision (see GC, T-201/04 [Microsoft I, 2007], 1251ff). The latter conclusion seems doubtful, however. It is submitted that Microsoft would only have risked a periodic penalty payment if it had completely refused to submit any proposals for the monitoring mechanism at all. The Commission could, however, not have sanctioned Microsoft on the ground that the proposals did not match its own expectations. The latter conclusion applies all the more in view of the fact that the 2004 decision described the requirements regarding the trustee that it contained expressly only as "guiding principles" (COMP/37792 [Microsoft, 2004], 1044). Therefore, the reviewable obligation that was imposed on Microsoft in the 2004 decision consisted merely of the obligation to make proposals for the monitoring mechanism. On the contrary, the "guiding principles" regarding the content that should be given to the proposals must be considered as a non-reviewable, preparatory act.

3.5.3.2.2.2.1 Conflict with the Public Interest in an Effective Enforcement of Competition Law

The Court argued in essence that the Commission had a responsibility for the effective implementation of a remedy and that it was incompatible with this responsibility if the implementation depended on the willingness or capacity of the concerned undertaking to bear the related costs.[1350] If this argument were pertinent, it would also oppose the absorption of monitoring costs by undertakings in consensual commitments. The rationale behind the argument is the public interest in an effective implementation of remedies. This public interest is, however, neither at the disposal of the Commission nor of an undertaking. Moreover, the risk of a payment default exists also where consensual remedies are concerned: Also where an undertaking has voluntarily committed to bear the costs in question, it may later not be capable or willing to fulfil the commitment.

The Court's argument is, however, from the outset not convincing.[1351] The threat of sanctions will usually provide a sufficient incentive for the concerned undertaking to comply with an obligation to bear monitoring costs, irrespective of whether the obligation predicates on a unilateral injunction or a consensual commitment. Should the undertaking really refuse to pay the trustee, the Commission can still fill the gap. Moreover, in the logic of the Court, also the costs for implementing the main obligations of a remedy could not be left to the undertaking, because the latter might be unwilling or unable to bear them.[1352]

3.5.3.2.2.2.2 Conflict with the Interest of the Undertaking That Has to Bear the Costs

The prohibition to inflict the costs of a monitoring mechanism on the undertaking upon which a remedy is imposed could also be justified by the individual interest of the undertaking in question. If this were the case, the undertaking could nevertheless absorb costs voluntarily in a consensual commitment, because it could waive the protection of its individual interest.

It is, however, submitted in any event that the prohibition to impose the costs of a monitoring mechanism on the undertaking cannot be justified in a persuasive manner with the interests of the latter. In fact, since a remedy merely aims at restoring a lawful situation, it should go without saying that the implementation costs must be borne by the undertaking having prompted its adoption. Also the General Court acknowledged in Microsoft I that implementation costs must be borne by the undertaking engaged by a remedy.[1353] If one accepts that the undertaking must bear the implementation costs, two reasons justify why it should also bear the monitoring costs: First, it seems doubtful

[1350] GC, T-201/04 (Microsoft I, 2007), 1275.

[1351] Critically also Brückner (2012), 136.

[1352] See Brückner (2012), 136.

[1353] GC, T-201/04 (Microsoft I, 2007), 1256.

whether a sufficiently clear distinction can at all be made between implementation and monitoring costs. If the Commission contents itself with requiring the undertaking to report itself on the compliance with a remedy, should the Commission then reimburse the additional costs caused by this obligation to the undertaking? On the other hand, if the Commission has recourse to external assistance, should mediation, arbitration or expert determination[1354] services be classified as implementation or as monitoring? The boundaries between implementation and monitoring often blur. Second, even if the costs of implementing and monitoring a remedy could be distinguished with sufficient clarity, the fact nonetheless remains that, like the remedy itself, also the necessity of its monitoring was prompted by the undertaking having acted unlawfully or, in the context of Article 9 Regulation 1/03, having caused anticompetitive concerns. The costs-by-cause principle justifies that the undertaking who prompted the monitoring also bears its costs.

3.5.3.2.2.3 Conclusion

The way the General Court dealt in Microsoft I with the Commission's order regarding the establishment of a monitoring mechanism has been criticised for its conservatism,[1355] in particular against the backdrop of the virtual success of the Microsoft trustee in his role as a mediator.[1356] In view of the arguments presented above, this criticism must be approved. An additional problem is the lack of clarity of the judgment. It conflates the various prongs of its reasoning, avoiding a statement whether they constitute independent or cumulative grounds for annulment.[1357] It is, for instance, impossible to infer from the judgment whether the imposition of the costs on Microsoft was in itself a sufficient ground for annulment or whether the imposition of costs lead to the annulment only in combination with the Court's findings regarding the trustee's investigative powers and his independence from the Commission.

[1354]In the IMS Health interim decision, the Commission ordered that the costs of the expert should be divided between the parties. It rejected IMS' argument that no costs should be imposed on it since the expert's task could lawfully only be exercised by the Commission (OJ 2002 L 59/18 [IMS Health, 2001], 219). Whether the IMS Health interim decision is compatible with the standard applied by the GC in Microsoft I is controversial: for compatibility Najar (2011), 4-028 fn 61; against Kerse/Khan (2012), 6-050 fn 147. If one counts the determination of a reasonable royalty rate as "implementation" of a remedy, as opposed to monitoring, then the allocation of costs in IMS Health is justified even under the standards applied by the GC in Microsoft I.

[1355]Economides/Lianos (2010), 378: "The conservatism showed by the Court in envisioning an effective compliance mechanism seems misplaced."

[1356]For the success of the Microsoft trustee as a factual mediator see Page/Childers (2008), 344; Economides/Lianos (2010), 379; Waller (2012), 589.

[1357]For the sake of completeness, it should still be pointed out that, besides the lines of argument presented above, the General Court also mentioned the fact that no time limit was provided for the monitoring mechanism. However, the Court did not annul the decision to that extent (see GC, T-201/04 [Microsoft I, 2007], 1270 and 1278). Therefore and for the sake of simplicity, the argument relating to the lack of a time limit has not been given further consideration in the present discussion.

Overall, it is submitted that the importance of the part of the Microsoft I judgment that deals with the monitoring trustee should not be overestimated. In Microsoft II, the General Court took a less rigid approach and clarified that the Commission could lawfully confer non-coercive investigative powers upon a trustee. In view of the arguments presented above, the Commission's recourse to trustees and ADR mechanisms should, in general and in the contours described above, be considered as lawful. This conclusion applies also to unilateral injunctions pursuant to Article 7 Regulation 1/03 and to the imposition of costs on the undertaking in question. It applies without prejudice to the necessity to assess each "outsourcing" constellation according to the individual circumstances of the case at hand. The main reasons why the Commission's practice should, in general, be considered as lawful can be summed up as follows: First, the Commission's own enforcement powers remain completely unaffected by all of the mechanisms described above. The actions of trustees, mediators, experts and arbiters do not bind the Commission. If necessary, the Commission can activate its own enforcement arsenal to correct unwarranted results. The effective implementation of remedies is therefore not at risk. Second, the powers that are conferred to external actors are sufficiently circumscribed. On the one hand, the scope of those powers is normally defined in rather precise terms in the remedy and the relevant derivative texts such as for instance the trustee mandate. On the other hand, the Commission typically has some sort of supervisory power. As far as trustees are concerned, the Commission can even give direct instructions. Certainly, when it comes to arbitration, direct interference of the Commission is less pronounced. However, even in this context the Commission is at least informed about the procedures and can, if need be, use its own enforcement powers. Finally, the undertakings have the possibility to complain about the action of the external actors to the Commission and to initiate court proceedings against the Commission, should the latter not provide for relief. Overall, this circumscription precludes potential risks for the institutional balance and the rights of the concerned undertakings in a satisfactorily manner. Third, the cost-by-cause principle justifies that the costs are either imposed on the undertaking engaged by the remedy or that the costs are split between the parties to a dispute or left to be determined by the external actor, as is the usual practice in arbitrations and expert determinations.[1358]

One final remark is still called for. All arguments made by the General Court in support of the partial annulment of the order regarding the monitoring mechanism were expressly subjected to the caveat that the Commission had acted without a legal basis.[1359] As was already briefly pointed out above,[1360] in the wake of the Microsoft I judgment, the Commission inserted a new provision into the implementing regulation of the Merger Regulation that now expressly allows for the use of trustees in the context of merger remedies. In view of the uncertainty created by the Microsoft I

[1358] See the IMS Health interim decision (Sect. 3.5.3.2.2.2.2, footnote 1354 above); COMP/39596 (BA/AA/IB, 2010); COMP/39654 (Reuters, 2012); Blanke (2011a), 30-104f and (2011b), 46-154.

[1359] GC, T-201/04 (Microsoft I, 2007), 1271 and 1278.

[1360] See Sect. 3.5.3.1.1 with footnote 1177 above.

judgment and the Commission's declared intention to make in the future even more frequent use of trustees,[1361] a similar provision could also be inserted into the implementing regulation of Regulation 1/03.[1362] It is submitted that Article 33(1), 1st sentence, Regulation 1/03 would provide a sufficient legal basis in this regard.[1363] A possible future statutory basis for the Commission's outsourcing practice would not have to be limited to trustees, but could also cover the other ADR mechanisms described above.[1364]

3.6 Fundamental Rights and the Scope of EU Law As Further Limitations to the Commission's Powers

3.6.1 Fundamental Rights

Remedies may affect fundamental rights. The most relevant are the freedom to conduct business, which includes the freedom to choose with whom to do business,[1365] and the right to property, laid down in Articles 16 and 17 of the Charter.[1366] The Court of Justice has held that the freedom to conduct business and the right to property "are subject to public interest restrictions and [...] cannot be relevant in the context of setting a fine for an infringement or EU competition law".[1367] Hellström et al. suggest applying this statement also to remedies.[1368] Inspite of its mistakable wording, the Court's dictum should, however, not be interpreted as meaning that the freedom to conduct business and the right to property are from the outset not at all applicable to competition law remedies. Rather, the statement must be understood as implying that interferences with the mentioned fundamental rights will as a rule be

---

1361 See Sect. 3.5.3.1.1 with footnote 1181 above.

1362 Regulation 773/2004.

1363 Article 33(1), 1st sentence, Regulation 1/03 provides a comprehensive legal basis for adopting provisions on implementation in regard of all aspects covered by Regulation 1/03 (see Dalheimer [2005], Art. 33, 1; Bischke [2008], Art. 33, 4-27-068). Therefore, it cannot be inferred from the fact that Article 33(1), 2nd sentence, Regulation 1/03 no longer explicitly refers to Article 7(1) Regulation 1/03, whilst Article 24 Regulation 17/62 referred without restriction to Article 3 Regulation 17/62, that the Commission no longer has the power to adopt provisions on implementation in regard of remedies (but see, in that direction, Weiß [2009], Art. 33, 3: "Entfallen ist [...] die Befugnis der Kommission zum Erlass von Durchführungsbestimmungen [...] zu Verbotsentscheidungen".)

1364 Bonnières/Vassileff (2014), 5f, have also suggested to provide for more detailed rules regarding the qualification and independence of trustees.

1365 CJ, C-307/91 (Luxlait, 1993), 14; Jarass (2013), Art. 17, 9.

1366 The right to property is also protected in Article 1 of the first protocol to the ECHR. The freedom to conduct a business is not recognised in the Convention. For the sake of simplicity, the present section will only refer to the Charter.

1367 CJ, C-308/04 P (SGL Carbon, 2006), 108.

1368 Hellström/Maier-Rigaud/Bulst (2009), 49.

justified as restrictions that take place in the public interest of preserving competition in the internal market. Certainly, it should be added that any public interest restriction of a fundamental right must nonetheless meet the threshold of the principle of proportionality. However, as long as that requirement is respected, the fact that a remedy encroaches upon a fundamental right offers no protection that would stretch further than the principle of proportionality. In view of the far-reaching parallel between the protection offered through fundamental rights and that offered through the principle of proportionality,[1369] the present work refrains from a detailed presentation of the ways in which competition remedies may interfere with the freedom to conduct business and the right to property.[1370] Only two selected questions shall briefly be touched upon: First, whether and to what extent the interference of a remedy with the right to property can necessitate compensation; second, what impact the consensual nature of Article 9 decisions has on the importance of fundamental rights.

3.6.1.1 The Right to Property and the Requirement of Compensation

The first question can be relevant in particular in the context of access[1371] and unbundling[1372] remedies. Its answer is traditionally anchored in the distinction between a deprivation of property and a mere restriction of use. Pursuant to Article 17(1), 2nd sentence, Charter, any deprivation must be subject to fair compensation being paid in good time. However, as mentioned above, the distinction between a deprivation of property and a mere restriction of its use is uncertain.[1373] Since not only formal transfers of title, but also restrictions that exclude any reasonable use are acknowledged as deprivations,[1374] the distinction depends to a large extent on value judgments how long remaining possibilities to use the property can be considered as reasonable. Yet, the difficult distinction between a deprivation of property and a mere restriction of its use loses much of its significance, if one takes into account that also mere restrictions of use can require compensation.[1375] The ultimate question is thus whether, in the absence of compensation, the burden imposed by the remedy

[1369]For criticism of the parallel between the fundamental right to property and the proportionality test see Calliess (2011), Art. 17, 21, who speaks of a "flight towards the proportionality test" (Flucht in die Verhältnismäßigkeitsprüfung).

[1370]For more detailed discussions see Müller-Tautphaeus (2003), 285ff; Hauser (2009), 167ff; Andreangeli (2010); Krings (2012), 244ff.

[1371]See Andreangeli (2010), 239, who infers from the fundamental right to property laid down in the ECHR that a compulsory license may only be imposed in exchange for adequate compensation.

[1372]For the discussion about whether an unbundling injunction necessitates compensation see eg Hauser (2009), 172f; MK (2010), 122 and 126; Kaiser/Wischmeyer (2010), 54ff; Voell (2014), 125ff.

[1373]See Sect. 3.4.1.1.4, footnote 801 above.

[1374]CJ, C-347/03 (ERSA, 2005), 122; Calliess (2011), Art. 17, 14ff; Jarass (2013), Art. 17, 19.

[1375]CJ, C-20/00 (Booker, 2003), 79; C-120/06 (Fiamm, 2008), 184; Jarass (2013), Art. 17, 19.

would be inadequate when compared to the benefits secured. Whether this is the case, cannot be answered abstractly. The following factors may, however, be of relevance:

First, the necessity of compensation will depend on whether the position that is affected by the remedy was attained lawfully. The creation of a joint venture in violation of Article 101 TFEU or the establishment of a standard through a patent ambush in violation of Article 102 TFEU may serve as examples for unlawfully attained positions. It is controversial whether unlawfully attained positions are from the outset excluded from protection under the fundamental right to property.[1376] The wording of Article 17(1), 1st sentence, Charter, which refers to "lawfully acquired possessions", and the case law of the Court of Justice[1377] point in that direction. However, even if one considers that unlawfully acquired positions can fall under the protection offered by Article 17 Charter, the fact that the relevant position was attained unlawfully will in any event reduce the need for compensation.[1378] On the other hand, compensation will more likely be necessary where the remedy affects a position that was acquired lawfully: The unbundling of a company in order to prevent future abusive conduct constitutes an example.

Second, the necessity of compensation will depend to a large extent on the concrete design of the remedy, for example on whether an unbundling remedy orders merely a separation of managements or accounts or a full ownership unbundling. Third, it results from the case law of the ECtHR that, if a compensation is necessary, "legitimate objectives of public interest [...] may call for less than reimbursement of the full market value"; the compensation must, however, be "reasonably related" to the market value.[1379] In the context of the expropriation of land, the ECtHR has considered a reimbursement of only 20% of the market value as sufficient, albeit in the light of the particular circumstances of the case.[1380] As far as competition law remedies are concerned, compulsory access obligations are typically imposed in exchange for reasonable remuneration. If an undertaking is ordered to divest parts of its business, it normally receives the purchase price.[1381] As a general rule, these payments will constitute a sufficient compensation for the purposes of Article 17 Charter.[1382]

[1376] See Hauser (2009), 171; Calliess (2011), Art. 17, 6 with references.

[1377] See CJ, C-277/10 (Luksan, 2012), 38f; C-283/11 (Sky Österreich, 2013), 34ff; see also von Danwitz (2013), 257.

[1378] See Jarass (2013), Art. 17, 7, 29 and 37.

[1379] ECtHR, n° 8793/79 (James, 1986), 54; n° 31423/96 (Papachelas, 1999), 48; see also n° 36813/97 (Scordino, 2006), 95 and 97; Kaiser/Wischmeyer (2010), 55; Jarass (2013), Art. 17, 29.

[1380] ECtHR, n° 28092/07 (Henne, 2009).

[1381] For details regarding the price setting in the context of divestiture commitments in merger cases see Hoeg (2014), 151f.

[1382] See, for the attainment of a similar result with a different reasoning, also Maier-Rigaud (2014), 6: "as structural remedies generate revenue from the sale of the relevant asset at current market value, a structural remedy is different from expropriation as the firm is remunerated".

3.6.1.2 Fundamental Rights and the Consensual Nature of Article 9 Decisions

The general question to what extent it is at all possible to waive fundamental rights cannot be discussed here in detail.[1383] It must suffice to state that there are certainly limits, but that these do not categorically exclude waivers and that the limits vary inter alia according to the type of fundamental right concerned and the circumstances in which the waiver is declared.[1384] The freedom to conduct business and the right to property that are relevant in the context of competition law remedies are classic subjective rights. They can more easily be waived than other fundamental rights that have a higher importance for the general public. Without entering into a more detailed discussion here, it is submitted that by voluntarily offering commitments, the undertakings concerned waive the potential protection that is provided against the remedy by fundamental rights. Since the concerned undertakings cannot declare a waiver at the expense of concerned third parties, the rights of the latter remain unaffected.

3.6.2 Scope of EU Law

3.6.2.1 The Internal Perspective: Appreciable Effect on Competition and on Trade Between Member States

In order to come within the prohibition of Article 101 TFEU, an agreement must have an appreciable effect on competition[1385] and on trade between member states.[1386] Similarly, also the prohibition of Article 102 TFEU applies only if the dominant position extends at least to a substantial part of the market[1387] and if its abuse appreciably affects trade between member states.[1388] In this context, the question arises whether the Commission must respect the said restrictions also when it imposes a remedy. May the Commission order compliance with the law only up to the mentioned boundaries?

[1383] For a detailed discussion of the possibility to waive fundamental rights under German constitutional law see Merten (2009). Winkler (2006), 112f, states that the possibility to waive fundamental rights under EU law remains to date largely unclear; see also the discussion by Bueren (2011), 752ff.

[1384] For example, Article 3(2) Charter appears to imply that the right to the integrity of the person may, in the area of medicine, be waived through "free and informed consent of the person concerned, according to the procedures laid down by law".

[1385] Jones/Sufrin (2011), 171ff.

[1386] Jones/Sufrin (2011), 177ff.

[1387] Jones/Sufrin (2011), 267ff.

[1388] Jones/Sufrin (2011), 269ff.

The Court of Justice rightly gave a negative answer when a similar question arose in the context of merger remedies. In Cementbouw, the Court rejected the argument that a remedy could not go further than needed to deprive the concentration of its community dimension and to bring it below the thresholds provided for in Article 1 Merger Regulation. In the view of the Court, the principle of proportionality does not withstand obligations that "entirely eliminate the competition problem that has been identified".[1389] AG Kokott used even stronger language. In her words, "[i]t would be absurd if the Commission were required to accept commitments [...] for the sole reason that they deprive the concentration of its Community dimension, without there being any need to examine whether those commitments are apt to resolve the competition problem identified by the Commission".[1390] It is submitted that the same conclusion applies mutatis mutandis also in the context of Articles 101 and 102 TFEU. It applies regardless of whether a remedy is adopted on the basis of Article 7 or Article 9.

3.6.2.2 The External Perspective: The International Dimension of Competition Law

The international dimension of competition law remedies is too complex to be treated here with any reasonable accuracy.[1391] Nevertheless, in view of its increasing importance, the subject cannot be completely neglected. At least some basic observations shall be made. In a first step, two elements of the international dimension of a case will be discussed that may set up limitations to the Commission's power to impose remedies. Thereafter, the subject of international cooperation, which extends also to competition law remedies, will briefly be touched upon. Finally, it will be stated that the Commission does not seem to use the Article 9 procedure to extract remedies that reach beyond its jurisdiction.

3.6.2.2.1 The International Dimension of a Case As a Limit for the Commission's Remedial Power

The international dimension of a case may limit the Commission's power to impose a certain remedy in particular under two aspects: First, it is questionable to what extent the Commission has jurisdiction to impose and enforce remedies with extra-territorial jurisdiction. Second, one must ask whether an existing foreign remedy can render the imposition of another remedy by the Commission unnecessary.

[1389] CJ, C-202/06 (Cementbouw, 2007), 54.

[1390] AG Kokott, opinion in C-202/06 (Cementbouw, 2007), 74.

[1391] For an overview of the international aspects of EU competition law in general see Whish/Bailey (2012), 487ff; Jones/Sufrin (2014), 1258ff. With respect to remedies see Roebling (2008), 1-5-046ff; Sofianatos (2009), 538ff.

3.6.2.2.1.1 Jurisdiction

Jurisdiction governs the ability of the Commission to apply the EU competition rules outside the territory of the EU. A distinction can be made between subject matter jurisdiction and enforcement jurisdiction. The former means the power to prescribe, the latter the power to give effect to a prescription.[1392] As regards both kinds of jurisdiction, it is necessary to differentiate between the perspectives of EU and public international law.[1393]

3.6.2.2.1.1.1 Subject Matter Jurisdiction

3.6.2.2.1.1.1.1 In General

Under EU law, the extraterritorial range of the Commission's procedural powers to adopt remedies pursuant to Articles 7 and 9 Regulation 1/03 follows the rules on the applicability of the substantive competition rules.[1394] The latter can be established by three different theories[1395]: The economic entity doctrine, the implementation doctrine or the effects doctrine. The economic entity doctrine, which was established by the Court of Justice in Dyestuffs, establishes jurisdiction by means of the nationality principle.[1396] It is essentially based on the idea that the anticompetitive conduct of a subsidiary situated in the EU may be imputed to a foreign parent company, as long as the latter can exercise decisive influence over the former.[1397] The economic entity doctrine leaves a gap in so far as it does not capture the conduct of purely non-European actors. The implementation doctrine, which was applied by the Court of Justice in Woodpulp, partially closes this gap.[1398] It is based on the territoriality principle[1399] and establishes jurisdiction over anticompetitive conduct that is implemented in the EU, whereby sales in the EU count as implementation.[1400] It is, however, controversial, whether the implementation doctrine captures also negative behaviour of actors situated outside the EU, such as an agreement not to sell within the EU or a refusal to supply to the EU by a dominant undertaking.[1401] The effects doctrine extends the applicability of EU law also to the latter practices.

[1392]See the opinion of AG Darmon in C-114/85 (Woodpulp, 1988), 28.

[1393]See the opinion of AG Darmon in C-114/85 (Woodpulp, 1988), 18; Jones/Sufrin (2014), 1270.

[1394]See Mestmäcker/Schweitzer (2004), § 6, 77; Rehbinder (2012), II.A., 73f; Lindemann (2014), 41.

[1395]For an overview of the three theories see eg Geradin/Reysen/Henry (2010), 25ff; Botteman/Patsa (2012), 367ff.

[1396]Geradin/Reysen/Henry (2010), 25.

[1397]CJ, 48/69 (Dyestuffs, 1972), 130ff.

[1398]Geradin/Reysen/Henry (2010), 25; Botteman/Patsa (2012), 371.

[1399]Geradin/Reysen/Henry (2010), 27.

[1400]CJ, 89/85 (Woodpulp, 1988), 11ff; see also GC, T-102/96 (Gencor, 1999), 87: "the criterion of the implementation of an agreement is satisfied by mere sale within the Community".

[1401]See Whish/Bailey (2012), 497; Jones/Sufrin (2014), 1277.

According to it, jurisdiction requires merely an effect on the internal market. The Commission has consistently relied on the effects doctrine to establish its jurisdiction.[1402] In a qualified version that requires a foreseeable, immediate and substantial effect, the doctrine has also been recognized by the General Court[1403] and several Advocates General.[1404] Also a strong strand of the literature favours it, albeit with certain restrictions.[1405] The Court of Justice avoided for a long time to establish jurisdiction on the basis of the effects doctrine, although it never expressly rejected the theory either.[1406] In Intel, the Court of Justice finally endorsed the qualified effects doctrine.[1407]

As far as public international law is concerned, it is broadly acknowledged that, as a rule, the principle of territoriality justifies the establishment of jurisdiction even under the broad standard of the effects doctrine.[1408] The exact limitations that must be applied to this general rule for various imperatives of public international law, such as in particular the ones of non-intervention and comity, are in their details controversial, both in the literature and between the subjects of public international law.[1409] Overall, it must be stated that, in the absence of existing rules on the matter, public international law leaves it to a large extent to its subjects to determine the range of the extraterritorial application of their competition laws.[1410]

3.6.2.2.1.1.1.2 Regarding Remedies

Against this backdrop, it is in principle uncontroversial that the Commission can adopt remedies with extraterritorial effects.[1411] The precise limits must be determined according to the circumstances of the individual case. Three examples shall be presented.

3.6.2.2.1.1.1.2.1. Commercial Solvents A first illustration is the already mentioned Commercial Solvents case.[1412] The Commission fixed the quantities it required Commercial Solvents to supply to Zoja to cover the latter's most urgent needs at the pre-rupture level. In doing so, the Commission did not take into account that

---

1402 Eg OJ 1985 L 85/1 (Woodpulp, 1985), 78f; Guidelines on the effect of trade concept (2004), 100; Rehbinder (2012), II.A., 11; Whish/Bailey (2012), 496; Lindemann (2014), 14.

1403 GC, T-102/96 (Gencor, 1999), 87; T-286/09 (Intel, 2014), 233, 236, 244.

1404 Opinions of AG Mayras in 48/69 (Dyestuffs, 1972), p. 694; AG Darmon in C-114/85 (Woodpulp, 1988), 17ff; AG Wahl in C-413/14 P (Intel, 2017), 296ff.

1405 See Rehbinder (2012), II.A., 26 and 12; Lindemann (2014), 15, both with further references.

1406 Whish/Bailey (2012), 496; Rehbinder (2012), II.A., 7; Jones/Sufrin (2014), 1276.

1407 CJ, C-413/14 P (Intel, 2017), 41ff. For a discussion see Prete (2018), 487.

1408 See Roebling (2008), 1-5-016; Rehbinder (2012), II.A., 15f and 26; Jones/Sufrin (2014), 1270f.

1409 For a detailed overview see Rehbinder (2012), II.A., 17ff.

1410 See Roebling (2008), 1-5-016.

1411 See Sofianatos (2009), 539.

1412 See Whish/Bailey (2012), 499 fn 86; for further discussion of the case also Sect. 3.3.1.4.1.2.2.1.1 with footnotes 325ff and Sect. 3.3.1.4.1.2.2.2 with footnote 353 above.

about 90% of Zoja's production was destined for export. On appeal, Commercial Solvents complained that the Commission thereby had applied Article 102 TFEU beyond the territory of the EU.[1413] The Commission argued that Zoja's overall viability depended also of its exports. AG Warner was inclined to follow the argument put forward by Commercial Solvents. In his view, the Commission had the power to order Commercial Solvents to resume supplies to Zoja only in so far as the cessation of such supplies could affect trade between member states. The AG did not completely discard the Commission's argument that Zoja's overall viability might depend also on its exports. However, he took a strict stance and required that the Commission should have shown that Zoja's exports were essential to the maintenance of its home trade.[1414] The Court of Justice was less strict and confirmed the Commission's order. The Court held that the criterion of the affection of trade between member states could not be interpreted as covering only domestic trade. In the view of the Court, the competition rules protected the competitive structure of a market and the elimination of a competitor had repercussions on that structure, irrespective of whether it was a result of an obstruction of domestic trade or of the exports of the competitor.[1415] In addition, the Court also found that a limitation of the order to supply to Zoja's needs for domestic trade would have put Zoja in a position in which its cost price would have been affected to such an extent that its production risked being unmarketable.[1416]

In Commercial Solvents, the Court of Justice did not explicitly rely on any of the above-mentioned theories to establish the Commission's jurisdiction.[1417] The facts of the case would probably have met the economic entity doctrine, because, prior to the rupture, Commercial Solvents had supplied Zoja through its EU subsidiary ICI. However, since the Court argued with the effects of the refusal to supply on structure of competition, the case can also be interpreted as an implicit recognition of the effects doctrine.

3.6.2.2.1.1.1.2.2. IBM In IBM, the Commission sent the company a statement of objections claiming that IBM had abused its dominant position in particular by refusing to make interface information available and by bundling various computer products.[1418] The US Department of Justice reportedly intervened in the case, requesting "that the Commission [should] not impose certain remedial measures on IBM because they would constitute a quasi-confiscatorial action that would be highly unfavorable to the US trade position".[1419] IBM appealed the statement of objections. It argued inter alia that the Commission had exceeded its jurisdiction,

---

[1413]See CJ, 6/73 (Commercial Solvents, 1974), 44.

[1414]See the opinion of AG Warner in CJ, 6/73 (Commercial Solvents, 1974), p. 272f.

[1415]CJ, 6/73 (Commercial Solvents, 1974), 48 together with 32f.

[1416]CJ, 6/73 (Commercial Solvents, 1974), 48 together with 34.

[1417]For various interpretations of the judgment with a view to jurisdiction see Schödemeier (1989), 24; Mestmäcker/Schweitzer (2004), § 6, 42 fn 49; Rehbinder (2012), II.A., 7 fn 8.

[1418]See XIVth Report on Competition Policy (1984), 94.

[1419]See Griffin (1993), 47; also Meng (1984), 714; Buchmann (2004), 49f.

because the conduct to which the Commission objected took place mostly outside the EU.[1420] The Court of Justice did not decide on the question of jurisdiction, but declared IBM's action inadmissible. It ruled that the statement of objections was no challengeable act.[1421] Ultimately, the Commission concluded the case with a settlement. However, in that settlement, the scope of the obligations engaged in by IBM to unbundle its products and to supply interface information was limited to the territory of the EU.[1422]

3.6.2.2.1.1.1.2.3. Microsoft Also in Microsoft I, the geographic scope of the remedies was problematic. The Commission found that both the tying of the Media Player and the refusal to disclose interoperability information concerned worldwide markets.[1423] Nonetheless, at least the geographic scope of the order to offer a version of Windows without the Media Player was limited to the EU.[1424] The geographic scope of the obligation to disclose interoperability information is not entirely clear. The decision itself does not contain any restrictions in that regard.[1425] However, in an accompanying press release, the Commission stated without distinguishing between the two remedies that it was "competent to ensure the maintenance of effective competition within the borders of the [EU]". Thus, "even if markets are defined as worldwide in the Decision, the geographical scope of the remedies is [EU]-wide".[1426] According to O'Donoghue and Padilla, complainants argued that, in line with the effects doctrine, the Commission should have extended the unbundling remedy also to Microsoft's sales outside the EU.[1427] It is not clear whether the Commission ultimately confined the geographic scope of the unbundling remedy to the EU because it considered that its jurisdiction did not reach further[1428] or "out of deference for the US authorities".[1429]

3.6.2.2.1.1.2 The Enforcement Problem

Neither public international nor EU law enables the Commission to exercise public power on foreign territory.[1430] Thus, while decisions imposing fines or periodic penalty payments for non-compliance with a remedy can in theory be sent to

---

[1420] CJ, 60/81 (IBM, 1981), p. 2643.

[1421] CJ, 60/81 (IBM, 1981), 9ff.

[1422] See XIVth Report on Competition Policy (1984), 95.

[1423] COMP/37792 (Microsoft, 2004), 427.

[1424] COMP/37792 (Microsoft, 2004), 1011; see Idot (2005), 49.

[1425] COMP/37792 (Microsoft, 2004), 999ff. Idot (2005), 49, states that the order to grant access to interoperability information was exposed to criticism due to its extraterritorial scope.

[1426] Memo/04/70; see also Fox (2005), 589 fn 103.

[1427] O'Donoghue/Padilla (2013), 942.

[1428] The wording of the press release (Sect. 3.6.2.2.1.1.1.2.3 footnote 1426 above) seems to point in that direction.

[1429] O'Donoghue/Padilla (2013), 942.

[1430] See AG Darmon in C-114/85 (Woodpulp, 1988), 28; Kruithof (1964), 88.

undertakings outside the EU, such decisions remain unenforceable unless the undertaking disposes of seizable assets within the EU.[1431] The impossibility to enforce injunctions abroad is a standard argument against the break up of foreign companies.[1432]

3.6.2.2.1.2 Lack of Necessity of a Domestic Remedy Due to an Existing Foreign Remedy

One might ask whether the fact that a foreign competition authority has already adopted a remedy can prevent the Commission from imposing another one. This can be exemplified with the Microsoft case.[1433] In defence against the unbundling remedy, the company relied on a prior commitment entered into vis-à-vis the US authorities.[1434] Under that commitment, Microsoft was not obliged to enable OEMs and consumers to completely remove the Media Player from Windows. Rather, Microsoft only had to provide for the possibility to hide the Media Player icon from the desktop and to disable automatic launches.[1435] Through this limitation, the US remedy addressed concerns that certain functions of Windows or of third party programs that relied on the Media Player would no longer operate properly, if the Media Player were completely removed.[1436] The Commission's remedy went further in that it required Microsoft to offer a fully functioning version of Windows without the Media Player.[1437] The General Court examined inter alia whether the prior US commitment deprived the later remedy of the Commission of its necessity.[1438] In order to confirm the necessity, the Court upheld the Commission's arguments that the US commitment did not fully restore the freedom of consumers to acquire Windows without the Media Player and that, in spite of the US commitment, the Media Player could override a default setting and reappear when a user used the Internet Explorer to access media files streamed over the internet.[1439] Overall, the imposition of a remedy by the Commission in the Microsoft case was hence justified by the fact that the US commitment did not fully address the infringement found by the Commission.

[1431] See Sofianatos (2009), 544; Whish/Bailey (2012), 499; Jones/Sufrin (2014), 1286; Lindemann (2014), 56.

[1432] See with respect to the discussion about a potential break up of Google, MK (2014), p. 70.

[1433] See Fox (2005), 590, who reports that the Commission's Microsoft decision was inter alia attacked as excessive, because the US courts had previously determined that no additional remedies were required or appropriate.

[1434] See GC, T-201/04 (Microsoft I, 2007), 53ff.

[1435] See GC, T-201/04 (Microsoft I, 2007), 959 and 974; Economides/Lianos (2010), 365.

[1436] See COMP/37792 (Microsoft I, 2004), 829; Economides/Lianos (2010), 365.

[1437] See Sect. 3.3.1.7 with footnote 557 above.

[1438] GC, T-201/04 (Microsoft I, 2007), 1227.

[1439] GC, T-201/04 (Microsoft I, 2007), 974.

The Rambus case can serve as another illustration. Here, the imposition of a remedy by the Commission in spite of the existence of another remedy that had previously been adopted by the US FTC was justified for a different reason. As explained above, Rambus was accused of having engaged in a so-called "patent ambush", intentionally concealing that it had patents which were relevant to a standard and subsequently claiming royalties for those patents. In both the US and the EU, the remedies consisted of obligations to license the patented technologies. The US remedy was only applicable to US patents and foreign patents to the extent that they related to import or export of relevant products into or from the US. In the statement of objections, the Commission considered that a further remedy was necessary, because Rambus was active worldwide, had obtained patent protection for the relevant technologies in Europe and was enforcing its patents against companies applying the relevant standards in Europe, so that these companies were exposed to litigation over the relevant European patents and could not seek relief on the basis of the US decision.[1440] Ultimately, the Commission accepted a commitment under Article 9 Regulation 1/03 that had a worldwide geographic scope.[1441]

Overall, the argument that a foreign remedy eliminates the necessity for the Commission to impose a further remedy is unlikely to succeed. Even if the geographic range of the foreign remedy covers also the territory of the EU and if it fully addresses the infringement found by the Commission, the latter could still rely on a risk that the foreign competition authority may not enforce the remedy in the EU.

3.6.2.2.2 International Cooperation

As long as authorities adopt remedies with an extraterritorial geographic scope, there remains a potential for conflict between them. Moreover, in view of the inability to enforce a remedy on foreign territory, the various competition authorities mutually depend on each other. There is hence a need for international cooperation. Such cooperation currently takes place mostly in two different ways[1442]:

On the one hand, there are bilateral cooperation agreements.[1443] A prominent example is the one between the EU and the US.[1444] It provides inter alia for the reciprocal notification of cases, exchanges of information and periodic meetings between competition officials and mutual assistance with and coordination of enforcement activities.[1445] Article II of the agreement expressly mentions remedies

[1440] See the press release regarding the statement of objections, Memo/07/330.

[1441] See Memo/09/544.

[1442] For a discussion of international cooperation regarding merger remedies see Hoeg (2014), 206ff.

[1443] An overview of the bilateral agreements concluded by the EU is available on the website of DG COMP.

[1444] 1995 OJ L 95/47.

[1445] See Jones/Sufrin (2014), 1287ff.

that would, in significant respects, require or prohibit conduct in the other party's territory as a case when enforcement activity requires notification because it may affect important interests of the other party. Moreover, Article VI of the agreement provides that important interests of the other party must be considered in decisions regarding the nature of the remedies. Finally, Article VII of the agreement provides for consultations between the competition authorities in all matters related to the agreement, hence also in matters related to remedies. Contrary to what has been posited in the literature,[1446] it is therefore submitted here that the cooperation agreement between the EU and the US extends also to consensual remedies, i.e. U.S. consent decrees and consent orders, and commitments under Article 9 Regulation 1/03. It bears mention, however, that there are limits to the effectiveness of the cooperation provided for in the agreement. As former Director General Schaub recognized, the agreement allows the EU and the US authorities to bring their respective approaches closer in cases of common interest, but there exists no mechanism for resolving conflicts in cases of substantial divergence of analysis.[1447]

On the other hand, there are several multilateral platforms that allow competition authorities to align their policies through the adoption of non binding comparative reports and best practices. Two prominent examples are the Competition Committee of the OECD and the ICN. Both institutions have published consultations on competition remedies, although these relate mostly to the field of merger control.[1448]

3.6.2.2.3 Does the Commission Use the Article 9 Procedure to Extract Remedies That Reach Beyond Its Jurisdiction?

Finally, it should be pointed out that, at least if one follows the qualified effects doctrine, the Commission does not appear to use the Article 9 procedure to extract remedies that reach beyond its jurisdiction. In general, the remedies made binding by the Commission only address effects within the EEA.[1449] In the Microsoft browser[1450] and the Standard & Poor's[1451] cases, the Commission explicitly rejected submissions that the remedies should have been worldwide in scope.

[1446]Georgiev (2007), 1031, who describes the "EU and US settlement procedures" as "one more area where coordination would be necessary and which is not covered by the 1991 Treaty".

[1447]Schaub (1998), 4.

[1448]See eg OECD (2006, 2011a, 2013); ICN (2005).

[1449]See for example: COMP/39.847 (E-Books, 2013): the obligations of the concerned undertakings covered only agreements relating to the sale of e-books in the EEA; COMP/39.692 (IBM, 2011): the obligation to make spare parts and technical information available extended only to the EEA; COMP/39.654 (Reuters, 2012): the license that had to be granted could be used worldwide provided that the customer had genuine business operations in the EEA; COMP/39.398 (Visa, 2014): Visa committed only to cap its Intra-EEA MIFs.

[1450]Comp/39.530 (Microsoft – tying, 2009), 88 together with fn 36.

[1451]COMP/39.592 (Standard & Poor's, 2011), 62ff.

3.7 Duration and Modification

A remedy may need to be adapted, in particular in case of a change of circumstances.[1452] When the necessary adaptation happens not at all or too slowly, the remedy risks creating inefficiencies[1453] or becoming disproportionate.[1454] There are two major ways to avoid that a change of circumstances renders a remedy inefficient or disproportionate: On the one hand, the effects of the remedy can be limited ex ante by providing for a maximum duration or by making the effects of the remedy dependent on the occurrence or lapse of a condition. On the other hand, the Commission can adapt the remedy ex post once the change of circumstances has occurred. The ex ante limitation of a remedy's effects is exposed to the difficulty of having to forecast future developments. At the same time, it saves the costs of a later reopening of the procedure.[1455]

3.7.1 Ex Ante Limitation of the Effects of a Remedy

3.7.1.1 In the Context of Article 7

Article 7 does not contain any prescription regarding the duration of the remedies that are imposed on its basis. The Commission's practice varies. Some decisions provide for explicit time limits,[1456] in particular with respect to ancillary obligations.[1457] Other decisions remain completely silent in that regard.[1458] At least in theory, instead of a time limit, also a condition that relates to market circumstances, in particular the continuity of a dominant position, may serve to limit a remedy's effects.

Some commentators infer from the principle of proportionality that remedies may not result in permanent control by the Commission.[1459] If this proposition were to be

[1452]As regards the controversial question to what extent the possibilities to limit the duration of a remedy ex ante or to adapt it ex post mitigate the risk of sub-optimal remedies see eg Wils (2008), 346; Wagner-Von Papp (2012), 950; Gerard (2013), 30.

[1453]Georgiev (2007), 1028.

[1454]Sofianatos (2009), 547: "Le marché est un tissu vivant qui se transforme constamment, de sorte qu'une mesure prononcée à un moment donnée peut ne pas correspondre à la situation du marché peu de temps après son édiction. Il se peut même que son exécution soit préjudiciable au marché ou qu'elle ne soit plus matériellement possible".

[1455]See, with regard to Article 9, Temple Lang (2006), 298: "The terms of a commitment can be altered only by a second formal commitment decision [. . .]. This is a troublesome and time-consuming procedure [. . .]". The same conclusion applies to Article 7 remedies.

[1456]OJ 1992 L 96/34 (British Midland, 1992); OJ 1993 L 183/19 (Langnese, 1992).

[1457]OJ 1985 L 374/1 (Akzo, 1985); COMP/38.233 (Wanadoo, 2003).

[1458]Eg OJ 1989 L 78/43 (Magill, 1988); COMP/37.792 (Microsoft I, 2004).

[1459]Bauer (2008), 4-7-029; Schütz (2013), Art. 7, 20. In the context of § 32 ARC also Jaeger (2010), § 32 ARC, 19.

understood as call for a general obligation to provide for limits regarding the duration of a remedy, it would have to be rejected as overbroad. It is submitted that the principle of proportionality may only require a limitation of the duration of a remedy according to the circumstances of the case. If a prognosis at the time of the adoption of the decision shows that the circumstances upon which the remedy predicates are not likely to change in the predictable future, the Commission can refrain from limiting the remedy's duration.[1460] For the sake of completeness, it should, however, also be pointed out that, in Microsoft I, the General Court based the partial annulment of the part of the Commission's decision that dealt with the monitoring trustee inter alia on the fact that that no limit in time was envisaged for the intervention of the monitoring trustee.[1461] The Court's reasoning should, however, not be construed as a general obligation for the Commission to provide for specific time limits in all Article 7 remedies.

On a sidenote, one observation regarding the duration of so-called structural remedies is called for. As structural remedies are sometimes considered to entail a permanent change in the market structure, one might argue that a time limit does not make sense for such remedies. Indeed, it has been suggested in the literature that the sole time limit that applies to divestiture remedies is the period that determines until when the divestiture has to be carried out.[1462] However, such a view neglects the importance that non-reacquisition obligations have for the duration of a divestiture remedy.[1463]

3.7.1.2 In the Context of Article 9

Article 9(1), 2nd sentence, provides that commitment decisions "may be adopted for a specified period". Alrosa argued before the General Court that these terms should be construed as requiring the Commission to make only commitments binding that provide for specific time limits.[1464] The General Court rejected that argument. The Court relied on the fact that the final wording of Article 9(1), 2nd sentence, differed from

[1460]As far as German law is concerned, this conclusion finds support in the jurisprudence of the Bundesverfassungsgericht, BVerfG, 1 BvR 1627/95 (Importarzneimittel, 2000), 45: The Bundesverfassungsgericht ruled that the Bundeskartellamt was not obliged to limit the duration of an obligation to supply or to provide for an express review clause. It argued in particular that German general administrative law provided for sufficient ways to revoke the decision or reopen the procedure ex post in case of a change of circumstances.

[1461]GC, T-201/04 (Microsoft I, 2007), 1270.

[1462]Kipiani (2014), 522f: "au sein des engagements structurels, aucune durée n'est fixée, il sera uniquement question du délai de mise en oeuvre de la cession"; similarly apparently also Gerard (2013), 29, who excludes structural remedies from his statistic regarding the duration of remedies as "obvious cases where remedies were of a one-off nature".

[1463]The Merger Remedies Notice (2008), 43, provides that commitments have to foresee that the merged entity cannot subsequently acquire influence over the divested business "[i]n order to maintain the structural effect of a remedy". Structural commitments adopted on the basis of Article 9 also typically provide for a non-reacquisition period, see eg COMP/39.388 (German electricity wholesale and balancing market, 2008), 57.

[1464]GC, T-170/06 (Alrosa, 2007), 46.

the wording which had been used at the stage of the Commission proposal for the Modernisation Regulation. The proposal had provided that commitment decisions had "to be adopted for a specified period".[1465] In her opinion on the case, Advocate General Kokott explicitly endorsed that aspect of the General Court's judgment.[1466] Even though the Court of Justice did not comment on the issue in its judgment, it can be considered as settled that there is no general obligation for the Commission to abstain from making commitments binding that do not contain any specific time limits.[1467]

A look at the Commission's actual practice reveals, however, that commitments of an indefinite duration are scarce. In the majority of cases, the duration of the commitment did not exceed 10 years.[1468] The average duration of Article 9 decisions is said to be around 5 years.[1469] Moreover, several commitment decisions contain conditions the occurrence or lapse of which decides about whether the remedy displays effects or not.[1470]

3.7.2 Ex Post Amendment of Remedies

Article 9(2) provides an explicit legal basis to reopen the procedure. No such legal basis is provided for remedies that are imposed on the basis of Article 7. Also in the literature, the possibility to reopen the procedure after an Article 7 remedy has been imposed is hardly ever discussed. Nevertheless, it should go without saying that also an Article 7 remedy may need to be revoked or amended. For instance, in the Microsoft interoperability case, the Commission repealed the part of the initially imposed remedy that concerned the monitoring trustee.[1471] In the absence of an

[1465]GC, T-170/06 (Alrosa, 2007), 91.

[1466]Opinion of AG Kokott, C-441/07 P (Alrosa, 2009), 217.

[1467]See eg Gerard (2013), 29 fn 157; Kipiani (2014), 520.

[1468]See for a good overview Kipiani (2014), 524f: 3 x indefinite duration; 2 x up to 20 years; 4 x up to ten years; 16 x between 3 and 7 years;

[1469]Gerard (2013), 30; Ortiz Blanco/Jörgens/Kellerbauer (2013), 13.17; Kipiani (2014), 540: "entre 5 et 10 ans".

[1470]In Coca-Cola, Distrigaz and Long-term electricity contracts France, the applicability of the commitments was conditional on the existence of a dominant position (see for the references Sect. 3.2.2.2.3, footnote 131 above). Prior to the enactment of Regulation 1/03, such a condition was already contained in the undertaking that was given in the Hilti case [OJ 1988 L 65/19 (Hilti, 1987)]. The Deutsche Bahn commitment was conditional on the acquisition of a certain market share by DB's competitors (Sect. 3.4.2.3.1, footnote 1144 above); when that market share was reached, the Commission decided that the commitments should cease prematurely (COMP/39.678, 2016). A premature termination of the commitments was also decided in COMP/39.317 (E.On Gas, 2016); approving with the latter decision von Kalben (2018), 444.

[1471]See COMP/37.792 (Microsoft, decision concerning the trustees, 2009). Since the General Court had only partially annulled the part of the initial remedy that dealt with the trustee, the GC's judgment cannot be considered to have been the only reason for the withdrawal. The Commission mentioned in particular constraints imposed by the Financial Regulation as reason for the complete

explicit legal basis, such an amendment of an Article 7 remedy must be based on the general principles of EU administrative law.

The following section will, in a first step, compare the different legal bases for the ex post amendment of remedies. It will in particular be asked whether the possibilities for an amendment of Article 9 decisions are narrower than those for an amendment of Article 7 decisions.[1472] If this were the case, it would be a reason why the risk of remedies that do not match competition concerns would be greater in the context of Article 9 than in the context of Article 7. It will, however, be argued below that, in spite of their different legal bases, the substantive conditions for the ex post amendment of remedies are the same, regardless of whether the remedy was adopted on the basis of Article 7 or Article 9. The rules that govern the revocation or amendment of commitments are therefore no reason to consider that Article 9 increases the risk of mismatch between harm and remedy. In a second step, some common problems that concern both Article 7 and Article 9 decisions will be addressed.

3.7.2.1 The Legal Bases for the Ex Post Amendment of Remedies

3.7.2.1.1 In the Context of Article 7: The General Principles of EU Administrative Law

In the absence of an explicit legal basis for the revocation or amendment of an Article 7 remedy the general principles of EU administrative law apply. Due to the existence of such general principles, there is no lacuna in the law that would justify an application of Article 9(2) by analogy. The EU Courts have developed a rather refined jurisprudence under what conditions an administrative act can be revoked or amended. For the details of that jurisprudence, reference is made to the specialised literature.[1473] For the present purposes, only the basic contours will be sketched. Overall, the possibility to revoke or amend an administrative act depends on the balancing of divergent principles that follow from the rule of law. On the one hand, the principle of legality requires that unlawful decisions should be rectified. On the other hand, the principle of legal certainty requires that acts become definitive and

withdrawal of the part of the initial remedy that dealt with the trustee (see Sect. 3.5.3.2.1 with footnotes 1320f above).

[1472] K. Schmidt (2003), 1242, criticises that there is no possibility for the concerned undertaking to rid themselves of the binding effects of an Article 9 decision: "Man wird [. . .] auf der Rechtsfolgenseite über Ausstiegsmöglichkeiten nachdenken müssen. So könnte dem an die Zusage gebundenen Unternehmen ein Ausstiegsinstrument an die Hand gegeben werden, das ihm gestattet, die Verpflichtung abzuschütteln und den Streit mit der Kommission auf der Verbotsebene nach Art. 9 Abs. 2 wieder beginnen zu lassen, ohne gleichzeitig Bußgelder riskieren zu müssen. Nicht alles scheint hier zu Ende gedacht".

[1473] See for a more detailed presentation eg Schwarze (2005); von Danwitz (2008), 401ff; Craig (2012), 556ff; Hofmann/Rowe/Türk (2012), 632ff.

that legitimate expectations of beneficiaries of an act are respected. The EU Courts have consistently ruled that neither of these divergent principles can be applied in an absolute manner. Rather, these principles must be balanced in accordance with the circumstances of the individual case.[1474]

As regards the more detailed rules that govern the revocation or modification of administrative acts, it is useful to make a distinction between whether an act was at the outset lawfully adopted or not.[1475] However, irrespective of this distinction, the revocation or amendment of an act is in any event unproblematic, if its effects on the addressee and potentially affected third parties are merely unfavourable. If an act produces only unfavourable effects, there is normally no interest that would justify its maintenance.[1476] Such acts can always be revoked or amended. Whether there is a corresponding obligation for the Commission to do so will be discussed below. Legitimate expectations that may necessitate the maintenance of an act exist only if the act produces beneficial effects, either for its addressee or for third parties. As far as competition law remedies are concerned, two situations in which legitimate expectations may justify the maintenance of a remedy can be distinguished. On the one hand, the Commission may envisage amending a remedy to the detriment of the addressee, i.e. to the detriment of the company upon which the remedy was unilaterally imposed or which offered the remedy. This would be the case if the Commission envisages imposing a remedy that is more intrusive for the addressee than the initial one. In this case, the addressee may have legitimate expectations in the maintenance of the initial remedy. On the other hand, the Commission may envisage an amendment or revocation in favour of the addressee. In this case, third parties who benefit from the remedy, for instance the beneficiary of an obligation to supply or the purchaser of an asset that had to be divested, may have legitimate expectations in the maintenance of the initial remedy. Whether, in either case, the legitimate expectations that oppose an amendment or revocation of the remedy prevail over the public interest in safeguarding the principle of legality depends on the circumstances of the individual case.

[1474]See CJ, C-49/59 (SNUPAT, 1961); Opinion of AG Léger, C-217/03 (Forum 187, 2006), 215: "the principle of respect for legal certainty, important as it may be, cannot be applied in an absolute manner, but its application must be combined with that of the principle of legality"; von Danwitz (2008), 401; Craig (2012), 563.

[1475]Von Danwitz (2008), 401ff; Craig (2012), 556ff; Hofmann/Rowe/Türk (2012), 633.

[1476]See GC, T-104/07 (BVGD, 2013), 68: "the necessary protection of legitimate expectations as to the legality and stability of a tainted measure has a *raison d'être* only in relation to measures which are favourable or grant individual rights to the applicant [;] it has none as regards measures imposing a burden or charge [. . .]. The principle of the protection of legitimate expectations applies by definition only to entitlements or advantages".

For unlawfully adopted acts, see von Danwitz (2008), 406: "die Aufhebung einer rechtswidrigen, belastenden Entscheidung [ist] regelmäßig sogar geboten, da insoweit der Rechtmäßigkeitsgrundsatz und das Individualinteresse übereinstimmen". For acts that were lawfully adopted see Craig (2012), 557: "the prohibition on retroactive revocation applies only in relation to unfavourable decisions".

3.7.2.1.1.1 Acts That Were Unlawfully Adopted

Acts that were unlawfully adopted can in principle be revoked or amended. It is, however, necessary to assess whether the beneficiaries of the act in question, i.e. either the addressee or third parties, have legitimate expectations in its maintenance and whether these expectations prevail over the public interest in the safeguard of the principle of legality.[1477] The beneficiary of an unlawfully adopted act cannot enjoy legitimate expectations in the maintenance of the remedy, if the beneficiary is or must have been aware of the unlawfulness. This is in particular the case if the act was adopted on the basis of false or incomplete information provided by the beneficiary.[1478] Even if the expectations of the beneficiary that the act be maintained are legitimate, these expectations must still be balanced against the public interest in the safeguard of the principle of legality. In that regard, the amount of time that lies between the initial adoption of the act and its revocation or amendment and the question whether the revocation or amendment applies ex nunc or ex tunc play a decisive role.[1479]

These principles apply also in the context of competition law remedies that have been adopted pursuant to Article 7. In AssiDomän the General Court had to deal with the question whether the Commission was empowered to repay an unlawfully imposed fine. The Court stated as follows:

> [...] while there are no specific provisions governing the withdrawal or revocation of decisions adopted by the Commission under [Article 3 and 15 Regulation 17/62], that regulation does not prevent the Commission from re-examining such a decision in relation to an individual when an element of it is unlawful. In that regard, it is helpful to recall the case-law regarding withdrawal of administrative acts conferring individual rights or similar benefits upon the addressee. The Court has acknowledged that the Community institutions are entitled, subject to the principles of the protection of legitimate expectations and of legal certainty, to withdraw, on the ground that it is unlawful, a decision granting a benefit to its addressee [...]. That case-law applies a fortiori in situations where [...] the decision in question merely imposes burdens or penalties on the individual. In such cases, the Commission is not precluded from withdrawing the decision by considerations relating to the protection of the legitimate expectations and vested rights of the person to whom the decision was addressed.[1480]

3.7.2.1.1.2 Acts That Were Lawfully Adopted

An act with favourable effects that was lawfully adopted can, in principle, not be revoked or amended, at least not with retroactive effect.[1481] A prospective

[1477]See eg GC, T-227/95 (AssiDomän, 1997), 89ff; T-267/08 (Région Nord-Pas-de-Calais, 2011), 188ff; Lübbig (2003), 236.

[1478]CJ, C-49/59 (SNUPAT, 1961), 87; C-90/95 P (De Compte, 1997), 37; T-25/04 (González y Diéz, 2007), 97; von Danwitz (2008), 405f; Craig (2012), 558 and 564f; Hofmann/Rowe/Türk (2012), 636.

[1479]See von Danwitz (2008), 404f with references.

[1480]GC, T-227/95 (AssiDomän, 1997), 89ff.

[1481]See GC, T-251/00 (Lagardère, 2000), 139; von Danwitz (2008), 402.

revocation or amendment can, however, be justified with a change of the circumstances on which the act was based. Although the EU Courts appear to have not yet explicitly endorsed the latter possibility, it is broadly accepted in the literature.[1482]

3.7.2.1.2 Article 9(2)

Article 9(2) provides three possibilities for the reopening of proceedings that have been closed with a commitment decision: (a) where there has been a material change in any of the facts on which the decision was based; (b) where the undertakings concerned act contrary to their commitments; (c) or where the decision was based on incomplete, incorrect or misleading information provided by the parties.

3.7.2.1.2.1 Exhaustiveness?

3.7.2.1.2.1.1 Article 9(2) Is More Restrictive Than the General Principles of EU Administrative Law

A comparison of Article 9(2) with the just described general principles of EU administrative law shows that option (c) is narrower than the conditions under which an act that was unlawfully adopted can be amended or revoked pursuant to the general principles of EU administrative law.[1483] In fact, Article 9(2)(c) permits the reopening of proceedings only where the decision was based on incomplete, incorrect or misleading information provided by the parties. According to the literature, "the parties" are only the addressees of the commitment decision.[1484] Under the general principles of EU administrative law, an act that was unlawfully adopted can, however, not only be revoked or amended if it predicates on incomplete, incorrect or misleading information provided by its addressee. It can generally be revoked or amended, unless the interest in safeguarding the principle of legality is outweighed by the legitimate expectations of any beneficiary of the act. Article 9(2)(c) does not allow the Commission to reopen the proceedings to the detriment of the addressee of the commitment where the commitment is unlawful for other reasons than the submission of incomplete, incorrect or misleading information by the addressee. This could, for instance, be the case where the Commission erroneously rejects a complaint or fails to take submissions made during the market test into account. Under the general principles of EU law, a revocation or

[1482]Lübbig (2003), 236; von Danwitz (2008), 402; Craig (2012), 559: "There can be cases where the initial decision was conditional, where the facts satisfied those conditions when the initial decision was made, but where they no longer do so because of subsequent events. Prospective revocation of the decision is clearly an option in these circumstances". See generally for the possibility to revoke a decision in case of a change of circumstances GC, T-186/98 (Inpesca, 2001), 47ff with further references.

[1483]See Hennig (2010), 246f.

[1484]See De Bronnet (2012), Art. 9, 22; Rachwol (2010), 173; see also Dalheimer (2005), Art. 9, 20; Ortiz Blanco/Jörgens/Kellerbauer (2013), 13.21.

amendment would in the latter cases be possible, subject the legitimate expectations of the addressee. The public interest in safeguarding the principle of legality might outweigh the legitimate expectations of the addressee, for instance where the time period between the adoption of the commitment and the reopening of proceedings would be sufficiently short and the commitment would only be amended ex nunc. Article 9(2)(c) also does not allow the Commission to reopen the proceedings in favour of the addressee of the commitment where the commitment is unlawful for other reasons than the submission of incomplete, incorrect or misleading information by the addressee. This could, for instance, be the case where the commitment predicates on false information submitted to the Commission by a complainant. Under the general principles of EU law, a revocation or amendment would in such a case be possible, subject to the legitimate expectations of other third parties than the complainant. Having provided false information, the complainant would not enjoy legitimate expectations.

Article 9(2)(a) and (b) cannot compensate for the deficits of Article 9(2)(c) in comparison to the general principles of EU administrative law. Article 9(2)(a) requires a material change in any of the facts on which the decision was based. Article 9(2)(b) requires that the undertakings concerned act contrary to their commitments.[1485] Neither of the two provisions covers constellations in which the commitment was merely unlawfully adopted.

3.7.2.1.2.1.2 Article 9(2) Is Not Exhaustive

This begs the question whether Article 9(2) is exhaustive or whether the general principles of EU administrative law remain applicable. In Alrosa, the General Court argued that the list of reasons to reopen procedures provided by Article 9(2) was exhaustive. The General Court concluded in particular that Alrosa could not have requested the procedure to be reopened on the ground that the remedy originally made binding was unlawful.[1486] This reasoning has met approval in the literature.[1487] It is, however, not convincing.

[1485]The scope of application of Article 9(2)(b) is difficult to comprehend. If the concerned undertakings act contrary to their commitments, the Commission can impose fines on the basis of Article 23(2)(c) and periodic penalties on the basis of Article 24(1)(c). Article 9(2)(b) is hence not necessary to impose fines and periodic penalties. Certainly, the Commission might want to adopt a prohibition decision pursuant to Article 7 as "punishment". However, in this case the Commission would face the heavier burden of proof required for an infringement procedure. For the discussion see eg Rachwol (2010), 169ff; Hennig (2010), 242f; De Bronnet (2012), Art. 9, 24: "Eine eigene praktische Bedeutung dieses Aufnahmegrundes ist [...] nicht ersichtlich".

[1486]GC, T-170/06 (Alrosa, 2007), 155: "Since the situations justifying a reopening are thus exhaustively listed, Alrosa could not request that the proceedings be reopened on grounds such as those set out in its application, in particular on the basis that the principle of proportionality had been infringed". Gippini-Fournier (2008), 413f.

[1487]Rachwol (2010), 174f; Sura (2014), Art. 9, 16. Similarly already Saitzek (2008), 276f; Bauer (2008), 4-9-057. De Smijter/Sinclair (2014), 2.144 consider that the authority of res judicata of the commitment decision precludes the Commission from reopening the proceedings to the detriment of the addressee save in the special circumstances set out in Article 9(2).

It is true that, in the proposal for Regulation 1/03, the Commission appears to have intended Article 9(2) to stipulate the reasons for which proceedings can be reopened in an exhaustive manner.[1488] However, as explained above, the reasons provided for in Article 9(2) are more restrictive than the general principles of EU administrative law. In the proposal for Regulation 1/03, the Commission did not explicitly state that it wanted to deviate from the general principles. The finally adopted wording of Article 9(2) does not exclude the parallel applicability of the general principles of EU administrative law. The principle of legality requires that, subject to the respect of legitimate expectations, the Commission has a possibility to revoke or amend a remedy that was unlawfully adopted. Overall, the better reasons thus militate for an approach that does not construe Article 9(2) as exhaustive, but permits the parallel applicability of the general principles of EU administrative law.[1489]

This conclusion is also supported by the General Court's jurisprudence in the area of state aid. Article 9 Regulation 659/1999 provides that the Commission may revoke certain decisions "where the decision was based on incorrect information provided during the procedure which was a determining factor for the decision". The General Court construed the provision as not exhaustive. It stated as follows:

> [..] the Commission's right to revoke a decision on State aid is not restricted solely to the situation referred to in Article 9 [Regulation 659/1999]. That provision is merely a specific expression of the general principle of law according to which retrospective withdrawal of an unlawful administrative act which has created subjective rights is permissible [. . .], in particular if the administrative act at issue was adopted on the basis of false or incomplete information provided by the party concerned [. . .]. The right to withdraw retroactively an unlawful administrative act which has created subjective rights is not, however, limited to that situation alone, since such a withdrawal may always be carried out provided that the institution which adopted the act complies with the conditions relating to reasonable time-limits and the legitimate expectations of beneficiaries of the act who have been entitled to rely on its lawfulness.[1490]

[1488]COM(2000) 582 final, p. 18: "[Article 9(2)] stipulates that the Commission is entitled to reopen the procedure only if [. . .]"; Saitzek (2008), 277 fn 109.

[1489]Unclear de Bronnet (2012), Art. 9, 22: "Die [. . .] Regelung ist abschließend. Will die Kommission aus anderen Gründen in den Bestand einer Entscheidung nach Art. 9 Abs. 1 eingreifen, muss sie auf allgemeine Grundsätze zurückgreifen"; Hennig (2010), 246f: "[E]iner über den Wortlaut des Art. 9 Abs. 2 [VO 1/03] hinausgehenden Wiederaufnahmepraxis [sollte] vehement entgegen getreten werden [. . .]. Die Wiederaufnahmegründe sind insoweit abschließend. [. . .] der Kommission [ist es] jedoch unbenommen, bei Vorliegen der entsprechenden Voraussetzungen unter Rückgriff auf die allgemeinen Grundsätze der Rücknahme von fehlerhaften Verwaltungsakten im Europäischen Recht in den Bestand einer Entscheidung einzugreifen [. . .]"; see also idem, 252: "Aus Gründen der Rechtssicherheit ist davon auszugehen, dass die Wiederaufnahmegründe des Art. 9 Abs. 2 [. . .] abschließend sind. Eine Erweiterung kommt damit nur im Rahmen eines erneuten Gesetzgebungsverfahrens in Betracht" and 263: "[Die Kommission kann] entweder das Verfahren nach Art 9 Abs. 2 [. . .] wiederaufnehmen oder ihre Entscheidung gegebenenfalls nach den Grundsätzen über die Rücknahme fehlerhafte Verwaltungsakte zurücknehmen. [. . .] Die Wiederaufnahmegründe des Art. 9 Abs. 2 [. . .] sind [. . .] abschließend".

[1490]GC, T-25/04 (González y Diéz, 2007), 97; Hofmann/Rowe/Türk (2012), 636.

3.7.2.1.2.2 *Not Only Power to Reopen, but Also Power to Modify*

It has been deplored in the literature that Article 9 "gives the Commission the power to reopen its investigation [. . .], but does not set out a procedure for the modification of a settlement".[1491] However, even if Article 9 does not expressly provide for the possibility to revoke or amend a commitment subsequent to the reopening of the procedure, it is clear that a revocation or amendment is one potential outcome.[1492] The reopening of a procedure that has been closed pursuant to Article 9 can have various consequences[1493]: It may lead to an infringement decision pursuant to Article 7, if appropriate accompanied by remedies and fines; to the modification of the initial commitment or its replacement by a new one; or to the withdrawal of the initial commitment without replacement.

Nevertheless, it must be conceded that the sole legal consequence that is explicitly provided for by Article 9(2) is the reopening of proceedings. New decisions taken subsequent to the reopening of proceedings therefore require an independent legal basis. For example, an infringement decision and a fine would need to be based on Articles 7 and 23 Regulation 1/03. A—if appropriate partial—revocation of the initial commitment would need to be based on the general principles of EU administrative law. The amendment of the initial commitment or the adoption of a new commitment would have to be based on Article 9(1). The respective decisions have to meet the requirements of the respective legal bases. In that connection, two issues merit particular emphasis:

3.7.2.1.2.2.1 *No Amendment of a Commitment Without the Consent of the Company That Offered It*

It is submitted that the Commission needs the consent of the company which offered the commitment to amend it or to substitute it with a new one. As explained above, the amendment of the initial commitment or the adoption of a new commitment would have to be based on Article 9(1). This provision requires consent. The Commission cannot rely on Article 7 to unilaterally amend a commitment to the detriment of the company that offered it. If that company refuses to consent to an amendment, the Commission can only unilaterally revoke the initial commitment and switch entirely to the Article 7 procedure. This implies in particular that the Commission must proof the existence of an infringement to the requisite standard and grant the undertaking concerned the procedural rights associated with an Article 7 decision.

If new circumstances give rise to new competition concerns and if these concerns are not closely related to the concerns that were addressed in the initial remedy, the Commission can, instead of reopening the procedure pursuant to Article 9(2)(a),

---

[1491] Georgiev (2007), 1021.

[1492] See Temple Lang (2006), 298: "Article 9 clearly envisages amendments, as well as termination, if circumstances alter".

[1493] See Wils (2006), 358; Saitzek (2008), 284; Hennig (2010), 250f; Ritter (2012), Art. 9, 32.

maintain the old remedy and address the new concerns in a new, separate procedure. If the investigated company refused to offer a commitment to address the new concerns, the Commission could then take a decision on the basis of Article 7.

3.7.2.1.2.2.2 Ex Nunc or Ex Tunc Revocation

Article 9(2) does not contain any statement regarding the question whether, subsequent to a reopening of the proceedings, a commitment may only be revoked ex nunc or also ex tunc. Given that the provision governs only the reopening of proceedings, but leaves the revocation to the general principles of EU administrative law, this is neither astonishing nor problematic. According to the general principles, a retroactive revocation is only possible if the commitment was unlawfully adopted and subject to potentially existing legitimate expectations of the beneficiaries. Thus, if the commitment was initially lawfully adopted and shall be revoked subsequent to a change of circumstances, in accordance with Article 9(2)(a), the revocation may only take effect ex nunc. These principles correspond also to Article 8(3) Regulation 17/62, which explicitly excluded an ex tunc revocation of an exemption decision subsequent to a change of circumstances.

3.7.2.2 Common Questions Regarding Articles 7 and 9

In the remainder of the present section, some common questions shall be addressed that concern the revocation or amendment of remedies irrespective of whether they have been adopted on the basis of Article 7 or Article 9. Particularities that apply to Article 9 decisions will be pointed out where necessary.

3.7.2.2.1 Discretion vs Obligation to Reopen the Procedure

In Alrosa, the General Court seems to have expressed the opinion that the Commission retains discretion to refuse to reopen a procedure, even if the remedy in question was unlawfully adopted or became unlawful subsequent to a change of circumstances.[1494] In her opinion on the case, Advocate General Kokott did not explicitly state that there could be an obligation for the Commission to reopen the procedure. However, she mentioned that, although the Commission was not required to apply a time-limit to commitment decisions, the undertakings concerned and third parties were "not left without protection", because the Commission had the possibility to reopen proceedings in case of a material change of the circumstances. Furthermore,

[1494]GC, T-170/06 (Alrosa, 2007), 155: "Since the situations justifying a reopening are thus exhaustively listed, Alrosa could not request that the proceedings be reopened on grounds such as those set out in its application, in particular on the basis that the principle of proportionality had been infringed. Furthermore, the Commission would have a discretion to refuse to reopen". Consenting Sofianatos (2009), 548.

the Advocate General explicitly stated that the principle of good administration laid down in Article 41 Charter required the Commission "to examine without delay any substantiated indication of a material change in the facts and to take a decision on the reopening of proceedings".[1495] Against this backdrop, the question must be raised whether and to what extent the Commission retains discretion to revoke or amend a remedy that was unlawfully adopted or that became unlawful subsequent to a change or circumstances.

According to the early case law of the Court of Justice, the balancing of the principles of legality and legal certainty is, in principle, the task of the authority that decides on the revocation or amendment of the act.[1496] However, in later cases, the EU Courts have made it clear that they are willing to engage in the balancing task themselves or that they exercise at least a close control.[1497] Hence, the Commission's discretion to revoke or amend a remedy is in any event not unlimited.[1498] Advocate General Colomer rightly explained that the Commission's discretion to withdraw a measure may become so insignificant that an obligation to withdraw must be envisaged.[1499] The existence of such an obligation is subject to review by the Courts.

3.7.2.2.1.1 Obligation to Withdraw or Amend an Unlawfully Adopted, Burdensome Remedy if There Are No Opposing Legitimate Expectations?

It is questionable whether the Commission is or at least can be obliged to revoke or amend a burdensome remedy that was unlawfully adopted, if there are no opposing legitimate expectations. In the already mentioned AssiDomän case, the General Court held that the Commission was not only empowered to repay a fine that had been unlawfully imposed. Rather, the Commission was also "required" to do so "in accordance with the principles of legality and of good administration".[1500] The Court of Justice set aside the judgment of the General Court and dismissed the appeal. In essence, the Court held that there was no obligation for the Commission to repay the fine, because the applicants had not challenged the decision imposing the fine within the limitation period provided for by Article 263(6).[1501] In his opinion on the case, Advocate General Colomer reached the same result as the Court of Justice. His line of reasoning was, however, more refined than that of the Court. According

[1495]Opinion of AG Kokott, C-441/07 P (Alrosa, 2009), 217ff.

[1496]CJ, C-49/59 (SNUPAT, 1961).

[1497]Craig (2012), 563; for an example see GC, T-416/04 (Anna Kontouli, 2006), 167: "[. . .] in the circumstances of the present case there is no public-policy interest [. . .] which overrides the beneficiary's interest in the maintenance of a situation which he was entitled to regard as stable".

[1498]See the opinion of AG Colomer in C-310/97 (AssiDomän, 1999), 48.

[1499]See the opinion of AG Colomer in C-310/97 (AssiDomän, 1999), 48.

[1500]GC, T-227/95 (AssiDomän, 1997), 92.

[1501]CJ, C-310/97 P (AssiDomän, 1999), 49ff; see also Neumayr/Kühnert (2011), 5f.

to the Advocate General, the general rule had to be that measures which had become final were not open to challenge.[1502] However, this general rule was subject to two reservations. First, the Commission was always entitled to reexamine and, if need be, to withdraw burdensome administrative acts, as long as it did not act arbitrarily.[1503] Second, the Advocate General suggested that the entitlement to reexamine could become an obligation to reexamine where there was any serious indication of irregularity, existing from the outset or becoming apparent subsequently, which could affect the measure in question.[1504] The view of the Advocate General differed from that of the General Court in that the Advocate General did not assume that any act which had been unlawfully adopted had to be revoked automatically. Rather, the Commission was obliged to balance a broad set of factors, including inter alia the severity of the burden imposed by the unlawful act on its addressee, the time which had elapsed since the act had became final and the degree of obviousness of the illegality.[1505] Only if the balancing of all the relevant factors led to the result that the maintenance of the unlawful act was "intolerable", there was an obligation for the Commission to withdraw it.[1506] In the case at hand, the Advocate General considered that this was not the case.[1507]

The AssiDomän judgment of the Court of Justice is problematic to the extent that it could imply a categorical exclusion of an obligation for the Commission to withdraw burdensome acts that were unlawfully adopted, but not challenged within the limitation period provided for by Article 263(6) TFEU. The more nuanced approach of the Advocate General is preferable.[1508] In any event, it is submitted that the restrictive approach taken by the Court of Justice regarding the question whether the Commission is obliged to repay an unlawfully imposed fine should not be transposed to injunctions and commitment decisions that were unlawfully adopted on the basis of Article 7 and 9. On the one hand, the negative effects of an unlawfully adopted injunction or commitment may affect the competitive process and thus the interest of the general public to a larger extent than an unlawfully

---

[1502] Opinion of AG Colomer, C-310/97 P (AssiDomän, 1999), 55ff.

[1503] Opinion of AG Colomer, C-310/97 P (AssiDomän, 1999), 66f.

[1504] Opinion of AG Colomer, C-310/97 P (AssiDomän, 1999), 68ff.

[1505] Opinion of AG Colomer, C-310/97 P (AssiDomän, 1999), 81.

[1506] Opinion of AG Colomer, C-310/97 P (AssiDomän, 1999), 81 and 96. The standard of "intolerability" is used in the same context also under German administrative law; the details are controversial: see eg Sachs (2014), § 48, 85: "Die Aufhebung des [Verwaltungsakts] ist allerdings geboten, soweit die *Aufrechterhaltung* eines [Verwaltungsakts] *schlechthin unerträglich* wäre; dies kann insbes. bei gleichheitswidriger Rücknahmepraxis, Sitten- oder Treuwidrigkeit der Berufung auf Unanfechtbarkeit sowie offensichtlicher Rechtswidrigkeit des [Verwaltungsakts] der Fall sein, ist aber nicht allein wegen Verfassungswidrigkeit anzunehmen".

[1507] Opinion of AG Colomer, C-310/97 P (AssiDomän, 1999), 98.

[1508] See, for a similar result, also Wessely (2000), 370; Neumayr/Kühnert (2011), 7f; more restrictive Moloney (2000), 980. See also CJ, 2/70 (Riva, 1971), 7, where the CJ held that considerations of equal treatment could justify a "duty to rectify all legal or factual errors and all assessments which experience showed to be inaccurate or incomplete", even though the act in question had become definitive.

adopted fine. On the other hand, injunctions and commitments normally have a certain duration during which they continue to burden the addressee. The interest in the withdrawal or amendment of such unlawful acts with permanent effects is higher than the interest in the withdrawal or amendment of an unlawful act the effects of which are limited to the past.[1509] In that connection, it should be pointed out that Advocate General Colomer explicitly stated in his opinion in AssiDomän that his analysis did not cover a set of unlawfully adopted commitments that the applicants had given to the Commission. These commitments were not the subject matter of the appeal and, in any event, the Commission and the applicants agreed that they did not display any legal effects.[1510]

Overall, it is hence submitted that, according to the circumstances of the case, there can be an obligation for the Commission to revoke or amend an unlawfully adopted remedy that produces merely burdensome effects, even if the addressee failed to challenge the remedy within the limitation period provided for by Article 263(6).

3.7.2.2.1.2 Obligation to Revoke or Amend a Remedy in Favour of the Addressee Despite Favourable Effects for Third Parties

The Commission can also be obliged to revoke or amend remedies that were unlawfully adopted and produce favourable effects for third parties. This can be the case if the interest in legal certainty and the legitimate expectations of the third parties do not outweigh the interest in the safeguard of the principle of legality and the interest of the remedy's addressee. The interest in a revocation or amendment of the remedy may for instance prevail if the remedy was adopted on the basis of false information that was provided by third party beneficiaries. In such a case, even a revocation ex tunc may be justified and required. Where the interests of the beneficiaries are more worthy of protection, it may still be necessary to revoke or amend the remedy ex nunc.

If the remedy becomes unlawful subsequent to a change of circumstances, there may a fortiori be an obligation for the Commission to revoke or amend it. In this case, since the circumstances that make the remedy unlawful arise only after its adoption, no reproach can be made to the addressee for not having challenged the initial decision in court. An obligation to revoke or amend a remedy that has become unlawful subsequent to a change of circumstances may in particular exist if the legitimate expectations of the third parties do not outweigh the public interest in the

---

[1509] Under German administrative law, authorities are obliged to revoke or amend an initially lawful act that produces permanent negative effects ("Dauerverwaltungsakt") for fundamental rights, if the act becomes unlawful due to a change of circumstances: see Bundesverwaltungsgericht, 6 C 9/10 (Widerruf einer Mobilfunkfrequenz, 2011), 55: "Ein subjektives Recht auf Widerruf (§ 49 I i. V. mit § 51 V VwVfG) kommt u. a. in Betracht, soweit ein grundrechtsbeschränkender Verwaltungsakt mit Dauerwirkung auf Grund veränderter Umstände nicht mehr erlassen werden dürfte"; Sachs (2014), § 48, 26 and 86.

[1510] Opinion of AG Colomer, C-310/97 P (AssiDomän, 1999), 51.

safeguard of the principle of legality and the interest of the remedy's addressee. However, since the remedy was lawful until the change of circumstances occurred, the revocation or amendment can in general only take effect ex nunc. Third party beneficiaries will normally not enjoy legitimate expectations in the future maintenance of the remedy. They have to expect that circumstances may change and that a change of circumstances may entail a revocation or amendment of the remedy.[1511]

Regardless of the existence of an obligation, the Commission itself does in any event not seem eager to maintain remedies in force that are no longer necessary subsequent to a change of circumstances.[1512] There are examples from the time before the entry into force of Regulation 1/03 in which the Commission revoked[1513] or amended[1514] conditions that had been attached to an exemption decision pursuant to Article 8(3)(a) Regulation 17/62 subsequent to a change of circumstances. In a memorandum dealing with Article 9 published in 2004, the Commission explained that it was possible for companies to ask the Commission to lift a commitment that was no longer appropriate.[1515] In the Distrigaz decision, the Commission indicated that it was going to lift or relax the commitment pursuant to Article 9(2)(a) upon the occurrence of certain predetermined conditions that would be considered as a material change of circumstances.[1516]

3.7.2.2.1.3 Obligation to Revoke or Amend a Remedy to the Detriment of the Addressee

The Commission can also be obliged to revoke or amend remedies to the detriment of the addressee in order to impose even further reaching obligations. The General Court

[1511]The preponderant view in the literature seems to be that the Commission is obliged to reopen proceedings if the conditions of Article 9(2)(a) are met: Schwarze/Weitbrecht (2004), § 6, Rn 82: "Ermessensreduktion auf Null"; Rab/Monnoyeur/Sukhtankar (2010), 172; "the undertaking may request that the Commission releases it from the commitments if a change in circumstances means that they are no longer required"; Hennig (2010), 250; Rachwol (2010), 176; Körber (2010), 86f with further references; similarly also Temple Lang (2006), 298: "[. . .] a refusal to amend is open to challenge in EU law"; see also Ortiz Blanco/Jörgens/Kellerbauer (2013), 13.25: "Whilst the Commission generally has discretion to refuse to reopen, it can be argued that there is an obligation to that effect where the commitments appear manifestly excessive in the light of the changed circumstances". For the contrary view see eg Saitzek (2008), 274ff: "Kein Anspruch auf Wiedereröffnung des Verfahrens".

[1512]See Kipiani (2014), 520: "Si la possibilité lui est laissée d'accepter des engagements à durée indéterminée, la Commission n'est pas contre leur levée. La volontée de ne pas enfermer imutilement les entreprises dans des engagements devenus inappropriés avec l'écoulement du temps est compréhensible".

[1513]OJ 2001 L 52/30 (Unisource, 2000); Sofianatos (2009), 548.

[1514]OJ 1994 L 174/34 (Bayer/BP Chemicals, 1994); for a detailed discussion see Müller-Tautphaeus (2003), 414.

[1515]MEMO/04/217; Kipiani (2014), 520.

[1516]COMP/37.966 (Distrigaz, 2007), 36f; Schweitzer (2010), 551; Rab/Monnoyeur/Sukhtankar (2010), 183.

recognised a comparable obligation in the context of Article 8(3) Regulation 17/62.[1517] The principles that have just been mentioned regarding the revocation or amendment of a remedy in favour of the addressee can in principle be transferred mutatis mutandis. One particularity nevertheless exists. An obligation to revoke or amend a remedy to the detriment of the addressee is not only subject to the legitimate expectations of the addressee. It is also subject to the discretion the Commission has in prioritising its cases. For instance, if a complainant requests the Commission to impose a further reaching remedy, because subsequent to a change of circumstances the initial remedy no longer suffices to address the now existing competition concerns,[1518] the Commission can rely on a lack of Union interest in order to reject the request.[1519]

3.7.2.2.2 Importance of the Change of Circumstances Required

According to the English version of Article 9(2)(a), a reopening of the proceedings is only justified if the change in the facts on which the decision was based is "material". The French version of the provision requires that "un des faits sur lesquels la décision repose subit un changement important". In these two languages, a reopening of the proceedings hence seems to be possible only if the change in circumstances is important enough to exceed a certain threshold. The German version points in a different direction. It allows for a reopening of the proceedings already "wenn sich die tatsächlichen Verhältnisse in einem für die Entscheidung wesentlichen Punkt geändert haben". The German version of Article 9 corresponds to the English version of Article 8(3)(a) Regulation 17/62 which permitted the revocation or amendment of an exemption decision "where there [had] been a change in any of the facts which were basic to the making of the decision".

Against this backdrop, the question arises whether, in order to justify the revocation or amendment of a remedy, a change of circumstances must only concern the facts upon which the initial decision was based or whether the change of circumstances must also be significant. The question arises also with respect to Article 7 remedies, for the revocation or amendment of which there is no statutory basis. The question shall not be discussed here comprehensively. The preponderant view in the

---

[1517]GC, T-65/98 (Van den Bergh, 2003), 195: "[...] even if the Commission had granted an exemption to HB, it would have had the power, and even the obligation, under Article 8(3) of Regulation [17/62], to revoke or amend that exemption if it had found that the exempted agreements nevertheless had certain effects that were incompatible with the conditions laid down in Article 85 (3) of the Treaty, and particularly if experience had shown that the changes made by HB to its distribution system had not brought about the expected results".

[1518]See Temple Lang (2006), 298: "[A] complainant may at any time file a new complaint to argue to the Commission that the company which gave the commitment is acting illegally in some way not prohibited by the commitment, and that the Commission should take further action".

[1519]See GC, T-342/11 (CEES, 2014), 47ff: The General Court decided that the Commission could rely on its right to prioritise cases in order to reject a request to reopen proceedings pursuant to Article 9(2). Although, in that case, the request was based on Article 9(2)(b), the Court's reasoning applies generally to all requests that are based on Article 9(2). The rationale of the judgment applies also to remedies that were adopted on the basis of Article 7.

literature regarding Article 9(2)(a) seems to be that the change of circumstances must not only concern the facts upon which the initial decision was based, but that it must also exceed a certain threshold in terms of significance.[1520] In principle, reasons of procedural economy justify this approach. This conclusion applies also in the context of Article 7 remedies. In that regard, it should be recalled that the revocation or amendment of a remedy is a deviation from the principle that acts that have become definitive should not be open to challenge.[1521] As such, it should be admitted only restrictively. On the other hand, the danger that a remedy becomes inefficient or disproportionate cautions against setting the threshold for a revocation or amendment too high. According to the case law of the Courts, only a change of circumstances that is substantial entails an obligation for the Commission to reconsider a decision that has become definitive.[1522] A new fact is "substantial", if it is capable of substantially altering the applicant's situation.[1523]

The market entry of a new competitor constitutes a change of circumstances that may justify the revocation or amendment of an existing remedy.[1524] The same applies if the implementation of the remedy has become impossible for the concerned undertaking.[1525] A revocation or amendment may also be justified if experience shows that the initial remedy does not attain its purpose.[1526] In the latter

[1520] See De Bronnet (2012), Art. 9, 23: "Die Änderung der tatsächlichen Verhältnisse muss im doppelten Sinne wesentlich sein: Die Änderung muss sich zumindest auf einen für die ursprüngliche Entscheidung wesentlichen Punkt beziehen und muss diesbezüglich selbst wesentlich sein"; Rachwol (2010), 168f, and Hennig (2010), 239f, follow De Bronnet; Sura (2014), Art. 9, 16: "Veränderungen im Bagatellbereich ermächtigen die Kommission im Lichte ihrer Bindung an den Verhältnismäßigkeitsgrundsatz nicht zur Wiederaufnahme des Verfahrens"; Kipiani (2014), 554: "Les textes sont très stricts sur cette révision qui est limitée notamment aux changements importants". Also the Merger Remedies Notice (2008), 74, states that "[e]xceptional circumstances justifying a waiver, modification or substitution [of a remedy] may [. . .] be accepted [. . .] if parties show that market circumstances have changed significantly and on a permanent basis. For showing this, a sufficient long time-span, normally at least several years, between the Commission decision and a request by the parties is required".

[1521] See opinion of AG Colomer, C-310/97 P (AssiDomän, 1999), 55; Sofianatos (2009), 550; De Bronnet (2012), Art. 9, 21.

[1522] GC, T-186/98 (Inpesca, 2001), 48; Neumayr/Kühnert (2011), 6.

[1523] GC, T-186/98 (Inpesca, 2001), 51.

[1524] See GC, T-9/93 (Schöller, 1995), 113.

[1525] Sofianatos (2009), 546f; Ritter (2012), Art. 9, 32.

[1526] GC, T-65/98 (Van den Bergh, 2003), 195: "[The Commission] would have had the power, and even the obligation, under Article 8(3) [Regulation 17/62], to revoke or amend that exemption [. . .] if experience had shown that the changes made by HB to its distribution system had not brought about the expected results"; Remedies Notice (2008), 75. But see De Smijter/Sinclair (2014), 2.139: "[. . .] proceedings cannot be reopened merely because experience shows that the commitments are ineffective or unnecessarily intrusive. There must be a material change in the relevant facts". See also Botteman/Patsa (2013), 373 together with fn 121: They consider that Article 9(2) does not cover the situation where "despite full implementation, the competition concerns that prompted the investigation remain largely unresolved". In their view, specific review clauses should be included in commitments to cover such situations.

situation, the outcome may be favourable or unfavourable for the addressee of the initial remedy. The preponderant view in the literature regarding Article 9(2)(a) denies that also a change in the law can justify the revocation or amendment of a remedy.[1527] It is submitted here that, regardless of the scope of Article 9(2)(a), a change in the law should, in any event, be allowed as a justification for the revocation or amendment of a remedy under the general principles of EU administrative law, subject to the protection of any existing legitimate expectations in the maintenance of the remedy.

3.7.2.2.3 Review Provisions

Both under Article 7 and Article 9, specific review provisions can be included in a remedy. Such specific provisions take precedence over the general principles that have been addressed above. In particular, review provisions can counteract the emergence of legitimate expectations.[1528] Recourse to review clauses is frequent in the context of merger remedies.[1529] It has also occurred in the context of Article 9 decisions.[1530] The review clauses that have been used in the context of Article 9 decisions mostly restate Article 9(2).[1531] The use of more specific review provisions depends on the circumstances of the individual case. For these reasons, review provisions will not further be discussed here.[1532] The absence of a review provision does, in any event, not exclude an ex post amendment of a remedy.[1533]

[1527] Against the possibility to reopen proceedings in case of a change of the law eg Bauer (2008), 4-9-057; Saitzek (2008), 277ff; Hennig (2010), 237ff; unclear Sura (2014), Art. 9, 17: "Änderungen der Rspr. der europäischen Gerichte und die damit einhergehende rechtliche Neubewertung eines Verhaltens [...] stellen hingegen keinen zulässigen Wiederaufnahmegrund dar. In solchen Fällen kann aber das gebundene Unternehmen bei der Kommission beantragen, die Zusagenentscheidung wieder aufzuheben. Im Lichte des Prinzips der Gesetzmäßigkeit der Verwaltung dürfte die Kommission dann verpflichtet sein, die Zusagenentscheidung einvernehmlich aufzuheben oder zumindest abzuändern".

[1528] See Hofmann/Rowe/Türk (2012), 635f.

[1529] See the Merger Remedies Notice (2008), 71ff; Sofianatos (2009), 553ff; Hoeg (2014), 154f; Kipiani (2014), 548.

[1530] See Kipiani (2014), 559, with three examples from the Commission's practice.

[1531] See the examples mentioned by Kipiani (2014), 559.

[1532] In the Manual of Procedure (2012), Module 16, 52, the Commission states that circumstances which are likely or at least possible to occur during the time of the implementation of the commitment should normally be addressed in the commitments themselves and not be left to the review clause. Moreover, the Commission emphasises that a review clause leaves the possibility of Article 9(2)(a) unaffected.

[1533] See Sofianatos (2009), 550; Ortiz Blanco/Jörgens/Kellerbauer (2013), 13.17.

3.8 Conclusion on the Relaxation of the Link Between Harm and Remedy

Summing up, it is submitted that the adoption of an Article 9 decision instead of an Article 7 decision relaxes the link between harm and remedy only to a modest extent. In the view defended here, the principle of proportionality and the required link between harm and remedy do not call into question the fact that the Commission enjoys broad and flexible powers under Article 7. On the basis of Article 7, the Commission can adopt remedies that are prescriptive and prospective; address on-going and imminent anticompetitive conduct; eliminate the causes of future anticompetitive conduct, in particular through recourse to the so-called "structural" remedies; eliminate the subsisting effects of past anticompetitive conduct; and impose ancillary obligations to ensure an effective implementation, in particular through recourse to monitoring trustees and ADR mechanisms.

At the same time, the principle of proportionality and the link between harm and remedy continue to play an important role also in the context of Article 9. It is true that the Article 9 procedure entails a risk that the Commission makes commitments binding which it could not have imposed under Article 7. This risk is due to the facts that Article 9 does not require the Commission to carry out a full investigation of the case and allows it—subject to the respect of the rights of third parties—to accept overbroad commitments where these have been proposed by the concerned undertakings. However, in the view defended here, the risk that the Commission makes commitments binding which it could not have imposed under Article 7 remains to date mostly abstract. The preceding analysis of the Commission's commitment practice against the benchmark of Article 7 has shown that overbroad commitments constitute rather isolated exceptions than the general rule.

Bibliography

Ackermann (2010): Vodafone: Price Regulation as a Substitute for Intervention under Article 102 TFEU, JECLP 2010, 426

Ackermann (2012): Excessive Pricing and the Goals of Competition Law, in: Zimmer (Ed.): The Goals of Competition Law, 2012, p. 349

Ackermann (2014a): The Interaction of Public and Private Antitrust Enforcement – The Calculation of Fines and Damages, in: Hüschelrath/Schweitzer (Eds.), Public and Private Enforcement of Competition Law in Europe. Legal and Economic Perspectives, 2014

Ackermann (2014b): State Aid for Banks in the Financial Crisis: The Commission's New and Stronger Role, in: Ringe/Huber (Eds.), Legal challenges in the global financial crisis. Bail-outs, the Euro, and regulation, 2014, p. 149

Ackermann/Petzold (2011): Energieregulierung und Kartellaufsicht, in: Baur/Salje/Schmidt-Preuß (Eds.), Regulierung in der Energiewirtschaft, 2011

Ahlborn/Evans (2009): The Microsoft judgment and its implications for competition policy towards dominant firms in Europe, 75 Antitrust L. J. 887 (2009)

Akman/Garrod (2011): When are excessive prices unfair?, JCLE 2011, 403

Al-Ameen (2009): Restitutionary Remedies in Competition Law: Bull in a China Shop?, World Competition 2009, 327

Alexiadis/Sependa (2013): Structural remedies under European Union antitrust rules, Concurrences 2013/2, 21

Andreangeli (2010): Between Economic Freedom and Effective Competition Enforcement: the impact of the antitrust remedies provided by the Modernisation Regulation on investigated parties' freedom to contract and to enjoy property, CLR 2010, 225

Anweiler (2009): in: Loewenheim/Meessen/Riesenkampff (Eds.), Kartellrecht. Kommentar, 2nd edition, 2009

Art/McCurdy (2004): The European Commission's media player remedy in its Microsoft decision: compulsory code removal despite the absence of tying or foreclosure, ECLR 2004, 694

Bansevic/Ryan/Wezenbeek (2014): Financial Services, in: Faull/Nikpay (Eds.), The EU Law of Competition, 3rd edition, 2014

Bauer (2008): in: Hirsch/Montag/Säcker (Eds.), Competition Law: European Community Practice and Procedure. Article-by-Article Commentary, 2008

Baumgart/Rasbach/Rudolph (2009): Eine brisante Mischung - Erste Erfahrungen mit § 29 GWB im Zusammenspiel mit §§ 32 und 64f. GWB, in: Baur/Sandrock/Scholtka/Shapira (Eds.), Festschrift für Gunther Kühne, 2009

Bechtold/Bosch/Brinker (2014): EU-Kartellrecht. Kommentar, 3rd edition, 2014

Bellis (2013): Article 102 TFEU: The case for a remedial enforcement model along the lines of Section 5 of the Federal Trade Commission Act, Concurrences 2013/1, 54

Bischke (2008): in: Hirsch/Montag/Säcker (Eds.), Competition Law: European Community Practice and Procedure. Article-by-Article Commentary, 2008

Blake/Browne/Sime (2011): A practical approach to alternative dispute resolution, 2011

Blanke (2011a): International Arbitration and ADR in Remedy Scenarios Arising under Articles 101 and 102 TFEU, in: Blanke/Landolt (Ed.), EU and US Antitrust Arbitration, 2011

Blanke (2011b): International Arbitration and ADR in Conditional EU Merger Clearance Decisions, in: Blanke/Landolt (Ed.), EU and US Antitrust Arbitration, 2011

Blanke (2013): in: Ortiz Blanco (Ed.), EU Competition Procedure, 3rd Edition, 2013

Blanke/Landolt (2011): EU and US Antitrust Arbitration, 2011

Bonnières/Vassileff (2014): Le mandataire: Vers un encadrement de la pratique, Concurrences 2014/1, 5

Bornkamm (2014): in: Langen/Bunte (Eds.), Kartellrecht, Volume 2, 12th edition, 2014

Bosch/Fritzsche (2013): Die 8. GWB-Novelle – Konvergenz und eigene wettbewerbspolitische Akzente, NJW 2013, 2225

Boscheck (2009): The EU's Third Internal Energy Market Legislative Package: Victory of Politics over Economic Rationality?, World Competition 2009, 593

Botteman/Patsa (2012): The jurisdictional reach of EU anti-cartel rules: unmuddling the limits, ECJ 2012, 365

Botteman/Patsa (2013): Towards a more sustainable use of commitment decisions in Article 102 TFEU cases, JAE 2013, 347

Bougette/Marty (2012): Quels remèdes pour les abus de position dominante? Une analyse économique des décisions de la Commission européenne, Concurrences 2012/3, 30

Bourgeois/Strievi (2010): EU Competition Remedies in Consumer Cases: Thinking Out of the Shopping Bag, World Competition 2010, 241

Brenner (2014): Regulierung mithilfe des Kartellrechts – Verpflichtungszusagen der Europäischen Kommission, EuR 2014, 671

Brisimi (2014): The interface between competition and the internal market, 2014

Brückner (2012): Der Treuhänder in der europäischen Fusionskontrolle, 2012

Brückner/Hoehn (2010): Monitoring Compliance with Merger Remedies – The Role of the Monitoring Trustee, Competition Law International 2010, 73

Buchmann (2004): Positive Comity im internationalen Kartellrecht, 2004

Budzinski/Kuchinke (2012): Deal or No Deal? Consensual arrangements as an Instrument of European Competition Policy, Review of Economics 2012, 265
Bueren (2011): Verständigungen – Settlements in Kartelbußgeldverfahren, 2011
Buhr/Bulst/Foucault/Kramler (2010): The Commission's decision in the Microsoft Internet Explorer case and recent developments in the area of interoperability, CPN 2010/1, 37
Bulst (2014): in: Langen/Bunte (Eds.), Kartellrecht, Volume 2, 12th edition, 2014
Calliess (2011): in: Calliess/Ruffert, EUV/AEUV, Kommentar, 4th Edition 2011
Carstensen (2012): Remedies for Monopolization from Standard Oil to Microsoft and Intel: The Changing Nature of Monopoly Law from Elimination of Market Power to Regulation of Its Use, 85 S. Cal. L. Rev. 815 (2012)
Carbone (2013): Antitrust commitments and arbitration in European competition law, in: Kronenberger/D'Alessio/Placco (Eds.), De Rome à Lisbonne: les juridictions de l'Union européenne à la croisée des chemins: Mélanges en l'honneur de Paolo Mengozzi, 2013
Cavicchi (2011): The European Commission's discretion as to the adoption of Article 9 commitment decisions: Lessons from Alrosa, Europa-Kolleg Hamburg, Institute for European Integration, Discussion paper 3/11, available online
Cengiz (2011): Judicial review and the rule of law in the EU competition law regime after Alrosa, ECJ 2011, 127
Chauve (2006): REPSOL: Opening up the fuel distribution system in Spain, CPN 2006/2, 25
Chauve/Godfried/Kovács/Langus/Nagy/Siebert (2009): The E.ON electricity cases: an antitrust decision with structural remedies, CPN 2009/1, 51
Cook (2006): Commitment Decisions: The Law and Practice under Article 9, World Competition 2006, 209
Cook (2011): Essentials of EU Merger Control for Arbitration Practitioners, in: Landolt/Blanke (eds.), EU and US Antitrust Arbitration
Craig (2012): EU administrative law, 2nd edition, 2012
Dalheimer (2005): in: Dalheimer/Feddersen/Miersch (Eds.), EU-Kartellverfahrensverordnung. Kommentar zur VO 1/2003. Sonderausgabe aus Grabitz/Hilf: Das Recht der Europäischen Union, nach Art. 83 EGV, 2005
Dannecker/Biermann (2012): in: Immenga/Mestmäcker (Eds.), EU-Wettbewerbsrecht, 5th Edition, 2012
Davies/Lyons (2007): Mergers and merger remedies in the EU: Assessing the consequences for competition, 2007
De Broca/Mielecka Riga/Subočs (2014): Transport, in: Faull/Nikpay (Eds.), The EU Law of Competition, 3rd edition, 2014
De Bronnet (2012): Europäisches Kartellverfahrensrecht. Kommentar zur VO 1/2003, 2nd edition, 2012
De Frutos/Fabra (2012): How to allocate forward contracts: The case of electricity markets, European Economic Review (2012), 451
De Hautecloque (2009): Legal Uncertainty and Competition Policy in European Deregulated Electricity Markets: the Case of Long-term Exclusive Supply Contracts, World Competition 2009, 91
De Hautecloque (2013): Market Building Through Antitrust. Long-term Contract Regulation in EU Electricity Markets, 2013
De Hautecloque/Hancher (2011): The Svenska Kraftnät case: introduction of bidding zones in Sweden, Network Industries Quarterly 2011/1, 20
De la Mano/Nazzini/Zenger (2014): Article 102, in: Faull/Nikpay (Eds.), The EU Law of Competition, 3rd edition, 2014
De Meese (2010): European Commission accepts commitments from Rambus in patent ambush case, JECLP 2010, 215
Derenne (2010): Round Up. October – December 2009, JECLP 2010, 162
Deselaers (1992): Selektiver Vertrieb und Kontrahierungszwang nach Art. 85 EWG-Vertrag, 1992
Deselaers (2011): in: Grabitz/Hilf/Nettesheim (Eds.), Das Recht der Europäischen Union

De Smijter/Sinclair (2014): The Enforcement System under Regulation 1/2003, in: Faull/Nikpay (Eds.), The EU Law of Competition, 3rd edition, 2014
De Valois Turk (2009): The EC's revised Remedies Notice - the trustee's perspective, ECLR 2009, 332
DiBrozolo (2004): Antitrust: a paradigm of the relations between mandatory rules and arbitration - a fresh look at the "second look", IALR 2004, 23
Dittert (2017): Abus de position dominante en matière de rabais de fidélité: une jurisprudence « précisée » en termes de compétence, de procécure et, surtout, d'analyse économique, Revue des Affaires européennes 2017, 583
Dohms/Rieder (2010): Commitment decision in the ship classification case: Paving the way for more competition, CPN 2010/1, 41
Dolmans/Graf (2004): Analysis of Tying under Article 82 EC: The European Commission's Microsoft Decision in Perspective, World Competition 2004, 225
Drauz (1997): Remedies under the Merger Regulation, in: Hawk (Ed), Annual proceedings of the Fordham Competition Law Institute 1996, 1997
Dreher/Thomas (2008): Die Beschränkung der Vertragsabschlussfreiheit durch kartellbehördliche Verfügung. Behördliche Wettbewerbsbeteiligungsverbote für Energielieferverträge, NJW 2008, 1557
Dreher (2009): Kurzkommentar zu BGH, KVR 67/07 (Gaslieferverträge, 2009), in: BGH EWiR § 1 GWB 1/09, 717
Drexl (2009): Deceptive Conduct in the Patent World – A Case for US Antitrust and EU Competition Law?, in: Prinz zu Waldeck und Pyrmont/Adelman/Brauneis/Drexl/Nack (Eds.), Patents and Technological Progress in a Globalized World – Liber Amicorum Joseph Straus, 2009
Drexl (2010): Ronald Dworkin, ökonomische Effizienz und das Kartellrech, in: Forschungsinstitut für Wirtschaftsverfassung und Wettbewerb e.V. (Ed.), Wettbewerbspolitik und Kartellrecht in der Marktwirtschaft – 50 Jahre FIW: 1960 bis 2010, Festschrift, 2010
Dunne (2014a): Between competition law and regulation: hybridized approaches to market control, JAE 2014, 225
Dunne (2014b): Commitment decisions in EU competition law, JCLE 2014, 399
Economides/Lianos (2009): The elusive antitrust standard on bundling in Europe and in the United States in the aftermath of the Microsoft cases, 76 Antitrust L. J. 483 (2009)
Economides/Lianos (2010): A critical appraisal of remedies in the E.U. Microsoft cases, 2010 Colum. Bus. L. Rev. 346
Ehricke/Pellmann (2005): Zur EG-kartellrechtlichen Bewertung der Unzulässigkeitskriterien langfristiger Gaslieferungsverträge, WuW 2005, 1104
Eilmansberger (2008): in: Hirsch/Montag/Säcker (Eds.), Competition Law: European Community Practice and Procedure. Article-by-Article Commentary, 2008
Elhauge (2009): Disgorgement as an antitrust remedy, 76 Antitrust L. J. 79 (2009)
Emde (2013): Anspruch von Vertriebsmittlern auf Zugang zum Vertriebssystem eines Unternehmers – Kontrahierungsanspruch, Belieferungsanspruch und ihr Verhältnis zum Schadensersatzanspruch, NZKart 2013, 355
Emmerich (2014): in: Immenga/Mestmäcker, GWB, 5th edition, 2014
Epstein (2007): Antitrust Consent Decrees in Theory and Practice. Why less is More, 2007
Epstein (2009): Monopolization Follies: The Dangers of Structural Remedies under Section 2 of the Sherman Act, 76 Antitrust L. J. 205 (2009)
Evans/Schmalensee (2005): The Economics of Interchange Fees and their Regulation: An Overview, MIT Sloan School of Management Working Paper 4548-05, 2005, available online
Ezrachi (2006): Behavioural Remedies in EC Merger Control – Scope and Limitations, World Competition 2006, 459
Ezrachi/Ioannidou (2011): Access to Justice in European Competition Law - Public Enforcement as a Supplementary Channel for "Corrective Compensation", 19 Asia Pac. L. Rev. 195 (2011)

Falconi (2011): Commitment decisions in the EU and UK – Developments, open issues and considerations for companies and competition authorities, Competition Law 2011, 41
First (1995): Is Antitrust "Law"?, 10 (1995) Antitrust 9
First (2008): Netscape is dead: Remedy Lessons from the Microsoft Litigation, NYU Law & Economics Research Paper Series, Working Paper n° 08-49, available online
Fletcher/Jardine (2008): Towards an appropriate policy for excessive pricing, in: Ehlermann/ Marquis (Eds.), European Competition Law Annual 2007, 2008
Fox (2005): Remedies and the Courage of Convictions in a Globalized World: How Globalization Corrupts Relief, 80 Tul. L. Rev. 571 (2005)
Forrester (2005): Article 82: Remedies in search of theories, in: Hawk (Ed.), Annual proceedings of the Fordham Competition Law Institute 2004, 2005
Forrester (2010): Creating New Rules or Closing Easy Cases? Policy Consequences for Public Enforcement of Settlements under Article 9 or Regulation 1/2003, in: Ehlermann/Marquis (Eds.), European Competition Law Annual 2008, 2010, p. 637
Franchoo/Pollard (2012): The Application of European Competition Law in the Financial Services Sector, JECLP 2012, 371
Frese (2011): Fines and Damages under EU Competition Law – Implications of the Accumulation of Liability, Amsterdam Center for Law & Economics Working Paper 2011-05, 2011, available online
Frese (2014): Sanctions in EU competition law. Principles and practice, 2014
Fuchs (2009): Die Anordnung von Wiedergutmachungszahlungen als Inhalt kartellbehördlicher Abstellungsverfügungen nach § 32 GWB?, ZWeR 2009, 176
Fuchs/Möschel (2012): in: Immenga/Mestmäcker (Eds.), EU-Wettbewerbsrecht, 5th Edition, 2012
Gasparon/Višnar (2005): Coca-Cola: Europe-wide remedies in fizzy drinks, CPN 2005/3, 60
Gauer/Kjølbye (2014): Energy, in: Faull/Nikpay (Eds.), The EU Law of Competition, 3rd edition, 2014
Gautier/Petit (2014): Optimal Enforcement of Competition Policy. The Commitments Procedure under Uncertainty, October 2014, available online
Georgiev (2007): Contagious Efficiency: The growing reliance on U.S.-style antitrust settlements in EU law, 2007 Utah L. Rev. 971
Geradin/Reysen/Henry (2010): Extraterritoriality, Comity, and Cooperation in EU Competition Law, in: Guzman (Ed.), Cooperation, Comity, and Competition Policy, 2010
Gerard (2013): Negotiated remedies in the modernization era: the limits of effectiveness, available online
Ginsburg/Wright (2013): Antitrust Settlements: The Culture of Consent, Concurrences 2013/2, 56
Gippini-Fournier (2008): The Modernisation of European Competition Law: First Experiences with Regulation 1/2003, in: Köck/Karollus (Eds.), The Modernisation of European Competition Law. FIDE Congress, 2008
Goyder (2012): The Lagardère Saga goes on, CLI 2012, n° 11, 16
Griffin (1993): EC and U.S. extraterritoriality: activism and cooperation, in: Hawk (Ed.), Annual proceedings of the Fordham Competition Law Institute 1992, 1993
Grzeszick (2006): in: Maunz/Dürig, GG, Kommentar
Gunther/Tayar (2008): L'arrêt Microsoft marque-t-il la fin de l'externalisation du contrôle des engagements en matière de concentration, RLC 2008 n° 14, 169
Gussone (2011): Entflechtung als Instrument des Kartellrechts – Neue Instrumente im GWB?, WuW 2011, 39
Gyselen (2005): Multilateral Interchange Fees under E.U. antitrust law: A one-sided view on a two-sided market?, 2005 Colum. Bus. L. Rev. 703
Gyselen (2014): The European Commission's commitments decisions in abuse of dominance cases, in: Hawk (Ed), Annual proceedings of the Fordham Competition Law Institute 2012, 2014
Hajnovicova/Lang/Usai (2019), Exclusivity Agreements and the Role of the As-Efficient-Competitor Test After Intel, JECLP 2019, 141

Hancher/De Hautecloque (2010): Manufacturing the EU energy markets: The current dynamics of regulatory practice, 11 Competition & Reg. Network Indus. 307 (2010)
Hellström/Maier-Rigaud/Bulst (2009): Remedies in European antitrust law, 76 Antitrust L. J. 43 (2009)
Hauser (2009): Strukturelle Maßnahmen im europäischen Kartellverfahrensrecht, 2009
Heinemann (2005): Compulsory Licences and Product Integration in European Competition Law – Assessment of the European Commission's Microsoft Decision, IIC 2005, 63
Heithecker (2002): Wettbewerbssicherung in der europäischen Fusionskontrolle durch Zusagen, 2002
Hennig (2010): Settlements im Europäischen Kartellverfahren, 2010
Hjelmeng (2012): Private Enforcement of Article 9 Commitment Decisions – "Objective" vs "Subjective" Direct effect, in: Andenas/Lilleholt (Eds.), Remedies and Substantive Law – European Dimensions of Economic and Private Law, EBLR 2012, 883
Hjelmeng (2013): Competition Law Remedies: Striving for Coherence or Finding New Ways, CMLR 2013, 1007
Hoeg (2014): European Merger Remedies, 2014
Hoehn (2012): The scope for errors, misconceptions and misunderstandings in the enforcement of European competition law, 19th St.Gallen International Competition Law Forum ICF, available online
Höppner (2017): Duty to Treat Downstream Rivals Equally: (Merely) a Natural Remedy to Google's Monopoly Leveraging Abuse, available online
Hofmann/Rowe/Türk (2012): Administrative Law and Policy of the European Union, 2012
Hovenkamp (2008): The Antitrust Enterprise, paperback edition, 2008
Ibanez Colomo (2010): On the Application of Competition Law as Regulation: Elements for a Theory, YEL 2010, 261
Ibanez Colomo (2014): Intel and Article 102 TFEU Case Law: Making Sense of a Perpetual Controversy, LSE Law, Society and Economy Working Papers 29/2014, available online
ICN (2005): Merger Remedies Review Project, Report for the fourth ICN annual conference, 2005, available online
Idot (2005): Les ventes liées après les affaires Microsoft et GE/Honeywell. Réflexions de juriste..., Concurrences 2005/2, 31
Idot (2010): Arbitration and Competition. Report for the OECD Competition Committee hearing on Competition and Arbitration, 2010, available online
Idot (2012): L'arbitrage et le contrôle des engagements en droit de la concurrence, Concurrences 2012/1
Idot (2016): Le contrôle exercé par le Tribunal sur une décision d'acceptation d'engagements est un contrôle restreint..., Europe 2016, 31
Idot/Momège (2001): Le rôle clef des engagements en matière de contrôle des concentrations: réflexions sur l'évolution de la pratique, Revue Lamy Droit des Affaires 2001, Supplément 37
Immenga (2011): Zusagen, Auflagen und Bedingungen der Kommission – Herausforderungen im Beihilferecht und nach Art. 9 VO 1/2003, in: Albach/Bechtold (Eds.), Recht, Ordnung und Wettbewerb, Festschrift zum 70. Geburtstag von Wernhard Möschel, 2011
Immenga/Mestmäcker (2012): Einleitung, in: Immenga/Mestmäcker (Eds.), EU-Wettbewerbsrecht, 5th Edition, 2012
Italianer (2012): Legal certainty, proportionality, effectiveness: the Commission's practice on remedies, Speech given in December 2012, available online
Jaecks/Säcker (2008): in: Hirsch/Montag/Säcker (Eds.), Competition Law: European Community Practice and Procedure. Article-by-Article Commentary, 2008
Jaeger (2008): Art. 7 VO 1/2003, in: Jaeger/Pohlmann/Schroeder (Ed.), Frankfurter Kommentar zum Kartellrecht
Jaeger (2009): Art. 81 Abs 2, in: Loewenheim, Meessen, Riesenkampff, Kartellrecht, 2nd edition, 2009

Jaeger (2010): § 32 ARC, in: Jaeger/Pohlmann/Schroeder (Ed.), Frankfurter Kommentar zum Kartellrecht
Jalabert-Doury/Nouvel (2007): Le suivi de l'exécution des engagements dans les concentrations francaises, Concurrences 2007/2, 29
Jarass (2013): Charta der Grundrechte der Europäischen Union. Kommentar, 2nd edition, 2013
Jenny (2015): Worst decision of the EU Court of Justice: The Alrosa judgment in context and the future of commitment decisions, Fordham Int'l L.J. 2015, 701
Johanns (2011): in: Mäger (Ed.), Europäisches Kartellrecht, 2nd Edition, 2011
Johnsten/Block (2012): EU Energy Law, 2012
Jones/Sufrin (2011): EU Competition Law, 4th edition, 2011
Jones/Sufrin (2014): EU Competition Law, 5th edition, 2014
Jung (2011): in: Grabitz/Hilf/Nettesheim (Eds.), Das Recht der Europäischen Union
Kadar (2019): Article 102 and exclusivity rebates in a post-Intel world: lessons from the Qualcomm and Google Android cases, available online
Kaiser/Wischmeyer (2010): Eigentumsrechtliche Entflechtung im Energiebereich. Zugleich ein Beitrag zur deutschen und europarechtlichen Eigentumsdogmatik, VerwArch 2010, 34
Kendall/Freedman/Farrell (2008): Expert determination, 4th Edition, 2008
Keßler (2008): in: Münchner Kommentar zum GWB, 2008
Keßler (2011): Die Zulässigkeit von Wiedergutmachungsverfügungen gem. § 32 Abs. 2 GWB – grundsätzliche Bemerkungen zu einem obiter dictum, in: Jost/Oetker/Paschke (Ed.), Festschrift für Franz Jürgen Säcker zum 70. Geburtstag, 2011, p. 771
Kellerbauer (2011): Playground instead of playpen: The Court of Justice of the European Union's Alrosa judgment on Art. 9 of Regulation 1/2003, ECLR 2011, 1
Kellezi (2010): Les mesures correctives dans les cas de concentrations d'entreprises et d'abus de position dominante, 2010
Kerse/Khan (2012): EU Antitrust Procedure, 6th edition, 2012
Kersten (2010): Herstellung von Wettbewerb als Verwaltungsaufgabe, in: Veröffentlichungen der Vereinigung der Deutschen Staatsrechtslehrer (VVDStRL) 69 (2010)
Kienapfel/Stein (2007): The application of Articles 81 and 82 EC in the sport sector, CPN 2007/3, 6
Killick/Berghe (2010): Closing Rambus. The implications for standard setting, and a thought about Tony Blair, CLI 2010, n° 9, 9
Kipiani (2014): Les engagements en matière de pratiques anticoncurrentielles. Analyse des droits français, européen et américain, 2014
Kirchner (2004): Competition policy vs. regulation: administration vs. judiciary, in: Neumann/Weigand (Eds.), The International Handbook of Competition, 2004
Klees (2005): Europäisches Kartellverfahrensrecht mit Fusionskontrollverfahren, 2005
Klees (2009): Das Instrument der Zusagenentscheidung der Kommission und der Fall E.On – Ein (weiterer) Sündenfall, WuW 2009, 374
Klees (2010): Freie Bahn für die Kommission in Kartellverfahren bei Anwendung des Art. 9 VO Nr. 1/2003, RIW 2010, 688
Klees (2011): Die Zusagenpraxis der Europäischen Kommission in Kartellverfahren – Eine kritische Analyse, EWS 2011, 14
Klees/Hauser (2007): Eigentumsrechtliche Entflechtung in der Energiewirtschaft als strukturelle Maßnahme i. S. des Art. 7 Abs. 1 Satz 2 VO 1/2003?, WuW 2007, 596
Kreße (2014): Die Verpflichtungszusage als Instrument der europäischen Wettbewerbsaufsicht, WRP 2014, 1261
Krings (2012): Möglichkeiten und Grenzen der Anordnung einer eigentumsrechtlichen Entflechtung nach Art. 7 VO 1/2003, 2012
Koch, A. (2008a): Eingriffe in die Struktur beherrschender Unternehmen, 2008
Koch, O. (2008b): in: Hirsch/Montag/Säcker (Eds.), Competition Law: European Community Practice and Procedure. Article-by-Article Commentary, 2008
Koch/Nagy/Pucinskaite-Kubik/Tretton (2009): The RWE gas foreclosure case: Another energy network divestiture to address foreclosure concerns, CPN 2009/2, 32

Körber (2010): Rechtliches Gehör, Verpflichtungszusagen nach Art. 9 VO 1/2003 und die Alrosa-Entscheidung, in: Weiß, Tagungsband zum 1. Speyerer Kartellrechtsforum, 2010, p. 73
Komninos (2013): Private enforcement in the EU with emphasis on damages actions, in: Lianos/Geradin (Ed.), Handbook on European Competition Law. Enforcement and Procedure, 2013, p. 228
Koska (2008): Zulassungsansprüche zu Vertriebssystemen und Belieferungsansprüche im Automobilsektor nach europäischen und deutschen Kartellrecht, 2008
Kruithof (1964): The application of the common market anti-trust provisions to international restraints of trade, CMLR 1964, 69
Kuik/Dawes (2014): Media, in: Faull/Nikpay (Eds.), The EU Law of Competition, 3rd edition, 2014
Larouche (2009): The European Microsoft case at the crossroads of competition policy and innovation: Comment on Ahlborn and Evans, 75 Antitrust L. J. 933 (2009)
Laumann (2007): Langfristige Bezugsbindungen in Gaslieferverträgen nach dem europäischen Kartellrecht, 2007
Lawrance (2012): Fair and reasonable. Perspectives from the General Court's 2012 Microsoft judgment, CPI 2012 n° 11, 8
Lenaerts/Maselis/Gutman (2014): in: Nowak (Ed.), EU Procedural Law, 2014
Lepsius (2010): in: Fehling/Ruffert (Eds.), Regulierungsrecht, 2010
Leschke (2010): in: Fehling/Ruffert (Eds.), Regulierungsrecht, 2010
Levêque (2000): The Conduct vs. Structural Remedies Controversy: An Irrelevant Dichotomy of Antitrust Policy Instruments, CERNA Working Paper, 2000, available online
Levy (1992): Case C-62/86, Akzo, CMLR 1992, 415
Lianos (2009): Categorical thinking in competition law and the "effects based" approach in Article 82 EC, in: Ezrachi (Ed.), Article 82 EC – Reflections on its recent evolution, 2009
Lianos (2012): Competition Law Remedies. In Search of a Theory, in: Lianos/Sokol (Eds.), The Global Limits of Competition Law, 2012
Lianos (2013): Competition law remedies in Europe, in: Lianos/Geradin (Eds.), Handbook on European Competition Law. Enforcement and Procedure, 2013
Liebscher (2013): Antitrust and arbitration: a status report, in: Klausegger/Klein et al. (Eds.), Austrian yearbook on international arbitration, 2013
Liesegang (2013): Kontrahierungszwang als Schadenersatz bei kartellverbotswidriger Lieferverweigerung, NZKart 2013, 233
Lista (2013): EU competition law and the financial services sector, 2013
Lindemann (2014): in: Jaeger/Pohlmann/Schroeder (Ed.), Frankfurter Kommentar zum Kartellrecht, C. Räumlicher Anwendungsbereich der EU-Wettbewerbsregeln
Lohse (2011): Preiskartelle als fehlerhafte Gesellschaften? Anmerkungen zu dem Kartellverwaltungsverfahren Nord-KS/Xella, in: Albach/Bechtold (Eds.), Recht, Ordnung und Wettbewerb, Festschrift zum 70. Geburtstag von Wernhard Möschel, 2011
Lowe/Maier-Rigaud (2008): Quo vadis antitrust remedies, in: Hawk (Ed.), Annual proceedings of the Fordham Competition Law Institute 2007, 2008, p. 597
Lübbig (2003): Die Aufhebung (Rücknahme und Widerruf) von Verwaltungsakten der Gemeinschaftsorgane, EuZW 2003, 233
Lübking (2007): Revision of the Notice on merger remedies, CPN 2007/2, 6
Lübking (2008): The European Commission's View on Arbitrating Competition Law Issues, EBLR 2008, 77
Lübking (2011): Konvergenz und ihre Grenzen bei Zusagen in der EU-Fusionskontrolle und nach Artikel 9 VO 1/2003, WuW 2011, 1223
Lübking (2019): Die Gazprom-Entscheidung der Kommission: Wettbewerbliche Preise und freie Lieferung von Gas in Mittel- und Osteuropa, WuW 2019, 434
Lugard/Möllmann (2013): The European Commission's Practice Under Article 9 Regulation 1/2003: A Commitment a Day Keeps the Court away?, CPI Antitrust Chronicle, March 2013(3)
Maier-Rigaud (2011): Excessive Prices, Background Paper, in: Excessive Prices, OECD Policy Roundtables, 2011, available online

Maier-Rigaud (2012): Zur Idee der Subsidiarität struktureller Maßnahmen im europäischen Wettbewerbsrecht, WuW 2012, 487
Maier-Rigaud (2014): Behavioural vs Structural Remedies in EU Competition Law, available online
Maier-Rigaud/Manca/von Koppenfels (2011): Strategic underinvestment and gas network foreclosure – the ENI case, CPN 2011/1, 18
Manoussakis (2009): Liberalization of the EU Electricity Market: Enough to Power Real Progress?, World Competition 2009, 228
Mariniello (2014): Commitments or prohibition. The EU antitrust dilemma, Bruegel Policy Brief, 2014/01, available online
Marty (2011): Éviction anticoncurrentielle – intégration verticale – engagements, Concurrences 2011/1, 97
Masing (2003): Grundstrukturen eines Regulierungsverwaltungsrechts, DöV 2003, 1
Masing (2006): Soll das Recht der Regulierungsverwaltung übergreifend geregelt werden? Gutachten D für den 66. Deutschen Juristentag, in: Verhandlungen des 66. Deutschen Juristentages, 2006
McGeown/Orologas (2013): You made a pledge, then keep your promise: Article 9 commitments decisions in European antitrust law, CPI Antitrust Chronicle, March 2013(3)
Melamed (1995): Antitrust: The New Regulation, 10 Antitrust 13 (1995)
Meng (1984): Völerrechtliche Zulässigkeit und Grenzen wirtschaftsverwaltungsrechtlicher Hoheitsakte, ZaöRV 1984, 675
Merten (2009): Grundrechtsverzicht, in: Merten/Papier (Eds.), Handbuch der Grundrechte, Volume 3, 2009
Messina/Ho (2011): Re-establishing the Orthodoxy of Commitment Decisions under Article 9 of Regulation 1/2003: Comment on Commission v Alrosa, ELR 2011, 737
Mestmäcker (1974): Europäisches Wettbewerbsrecht, 1974
Mestmäcker (1995): Zum Begriff des Mißbrauchs in Art. 86 des Vertrages über die Europäische Gemeinschaft, in: Schmidt/Schwark (Eds.), Festschrift für Peter Raisch, 1995
Mestmäcker/Schweitzer (2004): Europäisches Wettbewerbsrecht, 2nd edition, 2004
Mestmäcker/Schweitzer (2012): Art. 106(3), in: Immenga/Mestmäcker (Eds.), EU-Wettbewerbsrecht, 5th Edition, 2012
Mestmäcker/Schweitzer (2014): Europäisches Wettbewerbsrecht, 3rd edition, 2014
MK (1980): Monopolkommission: 3. Hauptgutachten, Fusionskontrolle bleibt vorrangig, 1980, BT-Drs
MK (2009): Monopolkommission: Sondergutachten, Strom und Gas 2009 – Energiemärkte im Spannungsfeld von Politik und Wettbewerb, 2009, BT-Drs 16/14060
MK (2010): Sondergutachten 58. Gestaltungsoptionen und Leistungsgrenzen einer kartellrechtlichen Unternehmensentflechtung, 2010, available online
MK (2014): Monopolkommission: 20. Hauptgutachten, Eine Wettbewerbsordnung für die Finanzmärkte, 2014, available online
Möschel (1979): Entflechtungen im Recht der Wettbewerbsbeschränkungen, 1979
Möschel (1986): Anforderungen an eine kartellbehördliche Missbrauchsverfügung bei Verkäufen unter Einkaufspreis, Betriebsberater 1986, 1785
Moloney (2000): Case C-310/97P, Commission of the European Communities v. AssiDomän Kraft Products AB, Iggesunds Bruk AB, Korsnäs AB, MoDo Paper AB, Södra Cell AB, Stora Kopparbergs Bergslags AB and Svenska Cellulosa AB ("Wood Pulp III"), Judgment of the Full Court of 14 September 1999, nyr, CMLR 2000, 970
Motta (2004): Competition Policy, 2004
Motta/Polo/Vasconcelos (2007): Merger Remedies in the European Union: An Overview, 52 Antitrust Bull. 603 (2007)
Mourre (2007): Opinions dissidentes sur un projet inutile et dangereux (à propos de l'intervention de la Commission comme amicus curiae dans les procédures arbitrales, RLC 2007 n° 12, 158

Muguet-Poullennec/Barbier de La Serre (2010): La procédure d'engagements en droit de l'Union: à la recherche du juste équilibre entre efficacité administrative et protection des entreprises, RLC 2010 n° 25, 36

Müller-Tautphaeus (2003): Abhilfebefugnisse der Europäischen Kommission im Wettbewerbsrecht, 2003

Najar (2011): Arbitrating Competition Law: The User's Perspective, in: Blanke/Landolt (Ed.), EU and US Antitrust Arbitration, 2011, p. 119

Nettesheim (2010): in: Grabitz/Hilf (Eds.), Das Recht der Europäischen Union

Neumayr/Kühnert (2011): The Repeal of Decisions by the European Commission Based on Considerations of Fact or Law, JECLP 2011, 4

Ngoc (2007): Entflechtungen nach Art. 7 Abs. 1 VO Nr. 1/2003. Grenzen der strukturellen Abhilfe, 2007

Nisser/Blanke (2006): Reflections on the Role of the European Commission as Amicus Curiae in International Arbitration Proceedings, ECLR 2006, 8

Nisser/Blanke (2007): Projet de lignes directrices de la Commission européenne intervenant en tant qu'amicus curiae dans les procédures d'arbitrage international, RLC 2007 n° 12, 148

Nothdurft (2014): Die Rückerstattungsanordnungen nach § 32 GWB – Fragen und Antworten zu einer guten Idee, in: Büscher et al. (Eds.), Festschrift für Joachim Bornkamm, 2014

O'Donoghue/Padilla (2006): The law and economics of Article 102 TFEU, 2006

O'Donoghue/Padilla (2013): The law and economics of Article 102 TFEU, 2nd edition, 2013

OECD (2004): Predatory foreclosure. OECD Policy Roundtables, 2004, available online

OECD (2006): Remedies and sanctions in abuse of dominance cases. OECD Policy Roundtables, 2006, available online

OECD (2011a): Excessive Prices, OECD Policy Roundtables, 2011, available online

OECD (2011b): Quantification of Harm to Competition by National Courts and Competition Agencies, OECD Policy Roundtables, 2011, available online

OECD (2011c): Remedies in Merger Cases, OECD Policy Roundtables, 2011, available online

OECD (2013): Remedies in Cross-Border Merger Cases, OECD Policy Roundtables, 2013, available online

OECD (2016): Commitment decisions in antitrust cases, OECD Policy Roundtables, 2016, available online

Oehler (1976): Entflechtung und Kontrahierungszwang. Methoden und Erfahrungen im amerikanischen Recht der Wettbewerbsbeschränkungen, 1976

Ortiz Blanco/Jörgens/Kellerbauer (2013): in: Ortiz Blanco (Ed.), EU Competition Procedure, 3rd Edition, 2013

Paas (2006): Non-structural remedies in EU merger control, ECLR 2006, 209

Paemen/Baltrusch (2017): Morningstar v Commission: Raising the Threshold for Challenging Commission Commitments Decisions, JECLP 2017, 99

Page/Childers (2008): Bargaining in the Shadow of the European Microsoft Decision: The Microsoft-Samba Protocol License, 102 NW. U. L. Rev. Coll. 332 (2008).

Papadimitriou (2005): Zum Belieferungsanspruch des Aussenseiters eines selektiven Vertriebsbindungssystems aus Art. 81 EG und deutschem Zivilrecht, 2005

Papandropoulos/Tajana (2006): The Merger Remedies Study – In Divestiture We Trust?, ECLR 2006, 443

Papon (2009): Structural versus Behavioural Remedies in Merger Control: A Case-By-Case Analysis, ECLR 2009, 36

Papy (2014): L'aviation commerciale et le droit antitrust, 2014

Peña Castellot (2003): Commission settles allegations of abuse and clears patent pools in the CD market, CPN 2003/3, 56

Petit/Neyrinck (2011): Back to Microsoft I and II: Tying and the Art of Secret Magic, JECLP 2011, 117

Petzold (2012): Die Kosten-Preis-Schere im EU-Kartellrecht, 2012

Picht (2013): Strategisches Verhalten bei der Nutzung von Patenten in Standardisierungsverfahren aus der Sicht des europäischen Kartellrechts, 2013
Picker (2005): Unbundling scope-of-permission goods: When should we invest in reducing entry barriers?, 72 U. Chi. L. Rev. 189 (2005)
Podszun (2012): Paradigmenwechsel in der kartellbehördlichen Befugnisausübung. Grundlagen, Gefahren, Grenzen, ZWeR 2012, 48
Pohlmann (1999): Der Unternehmensverbund im europäischen Kartellrecht, 1999
Pohlmann (2008): in: Hirsch/Montag/Säcker (Eds.), Competition Law: European Community Practice and Procedure. Article-by-Article Commentary, 2008
Polster/Petschko (2010): Nach Microsoft und E.On: Auf dem Weg zu Strukturpolitik duch die Europäische Missbrauchskontrolle?, ÖZK 2010, 108
Posner (2001): Antitrust Law, 2nd edition, 2001
Prete/Nucara (2005): Standard of proof and scope of judicial review in EC merger cases: everything clear after Tetra Laval?, ECLR 2005, 692
Prete (2018): On Implementation and Effects: The Recent Case-law on the Territorial (or Extraterritorial?) Application of EU Competition Rules, JECLP 2018, 487
Prümmer (2007): Verhältnismäßigkeitsaspekte der Zusagenpraxis in der Europäischen Fusionskontrolle, 2007
Rab/Monnoyeur/Sukhtankar (2010): Commitments in EU competition cases. Article 9 of Regulation 1/2003, its application, and the challenges ahead, JECLP 2010, 171
Rachwol (2010): Kartellrechtliche Zusagenentscheidungen nach Art. 9 Verordnung Nr. 1/2003, 2010
Rammerstorfer (2010): Constrained divestiture and ownership unbundling, 11 Competition & Reg. Network Indus. 264 (2010)
Rakovsky (2009): EC Merger Remedies (Interview), Concurrences 2009/1
Rapp/Jung (2008): in: Hirsch/Montag/Säcker (Eds.), Competition Law: European Community Practice and Procedure. Article-by-Article Commentary, 2008
Rato/Petit (2013): Abuse of Dominance in Technology-Enabled Markets: Established Standards Reconsidered?, ECJ 2013, 1
Rehbinder (2009): in: Loewenheim/Meessen/Riesenkampff (Eds.), Kartellrecht. Kommentar, 2nd edition, 2009
Rehbinder (2012): in: Immenga/Mestmäcker (Eds.), EU-Wettbewerbsrecht, 5th Edition, 2012
Reher/Haellmigk (2010): Die kartellrechtliche Rückzahlungsverpflichtung "nach § 32 Abs. 2 GWB", WuW 2010, 513
Rheinländer (2007a): Schadensersatz bei diskriminierender Lieferverweigerung – Klage auf Zulassung zum Vertriebssystem bei Verstoß gegen Art. 81 EGV, WRP 2007, 501
Rheinländer (2007b): Belieferungsanspruch eines diskriminierten Händlers aus Art. 81 II EG, GRUR 2007, 383
Rheinländer (2007c): Selektive Vertriebssysteme und Belieferungsansprüche ausgeschlossener Händler, 2007
Ridyard (2004): Compulsory access under EC competition law - a new doctrine of "convenient facilities" and the case for price regulation, ECLR 2004, 669
Ritter (2012): in: Immenga/Mestmäcker (Eds.), EU-Wettbewerbsrecht, 5th Edition, 2012
Roebling (2008): in: Hirsch/Montag/Säcker (Eds.), Competition Law: European Community Practice and Procedure. Article-by-Article Commentary, 2008
Roth (2007): Kartellrecht als Instrument der sicheren Energieversorgung, in: Leible/Lippert/Walter (Eds.), Die Sicherung der Energieversorgung auf globalisierten Märkten, 2007
Roth (2011): Entflechtung marktbeherrschender Unternehmen und Schranken des Unionsrechts - Eine Skizze, in: Albach/Bechthold (Eds.), Recht, Ordnung und Wettbewerb, Festschrift zum 70. Geburtstag von Wernhard Möschel, 2011
Rousseva (2010): Rethinking exclusionary abuses in EC competition law, 2010
Ruffert (2010): in: Fehling/Ruffert (Eds.), Regulierungsrecht, 2010

Rummel (2014): Der Betrachtungszeitraum in equally efficient competitor-Test – eine Analyse aus Anlass des Bahnstrombeschlusses der Kommission, NZKart 2014, 354

Sachs (2011): in: Sachs (Ed.), GG, Kommentar, 6th Edition 2011

Sachs (2014): in: Stelkens/Bonk/Sachs (Eds.), Verwaltungsverfahrensgesetz, Kommentar, 8th edition, 2014

Sadowska (2011): Energy Liberalization in an Antitrust Straitjacket: A Plant Too Far?, World Competition 2011, 449

Sadowska (2014): Committed to Reform? Pragmatic Antitrust Enforcement in Electricity Markets, 2014

Sadowska/Willems (2013): Power Markets Shaped by Antitrust, ECJ 2013, 131

Saecker/Jaecks (2002): Langfristige Energielieferverträge und Wettbewerbsrecht. Zur Leitbildfunktion der Schirm-GFVO für das deutsche Kartellverbot, 2002

Saitzek (2008): Verpflichtungszusagen im europäischen Kartellrecht, 2008

Salop/Romaine (1998): Preserving Monopoly: Economic Analysis, Legal Standards, and Microsoft, 7 Geo. Mason L. Rev. 617 (1998)

Sauer (2013): in: Ortiz Blanco (Ed.), EU Competition Procedure, 3rd Edition, 2013

Sauter (2014): Proportionality in EU competition law, ECLR 2014, 327

Schaub (1998): International cooperation in antitrust matters: making the point in the wake of the Boeing/MDD proceedings, CPN 1998, n° 1, p. 2

Schellingerhout/Cavicchi (2010): Patent ambush in standard-setting: the Commission accepts commitments from Rambus to lower memory chip royalty rates, CPN 2010/1, 32

Schild (2008): in: Hirsch/Montag/Säcker (Eds.), Competition Law: European Community Practice and Procedure. Article-by-Article Commentary, 2008

Schmidt, H. (2009): Competition law, innovation and antitrust, 2009

Schmidt, K. (2003): Umdenken um Kartellverfahrensrecht! Gedanken zur Europäischen VO Nr. 1/2003, Betriebs-Berater 2003, 1237

Schmidt, K. (2011): Gemeinschaftsunternehmen, Wettbewerbsverbote und Immanenztheorie – Zwei Lehrstücke zwischen Gesellschafts- und Kartellrecht: "Nord-KS/Xella" (2008) und "Gratiszeitung Hallo" (2009), in: Jost/Oetker/Paschke (Ed.), Festschrift für Franz Jürgen Säcker zum 70. Geburtstag, 2011, p. 949

Schmidt, K. (2012): in: Immenga/Mestmäcker (Eds.), EU-Wettbewerbsrecht, 5th Edition, 2012

Schödemeier (1989): Die vermiedene Auswirkung, WuW 1989, 21

Scholz/Purbs (2011): The application of EU competition law in the energy sector, JECLP 2011, 62

Schütz (2013): in Busche/Röhling (Eds.), Kölner Kommentar zum Kartellrecht, Band 4, 2013

Schulz (2018): Kartellrecht als Regulierungsinstrument, 2018

Schulze-Fielitz (2006): in: Dreier (Ed.), GG, Kommentar, 2nd Edition, 2006

Schwarze (2005): Europäisches Verwaltungsrecht: Entstehung und Entwicklung im Rahmen der Eurpäischen Gemeinschaft, 2nd edition, 2005

Schwarze/Weitbrecht (2004): Grundzüge des europäischen Kartellverfahrensrechts. Die Verordnung (EG) Nr. 1/2003, 2004

Schweitzer (2010): Commitment Decisions under Article 9 of Regulation 1/2003. The Developing EC Practice and Case Law, in: Ehlermann/Marquis (Eds.), European Competition Law Annual 2008, 2010, p. 547

Schweitzer (2011): Verpflichtungszusagen im Gemeinschaftsrecht, in: Albach/Bechthold (Eds.), Recht, Ordnung und Wettbewerb, Festschrift zum 70. Geburtstag von Wernhard Möschel, 2011

Schweitzer (2012): Commitment Decisions in the EU and in the Member States: Functions and Risks of a New Instrument of Competition Law Enforcement within a Federal Enforcement Regime, available online

Sessler/Leimert (2004): The Role of Expert Determination in Mergers and Acquisitions under German Law, AI 2004, 151

Shapiro (2009): Microsoft: A remedial failure, 75 Antitrust L. J. 739 (2009)

Smith/McComb (2013): Ebooks - European Commission has closed its anti-trust investigation, Ent. L. R. 2013, 78

Soames/Goeteyn/Camesasca/Hugmark (2006): EC competition law and aviation: "cautious optimism spreading its wings", ECLR 2006, 599
Sofianatos (2009): Injonctions et engagements en droit de la concurrence: étude de droit communautaire, français et grec, 2009
Sorinas/Moretti (2012): Remedies and fines, in: Siragusa/Rizza (Eds.), EU Competition Law, Vol. III, Cartels and collusive behaviour, 2nd edition, 2012
Steenbergen (2008): Proportionality in Competition Law and Policy, LIEI 2008, 259
Steinvorth (2014): Deutsche Bahn: Commitments end margin squeeze investigation, JECLP 2014, 628
Sullivan (2003): Antitrust remedies in the U.S. and the EU: advancing a standard of proportionality, 48 (2003) Antitrust Bull. 377
Sura (2014): in: Langen/Bunte (Eds.), Kartellrecht, Volume 2, 12th edition, 2014
Temple Lang (2003): Anti-competitive Non Pricing Abuses under European and National Antitrust Law, in: Hawk (Ed.), Annual proceedings of the Fordham Competition Law Institute 2002, 2003
Temple Lang (2006): Commitment decisions and settlements with antitrust authorities and private parties under European antitrust law, in: Hawk (Ed.), Annual proceedings of the Fordham Competition Law Institute 2005, 2006
Temple Lang (2009): Commitment decisions under Regulation 1/2003, in: Gheur/Petit (Eds.), Alternative enforcement techniques in EC competition law, 2009
Trstenjak/Beysen (2012): Das Prinzip der Verhältnismäßigkeit in der Unionsrechtsordnung, EuR 2012, 265
Turnbull/Holmes (2002): Remedies in Merger Cases: Recent Developments, ECLR 2002, 499
Ullrich (1984): Annotation to CJ, 228/82 (Ford I, 1984), CMLR 1984, 585
Ulshöfer (2011): Die Auflösung von Gemeinschaftsunternehmen im Lichte der Nord-KS-Entscheidung des BGH, WuW 2011, 820
Van Rompuy (2009): Fair access to exclusive sports rights still a long shot in UK pay TV market, Communications Law 2009, 118
Voell (2014): Entflechtungen als Abhilfemaßnahmen im europäischen und deutschen Missbrauchsrecht, 2014
Viscusi/Harrington/Vernon (2005): Economics of Regulation and Antitrust, 4th edition, 2005
Von Danwitz (2004): Was ist eigentlich Regulierung?, DöV 2004, 977
Von Danwitz (2008): Europäisches Verwaltungsrecht, 2008
Von Danwitz (2012): Thoughts on Proportionality and Coherence in the Jurisprudence of the Court of Justice, in: Cardonnel/Rosas/Wahl (Ed.), Constitutionalising the EU Judicial System, Essays in Honour of Pernilla Lindh, 2012, 367
Von Danwitz (2013): Verfassungsrechtliche Herausforderungen in der jüngeren Rechtsprechung des EuGH, EuGRZ 2013, 253
Von Kalben (2018): Verpflichtungszusagen im EU-Wettbewerbsrecht. Eine Untersuchung der Funktionen und Grenzen von Verpflichtungsbeschlüssen nach Art. 9 VO 1/2003 unter besonderer Berücksichtigung des Energiesektors, 2017
Von Koppenfels (2013): Les arrêts Odile Jacob de la Cour de Justice du 6 novembre 2012, Revue Lamy de la Concurrence 2013, n° 35, 8
Von Rosenberg (2009): Unbundling through the backdoor. . .The case of network divestiture as a remedy in the energy sector, ECLR 2009, 237
Wagner-Von Papp (2012): Best and even better practices in commitment procedures after Alrosa: the dangers of abandoning the "struggle for competition law", CMLR 2012, 929
Wallace (2009): RAMBUS v. F. T. C. in the context of standard-setting organizations, antitrust, and the patent hold-up problem, 24 Berkeley Tech. L.J. 661 (2009)
Waller (2009): The past, present, and future of monopolization remedies, 76 Antitrust L. J. 11 (2009)
Waller (2012): Access and information remedies in high-tech antitrust, JCLE 2012, 575

Wang/Rudanko (2012): EU Merger Remedies and Competition Concerns: An Empirical Assessment, ELJ 2012, 555
Wegener (2014): in: Rengeling/Middeke/Gellermann (Eds.), Handbuch des Rechtsschutzes in der Europäischen Union, 3rd edition, 2014
Went (2006): The Acceptability of Remedies under the EC Merger Regulation: Structural versus Behavioural, ECLR 2006, 455
Wernicke (2011): in: Grabitz/Hilf/Nettesheim (Eds.), Das Recht der Europäischen Union
Wernicke (2015): Das Intel-Urteil des EuG – ein Lehrstück dogmatischer Kontinuität, EuZW 2015, 19
Wertheimer (1984): Annotation to CJ, C-210/81 (Demo Studio, 1983), CMLR 1984, 724
Wessely (2000): EuGH schließt die vom EuG beschränkt zugelassene Anfechtung rechtskräftiger kartellrechtlicher Bußgelder aus. Zugleich eine Anmerkung zu EuGH, EuZW 1999, 660, EuZW 2000, 368
Whish (2006): Commitment Decisions under Article 9 of the EC Modernisation Regulation: Some Unanswered Questions, in: Johansson/Wahl/Bernitz (Eds.), Liber Amicorum in Honour of Sven Norberg, A European For All Seasons, 2006, p. 555
Whish (2015): Intel v Commission. Keep calm and carry on!, JECLP 2015, 1
Whish/Bailey (2012): Competition Law, 7th edition, 2012
Wilhelmi (2013): Strukturelle Abhilfemaßnahmen bis hin zur Entflechtung von Unternehmen bei Verstößen gegen das Kartell- oder Missbrauchsverbot, in: Bien (Ed.), Das deutsche Kartellrecht nach der 8. GWB-Novelle, 2013
Willis/Hughes (2008): Structural Remedies in Article 82 Energy Cases, CLR 2008, 147
Wils (2006): Settlements of EU Antitrust Investigations: Commitment Decisions under Article 9 of Regulation No. 1/2003, World Competition 2006, 345
Wils (2008): The Use of Settlements in Public Antitrust Enforcement: Objectives and Principles, World Competition 2008, 335
Wils (2009): The Relationship between Public Antitrust Enforcement and Private Actions for Damages, World Competition 2009, 3
Wils (2014): The Judgment of the EU General Court in Intel and the So-Called More Economic Approach to Abuse of Dominance, World Competition 2014, 405
Winkler (2006): Die Grundrechte der Europäischen Union. System und allgemeine Grundrechtslehren, 2006
Wirtz/Möller (2010): E.On: Commitment Decision-Gas Foreclosure, JECLP 2010, 419
Wollmann (2017): ARA Foreclosure: A Step Towards Consent Decrees in EU Antitrust Proceedings, JECLP 2017, 167
Wolter (2011): Zusagenentscheidungen als behördliche Maßnahmen gegen Wettbewerbsverstöße im europäischen und deutschen Kartellrecht, 2011
Wurmnest (2010): Marktmacht und Verdrängungsmissbrauch. Eine rechtsvergleichende Neubestimmung des Verhältnisses von Recht und Ökonomik in der Missbrauchsaufsicht über marktbeherrschende Unternehmen, 2010
Wright (2009): Why the Supreme Court was correct to deny certiorari in FTC v. Rambus, George Mason University Law and Economics Research Paper Series 09-14, available online
Zapfe/Mecke (2011): Evaluierung der Beschlüsse zu langfristigen Gaslieferverträgen, WuW 2011, 944

Chapter 4
The Relaxation of Procedural Safeguards

Critics of the Article 9 procedure deplore a relaxation of the procedural safeguards in comparison to the Article 7 procedure.[1] In order to assess to what extent this criticism is justified, it is useful to distinguish between, on the one hand, the procedural safeguards that exist during administrative procedure, and, on the other hand, the judicial review of remedies by the EU Courts.

4.1 Procedural Safeguards During the Administrative Procedure

The rights of defence, in particular the right to be heard and its corollary, the right of access to the file, constitute fundamental rights.[2] They apply, even in the absence of rules governing the procedure, wherever a measure of the administration adversely affects a particular person.[3] As far as the enforcement of Article 101 and 102 TFEU is concerned, the said rights are concretised in Article 27 Regulation 1/03 and Regulation 773/2004. According to these rules the scope of the said rights varies depending on the status of the affected undertaking. The strongest rights are granted to the so-called "concerned undertakings", i.e. those that are formally the subject of the proceedings conducted by the Commission. However, also "complainants" and "other natural or legal persons" may be adversely affected by a decision. Their rights

[1] See eg Gerard (2013), 30ff: "[. . .] choosing the commitment route has very much been a leap of faith so far, for the due process safeguards built into the process are virtually non-existent" (31); O'Donoghue/Padilla (2013), 907f: "At least four key safeguards [statement of objections, access to the file, oral hearing, judicial review] are absent from the Article 9 process"; see also Sadowska (2014), 51ff; von Kalben (2018), 79ff, 103ff.

[2] See Article 41(2) Charter.

[3] See eg CJ, C-68/94 (Kali + Salz, 1998), 174; Craig (2012), 290 with further references.

K. Reiter, *Market Design Powers of the European Commission?*, Munich Studies on Innovation and Competition 13, https://doi.org/10.1007/978-3-662-60711-4_4

of defence are, however, less strong than those of the concerned undertakings.[4] The following section will distinguish between the three categories of concerned undertakings, complainants, and other third parties and analyse respectively whether and to what extent the procedural rights granted in the context of an Article 9 procedure remain behind those granted in the context of an Article 7 procedure.

4.1.1 Concerned Undertakings

4.1.1.1 In the Context of Article 7

4.1.1.1.1 General Presentation of the Rights of Defence of the Concerned Undertakings

In an Article 7 procedure, the rights of defense of the concerned undertakings are ensured in three basic steps. Once it has completed the investigative phase, the Commission notifies a statement of objections to the investigated undertaking.[5] Next, the undertaking is granted access to the file[6] and replies in writing to the statement of objections.[7] Finally, upon request, an oral hearing takes place.[8] The details of these steps shall not be discussed here.[9] However, it must be pointed out that the rights of defence of the concerned undertakings do not only cover the "objections" on which the Commission wants to base its finding of an infringement. They extend to everything that "adversely affects" the concerned undertakings and thus also to the eventual imposition of fines and remedies.[10] The Commission's Best Practices state that the information given in the statement of objections should be sufficiently detailed to allow the parties to defend themselves as to the necessity and proportionality of the remedies envisaged.[11] It goes without saying that a remedy must not only be outlined with sufficient clarity in the statement of objections, but

[4]See also the opinion of AG Kokott in C-441/07 P (Alrosa, 2009), 167ff and 173.

[5]Article 27(1) Regulation 1/03; Article 10(1) Regulation 773/2004.

[6]Article 27(2) Regulation 1/03; Articles 15, 16 Regulation 773/2004.

[7]Article 10(2), (3) Regulation 773/2004.

[8]Article 12 Regulation 773/2004.

[9]For a more detailed presentation see eg the Commission's Best Practices (2011), 77ff; Manual of Procedures (2012), Modules 11, 12 and 13; Jones/Sufrin (2011), 1070ff; Körber (2010), 76; Whish/Bailey (2012), 283ff; Kerse/Khan (2012), chapters 2 III and 4.

[10]Commission, Best Practices (2011), 83ff; Müller-Tautphaeus (2003), 292ff. As is apparent from a press release (IP/03/1150), the Commission sent Microsoft a statement of objections giving the company the opportunity to comment on the remedies before the adoption of the 2004 decision.

[11]Commission, Best Practices (2011), 83.

that also the rights to access the file, to submit a written reply to the statement of objections and to a oral hearing extend to remedy related aspects.[12]

4.1.1.1.2 Transatlantic Container Line

The Transatlantic Container Line case constitutes an example in which the Commission did not give sufficiently detailed information about its remedies in the statement of objections. The case concerned an agreement between shipping companies to fix prices and capacity. In the statement of objections, the Commission merely indicated in abstract terms that it envisaged an order to bring an end to the infringement.[13] In the final decision, the Commission did not only prohibit the agreement that had been found to infringe Article 101 TFEU. It also ordered the infringing parties to offer customers the possibility to either renegotiate or terminate contracts, which had been concluded "in the context" of the prohibited agreement.[14] The General Court annulled the corresponding part of the order, inter alia because the Commission had failed to mention it in the statement of objections. The Court held that a statement of objections must set out, "briefly, but in sufficiently clear terms", the measures which the Commission intends to take in order to bring an end to an infringement and that the concerned undertakings must be given all the information necessary to defend themselves on that point. Against this benchmark, the Court considered the abstract indication that the Commission envisaged an order to bring the infringement to an end insufficient.[15] The Court found its conclusion to be confirmed by the fact that the concerned contracts had an important economic value, so that the obligation to renegotiate them could have significant consequences that could even be more severe than a fine.[16]

4.1.1.2 In the Context of Article 9

The scope of the procedural rights of the concerned undertakings during the administrative procedure in the context of an Article 9 decision varies according to whether the commitment decision is adopted subsequent to a preliminary assessment or to a statement of objections.

[12]See Müller-Tautphaeus (2003), 294 and Hellström/Maier-Rigaud/Bulst (2009), 62. The latter point out, however, that "[t]he quality of remedies might also be improved, if they were made a mandatory subject in the administrative hearing".

[13]See GC, T-395/94 (Transatlantic Container Line, 2002), 419.

[14]See GC, T-395/94 (Transatlantic Container Line, 2002), 35.

[15]See GC, T-395/94 (Transatlantic Container Line, 2002), 417ff.

[16]See GC, T-395/94 (Transatlantic Container Line, 2002), 418.

4.1.1.2.1 In Cases with a Statement of Objections

A commitment decision can be adopted subsequent to the notification of a statement of objections. If this is the case, the statement of objections replaces the otherwise necessary preliminary assessment.[17] It is not uncommon that the Commission adopts an Article 9 decision on the basis of a statement of objections.[18] In such cases, the notification of the statement of objections triggers the same procedural rights as in a procedure under Article 7. In particular, the Commission must grant the addressee of a statement of objections access to the file pursuant to Article 15(1) Regulation 773/2004.[19] The Commission's decisional practice shows that, upon request, it does grant access to the file in cases in which it issues a statement of objections, even if the case is ultimately resolved with a commitment decision.[20]

4.1.1.2.2 In Cases Without a Statement of Objections

4.1.1.2.2.1 Preliminary Assessment

Unlike the adoption of a decision pursuant to Article 7, the adoption of a commitment decision does not necessitate a statement of objections. Article 9 requires only a "preliminary assessment". Such a preliminary assessment is normally significantly shorter than a statement of objections. Reportedly, its length is only about one-tenth of the length of a statement of objections.[21] Nonetheless, in spite of its succinctness, a preliminary assessment must allow the addressee adequately to assess whether the essential facts are correctly stated and whether the provisional legal reasoning relied

[17]Best Practices (2011), 123; Manual of Procedures (2012), Module 16, 28.

[18]Eg COMP/38.173 (Premier League, 2006), 1f; COMP/38.126 (Santiago Agreement, no final commitments), 5 of the market test notice; COMP/39.530 (Microsoft – tying, 2009), 6; COMP/38.636 (Rambus, 2009), 2; COMP/39.315 (ENI, 2010), 2; COMP/39.398 (Visa MIF, 2010), 2; COMP/39.592 (Standard & Poor's, 2011), 2; Best Practices (2011), 123; Ortiz Blanco/Jörgens/Kellerbauer (2013), 13.12; Kipiani (2014), 163 with further references from the Commission's practice; Kipiani also states that 50% of the Commission's commitment decisions were adopted subsequent to a statement of objections.

[19]But see De Bronnet (2012), Art. 9, 8: "Auch wenn die Mitteilung [der Vorläufigen Beurteilung] in Form von Beschwerdepunkten erfolgt, sind an dieses Dokument nicht die Anforderungen zu stellen, die für Beschwerdepunkte gelten, sondern es handelt sich materiell um eine Vorläufige Beurteilung. Daraus folgt insbesondere, dass die Kommission keine Akteneinsicht gemäß Art. 27 Abs. 2 i.V.m. Art. 10 Verordnung Nr. 773/2004 zu gewähren hat".

De Bronnet's view is not persuasive. The procedural rights that are triggered by the statement of objections must come into existence with the notification of the statement of objections. They cannot depend on a retrospective requalification of the statement of objections as preliminary assessment if the case is ultimately resolved with a commitment decision; see Rachwol (2010), 76.

[20]See eg the Final Reports of the Hearing Officer in the following cases: COMP/38.636 (Rambus, 2009); COMP/39.530 (Microsoft – tying, 2009); COMP/39.315 (ENI, 2010); COMP/39.398 (Visa MIF, 2014).

[21]Ortiz Blanco/Jörgens/Kellerbauer (2013), 13.12.

on is well founded.[22] In its Manual of Procedures, the Commission points out that the actual preliminary assessment that is sent to the concerned undertakings will often contain considerably more detail than the commitment decision itself.[23]

4.1.1.2.2.2 Access to the File

It is controversial whether and to what extent the concerned undertakings have the right to access to the file, if the Commission intends to make a commitment binding without having issued a statement of objections.

4.1.1.2.2.2.1 Summary of the Controversy

Neither Regulation 1/03 nor Regulation 773/2004 expressly provide for a right of access to the file in the context of commitment decisions. Pursuant to Article 15 (1) Regulation 773/2004, access to the file is granted to the parties to whom the Commission has addressed a statement of objections after the notification of the statement of objections. The controversy about access to the file in commitment procedures without statement of objections concerns the question whether Article 15 (1) Regulation 772/2004 is exhaustive.

The Commission's Best Practices and the Notice on Access to the File do not expressly exclude the right of access to the file in commitment procedures without a statement of objections.[24] The Commission's position in its Manual of Procedures is ambiguous. On the one hand, the Commission states that access to the file is "only" granted to the addressees of a statement of objections.[25] In that regard the Commission explicitly underlines that access to the file is different from access to key documents.[26] According to the Best Practices, access to key documents comprises access at an early stage of the procedure to significant submissions of the complainant or interested third parties, but not, for example, to replies to requests for information.[27] On the other hand, in the section of the Manual of Procedures that deals with access to the file in the context of Article 9 decisions, the Commissions confines itself to stating that neither Regulation 1/03 nor Regulation 773/2004

[22]See Gippini-Fournier (2008), 403f; Hennig (2010a), 144f; De Bronnet (2012), Art. 9, 6; Ortiz Blanco/Jörgens/Kellerbauer (2013), 13.23; see also Temple Lang (2003), 351: He infers from the fact that the Commission can reopen the proceedings pursuant to Article 9(2)(a) in case of a change circumstances that "the Commission must set out in a commitment decision at least the most important facts on which it is based"; identically Sofianatos (2009), 548; Ortiz Blanco/Jörgens/Kellerbauer (2013), 13.25.

[23]Manual of Procedures (2012), Module 16, 18.

[24]In the Best Practices (2011), 92, the Commission states only positively that access to the file is granted to the addressee of a statement of objections. The Notice of Access to the File, 1, explicitly excludes access to documents in commitment procedures from its scope of application.

[25]Manual of Procedures (2012), Module 12, 7.

[26]Manual of Procedures (2012), Module 12, 8.

[27]Best Practices (2011), 73.

expressly provide a right of access to the file in the context of Article 9 proceedings. In a footnote, the Commission refers to the possibility to grant access to key documents.[28]

The General Court held in Alrosa that the concerned undertakings had a right to access to the file in commitment procedures.[29] In support of its conclusion, the General Court relied on Article 41(2) Charter,[30] Article 27(2) Regulation 1/03,[31] Recital 10 Regulation 773/2004[32] and on the jurisprudence of the Court of Justice according to which the right to be heard is, in all proceedings initiated against a person which are liable to culminate in a measure adversely affecting that person, a fundamental principle of EU law which must be guaranteed even in the absence of any rules governing the proceedings in question.[33] Advocate General Kokott and the Court of Justice did not have to take a decision on the matter. In their view, Alrosa was no concerned undertaking.[34] However, in an obiter dictum, AG Kokott construed Article 15(1) Regulation 773/2004 as exhaustive, stating that the right of access to the file could "only be exercised after the notification of the statement of objections".[35]

In the literature, views diverge whether the concerned undertakings have a right to access to the file in commitment procedures without statements of objections.[36] Several commentators have suggested an intermediate solution between not granting the concerned undertakings any access to the file at all and the full access to which the concerned undertakings are entitled after the notification of a statement of objections.[37] In particular, De Bronnet has suggested to apply Article 8 Regulation

---

[28]Manual of Procedures (2012), Module 12, 101; see also Module 16, 7: "no access to the file is expressly foreseen".

[29]GC, T-170/06 (Alrosa, 2007), 197 together with 188ff.

[30]Pursuant to Article 41(2), the right to good administration includes "the right of every person to be heard, before any individual measure which would affect him or her adversely is taken".

[31]Article 27(2) Regulation 1/03 provides that "the rights of defence of the parties concerned shall be fully respected in the proceedings" and that the parties concerned are to be "entitled to have access to the Commission's file".

[32]Recital 10 states that "in order to respect the rights of defence of undertakings, the Commission should give the parties concerned the right to be heard before it takes a decision".

[33]CJ, C-32/95 P (Lisrestal, 1996), 21.

[34]See Sect. 2.2.1.3.2 with footnote 45 and Sect. 2.2.1.4.2 with footnote 57 above.

[35]Opinion of AG Kokott, C-449/07 P (Alrosa, 2009), 182.

[36]On the one hand, eg Bauer (2008), 4-9-032; Rachwol (2010), 84 and 88f; Hennig (2010a), 145ff; Ortiz Blanco/Jörgens/Kellerbauer (2013), 13.23; Botteman/Patsa (2013), 370 claim that there is a right to access to the file even in the absence of a statement of objections; in that direction also Whish (2006), 566, according to whom the Commission's position that there is no access to the file in Article 9 procedures is "questionable". On the other hand, eg Bischke (2008), 4-27-012; Saitzek (2008), 175ff; Ritter (2012), Art. 9, 7; O'Donoghue/Padilla (2013), 907 and Kipiani (2014), 177, assume that there is no right to access to the file without a statement of objections.

[37]Bueren (2011), 461f: "Aus allgemeinen Grundsätzen und Art. 41 II 1 lit. b) GRCh folgt ein Einsichtsrecht nur in Bezug auf Dokumente, auf die das Organ seinen beschwerenden Beschluss stützt, bei Art. 9 also jene, die die vorläufigen Bedenken begründen. Der verfahrensökonomische

773/2004 by analogy and to grant the concerned undertakings access to the documents on which the Commission has based its preliminary assessment.[38]

4.1.1.2.2.2.2 Comment

4.1.1.2.2.2.2.1 Existence of a Right to Access to the File

It is preferable to grant the concerned undertakings a right to access to the file also in Article 9 procedures that do not involve a statement of objections. The necessity to protect the Commission's investigation does not oppose such a right. Certainly, the EU Courts acknowledge that the administrative procedure before the Commission is divided into two distinct and successive stages, each having its own internal logic, namely a preliminary investigation stage and an inter partes stage. According to the Courts, in Article 7 procedures, the inter partes stage starts only with the notification of the statement of objections. The Courts acknowledge that it is not until the beginning of the inter partes stage with the notification of the statement of objections that the concerned undertaking is able to rely in full on its rights of defence and that that undertaking has a right to access to the file. The EU Courts justify this restriction of the rights of defence during the preliminary investigation stage with the necessity to protect the Commission's investigation. In their view, if the rights of defence and in particular the right of access to the file were extended to the preliminary investigation stage, the effectiveness of the Commission's investigation would be compromised, since the undertaking concerned might use the gained insight into the Commission's investigation to conceal further information from the Commission.[39]

However, it is submitted that this reasoning cannot be applied to the Article 9 procedure after the issuance of a preliminary assessment. In an Article 9 procedure, the transmission of the preliminary assessment constitutes the end of the preliminary investigation stage and the beginning of the inter partes stage.[40] The transmission of

Zweck von Art. 9 VO 01/2003 und die zumindest formalrechtlich geringere Eingriffsintensität sprechen dafür, das Einsichtsrecht hierauf zu beschränken"; Kerse/Khan (2012), 4-047: "[...] since there is no [statement of objections] in Article 9 procedures, no statutory procedural rights exist for the addressee. However, general principles of sound administration require that the Commission provides the party concerned with sufficient information about the case against it in order for it to propose suitable commitments, without resorting to the formal procedure for access to the file"; Kipiani (2014), 181: "Idéalement, les parties devraient avoir un accès total à l'ensemble des pièces du dossier afin qu'elles puissent préparer de manière effective leur défense. [...] Toutefois, l'accès au dossier doit [...] être ciblé sur les éléments essentiels du dossier [...]".

[38]De Bronnet (2012), Art. 9, 8: "[...], dass die Kommission den Addressaten keine Akteneinsicht gemäß Art. 27 Abs. 2 i.V.m. Art. 10 Verordnung Nr. 773/2004 zu gewähren hat. Vielmehr besteht ein Recht auf Einsicht in die Unterlagen, die der vorläufigen Beurteilung der Kommission zugrunde liegen (Art. 8 Verordnung Nr. 773/2004 analog)".

[39]Eg GC, T-99/04 (AC Treuhand, 2004), 47f; T-292/11 (Cemex, 2014), 37f; see also CJ, C-521/09 P (Elf Aquitaine, 2011), 113f; Jones/Sufrin (2014), 938f.

[40]See Jones/Sufrin (2014), 966, who state that the Commission may proceed to a commitments decision "at the end of the investigative phase"; Dunne (2014), 403: "The choice to pursue a

a preliminary assessment implies that the Commission has completed its investigation to an extent that allows it to form a preliminary opinion on the scope of existing competition concerns. The transmission of a preliminary assessment expresses the Commission's willingness to engage into discussions about the adoption of a commitment decision. Once the Commission has transmitted a preliminary assessment, the question whether the procedure will be closed by the adoption of a commitment depends on whether the concerned undertaking offers a commitment that is sufficient to address the Commission's concerns and on the results of the market test. It does, however, not depend on further investigations by the Commission. The Commission issues a preliminary assessment only if it is convinced of the concerned undertaking's "genuine willingness to propose commitments which will effectively address the competition concerns".[41] There is hence no risk that companies which do not seriously pursue the commitment path will gain too early access to the Commission's investigative file.[42] Access to the file after the transmission of a preliminary assessment cannot therefore be denied with the argument that the Commission needs to protect its further investigations.

The only valid counter argument against the granting of a right to access to the file after the transmission of a preliminary assessment is that preparing a file for access to the file is a complex and time consuming exercise for the Commission.[43] It requires the assessment of confidentiality claims and hence a balancing of the interest of the investigated company in an effective defence with the interests of the authors of the documents in the file in the protection of their business secrets.[44] Therefore, the recognition of a right to access to the file runs to a certain extent counter to the objective of procedural economy that is pursued by Article 9. Nevertheless, the better reasons militate for a right to access to the file. In view of the fact that the

commitment decision is made after the initial assessment and investigation phases". In the Best Practices (2011), 75, the Commission states in essence that it may decide to engage in discussions with a view to an Article 9 decision once the investigation phase has allowed it to reach a preliminary view of the main issues raised by a case. Certainly, the Best Practices (2011), 118, state also that the concerned undertakings may contact the Commission at any time to explore the possibility of a commitment decision. This does, however, not contradict the conclusion that the transmission of the preliminary assessment constitutes the end of the investigation phase. The latter conclusion is also confirmed by Annex I to the Best Practices, in which the preliminary assessment is depicted clearly after the initial investigation stage.

[41] Best Practices (2011), 121; see also Manual of Procedures (2012), Module 16, 23.

[42] See Temple Lang (2006), 278, according to whom "the Commission may want to avoid allowing companies which do not really intend to offer commitments to see the Commission's file at an early stage".

[43] See Gippini-Fournier (2008), 408: "cumbersome exercise, resource- and time- consuming both for the Commission and for the undertakings involved"; Ritter (2012), Art. 27, 37: "[Die] Beurteilung der Vertraulichkeit [...] kann in Einzelfällen zu einer ganz erheblichen Belastung der Kommission [...] führen". But see Rachwol (2010), 89: "Durch Gewährung der Akteneinsicht steigt der administrative Aufwand nicht erheblich, insbesondere wenn man die durchschnittliche Dauer der Kommissionsverfahren (auch derjenigen, die mit Zusagenentscheidungen abgeschlossen wurden) berücksichtigt".

[44] Manual of Procedures (2012), Module 12, 1f.

Commission makes commitments binding also after a statement of objections has been issued and access to the file has been granted,[45] the just mentioned reasons of procedural economy seem not to be of decisive weight. More important are, however, the following reasons. Contrary to what is sometimes contended[46] and despite its consensual nature, a commitment decision is not merely beneficial for the concerned undertakings. Rather, given that a concerned undertaking has to comply with the commitment and risks getting sanctioned in case of non-compliance, a commitment decision produces adverse effects for the concerned undertakings.[47] As fundamental rights, the rights of defence apply even in the absence of rules governing the procedure, wherever an act produces adverse effects. This applies not only to the right to be heard, but also to the right of access to the file.[48] In fact, the right of access to the file ensures that the right to be heard can be exercised effectively.[49] In order to be able to assess effectively whether the Commission's allegations in the preliminary assessment are correct, the concerned undertakings must have access to the Commission's file. By enabling the concerned undertakings to effectively assess the correctness of the preliminary assessment, the right of access to the file reduces the risk of overbroad commitments.[50]

The intermediate solutions that are proposed in the literature[51] are not convincing. As long as the right to access to the file after a preliminary assessment is narrower than the full access to which the concerned undertakings are entitled subsequent to the notification of a statement of objections, there remain concerns that the Commission might withhold exculpatory information and extract overbroad remedies. According to the consistent jurisprudence of the EU Courts, "the right of access to the file means that the Commission must provide the undertaking concerned with the opportunity to examine all the documents in the investigation that might be relevant for its defence. Those documents comprise both inculpatory and exculpatory evidence, with the exception of business secrets of other undertakings, internal documents of the Commission and other confidential information".[52] Contrary to what is sometimes posited,[53] the obligation to grant access to all the documents on the Commission's file that might be relevant for the defence of the concerned undertaking does not follow only from secondary law, but from higher-ranking law that is not

---

[45] See Sect. 4.1.1.2.1, footnote 20 above.

[46] Ritter (2012), Art. 27, 4.

[47] See Wils (2006), 354; Gippini-Fournier (2008), 407; Ortiz Blanco/Jörgens/Kellerbauer (2013), 13.23.

[48] See Sect. 4.1, footnote 3 above.

[49] See GC, T-170/06 (Alrosa, 2007), 197.

[50] Temple Lang (2006), 277f; Wils (2006), 351 and 354; Schweitzer (2010), 572; Kipiani (2014), 180.

[51] See Sect. 4.1.1.2.2.2.1, footnote 37f above.

[52] Eg CJ, C-110/10 P (Solvay, 2011), 49 and the case law cited; Jones/Sufrin (2014), 971f.

[53] See Bueren (Sect. 4.1.1.2.2.2.1, footnote 37 above).

subject to amendments by the ordinary legislator.[54] Against this benchmark, it is not sufficient if the Commission grants the concerned undertakings access to the inculpatory documents upon which it bases the accusations contained in its preliminary assessment. Rather, the Commission must also grant access to all documents on its file that are potentially exculpatory. The logic of Article 8 Regulation 773/2004 is different, so that the provision cannot be applied by analogy. If the Commission rejects a complaint, it must grant the complainant access to the documents upon which it bases the rejection. These documents will mostly be of an exculpatory nature from the perspective of the investigated company. The Commission is, however, not obliged to grant the complainant also access to further potentially inculpatory evidence on its file. This restriction of the rights of a complainant in comparison to the rights of concerned undertakings is justified,[55] because the complainant does not need the documents to defend himself against action from the Commission. The complainant's access to documents pursues merely the objective to prompt the Commission to take action against the concerned undertaking.

4.1.1.2.2.2.2.2 Possibility for Concerned Undertakings to Waive Their Right to Access to the File

The existence of a right to access to the file does not mean that the concerned undertakings cannot waive this right in part or even completely.[56] In practice, this will normally happen if the Commission is likely to accept a proposed commitment. Access to the file is also costly for the undertakings involved.[57] The Commission should, however, not exert any pressure in that regard.[58] Initially, the reports of the Hearing Officers contained a statement that the concerned undertakings had declared to the Commission that they had received sufficient access to the file.[59] More recent reports state only that the Hearing Officer has not received any request or complaint

[54]It is true that the Court of Justice initially ruled that the Commission was not obliged to disclose the complete file, but only those documents on which it had based its decision [C-43/82 (VBVB, 1985), 24f]. The Commission later extended the concerned undertakings' right of access to the file to the entire file, stating expressly that it intended to go beyond the requirements laid down by the Court of Justice. Subsequently, the General Court held in Hercules [T-7/89 (1991), 52ff] only that the Commission had to stick to the rules which it had imposed on itself. However, in Solvay [GC, T-30/91 (1995), 83], the General Court inferred the necessity to grant a concerned undertaking access to the Commission's entire file directly from the general principle of equality of arms. See Jones/Sufrin (2011), 1074f; Craig (2014), Art. 41, 41.39; Sander (2014), Art. 41, 24.

[55]See for the argument that the procedural rights of complainants reach less far than those of the undertakings concerned also CJ, C-142/84 (BAT Reynolds, 1987), 19f.

[56]See Wils (2006), 354.

[57]Gippini-Fournier (2008), 408.

[58]Gippini-Fournier (2008), 409; Ortiz Blanco/Jörgens/Kellerbauer (2013), 13.23.

[59]Eg the final reports of the Hearing Officer in COMP/37.214 (Bundesliga, 2005); COMP/39.116 (Coca-Cola, 2005); COMP/38.348 (REPSOL, 2006); COMP/38.173 (Premier League, 2006); COMP/39.388 (German electricity wholesale and balancing market, 2008); COMP/38.636 (Rambus, 2009); COMP/39.315 (ENI, 2010). According to Gerard (2013), 32 fn 173, the final

from any party to the proceedings with respect to the proposed commitments.[60] If a concerned undertaking waives its right of access to the file in view of the envisaged acceptance of a proposed commitment and the commitment negotiations fail, the waiver does not extend to the subsequent infringement procedure. The concerned undertaking can therefore request access to the complete file of the Commission before the Commission adopts an infringement decision.

4.1.1.2.2.3 Hearing

In the Manual of Procedures, the Commission emphasises that the investigated undertaking does not have a right to a hearing pursuant to Article 12 Regulation 773/2004.[61] The undertaking can, however, submit a written reply to the preliminary assessment.[62] Moreover, discussions may take place between the Commission about the concrete design of the commitments that will be market tested. The Commission considers that these discussions are "crucial for the success of the remedies".[63]

O'Donoghue and Padilla have noted in relation to the lack of a hearing before the adoption of a commitment decision that, under the Article 7 procedure, the oral hearing represents an opportunity for the parties "to advocate their position before Member State representatives and to confront third party complainants directly".[64] It is submitted, however, that the lack of a hearing pursuant to Article 12 Regulation 773/2004 is no decisive reason against the commitment procedure.

On the one hand, under the Article 9 procedure, the so-called state of play meetings compensate to a certain extent for the lack of a hearing pursuant to Article 12 Regulation 773/2004. Such meetings provide the concerned undertaking with the opportunity to argue its case orally before the Commission. That the members of the College of the Commission that adopt the final commitment decision are not present at state of play meetings does not constitute a disadvantage of the Article 9 procedure in comparison to the Article 7 procedure. Also at a hearing pursuant to Article 12 Regulation 773/2004, those members are not present. The EU Courts have confirmed that the absence of the Commissioners from the oral hearing is no ground for annulling a prohibition decision.[65] Moreover, according to the Best Practices, state of play meetings may be held in a triangular setting with the parties and the

---

report of the Hearing Officer in the ENI case is the last one to mention such a declaration by the concerned undertakings.

[60]Eg the final reports of the Hearing Officer in COMP/39.692 (IBM, 2011); COMP/39.736 (Siemens/Areeva, 2012); COMP/39.654 (Reuters, 2012); COMP/39.678 (Deutsche Bahn I and II, 2013); COMP/39.398 (Visa, 2014).

[61]Manual of Procedures (2012), Module 16, 35.

[62]Manual of Procedures (2012), Module 16, 41.

[63]Manual of Procedures (2012), Module 16, 43.

[64]O'Donoghue/Padilla (2013), 907f.

[65]CJ, C-44/69 (Buchler, 1970), 20; GC, T-372/10 (Bolloré, 2012), 58ff; Kerse/Khan (2012), 4-117.

complainant or admitted third parties, albeit only at the Commission's discretion.[66] Where a triangular meeting takes place, the concerned undertaking has therefore an opportunity to directly confront complainants or other third parties.

On the other hand, the fact that the concerned undertaking is deprived of the possibility to plead its case orally before the representatives of the Member States that would attend a hearing pursuant to Article 12 Regulation 773/2004[67] does not appear to be a decisive disadvantage of the commitment procedure either. Pursuant to Article 14 Regulation 1/03, the Commission must nevertheless consult the Advisory Committee, composed of representatives of the competition authorities of the Member States, before it adopts a decision pursuant to Article 9. The sole fact that the concerned undertakings cannot plead their case orally to the representatives of the Member States should not be over-estimated. The influence of the Advisory Committee on the final decision is limited. The opinion of the Advisory Committee must be adopted by a majority of votes.[68] Although the Commission "shall take the utmost account of the opinion delivered by the Advisory Committee" and "inform the Committee of the manner in which its opinion has been taken into account",[69] the opinion of the Advisory Committee does not bind the Commission.

4.1.1.2.2.4 Information About Outcome of the Market Test

According to the Commission's Best Practices and the Manual of Procedures, the concerned undertakings are informed orally or in writing of the substance of the replies to the market test.[70] Subsequently, further discussions take place between the Commission and the concerned undertakings.[71]

Gerard criticises that the Commission provided the concerned undertakings sometimes only with a summary of the submissions received during the market test, whilst in other cases it provided the concerned undertakings with a full non-confidential version of the original submissions. According to Gerard, "[t]his variety of situations and treatment testifies altogether of the unsustainable character of the Court of Justice's position in Alrosa, of the wide discretion of the Commission and of the uncertain character of the procedural rights available in commitment proceedings".[72] Gerard calls for a departure from the Alrosa precedent. The suggested departure involves "consistently providing committing firms with a full

---

[66] Best Practices (2011), 129.

[67] See Article 14(3) Regulation 773/2004: "The Commission shall invite the competition authorities of the Member States to take part in the oral hearing. It may likewise invite officials and civil servants of other authorities of the Member States".

[68] Kerse/Khan (2012), 5-095.

[69] Article 14(5) Regulation 1/03.

[70] Best Practices (2011), 132; Manual of Procedures (2012), Module 16, 64; Ortiz Blanco/Jörgens/Kellerbauer (2013), 13.19.

[71] Manual of Procedures (2012), Module 16, 65.

[72] Gerard (2013), 33.

non-confidential version of the observations submitted by third parties in response to the market-test".[73]

This criticism is not convincing. The Alrosa judgment of the Court of Justice does not deal with the question whether and to what extent the concerned undertakings must be granted access to the submissions received by the Commission during the market test. More importantly, it appears unreasonable to request a "consistent" transmission of a "full non-confidential version" of these submissions. The way in which the Commission should inform the concerned undertakings about the outcome of the market test depends on the circumstances of the individual case. For instance, if there are no submissions or if the submissions only commend the tested commitment, it can be sufficient to inform the concerned undertaking orally about this outcome. The same may be true if the Commission considers that requests for further reaching commitments are manifestly unfounded. It will be more appropriate to inform the concerned undertakings in writing about the outcome of the market test, if the Commission considers that the test has revealed aspects that require a modification of the tested commitment. However, even in such a case, the transmission of a summary of the submission instead of a non-confidential version of the original document may be justified. Access to documents by the concerned undertakings is subject to the respect of the protection of the business secrets of third parties. If the original submissions provided by third parties contain important amounts of confidential information, it may be preferable from the perspective of the Commission and, for reasons of readability, also from the perspective of the concerned undertaking to provide the concerned undertaking with a summary of the substance of the submissions. According to the consistent case law of the Courts, the Commission can rely on summaries in order to ensure the respect of the business secrets of third parties.[74]

4.1.2 Complainants

4.1.2.1 In the Context of Article 7

By virtue of Article 27(1), 3rd sentence, Regulation 1/03, complainants shall be associated closely with the proceedings. If the Commission sends a statement of objections to the concerned undertakings, complainants are entitled to receive a non-confidential version, to submit written submissions, and, upon request and

---

[73]Gerard (2013), 34 and 36. See also Sadowska (2014), 52, who criticises that "it is unclear whether the Commission is required to give the undertaking access to third parties' observations submitted during the market test".

[74]See GC, T-108/07 (Spira, 2013), 71; T-286/09 (Intel, 2014), 1457 and the case law cited. See also the Commission's Notice on Access to the File, 17: "Access will be granted, where possible, to non-confidential versions of the original information. Where confidentiality can only be assured by summarising the relevant information, access will be granted to a summary".

where appropriate, to present their views at the oral hearing of the concerned undertakings.[75] Where the Commission intends to reject a complaint, it informs the complainant of its reasons in a so-called Article 7 letter.[76] In order to prevent that complaints are abused as a way to obtain internal information about competitors,[77] the complainant cannot request access to the full file of the Commission.[78] The complainant is, however, entitled to access the documents on which the Commission intends to base the rejection of the complaint.[79] It can then reply in writing to the Article 7 letter before the Commission adopts its decision on the complaint.[80]

As far as remedies are concerned, the rights of defence of a complainant become relevant if the Commission's remedy stays behind the expectations of the complainant. Although, in such a case, the Commission rejects the complaint only partially, no particularities arise with respect to the rights of defense.[81] As has just been pointed out, the complainant receives a non-confidential version of the statement of objections, in which the Commission must indicate the envisaged remedy with sufficient clarity. If the complainant maintains in his written observations and at the eventual oral hearing that the Commission's remedy does not go far enough and the Commission does not intend to follow the complainant, the Commission must set out its reasons in an Article 7 letter. The complainant can then access the documents on which the Commission intends to base the partial rejection of the complaint and present its observations before the Commission adopts its decision on the complaint.

4.1.2.2 In the Context of Article 9

If the Commission adopts a commitment decision on the basis of a statement of objections, the rights of complainants are the same as in the context of an Article 7 procedure.[82]

If the commitment decision is adopted on the basis of a preliminary assessment, the question arises whether the complainant has a right to receive a non-confidential version of the preliminary assessment or to a hearing. There is no express statutory basis for such rights.[83] In the Manual of Procedures, the Commission explicitly

---

[75] Article 6 Regulation 773/2004.

[76] Manual of Procedures, Module 21, 60; see Article 7 Regulation 773/2004.

[77] See Ritter (2012), Art. 27, 30; Jones/Sufrin (2011), 1079f; CJ, 53/85 (Akzo, 1986), 28.

[78] See the Commission's Notice on access to the file (2005), 29ff.

[79] Article 8 Regulation 773/2004.

[80] Article 7(1), (2) Regulation 773/2004.

[81] See also Müller-Tautphaeus (2003), 297.

[82] But see Whish (2006), 565, according to whom it is not clear whether complainants are entitled to receive a non-confidential version of the statement of objections in the context of an Article 9 procedure. See, as regards the rights of the concerned undertakings, Sect. 4.1.1.2.1, footnote 19 above.

[83] Ortiz Blanco/Jörgens/Kellerbauer (2013), 13.24.

excludes these rights.[84] At the same time, the Commission reserves itself the discretion to inform the complainant about the main content of the preliminary assessment, in particular if it can be expected that the complainant is able to provide important input for the subsequent discussions on the exact scope of the commitments. According to the Commission, potential advantages of granting complainants access to the main content of the preliminary assessment must be balanced against the risk that such access may undermine the commitment discussions.[85] The fact that complainants are not entitled to receive a non-confidential version of the preliminary assessment is also acknowledged in the literature.[86]

It bears mention that the lack of a right to receive a non-confidential version of the preliminary assessment does not put a complainant in a situation that is worse than the one he would be in if his complaint were rejected at a stage before the adoption of a statement of objections.[87] If the Commission adopts a commitment decision on the basis of a preliminary assessment and subsequently rejects a complaint, the procedural rights of the complainant pursuant to Article 7 and 8 Regulation 773/2004 remain unaffected. This means that the complainant receives an Article 7 letter in which the Commission informs him of the reasons for rejecting the complaint, that the complainant may request access to the documents on which the Commission intends to base the rejection and that the complainant can reply in writing to the Article 7 letter.

Nevertheless, the lack of a right to receive a non-confidential version of the preliminary assessment puts a complainant in a situation that is worse than the one he would be in if the Commission had adopted a decision on the basis of Article 7 subsequent to the notification of a statement of objections. The complainant is deprived of his right provided for in Article 6(1) Regulation 773/2004 to comment on the non-confidential version of the statement of objections. It is, however, submitted, that this difference between the Article 7 and the Article 9 procedure is no decisive argument against the use of commitments.

First, the BAT Reynolds judgment of the Court of Justice can be invoked as case law that militates against the necessity to grant the complainant access to a non-confidential version of the preliminary assessment.[88] In that case, BAT and Reynolds filed a complaint based on Article 101 TFEU with the Commission that was directed against the acquisition of Rothmans Tobacco by Philip Morris from Rembrandt. The Commission notified a statement of objections to Philip Morris and Rembrandt. BAT and Reynolds received a non-confidential copy of the statement of objections, had the opportunity of commenting on the replies of Philip Morris and

[84]Manual of Procedures (2012), Module 16, 36.

[85]Manual of Procedures (2012), Module 16, 37.

[86]Botteman/Patsa (2013), 370.

[87]On the fact that the Commission may reject a complaint before the adoption of a statement of objections see eg Ortiz Blanco/Jörgens/Kellerbauer (2013), 12.04.

[88]See also the discussion of the case by Saitzek (2008), 189ff.

Rembrandt to the statement of objections and took part in a hearing.[89] At a later stage of the administrative procedure, Philip Morris and Rembrandt replaced their initial agreements by new ones and entered into several undertakings to address the concerns raised by the Commission.[90] Having informed BAT and Reynolds of the new agreements and the undertakings entered into by Philip Morris and Rembrandt and having given them the opportunity to comment, the Commission rejected the complaints. BAT and Reynolds appealed the rejection decisions. They argued that they had not been sufficiently involved in the Commission's investigation and in particular that they should have been allowed to take part in the negotiations between the Commission and Philip Morris and Rembrandt or that they should at least have been sent minutes of the meetings and thus kept informed of the progress made.[91] The Court of Justice dismissed the appeals. The Court stated inter alia the following:

> [. . .] it should be recalled that the administrative procedure provides, among other things, an opportunity for the companies concerned to bring the agreements or practices complained of into conformity with the rules laid down in the Treaty. For such a possibility to be a real one the companies and the Commission must be entitled to enter into confidential negotiations in order to determine what alterations will remove the cause for the Commission's objections. Such a right would be imperilled if the complainants were to attend the negotiations or be kept informed of the progress made in order to submit their observations on the proposals put forward by one party or the other. The legitimate interests of the complainants are fully protected where they are informed of the outcome of the negotiations in the light of which the Commission proposes to close the proceedings.[92]

In BAT Reynolds, the Commission had notified a statement of objections to Philip Morris and Rembrandt and transmitted a non-confidential version of it to the complainants. Therefore, the case is no direct precedent regarding the question whether the Commission is obliged to grant complainants access to a non-confidential version of the preliminary assessment where it adopts a commitment decision without statement of objections. However, the Court recognised the necessity to allow the Commission and the concerned undertakings a certain amount of confidentiality in their negotiations. Moreover, the Court mentioned that the interests of complainants were fully protected where they were informed of the outcome of the negotiations. These statements can be construed as indication that the interests of complainants do not require the Commission to grant access to a non-confidential version of the preliminary assessment, if it wants to prevent an undermining of the commitment discussions. Rather, the interests of complainants are sufficiently protected if the Commission informs them in an Article 7 letter of the outcome of the negotiations.

Second, more important than the BAT Reynolds judgment is that the market test pursuant to Article 27(4) Regulation 1/03 compensates the complainants to a certain

[89]CJ, C-142/84 (BAT Reynolds, 1987), 16.

[90]CJ, C-142/84 (BAT Reynolds, 1987), 6ff.

[91]CJ, C-142/84 (BAT Reynolds, 1987), 18.

[92]CJ, C-142/84 (BAT Reynolds, 1987), 23f. See also GC, T-110/95 (IECC, 1998), 98; Kerse/Khan (2012), 4-039.

extent for the lapse of the access to a non-confidential version of the statement of objections and of the right to comment. Complainants have at least the right to present their observations in the context of the market test. The market test notice requires a publication of a concise summary of the case and the main content of the commitments. According to the Manual of Procedures, the concise summary of the case contains the suspected behaviour and the suspected infringement of competition law.[93] It is true that a market test notice is less detailed than the non-confidential version of a preliminary assessment.[94] However, the market test notice must allow third parties to understand the essential elements of the commitments and how they are intended to meet the competition concerns identified by the Commission.[95]

Third, Whish has raised the concern that not granting complainants access to the preliminary assessment would deteriorate their chances of successful damages actions when compared to the Article 7 procedure.[96] This concern is not pertinent. The access to the non-confidential version of a statement of objections that is granted by virtue of Article 6(1) Regulation 773/2004 does not pursue the objective to promote private damages actions. It serves merely the public interest in restoring compliance with the competition rules.[97] If one accepts the latter premise, then the deterioration of the complainant's chances of successful damages actions that is caused by the lack of access to the preliminary assessment is not decisive.

Finally, also the lapse of the possibility to participate in a hearing pursuant to Article 12 read in conjunction with Article 6(2) Regulation 773/2004 is no decisive argument against the use of the commitment procedure. Pursuant to Article 6(2), the Commission enjoys discretion whether it admits the complainant to the hearing of the concerned undertaking.[98] As explained above, in the context of commitment procedures, the Commission enjoys discretion to organise triangular state of play meetings that compensate to a certain extent for the lack of a hearing pursuant to Article 12 Regulation 773/2004.[99]

---

[93]Manual of Procedures (2012), Module 16, 57; see also Botteman/Patsa (2013), 370.

[94]See Whish (2006), 565.

[95]Manual of Procedures (2012), Module 16, 57.

[96]See Whish (2006), 565 and 568.

[97]Article 8(2) Regulation 773/2004 provides that the documents to which the complainant has had access in the context of proceedings conducted by the Commission under Articles 101 and 102 TFEU may only be used for the purposes of judicial or administrative proceedings for the application of those provisions. Article 8(2) Regulation 773/2004 must likely be construed as permitting a complainant to use the non-confidential version of the statement of objections that it received from the Commission in furtherance of an action for damages [see GC, T-12/07 R (Polimeri, 2007), 54; Kerse/Khan (2012), 4-038, fn 131]. This result does, however, not call into question the conclusion that the transmission of the non-confidential version of the statement of objections to a complainant pursuant to Article 6(1) does not pursue the objective to promote private enforcement.

[98]Sofianatos (2009), 631.

[99]See Sect. 4.1.1.2.2.3 with footnote 66 above.

4.1.3 Other Natural or Legal Persons

A remedy may also adversely affect other third parties than complainants. Such other third parties may consider the scope of the remedy as either too narrow or too broad. Examples of other third parties that may be affected by a remedy are: Potential beneficiaries of an obligation to grant access, who may feel that the terms of access provided for in the remedy are not advantageous enough; contractual partners of the addressee of the remedy, who may be affected by an order to modify or even completely terminate a commercial relation[100]; employees of a concerned undertaking.[101]

4.1.3.1 Grundig and Consten

The case Grundig and Consten constitutes an early example of a remedy that affected third parties. The Commission found that an agreement conferring absolute territorial protection upon a distributor violated Article 101 TFEU.[102] As remedy, the Commission required Grundig and Consten "to refrain from any measure likely to obstruct or impede the acquisition by third parties, in the exercise of their free choice, from wholesalers or retailers established in the [EU], of the products set out in the contract, with a view to their resale in the contract territory".[103] On appeal, Grundig and Consten complained that the Commission's order covered not only the exclusive supply relation between Grundig and Consten that constituted the subject of the proceedings, but also the export prohibitions contained in contracts with other distributors that were not the subject of the proceedings. They therefore argued that the order was overbroad and that the Commission violated third parties' right to be heard. Advocate General Roehmer was of the opinion that the Commission should at least have heard the concerned third parties and suggested annulling the order.[104] The Court of Justice nevertheless confirmed the remedy. It ruled that the prohibition to prevent other distributors from exporting was a mere corollary of the prohibition to grant absolute territorial protection to Consten. Moreover, in the view of the Court, the Commission's order did not directly affect the legal validity of the agreements between Grundig and the other distributors, but confined itself to restricting Grundig's freedom of action as regards the parallel imports of its

---

[100]See, for instance, the Grundig and Consten case outlined immediately below. With respect to Article 9 COMP/39.116 (Coca-Cola, 2005) and COMP/38.381 (Alrosa, 2006).

[101]The Merger Remedies Notice (2008), 80, makes explicit reference to the "recognised representatives of those employees whose positions are directly affected by the proposed remedies" as third parties who may, where appropriate, be consulted on a proposed remedy. It is submitted that the same possibility to consult representatives of employees exists also under Regulation 1/03.

[102]See eg Whish/Bailey (2012), 625.

[103]CJ, 56/64 (Consten & Grundig, 1966), p. 304.

[104]See the opinion of AG Roehmer (Consten & Grundig, 56/64, 1966), p. 381.

products. Hence, in the view of the Court, the order affected the other distributors only "de facto". The Court found it "desirable that the Commission should extend its enquiries as far as possible to those who may be affected by its decisions". However, ultimately it ruled that the mere "de facto" interest of the third parties did not suffice to grant them a right "to be called automatically by the Commission to take part in the proceedings concerning the relationship between Consten and Grundig".[105]

4.1.3.2 Procedural Rights During the Administrative Procedure Under Regulations 1/03 and 773/2004 de lege lata

In Grundig and Consten, the Court thus made it clear that the Commission is not obliged to take account of the interest of third parties "automatically", i.e. of its own motion. In principle, this merits approval. The contrary result would overstrain the Commission's investigative task. Nevertheless, the Court emphasised also that it was "desirable that the Commission should extend its enquiries as far as possible to those who may be affected by its decisions". The provisions in Regulation 1/03 and Regulation 773/2004 that concretise the right to be heard of "other natural or legal persons" today mirror this tension.

4.1.3.2.1 In the Context of Article 7

The Commission hears other natural or legal persons where it considers it necessary, upon request of the competition authority of a Member State, or upon request of the respective persons if the latter shows a sufficient interest.[106] While it is clear that the concept of sufficient interest pursuant to Article 27(3) Regulation 1/03 is broader than that of "individual concern" pursuant to Article 263(4) TFEU, the precise contours remain up to now vague.[107] Recital 11 Regulation 773/2004 provides that consumer associations should generally be regarded as having a sufficient interest, where the proceedings concern products or services used by the end-consumer or products or services that constitute a direct input into such products or services.[108] Experts may be heard, where the Commission deems this necessary or a national competition authority requests it.[109]

Once they are admitted to the administrative procedure, other natural or legal persons must be informed in writing about the "nature and subject matter" of the

---

[105] CJ, 56/64 (Consten & Grundig, 1966), p. 346; see also Müller-Tautphaeus (2003), 237f.

[106] Article 27(3) Regulation 1/03.

[107] See Kerse/Khan (2012), 4-034.

[108] See Kerse/Khan (2012), 4-034.

[109] See Kerse/Khan (2012), 4-036.

proceedings.[110] It results from the case law of the EU Courts that third parties other than complainants do not have any right in the context of an administrative procedure investigating infringements of Article 101 or 102 TFEU to have access to the documents in the Commission's file.[111] Although these parties also do not have a right to receive a non-confidential version of the statement of objections, the Commission may in practice nevertheless provide them with one.[112] It is submitted that, in any event, the information that must be transmitted to these parties must also cover an envisaged remedy. These parties are entitled to submit written observations and can, upon request and where appropriate, participate in the hearing of the addressees of the statement of objections.[113]

4.1.3.2.2 In the Context of Article 9

If the Commission adopts a commitment decision on the basis of a statement of objections, the rights of interested third parties are the same as in the context of an Article 7 procedure.[114]

Moreover, generally in the context of Article 9, the interests of third parties are in principle protected through the market test pursuant to Article 27(4) Regulation 1/03. The Commission must publish a concise summary of the case containing the suspected behaviour and the suspected infringement of competition law and the main content of the commitment proposal and give third parties a chance to submit their observations.[115] These "market test notices" are published in all official languages in the Official Journal. However, in its Best Practices, the Commission states that it will also publish the full text of commitments in the authentic language on the website of DG COMP.[116] In the Manual of Procedures, the Commission emphasises that the market test is not an opinion poll which determines the fate of the remedies. The Commission can take a commitment decision even in cases in which participants in the market test requested to reject the commitment offer.[117]

---

[110] Article 13(1) Regulation 773/2004 provides this explicitly only for parties who show a sufficient interest. However, also parties whose hearing is considered necessary by the Commission can only present observations, if the Commission informs them about the case.

[111] CJ, C-365/12 P (EnBW, 2014), 87; GC, T-534/11 (Schenker, 2014), 53.

[112] Commission Manual of Procedures (2012), Module 13, 11; see also Ritter (2012), Art. 27, 32. In the literature, demands that the Commission should provide interested third parties at least with a non-confidential version of the statement of objections have existed for some time, see Schweitzer (2010), 572; Körber (2010), 77.

[113] Article 13(2), (3) Regulation 773/2004.

[114] See, as regards the rights of the concerned undertakings and complainants, Sect. 4.1.1.2.1 with footnotes 17ff and Sect. 4.1.2.2 with footnote 82 above.

[115] Manual of Procedures (2012), Module 16, 56.

[116] Best Practices (2011), 129.

[117] Manual of Procedures (2012), Module 16, 66.

It is questionable whether interested third parties that have been admitted to the procedure pursuant to Article 27(3) Regulation 1/03 have any procedural rights besides the possibility to participate in the market test. In the literature, it has been suggested that the publication of a market test notice "can be insufficient in cases where a decision on commitments constitutes an individual measure which adversely affects specific third parties".[118] In that connection, it has been pointed out that the market test pursuant to Article 27(4) does not grant such third parties the right to receive feedback on their statement or to comment again if the commitments are revised in the light of the market test.[119] As a fundamental right, the right to a fair hearing is said to require the Commission to hear third parties more extensively upon request.[120] In that regard, it is submitted that two questions should be distinguished: First, whether interested third parties must be granted a more extensive right to be heard on a given commitment than the one that is granted in the context of the market test. Second, whether and to what extent interested third parties must be heard if commitments are revised in the light of the market test.

4.1.3.2.2.1 The Right of Interested Third Parties to Be Heard on a Given Commitment

As regards the first question, the better arguments seem to militate against granting interested third parties rights that go beyond the right to participate in the market test. The rights that an interested third party enjoys in connection with the market test are equivalent to the rights an interested third party enjoys by virtue of Article 13 (1) Regulation 773/2004 where a decision is adopted on the basis of Article 7. Article 13(1) Regulation 773/2004 provides a right for interested third parties to be informed about the "nature and subject matter" of the proceedings and to make known their views in writing. The information that is contained in a market test notice pursuant to Article 27(4) contains the suspected behaviour, the suspected infringement of competition law and the main content of the commitment proposal. Moreover, the Commission publishes the full text of the commitment proposal in the authentic language on its website. The amount of information that is provided to interested third parties in a market test notice does therefore not lag behind the one that is provided to them under Article 13(1) Regulation 773/2004. Also the possibility to submit comments is not restricted in the context of the market test when compared to Article 13(1) Regulation 773/2004. Finally, it is submitted that also under Article 13 (1) Regulation 773/2004, there is no right to receive feedback from the Commission. The Commission must only take the submissions of interested third parties into account when it adopts its final decision. Whether and to what extent the Commission is obliged to reply to the submissions of interested third parties in the grounds of the final decision depends on the scope of the Commission's obligation to state

[118] Ortiz Blanco/Jörgens/Kellerbauer (2013), 13.24.

[119] Kellerbauer (2011), 3f.

[120] Ortiz Blanco/Jörgens/Kellerbauer (2013), 13.24.

reasons laid down in Article 296 TFEU and is a question of the individual circumstances of the case.[121]

4.1.3.2.2.2 The Right of Interested Third Parties to Be Heard on a Revised Commitment

4.1.3.2.2.2.1 Alrosa

In the Alrosa case, Advocate General Kokott and the Court of Justice agreed that Alrosa should not be treated as a concerned undertaking, but merely as an interested third party. The Advocate General insisted that the Commission was required to hear Alrosa as an adversely affected interested third party on the change that was brought about by De Beers' individual commitment offer after the market test of the joint commitments. In her view, the Commission had complied with this obligation, because it had orally informed Alrosa of the insufficiency of the joint commitments and of its intention to accept only commitments leading to a complete cessation of the trading relations.[122] The Court of Justice took a more restrictive approach. It held that the Commission was not required to state to Alrosa the reasons for rejecting the joint commitments and to suggest to Alrosa that it should offer new joint commitments with De Beers. According to the Court of Justice, it followed from the Commission's discretion in regard of Article 9 decisions that the Commission's acceptance of the individual commitments offered by De Beers did not depend on the position of Alrosa or any other undertaking.[123]

In the literature, the judgment of the Court of Justice has been understood as denying interested third parties any procedural right if a commitment is amended after the market test.[124] For this reason, the judgment of the Court of Justice has been criticised.[125] This criticism must, in principle, be approved. The opinion of Advocate General Kokott is preferable. As the Advocate General rightly pointed out, the respect of the fundamental right to a fair hearing, which must be guaranteed even in the absence of any rules governing the proceedings, requires that a person that is

[121]According to the case law, the Commission is not obliged to adopt a position on all the arguments relied on by the parties concerned in support of their request, and need only set out the facts and legal considerations having decisive importance for the structure of the decision; see eg GC, T-231/99 (Joynson, 2002), 166; Kerse/Khan (2012), 6-012. The General Court has held "that the Commission enjoys some latitude in taking account [...] of the written observations and any oral observations presented by [third parties]", see GC, T-17/93/Matra-Hachette, 1994), 34.

[122]See Sect. 2.2.1.3.2 with footnote 48 above.

[123]See Sect. 2.2.1.4.2 with footnote 58 above.

[124]Muguet-Poullennec/Barbier de La Serre (2010), 43: "Les tiers intéressés n'ont donc, semble-t-il, que le droit de présenter des observations sur le résumé succinct de l'affaire et le principal contenu des engagements [...]: ils ne jouissent en apparence d'aucun droit procédural à un stade ultérieur si, sur le fondement des observations présentées, la Commission exige de nouveaux engagements et la ou les parties y consentent". Similarly Kipiani (2014), 183.

[125]Muguet-Poullennec/Barbier de La Serre (2010), 43f.

adversely affected by a measure must be heard.[126] If the amendment of a commitment decision after the market test adversely affects an interested third party, the latter must therefore be heard. This conclusion applies without prejudice to the fact that the right to be heard of interested third parties can be less extensive than the rights of the concerned undertaking.[127]

4.1.3.2.2.2.2 The Best Practices and the Manual of Procedures

Also the Commission's approach regarding the rights of interested third parties to be heard where a commitment is amended after the market test seems to reflect more the opinion of Advocate General Kokott and less the restrictive position of the Court of Justice in Alrosa. The Best Practices and the Manual of Procedures deal with the consequences of an amendment of commitments after the market test. The Best Practices contain only the succinct statement that a new market test will be conducted, if the amended version alters the very nature or scope of the commitments.[128] The Manual of Procedures contains more detailed information. It states as follows:

> [...] Smaller ("technical") changes to the commitment text do not require new procedural steps. In particular, no new market test is usually required in case of revised commitments, unless the revision of the commitments is substantial. A change is only substantial if the very nature or scope of the commitments changes. If, for instance, the parties originally offered to reduce the duration of non-compete obligations in contracts with third parties from 5 to 2 years and following the market test such duration is further reduced to 1 year, there is no need to repeat the market test.[129]

Albeit the cited passage from the Manual of Procedures is not unambiguous, it can be construed as implying three different situations. First, the change to the commitment can be merely technical. In this case, no further procedural steps are required at all. Interested third parties do not need to be heard again. Second, the change to the commitment can be substantial. In this case, a new market test must be carried out. Interested third parties can comment on the revised commitment in the context of the second market test.[130] Third, the Commission seems to assume that there is a grey area between the thresholds of "merely technical" and "substantial". Where the change to the commitment falls in that area, other procedural steps than a market test may be required.[131] It may hence be necessary to hear interested third parties again on the revised commitment. For instance, in the example of a further reduction of the duration of non-compete clauses to 1 year used by the Commission,

[126] Opinion of AG Kokott, C-441/07 (Alrosa, 2009), 191.

[127] Opinion of AG Kokott, C-441/07 (Alrosa, 2009), 192.

[128] Best Practices (2011), 133.

[129] Manual of Procedures (2012), Module 16, 67.

[130] A second market test was carried out in COMP/39.654 (Reuters, 2012).

[131] I infer this interpretation from the use of the term "in particular" at the beginning of the second sentence of the cited passage.

it is not necessary to carry out a new market test, because the change of the commitment is not substantial. However, if one considers that the change is also not merely technical, the Commission must hear interested third parties again before it makes the commitment binding.

It is submitted that this three-pronged approach is at the same time necessary and sufficient to protect the rights of interested third parties. On the one hand, the three-pronged approach is necessary. For reasons of procedural economy, it makes sense to set the substantiality threshold that indicates when the Commission must carry out a new market test at a comparatively high level. However, if the threshold for a new market test is high, the right of interested third parties to comment on a revised commitment cannot be confined to situations where this threshold is met. Rather, interested third parties must have a possibility to comment on the revised commitment also where the threshold for a new market test is not met, as long as the change to the commitment is not merely technical. On the other hand, the three-pronged approach is sufficient. If the change to a commitment is merely technical—in the sense that it does not alter the situation of the interested third party—there is no need to hear the third party again.

4.1.3.2.2.2.3 Intermediate Conclusion

Taken literally, the Alrosa judgment of the Court of Justice appears to exclude any rights of interested third parties to be heard if a commitment is changed after the market test. Such a restrictive approach must be criticised. It is not even pursued by the Commission in its Best Practices and the Manual of Procedures. According to the latter, the Commission will at least carry out a new market test if a commitment has been changed substantially.

However, it seems questionable whether the Court of Justice will pursue an equally restrictive approach in future cases. As explained above, the judgment of the Court of Justice is difficult to generalise. The reasoning of the judgment is very succinct and probably coined by the result that the Court wanted to achieve.[132] In the part of the judgment that deals with the action at first instance, the Court does not analyse whether the Commission respected Alrosa's rights as an interested third party. The Court rejects Alrosa's plea in law regarding the alleged violation of its rights of defence for the sole reason that all of Alrosa's criticism was based on the erroneous premise that Alrosa should have enjoyed more extensive procedural rights than those usually afforded to interested third parties.[133] In particular, the Court did not deal with the question under what conditions the Commission is obliged to carry out a new market test if the preceding market test leads to changes of the initial commitment.

More important than the statements of the Court of Justice that concern the scope of the rights of interested third parties are the statements that the Court makes

[132] See Sect. 2.2.2.2.1 with footnote 82 above.

[133] CJ, C-441/07 P (Alrosa, 2010), 119.

regarding the Commission's discretion in granting a company the status of a concerned undertaking or merely that of an interested third party. The Court made it clear that the Commission cannot choose arbitrarily between whether it grants a company the former or the latter status,[134] meaning that the Commission must give an objective reason for its decision.[135] However, the Court considered that it was objectively justified for the Commission to conduct two separate sets of administrative proceedings in view of their different material legal bases, Article 101 TFEU on the one hand and Article 102 TFEU on the other. With regard to the proceedings under Article 102 TFEU, only De Beers as the presumed dominant undertaking could be the addressee of the statement of objections and the Commission's final decision.[136] In the literature, this part of the Court's judgment has rightly been met with approval.[137]

4.1.3.3 De lege ferenda: A Need for Market Testing Article 7 Remedies?

In an Article 7 procedure, other natural and legal persons are only informed about the nature and subject matter of the proceedings once they are admitted. Before this happens, there is no formal procedure to inform them about the envisaged content of an Article 7 decision, so that they can decide whether they want to request to be admitted. This is different where the Commission intends to adopt a commitment decision pursuant to Article 9 or a finding of inapplicability pursuant to Article 10. In the latter cases, by virtue of Article 27(4) Regulation 1/03, the Commission is obliged to publish a concise summary of the case and the main content of the commitments or of the proposed course of action and to invite interested parties to present their observations. According to the unambiguous wording of Article 27 (4) Regulation 1/03, the market test is, however, not provided for decisions adopted on the basis of Article 7. Already under Regulation 17/62, it was criticised that the Commission was only obliged to market test negative clearance and exemption decisions.[138] It was suggested that the Commission should publish envisaged remedies in more complex cases.[139] Also with respect to Regulation 1/03, commentators have proposed to "formalize market testing for envisaged remedies similar to standard practice in merger proceedings" in more complex cases.[140]

This begs the question, whether the Commission's formal obligation, provided for in Article 27(4), to test commitments and findings of inapplicability on the market, should be extended to cases in which the Commission intends to impose a

[134]See Sect. 2.2.1.4.2 with footnote 57 above.

[135]See Ortiz Blanco/Jörgens/Kellerbauer (2013), 13.22.

[136]CJ, C-441/07 P (Alrosa, 2010), 89.

[137]Hennig (2010b), 452; Schweitzer (2011), 644f.

[138]See Article 19(3) Regulation 17/62.

[139]See Müller-Tautphaeus (2003), 295f.

[140]Hellström/Maier-Rigaud/Bulst (2009), 62.

remedy pursuant to Article 7(1). For the following reasons, the question has to be answered in the negative. First, it must be pointed out that the Commission normally publishes a press release when it addresses a statement of objections to the concerned undertakings.[141] At least where more complex remedies are concerned, such a press release may also cover the envisaged remedies.[142] Certainly, the succinct and often vague information contained in a press release is not comparable to the publication of the full text of proposed commitments on the website of DG COMP, which has evolved as the Commission's usual way to market test Article 9 commitments.[143] Nevertheless, a press release will normally contain at least first indications for third parties, allowing them to decide whether they want to request to be admitted to a procedure, which in turn will then lead to more detailed information about the "nature and subject matter of the procedure" or even a non-confidential version of the statement of objections being provided to them. Second, it is true that third parties may provide useful help for the Commission in the design of an appropriate remedy.[144] However, even the more complex Article 7 remedies will normally be

[141]See eg IP/03/1150 (Microsoft); MEMO/06/91 (Telefonica); IP/06/260 (Mastercard); IP/13/406 (Motorola). See also Best Practices (2011), 91: "In order to enhance the transparency of the proceedings, the Commission will, as a general rule, publish a press release setting out the key issues in the Statement of Objections shortly after it is received by its addressees"; Lübking/von Koppenfels (2012), 74.

[142]The Commission's practice regarding the provision of information about envisaged remedies in press releases about statements of objections is mixed.

The press release issued before the adoption of the 2004 Microsoft decision (Sect. 4.1.3.3, footnote 141 above) informed about the obligation to grant access; with respect to the tying abuse, it set out the untying and the must carry remedies as alternatives. The press release issued before the Mastercard decision (ibid.) indicated merely that the decision could prohibit the relevant MIF. The press releases issued before the adoption of the Telefonica and Motorola decisions (ibid.) did not contain any information regarding the remedies.

Some Article 9 cases in which the Commission initially sent statements of objections to the concerned undertakings can serve as further examples.

The press release in Rambus (MEMO/07/330) contained the information that "the appropriate remedy to [the] abuse would be that Rambus charge a reasonable and non-discriminatory royalty rate, the precise amount of which should be determined having regard to all the circumstances of the case". According to the press release in Standard and Poor's, the Commission envisaged to "require S&P to cease the abuse and [to] impose a fine". In the ENI case, which was ultimately closed by a structural commitment, the press release about the statement of objections (MEMO/09/120) did not contain any information regarding the envisaged remedy.

[143]As explained above, Article 27(4) requires the Commission only to publish a "concise summary of the case and the main content of the commitments". These "market test notices" are published in all official languages in the OJ. However, in its Best Practices (2011), 129, the Commission states that it will also publish the full text of commitments in the authentic language on the website of DG COMP. The "market test notices" required by Article 27(4) are far less detailed than the full text of the commitments published on the website.

[144]See Müller-Tautphaeus (2003), 295: "[d]ie Stellungnahmen sachkundiger Dritter und von Vereinigungen dürften der Kommission wertvolle Hinweise für die Ausgestaltung von Abhiflemaßnahmen geben"; Falconi (2011), 43: "As third parties [...] generally have a good knowledge of the case and of the relevant market dynamics, they can influence the Commission's decision-making process by helping to assess the appropriateness of the commitments"; Italianer

less detailed than Article 9 commitments. This is even more the case, if one compares the information about a remedy that must be contained in a statement of objections to the proposals for commitments that the parties submit to the Commission. In view of the lack of specificity of Article 7 remedies, the comments of third parties on the Commission's outline of an envisaged Article 7 remedy are hence from the outset of less use than comments on a proposal for an Article 9 commitment. At the same time, if the Commission intends to impose a remedy under Article 7 that is so complex and specific that the Commission deems it desirable to carry out a market test, Article 27(3), 1st sentence, leaves it sufficient room to do so. Third, it bears mention that, also in the context of merger control, the Commission retains a certain discretion whether it carries out a market test of proposed remedies.[145] Fourth, it must be emphasised that, by virtue of Article 30, the final Article 7 decision must in any event be published. Other natural and legal persons will thus at the latest learn of an Article 7 remedy through the publication of the decision. If they meet the requirements of Article 263 TFEU, they can then still seek judicial protection. At least where third parties could not foresee that an Article 7 remedy would aversely affect them, a lack of participation in the administrative procedure cannot lead to the inadmissibility of an application for annulment.

4.1.3.4 Necessity to Carry Out a Market Test for the Ex Post Revocation or Amendment of an Article 9 Remedy

It is questionable whether and to what extent the market test provided for by Article 27(4) Regulation 1/03 is also necessary where the Commission intends to revoke or amend a commitment. The Commission also carried out market tests pursuant to Article 19(3) Regulation 17/62 before it amended or revoked conditions that were attached to exemption decisions pursuant to Article 8(3) Regulation 17/62.[146] In the Merger Remedies Notice, the Commission states that it will take the views of third parties into account for any waiver, modification or substitution of commitments.[147]

(2012), 9: "Market-testing allows us to anticipate problems that could arise in the implementation phase. This is why we need to hear directly from industry which options are viable and which are not and why we encourage interested parties to reply to our market tests. This is very useful in achieving effective and proportionate remedies"; Gerard (2013), 14: "seeking the views of third-parties is an important step to balance the information asymmetry between firms and enforcers".

[145]The Merger Regulation does not contain a provision on the market testing of remedies that is comparable to Article 27(4) Regulation 1/03. Recital 30 Merger Regulation states merely in general terms that "[t]ransparency and the effective consultation of Member States as well as of interested third parties should be ensured". In the Merger Remedies Notice (2008), 80, the Commission states that it "will consult the authorities of the Member States on the proposed commitments and, when considered appropriate, also third parties in the form of a market test". See Cengiz (2011), 134; Jones/Sufrin (2011), 972; Körber (2012), Art. 8 FKVO, 115.

[146]OJ 1994 L 174/34 (Bayer/BP Chemicals, 1994); OJ 2001 L 52/30 (Unisource, 2000); Hennig (2010a), 251f.

[147]Merger Remedies Notice (2008), 75.

Since the revocation or amendment of a remedy may affect the interests of third parties as much as the initial adoption of the remedy, the better reasons seem, in principle, to militate for a second market test also in the context of Article 9.[148] Nonetheless, according to the circumstances of the case, a full-scale market test may not be appropriate. For example, if an amendment must be carried out particularly swiftly or if only minor changes are envisaged, the market test could be limited to those parties that submitted comments when the initial remedy was adopted or even to those that would be affected by the changes.

4.1.4 The Role of the Hearing Officer

The function of the Hearing Officer was created by the Commission in 1982 to meet some of the criticism related to the combination of prosecutorial and adjudicative powers.[149] His powers were continuously expanded.[150] His general mission is to safeguard the procedural rights throughout antitrust and merger proceedings before the Commission.[151] For this purpose, he acts independently.[152] The mandate extends also to the rights of complainants and third parties.[153]

The Hearing Officer has some limited decision making powers that concern essentially the admission of complainants and other third parties to an oral hearing[154]; the exercise of the right of access to the file[155]; and the extension of time limits.[156] The Hearing Officer is also responsible for the organisation and conduct of the oral hearing.[157] Besides that, he is confined to advisory and reporting powers that cover, however, both the investigative and the adversarial phase of the procedure. In Evonik Degussa, the Court of Justice strengthened the role of the hearing officer by finding that its power to rule on the disclosure of information was not limited to examining rules intended to afford specific protection against disclosure of the

[148]See also Kipiani (2014), 560: "[. . .] un second test de marché est préférable. À partir du moment où les engagements vont subir une modification, et dans une procédure où les tiers ont un droit de regard sur les engagements, la nouvelle consultation publique semble difficile à contourner"; differently Hennig (2010a), 252.

[149]Jones/Sufrin (2011), 1073.

[150]For detailed descriptions of the role of the Hearing Officer see Manual of Procedure (2012), Module 2; Albers/Jourdan (2011); Van Cleynenbreugel (2012); Wils (2012); Kellerbauer (2013).

[151]Article 1(2) Decision 2011/695/EU.

[152]Article 3(1) Decision 2011/695/EU.

[153]Recital 3 Decision 2011/695/EU.

[154]Articles 5 and 6 Decision 2011/695/EU.

[155]Articles 7 and 8 Decision 2011/695/EU.

[156]Article 9 Decision 2011/695/EU.

[157]Articles 10-13 Decision 2011/695/EU.

information to the public, such as the rules in Regulation 45/2001 and in Regulation 1049/2001, but extended also to the analysis of general principles of EU law.[158]

Also in the context of Article 9, the possibility to call upon the Hearing Officer existed since the adoption of the first commitment decision under Regulation 1/03.[159] To date, all decisions adopted on the basis of Article 9 have been accompanied by a report of the Hearing Officer.[160] A revision of the Hearing Officer's mandate in 2001 empowered the latter to report on the objectivity of the market tests conducted prior to the adoption of a commitment in merger and antitrust proceedings.[161] Since its revision in 2011, Article 15(1) of the Hearing Officer's mandate stipulates that parties offering commitments may call upon the Hearing Officer at any stage in the procedure, in order to ensure the effective exercise of their procedural rights.[162] This provision should not be construed as excluding the rights of complainants and third parties to call upon the Hearing Officer in commitment procedures. As is apparent from the final reports of the Hearing Officer, also in commitment procedures, the latter examines requests "from any party to the proceedings".[163]

4.1.5 Conclusion on the Administrative Procedure

Overall, the procedural safeguards are only modestly relaxed in the context of an Article 9 procedure. Gerard's statement that due process safeguards are "virtually non-existent"[164] clearly overshoots the mark. If the approach suggested above is followed, the concerned undertakings have a right to access to the file after the issuance of a preliminary assessment, or at least after the issuance of a statement of objections. The fact that the concerned undertakings receive sometimes only summaries of the submissions obtained by the Commission in the market test and the lapse of a formal hearing pursuant to Article 12 Regulation 1/03 are no decisive arguments against the Article 9 procedure. Complainants are sufficiently protected,

[158] CJ, C-162/15 P (Evonik Degussa, 2017), 39ff.

[159] See the report of the hearing officer in COMP/37.214 (Bundesliga, 2005): "No queries were raised before the Hearing Officer by the League Association or other companies as to the market test. No requests for additional information were made. The League Association has informed the Commission that the information necessary to assess the case was at its disposal. In the light of the above, the case does not call for any particular comments as regards the right to be heard".

[160] Gerard (2013), 32.

[161] Article 14 Decision 2001/462/EC; Albers/Jourdan (2011), 188 and 197.

[162] Van Cleynenbreugel (2012), 287; Wils (2012), 451; Ortiz Blanco/Jörgens/Kellerbauer (2013), 13.29.

[163] Eg the final reports of the Hearing Officer in COMP/39.736 (Siemens/Areeva, 2012); COMP/39.654 (Reuters, 2012); COMP/39.678 (Deutsche Bahn I and II, 2013); COMP/39.398 (Visa, 2014).

[164] See Sect. 4, footnote 1 above.

in particular because their rights pursuant to Article 7 and 8 Regulation 773/2004 remain unaffected. The interests of third parties are sufficiently protected through the market test. Moreover, according to the approach suggested above, the dictum of the Court of Justice in Alrosa that interested third parties do not have a right to be heard if commitments are amended after a market test must be rejected. Unless the change to the commitment is merely technical, the Commission must hear interested third parties subsequent to the amendment of a commitment. This can either be done by hearing the affected third parties individually or by conducting a new market test. Finally, also under the commitment procedure, the concerned undertakings, complainants and third parties have the possibility to call upon the Hearing Officer to ensure the effective exercise of their procedural rights.

4.2 Judicial Review

In order to answer the question whether and to what extent the judicial review of Article 9 decisions is restricted in comparison to the judicial review of Article 7 decisions, one must distinguish between admissibility questions and questions that concern the scope of review.

4.2.1 Admissibility

Like the procedural rights during the administrative procedure, also the admissibility of actions before the EU Courts must be examined from the perspective of the concerned undertakings, of complainants and of other third parties.

4.2.1.1 Concerned Undertakings

4.2.1.1.1 In the Context of Article 7

The admissibility of actions for annulment introduced by concerned undertakings against a decision adopted on the basis of Article 7 is unproblematic.[165] As will be explained in more detail below, like a decision that merely finds an infringement, also remedies that are imposed on the basis of Article 7 produce discrete legal effects. The entire Article 7 decision therefore constitutes an act that is reviewable

[165] See Sofianatos (2009), 648f.

under Article 263 TFEU.[166] As addressees of the Commission's decision, the concerned undertakings have standing pursuant to Article 263(4) TFEU.[167]

4.2.1.1.2 In the Context of Article 9

In the context of Article 9, a distinction must be made between actions that pursue the annulment of a commitment that was made binding by the Commission and actions that are directed against a refusal by the Commission to accept a commitment offer.

4.2.1.1.2.1 Actions Directed Against Commitments Made Binding by the Commission

The admissibility of an action against a decision by which the Commission has made a commitment binding can be questioned under two aspects.

4.2.1.1.2.1.1 Reviewable Act?

Isolated voices in the literature have raised the question whether a commitment decision constitutes a reviewable act. According to Sofianatos, the Commission's power to reopen the proceedings pursuant to Article 9(2) could justify the assumption that a commitment decision constitutes merely a preliminary step in the procedure that is not amenable to judicial review.[168] Similarly, Bechtold et al. have argued that the preliminary character of the assessment required for an Article 9 decision deprives a commitment decision of its finality.[169] Such arguments must be rejected.

---

[166]See Sect. 5.2.1.3.1 with footnote 318ff below. Doubts regarding the admissibility of an action for annulment could be raised, where the action is pointed towards an abstract like effects order. As explained below, there is a strand of case law that attributes them a purely declaratory value. According to the view taken here, like effects orders should be annulled for the sake of clarity. This result can only be achieved, if actions against them are declared admissible, although they do not produce any legal effects. The result is justified by the interest of the concerned undertaking to obtain legal certainty.

[167]See Kerse/Khan (2012), 8-096; Lenaerts/Maselis/Gutman (2014), 7.86.

[168]Sofianatos (2009), 654: "[. . .] la Commission se réserve le droit de rouvrir le dossier et d'adopter une décision de constatation d'infraction. La décision peut alors être considérée comme ne comportant pas sa position finale sur la procédure, condition nécessaire pour la considérer comme un acte attaquable". Sofianatos also claims that the Commission raised this argument before the General Court in Alrosa. This is not correct. As is apparent from the judgment (para 36), the Commission did not challenge the admissibility of Alrosa's action.

[169]Bechtold/Bosch/Brinker (2014), Art. 9, 6: "keine verfahrensbeendende und damit nach Art. 263 Abs. 4 AEUV anfechtbare Entscheidung". Bechtold et al. contradict themselves by stating (Art. 9, 14) that third parties can challenge a commitment decision with an action for annulment. If commitment decisions were no reviewable acts, then they could also not be challenged by third parties.

Unless it is revoked or amended, a commitment decision produces legally binding effects.[170] A commitment decision is no preparatory act that paves the way for a subsequent final decision.[171] The facts that the decision is adopted on the basis of a preliminary assessment and that the procedure can be reopened and the commitment revoked or amended do not call this conclusion into question. This can be illustrated with a comparative look at merger proceedings. Phase I clearance decisions that are adopted pursuant to Article 6(1)(b) or (2) Merger Regulation on the basis of a preliminary assessment constitute challengeable acts.[172] Moreover, the possibilities provided for in Articles 6(3) and 8(6) Merger Regulation to revoke a Phase I or Phase II clearance decision do not exclude that clearance decisions constitute challengeable acts. In accordance with the general principles of EU administrative law, every administrative act can under certain circumstances be revoked or amended.[173] It would be absurd to infer from this fact that all administrative acts are merely preliminary acts that are not amenable to judicial review.

4.2.1.1.2.1.2 Lack of Legal Interest in a Challenge Due to Consent?

It is sometimes contended that the consent of the concerned undertaking to a commitment decision excludes the possibility to appeal the decision.[174] According to the consistent case law of the EU Courts, actions brought under Article 263 TFEU require the existence of a legal interest in the action.[175] It could therefore be argued that the consent of the concerned undertakings excludes their legal interest in the challenge of a commitment decision, thus making an action inadmissible.[176] However, the better arguments militate against a categorical inadmissibility of actions brought by the addressees of a commitment decision. It is more convincing to grant a concerned undertaking the right to appeal a commitment decision, but to consider

---

[170]See Rachwol (2010), 144.

[171]See Kerse/Khan (2012), 8-105.

[172]See GC, T-151/05 (NVV, 2009), 65ff; Bengtsson/Carpi Badia/Kadar (2014), 5.1130; Boyd/von Lingen (2013), 18.06: "There is no question that Article 6(1)(b) decisions are open to review, since these are final clearance decisions".

[173]See Sect. 3.7.2.1.1 with footnotes 1473ff above.

[174]See eg Temple Lang (2006), 296; Cook (2006), 221; Bechtold/Bosch/Brinker (2014), Art. 9, 15; Sura (2014), Art. 9, 21.

[175]Eg CJ, C-362/05 P (Wunenburger, 2007), 42; C-269/12 P (Cañas, 2013), 15; GC, T-189/08 (Forum 187, 2010), 62; Kerse/Khan (2012), 8-096.

[176]For the classification of the impact of the voluntary nature of commitments on the admissibility of actions for annulment as a question of legal interest see eg Saitzek (2008), 293; Sofianatos (2009), 649; Körber (2010), 90; Hennig (2010a), 361ff. Schwarze/Weitbrecht (2004), 83f, Waelbroeck (2009), 235 fn 40 and Hennig (2010a), 365f, discuss the question also in connection with the estoppel principle of "venire contra factum proprium".

the grounds for review as restricted by the fact that the undertaking voluntarily offered the commitment.[177]

The Wood Pulp judgment of the Court of Justice militates against a categorical inadmissibility of an action brought by the addressee of a commitment decision.[178] In that case, the applicants had given an undertaking to the Commission and as a consequence obtained a reduction of their fine. On appeal, the applicants sought the annulment of the undertaking. The Commission asked the Court to declare the claim inadmissible, because the undertakings should be regarded as unilateral acts of the applicants.[179] The Court of Justice did not accept the Commission's submission. It held that the obligations imposed on the applicants by the undertaking had to be regarded in the same way as orders requiring an infringement to be brought to an end. In the view of the Court, in giving the undertaking, the applicants had merely assented, for their own reasons, to a decision which the Commission was empowered to adopt unilaterally.[180] Having declared the applicant's plea admissible, the Court partially annulled the undertaking.[181]

In Alrosa, the General Court relied on the Wood Pulp judgment of the Court of Justice in support of its conclusion that the consensual nature of Article 9 decisions did not restrict its proportionality review.[182] The Court of Justice did not follow that reasoning. As explained above, it considered that the consensual nature of commitment decisions necessitated a modification of the proportionality test.[183] However, it cannot be inferred from the Alrosa judgment of the Court of Justice that actions brought by addressees of a commitment decision are categorically inadmissible. Also after the Alrosa judgment of the Court of Justice, such actions must remain possible to the extent that the content of a commitment is not legitimised by the consent of the concerned undertaking. For instance, it must remain possible for the addressees of Article 9 decisions to argue that procedural guarantees have not been respected, that the commitment offered is not correctly reproduced in the commitment decision, that the commitment offer was induced by the Commission through deceitful conduct or exercise of illegitimate pressure or that the Commission

---

[177]See De Bronnet (2012), Art. 9, 20: "Entscheidungen nach Art. 9 können gemäß Art. 263 Abs. 4 AEUV durch den/die Adressaten [...] angefochten werden. Das Klagerecht der Adressaten ist jedoch dadurch eingeschränkt, dass sie die Zusagen angeboten haben"; Similarly eg Busse/Leopold (2005), 154; Wils (2006), 362f and (2008), 338f; Schweitzer (2010), 573. But see also Schweitzer (2012), 19, where she infers from the Alrosa judgment of the CJ that "undertakings which offer commitments will likely not enjoy standing to appeal a commitment decision"; similarly Hennig (2010a), 365.

[178]See eg Klees (2005), § 6, 153; Saitzek (2008), 294; Sofianatos (2009), 655; Hennig (2010a), 366f.

[179]CJ, C-89/85 (Wood Pulp, 1993), 178ff.

[180]CJ, C-89/85 (Wood Pulp, 1993), 181. For a detailed discussion of the parts of the judgment that concern the commitments see von Winterfeld (1995).

[181]See Sect. 3.3.1.3.2.1 with footnote 164 above.

[182]GC, T-170/06 (Alrosa, 2007), 105ff.

[183]See Sect. 2.2.2.2.2 with footnotes 83ff above.

committed an error in rejecting further commitment offers made by the concerned undertaking.[184]

The conclusion that the action brought by an addressee of an Article 9 decision is admissible, but that the grounds of review are restricted by the consent of the concerned undertaking, is further supported by the jurisprudence of the General Court in the context of merger control. In Cementbouw, the General Court examined the pleas brought by a notifying party which had offered commitments against the Commission's decision to make those commitments binding pursuant to Article 8 (2) Regulation 139/2004 without even raising the admissibility question.[185] On the substance, the Court rejected the pleas, in particular because the applicant had not shown that the Commission had "arbitrarily forced" it to offer the commitments in question.[186]

4.2.1.1.2.2 Actions Directed Against the Commission's Refusal to Accept a Commitment

It is broadly accepted that the Commission's refusal to accept a commitment offer is no challengeable act.[187] Such a refusal merely prepares a final decision, regardless of whether the procedure is ultimately closed with a decision adopted on the basis of Article 7 or Article 10 Regulation 1/03 or whether it is closed informally. As will be further explained below, the concerned undertaking can however challenge an Article 7 decision on the ground that the Commission committed a manifest error when balancing the respective pros and cons of the Article 7 and the Article 9 procedure. Moreover, the concerned undertaking can challenge a remedy imposed on the basis of Article 7 on the ground that the Commission should not have imposed a remedy that went beyond what the concerned undertaking offered as a commitment.[188]

[184]See Schwarze/Weitbrecht (2004), 84; Wils (2006), 362f; Körber (2010), 90; Hennig (2010a), 375; De Bronnet (2012); Art. 9, 20; De Smijter/Sinclair (2014), 2.143.

[185]GC, T-282/02 (Cementbouw, 2006), 293ff; see Ortiz Blanco/Jörgens/Kellerbauer (2013), 13.29 fn 128, who infer from the Cementbouw judgment that "it can be safely assumed that the addressee of an Article 9 decision is entitled to challenge the decision before the Court".

[186]GC, T-282/02 (Cementbouw, 2006), 319; see eg Waelbroeck (2009), 235; Sofianatos (2009), 650ff; Schweitzer (2010), 573; Rab/Monnoyeur/Sukhtankar (2010), 184; Ortiz Blanco/Jörgens/Kellerbauer (2013), 13.29.

[187]Wils (2006), 363; Saitzek (2008), 299ff; Hennig (2010a), 361; Kerse/Khan (2012), 8-106.

[188]See Sect. 5.1.2.3 with footnote 66 below.

4.2.1.2 Complainants

4.2.1.2.1 In the Context of Article 7

If the Commission merely rejects a complaint without at the same time adopting a decision against the undertakings that are the subject of the proceedings, the admissibility of an action for annulment is unproblematic. The rejection of the complaint is recognized as a reviewable act[189] and complainants have standing as addressees.[190] Complainants can therefore challenge the rejection decision.

Admissibility issues become a bit more complex, however, where the Commission rejects a complaint only partially. This would be the case where the Commission imposes a certain remedy on the concerned undertaking, but at the same time also rejects a complaint in so far as the complainant had requested a different remedy. It is unclear, whether, in such a constellation, the Commission would combine the imposition of an Article 7 remedy and the rejection of the complaint in a single decision or whether the Commission would adopt two separate decisions. The Commission's way of dealing with Article 9 commitments and the corresponding complaints seems to point in the latter direction.[191] If, however, the Commission adopts two separate decisions, the question arises whether the complainant can content himself with attacking only the rejection decision, or whether it must also challenge the decision that is addressed to the concerned undertakings.[192] The question is of importance due to the time delay that may lie between the two decisions. The Commission's practice regarding Article 9 decisions seems to evolve in the direction that the decision that makes commitments binding is adopted significantly earlier than the decision rejecting the complaint.[193] Applied to Article 7, this means that the remedy would be imposed before the rejection of the complaint. If the complainant then does not timely challenge the decision imposing the remedy, that decision becomes definitive. On the other hand, it is unreasonably difficult for the complainant to challenge the decision imposing the remedy, before he is told the reasons for the rejection of his complaint. There are several ways to

[189]See Lenaerts/Maselis/Gutman (2014), 7.43.

[190]See Kerse/Khan (2012), 8-096; Lenaerts/Maselis/Gutman (2014), 7.86.

[191]In BA/AA/IB (COMP/39596) and Rambus (COMP/38636), the Commission adopted separate decisions to make the respective commitments binding pursuant to Article 9 and to reject the respective complaints. See also De Smijter/Sinclair (2014), 2.144: "Although the complaint is rejected by separate decision, the two decisions are intrinsically linked".

[192]In the Rambus case, Hynix initially challenged the Article 9 commitment and the rejection decision in two separate applications (see GC, T-148/09 and T-149/09). Eventual admissibility issues could not be clarified, as Hynix later withdrew both applications; see also Botteman/Patsa (2013), 359 fn 61.

[193]In Rambus (Sect. 4.2.1.2.1, footnote 191), the rejection decision was adopted about a month after the commitments decision (December 2009/January 2010). In BA/AA/IB (Sect. 4.2.1.2.1, footnote 191), the rejection decision was adopted about a year after the commitments decision (July 2010/June 2011).

resolve this problem.[194] It must be left to the Commission and the EU Courts to find an appropriate solution. For the present purposes, it suffices to state that, if the Commission adopts two separate decisions, a complainant must be put in a position allowing it to raise the pleas against the rejection of its complaint also against the remedy decision.

4.2.1.2.2 In the Context of Article 9

The described principles apply mutatis mutandis also where the Commission partially rejects a complaint subsequent to the adoption of a commitment decision. No particularities arise in that regard.

4.2.1.3 Other Third Parties

The admissibility of actions for annulment instituted by other natural or legal persons against remedies adopted on the basis of Articles 7 and 9 was addressed by the General Court in Morningstar.[195] The admissibility of such actions causes problems in particular in so far as these persons must demonstrate that the contested decision is of "individual concern to them".[196] In this context, the differentiation of the

---

[194]The following ways may be considered, but would need further reflection:

First, the Commission could combine the remedy and the rejection of the complaint in a single decision, adopt the rejection decision before the remedy or at least adopt the two decisions on the same day.

Second, the complainant could be allowed to challenge only a later rejection decision. In case his application succeeds, the annulment of the rejection decision would in this case oblige the Commission to withdraw the remedy decision. The concerned undertakings could not put forward legitimate expectations against the withdrawal of the remedy decision due to the pending appeal against the rejection decision.

Third, the complainant could be obliged to challenge the remedy decision, either alone or in combination with a later rejection decision. In this case, the complainant would have to be allowed to put forward his arguments against the grounds of the later rejection decision in the proceedings against the remedies decision as new pleas in law that came to light in the course of the procedure, pursuant to Article 48(2) of the Rules of Procedure of the General Court.

De Smijter/Sinclair (2014), 2.144, consider that a complainant who does not challenge the commitment decision loses his right to challenge a rejection decision, because, in their view, Article 9(2) does not allow the Commission to reopen proceedings in such a case. In my view, this is not convincing. Regardless of whether Article 9(2) allows for a reopening of proceedings subsequent to the annulment of a rejection decision, the Commission could, in any event, base the revocation or amendment of the commitment decision on the general principles of EU administrative law (see Sect. 3.7.2.1.2.1.2 with footnotes 1487ff above).

[195]GC, T-76/14 (Morningstar, 2016). Although the case concerned only article 9, the considerations made by the General Court with regard to the admissibility apply also under article 7. For a discussion of the judgment see Idot (2016), 31, and Paemen/Baltrusch (2017), 99.

[196]Article 263(4) TFEU.

Plaumann formula[197] in the case law of the EU Courts shall not be treated here in all its details.[198] Rather, the following section will try to shed some light on the importance of the role played by an applicant during the administrative procedure. It is beyond doubt that the EU Courts consider this role to be an important factor for the assessment of a third party's individual concern. However, the questions whether or under what conditions the participation in the administrative procedure may constitute a necessary or sufficient condition to establish individual concern still merit a closer look.

It is not necessary to distinguish actions that are directed against injunctions adopted on the basis of Article 7 and actions that are directed against commitments adopted on the basis of Article 9. The assessment whether a third party is individually concerned by a commitment decision follows the general principles that apply for Article 7 decisions.[199] The consent of the concerned undertakings to a commitment cannot justify any restriction of rights of third parties to challenge a commitment.

4.2.1.3.1 Is the Exercise of a Procedural Right During the Administrative Procedure a Necessary Condition for Individual Concern?

It is questionable, whether the exercise of procedural rights during the administrative procedure is a necessary condition for individual concern or at least for the existence of a legal interest in an application.[200] Some voices in the literature contend with respect to Article 9 commitments that a failure to present observations during the market test pursuant to Article 27(4) forecloses a third party from a later action for annulment.[201] In support of their contention, most of these commentators rely on the Kruidvat case.[202] The case concerned the failure of an applicant to participate in a market test pursuant to Article 19(3) Regulation 17/62, which corresponded in essence to the market test that is now provided for in Article 27(4) Regulation 1/03. The contrary opinion denies that an applicant who fails to participate in the market test pursuant to Article 27(4) is barred from instituting an action against a

---

[197] According to the Plaumann formula (CJ, 25/62, 1963), in order to demonstrate "individual concern", applicants must show that a contested decision "affects them by reason of certain attributes which are peculiar to them or by reason of circumstances in which they are differentiated from all other persons and by virtue of these factors distinguishes them individually just as in the case of the person addressed."

[198] See instead eg Craig/De Búrca (2011), 494ff; Hofmann/Rowe/Türk (2012), 825ff; Lenaerts/Maselis/Gutman (2014), 7.111ff.

[199] See Klees (2005), § 6, 151; Saitzek (2008), 306ff; Rachwol (2010), 154.

[200] See Dervisopoulos (2014), § 7, 72.

[201] See Wolter (2011), 223; De Bronnet (2012), Art. 9, 20; Sura (2014), Art. 27, 49; Rachwol (2010), 154f with further references in fn 758.

[202] Rachwol (2010), 154; De Bronnet (2012), Art. 9, 20 fn 33; Sura (2014), Art. 27, 49.

commitments decision.[203] If the latter position were correct, this would a fortiori apply for actions against Article 7 decisions, for which no formal market test is prescribed.

4.2.1.3.1.1 The Development of the Case Law

4.2.1.3.1.1.1 Case Law Prior to the Kruidvat Case

There is a strand of case law predating the Kruidvat judgment of the Court of Justice, in which the General Court held both in the context of Article 19(3) Regulation 17/62 and in the context of merger control that, even where they enjoyed procedural rights in the administrative procedure, the capacity of third parties to institute an action for annulment could not be subjected to the exercise of these rights. The General Court argued that the contrary conclusion "would be tantamount to introducing an additional condition of admissibility in the form of a compulsory pre-litigation procedure, which is not provided for in Article [263 TFEU]".[204]

4.2.1.3.1.1.2 Kruidvat and Its Potential Scope of Application

4.2.1.3.1.1.2.1 The Case

In the Kruidvat case, the Commission granted an exemption for a selective distribution system. A trade union had submitted comments during the market test provided for by Article 19(3) Regulation 17/62. Kruidvat, a potential participant of the selective distribution system and member of the trade union, had not itself participated in the administrative procedure. Nevertheless, Kruidvat later instituted an action for annulment against the exemption decision. The General Court declared the action inadmissible. In the view of the General Court, Kruidvat had not sufficiently established the link between its individual position and the trade union's participation in the administrative procedure.[205] Referring to its prior case law, the General Court expressly confirmed that the absence of Kruidvat's participation in the administrative procedure did not suffice to declare the action inadmissible for lack of individual concern.[206] However, the General Court found that also the other circumstances of the case at hand were not sufficient to establish Kruidvat's individual concern.[207] On appeal, the Court of Justice confirmed the judgment. The ruling of the Court of Justice contains inter alia the following statement:

---

[203] Saitzek (2008), 314 and 317; Sofianatos (2009), 660; Hennig (2010a), 371.

[204] GC, T-528/93 (Métropole, 1996), 62, which concerned Article 19(3) Regulation 17/62; see also, in the context of merger control, GC, T-96/92 (CCESGGS, 1995), 36f; T-12/93, (CCESAV, 1995), 46f; Hennig (2010a), 371 fn 1543; Lenaerts/Maselis/Gutman (2014), 7.112 fn 433.

[205] GC, T-87/92 (Kruidvat, 1996), 66; confirmed by CJ, C-70/97 P (Kruidvat, 1998), 23; see also Lenaerts/Maselis/Gutman (2014), 7.112 fn 433.

[206] GC, T-87/92 (Kruidvat, 1996), 67.

[207] GC, T-87/92 (Kruidvat, 1996), 68ff.

> [. . .] there was an invitation to submit observations and interested parties had the opportunity to exercise their right to make their views known to the Commission. It is therefore not necessary for them to be regarded as individually concerned by the Decision in order for their interests to be judicially protected when they did not take advantage of that opportunity.[208]

In view of its wording and the previous judgment of the General Court, the cited passage could potentially be considered as ambiguous.[209] However, it results clearly from the opinion of Advocate General Fennelly, to which the Court of Justice expressly referred, that, contrary to the General Court, the Court considered a lack of participation in the administrative procedure as a sufficient reason to bar an applicant from an action for annulment. In fact, the Advocate General argued with the necessity of a balance between the interest of third parties to be heard and the interests of the Commission and the concerned undertakings in legal certainty. According to the Advocate General, in cases where there was an opportunity for third parties to present their views, that balance could be struck "by deeming only those who availed of that opportunity to be individually concerned by, and, thus, to have standing to challenge, the Decision".[210]

4.2.1.3.1.1.2.2 The Potential Scope of Application

The Kruidvat case concerned the failure to participate in a market test pursuant to Article 19(3) Regulation 17/62. One might therefore argue that the Kruidvat case is only of importance today with respect to the formal market test provided for by Article 27(4) Regulation 1/03, which only concerns Article 9 commitments and Article 10 findings of inapplicability, and which requires the Commission to publish a market test notice and to invite parties to comment. However, also as far as Article 7 decisions are concerned, Article 27(3) grants a procedural right to third parties to present their views. Article 27(3) only does not require the Commission to publish a market test notice and to invite parties to comment of its own motion. It goes without saying that a third party which does not have to be aware of an envisaged decision cannot be precluded from an application for annulment for lack of participation in the administrative procedure.[211] However, under the Kruidvat rationale, third parties might nevertheless be foreclosed in cases where they are or at least have to be aware of an envisaged Article 7 decision, for instance due to the announcement of the statement of objections in a press release, but who do not avail themselves of their right to request to be admitted to the administrative procedure pursuant to Article 27

---

[208] C-70/97 P (Kruidvat, 1998), 43.

[209] See Schütte (2008), § 49, 211 fn 395; Saitzek (2008), 314 and Hennig (2010a), 371 fn 1543, who all interpret the Kruidvat case as not implying that participation in the administrative procedure is a necessary condition for an action for annulment.

[210] Opinion of AG Fenelly, C-70/97 P (Kruidvat, 1998), 62.

[211] See Sect. 4.1.3.3, after footnote 144 above; also Schütte (2008), § 49, 211.

(3), 2nd sentence.[212] Moreover, in the context of Article 7 decisions, the Kruidvat rationale might be applied to parties who do not avail themselves of the opportunity to submit comments, if the Commission relies on the power granted in Article 27(3), 1st sentence, to hear third parties where it considers this necessary, to carry out a market test. It is hence submitted that the potential scope of application of the Kruidvat rationale is not limited to Article 27(4), but extends to Article 27(3).[213]

4.2.1.3.1.1.3 Case Law Following the Kruidvat Case

4.2.1.3.1.1.3.1 State Aid: Sniace

After Kruidvat, the Court of Justice had to treat the question again in Sniace, a judgment concerning state aids. According to the Court and contrary to what the Commission asserted, it did not follow from the case law that a participation in the administrative procedure was a necessary condition for a finding of individual concern. In the Court's view, the lack of participation in the administrative procedure did not preclude an applicant from putting forward other circumstances to establish its individual concern.[214]

4.2.1.3.1.1.3.2 Merger Control: ASBL

In ASBL, a judgment regarding merger control, the General Court applied a distinction between applications for annulment relying on defects of the substance of a decision and those relying merely on the infringement of a procedural right. The case concerned an action for annulment instituted by a consumer association against the clearance of a concentration subject to commitments by virtue of Article 6(2) Merger Regulation. In the context of merger control, it follows from Article 18(4) Merger Regulation and Article 11(c), second indent, Regulation 802/2004 that consumer associations are, upon request, entitled to a right to be heard, where the proposed concentration concerns products or services used by final consumers. The General Court held that "the locus standi of third parties concerned by a merger must be assessed differently depending on whether they, first, rely on defects affecting the substance of those decisions ('first category') or, second, submit that the Commission infringed procedural rights granted to them by the acts of [EU] law governing the monitoring of mergers ('second category')".[215] As regards the first category, the

---

[212]A fact that militates nevertheless for restricting the Kruidvat rationale only to Article 27(4) cases is that, different from market test notices pursuant to Article 27(4), press releases by DG COMP are not published in all official languages in the OJ. Moreover, although market test notices typically do not contain very detailed information, they are still more detailed than a press release.

[213]See also Dervisopoulos (2014), § 7, 72 fn 234, who interprets the CJ's Kruidvat judgment as a general statement that a failure to exercise procedural rights during the administrative procedure forecloses an applicant from a later action for annulment.

[214]CJ, C-260/05 P (Sniace, 2007), 57.

[215]GC, T-224/10 (ASBL, 2011), 27.

General Court stated that applicants had to show their individual concern in accordance with the conditions laid down in the Plaumann formula.[216] However, in the case at hand, the consumer association did not meet those conditions.[217] With respect to the second category, the Court examined whether the two conditions for the exercise of the procedural right to be heard during the administrative procedure were fulfilled, namely a sufficient interest and a valid request.[218] The Court found that the condition of a sufficient interest was met, because the concentration concerned products used by final consumers.[219] However, the Court also found that the consumer association had not submitted a valid request to be heard. In the view of the Court, requests to be heard could only be submitted after the notification of the concentration. In the case at hand, the consumer association had, however, only informed the Commission of its whish to be heard already 2 months prior to the notification. Holding that the Commission was not obliged to take such a request into account, the General Court declared the action for annulment inadmissible.[220]

The fact that the Court examined whether the consumer association was individually concerned according to the Plaumann formula although the consumer association had not submitted a valid request to be heard shows that the Court considered individual concern under the Plaumann formula to be independent from a participation in the administrative procedure. This is consistent with the ruling of the Court of Justice in Sniace.

4.2.1.3.1.2 Conclusion

Although the Kruidvat case contains a statement to the contrary, both the earlier and the later case law indicate that the failure to exercise a right to participate in the administrative procedure cannot foreclose an applicant from demonstrating its individual concern on the basis of other circumstances than the existence of the procedural participation right. In this respect, it is submitted that the rationale of the post Kruidvat case law is applicable also to the rights conferred by Article 27(3) and (4) Regulation 1/03, even if, strictly speaking, the two post Kruidvat cases described above concerned only the fields of state aid and merger control. There are no differences that could justify a different treatment. However, it must also be emphasised that, in so far as an applicant derives its individual concern from the existence of a right to participate in the administrative procedure, the exercise of this right is a necessary condition for a later action of annulment.

[216] GC, T-224/10 (ASBL, 2011), 28.
[217] GC, T-224/10 (ASBL, 2011), 32ff.
[218] GC, T-224/10 (ASBL, 2011), 36ff.
[219] GC, T-224/10 (ASBL, 2011), 40ff.
[220] GC, T-224/10 (ASBL, 2011), 46ff.

4.2.1.3.2 Is the Participation in the Administrative Procedure or a Right to Participate Sufficient to Establish Individual Concern?

4.2.1.3.2.1 Participation As Such Not Sufficient

The EU Courts assign the role played by an applicant in the process that leads to the adoption of an act of EU law an important influence for the assessment of the applicant's individual concern. Nevertheless, they have consistently ruled that mere participation alone is as such not decisive.[221] In the context of merger control, the General Court uses for instance the following formula:

> Whether a third party is individually concerned by a decision finding a concentration to be compatible with the common market depends, on the one hand, on that third party's participation in the administrative procedure and, on the other, on the effect on its market position. Whilst mere participation in the procedure is not sufficient to establish that the decision is of individual concern to the applicant, particularly in the field of merger control, the careful examination of which requires regular contact with numerous undertakings, active participation in the administrative procedure is a factor regularly taken into account in the case-law on competition, including in the more specific area of merger control, to establish, in conjunction with other specific circumstances, the admissibility of the action.[222]

In Morningstar, the General Court applied this strand of case law to a commitment decision. It considered that mere participation in the procedure was insufficient on its own to establish individual concern, but that active participation in the administrative procedure was a factor that could, in conjunction with other specific circumstances, such as a significant negative effect on the applicants business, render an application admissible.[223]

4.2.1.3.2.2 Existence of Participatory Right Sufficient

In the view of the EU Courts, mere participation in the administrative procedure as such hence does not suffice to establish individual concern. What is, however, sufficient, is a procedural rule that confers upon the applicant a specific participatory right.[224] Article 27(3) and (4) Regulation 1/03 and Article 13(1) Regulation 773/2004 must be considered to constitute such participatory rights. A third party who claims that its rights following from these provisions have been violated, for instance because the Commission did not recognise a sufficient interest to be heard or because the Commission failed to carry out a market test, is therefore in principle individually concerned.

---

[221] See CJ, C-342/04 P (Schmoldt, 2005), 39; GC, T-381/11 (Eurofer, 2012), 34; see also Ward (2007), 301f.

[222] GC, T-177/04 (Easyjet, 2006), 35; similarly T-114/02 (BaByliss, 2003), 95.

[223] GC, T 76/14 (Morningstar, 2016), 32ff. Similarly GC, T-873/16 (Canal+, 2018), 25, appeal pending under C-132/19 P.

[224] See CJ, C-342/04 P (Schmoldt, 2005), 39; GC, T-224/10 (ASBL, 2011), 29; T-381/11 (Eurofer, 2012), 34; see also Ward (2007), 304; Dörr (2012), Art. 263, 70; Hofmann/Rowe/Türk (2012), 829f.

However, several restrictive conditions nevertheless exist. First, it results from the ASBL judgment presented above[225] that the existence of a participatory right can only establish an individual concern if the third party actually benefits from the participatory right.[226] In the context of Article 27(3), 2nd sentence, and (4), this means that the third party must demonstrate a sufficient interest to be heard. Second, it also results from the said judgment that the third party must at least have tried to avail itself of its procedural right during the administrative procedure by presenting a valid submission. Third, where the individual concern of a third party predicates exclusively on the existence of a procedural right, the standing does not cover pleas in law that address the substance of a decision. Rather, the applicant is limited to putting forward a violation of his procedural right. This means that an application that is not based on a violation of the applicant's procedural right, but that only alleges a breach of the substantive rules, will be inadmissible.[227]

4.2.1.3.3 Individual Concern Irrespective of Procedural Rights

As explained above, irrespective of whether a third party has availed itself of its participatory rights in the administrative procedure, it can always establish its individual concern by showing that other circumstances distinguish it according to the Plaumann test. General statements when this will be the case are difficult to make and shall not be attempted here.[228] In any event, the fact that the adverse effect of a remedy on a third party constitutes merely a reflex of the obligation created for the addressee does as such not suffice to exclude the individual concern of third parties.[229] For instance, Alrosa's action against the Commission's decision to make De Beers' individual commitments binding was admissible,[230] even though the termination of the sales relation between Alrosa and DeBeers was merely a reflex of DeBeers commitment vis-à-vis the Commission.[231]

---

[225] See Sect. 4.2.1.3.1.1.3.2 with footnotes 215ff above.

[226] See also GC, T-91/07 (WWF-UK, 2008), 72; Dörr (2012), Art. 263, 70.

[227] See CJ, 355/08 P (WWF-UK, 2009), 44ff; GC, T-224/10 (ASBL, 2011), 29; T-381/11 (Eurofer, 2012), 37ff; Dörr (2012), Art. 263, 71 with further references. Different Saitzek (2008), 322.

[228] See for examples from the case law eg Jones/Sufrin (2011), 1134; Kerse/Khan (2012), 8-097; Ritter (2012), Anhang 1, 27.

[229] For cases in which the adverse effect of a remedy on third parties constitutes merely a reflex of the obligation created for the addressee see Sect. 3.2.2.2.3 with footnote 135 and Sect. 4.1.3.1 with footnotes 103ff above.

[230] CJ, C-441/07 P (Alrosa, 2010), 90. This passage of the judgment of the Court of Justice is construed in the literature as meaning that actions brought by affected third parties against a commitment decision are admissible: see Schweitzer (2012), 19 fn 97; De Smijter/Sinclair (2014), 2.144.

[231] Opinion of AG Kokott in C-441/07 P (Alrosa, 2009), 180.

4.2.2 *Scope of Review*

4.2.2.1 General Observations

The Commission's discretion in taking competition decisions and the corresponding restriction of the scope of judicial review are intensely debated. In a nutshell, the controversy focuses on the question whether the approach of the EU Courts to restrict their review in certain areas is compatible with the right to effective judicial protection laid down in Article 6(1) ECHR and Article 47 Charter.[232] A comprehensive presentation of the debate is beyond the scope of this work.[233] The following section must concentrate on some observations that have a bearing on the review of remedies. In this respect, it will deal with general considerations that apply irrespective of whether the remedy is unilaterally imposed on the basis of Article 7 or made binding upon proposition by the parties on the basis of Article 9. Particularities of the Article 9 procedure will be discussed below.

4.2.2.1.1 The Right to Effective Legal Protection Pursuant to Article 6(1) ECHR and Article 47 Charter

The right to effective judicial protection determines the minimum required intensity of judicial review. The right is laid down both in Article 6(1) ECHR and in Article 47 Charter. To date, the EU has not acceded to the ECHR. Different from the Charter, the Convention does therefore not yet produce direct effects for the EU institutions.[234] However, Article 6(3) TEU confirms that fundamental rights recognised by the ECHR constitute general principles of EU law. Moreover, Article 52(3) Charter requires rights contained in the Charter that correspond to rights guaranteed by the Convention to be construed as offering at least the same protection as those laid down by the Convention.[235] In order to determine the meaning and the scope of the rights laid down in the Charter, the EU Courts take not only the text of the Convention into account, but also the case law of the European Court of Human Rights.[236] As far as the right to effective judicial protection is concerned, the EU

[232]For the approach of the EU Courts with respect to decisions imposing a fine, see eg CJ, C-295/12 P (Telefonica, 2014), 36ff with further references.

[233]For the more recent discussion in the wake of the Menarini judgment of the European Court of Human Rights (n° 43509/08, 2011), see only Nazzini (2012); Schweitzer (2013); Andersson (2013); Waelbroeck/Frisch (2013); Forrester (2013); Wils (2014); Prek/Lefèvre (2016) and (2019); for the earlier discussion eg the contributions in Ehlermann/Marquis (2011) and Merola/Derenne (2012); Fritzsche (2008, 2010), Ackermann (2011), all with further references.

[234]See the opinion of the CJ [C-2/13 (Accession to ECHR, 2014)], in which the Court stated that the draft for the accession of the EU to the Convention was incompatible with the EU-Treaties.

[235]Pursuant to Article 52(3), 2nd sentence, Charter, Union law may offer more extensive protection than the Convention.

[236]See CJ, C-279/09 (DEB, 2010), 35; GC, T-286/09 (Intel, 2014), 1609.

Courts have confirmed that, in EU law, Article 47 Charter corresponds to Article 6 (1) ECHR.[237] Hence, although discrepancies between the European Court of Human Rights and the EU Courts in the interpretation of the right to effective legal protection can, in theory, not be excluded, they seem nevertheless rather unlikely. For the present purposes, a synchronism of the right to effective legal protection as laid down by the Charter and the Convention shall therefore be assumed.

4.2.2.1.1.1 General Remarks

Article 6(1), 1st sentence, ECHR provides that "[i]n the determination of his civil rights and obligations or of any criminal charge against him, everybody is entitled to a [. . .] hearing [. . .] by an independent and impartial tribunal [. . .]". In applying this right of access to court, the European Court of Human Rights follows a "sliding scale approach".[238] In order to determine the degree of judicial protection offered, the European Court of Human Rights distinguishes between cases that belong to the "hard core of criminal law", those that no longer belong to the hard core of criminal law, but still fall under the "criminal head" of Article 6(1),[239] and those that fall under the "civil head".[240] For the general distinction between the criminal and the civil head, the Court relies on three well-established criteria, commonly known as

---

[237]See CJ, C-386/10 P (Chalkor, 2011), 51; C-295/12 P (Telefonica, 2014), 40 with further references.

[238]Schweitzer (2013), 517 with further references; see also Jones/Sufrin (2014), 936.

Doubts regarding the sliding scale approach might result from ECtHR, n° 32181/04 (Sigma, 2011), 126f and 147ff. The ECtHR left the question open whether the sanction in question fell under the criminal head of Article 6(1), since the sanction fell in any event under the civil head of the provision [see also Kerse/Khan (2012), 8-090]. The ECtHR then simply confirmed that, in the case at hand, the degree of judicial review had been sufficient. However, if the ECtHR had considered that stricter standards of judicial review were required for cases that fall under the criminal head of Article 6(1), the Court could not have contented itself with such a statement. It would have had to decide whether the sanction in question fell under the criminal head and, in the affirmative, to assess whether the judicial review satisfied also the stricter standards of judicial review applicable under the criminal head. Taken literally, the Sigma judgment could therefore imply that there is only one uniform standard that is required for judicial review, regardless of whether the measure in question falls under the criminal or the civil head of Article 6 ECHR.

On the contrary, in the later case n° 36181/05 (Galina, 2013), 51ff, the ECtHR did not leave the question open whether the sanction in question fell under the civil or the criminal head of Article 6 (1). The Court found that the sanction fell under the civil head and held that the judicial review had been sufficient.

[239]For the distinction between "hard core" and other criminal law cases see in particular ECtHR, n° 73053/01 (Jussila, 2006), 43; n° 4837/06 (Segame, 2012), 59; n° 40820/12 (Marĉan, 2014), 37; n° 18640/10 (Grande Stevens, 2014), 120; at least implicitly, also n° 43509/08 (Menarini, 2011), 44 and 62. See also the opinion of AG Mengozzi in C-521/09 P (Elf Aquitaine, 2011), 30.

[240]The distinction between criminal law cases outside the "hard core" area and cases that fall under the civil head of Article 6(1) is particularly clear in ECtHR, n° 21539/07 (Steininger, 2012), 30ff, 45ff, 52ff; further cases, in which the scope of judicial review of an administrative decision was examined in regard of its compatibility with the civil head of Article 6(1) include n° 121235/86 (Zumtobel, 1993), 26ff; n° 33/1993/428/507 (Ortenberg, 1994), 25ff; n° 19178/91 (Bryan, 1995),

the Engel-criteria. These criteria are, first, the legal classification of the offence under national law, second, the nature of the offence and, third, the degree of severity of the penalty that the person concerned risks incurring.[241] The criteria to distinguish the "hard core" from the rest of criminal law are less clear. Traffic offences and tax surcharges are acknowledged examples of criminal cases that do not belong to the hard core of criminal law.[242] On a more abstract level, the judicature of the ECtHR does, however, not offer an unambiguous demarcation line. On the one hand, there is a strand of case law that seems to limit criminal law cases outside the hard-core area to "minor offences".[243] On the other hand, it results from the Jussila case that the hard core is not distinguished from the rest of criminal law solely by the seriousness of the offence, but also by what is traditionally considered as criminal law.[244] In any event, even cases in which the inflicted sanctions are severe may fall outside the area of hard core of criminal law.[245]

If a case belongs to the hard core of criminal law, the requirements of Article 6 (1) must be met already at first instance.[246] For all cases that fall outside the category of hard core criminal law, the Court has, however, accepted that decisions may initially be taken by a body that does not itself fulfil the requirements of Article 6(1), provided that such decisions are subject to subsequent control by a judicial body that has "full jurisdiction" and does provide the guarantees of Article 6(1).[247] The meaning of "full jurisdiction" varies, however, depending on whether a case falls under the civil head or the "soft"[248] criminal head of Article 6(1).

31ff; n° 48309/99 (Kilián, 2004), 27ff; n° 32181/04 (Sigma, 2011), 126f and 147ff; n° 36181/05 (Galina, 2013), 51ff; see also Meyer-Ladewig (2011), Art. 6, 33f.

[241]ECtHR, n° 21539/07 (Steininger, 2012), 34; Jones/Sufrin (2014), 936 with references.

[242]See Jones/Sufrin (2014), 936.

[243]ECtHR, n° 8544/79 (Öztürk, 1984), 56; n° 26138/95, (Lauko, 1998), 64; n° 27061/95, (Kadubec 1998), 57; n° 21539/07, (Steininger, 2012), 45.

[244]Section 4.2.2.1.1.1, footnote 239 above.

[245]See ECtHR n° 12547/86 (Bendenoun, 1994), 46; n° 34619/97 (Janosevic, 2002), 81; also Wils (2014), 8f.

[246]See ECtHR, n° 22107/93 (Findlay, 1997), 79, where the Court found that "serious charges classified as "criminal"" entitled a person to a first-instance tribunal which fully met the requirements of Article 6(1). In Jussila (Sect. 4.2.2.1.1.1, footnote 239 above), the Court stated that "in the criminal context, [. . .] generally there must be at first instance a tribunal which fully meets the requirements of Article 6" (40); at the same time, the Court confirmed that this did not apply for cases falling outside the area described as "hard core criminal law" (43). See also Schweitzer (2013), 517; Jones/Sufrin (2014), 936.

[247]For the civil head: ECtHR, (Zumtobel, 1993), 29; n° 33/1993/428/507 (Ortenberg, 1994), 31; n° 19178/91 (Bryan, 1995), 40; n° 48309/99 (Kilián, 2004), 27; n° 32181/04 (Sigma, 2011), 151. For the criminal head: see the references in Sect. 4.2.2.1.1.1, footnote 243 above and moreover n° 43509/08 (Menarini, 2011), 58; n° 18640/10 (Grande Stevens, 2014), 138.

[248]For the terminology see eg Forrester (2011a), 203f.

4.2.2.1.1.1.1 "Full Jurisdiction" Under the Civil Head of Article 6(1)

As far as cases falling under the civil head of Article 6(1) are concerned, the Court has expressly acknowledged that "full jurisdiction" only means "sufficient jurisdiction" or "sufficient review".[249] The Court justifies the latter conclusion with the fact that limited review of administrative decisions is common amongst the Member States of the Council of Europe and that "it is in the nature of review proceedings that the reviewing authority reviews the previous proceedings, rather than taking factual decisions".[250] In the view of the Court, "it is not the role of Article 6 of the Convention to give access to a level of jurisdiction which can substitute its opinion for that of the authorities".[251] This does, of course, not mean that there are no restrictions for the leeway that can be left to the administration. Rather, the Court assesses on a case-by-case basis[252] whether the judicial review was sufficient in a particular case. For that assessment, the Court takes in particular the following factors into consideration: The powers of the reviewing body in question; whether and to what extent the adoption of the challenged decision involved discretion or concerned a specialised subject matter that required expert knowledge; the procedural guarantees before the administrative body; the content of the dispute, including the desired and actual grounds of appeal.[253]

4.2.2.1.1.1.2 "Full Jurisdiction" Under the "Soft" Criminal Head of Article 6(1)

Whilst it results hence without ambiguity from the case law that Article 6(1) does not oppose a certain administrative discretion in cases that fall under the civil head of the provision, the legal situation is less obvious as regards the scope of review necessary for cases that fall under the soft criminal head. With respect to those cases, the Court does not—at last not expressly—apply the formula according to which the requirement of "full jurisdiction" merely means "sufficient review". Rather, the Court emphasises that the review must include "the power to quash in all respects, on questions of fact and law, the challenged decision".[254] Whether this categorically excludes all administrative discretion is, however, still unclear. On the one hand, the Court underlines that it follows different approaches regarding the required scope of judicial review, depending on whether a case falls under the civil or the criminal head of Article 6(1).[255] It can also be derived from the Court's case law that, under

[249] ECtHR, n° 42509/05 (Crompton, 2009), 71 and 79; n° 32181/04 (Sigma, 2011), 151; n° 36181/05 (Galina, 2013), 59; see also n° 21539/07 (Steininger, 2012), 49.

[250] ECtHR, n° 32181/04 (Sigma, 2011), 153.

[251] ECtHR, n° 32181/04 (Sigma, 2011), 153; n° 36181/05 (Galina, 2013), 59.

[252] ECtHR, n° 32181/04 (Sigma, 2011), 155; n° 36181/05 (Galina, 2013), 60.

[253] ECtHR, n° 32181/04 (Sigma, 2011), 154; n° 36181/05 (Galina, 2013), 59.

[254] ECtHR, n° 34619/97 (Janosevic, 2002), 81; n° 36985/97 (Vestbärga Taxi, 2002), 93; n° 47650/99 (Silvester's Horeca, 2004), 27; n° 70074/01 (Valico, 2006); n° 43509/08 (Menarini, 2011), 59; n° 21539/07 (Steininger, 2012), 45; n° 18640/10 (Grande Stevens, 2014), 139.

[255] See ECtHR, n° 21539/07 (Steininger, 2012), 52.

the criminal head, judicial review only meets the requisite standard, if it covers also the expediency and equity of the sanction and if the reviewing body can accord a complete or partial reduction.[256] On the other hand, in the Menarini judgment, the Court found that a standard of review that respected a certain administrative margin of discretion was still compatible with the requirements of the criminal head of Article 6(1).[257]

4.2.2.1.1.1.3 What Matters Is the Actual Exercise of "Full Jurisdiction"

Irrespective of whether there remains some room for administrative discretion even under the "soft" criminal head of Article 6(1), it must be underlined that, both under the civil and under the soft criminal head, the European Court of Human Rights analyses the requirement of "full jurisdiction" in a way that is "extremely flexible".[258] The flexibility in the Court's approach stems from the fact that the Court does not attribute much value to abstract statements by a reviewing body about whether its control is complete or restricted. Rather, with a strong focus on the circumstances of the particular case,[259] the Court examines how closely the reviewing body actually scrutinized a challenged decision.[260]

4.2.2.1.1.2 Applied to Competition Law Remedies

It shall not be discussed here, whether the Commission's competition decisions imposing fines fall outside the hard core of criminal law[261] and whether and under

---

[256]See ECtHR, n° 47650/99 (Silvester's Horeca, 2004), 28.

[257]See ECtHR, n° 43509/08 (Menarini, 2011): The judicial review of the decision imposing the fine was not confined to questions of law, but included a review of the facts. The review was only limited where the administration disposed of discretion. Where this was the case, the reviewing court was not allowed to substitute its own appreciation for that of the administration. The reviewing court could nevertheless assess whether the administration had made an appropriate use of its powers and check the logic and coherence of the decision (18, 21, 63). In particular, the reviewing court was allowed to examine whether "technical evaluations" were "reasonable, logic and coherent" (48, 64). Moreover, the reviewing court had the power to examine whether the fine was appropriate and could, where necessary, replace it (18, 48, 65).

Also Nehl (2012), 133f and 140, and Prek/Lefèvre (2016), 80f, interpret the Menarini judgment as not excluding all administrative discretion. See also Castillo de la Torre (2009), 573: "The language used by the ECtHR, both in civil and criminal cases, is that of 'sufficient examination' and does not suggest any need for the judge to substitute its own assessment for that of the authority".

[258]Opinion of AG Mengozzi (Mastercard, 2014), 121.

[259]See Sect. 4.2.2.1.1.1.1, footnote 252 above.

[260]See for the civil head: ECtHR, n° 32181/04 (Sigma, 2011), 156ff; for the criminal head: n° 43509/08 (Menarini, 2011), 63ff; also the opinion of AG Mengozzi (Mastercard, 2014), 122; Schweitzer (2013), 519; Wils (2014), 19.

[261]In her opinion in KME (C-272/09 P, 2011), 67, AG Sharpston suggested that competition decisions imposing fines should be considered as falling outside the hard core of criminal law. The case law of the ECtHR points in the same direction: In Jussila (Sect. 4.2.2.1.1.1, footnote 239 above), 43, the Court mentioned "competition law" as an area that did not belong to the hard

what conditions the judicial review of decisions imposing fines is still consistent with the requirements of Article 6(1) of the Convention, if a certain margin of discretion is granted to the administration. Different from fines, remedies that are based on Articles 7(1) and 9(1) Regulation 1/03 do in any event not pursue a punitive goal.[262] Assessed under the Engel criteria, they do not fall under the criminal head of Article 6(1) of the Convention, not even in its soft version. This conclusion is supported by the case law of the European Court of Human Rights.[263] In Neste, the Court found that powers of the Russian antimonopoly authorities comparable to those of the Commission under Article 7 Regulation 1/03[264] did not fall under the criminal head of Article 6(1) of the Convention. The Court considered that the powers in question, which ranged "from a simple warning to stop monopolistic activity to compulsory division of the company", belonged to a "regulatory field". The Court underlined that its conclusion applied also to "the confiscation of unlawfully gained profit" that was "intended as pecuniary compensation for damage rather than as a punishment to deter re-offending".[265] Hence, in so far as the judicial review of remedies based on Articles 7 and 9 Regulation 1/03 is concerned, the less strict standard of the civil head of Article 6(1) of the Convention applies. In France, the Cour de Cassation has confirmed that commitment procedures do not fall under the criminal head of Article 6(1) ECHR.[266]

---

core of criminal law. In Menarini (Sect. 4.2.2.1.1.1.2, footnote 257 above), 58, the Court confirmed that a competition law fine could at first instance be imposed by an administrative body. See also the opinion of AG Mengozzi in Elf Aquitaine (C-521/09 P, 2011), 30f. and 36. Ackermann (2011), 1409, argues that despite their increasing level, fines should not be subsumed under the hard core of criminal law because they have a narrower focus than traditional criminal sanctions. In his view, fines are "primarily designed to counteract economic incentives to engage in anticompetitive conduct by outweighing expected profits from such behaviour". For the opposing view see eg Forrester (2011a), 204, who emphasises an increased stigmatising effect that antitrust fines allegedly have when compared with tax penalties. Sceptical as regards the stigmatising effect of antitrust fines Castillo de la Torre (2009), 569.

[262]See Dalheimer (2005), Art. 7, 9; OECD (2006), 7, 18, 20ff; Saitzek (2008), 222; Lowe/Maier-Rigaud (2008), 600f; Koch (2008), 109; Sofianatos (2009), 191ff; Hellström/Maier-Rigaud/Bulst (2009), 44f and 50.

[263]See Sofianatos (2009), 410; Kipiani (2014), 172.

[264]The powers of the Russian authority examined by the ECtHR included: "prevention of activity which may violate antimonopoly laws; removal of consequences of violations of antimonopoly laws; restoration of the situation which existed before a violation of antimonopoly laws happened; compulsory division of a company. . .; amendment or rescission of contracts. . .; signing of contracts with business entities; payment to the State budget of proceeds gained as a result of a violation of antimonopoly laws; change or restricted use of a trade-mark; carrying out . . . measures aimed at prevention of discriminatory conditions; taking steps aimed at ensuring of competition. . ."; see ECtHR, n° 69042/01 (Neste, 2004), p. 5f.

[265]ECtHR, n° 69042/01 (Neste, 2004), p. 10; see also the opinion of AG Sharpston in C-272/09 P (KME, 2011), 65.

[266]Cass. com., n° 07-21.275 (Canal 9, 2008): The judgment did not concern the scope of judicial review, but the question whether commitment decisions must be adopted at first instance by a body that is fully independent in the sense of Article 6(1). The Cour de cassation denied this. For a

Certainly, voices in the literature have pointed out that remedies may be at least as burdensome for the concerned undertakings as a fine.[267] Also the Transatlantic Container Line judgment of the General Court contains a similar statement.[268] Nevertheless, under Article 6(1) of the Convention, even the strong intrusiveness of an administrative measure does not necessarily preclude all discretion. The European Court of Human Rights has, for instance, accepted an—albeit limited—discretion in cases that concerned the expropriation of land for road constructions,[269] the withdrawal of a license to operate a refuse tip,[270] the demolition of unlawfully erected buildings[271] and the removal from a list of persons qualified to act as liquidators of insolvent companies.[272] Transferred to competition law remedies this means that Article 6(1) does not exclude a certain degree of discretion, even where burdensome remedies such as an access obligation or the break up of a company are concerned.

4.2.2.1.2 The Current Practice of the EU Courts

4.2.2.1.2.1 General Remarks

The EU system of judicial review of competition decisions consists, on the one hand, of the legality review provided for by Article 263 TFEU, and, on the other hand, of the unlimited jurisdiction provided for by Article 261 TFEU in combination with Article 31 Regulation 1/03. The two kinds of judicial control have a different area of application and entail a different intensity of review. It is hence necessary to distinguish them. Both the legality review and the power of unlimited jurisdiction have, however, one important feature in common: Neither of them amounts to a review of the Court's own motion. With the exception of matters of public policy, the Court's assessment is from the outset limited to substantiated challenges, so-called "pleas in law", that must be raised by the applicant.[273] In order to trigger judicial control, the applicant has "to identify the impugned elements of the

---

detailed discussion see Sofianatos (2009), 410, and Kipiani (2014), 173, both with further references.

[267] Schweitzer (2013), 529; Jones/Sufrin (2014), 1044.

[268] The GC stated that an order to offer customers the possibility to either renegotiate or terminate contracts, which had been concluded in the context of the prohibited agreement, "could even amount to a penalty more serious than a fine" (see Sect. 4.1.1.1.2, footnote 16 above).

[269] See ECtHR, n° 121235/86 (Zumtobel, 1993), 31f; see also n° 21539/07 (Steininger, 2012), 50.

[270] See ECtHR, n° 16922/90 (Fischer, 1995), 34.

[271] See ECtHR, n° 19178/91 (Bryan, 1995), 44ff; see also n° 21539/07 (Steininger, 2012), 50.

[272] ECtHR, n° 36181/05 (Galina, 2013), 59ff.

[273] See generally 44(1)(c) and 48(2) of the Rules of Procedure of the General Court; von Danwitz (2008), 297f; Pohlmann (2011), 475f; Nehl (2012), 136; Schweitzer (2013), 497; Dervisopoulos (2014), 89. The EU Courts have repeatedly confirmed that the general rule applies also under the unlimited jurisdiction standard, see eg CJ, C-389/10 P (KME, 2011), 131; C-510/11 P (Kone, 2013), 32; GC, T-286/09 (Intel, 2014), 1643f.

contested decision, to formulate grounds of challenge in that regard and to adduce evidence – direct or circumstantial – to demonstrate that its objections are well founded".[274]

4.2.2.1.2.1.1 Legality Review

As a rule, the review of the legality of a contested decision comprises a full control of all legal and factual elements and of the application of the law to the facts to the extent that the applicant has challenged the decision.[275] However, in addition to the already mentioned fact that control is generally limited to an examination of substantiated pleas raised by the applicant, in particular three further aspects restrict the control of the EU Courts under the standard of legality review: First, as will be explained in more detail below, where the EU Courts find that the Commission has some sort of discretion, they take back the intensity of their review. Second, the legality of a contested decision must, in principle, be assessed on the basis of the elements of fact and of law existing at the time when the decision was adopted.[276] According to the case law, in particular complex assessments made by the Commission must be examined on the basis of the information available at the time when those assessments were made.[277] In Galp, the Court of Justice clarified the scope of this principle, holding that elements post-dating the contested decision needed to be taken into account where relevant to the review of the legality of the decision.[278] This judgement implies, in particular, that elements of proof, such as expert or witness testimonies, which post-date the decision, but relate to the period for which the Commission found an infringement, must be taken into account.[279] Third, pursuant to Article 264 TFEU, if they conclude that a contested decision is unlawful, the EU Courts may only declare it void, either partially[280] or in its entirety.

[274]CJ, C-389/10 P (KME, 2011), 132; C-510/11 P (Kone, 2013), 32; see also GC, T-352/09 (Novácke chemické, 2012), 117.

[275]See Schweitzer (2013), 504; see also GC, T-446/05 (Amann & Söhne, 2010), 131: "the question whether or not the conditions for the application of Article [101 TFEU] or Article [102 TFEU] are satisfied is, in principle, amenable to full review"; similarly also GC, T-271/03 (Deutsche Telekom, 2008), 185, and, with respect to Article 101(1) TFEU, T-28/03 (Holcim, 2005), 95; Fritzsche (2010), 393; Hofmann/Rowe/Türk (2012), 498f. For a different opinion see Cengiz (2011), 140: According to him, the entire legality review of a decision is limited in that the courts may not substitute their assessment for that of the Commission; similarly Nothdurft (2008), 288, who infers from Article 261 TFEU that full review is the exception and limited review the general rule.

[276]Eg T-322/01 (Roquette Frères, 2006), 325; T-23/09 (CNOP, 2010), 46; T-343/06 (Shell Petroleum, 2012), 104; see also Dörr (2012), Art. 263, 161; Dervisopoulos (2014), 106.

[277]CJ, C-449/98 P (IECC, 2001), 87; GC, T-349/03 (Corsica Ferries, 2005), 142.

[278]CJ, C-603/16 (Galp, 2016), 72. See also AG Bot, opinion in C-78/16 (Giovanni Pesce, 2016), 100ff, who points towards a more general tendency in the recent jurisprudence to allow, in certain specific circumstances, subsequent facts to be taken into consideration.

[279]See GC, T-582/15 (Silver Plastics, 2019), 38f.

[280]For the conditions of a partial annulment see eg CJ, C-441/11 P (Coppens, 2012), 37f and Dörr (2012), Art. 264, 5 with further references.

According to Article 266 TFEU, it is then for the institution concerned to take the measures needed to comply with the judgment. The EU Courts cannot, however, directly compel the institutions to issue a certain decision,[281] nor can they substitute their own decision for that of the Commission.[282]

4.2.2.1.2.1.2 Unlimited Jurisdiction

On the basis of Article 261 TFEU, Article 31 Regulation 1/03 vests the EU Courts with unlimited jurisdiction to review decisions whereby the Commission has fixed a fine or a periodic penalty payment. It is beyond doubt that the power of unlimited jurisdiction is broader than the power to review the legality of a decision. Nonetheless, the precise scope of the power of unlimited jurisdiction remains up to now vague. Pursuant to Article 31, 2nd sentence, Regulation 1/03, the EU Courts may cancel, reduce or increase the fine or the periodic penalty payment imposed. The Courts sometimes add that the power of unlimited jurisdiction enables them "to substitute their appraisal for the Commission's".[283] This is consistent with the wording of the German version of Article 261 TFEU, which leaves no doubt that the power of unlimited jurisdiction enlarges not only the power of the EU Courts to decide, but also their power to control.[284] At least in theory, there should therefore be no room for discretion under the unlimited jurisdiction standard at all.[285] However, as has frequently been pointed out, in practice the EU Courts concede the Commission discretion also in setting a fine and limit themselves to examining whether the Commission has not departed from the framework laid down in its Guidelines.[286] This approach may have its roots in an understanding according to which the power of unlimited jurisdiction is only triggered by the prior finding of an error in the Commission's decision.[287] According to such an understanding, where the Commission enjoys a margin of discretion in the context of the legality review, the power of unlimited jurisdiction would only enable the EU Courts to substitute their

---

[281]Eg T-120/10 (ClientEarth, 2011), 29 with further references; see also Dörr (2012), Art. 263, 27; Dervisopoulos (2014), 121.

[282]Jones/Sufrin (2014), 1045; see also Hofmann/Rowe/Türk (2012), 847.

[283]Eg CJ, C-386/10 P (Chalkor, 2011), 63; C-510/11 P (Kone, 2013), 23; GC, T-11/06 (Romana Tabacchi, 2011), 265; but see eg CJ, C-295/12 P (Telefonica, 2014), 44, where the Court of Justice did not repeat that statement.

[284]"Befugnis zu unbeschränkter Ermessensnachprüfung und zur Änderung oder Verhängung [von Zwangsmaßnahmen]"; see Dörr (2012), 196.

[285]See Ackermann (2011), 1412: "Starting from a natural understanding of Article 261 TFEU together with Article 31 Regulation 1/2003, one may be forgiven for thinking that the General Court regularly substitutes its own assessment of the fine under review for the Commission's assessment".

[286]See Ackermann (2011), 1412; Schweitzer (2011), 90 fn 52; Vesterdorf (2012), 140; Forrester (2011a), 194ff; Vilsmeier (2013), 58f; Jones/Sufrin (2014), 1040f.

[287]For a detailed account of the controversy whether the exercise of the power of unlimited jurisdiction requires the prior finding of an error in the Commission's decision see Nehl (2012), 143f with further references.

appraisal for the Commission's and subsequently cancel, reduce or increase the sanction once they have identified a defect of the decision under the manifest error standard.[288] Furthermore, the EU Courts seem not yet to have found a unanimous line regarding the question to what extent the power of unlimited jurisdiction allows them to take into account elements of fact and of law post-dating the adoption of a contested decision.[289] Be that as it may, confronted with a somewhat ambiguous wording of Article 261 TFEU and Article 31 Regulation 1/03, the Court of Justice has made it clear that the power of unlimited jurisdiction applies only to the part of a decision that imposes a fine or a periodic payment.[290]

---

[288]See the opinion of AG Warner in C-32/78 (BMW Belgium, 1979), p. 2493f: "[The power of unlimited jurisdiction] does not, however, in my opinion, mean that the Court should, in every case brought before it, substitute its own assessment of the appropriate fine for the Commission's. The Court should, in my opinion, alter the amount of a fine imposed by the Commission only if persuaded that the Commission has, in fixing the fine, made a material error of fact or of law".

See also GC, T-38/02 (Groupe Danone, 2005), 523f, where the GC exercised its unlimited jurisdiction only to correct a defect of the contested decision. The judgment was confirmed by CJ, C-3/06 P (Groupe Danone, 2007), 50ff.

See also CJ, C-328/05 P (SGL Carbon, 2007), 88, where the CJ held that the Commission enjoys a wide discretion in assessing the quality and usefulness of the cooperation provided by an undertaking in the context of a leniency application.

See also the GC's judgment in KME Germany (T-25/05, 2010), 97ff, where the GC assessed whether the Commission committed no error in determining the gravity of the fine by relying on the turnover of the concerned undertaking. The judgment was confirmed by CJ, C-389/10 P (KME, 2011), 58ff.

[289]See, on the one hand, GC, T-322/01 (Roquette Frères, 2006), 327: Within the GC's unlimited jurisdiction, the power to take into consideration additional information which was not mentioned in the contested decision must, in principle, be limited to taking into account information pre-dating the contested decision and which the Commission could have known at the time when it adopted that decision.

See, on the other hand, GC, T-11/06 (Romana Tabacchi, 2011), 282: The GC took into account that, after the adoption of the decision, the concerned undertaking was in a weak financial position. See also GC, T-343/06 (Shell Petroleum, 2012), 117: It is for the Court, in the exercise of its unlimited jurisdiction, to assess, on the date on which the Court adopts its decision, whether the applicants received a fine whose amount properly reflects the gravity of the infringement in question.

Generally on the problem see Castillo de la Torre (2009), 566f; Nehl (2012), 145f.

[290]See CJ, C-295/12 P (Telefonica, 2014), 42, 44 and in particular 45; see also Jones/Sufrin (2014), 1044.

In the literature, it is sometimes suggested that the General Court should exercise unlimited jurisdiction not only with respect to the level of the fine, but also with respect to the rest of a decision: eg Gerard (2010), 7ff; Forrester (2011b), 448f. The controversy can be associated with the divergent wording of Article 261 TFEU and Article 31 Regulation 1/03: While the former provision refers to the possibility of endowing the CJ with "unlimited jurisdiction *with regard to the penalties*", the latter mentions "unlimited jurisdiction to *review decisions* whereby the Commission has fixed a fine or periodic penalty payment".

4.2.2.1.2.1.3 In Particular: The Commission's Margin of Discretion Under the Standard of Legality Control

4.2.2.1.2.1.3.1 General Remarks

As already indicated above, at least in the context of the legality review of a decision, the EU Courts restrict their control wherever they recognize a margin of discretion on behalf of the Commission. The Courts do so in many areas that concern the enforcement of Articles 101 and 102 TFEU.[291] They have admitted margins of discretion during the investigative phase of the administrative procedure[292]; when the Commission assigns different priorities to the examination of complaints submitted to it[293]; where the Commission finds an infringement, for instance in the context of the market delimitation,[294] of the cost allocation necessary to carry out an AEC test,[295] of the assessment whether a restraint is ancillary[296] or of the application of Article 101(3) TFEU[297]; where the Commission imposes a remedy[298]; and finally also where the Commission imposes a fine, for instance in the context of determining the gravity of the infringement[299] or of assessing the quality and usefulness of the cooperation in the context of a leniency application.[300] The Court of Justice has made it clear that—at least under the standard of legality review—margins of discretion exist irrespective of whether the reviewed decision serves as the basis for imposing a fine.[301]

---

[291]For an overview including merger control see Schweitzer (2013), 506.

[292]CJ, 374/87 (Orkem, 1989), 15; GC, T-340/04 (France Télécom, 2007), 148; T-293/11 (Holcim, 2014), 110; see, in the context of merger control, also GC, T-145/06 (Omya, 2009), 32; M. Jaeger (2011), 301.

[293]See eg CJ, C-119/97 P (Ufex II, 1999), 87; GC, T-24/90 (Automec II, 1992), 80; T-60/05 (Ufex III, 2007), 65; T-427/08 (CEAHR, 2010), 65ff; T-119/09 (Protégé, 2012), 33ff; T-355/13 (EasyJet, 2015), 17ff; see also M. Jaeger (2011), 302.

[294]GC, T-65/96 (Kish Glass, 2000), 64ff; T-219/99 (British Airways, 2003), 107; T-111/08 (Mastercard, 2012), 169.

[295]GC, T-340/03 (France Telecom, 2007), 129ff; confirmed by CJ, C-202/07 P (France Telecom, 2009), 69ff.

[296]GC, T-112/99 (M6, 2001), 114; T-111/08 (Mastercard, 2012), 82.

[297]GC, T-168/01 (GlaxoSmithKline, 2006), 241; T-111/08 (Mastercard, 2012), 201.

[298]See GC, T-201/04 (Microsoft I, 2007), 379ff together with 151f, 208, 340 and 341; GC, T-170/06 (Alrosa, 2007), 110; CJ, C-441/07 P (Alrosa, 2009), 42.

[299]CJ, C-328/05 P (SGL Carbon, 2007), 43; GC, T-101/05 (BASF, 2007), 65; T-25/05 (KME, 2010), 99.

[300]CJ, C-328/05 P (SGL Carbon, 2007), 88; GC, T-141/08 (E.On, 2010), 287.

[301]CJ, C-295/12 P (Telefonica, 2014), 54 with further references.

It bears also mention that, at least up to now, the EU Courts seem to resist efforts[302] to categorise the Commission's discretion.[303] They do not make systematic terminological distinctions, but use terms such as "margin of discretion",[304] "margin of appreciation"[305] or "margin of assessment"[306] interchangeably.[307] Nor do they vary the intensity of review systematically in accordance with various potential rationales of restricted control, such as the structure of the norm in question, the respect for the EU's institutional balance, the political content of a decision or the superior expertise of the Commission.[308] In view of the fact that the various justifications for limited review are not mutually exclusive,[309] this is little surprising. The key term that is typically relied upon to justify the existence of a margin of discretion in competition law cases is "complex economic assessment".[310] However, in realty the term is merely a proxy: The EU Courts may refer to it as much out of respect for the EU's institutional balance as out of respect for the political content of a decision or the superior expertise of the Commission.[311]

---

[302]For a distinction between "political discretion" and "technical discretion" see the opinion of AG Léger, C-40/03 (Rica Foods, 2005), 45f; Dörr (2012), Art. 263, 187; Derenne (2012), 81ff.

For a distinction between a "margin of appreciation" and a "margin of discretion" see Bailey (2004), 1336f; Jones/Sufrin (2014), 1037 fn 674.

Craig (2012), 415ff, makes out a distinction in the modern case law between high and medium intensity review. He assigns risk regulation, competition and restrictive measures adopted in the context of the Common Foreign and Security Policy to the first category; the common policies in agriculture, fisheries and transport, state aids, and structural funds are assigned to the latter category.

For a distinction between, on the one hand, "discretion proper" or "power of appraisal", conferred on the administration by the Treaty or the legislature, and, on the other hand, "technical discretion" or "margin of appraisal" which merely results from judicial self-restraint in view of the complexity of the assessment carried out by the administration, see Prek/Lefèvre (2019), 339ff.

[303]See, in the context of competition law, Fritzsche (2008), 133: "Systematisierungsresistenz"; Pohlmann (2011), 476: "kein sachlich und systematisch stimmiges Konzept des Beurteilungsspielraums"; more generally, see Fritzsche (2010), 379; Dörr (2012), Art. 263, 187; Hofmann/Rowe/Türk (2012), 498f; Prek/Lefèvre (2019), 344.

[304]CJ, C-386/10 P (Chalkor, 2011), 54 and 62; C-295/12 P (Telefonica, 2014), 54 and 56.

[305]Eg GC, T-201/04 (Microsoft, 2007), 89; T-461/07 (Visa, 2011), 70.

[306]CJ, C-510/11 P (Kone, 2013), 53 and 56; GC, T-321/05 (AstraZeneca, 2010), 33; T-540/08 (Esso, 2014), 111.

[307]Schweitzer (2013), 492 fn 4; see also Dervisopoulos (2014), 117 with further references.

[308]For different rationales that may underlie a limitation of judicial review see Bailey (2004), 1333ff and (2012), 121ff; Fritzsche (2008), 120ff and (2010), 367ff; Derenne (2012), 78ff; Schweitzer (2013), 508; Vilsmeier (2013), 52f.

[309]Fritzsche (2008), 121.

[310]Eg CJ, 42/84 (Remia, 1985), 34; C-510/11 P (Kone, 2013), 28; GC, T-201/04 (Microsoft I, 2007), 87.

[311]For a critical discussion of the use of the term "complexity" in the context of discretion see Hofmann/Rowe/Türk (2012), 495f: They point out that the term is used as a proxy "for the requirement of undertaking a decision balancing up a combination of various factors, of evaluations and prognoses of future factual developments, and of interests and rights". In their view, this consideration as such does, however, not put a decision "beyond the intellectual reach of a court", since judges "are capable of [...] reconstructing complex situations". They consider that what lies

4.2.2.1.2.1.3.2 The Intensity of Limited Review in the Words of the EU Courts and Its Meaning

The fact that the EU Courts limit their review wherever they admit a margin of discretion does not mean that they refrain from a thorough control. In general, it can be stated that the restriction of control in regard of the substantive content of a particular aspect is compensated by an increase in the intensity of the review of the respect of procedural rules, in particular the obligation to state reasons.[312] The Courts assess "whether the relevant rules on procedure and on stating reasons have been complied with, whether the facts have been accurately stated and whether there has been a manifest error of assessment or a misuse of powers".[313] They "must, among other things, not only establish whether the evidence put forward is factually accurate, reliable and consistent, but must also determine whether that evidence contains all the relevant data that must be taken into consideration in appraising a complex situation and whether it is capable of substantiating the conclusions drawn from it".[314] They cannot, however, substitute their assessment for that of the Commission,[315] or, in other words, second-guess the Commission's conclusion.[316]

It has been shown convincingly that the EU Courts have over time increased the intensity of judicial review in areas in which they concede the Commission a margin of discretion[317] and that, at least today, even the reduced standard of review "entails an

behind the concept of complexity is actually the idea of institutional balance and separation of powers, namely "that policy decisions or decisions based on specific, non-legal expertise should be taken by the institutions which have both a competence and a mandate to do".

Similarly already Fritzsche (2008), 125 fn 763 and (2010), 379ff with further references. See also von Danwitz (2008), 300 and (2012), 376: "[. . .] the Court does not derive the restriction of its judicial review on proportionality requirements by a standard reference to its limited institutional legitimacy in comparison to the legislator. In fact it explicitly refers to the need for complex evaluations in order to justify its limited control".

The link between the use of the "complex economic appraisals" formula and the respect of the EU's institutional balance was also made by AG Tizzano in his opinion in C-12/03 P (Tetra Laval, 2005), 86 and 89.

312 See CJ, C-269/90 (TU München, 1991), 14: "[W]here the Community institutions have such a power of appraisal, respect for the rights guaranteed by the Community legal order in administrative procedures is of even more fundamental importance. Those guarantees include, in particular, the duty of the competent institution to examine carefully and impartially all the relevant aspects of the individual case, the right of the person concerned to make his views known and to have an adequately reasoned decision. Only in this way can the Court verify whether the factual and legal elements upon which the exercise of the power of appraisal depends were present." See also Fritzsche (2010), 378; Nehl (2012), 139.

313 Eg GC, T-201/04 (Microsoft I, 2007), 87; T-111/08 (Mastercard, 2012), 82.

314 Eg CJ, C-295/12 P (Telefonica, 2014), 54; GC, T-201/04 (Microsoft I, 2007), 89.

315 CJ, C-510/11 P (Kone, 2013), 26; critically with a view to the infliction of fines Wils (2014), 14f and in particular fn 71.

316 Bailey (2004), 1327; Schweitzer (2011), 100, and (2013), 495.

317 Fritzsche (2010), 377; Craig/De Búrca (2011), 552; Craig (2012), 416 and 420; Bailey (2012), 117; Lübking/von Koppenfels (2012), 83; Schweitzer (2013), 510f, who mentions that the

intensive strict degree of judicial scrutiny".[318] Along these lines, the Court of Justice has repeatedly underlined that the EU judicature cannot use the Commission's margin of discretion as a basis for dispensing with the conduct of an in-depth review of the law and of the facts.[319] Against the backdrop of the high intensity of the review actually carried out under the guise of the "margin of discretion"-doctrine, the EU Court's adherence to the latter has been criticised as misleading.[320] Several commentators have called for the abolition of the doctrine or at least for a clarification of its meaning.[321]

---

instauration of the General Court in 1989 and the decisions in Tetra Laval, Airtours and Schneider are considered as turning points.

[318]Geradin/Petit (2012), 53; see also eg Nothdurft (2008), 289: "bemerkenswerte Erhöhung der Kontrolldichte [...], auch wenn diese sich in den Obersätzen der Entscheidungen nur wenig niedergeschlagen hat"; Koch (2008), 111: "gewisse Tendenz [...], Kommissionsentscheidungen vollumfänglich sowohl in rechtlicher wie auch in tatsächlicher Hinsicht zu überprüfen"; Schroeder (2011), 281: "de facto standard of full control"; M. Jaeger (2011), 300ff: "the relevant case law reveals the willingness to apply an intense – though marginal – review when confronted with complex economic assessments"; Ackermann (2011), 1411: "the margin of appreciation doctrine has not prevented the General Court from looking into any economic or technical detail of a case that appeared remotely promising as a basis for a successful ground of appeal"; Pohlmann (2011), 474f; Whish/Bailey (2012), 292f: "the General Court has been prepared to exercise its power of review of the substance of Commission decisions in a comprehensive and exacting manner"; Schweitzer (2013), 522: "exacting and detailed judicial review of all legal and factual pleas raised"; Wils (2014), 15: "I do not have the impression that the General Court, even in those cases [...] where it stated that its review was limited to manifest errors, in fact abstained from exercising a full review in respect of all the pleas raised by the applicant against the Commission's decision".

For the opposing view, which, in my view, is not persuasive, see eg Gerard (2010), 5: "growing reliance on [a] deferential standard [;] the intensity of the judicial review [...] is perceived to have grown increasingly limited"; idem, (2013), 11: "[...] growing perception of the limits of the EU judicial review system, notably as it submits complex economic and technical appraisals inherent in modern substantive antitrust assessments, to a so-called "manifest error" standard, i.e., to limited review"; Forrester (2011a), 191ff: "seems clear that the Courts apply a more deferential level of review today than was the case in the first 30 years of the history of the European Community"; Waelbroeck/Frisch (2013), 670: "Il n'en demeure pas moins, en pratique, extrêmement exceptionnel que le juge de l'Union se livre à une analyse aussi minutieuse des décisions rendues par la Commission en droit de la concurrence"; Dunne (2014), 425: "significant margin of discretion granted to the Commission in respect of its economic assessments".

[319]CJ, C-386/10 P (Chalkor, 2011), 62; C-295/12 P (Telefonica, 2014), 56.

[320]See Craig (2012), 436: "The repeated articulation of manifest error conceals more than it reveals"; Castillo de la Torre (2009), 464.

[321]See Schweitzer (2011), 140: "It may therefore help the clarity and coherence of judicial review in EU competition cases [...] to abandon the [margin of appreciation] doctrine"; Schweitzer (2013): "the margin of appreciation rhetoric [has] become outdated and misleading [...] A clarification of the rationale, precise meaning and limits of this doctrine is highly desirable" (493); "[t]he ECJ should look for an opportunity to clarify the "margin of discretion" doctrine and language" (538); Ackermann (2011), 1411: "much would be won if the Court stopped paying lip-service to the old "complex appraisals" formula and searched for a more adequate description of what it actually does"; M. Jaeger (2011), 309: "A clear determination of the limits of the margin of appreciation doctrine [and] the type of situations where the judge applies a less intensive standard of review would probably be welcome"; Wils (2014): "It would therefore be preferable for the Courts to no

Although these suggestions cannot be discussed here in the depth they would deserve, some brief observations shall be made. It is true that, in competition cases, the latitude that is left to the Commission in areas where the Courts recognize the existence of discretion, is very restricted. Ultimately, it probably boils down to a preference for the Commission's choice where several equally valid options exist and where the Commission has reached its conclusion in a lawful way.[322] Whether the vocabulary of "discretion" and "manifest error" captures the high intensity of the review actually carried out in an adequate manner may of course be debated.[323] The formula according to which the EU Courts cannot substitute their assessment for that of the Commission[324] expresses the same idea. In any event, it is submitted that there is a fundamental difference between, on the one hand, a review by means of which the reviewing body substitutes its choice among several equally valid options for the choice of the decision taker at first instance and, on the other hand, a review that respects the initial choice.[325] In the former situation, the reviewing body takes a "de novo" decision. In the latter, the reviewing body merely controls whether the choice of the decision taker at first instance is consistent with a higher-ranking standard that can be either lax or strict.[326] This distinction is precisely the root of the legal idea of "discretion" and of the differentiation between "comprehensive" and "limited"

---

longer use the language of "manifest error", "discretion", "margin of appreciation", "complex economic assessments" and the like when reviewing decisions imposing fines, so as to avoid any confusion" (16); "potentially misleading general statements should be avoided" (19, 23).

[322]See Legal (2006), 115; Fritzsche (2008), 189f; Nothdurft (2008), 289; Ratliff (2011), 461; Schweitzer (2013), 512 and 538.

[323]See Castillo de la Torre (2009), 564f; Bailey (2012), 125.

[324]See Sect. 4.2.2.1.2.1.3.2, footnote 315 above.

[325]See, with regard to EU law in general, Craig (2012), 405ff and 408, who distinguishes between the Courts' general approach to "substitute judgment" and the qualification of the general approach in areas of discretion, where "review is cast in terms of manifest error rather than correctness"; idem, 433ff: "It is important that review does not collapse into substitution of judgment [. . .] It is however generally accepted that courts should not when reviewing legality substitute judgment about the relevant factual matter for that of the initial fact-finder".

But see Hofmann/Rowe/Türk (2012), 492, who seem to relativise the importance of the distinction. In their view, neither "totally bound" nor "totally free" administrative decision-making exists in reality. Rather, the two "ideas" constitute the respective ends of a spectrum, between which lie "various shades of more or less constrained decision making competence".

[326]In the UK, a comparable distinction seems to be expressed in the dichotomy between "judicial review" and "appeal on the merits": Under the former standard, a decision can be challenged only on limited grounds, in particular illegality, irrationality and procedural impropriety; under the latter standard, the appeal body may consider all aspects of the case and find that the decision was wrong, even where the decision was made in accordance with the law and where there was no irrationality or procedural impropriety. See the 2013 report by the UK Government, Streamlining Regulatory and Competition Appeals. Consultation on Options for Reform, available online, 2.17ff; judgment of the CAT [2014] CAT 16 (Skyscanner), 42: "[. . .] commitment decisions are subject under the Act to judicial review whilst infringement decisions are subject to full merits appeal". On the distinction between "judicial review" and "appeal on the merits" see also Barling (2014), 384f, who emphasises, however, that "a merits appeal [. . .] does not connote a full de novo re-hearing of the decision under appeal, in the manner of the German system".

review.[327] Even if the EU judicature has reached an intensity of review of "complex economic assessments" that comes very close to comprehensive review, it nevertheless still respects that distinction.[328] That the Courts subject the restriction of the control of discretion to fastidious limitations does not make their review comprehensive in the sense that it would amount to a full substitution of judgment.[329] Where they recognize a margin of discretion, the EU Courts do not take a de novo

[327]See Galligan (1990), 8: "According to its etymological origins, the idea of discretion is judgment, in particular good judgment. In its modern legal usage, however, discretion has come to connote, perhaps unfortunately, rather autonomy of judgment and decision. To have discretion, is, then, in its broadest sense, to have a sphere of autonomy within which one's decisions are in some degree a matter of personal judgment and assessment."

Engisch (2010), 207f: "Ermessen wird also von Recht und Gesetz dort eingeräumt, wo die letzte Entscheidung über das im konkreten Fall Richtige (Gerechte, Zweckmäßige, Angemessene) der individuellen Überzeugung (insbesondere: Wertung) der zur Einzelentscheidung Berufenen (eventuell durch Abstimmung innerhalb eines Gremiums sich "artikulierenden") Persönlichkeiten anvertraut und überantwortet wird [. . .]".

Fritzsche (2010), 386, defines discretion as "the competence of an institution to decide a certain question with highest authority". He emphasises that two conditions must be fulfilled for discretion to exist: Freedom of the decision maker and the recognition of that freedom by the courts (see 361f).

[328]See Fritzsche (2010), 399: "[T]he courts [. . .] limit their review to finding errors in the reasons given by the Commission. The more broadly the concept of error is interpreted in this context, the less the degree of discretion". Moreover M. Jaeger (Sect. 4.2.2.1.2.1.3.2, footnote 318 above), who insists that the standard of review in competition cases is "intense – though marginal"; Pohlmann (2011), 476 and 486, who recognises that questions of extent and degree that are not eligible for a precise evaluation ("Maß- und Gradfragen, die sich einer präzisen Bewertung entziehen") are not reviewed; Nehl (2012), 140: "nur strengere Anforderungen an die Verfahrens-, Tatsachen-, Beweis- und Plausibilitätsüberprüfung [. . .], die einer solchen Vollkontrolle zwar im Einzelfall recht nahe kommen können, aber keine vollständige Substitution der Ausübung des Verwaltungsermessens zum Gegenstand haben"; Kerse/Khan (2012), 8-093: "Although the [KME and Chalkor] judgments arguably mark a change of tone by the Court, they do not go further than confirming that the dictum in Tetra Laval applies to cartel cases as much as it applies to merger cases"; Schweitzer (2013), 511f and 538, who recognises that the EU Courts do not substitute their assessment for that of the Commission.

But see Wils (2014), 15f, who is of the opinion that the EU Courts actually engage in "full review" when reviewing decisions imposing fines. Wils seems to be of the opinion that, in the context of fining decisions, statements according to which the Courts do not substitute their assessment for that of the Commission's do not reflect the reality of the intensity of review.

[329]Craig (2012), 435, locates the modern margin of discretion doctrine close to comprehensive review implying substitution of judgment, because the General Court must not only establish whether the evidence put forward is factually accurate, reliable and consistent, but also determine whether it contains all the relevant data into consideration and whether it is capable of substantiating the conclusions drawn from it. In principle, Craig rightly argues that the elements of this test require themselves "complex findings [. . .] requiring a greater degree of evaluative judgment". It should be emphasised, however, that the mere fact that the EU Courts substitute judgment in respect of the said elements does not mean that they fully substitute their assessment for that of the Commission. In particular, the Courts merely ask whether the evidence in question "is capable" of substantiating the conclusions drawn from it. If taken seriously, this means that the Courts do not substitute judgment in respect of other conclusions that could equally be inferred from the evidence. In so far as Craig emphasises the use of the term "*establish*", it is noteworthy that the French version uses "vérifier" and not "établir".

decision.[330] The General Court will certainly examine all substantiated arguments put forward by an applicant. However, as long as the Commission's reasoning is at least equally plausible, so that no defect of the decision can be established, the Court will not overturn the decision, even if, as a first instance decider, it might have been of a different opinion.[331] Against this backdrop, it is submitted that, in spite of the high intensity of the review actually carried out, the margin of appreciation doctrine employed by the Courts does not constitute a mere "rhetoric"[332] or "lip service",[333] but still has a meaningful content.[334] It serves to distinguish the exceptional case of respect for the Commission's choice of one among several equally valid options from the general rule of substitution of judgment.

In the present context, it shall not be analysed any further whether it is really necessary and possible to define the content of the margin of discretion doctrine and in particular its areas of application and the existing limits to limited judicial review in a more precise manner than in the current practice of the EU Courts. In any event, it is submitted that a complete abolition of the margin of discretion doctrine in the text of the judgments would necessitate an important substantive shift to a truly comprehensive review implying substitution of judgment, i.e. "de novo decisions", also in matters of "complex economic appraisals".[335] Unless such a shift is really wanted, at least some variant of the margin of discretion formula should be maintained.

[330]Critically in that regard eg Waelbroeck/Frisch (2013), 670 and 674.

[331]In the words of AG Kokott: "If the factual and evidential position reasonably allows different assessments, there can be no legal objection if the Commission adopts one of them, even if it is not the one which the Court considers to be preferable. A manifest error of assessment exists only where the conclusions drawn by the Commission are no longer justifiable in the light of the factual and evidential position, that is to say if no reasonable basis can be discerned" (opinion in C-441/07 P [Alrosa, 2009], 84).

[332]But see Schweitzer (2013), 493 and 511; similarly already Nothdurft (2008), 289: "der Beurteilungsspielraum der Kommission im gesamten Gemeinschaftskartellrecht [ist] letztlich nur noch eine Formel [...], die als Reverenz gegeüber dem Primärrecht in die Obersätze der Entscheidungen aufgenommen wird, ohne allerdings den Prüfungsumfang des Gerichts faktisch merklich zu beeinflussen".

[333]But see Ackermann (2011), 1411; more carefully Fritzsche (2010), 399.

[334]See also Wahl (2011), 294: "[T]he limited review standard, after the Tetra Laval case, is brought somewhat closer to the comprehensive review standard without thereby being equivalent to it. In fact the two tests can never be similar since the conclusions to be proven under the limited review, like the choice of enforcement policy or predictions concerning future competitive pressure, may never be proven to the standard applicable under a comprehensive review, because there is in fact no single verifiable correct answer".

[335]But see Wils (Sect. 4.2.2.1.2.1.3.2, footnote 328 above). If his point of view were to be followed, at least in decisions imposing fines, no substantive shift would be necessary, since the EU Courts do allegedly already engage in full review and substitute their assessment for that of the Commission.

4.2.2.1.2.2 Applied to Remedies

As far as the judicial review of remedies is concerned, several consequences can be inferred from the general description presented above.

4.2.2.1.2.2.1 Only Review of Legality

Since the power of unlimited jurisdiction applies only to the part of a decision that relates to the level of the fine,[336] the judicial control of any remedy remains subject to the limitations of legality review.[337] This conclusion applies in the context of an Article 7 decision that imposes remedies and a fine simultaneously and all the more where no fine is imposed at all.

4.2.2.1.2.2.2 No Power to Reform a Remedy

Given that the review of remedies is a legality review, the EU Courts have only the power to annul a remedy, where appropriate only partially. They cannot reform the remedy.[338] It is noteworthy, however, that instead of annulling a remedy, the EU Courts sometimes interpret a remedy restrictively.[339]

4.2.2.1.2.2.3 Facts Posterior to the Adoption of the Decision Cannot Be Taken into Account

Furthermore, the nature of legality review entails the consequence that facts post-dating the adoption of a remedy cannot be taken into account.[340] For instance, in Microsoft I, the company argued that the lack of success of the unbundling remedy[341] showed the deficiency of the separate products test applied by the Commission. The General Court rejected the argument, ruling that the decision had to be assessed on the basis of the matters of fact and law existing at the time of its adoption.[342] This calls for some brief remarks.

---

[336] See Sect. 4.2.2.1.2.1.2 with footnote 290 above.

[337] See Sect. 4.2.2.1.2.1.1 with footnotes 275ff above; also Koch (2008), 109; Hauser (2009), 245; Brenner (2010), 1336.

[338] See Sect. 4.2.2.1.2.1.1 with footnotes 280ff above; also Koch (2008), 109; Hauser (2009), 245.

[339] See Sect. 3.3.1.6.1.1.2.3 with footnote 467 above and Sect. 5.2.1.1.2.1 with footnotes 303ff below.

[340] See Sect. 4.2.2.1.2.1.1, footnote 276 above; also Hauser (2009), 218. For a contrary opinion see Saitzek (2008), 297, who argues with respect to Article 9 commitments that, due to their prognostic character, the relevant time is the oral hearing in court.

[341] See Sect. 3.3.1.7 with footnotes 559ff above.

[342] See GC, T-201/04 (Microsoft I, 2007), 943; also Larouche (2009), 956; Jones/Sufrin (2014), 505 fn 596.

First, it must be underlined that the General Court did not examine Microsoft's argument in the context of the pleas in law pointed at the remedy, but in the context of the pleas in law aiming at the finding of an infringement. In theory, it would be possible to draw a distinction between these two situations, because—different from a remedy—the finding of an infringement relates only to the past, but does not create permanent obligations for the concerned undertaking.[343] However, the EU judicature decides also actions that aim at the annulment of acts that produce permanent effects on the basis of the circumstances that exist at the time of the adoption of the decision.[344] Had Microsoft relied on the retrospective lack of success of the remedy in the context of its plea pointed at the remedy, the Court would therefore have reached the same conclusion. This would also have been consistent with further case law according to which the legality of a measure "cannot depend on retrospective considerations of its efficacy".[345] Finally, as explained above, also the part of the Microsoft I judgment that deals with the monitoring trustee makes it unmistakeably clear that the Court examines the lawfulness of a remedy on the basis of the matters of fact and law existing at the time of its adoption.[346]

Second, it should be noted that, where the future effects of an act cannot be accurately foreseen at the time of its adoption, the EU Courts nonetheless control whether the act was manifestly incorrect in the light of the information available at that time.[347] As regards the unbundling remedy in Microsoft I, Economides and Lianos have claimed that the lack of success was "almost mathematically certain".[348] Be that as it may, it is in any event clear that if Microsoft had wanted to challenge the remedy for lack of its success, the company would have needed to show that the Commission carried out a flawed prognosis in that regard at the time the remedy was adopted.

Third, it must be pointed out that in cases of a change of circumstances after the remedy has been adopted, the concerned undertaking first has to approach the Commission and request a revocation or modification. The full or partial denial of such a request then constitutes a new decision that is itself amenable to judicial review.

---

[343]Such a distinction exists, for instance, in German administrative law: As a rule, the success for an action of annulment pursuant to Article 113 VwGO depends on the circumstances that existed at the time of the adoption of the contested decision. However, if the contested act produces permanent effects ("Dauerverwaltungsakt"), it must, in certain situations, be assessed on the basis of the circumstances that exist at the time of the oral hearing of the appeal. The details are controversial, see eg Gerhardt (1997), Art. 113, 21 fn 109 with references.

[344]See, for instance, regarding restrictive measures adopted in the context of the Common Foreign and Security Policy, GC, T-392/11 (Iran Transfo, 2013), 48.

[345]CJ, C-449/98 P (IECC, 2001), 87; GC, T-349/03 (Corsica Ferries, 2005), 143.

[346]See Sect. 3.5.3.2.2.1.2 with footnote 1348 above.

[347]See, in the context of the adoption of a legislative act, CJ, C-375/96 (Zaninotto, 1998), 66.

[348]Economides/Lianos (2010), 386.

4.2.2.1.2.2.4 The Commission's Margin of Discretion

Since the power of unlimited jurisdiction does not cover remedies,[349] any potential increase of the intensity of review that it may entail in regard of the amount of a fine is from the outset not applicable to the review of remedies. Rather, the ordinary standards of legality control apply. This means that, to the extent that the EU Courts recognize a margin of discretion, their control is limited. The necessity of a certain restriction when it comes to the judicial review of remedies is broadly acknowledged. It is accepted even by commentators who plead in general for a high intensity of judicial review, even for decisions that do not impose fines.[350]

4.2.2.1.2.2.4.1 A Particular Justification of Discretion: The Prospective Nature of Remedies

It has already been pointed out that several rationales can justify why the EU Courts concede discretion to the Commission, that these justifications are not necessarily mutually exclusive and that the key term "complex economic assessments" typically employed by the Courts serves merely as a proxy for these justifications.[351] As far as the Commission's discretion regarding remedies is concerned, it is worthwhile to point to one particular justification besides the already mentioned structure of a norm[352] and the respect for the EU's institutional balance, the political content of a decision or the superior expertise of the Commission: The prospective nature of remedies.

In the context of merger control, the EU Courts frequently justify the discretion that they concede to the Commission inter alia as regards the evaluation of remedies[353] with the prospective nature of the required assessment.[354] In Alrosa, the General Court argued that this reasoning was not transferable to remedies adopted on

---

[349]Section 4.2.2.1.2.1.2 with footnote 290 and Sect. 4.2.2.1.2.2.1 with footnotes 336f above.

[350]See Schweitzer (2013), 530 and 537.

[351]See Sect. 4.2.2.1.2.1.3.1 with footnotes 308ff above.

[352]Article 7(1) stipulates that the Commission "may" require the undertakings concerned to bring an infringement to an end and that the Commission "may" impose on them any behavioural or structural remedies which are proportionate to the infringement committed. Article 9(1) stipulates that the Commission "may" make proposed commitments binding. The Commission's discretion in adopting remedies follows hence already from the structure of the legal bases.

[353]CJ, C-202/06 P (Cementbouw, 2007), 53; opinion of AG Kokott in Cementbouw, 67; GC, T-119/02 (Royal Philips, 2003), 78; T-158/00 (ARD, 2003), 328.

[354]See GC, T-102/96 (Gencor, 1999), 163; T-464/04 (Impala, 2006), 250; T-79/12 (Cisco Systems, 2013), 63; see also GC, T-342/07 (Ryanair, 2010), 27 and 29; Hennig (2010a), 372.

But see also CJ, C-12/03 P (Tetra Laval, 2005), 39 and 42, where the Court emphasised that a prospective analysis nevertheless required great care and that there was "all the more" reason to apply the strict Tetra Laval formula for limited review as far as prospective assessments were concerned. Schweitzer (2013), 533, infers from the Tetra Laval case that "the Courts of the Union have explicitly rejected the prognostic character of merger decisions as a justification for judicial deference". In my view, this interpretation overstretches the actual content of the judgment. In any event, the post Tetra Laval case law of the General Court cited above confirms that at least the

the basis of Article 7 and 9 Regulation 1/03, because the latter concerned "existing practices". Although in the view of the General Court the latter conclusion did not generally exclude the existence of complex economic assessments, it nevertheless meant that, in the absence of such assessments, judicial review could not be limited to manifest errors.[355] During the procedure, the Commission had stated that the identification of alternative solutions to the commitments that were made binding would have required a complex economic assessment which Article 9 was intended to avoid. The General Court inferred from this statement that the Commission had carried out no complex economic assessment. The Court therefore applied a standard of comprehensive review.[356] On appeal, the Court of Justice stated in rather apodictic terms that the appropriate standard of review for a remedy adopted on the basis on Article 9 was the manifest error test. The Court of Justice did not explicitly deal with the question why it considered that this restriction of judicial control was justified.[357]

The opinion of AG Kokott, who also disagreed with the General Court, is more instructive. Suggesting that under the Article 9 procedure the Commission was not obliged to seek any alternatives to the proposed commitments of its own motion at all,[358] the AG rejected the General Court's finding that the Commission had abstained from a complex economic analysis.[359] The AG argued that there was no fundamental difference between remedies adopted on the basis of Article 9 Regulation 1/03 and those adopted under the Merger Regulation. In her view, in both cases the Commission must carry out a "futureoriented prospective economic analysis of the expected effects of commitments on market activities".[360] According to the AG:

> The crucial factor – which the [General Court] fails to recognise – is that before any decision under Article 9 of Regulation No 1/2003 is adopted the Commission must carry out an assessment of the market situation in which the commitments offered are embedded. It must examine what effects those commitments will have on future market activities and whether the alternatives known to it are equally appropriate for addressing the competition problem identified. This alone requires an appraisal of complex economic matters.[361]

In Morningstar, the General Court endorsed the approach of AG Kokott and justified the Commission's discretion in assessing the adequacy of commitments explicitly with the forward-looking character of the analysis that the Commission

---

General Court still uses the prospective character of merger control as a justification for the limitation of its review.

[355]GC, T-170/06 (Alrosa, 2007), 110.

[356]GC, T-170/06 (Alrosa, 2007), 125.

[357]CJ, C-441/07 P (Alrosa, 2009), 42. In my view, it can, however, be inferred from paragraph 67 of the judgment that the Court considered that the Commission had engaged in complex economic appraisals.

[358]Opinion in C-441/07 P (Alrosa, 2009), 56 and 73.

[359]Opinion in C-441/07 P (Alrosa, 2009), 73.

[360]Opinion in C-441/07 P (Alrosa, 2009), 71.

[361]Opinion in C-441/07 P (Alrosa, 2009), 74.

must undertake.[362] This logic is transferable to remedies adopted on the basis of Article 7 Regulation 1/03. Also the latter require a prospective analysis of their effects.[363] The reasoning of AG Kokott applies all the more, if one takes into account that in the context of Article 7 Regulation 1/03 the Commission must of its own motion identify less burdensome alternatives to a potential remedy and evaluate whether these are equally appropriate for addressing the found infringement.

Overall, the approach to justify the restriction of judicial review in regard of remedies with the latter's prospective nature must, in principle and without prejudice to other explanations, be approved of.[364] Different from a mere finding of an infringement for the past, most remedies are forward looking in that they terminate anticompetitive conduct for the future. The same conclusion applies all the more for remedies that aim at preventing imminent conduct. Also the assessment of whether it is sufficient to terminate only the anticompetitive conduct as such or whether it is necessary to address also its causes[365] necessitates a prognosis of the future conduct of the concerned undertaking. The prospective nature is in principle even inherent to remedies that aim at eliminating the subsisting effects of past anticompetitive conduct, albeit in a slightly attenuated form. In fact, as explained above,[366] while the existence of subsisting anticompetitive effects can be evaluated from an ex post perspective, the assessment of whether the remedy in question will adequately remove those effects, but go no further, will often depend on prognostic elements.[367] An exception applies only in respect of the termination of follow on contracts and of orders regarding the disgorgement or restitution of illicit profits. The fact that the

[362]GC, T-76/14 (Morningstar, 2016), 41.

[363]Hauser (2009), 218, states explicitly that the Commission's margin of discretion covers the "prognosis" that is necessary to assess the effectiveness of an Article 7 remedy; similarly Koch (2008), 112; Krings (2012), 218 and 222; see also Klees (2010), 694; Podszun (2012), 57f; Lianos (2013), 415, who recognise that Article 7 remedies may contain prospective elements. For a criticism of the view of AG Kokott see Klees (2011), 20: Along the lines of the Alrosa judgment of the General Court, he is of the opinion that neither under Article 7 nor under Article 9 do remedies necessarily have a prognostic character. According to Klees, it must always be assessed according to the circumstances of the case whether the Commission actually carried out complex economic assessments.

[364]That the prognostic character of remedies justifies a restriction of their judicial review is broadly acknowledged: See with respect to Article 7: Koch (2008), 112; Hauser (2009), 218; Krings (2012), 218 and 222. With respect to Article 9: Saitzek (2008), 297 and 323; Hennig (2010a), 372ff and (2010b), 452; Messina/Ho (2011), 746. But see also Jenny (2015), 761, who doubts that "commitment decisions always involve complex economic or technical analysis", but fails to take the prospective nature of remedies into account.

[365]For the discussion of remedies that eliminate the causes of anticompetitive conduct see Sect. 3.4.1.2.1.2 with footnotes 846ff above.

[366]See Sect. 3.3.4.1.1.3.2, after footnote 633 above.

[367]The following simple example may illustrate this: To what extent a refusal to deal abuse has increased the market share of the dominant undertaking on the downstream market can be evaluated ex post. However, the assessment whether an order to supply at a certain level will allow the competitor to eliminate the anticompetitive effects depends on prognostic elements.

latter do not have a prospective nature does, however, not preclude that a margin of discretion may be justified in their respect for a different reason.

4.2.2.1.2.2.4.2 The Test Applied

To the extent that the EU Courts admit a margin of discretion in regard of a remedy, the test is the ordinary one for limited review[368]: Although the Courts may not substitute their assessment for that of the Commission, they must in particular establish whether the evidence put forward is factually accurate, reliable and consistent, whether it contains all the relevant data and whether it is capable of substantiating the conclusions drawn from it.[369] As explained above, that test does not amount to a truly comprehensive control, because it preserves some room in which the Courts do not substitute their judgment for that of the Commission. Nonetheless, the test leads to a very intense control. The review carried out by the General Court in its two judgments regarding the interoperability remedy in the Microsoft case can serve as an example.

First, in its judgment regarding the 2004 decision, the General Court expressly limited its review with respect to the Commission's assessment of how much interoperability information Microsoft had to disclose in order to allow its competitors to remain "viably" on the market.[370] The Court saw in particular no manifest error in the Commission's assessment that, in order to allow for viable competition, Microsoft was required to disclose information that ensured interoperability "not only with Windows client PC operating systems but also, more generally, with the Windows domain architecture".[371] The Court did not substitute its assessment of the interpretation of the term "viably" for that of the Commission. It nonetheless engaged into an in-depth review of whether, in view of the arguments put forward by Microsoft, the evidence relied upon in the decision supported the Commission's conclusion.[372] Second, in the appeal against the 2008 penalties decision, Microsoft argued that the Commission had employed a too narrow definition of the concepts of "novelty" and "non-obviousness", which served to qualify the information for which Microsoft was allowed to charge remuneration without hampering "viable competition". Although the Court did not again expressly refer to the margin of appreciation formula, it abstained once more from substituting its assessment for that of the Commission. In the words of the Court, Microsoft had not put forward "a more appropriate definition of the concepts of novelty and non-obviousness" than the

[368]See Sect. 4.2.2.1.2.1.3.2 with footnotes 313ff above.

[369]In the context of remedies see in particular GC, T-201/04 (Microsoft I, 2007), 87ff together with 379ff and 151f, 208, 340 and 341; opinion of AG Kokott, C-441/07 P (Alrosa, 2009), 77, who points out in fn 45 that the Tetra-Laval-formula "can apply whenever Commission decisions are to be reviewed for manifest errors of assessment"; GC, T 76/14 (Morningstar, 2016), 41f; similarly Koch (2008), 109f; Hauser (2009), 245.

[370]GC, T-201/04 (Microsoft I, 2007), 379ff.

[371]See GC, T-201/04 (Microsoft I, 2007), 389ff.

[372]See GC, T-201/04 (Microsoft I, 2007), 397ff.

Commission.[373] However, the Court engaged in a thorough analysis of the arguments put forward by Microsoft and concluded that the company had failed to establish an error in the Commission's assessment.

4.2.2.2 Particularities Regarding the Review of Article 9 Decisions

In particular Lianos has posited that "[f]ollowing Alrosa, the distinction between voluntary and unilateral remedies leads to a different application of the proportionality principle [. . .], but also to a greater variation in the degree of judicial scrutiny of remedies and the remedial discretion of the Commission".[374] Lianos contrasts the manifest error test applied by the Court of Justice in Alrosa with the allegedly stricter Tetra Laval standard applied by the EU Courts in merger cases.[375] He concludes that "EU competition law operates with varying intensities of review, thus embodying a sliding scale, which goes from a more intensive judicial scrutiny of Article 7 decisions, then an intermediary intensity of review for merger decisions and finally a lower intensity of review for Article 9 decisions". Lianos emphasises that "the sliding scale of judicial review shows that the remedial discretion of the Commission remains important in the area of commitment decisions and that there is a risk of misfit between the remedies and the competition wrong they aim to address, possibly leading to broad prophylactic remedies of a regulatory nature".[376]

Lianos' criticism is not convincing. As has rightly been pointed out by Schweitzer, the outcome of the Alrosa judgment of the Court of Justice does not predicate on a softening of the standards of judicial review, but on a modification of the proportionality principle.[377] It is true that, in Alrosa, the Court of Justice did not expressly refer to the Tetra-Laval standard. The Court merely stated that the judicial review of Article 9 decisions was restricted to whether the Commission's assessment was manifestly incorrect[378] and that the General Court could have held that the Commission had committed a manifest error of assessment only if it had found that the Commission's conclusion was obviously unfounded, having regard to the facts

---

[373]See GC, T-167/08 (Microsoft II, 2012), 151.

[374]Lianos (2013), 443. See also Sadowska (2014), 53: Although she does not explicitly treat the question whether the standard of review of Article 9 decisions is lower than that of Article 7 decisions, she considers the limited review standard applied by the Court of Justice in Alrosa to contribute to the opportunity for the Commission to instrumentalise the Article 9 procedure for regulatory purposes.

[375]Lianos (2013), 447f, according to whom the Tetra-Laval standard "seems a higher intensity of review than the examination by the Court of the "obviously unfounded" character of the conclusions of the Commission with regard to the factual basis of remedies in Article 9 commitment decisions" or "goes far beyond looking to the "obviously unfounded" character of the Commission's conclusions in Article 9 of Regulation 1/2003 cases".

[376]Lianos (2013), 448f.

[377]See Schweitzer (2013), 535. See also GC, T 76/14 (Morningstar, 2016), 43-45.

[378]CJ, C-441/07 P (Alrosa, 2010), 42.

established by it.[379] However, the judgment of the Court of Justice must be read in the light of the opinion of Advocate General Kokott, who had explicitly referred to the Tetra Laval standard.[380] Against the backdrop of the opinion of the Advocate General, to which the Court of Justice explicitly referred in turn when it examined whether the Commission had committed a manifest error of assessment,[381] it becomes clear that the Court of Justice did not relax its standard of review any more than in other instances where it recognizes a margin of discretion in competition law cases. In Morningstar, the General Court explicitly endorsed the Tetra Laval standard to assess the adequacy of commitment decisions.[382] At the same time, it clarified that, if the Commission is reasonably entitled to conclude that the commitments served to dispel the concerns which had been identified in the preliminary assessment, the sole fact that other commitments could also have been accepted, or might even have been more favourable to competition, cannot, as such, establish a manifest error of assessment.[383]

Lianos' hypothesis that the intensity of judicial review varies in competition law cases according to whether a decision is adopted on the basis of Article 7 or Article 9 is also contradicted by the Kone judgment of the Court of Justice. In that judgment, the Court of Justice referred to the Alrosa case in support of the statement that, in the context of the legality review of decisions imposing fines, the General Court could not substitute its own assessment of complex economic circumstances for that of the Commission, but that it had to demonstrate that the way in which the Commission reached its conclusions was not justified in law. The Court went on by stating that "in that regard" the Tetra-Laval standard of judicial review applied.[384] The Kone judgment confirms therefore that the standard of review of matters for which the Commission enjoys discretion is in principle the same, irrespective of whether the

[379]CJ, C-441/07 P (Alrosa, 2010), 63.

[380]Opinion of AG Kokott, C-441/07 P (Alrosa, 2009), 77.

[381]CJ, C-441/07 P (Alrosa, 2010), 62.

[382]GC, T 76/14 (Morningstar, 2016), 42.

[383]GC, T 76/14 (Morningstar, 2016), 59.

[384]CJ, C-510/11 P (Kone, 2013), 27f: "[. . .] when it falls to the European Union judicature to review the legality of Commission decisions imposing fines for infringements of the EU competition rules, it cannot encroach upon the discretion available to the Commission in the administrative proceedings by substituting its own assessment of complex economic circumstances for that of the Commission, but, where relevant, must demonstrate that the way in which the Commission reached its conclusions was not justified in law (see, to that effect, Case C-441/07 P *Commission* v *Alrosa* [2010] ECR I-5949, paragraph 67). In that regard, whilst, in areas giving rise to complex economic assessments, the Commission has a margin of discretion with regard to economic matters, that does not mean that the Courts of the European Union must refrain from reviewing the Commission's interpretation of information of an economic nature. Those Courts must, among other things, not only establish whether the evidence relied on is factually accurate, reliable and consistent but also ascertain whether that evidence contains all the information which must be taken into account in order to assess a complex situation and whether it is capable of substantiating the conclusions drawn from it (see Case C-12/03 P *Commission* v *Tetra Laval* [2005] ECR I-987, paragraph 39 [. . .]".

decision subject to review was based on Article 7 or on Article 9.[385] In both instances, the appropriate standard of review is the Tetra-Laval standard. This conclusion applies without prejudice to the power of unlimited jurisdiction regarding fines.

As regards the judicial review of proportionality in general, von Danwitz has pointed out that, in the context of German constitutional law, the Bundesverfassungsgericht has developed an "extensive canonisation of factors relating to the intensity of scrutiny".[386] He reports that the standards employed by the Bundesverfassungsgericht to control the proportionality of legislative acts vary from "evidence control", "a control of tenability [...] to an intensive control with regard to content".[387] At the same time, he cautions that this canonisation "cannot be considered as a communis opinio amongst judicial traditions in Europe".[388] One might of course ponder whether it is desirable that the EU Courts should in the future develop similar nuances as regards the restriction of their control of the Commission's discretion in competition cases. This question shall not be treated here. For the present purposes, it must suffice to state that, at the current stage, the EU Courts have not yet developed varying standards of limited review in competition cases.[389] An alleged risk of a "misfit between the remedies and the competition wrong they aim to address" and of "broad prophylactic remedies of a regulatory nature" can therefore not be inferred from a non-existent relaxation of the standards of judicial review for Article 9 decisions when compared with the standards of review of Article 7 decisions.

One clarifying remark is still called for. It is not disputed here that the Article 9 procedure entails several important modifications in comparison with the Article 7 procedure. It is also not contested that these modifications may interact with the intensity of the review that must be applied by the General Court.[390] Under the Tetra Laval standard, the General Court must for instance determine whether the evidence relied on by the Commission contains all the relevant data.[391] This requirement will be met more easily in the context of Article 9 than in the context of Article

[385]Wils (2014), fn 71, criticises the reference to Alrosa contained in Kone. In his view, the reference is "misleading", because the EU Courts should not and do not grant any discretion in decisions imposing fines; see Sect. 4.2.2.1.2.1.3.2, footnotes 318 and 321 above.

[386]Von Danwitz (2012), 375.

[387]Von Danwitz (2012), 376 fn 34.

[388]Von Danwitz (2012), 376.

[389]See Castillo de la Torre (2009), 564: "Unlike certain national systems, case law has not developed analytical categories which would help the judge to decide the degree and type of judicial scrutiny where the courts will exercise some degree of self-restraint, even if I think that judges are probably conscious of the fact that different situations are not to be treated in the same way". See also Sect. 4.2.2.1.2.1.3.1 with footnotes 302ff above.

[390]See also GC, T 76/14 (Morningstar, 2016), 40-45, where the General Court refers to the modifications of the proportionality test brought about by article 9 in the context of the density of judicial control.

[391]See Sect. 4.2.2.1.2.2.4.2 with footnote 369 above.

7, precisely because the Commission's obligations to investigate the infringement and to ensure the proportionality of the remedies are reduced under the former provision. Similarly, any modification of the participatory rights during the administrative procedure in the context of Article 9 decisions will have an impact on the Tetra-Laval requirement that the General Court must assess whether the relevant rules of procedure have been complied with. These examples show that the standard of review of a decision is inextricably intertwined with the substantive and procedural requirements for the adoption of the decision. As already stated, this interaction is not disputed here. It is, however, contested that, in the context of Article 9, there is an independent, additional relaxation of the standard of review besides the modification of the substantive and procedural requirements for the adoption of a commitment decision.

For the sake of completeness, it should still be pointed out that the Skyscanner judgment of the UK Competition Appeal Tribunal contains a rather detailed discussion of the appropriate level of judicial scrutiny to which commitment decisions should be subject. In that connection, the Competition Appeal Tribunal closely considered the Alrosa judgment of the Court of Justice. The Tribunal concluded that "AG Kokott's description of the scope of review by the EU Courts is broadly analogous to that of the Tribunal in a judicial review".[392]

4.2.3 Conclusion on Judicial Review

If one follows the view the defended here, the adoption of an Article 9 decision instead of an Article 7 decision entails at best a modest relaxation of the standards for judicial review. The admissibility conditions for actions instituted by the concerned undertakings, complainants or third parties against a commitment decision are not more restrictive than those for bringing an action against an Article 7 decision. The voluntary nature of commitment decisions justifies that the grounds of review upon which the concerned undertakings can rely in actions against a commitment decision are limited to procedural and substantive aspects of a commitment decision that are not covered by the concerned undertaking's consent. The scope of review of Article 9 decisions is influenced by the slightly less strict requirements regarding the substantive and procedural requirements of the adoption of such a decision. Apart from that, the adoption of an Article 9 instead of an Article 7 decision does, however, not entail an additional relaxation of the scope of judicial review. Regardless of whether a remedy is adopted on the basis of Article 7 or 9, in particular the prospective nature of remedies justifies that judicial review is limited. However,

[392][2014] CAT 16 (Skyscanner), 41; see also Sect. 4.2.2.1.2.1.3.2, footnote 326 above. Also Lianos (2013), 446f, mentions that the standard of review applied by the Court of Justice in Alrosa corresponds to the UK standard of judicial review. He acknowledges that there is hence "a perception that the intensity of judicial review in this context should be limited".

also the limited standard of review still implies a strict judicial control according to the Tetra-Laval standard.

4.3 Conclusion on the Relaxation of Procedural Safeguards

Summing up, it is submitted that the adoption of an Article 9 instead of an Article 7 decision entails only a modest relaxation of the procedural safeguards. This conclusion applies both as regards the safeguards that exist during the administrative procedure and with a view to the judicial review exercised by the EU Courts.

Bibliography

Ackermann (2011): Towards a more judicial approach? EU antitrust fines under the scrutiny of fundamental rights, CMLR 2011, 1405

Albers/Jourdan (2011): The Role of Hearing Officers in EU Competition Proceedings: A Historical and Practical Perspective, JECLP 2011, 185

Andersson (2013): Judicial review after Menarini: any need for reform of the EU system, in: Bernitz/Groussot/Schulyok (Eds.), General Principles of EU Law and European Private Law, 2013

Bailey (2004): Scope of Judicial Review under Article 81 EC, CMLR 2004, 1327

Bailey (2012): Standard of Judicial Review under Articles 101 and 102 TFEU, in: Merola/Derenne (Eds): The Role of the Court of Justice of the European Union in Competition Law Cases. GCLC Annual Conference Series, 2012

Barling (2014): The role of the court in the public enforcement of competition law, in: Hawk (Ed), Annual proceedings of the Fordham Competition Law Institute 2013, 2014

Bauer (2008): in: Hirsch/Montag/Säcker (Eds.), Competition Law: European Community Practice and Procedure. Article-by-Article Commentary, 2008

Bechtold/Bosch/Brinker (2014): EU-Kartellrecht. Kommentar, 3rd edition, 2014

Bengtsson/Carpi Badia/Kadar (2014): Mergers, in: Faull/Nikpay (Eds.), The EU Law of Competition, 3rd edition, 2014

Bischke (2008): in: Hirsch/Montag/Säcker (Eds.), Competition Law: European Community Practice and Procedure. Article-by-Article Commentary, 2008

Botteman/Patsa (2013): Towards a more sustainable use of commitment decisions in Article 102 TFEU cases, JAE 2013, 347

Boyd/von Lingen (2013): in: Ortiz Blanco (Ed.), EU Competition Procedure, 3rd Edition, 2013

Brenner (2010): Wer freut sich, wenn zwei sich nicht streiten?, WRP 2010, 1333

Bueren (2011): Verständigungen – Settlements in Kartelbußgeldverfahren, 2011

Busse/Leopold (2005): Entscheidungen über Verpflichtungszusagen nach Art. 9 VO (EG) Nr. 1/2003, WuW 2005, 145

Castillo de la Torre (2009): Evidence, Proof and Judicial Review in Cartel Cases, World Competition 2009, 505

Cengiz (2011): Judicial review and the rule of law in the EU competition law regime after Alrosa, ECJ 2011, 127

Cook (2006): Commitment Decisions: The Law and Practice under Article 9, World Competition 2006, 209

Craig (2012): EU administrative law, 2nd edition, 2012

Craig (2014): in: Peers/Hervey/Kenner/Ward (Eds.), The EU Charter of Fundamental Rights. A Commentary, 2014
Craig/De Búrca (2011): EU law. Text, cases and materials, 5th edition, 2011
Dalheimer (2005): in: Dalheimer/Feddersen/Miersch (Eds.), EU-Kartellverfahrensverordnung. Kommentar zur VO 1/2003. Sonderausgabe aus Grabitz/Hilf: Das Recht der Europäischen Union, nach Art. 83 EGV, 2005
De Bronnet (2012): Europäisches Kartellverfahrensrecht. Kommentar zur VO 1/2003, 2nd edition, 2012
Derenne (2012): The scope of judicial review in EU economic cases, in: Merola/Derenne (Eds): The Role of the Court of Justice of the European Union in Competition Law Cases. GCLC Annual Conference Series, 2012
Dervisopoulos (2014): in: Rengeling/Middeke/Gellermann (Eds.), Handbuch des Rechtsschutzes in der Europäischen Union, 3rd edition, 2014
De Smijter/Sinclair (2014): The Enforcement System under Regulation 1/2003, in: Faull/Nikpay (Eds.), The EU Law of Competition, 3rd edition, 2014
Dörr (2012): in: Grabitz/Hilf/Nettesheim (Eds.), Das Recht der Europäischen Union
Dunne (2014): Commitment decisions in EU competition law, JCLE 2014, 399
Economides/Lianos (2010): A critical appraisal of remedies in the E.U. Microsoft cases, 2010 Colum. Bus. L. Rev. 346
Ehlermann/Marquis (2011): European Competition Law Annual 2009: The Evaluation of Evidence and its Judicial Review in Competition cases
Engisch (2010): Einführung in das juristische Denken, 11th edition, 2010
Falconi (2011): Commitment decisions in the EU and UK – Developments, open issues and considerations for companies and competition authorities, Competition Law 2011, 41
Forrester (2011a): A challenge for Europe's judges: the review of fines in competition cases, ELR 2011, 185
Forrester (2011b): A Bush in Need of Pruning: the Luxuriant Growth of "Light Judicial Review", in: Ehlermann/Marquis (Eds.), European Competition Law Annual 2009, 2011
Forrester (2013): From Regulation 17/62 to Article 52 of the Charter of Fundamental Rights, in: Bernitz/Groussot/Schulyok (Eds.), General Principles of EU Law and European Private Law, 2013
Fritzsche (2008): Ermessen und institutionelles Gleichgewicht, 2008
Fritzsche (2010): Discretion, scope of judicial review and institutional balance in European Law, CMLR 2010, 361
Galligan (1990): Discretionary Powers, 1990
Geradin/Petit (2012): Judicial Review in European Union Competition Law: A Quantitative and Qualitative Assessment, in: Merola/Derenne (Eds): The Role of the Court of Justice of the European Union in Competition Law Cases. GCLC Annual Conference Series, 2012
Gerard (2010): EU Antitrust Enforcement in 2025: "Why Wait? Full Appellate Jurisdiction, Now", CPI Antitrust Journal December 2010/1
Gerard (2013): Negotiated remedies in the modernization era: the limits of effectiveness, available online
Gerhardt (1997): in: Schoch/Schneider/Bier, VwGO, Kommentar
Gippini-Fournier (2008): The Modernisation of European Competition Law: First Experiences with Regulation 1/2003, in: Köck/Karollus (Eds.), The Modernisation of European Competition Law. FIDE Congress, 2008
Hellström/Maier-Rigaud/Bulst (2009): Remedies in European antitrust law, 76 Antitrust L. J. 43 (2009)
Hauser (2009): Strukturelle Maßnahmen im europäischen Kartellverfahrensrecht, 2009
Hennig (2010a): Settlements im Europäischen Kartellverfahren, 2010
Hennig (2010b): Die Bedeutung des Verhältnismäßigkeitsgrundsatzes bei der Annahme von Verpflichtungszusagen durch die Kommission nach Art. 9 VO (EG) Nr. 1/2003, ZWeR 2010, 440

Hofmann/Rowe/Türk (2012): Administrative Law and Policy of the European Union, 2012
Idot (2016): Le contrôle exercé par le Tribunal sur une décision d'acceptation d'engagements est un contrôle restreint..., Europe 2016, 31
Italianer (2012): Legal certainty, proportionality, effectiveness: the Commission's practice on remedies, Speech given in December 2012, available online
Jaeger, M. (2011): The Standard of Review in Competition Cases Involving Complex Economic Assessments: Towards the Marginalisation of the Marginal Review?, JECLP 2011, 295
Jenny (2015): Worst decision of the EU Court of Justice: The Alrosa judgment in context and the future of commitment decisions, Fordham Int'l L.J. 2015, 701
Jones/Sufrin (2011): EU Competition Law, 4th edition, 2011
Jones/Sufrin (2014): EU Competition Law, 5th edition, 2014
Kellerbauer (2011): Playground instead of playpen: The Court of Justice of the European Union's Alrosa judgment on Art. 9 of Regulation 1/2003, ECLR 2011, 1
Kellerbauer (2013): Das neue Mandat des Anhörungsbeauftragten für EU-Wettbewerbsverfahren, EuZW 2013, 10
Kerse/Khan (2012): EU Antitrust Procedure, 6th edition, 2012
Kipiani (2014): Les engagements en matière de pratiques anticoncurrentielles. Analyse des droits français, européen et américain, 2014
Klees (2005): Europäisches Kartellverfahrensrecht mit Fusionskontrollverfahren, 2005
Klees (2010): Freie Bahn für die Kommission in Kartellverfahren bei Anwendung des Art. 9 VO Nr. 1/2003, RIW 2010, 688
Klees (2011): Die Zusagenpraxis der Europäischen Kommission in Kartellverfahren – Eine kritische Analyse, EWS 2011, 14
Krings (2012): Möglichkeiten und Grenzen der Anordnung einer eigentumsrechtlichen Entflechtung nach Art. 7 VO 1/2003, 2012
Koch, A. (2008): Eingriffe in die Struktur beherrschender Unternehmen, 2008
Körber (2010): Rechtliches Gehör, Verpflichtungszusagen nach Art. 9 VO 1/2003 und die Alrosa-Entscheidung, in: Weiß, Tagungsband zum 1. Speyerer Kartellrechtsforum, 2010, p. 73
Körber (2012): in: Immenga/Mestmäcker (Eds.), EU-Wettbewerbsrecht, 5th Edition, 2012
Larouche (2009): The European Microsoft case at the crossroads of competition policy and innovation: Comment on Ahlborn and Evans, 75 Antitrust L. J. 933 (2009)
Legal (2006): Standards of proof and standards of judicial review in EU competition law, in: Hawk (Ed.), Annual proceedings of the Fordham Competition Law Institute 2005, 2006
Lenaerts/Maselis/Gutman (2014): in: Nowak (Ed.), EU Procedural Law, 2014
Lianos (2013): Competition law remedies in Europe, in: Lianos/Geradin (Eds.), Handbook on European Competition Law. Enforcement and Procedure, 2013
Lowe/Maier-Rigaud (2008): Quo vadis antitrust remedies, in: Hawk (Ed.), Annual proceedings of the Fordham Competition Law Institute 2007, 2008, p. 597
Lübking/von Koppenfels (2012): Effektive Durchsetzung des EU-Wettbewerbsrechts und Verfahrensgarantien – Die Kommission zwischen Gestaltungsmacht und Rechtsbindung, in: Immenga/Körber (Eds.): Die Kommission zwischen zwischen Gestaltungsmacht und Rechtsbindung, 2012
Merola/Derenne (2012): The Role of the Court of Justice of the European Union in Competition Law Cases. GCLC Annual Conference Series, 2012
Messina/Ho (2011): Re-establishing the Orthodoxy of Commitment Decisions under Article 9 of Regulation 1/2003: Comment on Commission v Alrosa, ELR 2011, 737
Meyer-Ladewig (2011): Europäische Menschenrechtskonvention. Handkommentar, 3rd edition, 2011
Muguet-Poullennec/Barbier de La Serre (2010): La procédure d'engagements en droit de l'Union: à la recherche du juste équilibre entre efficacité administrative et protection des entreprises, RLC 2010 n° 25, 36
Müller-Tautphaeus (2003): Abhilfebefugnisse der Europäischen Kommission im Wettbewerbsrecht, 2003

Nazzini (2012): Administrative Enforcement, Judicial Review and Fundamental Rights in EU Competition Law: A Comparative Contextual-Functionalist Perspective, CMLR 2012, 971
Nehl (2012): Kontrolle kartellrechtlicher Sanktionsentscheidungen der Kommission durch die Unionsgerichte, in: Immenga/Körber (Ed.), Die Kommission zwischen Gestaltungsmacht und Rechtsbindung, 2012, p. 113
Nothdurft (2008): Ökonomie vor Gericht. Richterliche Überprüfung wirtschaftlicher Fragen im deutschen und europäischen Kartellverwaltungsprozess, in: Müller/Osterloh/Stein (Eds.), Festschrift für Günter Hirsch, 2008
O'Donoghue/Padilla (2013): The law and economics of Article 102 TFEU, 2nd edition, 2013
OECD (2006): Remedies and sanctions in abuse of dominance cases. OECD Policy Roundtables, 2006, available online
Ortiz Blanco/Jörgens/Kellerbauer (2013): in: Ortiz Blanco (Ed.), EU Competition Procedure, 3rd Edition, 2013
Paemen/Baltrusch (2017): Morningstar v Commission: Raising the Threshold for Challenging Commission Commitments Decisions, JECLP 2017, 99
Podszun (2012): Paradigmenwechsel in der kartellbehördlichen Befugnisausübung. Grundlagen, Gefahren, Grenzen, ZWeR 2012, 48
Pohlmann (2011): Verfahrensrecht für ein ökonomisiertes Kartellrecht: Der Beurteilungsspielraum der Kommission, in: in: Albach/Bechthold (Eds.), Recht, Ordnung und Wettbewerb, Festschrift zum 70. Geburtstag von Wernhard Möschel, 2011
Prek/Lefèvre (2016): Competition litigation before the General Court: Quality if not quantity, CMLR 2016, 65
Prek/Lefèvre (2019): Administrative discretion, Power of appraisal, and Margin of appraisal in judicial review proceedings before the General Court, CMLR 2019, 339
Rab/Monnoyeur/Sukhtankar (2010): Commitments in EU competition cases. Article 9 of Regulation 1/2003, its application, and the challenges ahead, JECLP 2010, 171
Rachwol (2010): Kartellrechtliche Zusagenentscheidungen nach Art. 9 Verordnung Nr. 1/2003, 2010
Ratliff (2011): Judicial Review in EC competition cases before the European Courts: Avoiding double renvoi, in: Ehlermann/Marquis (Eds.), European Competition Law Annual 2009, 2011, p. 453
Ritter (2012): in: Immenga/Mestmäcker (Eds.), EU-Wettbewerbsrecht, 5th Edition, 2012
Sadowska (2014): Committed to Reform? Pragmatic Antitrust Enforcement in Electricity Markets, 2014
Saitzek (2008): Verpflichtungszusagen im europäischen Kartellrecht, 2008
Sander (2014): in: Holoubek/Lienbacher (Eds.), GRC. Kommentar, 2014
Schroeder (2011): Normative and institutional limitations to a more economic approach, in: Drexl/Podszun/Kerber (Eds.), Competition Policy and the Economic Approach. Foundations and Limitations, 2011
Schütte (2008): in: Wiedemann (Ed.), Handbuch des Kartellrechts, 2nd edition, 2008
Schwarze/Weitbrecht (2004): Grundzüge des europäischen Kartellverfahrensrechts. Die Verordnung (EG) Nr. 1/2003, 2004
Schweitzer (2010): Commitment Decisions under Article 9 of Regulation 1/2003. The Developing EC Practice and Case Law, in: Ehlermann/Marquis (Eds.), European Competition Law Annual 2008, 2010, p. 547
Schweitzer (2011): Verpflichtungszusagen im Gemeinschaftsrecht, in: Albach/Bechthold (Eds.), Recht, Ordnung und Wettbewerb, Festschrift zum 70. Geburtstag von Wernhard Möschel, 2011
Schweitzer (2012): Commitment Decisions in the EU and in the Member States: Functions and Risks of a New Instrument of Competition Law Enforcement within a Federal Enforcement Regime, available online
Schweitzer (2013): Judicial review in EU competition law, in: Lianos/Geradin (Ed.), Handbook on European Competition Law. Enforcement and Procedure, 2013, p. 491

Sofianatos (2009): Injonctions et engagements en droit de la concurrence: étude de droit communautaire, français et grec, 2009
Sura (2014): in: Langen/Bunte (Eds.), Kartellrecht, Volume 2, 12th edition, 2014
Temple Lang (2003): Commitment decisions under Regulation 1/2003: legal aspects of a new kind of competition decision, ECLR 2003, 347
Temple Lang (2006): Commitment decisions and settlements with antitrust authorities and private parties under European antitrust law, in: Hawk (Ed.), Annual proceedings of the Fordham Competition Law Institute 2005, 2006
Van Cleynenbreugel (2012): The hearing officer's extended mandate: whose special friend in the conduct of EU competition proceedings?, ECLR 2012, 286
Vesterdorf (2012): The General Court's Unlimited Jurisdiction over Fines, in: Merola/Derenne (2012): The Role of the Court of Justice of the European Union in Competition Law Cases. GCLC Annual Conference Series, 2012
Vilsmeier (2013): Tatsachenkontrolle und Beweisführung im EU-Kartellrecht auf dem Prüfstand der EMRK, 2013
Von Danwitz (2008): Europäisches Verwaltungsrecht, 2008
Von Danwitz (2012): Thoughts on Proportionality and Coherence in the Jurisprudence of the Court of Justice, in: Cardonnel/Rosas/Wahl (Ed.), Constitutionalising the EU Judicial System, Essays in Honour of Pernilla Lindh, 2012, 367
Von Kalben (2018): Verpflichtungszusagen im EU-Wettbewerbsrecht. Eine Untersuchung der Funktionen und Grenzen von Verpflichtungsbeschlüssen nach Art. 9 VO 1/2003 unter besonderer Berücksichtigung des Energiesektors, 2017
Von Winterfeld (1995): Verpflichtungserklärungen in europäischen Kartellverfahren, in: Due/Lutter/Schwarze (Eds.), Festschrift für Everling, Volume II, 1995, p. 1689
Waelbroeck (2009): The development of a new "settlement culture" in competition cases. What is left to the Courts?, in: Gheur/Petit (Eds.), Alternative enforcement techniques in EC competition law. Settlements, commitments and other novel instruments, 2009
Waelbroeck/Frisch (2013): Après l'arrêt Menarini: l'impact de la Convention européenne de sauvegarde des droits de l'homme et des libertés fondamentales sur les procédures en droit de la concurrence, in: Govaere/Hanf (Eds.), Scrutinizing internal and external dimensions of European law. Les dimensions internes et externes du droit européen à l'épreuve. Liber amicorum Paul Demaret. Vol. II (2013), p. 663
Wahl (2011): Standard of Review – Comprehensive or Limited, in: Ehlermann/Marquis (Eds.), European Competition Law Annual 2009, 2011
Ward (2007): Judicial review and the rights of private parties in EU law, 2007
Whish (2006): Commitment Decisions under Article 9 of the EC Modernisation Regulation: Some Unanswered Questions, in: Johansson/Wahl/Bernitz (Eds.), Liber Amicorum in Honour of Sven Norberg, A European For All Seasons, 2006, p. 555
Whish/Bailey (2012): Competition Law, 7th edition, 2012
Wils (2006): Settlements of EU Antitrust Investigations: Commitment Decisions under Article 9 of Regulation No. 1/2003, World Competition 2006, 345
Wils (2008): The Use of Settlements in Public Antitrust Enforcement: Objectives and Principles, World Competition 2008, 335
Wils (2012): The Role of the Hearing Officer in Competition Proceedings before the European Commission, World Competition 2012, 431
Wils (2014): The Compatibility with Fundamental Rights of the EU Antitrust Enforcement System in which the European Commission Acts both as Investigator and as First-instance Decision Maker, World Competition 2014, 5
Wolter (2011): Zusagenentscheidungen als behördliche Maßnahmen gegen Wettbewerbsverstöße im europäischen und deutschen Kartellrecht, 2011

Chapter 5
The Impact of Commitments on Legal Certainty

The criticism that the recourse to Article 9 instead of Article 7 has a negative impact on legal certainty has several facets. The most important aspect is certainly that commitment decisions are de facto only scarcely appealed. Critics stress above all that the use of commitments reduces the likeliness that a judicial precedent is created which contributes to the clarification of the law. However, there are also other issues that raise commentators' concerns: The absence of clear criteria when the commitment procedure applies; the lack of a right of the concerned undertaking to a commitment decision; the room left by Article 9 to the Commission's power to prioritise cases; and the effects of commitment decisions on the practice of the competition authorities and courts of the Member States. The present chapter will organise the assessment of the mentioned aspects in a first section that deals with the disadvantages of the Article 9 procedure in terms of legal certainty. The second section will then place an emphasis on an advantage of the adoption of a commitment decision in terms of legal certainty that, it is submitted, has to date been paid too little attention: The fact that a commitment results in precise and enforceable obligations.

On a sidenote, it bears mention that commentators sometimes mention the closure of an investigation by means of a formal decision and the resulting certainty for the concerned undertakings that the Commission will not take further action against them as an advantage of Article 9 decisions in terms of legal certainty.[1] However, it is clear that the closure of an investigation by means of a formal decision constitutes only an advantage of Article 9 decisions when compared to the informal closure of procedures, but not when compared to the closure of an investigation by means of an Article 7 decision. Since the present study aims at comparing the standards of Article 7 and Article 9 decisions, the said advantage will not be addressed in more detail.

[1] Eg Sadowska (2014), 10.

K. Reiter, *Market Design Powers of the European Commission?*, Munich Studies on Innovation and Competition 13, https://doi.org/10.1007/978-3-662-60711-4_5

5.1 Disadvantages of Commitments in Terms of Legal Certainty

The present section will address the criticism of the Article 9 procedure that relies on the disadvantages of the procedure in terms of legal certainty.

5.1.1 Lack of Clear Criteria When the Article 9 Procedure Applies

Many commentators deplore the lack of clear criteria for the selection of cases that can be resolved with an Article 9 decision.[2] The following section will therefore discuss the scope of application of the Article 9 procedure and whether this scope of application should be defined in more precise terms.

5.1.1.1 The Last Sentence of Recital 13 Regulation 1/03

Pursuant to the last sentence of Recital 13 Regulation 1/03, "[c]ommitment decisions are not appropriate in cases where the Commission intends to impose a fine". The meaning of this sentence is controversial. According to one view, the sentence has a purely declaratory importance and does not limit the scope of application of the Article 9 procedure at all. According to this view, the sentence merely clarifies that the Commission cannot combine the adoption of a commitment decision with the imposition of a fine. The sentence is hence said not to exclude the acceptance of commitments even where serious infringements are concerned.[3] The contrary view construes the last sentence of Recital 13 Regulation 1/03 as implying some sort of substantive restriction of the scope of application of the Article 9 procedure.[4] Within this view, opinions diverge to a certain extent. On the one hand, the following results seem to be uncontroversial: First, the mere possibility for the Commission to impose a fine cannot suffice to exclude the application of Article 9. By virtue of Article 23 (2) Regulation 1/03, the Commission may impose fines for any infringement of the competition rules that is committed at least negligently. Excluding all cases that can potentially be fined from the scope of application of Article 9 would hence unduly

---

[2]Eg Schweitzer (2011), 638 and (2012), 6; Falconi (2011), 53f; Wagner-Von Papp (2012), 932; Lugard/Möllmann (2013), 10f; Botteman/Patsa (2013), 358f; Jones/Sufrin (2014), 982; Gyselen (2014), 251; Mariniello (2014), 2.

[3]See Kahlenberg/Neuhaus (2005), 621; Hirsbrunner/Rhomberg (2005), 62f; Hennig (2010), 120f; Brenner (2012), 324ff.

[4]See Gippini-Fournier (2008), 399: "it seems reasonable to attach to this recital a minimum content".

restrict the latter provision.[5] Second, the sole fact that the Commission indicates its intention to impose a fine in a statement of objections does not hinder the later adoption of a commitment decision.[6] Third, hard-core cartels are excluded from the scope of application of Article 9.[7] On the other hand, the following issues seem to be controversial or at least unclear: First, whether the last sentence of Recital 13 Regulation 1/03 prevents the Commission from discriminating between companies that are concerned by an identical investigation or between similar groups of cases.[8] Second, whether other categories of infringements than hard-core cartels, in particular categories of abuses of a dominant position, can be made out that are excluded from the scope of application of Article 9.[9] Predatory pricing practices constitute a type of abuse that could, for instance, be excluded.[10] In its Best Practices and in the Manual of Procedures, the Commission sides with those commentators that interpret the last sentence of Recital 13 Regulation 1/03 as implying a substantive restriction of the scope of application of the Article 9 procedure. It construes the sentence as excluding the adoption of commitment decisions in "secret cartel" cases that fall under the Leniency Notice.[11]

It appears preferable, however, to follow the first view presented above and to assign the last sentence of Recital 13 Regulation 1/03 the purely declaratory meaning that the Commission cannot combine the adoption of a commitment decision with the imposition of a fine. As has been pointed out by Kellerbauer, this interpretation seems to be more in line with the preparatory work for Regulation 1/03 and thus with the intent of the legislator.[12] Recital 39, second sentence, of directive 2019/1 seems to further support this conclusion. It states that commitment decisions are, in principle, not appropriate in the case of secret cartels, in respect of which NCAs

---

[5]Hirsbrunner/Rhomberg (2005), 62; Saitzek (2008), 97; Rachwol (2010), 96; De Bronnet (2012), Art. 9, 12.

[6]Kahlenberg/Neuhaus (2005), 621; Hirsbrunner/Rhomberg (2005), 62; Saitzek (2008), 97f; Bauer (2008), Art. 9, 4-9-028f; Rachwol (2010), 97; De Smijter/Sinclair (2014), 2.128.

[7]Dalheimer (2005), Art. 9, 4; Anweiler (2009), Art. 9, 9; Saitzek (2008), 97; De Smijter/Sinclair (2014), 2.128.

[8]For a prohibition to discriminate De Smijter/Sinclair (2014), 2.128: "The intention behind recital 13 [. . .] is to avoid a situation where, in the same case or group of cases, commitment decisions are adopted in respect of some undertakings but fines are imposed on others"; for the possibility to discriminate Temple Lang (2003), 348; Bauer (2008), 4-9-30; Anweiler (2009), Art. 9, 8f.

[9]See Forrester (2010), 643; Schweitzer (2012), 6f; Kipiani (2014), 127.

[10]In the UK, the OFT states in its Enforcement Guidelines (2004), 4.4 fn 16, that "as a general rule, it will regard predatory pricing as a serious abuse" for which the adoption of commitments is excluded; see Forrester (2010), 643 fn 19; Schweitzer (2012), fn 26.

[11]Best Practices (2011), 116; Manual of Procedures (2012), Module 16, 13.

[12]See Kellerbauer (2011), 2, and Ortiz Blanco/Jörgens/Kellerbauer (2013), 13.09 fn 31, who refer to: Council of the European Union, *Report of the Competition Working Party of 8 November 2002* (2000/0243(CNS)): "[. . .] the possibility for the Commission to adopt commitment decisions has been limited to cases in which it does not intend to impose a fine. This is however logical given that the regulation does not provide for a possibility to settle on the payment of an amount of money". See also Wagner-von Papp (2012), 945 fn 65, with further references.

should impose fines. The use of a "principle" with the possibility of exceptions shows that, as far as the NCA's are concerned, the EU legislator did not even want to exclude the area of secret cartels from the scope of application of commitment decisions.

5.1.1.2 Guidance Provided by the Best Practices and the Manual of Procedures

The fact that the last sentence of Recital 13 Regulation 1/03 does not restrict the scope of application of Article 9 does not prevent the Commission from limiting the use it makes of the commitment procedure or from providing further guidance when a commitment decision may be adopted. As already mentioned, in its Best Practices and the Manual of Procedures, the Commission expressly excludes secret cartels that fall under the Leniency Notice from the scope of application of Article 9.[13] The latter restriction of the scope of application of Article 9 appears, in principle, justified, because in cases involving secret cartels, the benefits of an Article 7 decision accompanied by a fine will, as a general rule, clearly outweigh the benefits of an Article 9 procedure. The serious nature of the infringements requires the imposition of a fine in order to deter. Moreover, secret cartels do not require any complex remedies, so that there is no benefit from the consensual design and implementation of a remedy.[14]

Besides the exclusion of secret cartels from the scope of application of the Article 9 procedure, the Best Practices and the Manual of Procedures provide little concrete guidance regarding any further boundaries of the scope of application of the Article 9 procedure. In both documents, the Commission excludes commitments in cases in which it considers itself "that the nature of the infringement calls for the imposition of a fine".[15] The Manual of Procedures contains also the following hints: First, the Commission states in essence that it may prefer an Article 7 decision, where it wants to establish an important precedent[16] and that it may take the necessity to deter third undertakings and to facilitate private damages claims into account.[17] Second, the Commission considers it "preferable" to explain why a fine was no longer necessary, if the Commission adopts a commitment after having indicated its intention to impose a fine in the statement of objections.[18] Third, in order to ensure that a

---

[13]The Commission had already explicitly excluded "hardcore cartels" from the scope of application of Article 9 in a memorandum dealing with the commitment procedure published in 2004 (MEMO/04/217).

[14]See also the Commission's staff working document accompanying the report on the functioning of Regulation 1/03, COM(2009)206 final, 95: "in hard-core cartel cases fines are necessary, as the emphasis of enforcement is on punishing past behaviour and deterring anti-competitive practices".

[15]Best Practices (2011), 116; Manual of Procedures (2012), Module 16, 13.

[16]Manual of Procedures (2012), Module 16, 11.

[17]Manual of Procedures (2012), Module 16, 12.

[18]Manual of Procedures (2012), Module 16, 14.

company will abide by the competition rules in the future, a commitment decision may still be adopted where the investigated practices have been discontinued.[19] In a speech given in 2013, Italianer, at the time director of DG COMP, stated that in order to choose between the adoption of an Article 7 and of an Article 9 decision, the Commission would take account of the need to punish, to deter and to set a precedent.[20]

5.1.1.3 The Commission's Practice and Its Criticism: Should the Scope of Application of the Article 9 Procedure Be Further Restricted?

Commentators decry the fact that the Commission is not sticking to the restrictions for the application of the Article 9 procedure that it has imposed on itself.[21] In that regard, they criticise, first, that the Commission accepted commitments in "hard-core horizontal collusion" cases. This criticism is not persuasive. As far as can be ascertained, only the Alrosa and the Ebooks case are put forward in its support.[22] However, the commitments finally made binding in Alrosa addressed concerns raised by the Commission under Article 102 TFEU. The case hence cannot be counted as a secret cartel case for which the Commission excluded the application of the Article 9 procedure. As regards the Ebooks case, the Commission explained in a memorandum why it had accepted commitments despite allegations of collusion between competitors. The Commission considered that the market for e-books was a nascent and fast-moving market and that the Commission's priority therefore should be to put an end to the potential infringement and restore the normal conditions of

---

[19]Manual of Procedures (2012), Module 16, 15.

[20]Italianer (2013), 3f; similarly also Commission, Competition Policy Brief, Issue 3, March 2014, 2.

[21]See eg Lugard/Möllmann (2013), 10: "contrary to what the Regulation states, the Commission does not restrict the use of commitments to procedures where a fine is not envisaged"; Mariniello (2014), 2, according to whom the Commission's claim "that prohibition decisions are made whenever there is a significant need for deterrence, punishment and legal precedent [. . .] is not fully supported by the facts".

[22]See Cengiz (2011), 146 fn 78, who is of the opinion that the horizontal concerns raised by the Commission in Alrosa amounted "to a hard-core horizontal collusion under the EU competition rules which would not be suitable to be addressed by a commitment decision in the first place under Regulation 1/2003, Recital 13"; Jones/Sufrin (2014), 982: "[. . .] in Ebooks commitments were taken in a case which in effect involved price-fixing and resale maintenance"; Lugard/Möllmann (2013), 10, criticise that the Commission "accepted commitments in cases that might be considered akin to cartels". In support of their allegation, they only point to the Ebooks case. Also Botteman/ Patsa (2013), 359 fn 57, and Brenner (2014), 680, criticise the Commission for having accepted commitments in the Ebooks case.

competition as quickly as possible. Given the particularities of the Ebooks case,[23] this reasoning cannot be criticised.[24]

Second, commentators criticise that the Commission has accepted commitments in several serious abuse cases for which fines could have been imposed. Cases that raise commentators' concerns are in particular RWE, Microsoft Internet Explorer, Rambus and IBM Maintenance Services.[25] One could mention the Deutsche Bahn commitment decision as a further example: As is apparent from the decision, participants in the market test claimed that a commitment was inappropriate for an alleged margin squeeze of a duration of 10 years, taking into account that a commitment did not facilitate private damages actions.[26] The Commission did not expressly address this submission in its reasoning. It merely stated in abstract terms that it had taken the interests of third parties into account.[27] Third, commentators deplore that the Commission settles cases that involve novel or controversial theories and would hence require the setting of a precedent.[28] Cases that raise commentators' concerns are in particular Rambus,[29] RWE, ENI, and E.On Gas foreclosure.[30]

As regards the last two points of criticism, i.e. the acceptance of commitments in serious abuse cases and in cases involving novel or controversial theories of harm, two remarks are called for. First, nothing indicates that the adoption of the criticised commitments is inconsistent with the principles laid down in the Commission's Best Practices or the Manual of Procedures. Outside the area of secret cartels, the Best Practices do not provide for concrete criteria that would restrict the Commission's discretion in choosing between an Article 7 and an Article 9 decision. The Manual of Procedures merely states that the Commission will take account of the necessity to establish a precedent, to deter third undertakings and to facilitate private damages claims. It does, however, not contain any more precise statements when these three factors that militate for an Article 7 decision will outweigh the potential benefits of the Article 9 procedure that must also be taken into account, in particular the simplification of the procedure, a swifter resolution of the competitive concerns and a more effective implementation of the remedy.[31]

---

[23]See the more detailed discussion of the case above (Sect. 3.3.4.2.1.1 with footnotes 706ff).

[24]See Voss (2013), 153f, who considers that the Ebooks case concerned an "open business arrangement rather than a secret cartel" and that the case was hence "suitable for a commitment decision".

[25]See Schweitzer (2011), 638; Wagner-von Papp (2012), 945 fn 65; Botteman/Patsa (2013), 360; Mariniello (2014), 2; Jones/Sufrin (2014), 982 fn 351.

[26]COMP/39.678 (Deutsche Bahn I and II, 2013), 72.

[27]COMP/39.678 (Deutsche Bahn I and II, 2013), 101.

[28]Eg Schweitzer (2012), 6; Botteman/Patsa (2013), 348; Marsden (2013), 3f; Mariniello (2014), 2f; Dunne (2014), 415.

[29]Eg Wagner-von Papp (2012), 963; Dunne (2014), 409 and 415 fn 89; Mariniello (2014), 2f.

[30]See the discussion of those cases above (in particular Sect. 3.4.2.1.1.1.2.2 with footnotes 973ff, Sect. 3.4.2.1.1.1.3.2 with footnotes 990ff and Sect. 3.4.2.1.2.2.2 with footnotes 1066ff).

[31]See Manual of Procedures (2012), Module 16, 7f: "[...] commitment decisions involve less procedural steps [...] As a result, the commitment path can bring a swifter change to the market.

Second, the sole fact that the Commission's practice does not seem inconsistent with the approach laid out in the Best Practices and the Manual of Procedures does of course not mean that the latter approach is correct. This begs the question whether further restrictions should be introduced—regardless of whether by soft- or hard-law—to limit the scope of application of the Article 9 procedure.[32] It is submitted, however, that the introduction of such further restrictions should be met with caution. The decisive counter argument is that it is too difficult to develop abstract criteria when a commitment procedure should be excluded.[33] Whether the adoption of a commitment instead of an infringement decision is appropriate depends primarily on the circumstances of the individual case at hand.

This conclusion applies, on the one hand, in the context of criteria that would seek to exclude the application of Article 9 in cases of serious infringements. For instance, inspired by the enforcement guidelines of the UK OFT, Botteman and Patsa have suggested to take account of the nature of the conduct, the market structure and market shares, the effect on competitors and third parties and the direct or indirect damage caused to consumers in order to assess whether the gravity of an infringement calls for the adoption of an Article 7 decision. In order to evaluate whether the necessity to deter calls for the adoption of an Article 7 decision, they propose to look at the duration of the alleged infringement.[34] Also Schweitzer has pointed out that "some [competition authorities of the Member States] try to set stricter limits to the use of commitment decisions" than the Commission.[35] It shall not be disputed that the criteria relied on by Botteman and Patsa or those contained in the enforcement guidelines of some of the competition authorities of the Member States are relevant factors that ought to be taken into consideration when the Commission chooses between the Article 7 and the Article 9 procedure. However, it is submitted that none of these factors can or should be given an absolute priority. They must always be balanced against the advantages of the Article 9 procedure. For example, even where

---

The fact that the commitments are not imposed by the Commission but voluntarily submitted and implemented only after discussions with the parties *as well as* a market test may also facilitate the later implementation of the commitments".

[32]For the introduction of criteria that further restrict the scope of application of Article 9 see eg Petit (2010), 49; Voss (2013), 164; Lugard/Möllmann (2013), 10f; Botteman/Patsa (2013), 368f; Mestmäcker/Schweitzer (2014), § 21, 61; Jenny (2015), 768f; von Kalben (2018), 436ff, and the references cited further below.

[33]See Rachwol (2010), 112ff: "Die Schwierigkeiten, allgemein handhabbare Abgrenzungskriterien zwischen dem Anwendungsbereich von Untersagungs- und Zusagenentscheidungen zu finden, lassen diesbezüglich nur beschränkte Aussagen zu. Dennoch sollte ein wesentliches – obwohl wenig trennscharfes – Merkmal für die Kommission bei der Ausübung ihres Ermessens bezüglich der Wahl zwischen diesen beiden Entscheidungsarten vor allem die Schwere des vermuteten Wettbewerbsverstoßes sein. [. . .] Eine pauschale, abstrakte und weitergehende Abgrenzung des Anwendungsbereichs von Art. 7 und Art. 9 VO 1/2003 lässt sich – wenn überhaupt – nur sehr schwer vornehmen. [. . .] Es sind die konkreten Fälle, in denen die [. . .] allgemeinen Kriterien bei der Wahl der Entscheidungsart durch die Kommission abzuwägen sind".

[34]Botteman/Patsa (2013), 368.

[35]See Schweitzer (2012), 6ff, with a detailed overview of the practice in the Member States.

an infringement of a serious nature, for example a margin squeeze, is of a long duration and has likely had a strong impact on third parties who may thus have an interest in follow on action, the benefit of swiftly resolving the competition concerns or the prospect of an effective implementation of the remedy may nevertheless tilt the balance in favour of the commitment procedure. The conclusion defended here is corroborated by the fact that also the enforcement guidelines of the competition authorities of the Member States that are invoked as models by the supporters of a stronger restriction of the Commission's power to accept commitments in cases of serious infringements contain only vague and flexible formulations that leave room for an assessment according to the circumstances of the individual case.[36]

On the other hand, the conclusion that it is too difficult to develop abstract criteria to restrict the scope of application of Article 9 applies also in so far as commentators stress that commitments should be excluded in cases involving novel or controversial theories of harm.[37] To start with, there is the difficulty to define when a theory of harm is truly novel or controversial. For example, Dunne classifies the theories of harm of excessive pricing and refusal to supply as controversial and considers that the use of commitments is problematic where such theories of harm are concerned.[38] Is this supposed to mean that the Commission should never accept commitments in refusal to deal and excessive pricing cases? Should the Commission refrain from doing so as a general rule? Wagner-von Papp suggests that a theory of harm should be considered as novel and the Commission prevented from applying the Article 9 procedure where the Commission is not able to support the stated theories of harm with precedent.[39] Wagner-von Papp's suggestion sounds at first blush tempting in view of its simplicity. However, at second thought his suggestion faces the objection

[36]See Autorité de la concurrence, Communiqué de procédure du 2 mars 2009 relatif aux engagements en matière de concurrence, 11: "L'Autorité n'applique pas la procédure d'engagements dans les cas où, en tout état de cause, l'atteinte à l'ordre public économique impose le prononcé de sanctions pécuniaires, ce qui exclut notamment *a priori* les ententes particulièrement graves comme les cartels et certains abus de position dominante ayant déjà causé un dommage à l'économie important".

OFT Enforcement Guidelines (2004), 4.4 fn 16: "The OFT will not accept, other than in very exceptional circumstances, binding commitments in cases involving secret cartels [...] Nor will the OFT accept binding commitments in cases involving serious abuse of a dominant position. It is the OFT's assessment of the seriousness of an abuse and its effect on competition which will be taken into account in determining whether commitments are appropriate in a particular case. When making its assessment, the OFT will consider a number of factors, including the nature of the product, the structure of the market, the market share(s) of the undertaking(s) involved, entry conditions and the effect on competitors and third parties (the term product would be interpreted to include goods, services and property rights). The damage caused to consumers whether directly or indirectly will also be an important consideration. This assessment will be made on a case by case basis, taking account of all the circumstances of the case. However, as a general rule, the OFT will regard predatory pricing as a serious abuse".

[37]For such claims see eg Gippini-Fournier (2008), 411; Wagner-Von Papp (2012), 969; Schweitzer (2012), 22; Marsden (2013), 11; Botteman/Patsa (2013), 369; von Kalben (2018), 437f.

[38]Dunne (2014), 415.

[39]Wagner-von Papp (2012), 968f.

that it does not deliver a criterion to distinguish when an existing precedent is strong enough to permit the application of the Article 9 procedure[40]: Should a controversial precedent like the Microsoft I judgment of the General Court be sufficient to permit the application of the Article 9 procedure or does the precedent have to be confirmed by the Court of Justice? Is one judgment sufficient or does there have to be a consistent line of case law? What about cases, in which the Commission applies precedents by analogy, as is frequently the case in law, where cases are hardly ever identical?

The difficulty to determine when a theory of harm is truly novel is well illustrated by the Google Search case, in which the Commission, after having negotiated three different sets of commitments, finally reverted to the article 7 procedure[41]: Although the abusive conduct identified by the Commission did not fit into an established abuse category such as tying, discrimination or refusal to supply, the Commission rejected the novelty of the abuse by referring to the rather abstract theory of harm of extending a dominant position to adjacent markets ("leveraging"), which it qualified as a "well established, independent, form of abuse falling outside the scope of competition on the merits".[42]

More important than this difficulty is, however, that even in novel or controversial cases the benefits of setting a precedent will not necessarily outweigh the benefits of the Article 9 procedure. For example, a novel or controversial case may be of limited precedential value because it predicates on factual circumstances that are unlikely to arise again. Furthermore, in particular in a dynamic market, the

[40]Legal certainty cannot be measured in a simple binary code that only distinguishes between whether a precedent exists or not. Gautier/Petit (2014), 8, rightly point out that legal certainty "depends on a range of factors". They mention inter alia: "absence of judicial precedent, divergences in precedents, weakness of precedent, inaccuracy of precedent, age of precedent, inconsistency in precedents".

[41]The legal qualification of the "naked restrictions" in the Intel judgment of the General Court (T-286/09, 2014) may serve as a further example: The Court ruled that three practices applied by Intel clearly fell outside the scope of competition on the merits (209), because they were targeted directly against the products of Intel's competitor AMD (204f). Although there was no direct precedent in the case law, the Court relied on the British Sugar judgment, holding that the rationale underlying that judgment supported its conclusion in the Intel case (207). The Court also rejected Intel's argument that the alleged novelty of the type of abuse should have prevented the Commission from imposing a fine. In the view of the Court, the fact that the practices clearly fell outside the scope of competition on the merits excluded that their prohibition could be considered as novel (219 and 1602). In the light of the Court's reasoning, one might of course argue that the concerns resulting from the naked restrictions could not have been addressed in a commitment decision due to their seriousness. It seems, however, difficult to argue that the "novelty" or the "lack of precedent" should have excluded the adoption of a commitment decision.

[42]COMP/39.740 (Google Search, 2017), 649, appeal pending under T-612/17. For the controversy about the novelty of the Commission's theory of harm see, on the one hand, Akman (2017); Höppner (2017); Vesterdorf/Fountoukakos (2018), 6; Kuenzler (2019).

benefit of bringing about a rapid solution may outweigh the benefit of setting a precedent.[43]

Overall, it is hence submitted that there is little to be gained from introducing further criteria that constrain the Commission's power to apply the Article 9 procedure in serious, novel or controversial cases. For the avoidance of misunderstandings: This conclusion does not mean that the Commission should be relieved of having to take account of the need to set a precedent, to deter third parties or to facilitate follow on actions. However, these factors, which militate for an Article 7 decision, must always be balanced against the advantages of the Article 9 procedure, in particular the simplification of the procedure, a swifter resolution of the competitive concerns and a more effective implementation of the remedy. Outside the area of secret cartels, this balancing exercise depends to an extent of the circumstances of the individual case that makes generalised statements when the application of the Article 9 procedure should be excluded too difficult.

5.1.1.4 Manifest Error in Choosing the Article 9 Procedure As a Ground for Judicial Review

In the action brought by Hynix against the Rambus commitments, the former company argued inter alia that the Commission should not have adopted a commitment decision in view of the seriousness of the infringement.[44] As explained above, the General Court did not have to decide the question, because Hynix later withdrew its action.[45] In Morningstar, the General Court seems to have ruled that the Commission does not have to set out reasons why it adopted an article 9 and not an article 7 decision.[46] This jurisprudence must be seen critically. The requirement of effective legal protection, the rule of law and the public interest in an effective enforcement of EU competition law militate in favour of the possibility to challenge a commitment decision on the ground that the Commission should have adopted an Article 7 decision instead. Such a plea in law is, however, from the outset made impossible, if the Commission is not even obliged to state the reasons why it went for an article 7 and not for an article 9 decision. It is also submitted that the EU Courts should consider the balancing of the respective pros and cons of the Article 7 and the Article 9 procedure as a "complex assessment" that implies discretion for the Commission. An applicant should therefore have to show that the Commission violated the Tetra

---

[43]That the advantages of a quick resolution of the competition concerns may outweigh the benefit of setting a precedent in a novel or controversial case is acknowledged by some proponents of a restriction of the Commission's power to adopt commitment decisions in novel cases: eg Gippini-Fournier (2008), 411; Botteman/Patsa (2013), 369, who suggest a "caveat for cases which, despite involving novel legal issues or untested theories of harm necessitate immediate intervention (eg certain fast evolving markets)".

[44]See the summary of the application in T-148/10 (Hynix); Botteman/Patsa (2013), 359f.

[45]See Sect. 2.3.1.1.2 with footnotes 158f above.

[46]GC, T-76/14 (Morningstar, 2016), 97 and 101.

Laval standard when it decided to adopt a commitment decision instead of an Article 7 decision.

5.1.2 *No Right to a Commitment Decision?*

In the context of merger control, the notifying parties have a right that the Commission accepts their commitments, if these suffice to eliminate the competition concerns.[47] However, contrary to what is sometimes contended,[48] the existence of this right under the Merger Regulation does not permit the conclusion that a comparable right exists also under Regulation 1/03.[49] The enforcement mechanism of the Merger Regulation is different from that of Regulation 1/03. A concentration that falls under the scope of the Merger Regulation is prohibited unless it is declared compatible with the common market. As a corollary of this broad prohibition, the notifying parties have a right that the Commission declares the concentration compatible with the common market if the concentration does not raise competition concerns. The Commission can, however, not modify a concentration unilaterally to make it compatible with the common market. The Commission can only accept commitments offered by the notifying parties or prohibit the entire concentration.[50] If initially existing competition concerns can be eliminated by commitments, the Commission must hence accept these and declare the concentration compatible with the common market. In the context of Regulation 1/03, the behaviour of the undertakings is at the outset free. Intervention by the Commission is limited to cases with competition concerns. In order to eliminate existing competition concerns, the Commission can either accept commitments on the basis of Article 9 or impose an injunction on the basis of Article 7.

Under Regulation 1/03, it follows from the wording of Article 9, which stipulates that the Commission "may" adopt a commitment decision, that the Commission enjoys discretion to reject a commitment offer in favour of an Article 7 decision, even if the commitment would eliminate the competition concerns.[51] Also Recital

---

[47]See Saitzek (2008), 155; Körber (2012), Art. 8 FKVO, 125; also GC, T-342/07 (Ryanair, 2010), 28: "Where commitments have been validly proposed by the parties to the concentration during the administrative procedure in order to obtain a decision that the concentration is compatible with the common market, the Commission is required to examine the concentration as modified by those commitments. It is then for the Commission to demonstrate that those commitments do not render the concentration, as modified by the commitments, compatible with the common market".

[48]See Ritter (2012), Art. 9, 15 together with fn 79; Schütz (2013), Art. 9, 7.

[49]See Saitzek (2008), 156; Hennig (2010), 160.

[50]Merger Remedies Study (2008), 6.

[51]Wils (2006), 350; Rachwol (2010), 107.

13, 1st sentence, Regulation 1/03, which states that the Commission "should be able" to adopt commitment decisions, militates for discretion.[52] Nevertheless, the sole fact that the Commission enjoys discretion in rejecting commitments does not necessarily mean that this discretion is unlimited. This begs the question, whether there are any limits to the Commission's discretion to reject commitment decisions.

5.1.2.1 Position of the Commission and the EU Courts

In the Manual of Procedures, the Commission emphasises that undertakings are by no means entitled to a commitment decision, even if the Commission previously settled a similar case.[53] In Alrosa, the General Court stated that the Commission was "never obliged" under Article 9(1) to decide to make commitments binding instead of proceedings under Article 7. In the view of the Court, it followed that the Commission was also "not required to give the reasons" why it decided not to accept a commitment.[54] Even though the Court of Justice did not expressly endorse that statement, the Alrosa judgment points in a similar direction.[55] In Cartes Bancaires, the General Court confirmed that the Commission had discretion in choosing between the Article 7 and the Article 9 procedure.[56] Moreover, the General Court ruled that a commitment offer that was rejected by the Commission could not serve as a point of reference for the assessment of the proportionality of an Article 7 decision.[57]

5.1.2.2 Doctrine

In the literature, it is controversial whether the Commission's discretion to reject commitments can turn into an obligation to accept commitments, if these eliminate the existing competition concerns. Three approaches can be distinguished. According to the first approach, there are no limits to the Commission's discretion in rejecting commitments. In particular Wils argues that "it is essential that the undertakings concerned are not given any right to a commitment decision".[58] In his

[52]Ortiz Blanco/Jörgens/Kellerbauer (2013), 13.09 fn 29. Schütz (2013), Art. 9, 7, construes Recital 13 Regulation 1/03 as meaning that the Commission "should" adopt commitment decisions. As explained by Hennig (2010), 159 fn 759, this interpretation is incorrect.

[53]Manual of Procedures (2012), Module 16, 16.

[54]GC, T-170/06 (Alrosa, 2007), 130.

[55]Wils (2011), fn 45. See also COMP/39.740 (Google Search, 2017), 125 and 730ff.

[56]GC, T-491/07 (Cartes Bancaires, 2012), 430.

[57]GC, T-491/07 (Cartes Bancaires, 2012), 429.

[58]Wils (2006), 350; consenting Choné/Souam/Vialfont (2014), 177; see also Wils (2008), 338 and 345 and (2011), fn 45; similarly de Bronnet (2012), Art. 9, 14: "Die Kommission ist unter keinen Umständen verpflichtet, angebotene Verpflichtungszusagen anzunehmen. [. . .] Sie hat das Angebot weder formell zurückzuweisen, noch die Ablehnung in einer möglichen späteren Entscheidung

view, the exclusion of any right for the concerned undertakings to a commitment decision is necessary "[i]n order to ensure that the benefits of infringement decisions [...] are adequately weighed in the choice between commitment decisions and infringement decisions".[59] The second approach posits that the principle of proportionality requires the Commission to accept commitments that eliminate the existing competition concerns. Proponents of this view argue in particular that commitments that eliminate the competition concerns are equally effective and less burdensome than the adoption of Article 7 decisions, potentially accompanied by fines. In that connection, they emphasise the consensual nature of a commitment decision, the absence of fines and the absence of a facilitation of damages actions.[60] According to the third approach, the Commission's discretion to reject commitments is or at least should be limited by the principle of equal treatment.[61]

5.1.2.3 Comment

On the one hand, the approach according to which the principle of proportionality requires the Commission to accept commitments that eliminate the competition concerns is not convincing. When the Commission chooses between an Article 7 and an Article 9 decision, its assessment is not limited to the question whether a commitment would have eliminated the competition concerns in an equally effective, but less burdensome manner than an Article 7 decision, potentially accompanied by a fine. Rather, the Commission must also take the other benefits of an Article 7 decision and a fine into account, in particular the need to deter third parties, to facilitate private damages actions and to clarify the law by setting a precedent.[62]

On the other hand, it is, however, also not persuasive to grant the Commission unlimited leeway in choosing between an Article 7 and an Article 9 decision. If the Commission could choose at will between the two procedures without having to give reasons, this would amount to arbitrariness and run counter to the rule of law.[63]

---

nach Art. 7 Abs. 1 zu begründen"; Gippini-Fournier (2008), 419: "it is a discretionary choice to engage in commitment discussions, and the Commission does not need a particular reason to refuse to accept commitments".

[59] Wils (2006), 350.

[60] Saitzek (2008), 156ff; Anweiler (2009), Art. 9, 19; Schütz (2013), Art. 9, 2 and 7.

[61] See De Smijter/Sinclair (2014), 2.128.

[62] Similarly Hennig (2010), 159: "Die [...] Ansicht, wonach aus dem Verhältnismäßigkeitsgrundsatz folge, dass die Kommission verpflichtet sei, geeignete Verpflichtungszusagen anzunehmen, ist abzulehnen. [...] Die Entscheidung, ob die Kommission eine Verpflichtungszusageentscheidung oder eine Abstellungsentscheidung erlässt, hängt [...] nicht allein vom Grundsatz der Verhältnismäßigkeit ab. Vielmehr wird die Kommission in jedem Einzelfall prüfen, mit welcher Entscheidung [...] der Durchsetzung der Artt. 101 und 102 AEUV am besten gedient ist".

[63] See Wils (2011), text accompanying fn 4: "Discretion may be narrower or wider but is unlikely ever to be unlimited. The rule of law requires that no discretion should be unconstrained so as to be potentially arbitrary".

Contrary to what the General Court stated in Alrosa, it is hence submitted that the Commission must give reasons if it wants to reject a commitment decision.[64] This conclusion applies without prejudice to the fact that the Commission may reject a commitment offer that would eliminate the competition concerns, for instance because the Commission considers that there is a need to deter third parties, to facilitate private damages actions or to clarify the law by setting a precedent. If a concerned undertaking wants to challenge the Commission's rejection of a commitment, it must bring an action against the final Article 7 decision. As explained above, the rejection of the commitment offer is merely a preparatory act that is not amenable to judicial review.[65] In an action against the final decision, the concerned undertaking should have the possibility to argue that the Commission violated the Tetra-Laval standard for limited review[66] when it balanced the respective pros and cons of an Article 7 and an Article 9 decision. Admittedly, in view of the many factors that need to be balanced, such an argument would in practice have only limited chances of success. Even if the Commission has not committed an error of assessment in deciding to adopt an Article 7 decision, the concerned undertakings should, however, still have the possibility to argue that the remedy that was adopted by the Commission on the basis of Article 7 should not have gone beyond what the undertaking offered as a commitment decision.[67] In that regard, the statement of the General Court that a rejected commitment offer cannot serve as a point of reference for the assessment of the proportionality of an Article 7 decision must be criticised.

Finally, it is submitted that the Commission's discretion to reject commitment decisions is limited by the principle of equal treatment. To the extent that the Manual of Procedures[68] and some voices in the literature[69] categorically exclude such a limitation, their positions are inconsistent with higher-ranking law. Nonetheless, the doubts that have been raised in the literature as regards the compatibility of the Commission's actual decisional practice with the principle of equal treatment[70] appear unfounded. In the context of fines, the EU Courts rightly apply the principle of equal treatment in a restrictive manner. The principle applies only if an applicant shows that the facts underlying his case are comparable to the facts of the cases relied

[64]For such an obligation also Gerard (2013), 34. See also the Commission decision in COMP/39.740 (Google Search, 2017), 126ff, which contains an obiter dictum in which the Commission explains in a rather detailed manner why it reverted to the article 7 procedure after having negotiated three sets of commitments.

[65]See Sect. 4.2.1.1.2.1.2 with footnote 177 above.

[66]See Sect. 4.2.2.1.2.1.3.2 with footnotes 313f above.

[67]In that direction also de Bronnet (2012), Art. 9, 14, who states that the reasoning of the final Article 7 decision will enable the concerned undertaking to evaluate the legality of the Article 7 decision also in comparison to a rejected commitment offer.

[68]See Sect. 5.1.2.1 with footnote 53 above.

[69]See the references in Sect. 5.1.1.1, footnote 8 above.

[70]See Petit (2010), 41; Podszun (2012), 63f; also, albeit not explicitly raising equal treatment concerns, Gerard (2013), 12; Gyselen (2014), 251.

on in support of his claim. In order to establish comparability, it is not sufficient to demonstrate that the types of infringement are similar. Rather, all relevant factors, such as the markets, the products, the countries, the undertakings and the periods concerned must be taken into account.[71] It is true that under this restrictive standard, the importance of the principle of equal treatment is mostly confined to situations where several undertakings are concerned by the same case.[72] Nonetheless, it is submitted that this restrictive standard should be applied mutatis mutandis also in the context of the Commission's discretion to reject commitment decisions.[73] The principle of equal treatment should hence only be applied, if the factors that are relevant for the choice between an Article 7 and an Article 9 decision coincide to a sufficiently large extent to make the invoked cases comparable. If one follows this suggestion, the criticism that is levied at the Commission's decisional practice is unfounded, because the cases relied on by the critics are not comparable.[74]

5.1.3 Remedies and the Commission's Power to Prioritise Cases

It is an inherent feature of the task to define and implement the competition policy of the EU that the Commission retains discretion as to whether and to what extent it takes action in a particular case.[75] This discretion allows the Commission not only to discontinue an entire case, but also to drop certain aspects.[76] The Commission may

---

[71]See eg GC, T-286/09 (Intel, 2014), 1614ff, in particular 1619; T-332/09 (Electrabel, 2012), 274.

[72]See Voss (2013), 163.

[73]Similarly Voss (2013), 162f.

[74]For instance, Podszun (2012), 63f, compares the fine in COMP/37.990 (Intel, 2009), on the one hand, and, on the other hand, the commitments in COMP/39.317 (E.On Gas, 2010) and COMP/39.386 39.386 (Long-term electricity contracts France, 2010). He argues that the Commission violated the principle of equal treatment, because all mentioned cases involved "large scale market foreclosure" ("großflächige Marktabschottung"). Similarly, Gyselen (2014), 251, asks why the Commission imposed fines in COMP/38.784 (Telefonica, 2007) and COMP/39.525 (Telekomunikacja Polska, 2011), but accepted commitments in COMP/39.402 (RWE Gas Foreclosure, 2009), although all three cases were margin squeeze cases. Gyselen also asks why the Commission accepted commitments in COMP/39.116 (Coca-Cola, 2005), but imposed fines in COMP/38.113 (Tomra, 2006) and COMP/37.990 (Intel, 2009), although all three cases related to loyalty rebates and exclusive dealing. Gerard (2013), 12, contrasts the commitment accepted in COMP/39736 (Siemens/Areva, 2012) to address concerns resulting from a non-compete obligation to the fine imposed in COMP/39839 (Telefonica/Portugal Telecom, 2013) for the use of a non-compete obligation. According to the restrictive approach suggested here, the mentioned pairs of cases are not comparable.

[75]See GC, T-24/90 (Automec II, 1992), 77; T-712/14 (CEAHR, 2017), 34f; T-480/15 (Agria Polska, 2018), 34f. Generally on the Commission's power to prioritise cases see eg Jones/Sufrin (2014), 1072ff. As regards the power of the national competition authorities to prioritise case see recital 23 and article 10, paragraph 2, Regulation 2019/1.

[76]See Wils (2011), 12.

decline action in particular where it finds that there is no sufficient Union interest to warrant the necessary time and resources.[77] This may be the case, for instance, where the Commission finds that an alleged infringement is not serious enough or that enforcement by national competition authorities or national courts is in any event sufficient.[78] The Commission's discretion as regards this power to prioritise cases is, however, not unlimited. The Commission must in particular take into consideration all the relevant matters of law brought to its attention and state sufficient reasons why it decides not to take further action.[79]

The power of the Commission to prioritise cases can influence the content of a remedy in two ways. The more important one is certainly a potential enlargement of the Commission's leeway. Where complainants or other individually concerned third parties claim that a remedy does not reach far enough, the question arises whether the Commission can rely on its power to prioritise cases in defence of the remedy. On the other hand, at least in theory, the exercise of the power to prioritise cases also sets up certain limits to the Commission's remedial powers as regards future cases.

5.1.3.1 Enlargement of the Commission's Discretion

In the context of Article 9, it is controversial whether the Commission may only accept commitments that fully eliminate its concerns[80] or whether it is sufficient that commitments reduce the concerns to such a degree that the case no longer is a matter of administrative priority.[81] The question arises also in the context of Article 7: Can the Commission content itself with imposing a remedy that brings an infringement outside the scope of its priorities?[82] In the context of Article 9, Recital 13, 2nd sentence, states that commitment decisions should find that there are no longer grounds for action by the Commission without concluding whether or not there has been or still is an infringement. This language clearly indicates that the Commission can content itself with a commitment that brings the infringement outside

[77] See Recital 18 Regulation 1/03; GC, T-119/09 (Protégé, 2012), 34.

[78] See Commission's Notice on the handling of complaints (2004), 44; Best Practices (2011), 136 and 138.

[79] See GC, T-427/08 (CEAHR, 2010), 28; Lübking/von Koppenfels (2012), 80.

[80] This view is defended by Klees (2005), 125; Saitzek (2008), 126ff; Jaeger (2009), Art. 9, 17; Hennig (2010), 171ff; Schweitzer (2010), 574ff and (2011), 646.

[81] This view is defended by Temple Lang (2003), 349 and (2006), 290; Dalheimer (2005), Art. 9, 5; Busse/Leopold (2005), 151; Sousa Ferro (2005), 456; Whish (2006), 569; Wils (2006), 357f; von Rosenberg (2009), 246f; Botteman/Patsa (2013), 371.

[82] See Schweitzer (2010), 575, who bases her argument that an Article 9 commitment must "address the alleged infringement of the competition rules in full" on the "parallels between Article 7 procedures and Article 9 procedures" drawn by the GC in Alrosa. Schweitzer hence appears to be of the opinion that, in the context of an Article 7 remedy, the Commission cannot rely on its right to prioritise, but must eliminate the alleged infringement in full.

the scope of its priorities. Also the Commission's decisional practice[83] and its Manual of Procedures[84] point in the latter direction. The approach finds also support in the case law of the Courts. In their view, "the Commission may decide that it is not appropriate to act upon a complaint where the undertakings concerned agree to change their conduct so that there is no longer sufficient Community interest in acting".[85] Moreover, the General Court decided that the Commission could rely on its right to prioritise cases in order to reject a complaint that had requested a reopening of proceedings pursuant to Article 9(2), because the concerned undertaking allegedly failed to comply with the commitment that had been made binding.[86]

It is submitted that the latter approach is correct. Irrespective of whether it is adopted on the basis of Article 7 or 9, the Commission can defend a remedy against pleas alleging its insufficiency by relying on the right to prioritise cases. In fact, any obligation of the Commission to pursue alleged violations of Articles 101 and 102 TFEU is subject to the Commission's right to prioritise. However, where the Commission lawfully decides not to investigate a certain aspect of a case any further because it does not assign a priority to it, the Commission cannot be obliged to request or impose a remedy.[87] Moreover, even where the Commission finds that a certain aspect of a case amounts to an infringement, it retains discretion not to impose a remedy in that regard. This results from the structure of Article 7, which provides that the Commission "may" require the concerned undertaking to bring a found infringement to an end. As explained above, the Commission's discretion is not unlimited, but merely subject to a restricted judicial control.

---

[83]See the rejection decision in BA/AA/IB (COMP/39596): "The Commission has come to the conclusion that by virtue of [the commitments] the identified competition concerns are met in a satisfactory way and there is no sufficient European Union interest in the further investigation of the present complaint." The rejection decision in Rambus (COMP/38636), 92, is even more clear: "[E]ven if the possible, minor shortcomings of certain aspects of the remedies were to be considered to be substantiated, the whole package of Commitments substantially addresses the concerns expressed by the Commission in the present case. In this context [. . .] the Commission considers that the Community interest does not warrant continuing the investigation any further."

[84]See the Manual of Procedures (2012), Module 21, 47 together with 54: "When deciding whether there is a sufficient degree of European Union interest for acting, the Commission will normally look at [. . .] the cessation or modification of the conduct complained of, in particular where commitments have been made binding by a Commission decision pursuant to Article 9 of Regulation 1/03 [. . .], provided that neither significant persisting anti-competitive effects nor the seriousness of the alleged infringement(s) constitute sufficient grounds for conducting a further investigation in spite of the cessation or modification".

[85]GC, T-108/07 (Spira, 2013), 196; see also para 156 of the said judgment and CJ, C-449/98 P (IECC, 2001), 48f: "there is no longer sufficient Community interest where the undertakings concerned agree to change their conduct in a manner conducive to the general interest"; see also the Commission's Notice on the handling of complaints (2004), 44.

[86]See GC, T-342/11 (CEES, 2014), 47ff.

[87]See Wils (2006), 357f and von Rosenberg (2009), 246f: In their view, it follows from the Commission's right not to investigate cases without priority at all that the Commission may accept commitments under Article 9 that merely bring an alleged infringement outside the scope of the Commission's enforcement priorities.

Restitutionary orders shall serve as a first example. It was argued above[88] that Article 7 empowers the Commission to order the restitution of anticompetitive profits. A complainant might therefore argue that the Commission should have imposed such an order.[89] However, in most cases there will be no corresponding obligation for the Commission. The Commission can rely on its right to prioritise in order to abstain from imposing a restitutionary order, for instance by declining an EU interest in view of the possibility of private enforcement. Loyalty rebates can serve as a further illustration. According to the interpretation given to Article 102 TFEU by the Courts, loyalty rebates may be prohibited even if they do not result in a setting of prices below cost by the dominant undertaking.[90] In the 2008 Guidance,[91] the Commission states, however, that it will concentrate its activity on such loyalty rebates that lead to below cost pricing.[92] If one assumes that the Commission can lawfully confine its enforcement priorities to the content set out in the Guidance,[93] then the Commission could limit its remedy to an order to raise the rebate to an above cost level, even though the rebate could be prohibited further according to the case law of the Courts.

5.1.3.2 A Limit to the Commission's Powers

In exceptional circumstances, the Commission's enforcement priorities may also limit its margin of manoeuvre with respect to remedies. On the one hand, the indirect binding effect of soft-law instruments recognised by the Courts[94] also applies to the

[88] See Sect. 3.3.4.1.3 with footnotes 670ff above.

[89] See also GC, T-213/01 (Österreichische Postsparkasse, 2006), 114, where the Court considered that a final consumer who shows that his economic interests have been harmed or are likely to be harmed as a result of a restriction of competition has a legitimate interest pursuant to Article 7(2) to act as a complainant.

[90] See CJ, C-549/10 P (Tomra, 2012), 73; GC, T-286/09 (Intel, 2014), 144f.

[91] Pursuant to paras 2 and 3, the Guidance paper merely sets out the Commission's enforcement priorities. It does not constitute a statement of law and does not influence the interpretation of Article 102 TFEU by the Courts. Generally on the Guidance see Whish/Bailey (2012); Jones/Sufrin (2014), 289ff.

[92] See Guidance (2008), 41ff: In essence, the Commission wants to estimate what price a competitor would have to offer in order to compensate the customer for the loss of the conditional rebate in case of a partial switch away from the dominant undertaking. The Commission will prosecute the rebate if that price is below a certain measure of the costs of the dominant undertaking.

[93] In view of the Commission's task to ensure the application of the Treaties pursuant to Article 17 (1) TEU and the discrepancy between the interpretation of Article 102 TFEU by the Courts and the content of the Commission's Guidance, this assumption appears questionable. The question shall, however, not be further discussed here. Critically eg Ackermann (2010), 11, who raises concerns against the Commission's effort to reshape the substantive competition rules in a document disguised as mere enforcement priorities.

[94] See Sect. 1.3 with footnotes 48f above.

2008 Guidance.[95] The latter may therefore prevent the Commission from imposing remedies that go beyond the enforcement priorities laid down in it. On the other hand, also where no abstract soft law exists, the Commission's decisional practice must observe the principle of equal treatment. In general, the Commission may therefore only impose different remedies in comparable cases where an objective justification exists.[96]

Nevertheless, in practice, the Commission's enforcement priorities will hardly ever serve as a limit to the Commission' remedial discretion. The 2008 Guidance is phrased in careful terms that leave ample room for the Commission to take action also in cases that are described in the paper as not typically belonging to the Commission's enforcement priorities.[97] As far as the binding effect of the Commission's prior decisional practice is concerned, the exigencies for showing that two cases are comparable are strict. In the context of fines, the Courts request an applicant to demonstrate the comparability by taking account of the concerned markets, products, countries, undertakings, periods and the evolution of the Commission's policy.[98] These requirements apply mutatis mutandis for the imposition of remedies.[99]

5.1.3.3 Article 9 Does Not Increase the Commission's Power to Prioritise Cases

In any event, it is submitted that the Article 9 procedure does not increase the Commission's discretion in prioritising cases in comparison to the Article 7 procedure. As explained above, also where the Commission imposes a remedy on the basis of Article 7, the remedy does not need to fully eliminate all existing competition concerns. Rather, the Commission can confine itself to addressing the concerns that are covered by its enforcement priorities. The fact that the Commission may adopt commitments that only bring a case outside the scope of the Commission's enforcement priorities is therefore no disadvantage of the Article 9 procedure in terms of legal certainty.

[95] See Jones/Sufrin (2011), 1107; Fuchs/Möschel (2012), Art. 102, 15.

[96] See, as regards decisions imposing fines, GC, T-360/09 (E.ON Ruhrgas, 2012), 261f; T-286/09 (Intel 2014), 1615.

[97] See Kellerbauer (2010), 184; Jones/Sufrin (2011), 277. In particular, the Commission states in para 8 of the Guidance that it will apply the "general enforcement principles" set out only where this suits the circumstances of a given case and that it may, where appropriate, adapt its approach.

[98] See GC, T-286/09 (Intel, 2014), 1614ff.

[99] See Sect. 5.1.2.3 with footnotes 68ff above.

5.1.4 Effects on Competition Authorities and Courts of the Member States

The effects of Article 9 decisions on competition authorities and courts of the Member States were initially discussed intensely and controversially.[100] The judgment of the Court of Justice in Gasorba[101] has in the meantime contributed significantly to clarify the question. Further clarifications will result from the appeal in Canal+,[102] which is still pending at the time of writing. On the contrary, the effects of Article 7 decisions on competition authorities and courts of the Member States have been discussed only sparsely.[103]

The text of Regulation 1/03 does not contain a clear statement as regards the effects of decisions adopted on the basis of Article 7 and Article 9 on the competition authorities and courts of the Member States. In order to ensure the uniform application of EU competition law, Article 16(1) Regulation 1/03 provides that national courts cannot take decisions running counter to the decision adopted by the Commission, when they rule on practices under Article 101 or 102 TFEU which are already the subject of a Commission decision. According to Article 16(2) Regulation 1/03, the same applies also to competition authorities of the Member States. According to Recital 13, 2nd sentence, Regulation 1/03, commitment decisions should find that there are no longer grounds for action by the Commission without concluding whether there has been or still is an infringement. Recital 13, 3rd sentence, and Recital 22, 3rd sentence, Regulation 1/03, stipulate that commitment decisions do not affect the powers of the national courts and competition authorities to apply Articles 101 and 102 TFEU. Since these provisions leave room for interpretation, it is necessary to analyse the effects of decisions adopted on the basis of Article 7 and Article 9 on the competition authorities and courts of the Member States in more detail. In that regard, it appears useful to distinguish between the effects on the power to impose fines; the effects on the power to adopt further injunctions or commitments; the effects on private damages claims; and the question whether remedies that have been adopted on the basis of Article 7 or Article 9 can be enforced by competition authorities and courts of the Member States.

Two preliminary remarks are called for. First, by virtue of Article 11(6) Regulation 1/03, the initiation of proceedings by the Commission relieves the national competition authorities of their competence to apply Articles 101 and 102 TFEU. Article 11(6) Regulation 1/03 does, however, not apply to national courts, except

[100] For overviews see eg Saitzek (2008), 208ff; Rachwol (2010), 200ff; Hennig (2010), 253ff; Imgrund (2011), 139ff.

[101] CJ, C-547/16 (Gasorba, 2017). For a discussion of the judgment see Paulus (2017), 236; Fasoula (2018), 60; Nijhof (2018), 9; Makris/Feases (2018), 1959; Hartlieb (2018), 46.

[102] C-132/19 P (Canal+, pending).

[103] But see eg Dohrn (2010), 56f; Imgrund (2011), 136f.

when they act as competition authorities.[104] Moreover, the provision removes the power of the national competition authorities not on a permanent basis, but only for the duration of the procedure before the Commission.[105] In view of the limited effects of Article 11(6) TFEU, the provision will not be discussed in more detail here. Second, it should be recalled that pursuant to Article 3(2), last sentence, Regulation 1/03, Member States are not precluded from adopting and applying on their territory national law that is stricter than EU law in respect of unilateral conduct. Decisions adopted by the Commission on the basis of Article 7 or 9 hence leave the powers of the Member States unaffected to apply stricter national law in regard of unilateral conduct.[106]

5.1.4.1 Effects on Power to Find an Infringement and Impose a Fine

The question arises whether Commission decisions adopted on the basis of Article 7 or Article 9 preclude the imposition of a fine by a national competition authority or court. In that regard, the ne bis in idem principle laid down in Article 50 Charter must be respected in addition to Article 16 Regulation 1/03. According to the jurisprudence of the EU Courts, the ne bis in idem principle must be observed in proceedings for the imposition of fines under competition law.[107] It precludes an undertaking being found liable or proceedings being brought against it afresh on the grounds of anti-competitive conduct for which it has been penalised or declared not liable by an earlier decision that can no longer be challenged.[108] However, the principle of ne bis in idem applies only to proceedings that are of a criminal nature.[109] If either the first or the second procedure is not of a criminal nature, the principle is not applicable.

5.1.4.1.1 Article 7 Decisions

If the Commission adopts a decision on the basis of Article 7 that is accompanied by a fine pursuant to Article 23(2), the ne bis in idem principle precludes the imposition of a second fine for the same infringement by a national competition authority or court. It is submitted that the same applies also where the Commission merely adopts

---

[104]See Article 35(3) Regulation 1/03; Saitzek (2008), 235ff; Ritter (2012), Art. 11, 27 and Art. 35, 1; for the contrary view see Rab/Monnoyeur/Sukhtankar (2010), 185.

[105]GC, T-342/11 (CEES), 67; see also CJ, C-17/10 (Toshiba, 2012), 78f with 85; Gippini-Fournier (2008), 401f.

[106]See eg Whish (2006), 567f; Wils (2006), 362; Kellezi (2010), 383f.

[107]GC, T-128/11 (LG Display, 2014), 214.

[108]CJ, C-238/99 P (LVM, 2002), 59; C-17/10 (Toshiba, 2012), 94; GC, T-128/11 (LG Display, 2014), 214.

[109]Jarass (2013), Art. 50, 5a and 8; see also ECtHR, n° 46410/99 (Üner, 2006), 56; CJ, C-150/10 (Beneo, 2011), 70ff; C-489/10 (Bonda, 2012), 26ff; opinion of AG Kokott in C-526/08 (Commission/Luxemburg, 2010), 31ff.

an Article 7 decision without imposing a fine. An Article 7 decision in which the Commission abstains from imposing a fine must be considered as a substantive decision that no fine should be imposed. This is evident if the Commission states the reasons why it refrains from imposing a fine.[110] However, for reasons of legal certainty, also decisions in which the Commission does not expressly state the reasons why it does not impose a fine[111] should be considered as substantive decisions that no fine should be imposed. The latter conclusion is supported by the case law of the Court of Justice according to which the decision not to impose a fine on an undertaking having entered into an anticompetitive agreement constitutes an exceptional departure from the principles set out in Article 101 TFEU that must be based on objective reasons.[112]

It was argued above that the Commission could adopt decisions on the basis of Article 7 that do not fully eliminate all existing competition concerns, but merely bring an infringement outside the scope of its enforcement priorities. This raises the question whether, for the period after the adoption of the Article 7 decision, compliance with the Article 7 decision bars the national competition authorities and courts from the finding of an infringement and the imposition of fines. Since this question arises equally in the context of Article 9, it will be addressed below.

5.1.4.1.2 Article 9 Decisions

It is broadly accepted in the literature that the adoption of a commitment decision does not preclude the finding of an infringement and the imposition of a fine for the period before the commitment decision was adopted.[113] In Gasorba, the Court of Justice endorsed that position.[114] Contrary opinions are from the outset not convincing. For instance, Gruber argues that the ne bis in idem principle excludes the imposition of a fine. In his view, the adoption of a commitment decision implies a substantive decision by the Commission not to impose a fine.[115] However, Gruber ignores that the Article 9 procedure is not of a criminal nature. Moreover, the Commission does not take a substantive decision whether a fine should be imposed

---

[110]Eg OJ 1978 L 70/54 (Vegetable Parchment, 1977), 82f; OJ 1990 L 220/28 (Stainless Steel, 1990), X.14; COMP/38.096 (Clearstream, 2004); 344f; COMP/39.985 (Motorola, 2014), 559ff.

[111]OJ 1990 L 351/46 (Bayer Dental, 1990); OJ 1998 L 246/1 (Van den Bergh Foods, 1998); COMP/34.493 (Duales System Deutschland, 2001); COMP/38.606 (Cartes Bancaires, 2007); COMP/38.698 (CISAC, 2008).

[112]CJ, C-499/11 P (Dow Chemical, 2013), 47; COMP/39.985 (Motorola, 2014), 559.

[113]See eg Nazzini (2004), 7.32; Wils (2006), 360f; Whish (2006), 567; Armengol/Pascual (2006), 126; Bauer (2008), 4-9-046; Saitzek (2008), 216; Jaeger (2009), Art. 9, 37; Körber (2010), 80; Rab/Monnoyeur/Sukhtankar (2010), 185; Kellezi (2010), 383; Hennig (2010), 260f; Falconi (2011), 43; Schweitzer (2011), 654; Messina/Ho (2011), 749f; Wagner-von Papp (2012), 953 fn 89.

[114]CJ, C-547/16 (Gasorba, 2017), in particular 28.

[115]Gruber (2005), 313f; similarly Sousa Ferro (2005), 456f; Jaecks/Säcker (2008), 2-8-037.

or not. The principle of ne bis in idem cannot therefore exclude the imposition of a fine subsequent to the adoption of a commitment decision.[116]

As far as the period after the adoption of a commitment decision is concerned, different positions have been expressed in the literature whether compliance with the commitment bars the finding of an infringement and the imposition of a fine.[117] According to a first view, this is always the case. According to this view, the fact that compliance with a commitment decision eliminates the Commission's competition concerns is sufficient to bar national competition authorities and courts from further action.[118] A second view suggests that national competition authorities and courts can take further action to the extent that their findings go beyond the factual assessment made by the Commission in the commitment decision.[119] A third view extends the scope of action for national competition authorities and courts to factual and legal findings that go beyond the Commission's assessment in the commitment decision.[120] A fourth view assumes that compliance with a commitment decision does not at all affect the powers of the national competition authorities and courts to find an infringement and impose a fine.[121]

The third and fourth views lead to identical results. National competition authorities and courts cannot be considered to be barred from further action, if they can intervene not only when their factual assessment goes beyond that of the Commission, but also when their legal assessment diverges from that of the Commission.

[116] See Gippini-Fournier (2008), 401; Saitzek (2008), 221ff; Hennig (2010), 260; Ritter (2012), Art. 9, 31 fn 121.

[117] See, besides the references immediately below, also the detailed discussion by Temple Lang (2003), 348ff and (2006), 287ff; Waelbroeck (2009), 228ff.

[118] Montag/Rosenfeld (2003), 132; Nazzini (2004), 7.32; Gruber (2005), 313; Jaecks/Säcker (2008), 2-8-037; de Bronnet (2012), Art. 9, 18; for national competition authorities, but not for national courts, also Ortiz Blanco/Jörgens/Kellerbauer (2013), 13.36f: In their view, it follows from Articles 13(2), 11(6) and 16(2) that the NCAs must either reject the claim brought against the agreement in question or reach the same decision as the Commission, if the Commission has reached a decision concerning a case.

[119] See Hennig (2010), 261: "Mit einer Verpflichtungszusageentscheidung wird [...], für den Zeitraum nach Erlass der Entscheidung, eine zumindest eingeschränkte Sachentscheidung getroffen. Diese ist für die nationalen Behörden und Gerichte gemäß Art. 16 [VO 1/03] soweit verbindlich, wie die tatsächlichen Umstände mit der vorläufigen Beurteilung der Kommission übereinstimmen".

[120] Schweitzer (2011), 655: "[Dass eine Verpflichtungsentscheidung nach Art. 9 keine Feststellung einer Zuwiderhandlung beinhaltet] spricht dafür, dass ein Konflikt i.S.d. Art. 16 Abs. 1 bzw. Abs. 2 VO 1/2003 jedenfalls dann nicht vorliegt, wenn ein nationales Gericht oder eine nationale Behörde auf der Grundlage weitergehender tatsächlicher und/oder rechtlicher Feststellungen und der darauf gründenden Feststellung eines Wettbewerbsverstoßes weiterreichende Auflagen oder Verbote verhängt". See also Schweitzer (2010), 575f with fn 121, where she argues that commitment decisions should bar national competition authorities and courts in so far as their actions do not fall outside the scope of the competition concerns addressed by the commitment decision.

[121] Whish (2006), 569; Wils (2006), 361; Armengol/Pascual (2006), 126; Saitzek (2008), 214ff; Bauer (2008), 4-9-046; Gippini-Fournier (2008), 402; Jaeger (2009), Art. 9, 37; Dohrn (2010), 61; Rab/Monnoyeur/Sukhtankar (2010), 185; Imgrund (2011), 146f.

These views are also preferable to the first and the second view. The first view must at the outset be rejected. As explained above, a commitment decision does not necessarily eliminate all existing competition concerns. Rather, it can also bring the investigated conduct only outside the scope of the Commission's enforcement priorities.[122] Compliance with a commitment therefore only means that the investigated conduct no longer falls under the Commission's enforcement priorities. It does not mean that there is no longer an infringement of competition law. The second view limits the scope of further action for national competition authorities and courts to factual findings that go beyond the Commission's assessment in the commitment decision. This limitation is not persuasive for two reasons. First, it is difficult to determine which facts are covered by the Commission's assessment and which may still be addressed by a national competition authority or a court.[123] Second, the Commission's enforcement priorities may also touch upon legal questions. For example, in the 2008 Guidance Paper on the enforcement of Article 102 TFEU, the Commission stated that it would apply a case-by-case approach to exclusive purchasing obligations[124] and focus its action against loyalty rebates on those that lead to below cost pricing.[125] These criteria diverged, at least initially, from the case law of the EU Courts on exclusive purchasing[126] and loyalty rebates.[127] Where the legal assessment in a commitment decision expresses only the Commission's enforcement priorities, it cannot bar national competition authorities and courts from finding an infringement and imposing a fine.

The approach defended here corresponds also to the jurisprudence of the EU Courts. In Gasorba, the Court of Justice ruled that a commitment decision does not certify that the practice, which was the subject of concern, complies with the EU competition rules and that such a decision cannot 'legalise' the market behaviour of the undertaking concerned. Hence, a commitment decision does not preclude national competition authorities and courts from examining whether an undertaking complies with the competition rules and, if necessary, taking the adequate steps.[128] The Gasorba judgment is consistent with earlier case law. In Toshiba, the Court of Justice had already held that Article 16(2) Regulation 1/03 did not relieve the national authorities of their competence to take action after the Commission had intervened, but merely prohibited them from contradicting a previous Commission

[122]See Sect. 5.1.3.1 with footnotes 80ff above.

[123]See Wagner-von Papp (2012), 953 with fn 92, who points out that the determination to what extent the commitment decision completely removed the competitive concerns and to what extent the infringements remain is impracticable.

[124]Guidance (2008), 33ff.

[125]Guidance (2008), 41ff.

[126]GC, T-286/09 (Intel, 2014), 80ff. But see the reversal of the Court's case law in CJ, C-413/14 P (Intel, 2017), 138ff.

[127]CJ, C-549/10 P (Tomra, 2012), 73f; C-23/14 (Post Danmark, 2015), 51ff; GC, T-286/09 (Intel, 2014), 144f. But see the reversal of the Court's case law in CJ, C-413/14 P (Intel, 2017), 138ff.

[128]CJ, C-547/16 (Gasorba, 2017), 25ff.

decision.[129] In CEES, the General Court had stated that the parallel jurisdiction of the national competition authorities for the application of Articles 101 and 102 TFEU was not called into question by the adoption of a commitments decision by the Commission.[130]

The conclusion that compliance with a remedy does not bar the national competition authorities and courts of the member states from finding an infringement and imposing a fine must also apply in the context of Article 7. For example, if a dominant undertaking violated Article 102 TFEU by granting loyalty rebates, the Commission could limit its remedy under Article 7 to an order to raise the rebates to an above cost level.[131] Such an order would correspond to the Commission's enforcement priorities. Nonetheless, compliance with the Commission's remedy would not prevent the national competition authorities from finding an infringement and imposing a fine on the basis of stricter case law of the EU Courts. Even if the Commission's original decision had already included a fine, the ne bis in idem principle would not apply, because the fine imposed by the Commission would concern conduct prior to the adoption of the Commission's decision, whilst the fine imposed by the national competition authority would concern conduct postdating the adoption of the Commission's decision.

National competition authorities and courts cannot, however, find an infringement and impose a fine for conduct that is required by a remedy that was adopted by the Commission on the basis of Article 7 or Article 9. Otherwise their decision would run counter to the Commission's decision and thus violate Article 16 Regulation 1/03.[132] On the other hand, the General Court held, in Canal+, that an undertaking which had committed to the Commission no longer to honour certain territorial exclusivity clauses could, without violating the latter provision, be obliged by a national court to execute these clauses, if the national court found that they were compatible with article 101 TFUE. The General Court justified this approach in particular with the fact that the commitment decision was not binding upon the contractual partners of the undertaking which had entered into the commitment vis-à-vis the Commission. Moreover, the General Court considered that a resulting duty of the undertaking to breach the commitment needed to be addressed by the Commission by reopening its investigation in accordance with Article 9(2)(b).[133]

[129]CJ, C-17/10 (Toshiba, 2012), 85; see also the opinion of AG Kokott in the case, 84.

[130]GC, T-342/11 (CEES, 2014), 67.

[131]See Sect. 5.1.3.1 with footnote 93 above.

[132]In the context of Article 9 decisions: eg Cook (2006), 225; Gippini-Fournier (2008), 402; Rab/Monnoyeur/Sukhtankar (2010), 184; Kellezi (2010), 383; Messina/Ho (2011), 750; Schweitzer (2011), 655; Wagner-Von Papp (2012), 952.

[133]GC, T-873/16 (Canal+, 2018), 100-104, appeal pending under C-132/19 P. For a discussion of the case see Idot (2019), 73; Bernault (2019), 42; Debroux (2019), 70, who all point out that, in practice, it is rather unlikely that a national court declares an agreement compatible with 101 TFUE after the Commission has expressed concerns regarding this agreement in a commitment decision.

5.1.4.1.3 De Facto Effects of Commission Decisions

Commentators generally agree that, for various reasons, additional enforcement action by a national competition authority is in practice unlikely to happen once the Commission has adopted a commitment decision.[134] Additional enforcement by national competition authorities could be considered as a squandering of resources in view of the fact that the Commission has already dealt with the case.[135] It would require the national competition authorities to set its enforcement priorities different from those of the Commission.[136] In particular the finding of an infringement for the past and the imposition of a fine would undermine the attractiveness of the Commission's commitment procedure.[137] As regards the future conduct of the concerned undertaking, the Commission will normally address competition concerns in such a way that additional enforcement is not necessary.[138] For all these reasons and in view of the cooperation between the competition authorities that takes place within the network, it appears indeed unlikely that national competition authorities will take further enforcement action once the Commission has adopted a commitment decision.[139]

5.1.4.2 Effects on Power to Adopt Further Injunctions or Commitments

In the light of what has been mentioned so far, also the power of national competition authorities and courts to adopt further injunctions or commitment decisions is de jure not affected by a prior decision of the Commission, regardless of whether the latter has been adopted on the basis of Article 7 or Article 9. Article 16 Regulation 1/03 requires only that further injunctions or commitments do not make compliance with the remedy that was imposed by the Commission more difficult or even

[134] Wils (2006), 362; Cook (2006), 226; Whish (2006), 567f; Armengol/Pascual (2006), 328; Georgiev (2007), 1030; Körber (2010), 80f; Schweitzer (2011), 654 fn 38; Ritter (2012), Art. 9, 31; Wagner-Von Papp (2012), 954; Ortiz Blanco/Jörgens/Kellerbauer (2013), 13.37; O'Donoghue/Padilla (2013), 914; De Smijter/Sinclair (2014), 2.122.

[135] See Wagner-von Papp (2012), 954: "it is hardly the best use of scarce enforcement resources to look into a case which was already looked into and discarded by another enforcer".

[136] See Cook (2006), 226.

[137] See also Whish (2006), 568: "It would be reasonable to expect that, within the network of competition authorities, the Commission would attempt to dissuade national authorities from beginning their own proceedings in relation to past conduct".

[138] See the Commission's staff working document accompanying the report on the functioning of Regulation 1/03, COM(2009)206 final, 108; De Smijter/Sinclair (2014), 2.122.

[139] The Commission's staff working document accompanying the report on the functioning of Regulation 1/03, COM(2009)206 final, 108, mentions that the Greek competition authority had adopted a prohibition decision against Coca Cola under Greek competition law in 2002 and imposed periodic penalty payments for non-compliance with that decision in 2006, i.e. after the Commission had adopted its commitment decision.

impossible.[140] The ne bis in idem principle does from the outset not protect against the adoption of further injunctions or commitments, because the latter are not of a criminal nature. However, also in this context, additional action by a national competition is de facto unlikely once the Commission has adopted a remedy on the basis of Article 7 or 9.

5.1.4.3 Effects on Private Damages Actions

5.1.4.3.1 Article 7 Decisions

It is broadly accepted that the finding of an infringement contained in an Article 7 decision is binding for the courts of the Member States when they have to decide about private damages claims. The company claiming the damages must merely prove the quantum of damage and the causation between the infringement and the damage.[141] In the light of what was argued above, compliance with an Article 7 remedy does not shield the concerned undertaking from a finding of an infringement and the award of damages by a national court for the time after the adoption of the Commission's decision. However, in that regard, the company claiming the damages cannot rely on the Article 7 decision, but must establish that there is an infringement despite the compliance with the Article 7 remedy. Moreover, a national court can take the compliance with an injunction into account as a factual element in the assessment whether there is an infringement.[142]

5.1.4.3.2 Article 9 Decisions

An Article 9 decision does not establish whether there has been or still is an infringement. A company claiming damages must therefore establish the infringement itself. A national court can, however, take a commitment decision into account as a factual element in the assessment whether there was an infringement prior to the adoption of the commitment decision.[143] According to the Gasorba judgment, the

---

[140]See the references in Sect. 5.1.4.1.2, footnote 132 above.

[141]Eg IP/10/1487: "a Commission decision is binding proof that the behaviour took place and was illegal"; Temple Lang (2003), 350; Dalheimer (2005), Art. 7, 19; Saitzek (2008), 240; Dohrn (2010), 57; Imgrund (2011), 137; Jones/Sufrin (2011), 125; Ritter (2012), Art. 16, 3; Ortiz Blanco/Jörgens/Kellerbauer (2013), 13.34 fn 145. See also the decision by the English High Court in Iberian UK Ltd vs BPB Industries plc, summarised by Mitropoulos (1996), 28f, and § 33(4) of the German ARC.

[142]See, in the context of Article 9, Busse/Leopold (2005), 151; Kahlenberg/Neuhaus (2005), 620; Hennig (2010), 1251; similarly De Smijter/Sinclair (2014), 2.122.

[143]Wils (2006), 360; Saitzek (2008), 241; Hennig (2010), 289; Imgrund (2011), 143; De Smijter/Sinclair (2014), 2.126; for a concrete example from French law see Duron (2016), 125ff; Olmedo-Peralta (2019), 990.

principle of sincere cooperation and the effective and uniform application of EU competition law even require a national court to take into account the preliminary assessment carried out by the Commission and to regard it as an indication, if not prima facie evidence, of the anticompetitive nature of conduct in question.[144]

As explained above, compliance with a commitment does not shield the concerned undertaking from a finding of an infringement and the award of damages by a national court for the time after the adoption of the Commission's decision. However, like in the context of Article 7, a national court can take the compliance with a commitment decision into account as a factual element in the assessment whether there is an infringement.[145]

5.1.4.4 Can Decisions Be Enforced by National Courts or by National Competition Authorities?

As opposed to enforcement of Articles 101 and 102 TFEU, enforcement of a decision adopted on the basis of Article 7 or 9 means that the body enforcing the decision does not have to find an infringement of Articles 101 or 102 TFEU, but merely of the decision in question. EU law does not exclude that national law enables the national competition authorities and courts to enforce remedies that have been adopted by the Commission on the basis of Article 7 and Article 9. It is however questionable, whether EU law requires that such decisions can be enforced by national competition authorities and courts.[146]

5.1.4.4.1 Enforcement of Article 7 and Article 9 Decisions by National Courts

5.1.4.4.1.1 Preparatory Works of Regulation 1/03

The preparatory works of what is now Regulation 1/03 do not contain any statement regarding the question whether remedies adopted on the basis of Article 7 are enforceable by national courts. However, the preparatory works contain some statements regarding commitments. In its White Paper on the modernisation of the rules implementing Articles 101 and 102 TFEU, the Commission envisaged that third parties should be able to invoke commitment decisions before national bodies.[147] Recital 12 of the Commission's proposal for Regulation 1/03 stated that the

---

[144] CJ, C-547/16 (Gasorba, 2017), 29; similarly GC, T-873/16 (Canal+, 2018), 100, under appeal in C-132/19 P, pending.

[145] See the references in Sect. 5.1.4.3.1, footnote 142 above.

[146] See, in the context of Article 9, Wils (2006), 358.

[147] OJ 1999 C 132/1, 90; Saitzek (2008), 216f; Sofianatos (2009), 574; Hjelmeng (2012), 884. The English version states that third parties should be able to invoke commitments before "national courts". This seems to be a translation error, see the German (vor einer staatlichen Instanz), French

Commission should have the power to make commitments binding "so that the commitments can be relied upon by third parties before national courts".[148] The version of Regulation 1/03 that was finally adopted is, however, silent on the question whether commitment decisions can be invoked before national bodies in general or at least before national courts. In the literature, it has been suggested that the deletion of the initially envisaged passage could possibly imply that the legislator intended that commitment decisions could not be invoked before national bodies.[149] Some commentators go further and conclude that the legislator actually wanted to exclude that commitment decisions could be invoked before national bodies.[150] It appears preferable, however, to infer from the silence of Regulation 1/03 only that the legislator wanted to leave the question to the EU Courts.[151] Ultimately, it is broadly accepted that the silence of Regulation 1/03 on whether commitment decisions can be invoked before national bodies is not decisive.[152] Overall, the preparatory works of Regulation 1/03 do hence not permit a conclusion whether remedies that have been adopted on the basis of Article 7 or Article 9 can be enforced by national courts.

5.1.4.4.1.2 Overview Over Opinions

In its Notice on cooperation with national courts, the Commission states that national courts are competent to apply acts adopted by EU institutions to the extent that these acts have direct effect and that national courts may thus have to enforce inter alia decisions taken pursuant to Articles 7 and 9.[153] In a memorandum on the Article 9 procedure published in 2004, the Commission insisted that "national courts must enforce the commitments by any means provided for by national law, including the adoption of interim measures".[154]

In the literature, the question whether remedies that have been adopted on the basis of Article 7 can be enforced by national courts is only scarcely addressed. Müller-Tautphaeus suggests that third parties can invoke an Article 7 decision before the national courts if the decision confers a subjective right on them. At the same time he argues that the civil law consequences of the violation of an Article

(devant une instance nationale), Italian (davanti a un organo nazionale), Spanish (ante un órgano nacional) and Dutch (voor een nationale instantie) versions.

[148]Com(2000) 582 final; Wils (2006), 359f; Saitzek (2008), 217; Sofianatos (2009), 574; Hjelmeng (2012), 884.

[149]See Davies/Das (2006), 201; Sofianatos (2009), 574.

[150]See Wils (2006), 359f; Hennig (2010), 286f; Ortiz Blanco/Jörgens/Kellerbauer (2013), 13.35.

[151]Hossenfelder/Lutz (2003), 122; Klees (2005), § 6, 132; Anweiler (2009), Art. 9, 33; De Smijter/Sinclair (2014), 2.125 with fn 136.

[152]Davies/Das (2006), 202; Wils (2006), 359; Rachwol (2010), 248.

[153]Notice on cooperation with national courts (2004), 7; Wils (2006), 359; Ortiz Blanco/Jörgens/Kellerbauer (2013), 13.35.

[154]Memo/04/217; Davies/Das (2006), 200; Wils (2006), 359; Sofianatos (2009), 574; Olmedo-Peralta (2019), 985.

7 decision are a matter of national law.[155] On the contrary, the question whether Article 9 decisions can be enforced by national courts has been abundantly discussed and remains controversial.[156] Some commentators remain at least sceptical.[157] Others clearly deny that commitment decisions can at all be enforced in national courts.[158] Besides the alleged intent of the legislator, in particular the following arguments are put forward against the enforcement of commitment decisions by national courts: Commitment decisions are said not to determine the rights and obligations between private parties[159] or not to aim at the protection of third parties.[160] Enforcement of commitment decisions in national courts is said to undermine the attractiveness of the commitment procedure, because the concerned undertakings cannot predict the claims to which they are exposed.[161] The Commission itself is considered to be best placed to enforce commitments that it made binding.[162] The contrary view posits that commitment decisions can be enforced before national courts. Within that view, opinions diverge. Some commentators appear to argue in favour of an enforceability of commitments in national courts without further reservations.[163] Hjelmeng argues that national courts must always enforce a commitment by means of injunctions, but only award damages if the commitment was intended to grant the company claiming the damages a subjective right.[164] The preponderant view appears to be that the enforcement of a commitment in national courts by means of injunctions and by means of the award of damages depends on whether the commitment was intended to grant a subjective right.[165] Finally, it has also been suggested that commitments should be enforceable by the national courts by means of injunctions where they aim at granting a subjective right, but not at all by the award of damages.[166]

---

[155] Müller-Tautphaeus (2003), 300 with 158f.

[156] For an overview see also the references in Imgrund (2011), 149 fn 614 and 615.

[157] Wils (2006), 359f; Hahn (2006), 83; Imgrund (2011), 150ff; Ortiz Blanco/Jörgens/Kellerbauer (2013), 13.35.

[158] Busse/Leopold (2005), 154; Saitzek (2008), 247; Jaeger (2009), Art. 9, 38; Hennig (2010), 286.

[159] Busse/Leopold (2005), 154; Saitzek (2008), 247.

[160] Jaeger (2009), Art. 9, 38.

[161] Hennig (2010), 287.

[162] Wils (2006), 360; Ortiz Blanco/Jörgens/Kellerbauer (2013), 13.35; Imgrund (2011), 151.

[163] Schwarze/Weitbrecht (2004), § 6, 92; De Smijter/Sinclair (2014), 2.125; Olmedo-Peralta (2019), 986: "their direct effect – and hence their enforceability by national courts – is evident".

[164] Hjelmeng (2012), 887f; similarly Hjelmeng (2013), 1011f.

[165] See Temple Lang (2003), 351; Temple Lang (2006), 286; Davies/Das (2006); Anweiler (2009), Art. 9, 33; Sofianatos (2009), 575ff; Kellezi (2010), 385; Ritter (2012), Art. 9, 26; Schweitzer (2012), 17.

[166] Rachwol (2010), 248ff.

5.1.4.4.1.3 Comment

As the Commission rightly states in its Notice on cooperation with national courts, the enforceability of remedies that have been adopted on the basis of Article 7 or Article 9 by national courts depends on whether the remedy in question produces direct effects. In the context of Article 9 decisions, Davies and Das[167] have inferred four criteria from the case law of the EU Courts[168] to assess whether a commitment decision produces direct effects.[169] The same criteria can also be used in the context of Article 7 decisions. The following closer analysis of those criteria will show that, both in the context of Article 7 and Article 9, the decisive question is whether the remedy in question confers a subjective right on the person who invokes it.

5.1.4.4.1.3.1 Binding Nature of the Remedy

In order to produce direct effects, remedies must be of a binding nature. There is no doubt that this is the case, regardless of whether the remedy has been adopted on the basis of Article 7 or Article 9.[170] By virtue of Article 288(5), second sentence, TFEU, a decision that specifies those to whom it is addressed shall be binding on them. By virtue of Article 7(1), the Commission "may by decision require" an undertaking to bring an infringement to an end. Pursuant to Article 9(1), the Commission may make commitments binding on the undertakings. The fact that Article 7 and Article 9 decisions do not bind third parties who are not the addressees does not exclude that such third parties may be entitled by the binding effects the decisions produce on the undertakings concerned.[171]

[167] Davies/Das (2006), 204ff; Sofianatos (2009), 574ff follows Davies/Das; Hahn (2006), 79ff applies exactly the same four criteria, albeit without referring to Davies/Das.

[168] Davies/Das rely in particular on CJ, C-9/70 (Franz Grad, 1970), 5f. That judgment is broadly used in the literature as a precedent to discuss the enforceability of commitment decisions by national courts: see eg Müller-Tautphaeus (2003), 300 with 157f; Temple Lang (2006), 286 fn 27; Hahn (2006), 78; Sofianatos (2009), 576; Imgrund (2011), 150; Hjelmeng (2012), 884f.

[169] In the context of Article 9 decisions, it is sometimes suggested that the possibility to invoke a commitment before national courts could be derived from an understanding of the commitments as a contract between the Commission and the concerned undertaking containing stipulations in favour of a third party [see Hennig (2010), 285, and Ritter (2012), Art. 9, 26, both with references to US law; in the context of merger remedies eg Müller-Tautphaeus (2003), 160]. In my view, it is preferable to construct the possibility to invoke a remedy through recourse to the principle of direct effects and subjective rights. As Schweitzer (2012), 17, rightly points out, "[d]espite the consensual character of the commitments, a commitment decision [. . .] is, by its very nature, a unilateral act of state as opposed to a contract".

[170] In the context of Article 9 see Davies/Das (2006), 206f; Hahn (2006), 79; Sofianatos (2009), 576.

[171] See Craig/De Búrca (2011), 191: "A decision can [. . .] be addressed to a private party, in which case it will bind the addressee [. . .]. In such cases the decision may create horizontal direct effect between private parties, provided that the obligation specified is sufficiently precise, certain, and unconditional".

5.1.4.4.1.3.2 Enforcement in National Courts Contributes to the Effectiveness of EU Law (Effet Utile)

The effet utile criterion requires that the full effectiveness of EU law would be put at risk, if it were not possible to enforce a remedy in national courts.[172] In that connection, two questions should be distinguished.

First, some commentators seem to suggest that the enforcement of remedies by national courts must not only contribute[173] to the effectiveness of EU law. They seem to be of the opinion that the enforcement by national courts must be indispensable. In view of the Commission's own enforcement powers, they raise doubts as regards the necessity of enforcement by national courts.[174] These doubts are not persuasive. In the judgments that recognised the possibility of private enforcement, the Court of Justice has consistently argued that private enforcement would "strengthen" the working of the EU competition rules, "thereby making a significant contribution to the maintenance of effective competition".[175] It can hence be inferred from these judgments that the effet utile criterion is met not only if private enforcement is indispensable, but already if it contributes to the effectiveness of EU law.

Second, the act that shall be enforced must apply EU law. In the context of Article 7 decisions, there is no doubt that this criterion is met. Article 7 decisions apply Articles 101 and 102 TFEU. The enforcement of such decisions by national courts thus contributes to the effectiveness of EU competition law.[176] Davies and Das have raised doubts, however, whether the same conclusion applies also in the context of Article 9. They argue in essence that commitment decisions do in principle not establish whether there has been or still is an infringement, so that such decisions do not apply Articles 101 and 102 TFEU and that their enforcement by national courts cannot ensure the effectiveness of EU law.[177] In their view, the condition that the possibility to enforce commitment decisions in national courts must ensure the effectiveness of EU law is only met, if the commitment decision "spells out in considerable detail the competition infringement that would have been found [...] but for the offering of the commitment".[178]

[172]See Davies/Das (2006), 207ff; Hahn (2006), 79; Sofianatos (2009), 576; Imgrund (2011), 150.

[173]In that direction Hahn (2006), 79 and Imgrund (2011), 150: "Voraussetzung für eine unmittelbare Drittwirkung ist [...], dass anderenfalls die praktische Wirksamkeit der Maßnahme abgeschwächt würde".

[174]See Wils (2006), 359; Rachwol (2010), 254; Ortiz Blanco/Jörgens/Kellerbauer (2013), 13.35.

[175]C-453/99 (Courage, 2001), 27; C-295/04 (Manfredi, 2006), 91; C-557/12 (Kone, 2014), 21.

[176]See Davies/Das (2006), 209: "If commitment decisions were based on a finding of infringement of [Article 101 or 102 TFEU], their purpose would be clear: the protection of competition by the application of the prohibitions contained in those provisions"; Hahn (2006), 80; Sofianatos (2009), 576.

[177]See Davies/Das (2006), 210; Hahn (2006), 80. Similar concerns have also been raised by Wils (2006), 359; Sofianatos (2009), 576; Rachwol (2010), 254; Ortiz Blanco/Jörgens/Kellerbauer (2013), 13.35: They all point out that failure to comply with a commitment decision does not necessarily imply that Articles 101 or 102 TFEU are being infringed.

[178]Davies/Das (2006), 210; Hahn (2006), 80.

The doubts raised by Davies and Das are not convincing. Despite the fact that commitment decisions do not establish whether there has been or still is an infringement, such decisions nevertheless apply Articles 101 and 102 TFEU. In fact, an Article 9 decision predicates always on concerns that have been raised by the Commission on the basis of Article 101 or 102 TFEU. The absence of a full proof of an infringement for the past does not exclude that the Commission applies EU competition law, because by offering a commitment, the concerned undertaking engages itself in a binding manner to eliminate the concerns that have been raised by the Commission on the basis of Article 101 or 102 TFEU. Nor does the fact that a commitment decision must only bring the investigated conduct outside the scope of the Commission's enforcement priorities exclude that the Commission applies EU competition law. Even where Articles 101 and 102 TFEU grant rights that reach further than a commitment decision, the commitment decision still implements competition law. Otherwise, Article 7 decisions that do not fully eliminate all competition concerns, but merely bring the infringement outside the scope of the Commission's enforcement priorities would have to be considered as not applying EU competition law.

Davies and Das have also relied on the rationale of procedural economy that underlies Article 9 in order to doubt that commitments serve the effective enforcement of EU competition law.[179] Also these concerns are not persuasive. The fact that Article 9 pursues the objective of procedural economy does not exclude that the Commission applies Articles 101 and 102 TFEU when it adopts a commitment decision. Overall, it is hence submitted that both Article 7 and Article 9 decisions apply Articles 101 and 102 TFEU. The enforcement of both kinds of decisions by national courts contributes therefore to the effectiveness of EU law.

5.1.4.4.1.3.3 Unconditionality and Sufficient Precision

Third, the remedy must be unconditional and sufficiently precise.[180] Whether this criterion is met depends on the circumstances of the individual case. Generally, the criterion will, however, be met.[181] The Court of Justice has consistently confirmed that Articles 101(1) and 102 TFEU are sufficiently precise to produce direct effects.[182] As long as the precision of remedies does not lag behind that of the latter provisions, also remedies must hence be considered as sufficiently precise to be enforced by national courts. Normally, remedies will be more specific than Articles 101 and 102 TFEU. As far as Article 9 decisions are concerned, the Commission

[179]Davies/Das (2006), 212ff; Hahn (2006), 81; Imgrund (2011), 151.

[180]Davies/Das (2006), 218f; Hahn (2006), 82; Sofianatos (2009), 576; Imgrund (2011), 151.

[181]In the context of Article 9 see Hahn (2006), 82f; Imgrund (2011), 150.

[182]CJ, C-127/73 (BRT, 1974), 15ff; C-282/95 P (Guérin, 1997), 39; C-453/99 (Courage, 2001), 23; C-295/04 (Manfredi, 2006), 39; C-557/12 (Kone, 2014), 20; von Danwitz (2008), 512; Whish/Bailey (2012), 297; Jones/Sufrin (2014), 108.

states in its Best Practices and in the Manual of Procedures that commitments have to be "unambiguous and self-executing".[183]

5.1.4.4.1.3.4 Creation of Rights in Favour of Third Parties

The question whether and to what extent the possibility to invoke an act of EU law before the national courts depends on the conferral of a subjective right is to date not settled.[184] The question cannot be treated here in detail. It is submitted that, at least in the context of competition law remedies adopted on the basis of Article 7 or 9, EU law does not exclude that national law makes the possibility to invoke such a remedy before the national courts dependant on the existence of a subjective right.[185] It is true that the Court of Justice generally seems to pursue a generous approach as regards the possibility to invoke Articles 101 and 102 TFEU before the national courts. In Courage, the Court of Justice ruled that subjective rights arise not only where they are expressly granted by the Treaty, but also by virtue of clearly defined obligations.[186] The Court recognised that "any individual" must have the possibility to claim damages for infringements of the competition rules.[187] In Kone, the Court held that national law could not categorically exclude actions brought against cartel members by persons who have suffered damages as a result of umbrella pricing.[188] The generous approach of the Court of Justice can be linked back to the idea expressed already in van Gend en Loos that the "vigilance of individuals" can contribute to the effective enforcement of EU law and that it is therefore useful to award individuals broad rights to invoke EU law before their national courts.[189]

However, it is submitted that the generous jurisprudence of the Court of Justice regarding the possibility to invoke Articles 101 and 102 TFEU to claim damages should not be interpreted as meaning that EU law requires national law to provide every individual with a possibility to invoke every clearly defined obligation under the competition rules before the national courts. In fact, in the absence of EU rules governing the matter, the detailed rules how an act of EU law is given effect within the legal orders of the Member States fall in principle under the procedural autonomy of the Member States, provided that the principles of equivalence and effectiveness

[183]Best Practices (2011), 128; Manual of Procedures (2012), Module 16, 47; Dunne (2014), 403.

[184]See Davies/Das (2006), 214; von Danwitz (2008), 510ff; Craig/De Búrca (2011), 181f.

[185]See Davies/Das (2006), 210; Hahn (2006), 81f; Sofianatos (2009), 576 and the references cited in Sect. 5.1.4.4.1.2, footnotes 155 and 165 above.

[186]CJ, C-453/99 (Courage, 2001), 19; Davies/Das (2006), 217; Hahn (2006), 82; Sofianatos (2009), 576; Rachwol (2010), 250.

[187]CJ, C-453/99 (Courage, 2001), 26f.

[188]CJ, C-557/12 (Kone, 2014), 27ff.

[189]See CJ, C-26/62 (Van Gend en Loos, 1963), p. 13; Masing (1996), 42ff and 50ff; von Danwitz (2008), 515f. Schwarze/Weitbrecht (2004), § 6, 92, and Hennig (2010), 286, refer to the image of the individual as auxiliary policeman (Hilfspolizist).

are observed.[190] As regards the principle of effectiveness, the Court of Justice has never required that national law provides for an actio popularis in which individuals can demand compliance with acts of EU law in national courts merely in the public interest, without having to show any subjective interest at all.[191] Although the jurisprudence is not free from ambiguity, there are several cases in which the Court of Justice seems to have acknowledged that the possibility to invoke an act of EU law can be made dependant on the existence of a subjective interest of the party invoking the act.[192] In the area of state liability, the Court requests that there is a violation of a rule "intended to confer rights on individuals".[193] The General Court has confirmed that a provision in a decision has direct effect on a person other than the addressee only if that provision imposes a sufficiently clear obligation "vis-à-vis the person concerned".[194]

If EU law would require national law to provide every individual with the opportunity to invoke every sufficiently precise obligation contained in a decision that was adopted on the basis of Article 7 or 9, this would lead to bizarre results.[195] Everybody could invoke for instance an obligation to grant access to a third party, an obligation to divest parts of a business to a third party, an obligation to appoint a monitoring trustee, or an obligation to report on the implementation of a remedy to the Commission. Against this backdrop, the position of Hjelmeng that actions that seek the enforcement of a competition law remedy before the national courts by means of an injunction "cannot be made conditional on a subjective right"[196] must be rejected. This conclusion is also corroborated by Recital 7 of Regulation 1/03, according to which national courts contribute to the effective application of EU competition law by enforcing the "subjective rights" of private individuals.[197]

At the same time, also Rachwol's suggestion that remedies should be enforceable by the national courts by means of injunctions where they aim at granting a subjective right, but not at all by the award of damages[198] is not persuasive.

---

[190]See eg CJ, C-453/99 (Courage, 2001), 29; C-557/12 (Kone, 2014), 24f; von Danwitz (2008), 517f.

[191]See von Danwitz (2008), 520: "Einigkeit besteht [. . .] wohl darin, dass es gemeinschaftsrechtlich keineswegs geboten ist, dass die Mitgliedstaaten dem Einzelnen ein im Wege der Popularklage durchsetzbares Recht auf Einhaltung des objektiven Gemeinschaftsrechts gewähren".

[192]See in particular CJ, C-9/70 (Franz Grad, 1970), 6: "[. . .] in each particular case, it must be ascertained whether the nature, background and wording of the provision in question are capable of producing direct effects in the legal relationships between the addressee of the act and third parties"; CJ, C-174/84 (Bulk Oil, 1986), 61f, relied on by Davies/Das (2006), 215; CJ, C-235/95 (AGS Assedic, 1998), 32, relied on by van Gerven (2000), 508.

[193]CJ, C-46/93 (Brasserie du Pêcheur, 1996), 51; van Gerven (2000), 511; Hjelmeng (2012), 886 with fn 49.

[194]GC, T-254/97 (Fruchthandelsgesellschaft, 1999), 29.

[195]See Davies/Das (2006), 217; Hahn (2006), 82.

[196]Hjelmeng (2012), 887.

[197]See Davies/Das (2006), 214; Hahn (2006), 81.

[198]See Sect. 5.1.4.4.1.2, footnote 166 above.

Where a remedy confers a subjective right to an individual, it is contradictory to award the individual the possibility to enforce compliance with the remedy by means of injunctions, but to deny the individual the possibility to claim damages for non-compliance with the remedy.

Finally, the question must be raised when a remedy awards a subjective right. As stated above, in the absence of EU rules, this is a matter of national law, provided that the principles of equivalence and effectiveness are complied with. It is submitted that the principle of effectiveness of EU law requires that the requirements that must be met in order to infer a subjective right from a decision adopted on the basis of Article 7 or Article 9 cannot be overly restrictive. Suggestions that only parties who are expressly determined in a remedy as beneficiaries dispose of a subjective right to enforce the remedy before the national courts[199] are too narrow. A subjective right to invoke a remedy before the national courts should already be acknowledged where non-compliance with the remedy adversely affects the interests of the individual in question.[200]

5.1.4.4.2 Enforcement of Article 7 and Article 9 Decisions by National Competition Authorities

5.1.4.4.2.1 Preparatory Works of Regulation 1/03

The preparatory works of Regulation 1/03 are silent on the question whether national competition authorities should have the power to enforce Article 7 decisions of the Commission. The White Paper on the modernisation of the rules implementing Articles 101 and 102 TFEU contains only the statement that third parties should be able to invoke Article 9 decisions before national bodies.[201] While the term national bodies used in the White Paper covers also competition authorities, the Commission's proposal for Regulation 1/03 mentioned merely that commitment decisions should be enforceable by national courts. As explained above, the version of Regulation 1/03 that was finally adopted is completely silent on the question whether national competition authorities and courts should have the power to

[199]In that direction Hahn (2006), 82; Imgrund (2011), 151f.

[200]See von Danwitz (2008), 513f, with references: "Abweichend von der deutschen Schutznormtheorie bejaht der Gerichtshof ein subjektives Recht nicht nur dann, wenn der [...] Zweck der Norm gerade im Schutz der Rechtsgüter einzelner, bzw. eines zahlenmäßig begrenzten Personenkreises zu sehen ist, sondern auch, wenn die Norm auf den Schutz eines typisierten Interesses der Gesamtheit [...] gerichtet ist. Darüber hinaus ist eine – tendenziell weit zu verstehende – faktische Betroffenheit des Einzelnen erforderlich, die schon anzunehmen ist, wenn dem Einzelnen infolge der Missachtung der einschlägigen Rechtsnorm tatsächliche Nachteile hinsichtlich seiner geschützten Individualinteressen entstehen". See also Ritter (2012), Art. 9, 26, who suggests that an individual must be at least "identifiable" (bestimmbar) – as opposed to "identified" (bestimmt) – as a beneficiary of a remedy in order to be able to invoke it before the national courts.

[201]See Sect. 5.1.4.4.1.1, footnote 147 above.

enforce commitment decisions. The silence of Regulation 1/03 regarding the question whether Article 7 and Article 9 decisions can be enforced by national competition authorities should, however, not be understood as meaning that such enforcement is excluded by Regulation 1/03. Rather, the Regulation leaves the question open.

5.1.4.4.2.2 Overview Over Opinions

The question whether national competition authorities can or even must enforce decisions adopted by the Commission on the basis of Article 7 or 9 is only rarely treated in the literature. Temple Lang has suggested that Article 4(3) TEU imposes an obligation on national competition authorities to enforce commitment decisions adopted by the Commission.[202] O'Donoghue and Padilla suggest that national competition authorities may enforce commitment decisions "through whatever powers are available under their national laws".[203] Sousa Ferro has dealt with the question whether the competition authorities of the Member States can enforce Article 9 decisions more extensively.[204] He concludes that the answer is uncertain.[205] Besides the obligation to cooperate with the Commission pursuant to Article 4(3) TEU and Article 11(1) Regulation 1/03, Sousa Ferro refers in particular to the Fiammiferi[206] case of the Court of Justice in support of an obligation for national competition authorities to enforce commitment decisions adopted by the Commission.[207] Moreover, he points out that enforcement by a national competition authority may be "more efficient, and within the spirit of the co-operation in the European Competition Network", if the infringement of the Commission's commitment decision relates only or mainly to the Member State in question.[208] The major counter arguments relied on by Sousa Ferro are that neither Regulation 1/03 nor the Notice on cooperation within the network of competition authorities refers to a possibility or duty for national competition authorities to enforce commitment decisions adopted by the Commission and that national laws in the Member States do not provide legal bases for the enforcement of such commitments.[209]

[202] Temple Lang (2006), 286 fn 27.

[203] O'Donoghue/Padilla (2013), 912.

[204] Sousa Ferro (2005), 455; Sofianatos (2009), 579 follows Sousa Ferro. See also the discussion by Whish (2006), 569f and Messina/Ho (2011), 750.

[205] Sousa Ferro (2005), 455.

[206] CJ, C-198/01 (Fiammiferi, 2003).

[207] Sousa Ferro (2005), 455; Sofianatos (2009), 579.

[208] Sousa Ferro (2005), 455.

[209] Sousa Ferro (2005), 455; Sofianatos (2009), 579.

5.1.4.4.2.3 Comment

In the light of what was argued above in relation to the enforcement of remedies by national courts, it is submitted that also national competition authorities must in principle enforce a remedy that was adopted by the Commission on the basis of Article 7 or 9 and that produces direct effects. In Fratelli Constanzo, the Court of Justice ruled that all organs of the administration had to apply acts of EU law that produce direct effects. The Court argued that it would be contradictory, if an act that produces direct effects could be invoked before the national courts, but did not have to be followed by the administration.[210] In Fiammiferi, the Court confirmed that dictum, adding that there was an obligation to take all appropriate measures to enable EU law to be fully applied, if the circumstances so required.[211] Although these judgments concerned the duty of the administration to disapply national legislation that was in conflict with EU law producing direct effects, the underlying rationale can be transferred to the present question.

At the same time, national competition authorities cannot enforce remedies adopted by the Commission as long as there is no legal basis for such enforcement. If a national competition authority enforced remedies adopted by the Commission, it would implement EU law. The Charter would hence apply pursuant to its Article 51 (1). According to Article 52(1) Charter, any limitation on the exercise of the rights and freedoms recognised must be provided for by the law. Regardless of whether a national competition authority would enforce a remedy adopted by the Commission by means of an injunction, periodic penalty payments or a fine, all such enforcement measures would restrict fundamental rights provided for by the Charter. They could hence only be taken if there was a legal basis. However, EU law does not provide an independent legal basis that would allow national competition authorities to enforce remedies adopted by the Commission. The powers granted by Regulation 1/03 apply only to the Commission.[212] In so far as the national laws of the Member States do not provide a basis to enforce decisions that have been adopted by the Commission on the basis of Article 7 or 9 Regulation 1/03, such enforcement is hence not possible. For Germany, this is for instance the case: § 32 ARC permits the Bundeskartellamt only to issue injunctions to bring infringements of the ARC or of Articles 101 or 102 TFEU to an end. § 81 ARC allows the imposition of fines only for infringements of the ARC and Articles 101 or 102 TFEU and for non-compliance with orders or commitment decisions adopted by the Bundeskartellamt. At least with respect to fines, an extensive interpretation or analogous application of the enforcement powers

---

[210] CJ, C-103/88 (Fratelli Constanzo, 1989), 39; von Danwitz (2008), 505: "Der Rechtsprechung des Gerichtshofs liegt [...] der Gedanke zu Grunde, dass sich die Verbindlichkeit des Gemeinschaftsrechts in gleicher Weise auf der Ebene der Exekutive wie auf der Ebene der Judikative auswirken muss".

[211] CJ, C-198/01 (Fiammiferi, 2003), 49.

[212] See Ritter (2012), Art. 5, 1f.

granted to national competition authorities should be excluded in view of the punitive nature of fines.[213]

The question whether the Member States are obliged to amend their national legislation so that remedies adopted by the Commission can be enforced shall not be discussed here. Ultimately, the question appears to be of little practical relevance. Certainly, where non-compliance with a remedy that was adopted on the basis of Article 7 or 9 affects mainly or only a particular Member State, the Commission may theoretically want to leave the enforcement of the remedy to the national competition authority in question. However, Sousa Ferro's suggestion that, in such a case, enforcement by the national competition authority is more efficient and in the spirit of the repartition of work within the European Competition Network is not necessarily pertinent. Even if non-compliance with a commitment affects only a single Member States, the Commission will normally be able to deal with the case more efficiently than the concerned national competition authority due to its closer familiarity with the facts of the case. It seems therefore rather unlikely that the European Competition Network would assign the enforcement of a remedy that has been adopted by the Commission to a national competition authority.[214]

5.1.4.5 Intermediate Conclusion: Comparison of Article 7 and Article 9 Decisions and Comment

The preceding analysis reveals that there are only two important differences between Article 7 and Article 9 decisions in relation to the effects on the competition authorities and courts of the Member States: First, at least de jure a commitment decision does not shield the concerned undertaking from the imposition of a fine for the conduct that predates the adoption of the commitment decision. Second, a commitment decision does not facilitate private damages claims to the same extent as an Article 7 decision. The other aspects regarding the effects of a remedy on the competition authorities and courts of the Member states are the same for remedies adopted under Article 7 and under Article 9: First, at least de jure neither compliance with an Article 7 decision nor compliance with an Article 9 decision protects the concerned undertaking from a finding of an infringement and the imposition of a fine or the award of damages as far as the period after the adoption of the Commission's

[213]Sofianatos (2009), 579; even more restrictive Sousa Ferro (2005), 455, who seems to exclude an extensive interpretation or analogous interpretation also for other enforcement measures such as injunctions or periodic penalty payments.

[214]But see GC, T-342/11 (CEES, 2014): The Commission rejected a complaint that Repsol was not complying with a commitment given to the Commission on the ground that the Spanish competition authority had already sanctioned the conduct in question. The case does not allow any conclusion as regards a power or duty of national competition authorities to enforce remedies adopted by the Commission, since the Spanish competition authority had not acted on the basis of the Commission's commitment decision, but directly on the basis of Article 101 TFEU and of Spanish competition law (13).

decision is concerned. Second, the conditions for the enforcement of a remedy by national competition authorities and courts are the same, regardless of whether the remedy has been adopted on the basis of Article 7 or 9. The remaining part of the present section shall briefly address the question whether the two mentioned differences between Article 7 and Article 9 decisions regarding the effects on the competition authorities and courts of the Member States are decisive arguments against the use of the Article 9 instead of the Article 7 procedure.

5.1.4.5.1 Uncertainty Regarding the Imposition of a Fine for Conduct That Predates the Commitment Decision

The uncertainty to which a commitment decision exposes the concerned undertaking in that it does not preclude the finding of an infringement and the imposition of a fine for the conduct that predates the adoption of the commitment decision is no decisive argument against the use of the Article 9 instead of the Article 7 procedure. If a national competition authority succeeds in proving an infringement and imposing a fine, there is a high likeliness that also the Commission would have been able to establish an infringement and impose a fine if the concerned undertaking had refused to offer a commitment. By offering the commitment, the concerned undertaking gains at least the certainty that no infringement will be found and no fine will be imposed by the Commission. Moreover, as explained above, de facto it is unlikely that a national competition authority will take further action once the Commission has adopted a commitment decision.

5.1.4.5.2 Reduced Facilitation of Follow on Action

In the view of several commentators, the Commission's use of commitment decisions undermines the goal of private enforcement and therefore contradicts one of the goals pursued with the enactment of Regulation 1/03.[215] This criticism calls for some relativising remarks. First, it must be emphasised that a commitment decision does not exclude private enforcement. A commitment decision merely does not facilitate private damages claims to the same extent as an infringement decision, because the person claiming the damages must prove the existence of an infringement. Even if there is an infringement decision, private enforcement remains still difficult because the person claiming the damage must in any event prove the quantum of damage and the causation between infringement and damage. Second, McGeown and Orologas have rightly pointed out that the most relevant cases for follow-on actions, namely secret cartels, are from the outset not eligible for the

[215] See Georgiev (2007), 1030 and 1035; Podszun (2012), 368; Botteman/Patsa (2013), 365.

commitment procedure.[216] Third, potential welfare losses for society that result from the lack of a facilitation of private enforcement must be balanced against the benefits of an Article 9 decision, in particular the simplification of the procedure, a swifter resolution of the competitive concerns and a more effective implementation of the remedy.[217] Against this backdrop, it is submitted that the lack of facilitation of follow-on actions is at least not always a decisive argument against the use of the commitment procedure. Rather, it is only one of the factors that must be taken into account when deciding whether to adopt an Article 7 or an Article 9 decision.

5.1.5 Loss of the Positive Externalities of Adjudication

It is broadly accepted that the use of the Article 9 instead of the Article 7 procedure negatively affects legal certainty in that it reduces the likeliness of an appeal before the EU Courts and thereby reduces the amount of precedents that contribute to the clarification of the law.[218] The reduction in precedents is a standard argument against the use of consensual dispute resolution instead of adversarial adjudication in general.[219] Posner cautioned already in the 1970s that "beyond a certain point [. . .] a further increase in the settlement rate would increase the total costs of dispute resolution by reducing the production of precedents below the optimal level".[220] In a paper published in 1986, Silver and Coleman explained at length that, by creating precedents, adversarial adjudication benefits not only the parties to a lawsuit, but third parties as well. Adversarial adjudication hence creates positive externalities that

[216]McGeown/Orologas (2013), 6. See also Forrester (2010), 647, who considers that the lack of facilitation of follow-on actions "is a very hypothetical problem" of the commitment procedure.

[217]See McGeown/Orologas (2013), 6: "[. . .] as long as there are – Article 7 decision or not – many unsolved obstacles to private damages actions in the European Union based on a breach of competition law, in the foreseeable future any welfare loss that society might suffer is likely to be outweighed by the quicker correction of anticompetitive effects on the market through Article 9 commitments"; Hjelmeng (2013), 1033: "[. . .] remedies aimed at reversing harmful effects in the marketplace should focus on market entry, while protective measures in favour of specific competitors should only be employed cautiously. Against this background, a more widespread use of commitment decisions making damages suits more difficult is a decent price to pay for increased flexibility with regard to the design of a remedy". But see also Botteman/Patsa (2013), 366: "Notwithstanding such considerations, one should not loose sight of the need of effective private enforcement of EU competition law, as the latter serves a different purpose than the swift resolution of competition concerns through commitment decisions".

[218]See eg Wils (2006), 351; Georgiev (2007), 1016 and 1027f; Waelbroeck (2009), 224; Forrester (2010), 647; Cengiz (2011), 137; Schweitzer (2011), 648 and 657 and (2012), 22; Barbier de la Serre (2012b), 99; Wagner-von Papp (2012), 930 and 961ff; Podszun (2012), 67f; Marsden (2013), 10; Gerard (2013), 23; Botteman/Patsa (2013), 363f; Hjelmeng (2013), 1029f; Jones/Sufrin (2014) 273f; Dunne (2014), 415f; Mestmäcker/Schweitzer (2014), § 21, 61; Brenner (2014), 693; OECD (2016), 44f.

[219]See Georgiev (2007), 1015f; Wagner-von Papp (2012), 961, with further references.

[220]Posner (1977), 434.

are lost if the dispute is resolved consensually.[221] Wagner-von Papp wants to link the concerns raised in the context of the commitment procedure even back to Rudolf von Jhering's speech "The struggle for law", delivered in 1872.[222]

Commentators mention various reasons why commitment decisions reduce the likeliness of appeals before the EU Courts, even though appeals are theoretically not excluded. According to Klees[223] and Wagner-von Papp,[224] the concerned undertakings fear that a successful challenge of a commitment decision would lead to an infringement decision. Körber argues that the concerned undertakings want to avoid that the Commission loses its proclivity to engage in settlement discussions in future cases.[225] Moreover, the deferential standard of review applied by the Court of Justice in the Alrosa case is considered to scare off the concerned undertakings and third parties from potential appeals.[226] It shall not be disputed here that the said reasons may all have a role to play. Nevertheless, it is submitted that the most important reason for the concerned undertakings and third parties not to challenge an Article 9 decision is their involvement in the remedy design through the offering of the commitments and submission of comments during the market test, combined with the saving of litigation costs.[227] In that regard, it has rightly been emphasised that the Article 9 procedure constitutes the manifestation of a cooperative administrative practice that avoids further dispute.[228]

---

[221]Coleman/Silver (1986), 114 and 116ff.

[222]Wagner-Von Papp (2012), 961.

[223]Klees (2011), 19: "Das betroffene Unternehmen als Adressat der Entscheidung ist zwar klagebefugt, es wird in aller Regel jedoch kein Interesse haben, Klage zu erheben. [...] Nach Nichtigerklärung einer Zusagenentscheidung würde das Verfahren voraussichtlich auf Verbotsebene fortgeführt".

[224]Wagner-von Papp (2012), 939: "[...] addressees are unlikely to challenge a commitment decision to which they agreed. A successful challenge would risk an infringement procedure, so that the reasons that made the addressees offer commitments in the first place argue against challenging the commitment decision as well. The only difference to the initial position would be that the appellant would have antagonized the Commission in the process".

[225]Körber (2010), 90: "[...] wenn ein Unternehmen sich zunächst auf das Artikel 9-Verfahren einlässt, um der Verhängung eines Bußgeldes zu entgehen und dann versucht, sich über eine Nichtigkeitsklage auch von der Bindung an die eigenen Zusagen zu lösen, wird die Kommission es sich in künftigen Fällen zweimal überlegen, mit diesm Unternehmen [...] in Verhandlungen nach Art. 9 zu treten".

[226]Barbier de la Serre (2012b), 99; Podszun (2012), 68; Dunne (2014), 425.

[227]For the voluntary nature of commitments as reasons why these are not appealed: Whish (2006), 570; Wils (2008), 339; Mariniello (2014), 3.

[228]K. Schmidt (2003), 1242: "wirksame kooperative Verwaltungspraxis"; Podszun (2012), 59: "Ausdruck einer kooperativen [...] Konfliktlösung, die weitere Streitigkeiten zu vermeiden geeignet ist".

5.1.5.1 The Criticism

The negative impact of the Article 9 procedure on the creation of precedents is considered to be a particularly serious reason against the use of commitment decisions.[229] Concerns have been raised that the EU Courts will in the future only have a word to say on the Commission's fining policy, but not on the substantive development of EU competition law.[230] Commentators emphasise that a lack of litigated precedents is worrying in a system of competition enforcement where companies are required to self-assess their business conduct[231] and that clarification of the interpretation of the EU competition rules has become more important than ever in times of the more economic approach.[232] Moreover, it is pointed out that the legal uncertainty entailed by the use of the Article 9 procedure brings about a negative feedback effect for the adoption of future commitment decisions, because effective negotiation is said to be possible only "in the shadow of the law".[233] The negative impact of the Article 9 procedure on legal certainty is considered to be particularly alarming where controversial or novel cases are concerned. In that connection, the Commission is criticised for settling precisely the wrong cases, namely the controversial or novel ones.[234]

From a broader perspective, two additional concerns are being raised. First, the Commission has acknowledged that its commitment practice can serve as a model for other market participants and national competition authorities.[235] Cases where national competition authorities followed the approach pursued in commitment decisions adopted by the Commission concerned for example the central marketing of media rights for popular sports events, the energy sector and the payments sector.[236] Commentators hence fear that the unchecked standards used in Article

[229]See Wagner-von Papp (2012), 930: "main criticism".

[230]See Podszun (2012), 68: "Die Richter brauchen sich nicht zu wundern, wenn sie eines Tages Kartellrecht nur noch in Form von Bußgeldregulierung betreiben".

[231]Wagner-von Papp (2012), 966; Lugard/Möllmann (2013), 8.

[232]Cengiz (2011), 137; Wagner-von Papp (2012), 966.

[233]Gerard (2013), 24. The term was originally coined by Mnookin/Kornhauser (1979) in the context of divorce. It has repeatedly been used when discussing the Article 9 procedure, albeit in contexts that slightly differ from the one in which the term is used by Gerard; see Georgiev (2007), 1018; Wagner-von Papp (2012), 947.

[234]Cengiz (2011), 138; Wagner-Von Papp (2012), 962f; Botteman/Patsa (2013), 369; Hjelmeng (2013), 1021 with 1030; Dunne (2014), 425; Mariniello (2014), 4.

[235]Staff working document accompanying the report on the functioning of Regulation 1/03, COM (2009)206 final, 109; Manual of Procedures (2012), Module 16, 7: "Commitment decisions also serve to clarify the Commission's competition policy [. . .]. Other market participants can learn from the decision and the commitments what was considered by the Commission sufficient to remove the competition concerns".

[236]Schweitzer (2012), 12ff.

9 decisions become soft-law relied on by other market participants and national competition authorities, so that potential enforcement errors are multiplied.[237]

Second, commentators are worried about a politicisation of competition policy. As Dunne explains, once enforcement is no longer legalistic, it becomes prone to regulatory capture.[238] Echoing voices raised in the mid 1990s in the US,[239] commentators criticise that EU competition law runs the risk of coming to the point where what matters is not what the law requires, but rather what the government wants.[240]

5.1.5.2 Comment

The loss of the positive externalities of adjudication is undeniably an important argument against the use of the commitment procedure. Like any consensual dispute resolution, also the Article 9 procedure raises valid concerns regarding the rule of law. Nevertheless, some moderating remarks are called for.

First, the fear that there will in the future be no more judgments on the substantive rules of competition law appears at least exaggerated. Cases like Peugeot,[241] Tomra,[242] AstraZeneca,[243] Visa,[244] Telefonica,[245] Mastercard,[246] Cartes Bancaires,[247] CISAC,[248] Intel,[249] Orange Polska,[250] Deutsche Telekom,[251]

---

[237] See Schweitzer (2012), 15 and 22; Gerard (2013), 22f; Hjelmeng (2013), 1029; Marsden (2013), 5.

[238] Dunne (2014), 440ff.

[239] Melamed (1995), 14.

[240] Georgiev (2007), 1028; Marsden (2013), 11. See also MK (2009), 496: "gerade für vergleichsweise politisch orientierte Aufsichtsbehörden wie die Europäische Kommission bedenkliche Möglichkeiten gegeben, eigene politische Ziele durchzusetzen, die jenseits des begründeten Interesses an einer nachhaltigen Abstellung wettbewerbswidriger Verhaltensweisen liegen".

[241] GC, T-450/05 (Peugeot, 2009).

[242] GC, T-155/06 (Tomra, 2010); CJ, C-549/10 P (Tomra, 2012).

[243] GC, T-321/05 (AstraZeneca, 2010); CJ, C-457/10 P (AstraZeneca, 2012).

[244] GC, T-461/07 (Visa, 2011).

[245] GC, T-336/07 (Telefonica, 2012); CJ, C-295/12 P (Telefonica, 2014).

[246] GC, T-111/08 (Mastercard, 2012); CJ, C-382/12 P (Mastercard, 2014).

[247] GC, T-491/12 (Cartes Bancaires, 2012); CJ, C-67/13 P (Cartes Bancaires, 2014).

[248] GC, T-442/08 (CISAC, 2013).

[249] GC, T-286/09 (Intel, 2014); CJ, C-413/14 P (Intel, 2017).

[250] GC, T-486/11 (Orange Polska, 2015); CJ, C-123/16 P (Orange Polska, 2018).

[251] GC, T-827/14 (Deutsche Telekom, 2018), under appeal in C-152/19 P.

Servier,[252] Qualcomm[253] and Google[254] show that also after the introduction of the Article 9 procedure the Commission still adopts infringement decisions under Article 7 outside the area of secret cartels that are challenged in court. Moreover, there continues to be a significant amount of preliminary reference procedures outside the cartel area in which the Court of Justice interprets the substantive competition rules.[255] I am not aware of any reliable figures that would show that the number of direct actions and preliminary references filed with the EU Courts that deal with the interpretation of Articles 101 and 102 TFEU have significantly declined as a result of the introduction of commitment procedures on the EU and the Member State level.[256]

Second, in particular in complex cases, infringement decisions do not necessarily provide guidance to the industry.[257] Moreover, although an infringement decision increases the likeliness of an appeal, infringement decisions are not necessarily challenged in court. A prominent example is the Commission's Motorola decision, which concerned the abusive use of injunctions based on standard essential patents. Prior to the adoption of the Commission's decision, commentators raised concerns that a commitment decision would not bring about the necessary clarification of the

[252]GC, T-691/14 (Servier, 2018), under appeal in C-176/19 P and C-201/19 P.

[253]GC, T-235/18 (Qualcomm, pending).

[254]GC, T-612/17 (Google Search, pending); T-604/18 (Google Android, pending); T-334/19 (Google Adsense, pending).

[255]Eg CJ, C-52/07 (Kanal 5, 2008); C-260/07 (Pedro IV, 2009); C-506/07 (Lubricantes y Carburantes, 2009); C-8/08 (T-Mobile Netherlands, 2009); C-403/09 (Premier League, 2011); C-52/09 (TeliaSonera, 2011); C-437/09 (AG2R Prévoyance, 2011); C-439/09 (Pierre Fabre, 2011); C-209/10 (Post Danmark, 2012); C-138/11 (Compass Datenbank, 2012); C-158/11 (Auto 24, 2012); C-117/12 (La Retoucherie de Manuela, 2013); C-32/11 (Allianz Hungária, 2013); C-384/13 (Estación de Servicio Pozuelo, 2014); C-142/13 (Bright Service, 2014); C-413/13 (FNV Kunsten, 2014); C-170/13 (Huawei, 2015); C-345/14 (SIA Maxima Latvija, 2015); C-23/14 (Post Danmark II, 2015); C-542/14 (VM Remonts, 2016); C-74/14 (Eturas, 2016); C-567/14 (Genentech, 2016); C-177/16 (AKKA/LAA, 2017); C-179/16 (Hoffmann-La Roche, 2017); C-230/16 (Coty Germany, 2017); C-427/16 (CHEZ, 2017). See also Prek/Lefèvre (2016), 66, who rightly point out that, as a consequence of the decentralisation of the application of EU competition law entailed by Regulation 1/2003, important competition cases arrive nowadays often before the Court of Justice under the preliminary reference procedure.

[256]For the conclusion that the introduction of the article 9 procedure has not brought about a significant decrease in annulment cases, based on statistical evidence, also Blockx (2018), 96. Barbier de la Serre (2012b), 93ff, presents data from which he infers that the "well" of competition cases before the EU Courts may be "running dry". However, in particular for the following two reasons this data cannot be used to support the conclusion that the introduction of commitment procedures has led to a decline in competition law cases before the EU courts. First, Barbier de la Serre observes that the number of direct actions and preliminary references in competition cases has remained stable between 1997 and 2009. His conclusion that the well is running dry is merely based on the assumption that, for several reasons that shall not further be discussed here, there should have been an increase in competition law cases. Second, the data presented by Barbier de la Serre only covers the overall amount of competition cases. It does not exclude secret cartels.

[257]See Falconi (2011), 53.

law.[258] Ultimately, the Commission adopted an Article 7 decision without fine,[259] arguing inter alia that there was no Commission decisional practice or case law of the EU Courts.[260] Despite the need for legal certainty perceived in the literature, Motorola abstained from bringing an action for annulment. However, the preliminary reference procedure in Huawei[261] concerned a similar subject, so that the Court of Justice had an opportunity to clarify open questions.[262]

Third, also the danger that Article 9 decisions act as models and thereby multiply potential enforcement errors appears over-stated. In its Manual of Procedures, the Commission emphasises that the "precedent value" of commitment decisions differs from that of infringement decisions.[263] It is submitted that other market participants and in particular competition authorities of the Member States are able to take this difference in precedent value into account when they decide whether to align their own actions with the model of a commitment decision adopted by the Commission.

Fourth, as regards the risk of an increasing politicisation of competition law, two remarks bear mention. On the one hand, on an abstract level, the concerns regarding the politicisation of competition law must be contrasted with concerns that EU competition law faces a democracy deficit.[264] From the latter perspective, the active role of the concerned undertakings offering the commitments and the opportunities for third parties to make submissions during the market test appear more as a form of cooperative governance mechanism that strengthens the legitimacy of the Commission's action than as an opportunity for regulatory capture. At least to a certain extent, the potential disadvantages of the Article 9 procedure related to the politicisation of competition policy are hence compensated by an increase in democratic legitimacy. On the other hand, on a more practical level, it must be stressed that the analysis of the Commission's decisions throughout the present work has not revealed any concrete signs that Article 9 decisions predicate to a larger extent on political considerations that are unrelated to competition law than Article 7 decisions.

Fifth, it should be recalled that the Commission acknowledges in its Manual of Procedures that an Article 9 decision is less likely going to be appealed and that such a decision therefore reduces the chance to have contentious legal issues clarified in

[258]Eg Marsden (2013), 5; Mariniello (2014), 3.

[259]COMP/39.985 (Motorola, 2014).

[260]MEMO/14/322.

[261]CJ, C-170/13 (Huawei, 2015).

[262]See Whish (2014), 604; Wathelet (2015), 554f, who concludes that "the paucity of precedent may be overstated".

[263]Manual of Procedures (2012), Module 16, 11.

[264]For the EU see Dann (2013), who criticises that the EU Parliament does not have a decisive role to play in the development of EU competition policy: "Kritisch zu sehen ist [. . .] das [. . .] nach wie vor ernsthafte Legitimationsproblem in Form des parlamentarisch demokratischen Defizits in der Wettbewerbspolitik. Sie wirkt eher wie die parlamentarisch umzingelte letzte Hochburg der Exekutive denn als Paradebeispiel europäischer Kompetenzverteilung" (108). For the US see First/Waller (2013).

court. The Commission states that it may hence prefer the path of an Article 7 decision, if it wants to establish an important precedent.[265] Such consideration of the need to clarify legal issues in court is necessary. However, as was already submitted above,[266] the need to establish a precedent is only one of the factors that must be taken into account when deciding whether to adopt an Article 7 instead of an Article 9 decision. The disadvantage that derives from the lack of a precedent must always be balanced against the benefits of the Article 9 procedure according to the circumstances of the individual case at hand.

5.2 Advantage: Precise and Enforceable Obligations

The following section will turn to one particular advantage of Article 9 decisions that has, it is submitted, received to date too little attention: While the precision of injunctions adopted unilaterally on the basis of Article 7 is problematic, a commitment results in precise and enforceable obligations.

5.2.1 The Problematic Precision of Injunctions Adopted on the Basis of Article 7

In order to assess whether a remedy that was adopted on the basis of Article 7 meets the requirements of the principle of legal certainty, the EU Courts typically examine whether an interpretation of the operative part in the light of the grounds of the decision permits the concerned undertaking to know what it is required to do.[267] As will be shown in more detail below, the EU Courts take a rather lax stance in applying that test. Although at least two Advocate Generals[268] and voices in the literature[269] have emphasised that imprecise remedies are problematic in view of potential periodic penalty payments, the Courts have to my knowledge so far never annulled a remedy for lack of sufficient clarity. This can possibly be explained with the fact that at least until recently, the unilateral enforcement of remedies by means of periodic penalties has not played a significant role in the Commission's decisional practice. When the Commission imposed periodic penalty payments upon Microsoft

---

[265] Manual of Procedures (2012), 11.

[266] See Sect. 5.1.1.3 with footnotes 37ff above.

[267] See GC, T-167/08 (Microsoft II, 2012), 84f; T-491/07 (Cartes Bancaires, 2012), 443ff; also eg Craig (2012), 549f; Sauer (2013), 11.06.

[268] Opinion of AG Roehmer, 56/64 (Consten & Grundig, 1966), p. 380f; opinion of AG Warner, 6/73 (Commercial Solvents, 1974), p. 272.

[269] Klees (2005), § 6, 74; Bauer (2008), 4-7-035; Hauser (2009), 211 and 242; Krings (2012), 252; Ritter (2012), Art. 9, 27; Akman (2017); Vesterdorf/Fountoukakos (2018), 6ff.

in 2008 for failure to comply with the 2004 decision, then Competition Commissioner Neelie Kroes stated that Microsoft was "the first company in fifty years of EU competition policy that the Commission has had to fine for failure to comply with an antitrust decision".[270]

There are several potential reasons why the unilateral enforcement of remedies by means of periodic penalty payments has so far only been of minor importance in EU competition law. One reason may lie in a lack of monitoring and enforcement by the Commission. Another explanation may be the success of a remedy design that does not focus on unilateral prescription and enforcement, but rather on market-based solutions that are developed by the concerned undertakings themselves. Which of the two explanations is more plausible shall not be answered here. What can be stated is that the Commission is reluctant to impose remedies containing precise prescriptions unilaterally under Article 7 and that this reluctance predicates on a preference for market based solutions. In principle, this is commendable. In fact, at least as long as the parties are willing to cooperate, there is a universal interest to leave the question how to put an infringement to an end mostly to the concerned parties[271]: The parties benefit from being able to tailor a solution according to their needs and the Commission avoids the difficult and resource consuming task of having to craft precise prescriptions unilaterally and enforce them subsequently. Nevertheless, it is also obvious that market based solutions are only possible to the extent the parties and the Commission cooperate. As long as this is the case, unilateral enforcement is superfluous and the question whether the remedy is sufficiently precise to serve as the basis for the imposition of penalties does not arise. This is different, however, if the parties do not reach a solution or if their solution falls short of the Commission's expectations. In such a case, the question of when a remedy is sufficiently precise to be unilaterally enforced by the Commission by means of periodic penalty payments becomes paramount. When Microsoft appealed the 2008 penalties decision, the General Court had to deal with this question for the first time. The Court decided to apply the lax standards regarding the principle of legal certainty known from earlier cases also to constellations that concerned the imposition of periodic penalties. Backed up by this judgment, the Commission imposed periodic penalty payments also in Google Search, although the injunction imposed on Google consisted only of a rather abstract cease and desist- and like effects order.

The following section will in a first step give an overview over the case law of the EU Courts that concerns the compatibility of remedies with the principle of legal certainty. In a second step, a brief comparative look to German competition law will

---

[270]Commission, IP/08/318; see also Kerse/Khan (2012), 7-261; Hinds/Eaton (2014), 33 and 35ff; Lugard/Möllmann (2013), 11 fn 51 point out that several national competition authorities have imposed fines for non-compliance with a commitment decision prior to the fine imposed by the Commission in Microsoft.

[271]That "negotiated solutions" for remedies found by market participants are preferable to unilateral prescriptions imposed by competition authorities or courts is emphasised eg by Podszun (2012), 56f and 65f; O'Donoghue/Padilla (2013), 933 and 941.

show that German courts apply stricter standards. The final part of this section will then consist of a discussion of the standards applied by the EU Courts in general and of the Microsoft penalties judgment in particular. Finally, a quick glance will be cast at the Commission's Google Search decision.

5.2.1.1 The EU Case Law

As has already been mentioned, the EU courts have consistently accepted that the Commission may require undertakings that have infringed the competition rules in abstract terms "to put the infringement to an end".[272] Such abstract cease and desist orders are not problematic under the aspect of the principle of legal certainty: The finding of an infringement requires a precise description of the incriminated conduct and an order "to put the infringement to an end" only prohibits precisely the behaviour that has been found to constitute the infringement. The compatibility of remedies with the principle of legal certainty has, however, become a matter of controversy were the Commission used different terms.

5.2.1.1.1 Cease and Desist Orders

5.2.1.1.1.1 Grundig and Consten

As pointed out above, in Grundig and Consten, the Court of Justice upheld an order in which the Commission required the said undertakings "to refrain from any measure likely to obstruct or impede the acquisition by third parties, in the exercise of their free choice, from wholesalers or retailers established in the [EU], of the products set out in the contract, with a view to their resale in the contract territory".[273] Previously, AG Roehmer had suggested annulling the order, inter alia because it violated the principle of legal certainty. According to the AG, the wording of the order did not only capture the absolute territorial protection clause that constituted the subject of the procedure under Article 101 TFEU, but also a multitude of unilateral practices that the Commission could only assess under Article 102 TFEU. The Advocate General acknowledged that the grounds of the decision were limited to criticising the absolute territorial protection clause and the steps to ensure that protection. Nevertheless, in view of the "categoric wording" of the operative part of the decision and in view of the potential imposition of penalties, the Advocate General argued that there was an unwarranted uncertainty for the concerned undertakings.[274] The Court of Justice confirmed the order without dealing

[272]See Sect. 3.3.1.1 with footnote 142 above.

[273]See Sect. 4.1.3.1 with footnote 103 above.

[274]Opinion of AG Roehmer (Consten & Grundig, 56/64, 1966), p. 380f.

with the Advocate General's concerns regarding the principle of legal certainty.[275] In the literature, the judgment is interpreted as meaning that an imprecise order cannot be annulled for lack of legal certainty, if its meaning can be inferred from the grounds of the decision.[276]

5.2.1.1.1.2 Aéroports de Paris

A second example for a cease and desist order that raised concerns regarding its compatibility with the principle of legal certainty is Aéroports de Paris. As pointed out above, in that case the General Court upheld an abstract order to apply a non-discriminatory fee scheme.[277] According to the Court, the order was sufficiently precise, since it required ADP to achieve the result of applying non-discriminatory fees, while recognising the parties' freedom of contract. In the view of the Court, the Commission was "not required to stipulate for ADP the means whereby a non-discriminatory scheme of commercial fees was to be put in place".[278]

5.2.1.1.1.3 Microsoft II: Sufficient Precision of an Obligation to Grant Access on "Reasonable Terms"

5.2.1.1.1.3.1 The Case[279]

In the operative part of the 2004 decision, the Commission ordered Microsoft inter alia to make interoperability information available and to allow for its use on reasonable and non-discriminatory terms.[280] According to the grounds of the decision, the objective of the order was to allow competitors to "viably compete" with Microsoft[281] and the remuneration "should not reflect the strategic value stemming from Microsoft's market power".[282] In 2005, Microsoft submitted proposals for license agreements to the Commission, which also contained principles for pricing the interoperability information.[283] These pricing principles were to guide a monitoring trustee and the High Court of Justice of England and Wales in case of a dispute about whether Microsoft's royalties were reasonable.[284] These principles provided that, "in order to assess whether the interoperability information [did not consist in

---

[275]See for a more detailed description of the Court's reasoning Sect. 4.1.3.1 with footnotes 103ff above.

[276]See Mestmäcker (1974), 530.

[277]See Sect. 3.3.1.4.1.2.1 with footnotes 316f above.

[278]GC, T-128/98 (Aeroports de Paris, 2000), 83.

[279]For an overview see also Haslinger (2012); Kerse/Khan (2012), 7-261; O'Donoghue/Padilla (2013), 938ff; Mestmäcker/Schweitzer (2014), § 21, 40ff.

[280]COMP/C-3/37.792 (Microsoft, 2004), Article 5 a) of the operative part.

[281]COMP/C-3/37.792 (Microsoft, 2004), 1003; see also GC, T-167/08 (Microsoft II, 2012), 29.

[282]COMP/C-3/37.792 (Microsoft, 2004), 1008(ii); see also GC, T-167/08 (Microsoft II, 2012), 29.

[283]See GC, T-167/08 (Microsoft II, 2012), 22ff.

[284]See GC, T-167/08 (Microsoft II, 2012), 25.

the strategic value stemming from Microsoft's market power], it [was] necessary (i) to examine whether the protocols concerned [were] Microsoft's own creations, (ii) to examine whether those creations constitute[d] innovation and (iii) to take into account a market valuation of comparable technologies, excluding the strategic value stemming from the dominant position of any such technologies".[285] Still in 2005, the Commission issued a decision, in which it found that the interoperability information provided by Microsoft was inaccurate and incomplete and that the remuneration rates were unreasonable. In this decision, the Commission ordered Microsoft to comply with the 2004 decision and imposed a periodic penalty payment in case of future non-compliance.[286] In 2006, the Commission imposed a first periodic penalty payment of 280.5 million euro, because the interoperability information provided by Microsoft was still inaccurate and incomplete.[287] In 2008, the Commission imposed a second periodic penalty payment of 899 million euro, because Microsoft had failed to comply with the obligation to make the interoperability information available at reasonable remuneration rates.[288]

Microsoft appealed the 2008 periodic penalty decision. It argued, inter alia, that the Commission had "infringed its obligation to specify positively what Microsoft had to do in order to comply with [the order contained in the 2004 decision]".[289] This argument was, however, not pointed against the 2004 decision. In the appeal against the latter decision, Microsoft had not pleaded a violation of the principle of legal certainty. Instead, Microsoft now argued that the Commission could not impose periodic penalties without having determined the rate of royalty that the Commission considered reasonable.[290]

The General Court examined this argument against the benchmark of its case law, according to which the use of imprecise rules does not withstand the imposition of a remedial measure, if the individual concerned is in a position to know, on the basis of the wording and, if need be, with the help of the interpretation given to it by the courts, which acts or omissions will make him liable.[291] The Court found that the latter was the case, in particular for two reasons: On the one hand, it argued, in essence, that the term "reasonable" had been concretised in the grounds of the decision and in the pricing principles, which the Court found to provide sufficiently precise criteria to assess whether a given technology had merely a strategic value.[292] According to the Court, "nothing permitted the inference that [the] pricing principles [were] suitable for application by the monitoring trustee and the High Court of Justice but [were] not sufficient for Microsoft to adopt a course of conduct that

[285]See GC, T-167/08 (Microsoft II, 2012), 31.

[286]COMP/C-3/37.792 (Microsoft, 2005); see also GC, T-167/08 (Microsoft II, 2012), 15.

[287]COMP/C-3/37.792 (Microsoft, 2006); see also GC, T-167/08 (Microsoft II, 2012), 16.

[288]COMP/C-3/37.792 (Microsoft, 2008); see also GC, T-167/08 (Microsoft II, 2012), 20f.

[289]GC, T-167/08 (Microsoft II, 2012), 74.

[290]GC, T-167/08 (Microsoft II, 2012), 82.

[291]GC, T-167/08 (Microsoft II, 2012), 84.

[292]GC, T-167/08 (Microsoft II, 2012), 85 to 88.

[complied with the order of the 2004 decision] or for the Commission to carry out its task of monitoring that conduct".[293] On the other hand, the Court considered Microsoft's argument that there was more than one correct reasonable rate to confirm that it was not for the Commission to choose a reasonable rate and to impose it on Microsoft. In this respect, the Court relied on its Automec jurisprudence,[294] according to which, "where several remedies exist [. . .], it is not for the Commission to impose [. . .] its own choice from among all the various potential courses of action which are in conformity with [EU competition law][295]".

5.2.1.1.1.3.2 Preliminary Comment

It must be noted that the Court's finding of a sufficient concretisation of the term "reasonable" predicated neither on the 2005 nor the 2006 decision, but exclusively on the grounds of the 2004 decision and the pricing principles. One must thus assume that the 2005 and 2006 decisions were not relevant for the concretisation of the term reasonable. However, there are good arguments to contest the General Court's finding that the term "reasonable" was concretised to a sufficient degree in the grounds of the 2004 decision and in the pricing principles in order to enable Microsoft to know what it was required to do. The grounds of the decision only stated that the objective of the order to grant access was to allow competitors to "viably compete" with Microsoft and that the remuneration "should not reflect the strategic value stemming from Microsoft's market power". In order to examine whether this was the case, the pricing principles merely provided for three criteria: the concerned protocols had to be Microsoft's "own creations", they had to constitute "innovation" and their value had to be compared to like technologies. Even if these requirements are considered together, it is difficult to share the General Court's reasoning that they enabled Microsoft to know what it was expected to do.[296] The notions "viably compete", "strategic value" and in particular "innovation" are themselves open to so many different interpretations that they can hardly be considered as a sufficiently precise legal basis for the imposition of a periodic penalty payment. The controversy between Microsoft and the Commission about the interpretation of the notion of "innovation" illustrates this well. The Commission interpreted innovation restrictively in the light of patent law and requested that remuneration be charged only for information that fulfilled the conditions of "novelty" and "non-obviousness". On the contrary, Microsoft argued that a less strict interpretation should be applied and that it should be allowed to charge remuneration

[293] GC, T-167/08 (Microsoft II, 2012), 87.

[294] GC, T-167/08 (Microsoft II, 2012), 95.

[295] GC, T-24/90 (Automec II, 1992), 52.

[296] See Barbier de la Serre (2012a), 64: "Le moins que l'on puisse dire est que ces dispositions ne sont pas de la plus grande clarté [. . .] après s'être accordés sur ces principes généraux, Microsoft et la Commission restaient en désaccord sur leur interprétation, notamment sur ce qui constitue une innovation. Il était dès lors difficile d'en conclure que ces principes étaient univoques, voire simplement clairs".

also for information that was only protected as a trade secret. The General Court followed the Commission's interpretation.[297] It is beyond the scope of the present work to evaluate which of the two interpretations of "innovation" was actually appropriate for examining Microsoft's conduct. In any event, the fact that several possible interpretations exist shows that the term innovation as such did not allow Microsoft to know what it was required to do.

Moreover, the General Court also errs in so far as it bases the finding that Microsoft could know what it was required to do on the fact that the pricing principles "are suitable for application by the monitoring trustee and the High Court of Justice".[298] Surveillance or dispute resolution bodies like monitoring trustees, arbitration panels or courts do not only apply precise rules. Rather, they also apply imprecise rules by giving them a particular interpretation for the first time. They thus contribute to the concretisation of a rule, which was imprecise beforehand. This does, however, not mean that the respective interpretation was foreseeable for the concerned undertakings. Certainly, in order to assess whether an undertaking can know what it is required to do, the Courts do not only take into account the wording of the respective legal act, but also "the interpretation given to it by the courts".[299] This passage should, however, not be understood as referring to future interpretations that take place after a sanction has been imposed, but only to interpretations that already exist.

5.2.1.1.1.4 Excursus: Langnese

In Langnese, the Court of Justice used the principle of legal certainty to confirm the annulment of the Commission's order to refrain from any conclusion of future exclusive purchase agreements.[300] Against the backdrop of the annulment of its order by the General Court for lack of proportionality, the Commission tried to argue before the Court of Justice that the order should be interpreted as merely prohibiting the re-establishment of the same network of exclusive purchasing agreements that had been found to constitute an infringement, without, however, prohibiting the conclusion of new exclusive purchasing agreements with other retail distributors. However, in view of the grounds of the decision, the wording of the operative part of the decision, the stance the Commission had taken in front of the General Court and

[297] See GC, T-167/08 (Microsoft II, 2012), 123ff. In this context, it is noteworthy that, in Microsoft I (T-201/04, 2007), 810, the General Court had emphasised that the 2004 decision did not prevent Microsoft from charging reasonable remuneration where the interoperability information sought related "to a technology covered by a patent (or by another form of intellectual property right)". For further problems regarding the interpretation of the term "innovative" in the Microsoft II case see O'Donoghue/Padilla (2013), 939f.

[298] See Sect. 5.2.1.1.1.3.1 with footnote 293 above.

[299] See Sect. 5.2.1.1.1.3.1 with footnote 291 above.

[300] See for a more detailed description of the case Sect. 3.3.1.3.2.3.1.1 with footnotes 170ff above.

finally of the requirements of the principle of legal certainty, the Court of Justice rejected such a reinterpretation.[301] The judgment shows that the principle of legal certainty cannot only be used to attack imprecise orders. It also sets a limit to any potential reinterpretations of orders that are sufficiently precise. Due to the particular constellation, the judgment must, however, not be understood as a deviation from the generally low standards of the EU courts regarding the sufficient clarity of remedies.

5.2.1.1.2 Abstract Like Effects Orders

The General Court does not pursue a uniform approach in dealing with pleas in law challenging abstract like effects orders on the ground of their insufficient precision. As far as can be ascertained, the Court of Justice has to date never had to address the issue.

5.2.1.1.2.1 Purely Declaratory Value

A first strand of case law rejects the argument that abstract like effects orders are not sufficiently precise by ruling that such orders have a "purely declaratory value".[302] As regards the risk of getting sanctioned for non-compliance with a like effects order, the General Court holds that, if the Commission wanted to impose such a sanction, it would need to prove that the behaviour of the concerned undertaking constitutes an infringement.[303] According to the Court, the undertaking can appeal a decision imposing a sanction by relying on the ambiguity of the underlying order.[304]

5.2.1.1.2.2 Restrictive Interpretation

A second strand of case law rejects the argument that like effects orders are not sufficiently precise by giving such orders a restrictive interpretation.[305] According to this approach, like effects orders are "aimed solely at preventing the undertakings from repeating the behaviour found to be unlawful".[306] Emphasising that such orders must be interpreted "in the lights of the grounds of the decision", the General

[301] See CJ, C-279/95 P (Langnese, 1998), 74ff.

[302] GC, T-34/92 (Fiatagri, 1994), 39; T-136/94 (Eurofer, 1999), 226; T-422/08 R (Sacem, 2008), 46; T-425/08 R (Koda, 2008), 48. See also Müller-Tautphaeus (2003), 263, who approves that like effects orders have only a declaratory nature.

[303] GC, T-422/08 R (Sacem, 2008), 47; T-425/08 R (Koda, 2008), 49.

[304] GC, T-422/08 R (Sacem, 2008), 47; T-425/08 R (Koda, 2008), 49.

[305] See Sect. 3.3.1.5.1.2 with footnotes 390ff above for a more detailed description of the restrictive interpretation of the like effects order in Cartes Bancaires.

[306] GC, T-310/94 (Gruber + Weber, 1998), 167; T-491/07 (Cartes Bancaires, 2012), 439; see also T-305/94 (PVC II, 1999), 1249; T-25/95 (Cimenteries, 2000), 4704; T-45/98 (Krupp Thyssen, 2001), 311; De Bronnet (2012), Art. 7, 10.

Court understands their scope as limited to a prohibition of what has been found to be unlawful in the decision.[307]

5.2.1.2 The Stricter Standards Under German Law: Fährhafen Puttgarden

In Germany, the standards regarding the required degree of precision of orders to put an infringement to an end are stricter than those established by the EU Courts.[308] The Bundesgerichtshof has expressly stated that like effects orders comparable to the ones used by the Commission are not compatible with the requirements of the German understanding of the principle of legal certainty; they are hence not admissible under Article 32 ARC, which corresponds to Article 7 Regulation 1/03.[309] Strict standards regarding the principle of legal certainty do not only apply in respect of like effects orders, but also for instance where remedies regarding predatory pricing[310] and obligations to grant access are concerned. Regarding the latter, the case Fährhafen Puttgarden is of importance. Due to its comparability with the Microsoft penalties decision, it shall be presented here in more detail.

The Bundeskartellamt found that Scandlines had violated Article 102 TFEU by refusing to grant two ferry lines access to the infrastructure of its harbour.[311] As remedy, the Bundeskartellamt required Scandlines to grant at least one of the two ferry lines access in exchange for reasonable remuneration.[312] The court of appeal quashed the decision for lack of sufficient clarity. It found that the notion "reasonable remuneration" was as such not sufficiently precise and that, even taking the need for a margin of negotiation into account, the Bundeskartellamt would at least have been required to define a maximum amount up to which remuneration was

---

[307]See GC, T-491/07 (Cartes Bancaires, 2012), 440: "l'injonction en cause visant simplement à empêcher que le Groupement n'adopte à nouveau des mesures telles que celles dont l'illégalité a été constatée dans la décision attaquée"; "seule l'adoption de mesures ayant pour objet ou pour effets l'exclusion de certains opérateurs nouveaux entrants sur le marché de l'émission et la limitation de la concurrence intrasystème, telles que décrites dans la décision attaquée est interdite".

[308]By contrast, in the UK, the CAT has upheld a like effects order, arguing that such an order corresponds to the practice of the EU Commission. In the view of the CAT, any doubt in respect of the scope of such an order must be resolved at the stage of its enforcement. See CAT, Case 1001/1/1/01 (Napp Pharmaceutical, 2002), 553; Frese (2014), 182.

[309]BGH, KVR 67/07 (Gasliefervertäge, 2009), 52 and Jaeger (2010), § 32 ARC, 18. See also Frese (2014), 175f and 183, who explains the strict stance of the Bundesgerichtshof with the fact that, unlike under Regulation 1/03, under German law a violation of a remedy is directly punishable with a fine.

[310]For an example of strict standards as regards the precision of an order putting predatory pricing behaviour to an end see BGH, KVR 12/83 (Kaufmarkt, 1984), 13ff, and the discussion by Kirchhof (1986), Möschel (1986) and Bruglacher (1987), 141ff.

[311]See BGH, KVR 15/01 (Puttgarden, 2002), 7.

[312]See BGH, KVR 15/01 (Puttgarden, 2002), 3.

reasonable.[313] The Bundesgerichtshof overturned the judgment, ruling that the order of the Bundeskartellamt was sufficiently precise.[314] The Bundesgerichtshof argued that, where several ways exist to put an infringement to an end, a competition authority may not restrict the existing margin of negotiation of the concerned parties more than necessary to put the infringement to an end.[315] However, the Court did not stop there. It also interpreted the order of the Bundeskartellamt restrictively. According to the Bundesgerichtshof, the order did not go further than requiring Scandlines to generally grant access, to make proposals for a remuneration which Scandlines deemed reasonable and to enter into negotiations. The evaluation of whether the proposals made by Scandlines were actually "reasonable" had to be reserved to an independent abuse procedure or to civil law litigation before courts.[316] The Bundesgerichtshof refuted the court of appeal's argument that the Bundeskartellamt was required to define the maximum amount that was still reasonable. The Bundesgerichtshof acknowledged that such a definition of a maximum amount would have the benefit of avoiding a second abuse procedure or civil law litigation. It argued, however, that the latter benefit was outbalanced by the additional burden, which the difficulties of defining maximum amounts implied for the first abuse procedure. The Bundesgerichtshof considered that it was not justified to impose such an additional burden on the first abuse procedure as long as it was still open whether the parties would not find a negotiated solution themselves, once Scandline's basic obligation to grant access had been clarified.[317]

[313]See BGH, KVR 15/01 (Puttgarden, 2002), 15.

[314]See BGH, KVR 15/01 (Puttgarden, 2002), 16ff.

[315]See BGH, KVR 15/01 (Puttgarden, 2002), 36.

[316]See BGH, KVR 15/01 (Puttgarden, 2002), 22: "Das Bundeskartellamt hat sich [...] darauf beschränkt, es [Scandlines] "im ersten Zugriff" zu untersagen, sich - weil sie einen Zugangsanspruch der Beigeladenen überhaupt verneint - zu weigern, die aus ihrer Sicht angemessenen Bedingungen eines solchen Zugangs zu formulieren und gegebenenfalls auszuhandeln. Es bleibt damit erforderlichenfalls einem weiteren kartellbehördlichen Verfahren oder auch einer zivilrechtlichen Auseinandersetzung vorbehalten, zu klären, ob von [Scandlines] letztlich angebotene Bedingungen tatsächlich angemessen sind oder nicht."

[317]See BGH, KVR 15/01 (Puttgarden, 2002), 38: "Zwar mag eine solche Festsetzung [von Höchstpreisen] im Einzelfall geeignet sein, ein weiteres kartellbehördliches Verfahren oder eine zivilrechtliche Auseinandersetzung zwischen den beteiligten Unternehmen über die angemessene Höhe des von dem Zugang suchenden Unternehmen zu zahlenden Entgelts auszuschließen. Dieser Vorteil müsste jedoch vielfach durch eine erhebliche zusätzliche Belastung des Ausgangsverfahrens erkauft werden. [...] Ein derartiger Aufwand und die damit verbundene zeitliche Verzögerung wären unabhängig davon aufzubringen, ob sich die Beteiligten nicht viel besser im Verhandlungswege über die angemessenen Bedingungen verständigen könnten, sofern erst verbindlich feststeht, dass das marktbeherrschende Unternehmen den Zugang zu seinen Infrastruktureinrichtungen nicht schlechthin verweigern darf."

5.2.1.3 Discussion

Three points that arise from the described cases shall be discussed. First, it will be asked whether remedies in general do produce discrete legal effects at all or whether they merely have a declaratory function. It will be argued that one discrete legal effect of a remedy is to concretise the abstract competition rules so that these become enforceable by means of periodic penalty payments. However, as will be pointed out, only sufficiently precise remedies can achieve this function. Second, a closer look shall be had at the question how to assess whether a remedy is sufficiently precise in order to serve as the basis for the imposition of periodic penalty payments. Third, it will be reflected when an imprecise remedy should be annulled and when it may be upheld by means of restrictive interpretation.

5.2.1.3.1 Imprecise Orders to Put an Infringement to an End Do Not Produce Any Discrete Legal Effects

Within the literature, it is controversial whether orders to put an infringement to an end produce discrete legal effects at all. One commentator argues that such orders generally only have a "declaratory effect", because the respective obligations of the concerned undertakings follow already directly from the competition rules of the Treaty.[318] Other commentators generally assign a "constitutive effect" to orders to put an infringement to an end.[319] It is submitted that a distinction must be made between precise and imprecise orders.[320]

On the one hand, sufficiently precise orders cannot be said to have a merely declaratory nature. Certainly, the obligations of the concerned undertakings follow already directly from the rules of the treaty or the pertinent secondary legislation, given that these are directly applicable. Nevertheless, like a finding of an infringement,[321] sufficiently precise orders concretise the abstractly formulated competition rules by translating them into concrete obligations to act for individualised

[318]Bulst (2014), Art. 102, 387: "Wie die Feststellung des Verstoßes dürfte auch die Anordnung der Einstellung des Verstoßes rein deklaratorischer Natur sein, da sich die Pflicht zur Einstellung der Praxis bereits unmittelbar aus Art. 102 ergibt". For a declaratory nature of Article 7 and Article 9 decisions also Schütz (2013), Art. 9, 8.

[319]Fuchs/Möschel (2012), Art. 102, 408.

[320]See also Müller-Tautphaeus (2003), 260ff, who states that general cease and desist have no discrete substantive significance ("keine materiell eigenständige Bedeutung"); he acknowledges, however, that such orders have the procedural effect of concretising the competition rules in a binding manner for the individual case and of acquiring res judicata status.

[321]On the fact that the finding of an infringement constitutes an administrative act with independent legal effects that is reviewable under Article 263 TFEU, see eg Schwarze (2005), 929ff; Lenaerts/ Maselis/Gutman (2014), 7.41. See also Whish/Bailey (2012), 291: "Formal decisions of the Commission applying Articles 101 and 102 of course can be challenged".

undertakings.[322] There will often be several ways to put an infringement to an end. Where this is the case, the discrete legal effect of a remedy may consist in determining one particular way how to put the infringement to an end. Furthermore, the obligations laid down in a sufficiently precise remedy may become definitive or acquire res judicata status. Once this is the case, the remedy defines the scope of the concerned undertakings rights and obligations in an authoritative manner, independently of the scope of the abstract competition rules. Finally, the concretisation of the abstract competition rules in a sufficiently precise remedy entails the possibility to impose periodic penalty payments. Pursuant to Article 24(1)(a)–(c) Regulation 1/03, the imposition of periodic penalty payments is not possible without a prior or simultaneous imposition of an Article 7 order to put the infringement to an end, an Article 8 interim order or an Article 9 commitment decision. In accordance with Articles 23(2) Regulation 1/03, only fines can be imposed directly on the basis of the competition rules.[323]

On the other hand, none of the said characteristics apply to imprecise orders to put an infringement to an end. In particular, imprecise orders lack the effect of making the competition rules enforceable by means of periodic penalty payments. Several commentators have rightly pointed out that a periodic penalty payment may only be imposed on the basis of a sufficiently precise order.[324] For instance, Ritter emphasises that abstract like effects orders cannot automatically lead to sanctions. In his view, the Commission must open new proceedings in order to examine whether the new behaviour is "similar" to the one identified in a past decision and constitutes therefore a new infringement.[325] Ritter hence suggests that abstract like effects orders should merely be understood as announcement of a higher fine in case of recidivism.[326] More generally, in order to explain why the Commission should have the power to issue precise orders under Article 7, AG Warner emphasised in his opinion in Commercial Solvents that it was "in general unfair to a person to make an order against him requiring him to do something positive without specifying in the

[322]See Mestmäcker/Schweitzer (2014), § 20, 2: "Art. 7 VO 1/03 dient [...] dem Zweck, die wettbewerbsrechtlichen Verbotsnormen durch Abstellungsbeschlüsse durchzusetzen. [...] Die Wettbewerbsregeln werden durch diese Beschlüsse in konkrete Handlungspflichten übersetzt."

[323]See Schneider (2008), 4-24-011; Dannecker/Biermann (2012), Art. 24, 1, 10.

[324]Klees (2005), § 6, 74; Bauer (2008), 4-7-035; Hauser (2009), 211 and 242; Krings (2012), 252.

[325]See Ritter (2012), Art. 7, 39: "Unbestimmte Anordnungen können keinen Sanktionsautomatismus auslösen; erforderlich ist in jedem Fall die Einleitung eines neuen Verfahrens, um festzustellen, ob das neue Marktverhalten dem in der Entscheidung festgestellten vergleichbar ist und deshalb eine (neue) Zuwiderhandlung darstellt". See also Ritter (2012), Art. 9, 27 fn 107.

[326]See Ritter (2012), Art. 7, 39: "Solche Anordnungen sind daher eher als *Ankündigung* eines höheren Bußgelds im Wiederholungsfall zu sehen."

By virtue of para 28 of the Commission's 2006 Guidelines on fines, the fact that an undertaking continues or repeats the same or a similar infringement after the Commission or a national competition authority has made a finding of infringement of the competition rules constitutes an aggravating circumstance; for each such infringement established, the basic amount of the fine may be increased by up to 100%.

order exactly what he must do in order to comply with it".[327] Applied to the case, this meant that, in view of the periodic penalties imposed with the order, an imprecisely formulated order to supply would have put the dominant undertaking in an "intolerable position".[328]

The distinction between imprecise and precise orders also seems to underlie the case law of the EU courts, although the latter is not free from ambiguity. On the one hand, as mentioned above, in some judgments, the General Court has expressly assigned a purely declaratory value to abstract like effects orders. In this respect, the Court even states expressly that the Commission must first prove that the conduct in question constitutes an infringement, if it wants to impose a sanction for non-compliance with a like effects order. The approach of the EU courts to deal with imprecise orders by means of restrictive interpretation leads to a similar result. If they interpret an imprecise order restrictively, the Courts confine its legally relevant content; in so far as the wording of the order is broader, it does not produce any discrete legal effects. On the other hand, the case law also indicates that sufficiently precise orders do produce discrete legal effects. The Microsoft case shows that the Commission may impose a periodic penalty payment for non-compliance with a previous Article 7 order that is considered sufficiently precise without having to prove first that the behaviour in question constitutes an infringement of the competition rules.[329] In a similar vein, the General Court has explicitly acknowledged that the Commission may inflict penalties for violation of an Article 9 commitment without having to prove first that the behaviour in question constitutes an infringement.[330]

---

[327] AG Warner, 6/73 (Commercial Solvents, 1974), p. 272.

[328] AG Warner, ibid.

[329] In order to assess the lawfulness of the decision imposing the penalties, the General Court did not examine whether Microsoft's conduct infringed Article 102 TFEU. The Court merely examined whether Microsoft had complied with the remedy imposed in the 2004 decision; see in particular GC, T-167/08 (Microsoft II, 2012), 113ff, 142, 145f, 150.

[330] GC, T-342/11 (CEEES, 2014), 56 et 98: "[...] lorsqu'une entreprise ne respecte pas les engagements qu'elle a formulés et qui ont été rendus obligatoires par la Commission, cette dernière peut rouvrir la procédure et lui infliger une astreinte ou une amende en se limitant à démontrer le non-respect de la décision sur les engagements, sans devoir constater auparavant une violation des articles 101 TFUE ou 102 TFUE". See, however, also Ritter (2012), Art. 9, 37 and 30, where he highlights that the use of imprecise terms such as "reasonable" in a commitment to grant access cannot be automatically enforced.

In the context of merger control, Article 15(1)(c), (d) Regulation 139/2004 provides that the Commission can impose penalties directly for non compliance with injunctions or commitments. The General Court held in ARD (T-158/00 [ARD, 2003], 202f) that, due to the "detailed obligations" imposed by them, commitments offered "far greater legal certainty" than the normal monitoring of abusive conduct under Article 102 TFEU. In this respect, the Court argued that commitments had the advantage of reversing the burden of proof for abusive conduct.

5.2.1.3.2 How to Assess Whether a Remedy Is Sufficiently Precise in Order to Serve As the Basis for the Imposition of Periodic Penalty Payments?

It follows from the above that a remedy only produces discrete legal effects, if it is sufficiently precise. In particular, only if it is sufficiently precise, the remedy will have the effect of creating obligations to act that are enforceable by means of periodic penalty payments. Hence, the important question remains how to assess whether this is the case. The EU Courts rely on the general formula that "the individual concerned [must be] in a position, on the basis of the wording of the relevant provision and, if need be, with the help of the interpretation of it given by the courts, to know which acts or omissions will make him liable".[331] They also state that it is necessary to interpret the operative part in the light of the grounds of the decision.[332] Apart from these general formulae, the question how to assess whether an order is sufficiently precise cannot be answered in the abstract, but depends to a large extent on the circumstances of the case at hand. A general answer to the said question shall therefore not be attempted here. However, in the following section, it will be argued that, in Microsoft II, the General Court applied a too soft standard for assessing whether the penalties were imposed on a sufficiently precise basis. In this respect, in addition to the observations presented above that relate more to the particularities of the case of Microsoft,[333] two more general arguments will be criticised, that were both used by the General Court to justify the alleged sufficient precision of the order to grant access on reasonable terms. The first is the General Court's argument that the degree of precision required for a decision that serves as the basis for the imposition of periodic penalty payments is not higher than the degree of precision that is required of a legal rule that serves as the basis for the imposition of a fine. Secondly, it will be shown that also the Court's reliance on the Automec judgment and the necessity to preserve the concerned undertakings' freedom of choice is not convincing.

5.2.1.3.2.1 Periodic Penalties Require a More Precise Basis Than Fines

In the penalties judgment, the General Court rejects "Microsoft's argument that the Commission should itself first have established, by means of a decision amenable to judicial review, the appropriate remuneration rate before it could impose a periodic penalty payment".[334] In this respect, Microsoft had argued, inter alia, that a periodic penalty payment, which is "designed to compel a person to adopt a certain course of action", cannot be imposed, unless "the obligations of the person in question have

[331] GC, T-167/08 (Microsoft II, 2012), 84 with further references.

[332] GC, T-167/08 (Microsoft II, 2012), 85 with further references.

[333] See Sect. 5.2.1.1.1.3.2 with footnotes 296ff.

[334] GC, T-167/08 (Microsoft II, 2012), 90.

been specified exactly".[335] The Court discards this argument in particular with the following reasoning: It refers back to the case law according to which the use of imprecise legal concepts in making rules does not preclude the imposition of a remedial measure as long as the individual concerned is in a position to know which acts or omissions will make him liable. Next, the Court restates this case law in a curtailed manner as meaning that "the use of imprecise legal concepts within a provision does not prevent liability being established as against a person who contravenes it". In this respect, the Court then embraces the Commission's argument that, "if it were otherwise, an infringement of Article 101 or 102 TFEU – which are themselves drawn up using imprecise legal concepts, such as distortion of competition or abuse of a dominant position – could not give rise to a fine without the prior adoption of a decision establishing the infringement".[336] The Court goes on by stating that "the distinction between a fine and a periodic penalty payment [. . .] is of no relevance [. . .and that. . .] there is no reason to state with different degrees of precision what an undertaking must do or not do to comply with the competition rules before either a decision imposing a fine or a decision imposing a definitive periodic penalty payment is adopted in its regard".[337]

It is submitted that this reasoning erroneously evens out the difference between fines and periodic penalty payments. Taken to the extreme, the General Court's reasoning implies that the Commission can impose periodic penalty payments for non-compliance with an order that is as imprecise as the competition rules of the Treaty. The General Court's reasoning thereby leads to a too soft standard as regards the degree of precision required for a rule that serves as basis for a periodic penalty payment.[338] Periodic penalty payments are distinct from fines. The distinction can already be inferred from the terms of Articles 23(2) and 24(1)(a) Regulation 1/03: Only fines may be inflicted on the basis of the abstract competition rules; a periodic penalty payment always needs "a decision taken pursuant to Article 7" as its basis.[339] If the General Court's argument were correct and periodic penalty payments could be imposed for non-compliance with an order that is as imprecise as the competition rules of the treaty, then this distinction would be meaningless. If the necessity of "a decision taken pursuant to Article 7" does not serve the purpose of concretising the competition rules, why does the imposition of penalties require such a decision at all and why can penalties not be imposed like fines directly on the basis of the abstract competition rules?

---

[335]GC, T-167/08 (Microsoft II, 2012), 76.

[336]GC, T-167/08 (Microsoft II, 2012), 91.

[337]GC, T-167/08 (Microsoft II, 2012), 94.

[338]Also Barbier de la Serre (2012a), 64, criticises this argument of the General Court, albeit with a slightly different reasoning. According to him, the General Court's argument is circular and the latter should have examined under which conditions the vagueness of Articles 101 or 102 TFEU can, in certain circumstances, preclude the infliction of a fine. Critically also Mestmäcker/Schweitzer (2014), § 21, 42. By contrast, Cardonnel (2012) agrees with the General Court.

[339]See Sect. 5.2.1.3.1, footnote 323 above.

The difference that is, however, even more important, is that the imposition of a fine presupposes a finding of negligence or intent, while this is not the case for periodic penalty payments. The reason behind this distinction is that fines and periodic penalty payments serve different functions. Fines are punishments for past behaviour and therefore presuppose fault, i.e. intent or negligence. Periodic penalty payments are means of administrative coercion; they compel the concerned individual for the future to comply with an obligation,[340] irrespective of the presence of any fault.[341] The divergence of fines and penalty payments as to whether a finding of fault is a precondition for their infliction necessitates different standards as regards the degree of precision required of the rules that serve as basis for their imposition. In fact, the requirement of negligence protects an undertaking against the imposition of a fine, where there is uncertainty how an imprecise rule must be interpreted. If the concerned undertaking succeeds in demonstrating that it committed an unavoidable error of law, the condition of negligence is not met and the undertaking is exempted from liability.[342] In the context of fines, the negligence requirement therefore serves as a corrective to eventual uncertainty regarding the interpretation of Article 101 or 102 TFEU. Irrespective of whether the rule that serves as the basis for the imposition of a fine is in itself sufficiently precise or not, this corrective guarantees that a fine is only inflicted where the concerned undertaking could not be unaware of the anti-competitive nature of its conduct.[343] However, no comparable filter exists with

[340]See COMP/C-3/37.792 (Microsoft, 2008), 295: "The procedure pursuant to Article 24 of Regulation [1/03] aims at compelling undertakings to comply with their obligations." For the distinction between fines and penalty payments see also A. Koch (2011), 74f and 301f; Haslinger (2012), 93f.

[341]See the wording of Articles 23(2) and 24; Mestmäcker/Schweitzer (2014), § 22, 2; Hauser (2009), 242; Dannecker/Biermann (2012), Art. 24, 43ff; Kerse/Khan (2012), 7-260. For the sake of completeness, it must be pointed out that, according to a minority view, also the imposition of periodic penalty payments can, under certain circumstances, presuppose negligence, see Dannecker/Biermann (2012), Art. 24, 44, who nevertheless share the contrary opinion. For the analogous discussion under German administrative law see Waldhoff (2013), § 46, 132; Troidl (2014), § 11 VwVG, 1.

[342]The precise conditions under which such an "unavoidable error in law" can be assumed are controversial. In the Schenker case (C-681/11, 2012), AG Kokott suggested to assume an unavoidable error in law under certain restrictive conditions, where an undertaking has relied on independent and qualified legal advice (see 38ff of the opinion). The Court of Justice did not follow the AG's opinion and simply held that "[u]ndertakings which directly coordinate their behaviour in respect of their selling prices quite evidently cannot be unaware of the anti-competitive nature of their conduct" (39 of the judgment). The judgment confirms the general reluctance of the EU courts to assume unavoidable errors in law. Nevertheless, I argue that the test applied by the CJ unequivocally shows that the concept of an error in law precluding liability is as such recognised in EU competition law. In fact, according to the CJ, an undertaking only acts negligently if it "cannot be unaware of the anti-competitive nature of its conduct".

[343]Although the EU Courts are very reluctant to assume an unavoidable error of law, its existence and the resulting exemption from liability are not purely hypothetical. In a series of decisions [eg OJ 1978 L 70/54 (Vegetable Parchment, 1977), 82f; OJ 1990 L 220/28 (Stainless Steel, 1990), X.14; COMP/38.096 (Clearstream, 2004); 344f; COMP/39.985 (Motorola, 2014), 559ff], the Commission abstained from imposing a fine, because it had not been clarified beforehand whether the

respect to periodic penalty payments. The decision serving as a basis for a periodic penalty payment must therefore in itself be sufficiently precise to guarantee that the concerned undertaking cannot be unaware of what constitutes anticompetitive conduct and what does not. Overall, this shows that decisions that serve as basis for the imposition of a periodic penalty payment must be more precise than rules that serve as basis for the infliction of a fine.

5.2.1.3.2.2 The Freedom of Choice of the Concerned Undertakings Cannot Justify the Use of Imprecise Orders As the Basis for Periodic Penalty Payments

Also the General Court's reliance on the Automec jurisprudence is flawed.[344] The gist of the Court's argument seems to be based on two assumptions: First, that the existence of several ways to put an infringement to an end justifies or even requires the imposition of an imprecisely formulated injunction. Second, that, in such a case, the imprecision of the injunction does not hinder the infliction of a periodic penalty payment. In order to explain why at least the second assumption is not convincing, it is useful to compare the General Court's reasoning with that of the Bundesgerichtshof in the Puttgarden case.

The reasoning of the two judgments is at best superficially consistent. Certainly, on the surface, both courts agree that an order to grant access on reasonable terms is sufficiently precise. In support of this conclusion, both courts rely unanimously on the fact that competition authorities must respect the concerned parties freedom of action where there are several ways to comply with the law. Hence, there is common ground as regards the first assumption mentioned above, namely that the existence of several ways to put an infringement to an end justifies or even requires the imposition of an imprecisely formulated injunction.[345] This is, however, also where the common ground between the General Court and the Bundesgerichtshof ends. The General Court does not shy away from drawing the consequences of the admissibility of the use of the imprecise term "reasonable" and allows the infliction of a

practices in question constituted infringements of the competition rules. It is submitted that this reasoning for not imposing a fine comes at least close to accepting that the concerned undertakings could not be aware that their conduct amounted to an infringement, i.e. that the undertakings committed an unavoidable error in law. Generally on the problem of unavoidable errors in law under EU competition law see eg Engelsing/Schneider (2008), 4-23-031f; Jones/Sufrin (2014), 997ff; Dannecker/Biermann (2012), before Art. 23, 200ff; von Danwitz (2013); Fleischer (2013).

[344] For the general discussion of the Automec case see Sect. 3.3.1.4.1.1.1.3 with footnotes 274ff and Sect. 3.3.1.4.1.1.2.1 with footnotes 286ff above.

[345] See, for analogous statements regarding German law, von Ungern-Sternberg (2000), 664; Bornkamm (2014), § 32, 50; see also BGH, KVR 15/01 (Puttgarden, 2002), 28: "[Es kann] insbesondere dann, wenn das Bestimmtheitsgebot einerseits und verfassungsrechtlich geschützte Freiheitsrechte des Adressaten, die es ihm überlassen, in welcher Weise er einer gesetzlichen, durch den Verwaltungsakt konkretisierten Verpflichtung nachkommen will, andererseits in Widerstreit miteinander treten, geboten sein, die Anforderungen an die Bestimmtheit der behördlichen Anordnung gering zu halten".

periodic penalty payment where the Commission finds that the concerned undertaking has not complied with this term. In this regard, the General Court explicitly emphasizes that "the purpose of [the order to grant access on reasonable terms] is not only to oblige Microsoft to negotiate [...] but also to compel it to make the interoperability information available [...] and to allow the use of it [...] on reasonable [...] terms" and that "Microsoft was obliged to propose such terms on its own initiative".[346]

The Bundesgerichtshof takes a different path. It reinterprets the order to grant access on reasonable terms restrictively as only requiring the dominant undertaking generally to grant access and to make a proposal and to enter into negotiations with respect to the remuneration. Only the content read into the order by the Bundesgerichtshof is enforceable by means of a periodic penalty payment. This means that the prescribed conduct to which the dominant undertaking can be compelled by means of a periodic penalty payment consists only of the general granting of access, of making a proposal regarding the remuneration and of entering into negotiations. Under the restrictive interpretation of the Bundesgerichtshof, the use of the term "in exchange for reasonable remuneration" in the decision of the Bundeskartellamt has no—or at most a very limited—enforceable content. The Bundesgerichtshof explicitly states that the use of this term serves merely two functions: On the one hand, the term clarifies that Scandlines is not obliged to grant access for free; on the other hand, it allows to capture the charging of rates that are so manifestly unreasonable that they must objectively be considered as a general refusal to grant access at all.[347] Different from the General Court, the Bundesgerichtshof does not allow the immediate infliction of a periodic penalty payment where the Bundeskartellamt finds that the proposal made by the dominant undertaking is not reasonable. Rather, the intermediate step of a second abuse procedure is necessary.

Both judgments are not fully persuasive in so far as they share the assumption that the existence of several ways to put an infringement to an end justifies or even requires the imposition of an imprecisely formulated injunction. A competition authority's obligation to respect an undertaking's freedom of action is limited to the area within the boundaries of what is lawful. Such an obligation does, however, not hinder the competition authority to define precisely where those boundaries are.[348] As regards the imposition of an order to grant access in exchange for

---

[346]GC, T-167/08 (Microsoft II, 2012), 113f.

[347]See BGH, KVR 15/01 (Puttgarden, 2002), 27: "Die Erwähnung des angemessenen Entgelts im Entscheidungssatz hat hiernach zum einen [...] die Funktion, [...] klarzustellen, dass es [Scandlines] nicht untersagt ist, die unentgeltliche Mitbenutzung zu verweigern. Zum anderen erlaubte sie es, unter "Weigerung" im Sinne des Entscheidungssatzes auch die Forderung eines Entgelts zu fassen, das so offensichtlich unangemessen wäre, dass sich die Forderung bei objektiver Wertung als nicht ernst gemeint und damit als Fortsetzung der grundsätzlichen Weigerung darstellte, überhaupt einem der Beigeladenen die Mitbenutzung zu gestatten."

[348]In the case of Microsoft, the fact that it is not for the Commission to choose a particular rate from among the plurality of rates that must be considered as reasonable and therefore lawful does not

reasonable remuneration, the definition of maximum amounts of what is reasonable allows reconciling the needs to preserve the concerned parties margin of negotiation and to provide for sufficient clarity of an injunction.

Certainly, the definition of such maximum amounts can be difficult for competition authorities to accomplish. Nevertheless, although this difficulty may possibly justify the use of an imprecise order to put the infringement to an end, it cannot warrant the imposition of a periodic penalty payment on its basis. In this regard, the judgment of the Bundesgerichtshof is more convincing than the one of the General Court: Where competition authorities cannot or do not want to define a maximum amount of what is reasonable, they must confine themselves to a general order to grant access and to enter into negotiations—with the consequence that only the latter obligations can be enforced by means of a periodic penalty payment. Whether such a general order to grant access and to enter into negotiations is in the long run preferable to an order defining a maximum amount depends on the likeliness of the necessity of a second abuse procedure. If chances are good that a general order will suffice to stop the abusive behaviour, competition authorities can unburden the first procedure by abstaining from the difficult task to define a maximum amount. On the contrary, the likeliness that a general order will only lead to the dominant undertaking charging unreasonable prices and thus to a continuation of the abusive conduct militates for defining a maximum amount from the outset.

Overall, it is hence submitted that the endeavour to preserve the concerned undertakings' freedom of choice does not warrant the imposition of a periodic penalty payment on the basis of an imprecise order. Certainly, the Commission may resort to vague terms, if the formulation of more precise prescriptions is too costly. However, the vague term will then only be of a declaratory nature; it will not be enforceable by means of periodic penalty payments.[349] Many examples of the decisional practice of the Commission and the EU Courts support this result. In fact, although the Commission has frequently used vague terms in its orders, until the Microsoft II case, it never relied on such terms to impose periodic penalties. Before Microsoft II, wherever the Courts have upheld orders containing vague terms, they did not decide about their enforceability by means of penalties. The penalties imposed in the Commercial Solvents case related, on the one hand, to an order to supply of which the price and quantity had been fixed in a precise manner. On the

---

preclude the Commission from precisely defining the demarcation line beyond which a rate can no longer be considered reasonable. Certainly, strictly speaking one might argue that the General Court relied on the Automec case law only to reject Microsoft's argument "that the Commission should itself first have established [...] the appropriate remuneration rate" (see Sect. 5.2.1.3.2.1, footnote 334 above). As the Commission cannot fix the appropriate rate itself, but only the outer boundaries of what constitutes lawful conduct, this argument would indeed have to be rejected. However, it is apparent from the judgment that Microsoft's did not literally request that the Commission should "fix the appropriate remuneration rate", but merely that the Commission should specify Microsoft's obligations more precisely (see GC, T-167/08 [Microsoft II, 2012], 73ff).

[349] See also Jaeger (2010), § 32 ARC, 23, who enumerates several possibilities for a competition authority to obtain an enforceable order in cases in which there are several ways to put the infringement to an end.

other hand, those penalties related only to the obligation to submit proposals to the Commission.[350] In Aéroports de Paris, the General Court upheld an abstractly formulated order to apply a non-discriminatory scheme of fees.[351] However, in the contested decision, the Commission had abstained from imposing penalties.[352] In Magill, the Court confirmed an order to supply on non-discriminatory terms. However, in that order, the Commission had specified that the parties were "therefore required to submit proposals for approval by the Commission" and had abstained from imposing penalties.[353] The IMS Health interim order contained periodic penalties to ensure compliance with an abstract order to license IP on reasonable terms.[354] However, the decision provided that an independent expert should determine the appropriate royalties, if the parties could not find an agreement. The penalties hence related only to compliance with that dispute resolution mechanism.

5.2.1.3.3 Restrictive Interpretation or Annulment?

It must be emphasised that not all orders that leave it to the undertakings how to put an infringement to an end are completely devoid of enforceable content. For instance, an abstract order to put the infringement to an end has a precise content and is enforceable in so far as it implies that the concerned undertaking may not continue the practice that has been found to constitute the infringement. On the contrary, such an order cannot be used to compel the undertaking to modify a practice in a certain way or to abandon the practice completely. Similarly, on the basis of an order to submit proposals, an undertaking can be compelled to submit proposals. The undertaking cannot, however, be forced to give its proposals a certain content.[355] Where such a precise enforceable content can be given to an order at least

[350] See Sect. 3.3.1.4.1.2.2.1.1 with footnotes 325ff above.

[351] See Sect. 3.3.1.4.1.2.1 with footnotes 316f above.

[352] OJ 1998 L 230/10 (Aéroports de Paris, 1998).

[353] See Sect. 3.3.1.4.1.2.2.1.2 with footnotes 331ff above.

[354] See Sect. 3.3.1.4.1.2.2.1.3 with footnotes 339ff above.

[355] In Article 5(d) of the operative part of the 2004 decision, the Commission required Microsoft to communicate to it the measures Microsoft intended to take in order to comply with the obligation to grant access on reasonable terms. That communication had to be "sufficiently detailed to enable the Commission to make a preliminarily assessment as to whether the [. . .] measures [would] ensure effective compliance with the [d]ecision". On appeal, Microsoft argued that it followed from Article 5(d) that the Commission was obliged to specify Microsoft's obligations more precisely before any penalties could be imposed. The General Court rejected this argument, stating that Article 5(d) did not imply that the Commission had undertaken to specify Microsoft's obligations more precisely. Furthermore, the Court was concerned that Microsoft would otherwise obtain "a right of veto over enforcement of the 2004 decision", because it could block the enforcement of the obligation to grant access by not complying with Article 5(d); see GC, T-167/08 (Microsoft II, 2012), 75, 92 and 205.

The argument of the Court is not convincing. Against the background of the vague terms in which the obligation to grant access was formulated in Article 5(a) of the operative part of the decision, Article 5(d) must be understood as sign of a certain flexibility regarding the

by means of restrictive interpretation, the courts do not necessarily have to annul the order for lack of sufficient clarity. In view of the interest to leave it to the undertakings how to put an infringement to an end, it may suffice to ensure that the Commission does not enforce conduct that is not covered.

This is different, however, if an imprecise order does not contain any enforceable content at all, as is the case with abstract like effects orders. It is submitted that even under the strand of case law that interprets them restrictively as "aimed solely at preventing the undertakings from repeating the behaviour found to be unlawful",[356] abstract like effects orders do not contain any independent enforceable content. The prohibition of a repetition of the behaviour found to be unlawful is already encapsulated in the order to put the infringement to an end. Under the strand of case law that assigns abstract like effects orders a "purely declaratory value", the lack of independent enforceable content is even more obvious. Certainly, one might nevertheless refute the criticism that is pointed against abstract like effects orders[357] with the argument that, in the way they are interpreted by the General Court, such orders cause at least no legal harm and thus do not need to be annulled. Moreover, one might even hope that abstract like effects orders produce an informal deterrent effect on the concerned undertakings that promotes compliance with the competition rules. Nevertheless, without any discrete legal effects at all, abstract like effects are legally superfluous. They do not fulfil the function that is typically assigned to them: If they are not enforceable, they cannot prevent the circumvention of the actual order to put the infringement to an end any more than the general competition rules.[358] It is hence submitted that, for the sake of clarity, the Commission should stop using such orders. In court, they should be considered not sufficiently precise and be annulled for violation of the principle of legal certainty.

---

implementation of the remedy and as a mechanism of coordination between Microsoft and the Commission. This conclusion is supported by the fact that the decision provided for a time limit of only 60 days until Microsoft had to communicate its proposals to the Commission and of 120 days until Microsoft was obliged to grant access. The existence of this flexibility regarding the implementation of the remedy constitutes yet another indication that the original decision was not sufficiently precise to serve directly as basis for the imposition of periodic penalty payments.

It is submitted that the Commission could have imposed penalties in order to compel Microsoft to comply with the obligation to make proposals. However, as long as Microsoft complied with that obligation, the Commission could not directly justify the imposition of penalties on Microsoft with the fact that Microsoft's proposals did not comply with the obligation laid down in Article 5(a) to grant access on reasonable terms. In order to do the latter, the Commission would have needed to specify first more precisely, what "access on reasonable terms" meant.

[356]See Sect. 5.2.1.1.2.2, footnote 306 above.

[357]Eg Bauer (2008), 4-7-035: "[C]onsiderable doubts as to whether such an operative part complies with the principle [. . .] that measures should be sufficiently clear"; Jaeger (2008), Art. 7, 11: "[E] ntspricht [. . .] nicht mehr dem aus dem Rechtsstaatsprinzip resultierenden Bestimmtheitsgebot"; Jaeger considers, however, that orders that require an undertaking to abstain from conduct having "the same object or effect" are still tolerable – as opposed to orders requiring an undertaking to abstain from conduct having "a similar" object or effect; Schütz (2013), 14: "[U]nter Bestimmtheitsgesichtspunkten nicht unproblematisch".

[358]Similarly Müller-Tautphaeus (2003), 263.

5.2.1.3.4 Concluding Example: Google Search

The Google Search decision may serve as a concluding example to illustrate the difficulties in terms of legal certainty brought about by imprecise injunctions. The Commission limited itself to an abstract cease and desist- and like effects order, sided by an obligation to report to the Commission on the implementation of the remedy. At the same time, the Commission imposed periodic penalty payments, if Google were to fail to comply with these injunctions.[359] In the decision, the Commission explicitly explained that, since there were several ways how to put the infringement to an end, it was for Google to choose between those various ways. Moreover, the Commission specified some rather abstract principles that any chosen remedy had to observe. According to those principles, the remedy has to treat competing comparison shopping services no less favourably than Google's own comparison shopping service within its general search results pages. The equal treatment must apply to all devices and to all consumers in the concerned geographic area and extend to all elements having an impact on the visibility, triggering, ranking or graphical format of a search result. Furthermore, the remedy may not lead to competing comparison shopping services being charged a fee or another form of consideration having the same or an equivalent object or effect as the infringement established by the decision.[360]

In order to comply with the Commission's injunction, Google introduced an auction mechanism enabling competing comparison shopping services to bid in competition with Google Shopping for access to the Shopping Unit for the placement of product ads. Whether this auction mechanism complies with the Commission's decision remains, at the time of writing, controversial[361] and shall not be discussed here in detail. On the basis of the arguments developed above, it is, however, submitted that the remedy imposed in the decision produces only limited discrete legal effects and can only to a limited extent serve as the basis for the imposition of periodic penalty payments. In particular, given the lack of more precise prescriptions regarding the auction prices, it would be contrary to the principle of legal certainty, if the Commission imposed periodic penalty payments for those prices directly on the basis of the decision. The same applies to an eventual insufficiency of the measures taken to separate Google Shopping from the rest of Googles business and to prevent cross subsidisation.

---

[359] See articles 3 and 4 of the operative part of COMP/39.740 (Google Search, 2017).

[360] COMP/39.740 (Google Search, 2017), 693ff.

[361] For compliance with the Commission's decision in particular Vesterdorf/Fountoukakos (2018), 4ff; for non compliance see the open letters addressed by competing comparison shopping services to the Commission on 28 February and 22 November 2018, available on www.searchneutrality.org.

5.2.2 *Precision in the Context of Article 9*

The Microsoft penalties judgment and the Commission's Google Search decision demonstrate particularly well that the implementation of Article 7 remedies causes difficulties.[362] The Mastercard 2007 decision constitutes another example[363]: As explained above, the decision did not set out a methodology how Mastercard could have made its MIFs compatible with Article 101(3) TFEU. When Mastercard reimposed modified MIFs subsequent to the Commission's decision, the Commission was concerned that this would constitute a violation of the 2007 decision or of the competition rules. Ultimately, Mastercard and the Commission were able to resolve the dispute only by means of an informal settlement.[364] Also Tetra Pak II and Aéroports de Paris confirm the concerned undertaking's distress that they did not know what the respective Article 7 remedies required them to do.[365] One reason for the lack of specifity of Article 7 decisions that causes the described implementation problems is precisely the want of the Commission to preserve the concerned undertaking's freedom to choose how to put the infringement to an end.

Commitments made binding on the basis of Article 9 are normally significantly more specific than Article 7 remedies. The Commission requests that commitments have to be "unambiguous and self-executing".[366] Examples of commitments that are more precise than the injunction to grant access on reasonable terms used in the Microsoft 2004 decision are the Rambus,[367] Standard & Poor's[368] and Reuters[369] commitments, all of which contain specific provisions as regards the licensing fees of the concerned products. The Visa commitment decisions and the informal settlement with Mastercard subsequent to the adoption of the Commission's infringement decision included specific caps for the MIFs in question.[370] One explanation for the increased precision of Article 9 decisions is precisely their consensual nature. As explained above, due to the consensual nature of commitments, the argument used in the context of Article 7 that the use of imprecise orders is necessary to preserve the concerned undertaking's freedom of choice is only of limited importance in the context of Article 9.[371]

---

[362] See Botteman/Patsa (2013), 355: "remedies imposed as part of an infringement decision may be prone to implementation problems, and, ultimately, result in litigation over the defendant's precise obligations"; Mestmäcker/Schweitzer (2014), § 21, 40.

[363] See also Vesterdorf/Fountoukakos (2018), 4ff.

[364] See Sect. 3.3.1.5.1.1.1 with footnote 379 above.

[365] See Sect. 3.3.1.4.1.2.1 with footnote 316 (Aéroports de Paris) and Sect. 3.3.1.6.1.1.2.1 with footnote 455 (Tetra Pak II) above.

[366] See Sect. 5.1.4.4.1.3.3, footnote 183 above.

[367] COMP/38.636 (Rambus, 2009).

[368] COMP/39.592 (Standard & Poor's, 2011).

[369] COMP/39.654 (Reuters, 2012).

[370] See Sect. 3.3.1.5.1.1.1 with footnotes 379f above.

[371] See Sect. 3.3.1.4.2 with footnote 367 above.

The higher degree of precision of Article 9 decisions constitutes an advantage in terms of legal certainty. The Commission obtains a decision that is sufficiently precise to be enforced without problems by means of periodic penalty payments. The concerned undertakings know what they are required to do in order to avoid being sanctioned by the Commission.[372] Third parties know what they can request of the concerned undertakings. Overall, the use of an Article 9 instead of an Article 7 decision hence creates an advantage in terms of legal certainty without sacrificing the freedom of choice of the concerned undertaking how to put the infringement to an end.

5.3 Conclusion on the Impact of Commitments on Legal Certainty

Summing up, it is submitted that the overall impact of the recourse to an Article 9 instead of an Article 7 decision on legal certainty is only modestly negative. The most valid concern remains that the use of commitments does not entail the positive externalities of adjudication. However, for the reasons set out above, this concern appears less alarming than is often contended. Moreover, all potential disadvantages of the Article 9 procedure in terms of legal certainty must be balanced against an important advantage: The fact that commitments result in precise and enforceable obligations.

Bibliography

Ackermann (2010): Europäisches Kartellrecht, in: Riesenhuber (Ed.), Europäische Methodenlehre, 2nd edition, 2010

Akman (2017): A preliminary assessment of the EC's Google Search decision, available online

Anweiler (2009): in: Loewenheim/Meessen/Riesenkampff (Eds.), Kartellrecht. Kommentar, 2nd edition, 2009

Armengol/Pascual (2006): Some reflections on Article 9 commitment decisions in the light of the Coca-Cola case, ECLR 2006, 124

Barbier de la Serre (2012a): Sois raisonnable ou tu seras puni, RLC 2012/33, 63

[372]See Cook (2006), 210: "opportunity [. . .] to develop an acceptable set of conduct guidelines, approved by the competition authority, according to which the company can run its business in the future"; identically O'Donoghue/Padilla (2013), 897; Rab/Monnoyeur/Sukhtankar (2010), 175: "opportunity to develop a clear set of Commission-approved guidelines"; Falconi (2011), 51: "opportunity to [. . .] seek clarification on key business practices"; similarly Temple Lang (2006), 272f; Rachwol (2010), 52: "Verpflichtungszusagen schaffen [. . .] einen Gewinn an Rechtssicherheit für die gebundenen Unternehmen, denn sie bilden einen Satz von Regeln und Richtlinien, die von der Kommission akzeptiert worden sind und an denen sich die Unternehmen orientieren können bzw. müssen".

Barbier de la Serre (2012b): Competition law cases before the EU Courts: Is the well running dry?, in: Merola/Derenne (2012): The Role of the Court of Justice of the European Union in Competition Law Cases. GCLC Annual Conference Series, 2012
Bauer (2008): in: Hirsch/Montag/Säcker (Eds.), Competition Law: European Community Practice and Procedure. Article-by-Article Commentary, 2008
Bernault (2019): Accès transfrontalier à la télévision payante - Cloisonnement des marchés nationaux - Droit de la concurrence, Propriétés intellectuelles 2019, 42
Blockx (2018): The Impact of EU Antitrust Procedure on the Role of the EU Courts (1997-2016), JECLP 2018, 92
Bornkamm (2014): in: Langen/Bunte (Eds.), Kartellrecht, Volume 2, 12th edition, 2014
Botteman/Patsa (2013): Towards a more sustainable use of commitment decisions in Article 102 TFEU cases, JAE 2013, 347
Brenner (2012): Das Vergleichsverfahren der Europäischen Kommission in Kartellfällen, 2012
Brenner (2014): Regulierung mithilfe des Kartellrechts – Verpflichtungszusagen der Europäischen Kommission, EuR 2014, 671
Bruglacher (1987): Das Bestimmtheitsgebot im Rahmen der kartellrechtlichen Preismißbrauchsaufsicht. Die Bestimmtheit von Untersagungsverfügungen auf der Grundlage der §§ 22, 26 und 37a Abs. 3 GWB, 1987
Bulst (2014): in: Langen/Bunte (Eds.), Kartellrecht, Volume 2, 12th edition, 2014
Busse/Leopold (2005): Entscheidungen über Verpflichtungszusagen nach Art. 9 VO (EG) Nr. 1/2003, WuW 2005, 145
Cardonnel (2012): Astreinte: Le Tribunal de l'UE réduit légèrement le montant d'une astreinte imposée en 2008, Concurrences 2012/4, 145
Cengiz (2011): Judicial review and the rule of law in the EU competition law regime after Alrosa, ECJ 2011, 127
Choné/Souam/Vialfont (2014): On the optimal use of commitment decisions under European competition law, IRLE 2014, 169
Coleman/Silver (1986): Justice in settlements, Social Philosophy and Policy 1986, 102
Cook (2006): Commitment Decisions: The Law and Practice under Article 9, World Competition 2006, 209
Craig (2012): EU administrative law, 2nd edition, 2012
Craig/De Búrca (2011): EU law. Text, cases and materials, 5th edition, 2011
Dalheimer (2005): in: Dalheimer/Feddersen/Miersch (Eds.), EU-Kartellverfahrensverordnung. Kommentar zur VO 1/2003. Sonderausgabe aus Grabitz/Hilf: Das Recht der Europäischen Union, nach Art. 83 EGV, 2005
Dann (2013): Parlamentarische Legitimation der Binnenmarkt- und Wettbewerbspolitik der EU, EuR-Bei 2013, 93
Dannecker/Biermann (2012): in: Immenga/Mestmäcker (Eds.), EU-Wettbewerbsrecht, 5th Edition, 2012
Davies/Das (2006): Private enforcement of Commission commitment decisions: a steep climb, not a gentle stroll, in: Hawk (Ed), Annual proceedings of the Fordham Competition Law Institute 2005, 2006
De Bronnet (2012): Europäisches Kartellverfahrensrecht. Kommentar zur VO 1/2003, 2nd edition, 2012
Debroux (2019): Comment on GC, T-873/16 (canal+, 2018), Concurrences 2019, n° 1, 70
De Smijter/Sinclair (2014): The Enforcement System under Regulation 1/2003, in: Faull/Nikpay (Eds.), The EU Law of Competition, 3rd edition, 2014
Dohrn (2010): Die Bindungswirkung kartellrechtlicher Entscheidungen der Kommission sowie deutscher und mitgliedstaatlicher Kartellbehörden und Gerichte im deutschen Zivilprozess, 2010
Dunne (2014): Commitment decisions in EU competition law, JCLE 2014, 399
Duron (2016): Private Damages Actions in the Wake of a Commitment Decision: New Risks after the Judgment of the Paris Commercial Court in Eco-Emballages, JECLP 2016, 125

Engelsing/Schneider (2008): in: Hirsch/Montag/Säcker (Eds.), Competition Law: European Community Practice and Procedure. Article-by-Article Commentary, 2008

Falconi (2011): Commitment decisions in the EU and UK – Developments, open issues and considerations for companies and competition authorities, Competition Law 2011, 41

Fasoula (2018): The legal effects of commitment decisions under Article 9(1) of regulation 1/2003 on antitrust proceedings before national Courts, European Competition and Regulatory Law Review 2018, 60

First/Waller (2013): Antitrust's democracy deficit, Fordham Law Review 2013, 2543

Fleischer (2013): Verbotsirrtum und Vertrauen auf Rechtsrat im europäischen Wettbewerbsrecht, EuZW 2013, 326

Forrester (2010): Creating New Rules or Closing Easy Cases? Policy Consequences for Public Enforcement of Settlements under Article 9 or Regulation 1/2003, in: Ehlermann/Marquis (Eds.), European Competition Law Annual 2008, 2010, p. 637

Frese (2014): Sanctions in EU competition law. Principles and practice, 2014

Fuchs/Möschel (2012): in: Immenga/Mestmäcker (Eds.), EU-Wettbewerbsrecht, 5th Edition, 2012

Gautier/Petit (2014): Optimal Enforcement of Competition Policy. The Commitments Procedure under Uncertainty, October 2014, available online

Georgiev (2007): Contagious Efficiency: The growing reliance on U.S.-style antitrust settlements in EU law, 2007 Utah L. Rev. 971

Gerard (2013): Negotiated remedies in the modernization era: the limits of effectiveness, available online

Gippini-Fournier (2008): The Modernisation of European Competition Law: First Experiences with Regulation 1/2003, in: Köck/Karollus (Eds.), The Modernisation of European Competition Law. FIDE Congress, 2008

Gruber (2005): Verpflichtungszusagen im europäischen Kartellrecht, EWS 2005, 310

Gyselen (2014): The European Commission's commitments decisions in abuse of dominance cases, in: Hawk (Ed), Annual proceedings of the Fordham Competition Law Institute 2012, 2014

Haslinger (2012): Kartellrecht: Missbrauch einer marktbeherrschenden Stellung durch Microsoft – Verfahren und Herabsetzung der Höhe des Zwangsgelds, EuZW 2012, 673

Hahn (2006): Drittwirkungen von Zusagenentscheidungen nach der VO 1/2003, in: Boesche/Füller/Wolf (Eds.), Variationen im Recht – Festbeigabe für Franz Jürgen Säcker zum 65. Geburtstag, 2006, p. 77

Hartlieb (2018): Kartellrecht: Verpflichtung zur Überprüfung von Wettbewerbsregeln für Vereinbarungen, EuZW 2018, 46

Hirsbrunner/Rhomberg (2005): Verpflichtungszusagen im EG-Kartellrechtsverfahren – Erste praktische Erfahrungen mit der Neuregelung der Kartellverfahrensverordnung 1/2003, EWS 2005, 61

Hauser (2009): Strukturelle Maßnahmen im europäischen Kartellverfahrensrecht, 2009

Hennig (2010): Settlements im Europäischen Kartellverfahren, 2010

Hinds/Eaton (2014): Commitment issues - new developments in EU and Irish competition law, ECLR 2014, 33

Hjelmeng (2012): Private Enforcement of Article 9 Commitment Decisions – "Objective" vs "Subjective" Direct effect, in: Andenas/Lilleholt (Eds.), Remedies and Substantive Law – European Dimensions of Economic and Private Law, EBLR 2012, 883

Hjelmeng (2013): Competition Law Remedies: Striving for Coherence or Finding New Ways, CMLR 2013, 1007

Höppner (2017): Duty to Treat Downstream Rivals Equally: (Merely) a Natural Remedy to Google's Monopoly Leveraging Abuse, available online

Hossenfelder/Lutz (2003): Die neue Durchführungsverordnung zu den Artikeln 81 und 82 EG-Vertrag, WuW 2003, 118

Idot (2019): Effets à l'égard des tiers d'une décision d'acceptation d'engagements, Revue des contrats 2019, 70

Imgrund (2011): Die Bindung der deutschen Zivilgerichte an Beschlüsse von Kommission und Behörden der Europäischen Union im Kartellrecht, 2011

Italianer (2013): To commit or not to commit, that is the question, Speech given in December 2013, available online

Jaecks/Säcker (2008): in: Hirsch/Montag/Säcker (Eds.), Competition Law: European Community Practice and Procedure. Article-by-Article Commentary, 2008

Jaeger (2008): Art. 7 VO 1/2003, in: Jaeger/Pohlmann/Schroeder (Ed.), Frankfurter Kommentar zum Kartellrecht

Jaeger (2009): Art. 9 VO 1/2003, in: Jaeger/Pohlmann/Schroeder (Ed.), Frankfurter Kommentar zum Kartellrecht

Jaeger (2010): § 32 ARC, in: Jaeger/Pohlmann/Schroeder (Ed.), Frankfurter Kommentar zum Kartellrecht

Jarass (2013): Charta der Grundrechte der Europäischen Union. Kommentar, 2nd edition, 2013

Jenny (2015): Worst decision of the EU Court of Justice: The Alrosa judgment in context and the future of commitment decisions, Fordham Int'l L.J. 2015, 701

Jones/Sufrin (2011): EU Competition Law, 4th edition, 2011

Jones/Sufrin (2014): EU Competition Law, 5th edition, 2014

Kahlenberg/Neuhaus (2005): Erste praktische Erfahrungen mit Zusagenentscheidungen nach Art. 9 Verordnung (EG) Nr. 1/2003, EuZW 2005, 620

Kellerbauer (2010): The Commission's new enforcement priorities in applying article 82 EC to dominant companies' exclusionary conduct: a shift towards a more economic approach?, ECLR 2010, 175

Kellerbauer (2011): Playground instead of playpen: The Court of Justice of the European Union's Alrosa judgment on Art. 9 of Regulation 1/2003, ECLR 2011, 1

Kellezi (2010): Les mesures correctives dans les cas de concentrations d'entreprises et d'abus de position dominante, 2010

Kerse/Khan (2012): EU Antitrust Procedure, 6th edition, 2012

Kipiani (2014): Les engagements en matière de pratiques anticoncurrentielles. Analyse des droits français, européen et américain, 2014

Kirchhof (1986): Die Bestimmtheit von Ermächtigungsgrundlage und Inhalt eines Verwaltungsakts nach § 37a Abs. 3 GWB, ZHR 1986, 303

Klees (2005): Europäisches Kartellverfahrensrecht mit Fusionskontrollverfahren, 2005

Klees (2011): Die Zusagenpraxis der Europäischen Kommission in Kartellverfahren – Eine kritische Analyse, EWS 2011, 14

Krings (2012): Möglichkeiten und Grenzen der Anordnung einer eigentumsrechtlichen Entflechtung nach Art. 7 VO 1/2003, 2012

Koch, A. (2011): Verwaltungssanktionen im europäischen und niederländischen Verwaltungs- und Kartelrecht, 2011

Körber (2010): Rechtliches Gehör, Verpflichtungszusagen nach Art. 9 VO 1/2003 und die Alrosa-Entscheidung, in: Weiß, Tagungsband zum 1. Speyerer Kartellrechtsforum, 2010, p. 73

Körber (2012): in: Immenga/Mestmäcker (Eds.), EU-Wettbewerbsrecht, 5th Edition, 2012

Kuenzler (2019): Promoting Quality Competition in Big Data Markets: What the European Commission's Decision in Google Search (Shopping) Achieves, available online

Lenaerts/Maselis/Gutman (2014): in: Nowak (Ed.), EU Procedural Law, 2014

Lübking/von Koppenfels (2012): Effektive Durchsetzung des EU-Wettbewerbsrechts und Verfahrensgarantien – Die Kommission zwischen Gestaltungsmacht und Rechtsbindung, in: Immenga/Körber (Eds.): Die Kommission zwischen zwischen Gestaltungsmacht und Rechtsbindung, 2012

Lugard/Möllmann (2013): The European Commission's Practice Under Article 9 Regulation 1/2003: A Commitment a Day Keeps the Court away?, CPI Antitrust Chronicle, March 2013(3)

Makris/Feases (2018): Commitments and network governance in EU antitrust: Gasorba, CMLR 2018, 1959

Mariniello (2014): Commitments or prohibition. The EU antitrust dilemma, Bruegel Policy Brief, 2014/01, available online
Marsden (2013): The Emperor's Clothes Laid Bare: Commitments Creating the Appearance of Law, While Denying Access to Law, CPI Antitrust Chronicle, October 2013 (1)
Masing (1996): Die Mobilisierung des Bürgers für die Durchsetzung des Rechts: europäische Impulse für eine Revision der Lehre vom subjektiv-öffentlichen Recht, 1996
McGeown/Orologas (2013): You made a pledge, then keep your promise: Article 9 commitments decisions in European antitrust law, CPI Antitrust Chronicle, March 2013(3)
Melamed (1995): Antitrust: The New Regulation, 10 Antitrust 13 (1995)
Messina/Ho (2011): Re-establishing the Orthodoxy of Commitment Decisions under Article 9 of Regulation 1/2003: Comment on Commission v Alrosa, ELR 2011, 737
Mestmäcker (1974): Europäisches Wettbewerbsrecht, 1974
Mestmäcker/Schweitzer (2014): Europäisches Wettbewerbsrecht, 3rd edition, 2014
Mitropoulos (1996): The English High Court's judgment in Iberia UK Ltd v (1) BPB Industries ply and (2) British Gypsum Ltd, CPN 1996/2, 28
MK (2009): Monopolkommission: Sondergutachten, Strom und Gas 2009 – Energiemärkte im Spannungsfeld von Politik und Wettbewerb, 2009, BT-Drs 16/14060
Mnookin/Kornhauser (1979): Bargaining in the Shadow of the Law: The Case of Divorce, 88 Yale L.J. 950 1978
Möschel (1986): Anforderungen an eine kartellbehördliche Missbrauchsverfügung bei Verkäufen unter Einkaufspreis, Betriebsberater 1986, 1785
Montag/Rosenfeld (2003): A solution to the problems? Regulation 1/2003 and the modernization of competition procedure, ZWeR 2003, 107
Müller-Tautphaeus (2003): Abhilfebefugnisse der Europäischen Kommission im Wettbewerbsrecht, 2003
Nazzini (2004): Concurrent Proceedings in Competition Law. Procedure, Evidence and Remedies, 2004
Nijhof (2018): Gasorba: "stating the obvious" over parallelle handhaving, Nederlands tijdschrift voor Europees recht 2018, 9
O'Donoghue/Padilla (2013): The law and economics of Article 102 TFEU, 2nd edition, 2013
OECD (2016): Commitment decisions in antitrust cases, OECD Policy Roundtables, 2016, available online
Olmedo-Peralta (2019): The evidential effect of commitment decisions in damage claims. What is the assumptive value of a pledge, CMLR 2019, 979
Ortiz Blanco/Jörgens/Kellerbauer (2013): in: Ortiz Blanco (Ed.), EU Competition Procedure, 3rd Edition, 2013
Paulus (2017): Safe Harbor durch Verpflichtungsentscheidung der Europäischen Kommission?, ÖZK 2017, 236
Petit (2010): How much discretion do, and should, competition authorities enjoy in the course of their enforcement activities? A multi-jurisdictional assessment, Concurrences 2010/1, 44
Podszun (2012): Paradigmenwechsel in der kartellbehördlichen Befugnisausübung. Grundlagen, Gefahren, Grenzen, ZWeR 2012, 48
Posner (1977): Economic analysis of law, 2nd edition, 1977
Prek/Lefèvre (2016): Competition litigation before the General Court: Quality if not quantity, CMLR 2016, 65
Rab/Monnoyeur/Sukhtankar (2010): Commitments in EU competition cases. Article 9 of Regulation 1/2003, its application, and the challenges ahead, JECLP 2010, 171
Rachwol (2010): Kartellrechtliche Zusagenentscheidungen nach Art. 9 Verordnung Nr. 1/2003, 2010
Ritter (2012): in: Immenga/Mestmäcker (Eds.), EU-Wettbewerbsrecht, 5th Edition, 2012
Sadowska (2014): Committed to Reform? Pragmatic Antitrust Enforcement in Electricity Markets, 2014
Saitzek (2008): Verpflichtungszusagen im europäischen Kartellrecht, 2008

Sauer (2013): in: Ortiz Blanco (Ed.), EU Competition Procedure, 3rd Edition, 2013
Schmidt, K. (2003): Umdenken um Kartellverfahrensrecht! Gedanken zur Europäischen VO Nr. 1/2003, Betriebs-Berater 2003, 1237
Schneider (2008): in: Hirsch/Montag/Säcker (Eds.), Competition Law: European Community Practice and Procedure. Article-by-Article Commentary, 2008
Schütz (2013): in Busche/Röhling (Eds.), Kölner Kommentar zum Kartellrecht, Band 4, 2013
Schwarze (2005): Europäisches Verwaltungsrecht: Entstehung und Entwicklung im Rahmen der Eurpäischen Gemeinschaft, 2nd edition, 2005
Schwarze/Weitbrecht (2004): Grundzüge des europäischen Kartellverfahrensrechts. Die Verordnung (EG) Nr. 1/2003, 2004
Schweitzer (2010): Commitment Decisions under Article 9 of Regulation 1/2003. The Developing EC Practice and Case Law, in: Ehlermann/Marquis (Eds.), European Competition Law Annual 2008, 2010, p. 547
Schweitzer (2011): Verpflichtungszusagen im Gemeinschaftsrecht, in: Albach/Bechthold (Eds.), Recht, Ordnung und Wettbewerb, Festschrift zum 70. Geburtstag von Wernhard Möschel, 2011
Schweitzer (2012): Commitment Decisions in the EU and in the Member States: Functions and Risks of a New Instrument of Competition Law Enforcement within a Federal Enforcement Regime, available online
Sofianatos (2009): Injonctions et engagements en droit de la concurrence: étude de droit communautaire, français et grec, 2009
Sousa Ferro (2005): Committing to commitment decisions - unanswered questions on Article 9 decisions, ECLR 2005, 451
Temple Lang (2003): Commitment decisions under Regulation 1/2003: legal aspects of a new kind of competition decision, ECLR 2003, 347
Temple Lang (2006): Commitment decisions and settlements with antitrust authorities and private parties under European antitrust law, in: Hawk (Ed.), Annual proceedings of the Fordham Competition Law Institute 2005, 2006
Troidl (2014): in: Engelhardt/App/Schlatmann (Eds.), VwVG, VwZG. Kommentar, 10th edition, 2014
Van Gerven (2000): Of Rights, Remedies and Procedures, CMLR 2000, 501
Vesterdorf/Fountoukakos (2018): An Appraisal of the Remedy in the Commission's Google Search (Shopping) Decision and a Guide to its Interpretation in Light of an Analytical Reading of the Case Law, JECLP 2018, 3
Von Danwitz (2008): Europäisches Verwaltungsrecht, 2008
Von Danwitz (2013): Ignorantia Legis Non Excusat, JECLP 2013, 389
Von Kalben (2018): Verpflichtungszusagen im EU-Wettbewerbsrecht. Eine Untersuchung der Funktionen und Grenzen von Verpflichtungsbeschlüssen nach Art. 9 VO 1/2003 unter besonderer Berücksichtigung des Energiesektors, 2017
Von Rosenberg (2009): Unbundling through the backdoor...The case of network divestiture as a remedy in the energy sector, ECLR 2009, 237
Von Ungern-Sternberg (2000): Zur inhaltlichen Bestimmtheit von Kartellverwaltungsakten, in: Brandner/Hagen/Stürner (Eds.), Festschrift für Karlmann Geiß, 2000, p. 655
Voss (2013): The Principle of Equality: A Limit to the Commission's Discretion in EU Competition Law Enforcement?, Global Antitrust Review 2013, 149
Waelbroeck (2009): The development of a new "settlement culture" in competition cases. What is left to the Courts?, in: Gheur/Petit (Eds.), Alternative enforcement techniques in EC competition law. Settlements, commitments and other novel instruments, 2009
Wagner-Von Papp (2012): Best and even better practices in commitment procedures after Alrosa: the dangers of abandoning the "struggle for competition law", CMLR 2012, 929
Waldhoff (2013): Vollstreckung und Sanktionen, in: Hoffmann-Riem/Schmidt-Aßmann/Voßkuhle (Eds), Grundlagen des Verwaltungsrechts, Volume 3, 2nd edition, 2013
Wathelet (2015): Commitment Decisions and the Paucity of Precedent. Editorial, JECLP 2015, 553

Whish (2006): Commitment Decisions under Article 9 of the EC Modernisation Regulation: Some Unanswered Questions, in: Johansson/Wahl/Bernitz (Eds.), Liber Amicorum in Honour of Sven Norberg, A European For All Seasons, 2006, p. 555

Whish (2014): Motorola and Samsung: An Effective Use of Article 7 and Article 9 of Regulation 1/2003, JECLP 2014, 603

Whish/Bailey (2012): Competition Law, 7th edition, 2012

Wils (2006): Settlements of EU Antitrust Investigations: Commitment Decisions under Article 9 of Regulation No. 1/2003, World Competition 2006, 345

Wils (2008): The Use of Settlements in Public Antitrust Enforcement: Objectives and Principles, World Competition 2008, 335

Wils (2011): Discretion and Prioritisation in Public Antitrust Enforcement, in Particular EU Antitrust Enforcement, World Competition 2011, 353

Chapter 6
Outlook: Discussion of Reform Proposals

So far, the present study has argued that most of the criticism that is levelled at the Commission's use of commitment decisions is not justified. In the view defended here, the recourse to the Article 9 instead of the Article 7 procedure entails only a modest relaxation of the link between harm and remedy and of the procedural safeguards; it entails also only a modest negative impact on legal certainty. It is submitted that these modest shortcomings are, from an abstract point of view, acceptable in view of the consensual nature of commitments and of their underlying goal of procedural economy. This conclusion applies without prejudice to the necessity to balance the respective costs and benefits of Article 7 and Article 9 in each individual case according to the circumstances of the case at hand.

The conclusion that the criticism that is levelled at the Commission's use of commitment decisions is not justified does, however, not yet mean that there is no need for reform. The final chapter of the present study will therefore discuss a selection[1] of proposals that have been made to improve the legal framework for the adoption of competition law remedies under Regulation 1/03. Most of these proposals address disadvantages of the Article 9 procedure. Some of them have already been discussed throughout the present work. To that extent they will only be repeated here briefly for the sake of completeness.

[1]For instance the following proposals will not further be discussed here:

McGeown/Orologas (2013), 4, suggest that "the most that can [. . .] be asked of the Commission is that it communicates more extensively on Article 9 cases. [. . .] there is surely room for senior officials or members of the case team to flesh out the Commission's thinking in presentations or articles in the house magazine, Competition Policy Newsletter (especially once the two-month time limit for appeals to the General Court has elapsed)".

Brenner (2010), 1336, suggests that there should be clearly defined criteria subject to unrestricted judicial control when the Commission is allowed to discontinue commitment negotiations.

Von Kalben (2018), 435f is of the view that the establishment of a European "Monopolies Commission" along the lines of the model of the German "Monopolies Commission" would be a reasonable complement to stricter procedural and judicial control of commitment decisions.

K. Reiter, *Market Design Powers of the European Commission?*, Munich Studies on Innovation and Competition 13, https://doi.org/10.1007/978-3-662-60711-4_6

Three preliminary points shall be mentioned. First, several commentators have called for a remedies study comparable to the Merger Remedies Study conducted by the Commission in 2005.[2] In principle, such an ex post review of the remedies adopted under Regulation 1/03 is desirable. However, at the time of writing, it seems questionable whether the existing amount of decisions is already large enough to conduct a meaningful study. Since the enactment of Regulation 1/03, the Commission has only adopted around 40 commitment decisions. Apart from the Microsoft 2004 decision, there are hardly any decisions in which remedies have been imposed on the basis of Article 7 that are interesting enough to provide material for a remedies study. The Commission's Merger Remedies Study analysed 40 decisions that were selected out of an overall stock of 190 decisions including remedies.[3] Against this backdrop, it appears preferable to wait with a study of remedies adopted under Regulation 1/03 until a larger stock of decisions exists that can provide material for the study. Moreover, it should be recalled that the insight that can be gained as regards the overall impact of remedies on markets is from the outset limited, due to the methodological constraints that exist in that regard.[4]

Second, several commentators have invited the Commission to adopt a guidance paper similar to the Merger Remedies Notice.[5] In that regard, the just mentioned observations apply: While such a guidance is in principle commendable, the Commission's decisional practice probably does not yet provide sufficient material for its draft. Moreover, there seems to be no urgent need for yet another soft-law instrument. The Commission's Best Practices and the Manual of Procedures provide already some information. Many of the statements made in the Merger Remedies Notice can be applied mutatis mutandis also to remedies under Regulation 1/03.

Third, it should be recalled that, pursuant to Article 17(2) TEU and Article 103 (1) TFEU, the Commission retains the right of legislative initiative for regulations or directives that give effect to the principles set out in Articles 101 and 102 TFEU. To the extent that the reform proposals discussed below would require an amendment of Regulation 1/03, they can hence not be enacted against the will of the Commission.[6]

6.1 Reform Proposals Relating to Article 9 Decisions

The most important reform proposal regarding Article 9 decisions concerns probably the increase of judicial control. While the focus of the present section lies clearly on that aspect, some further suggestions regarding the scope of application of the

[2] See Polster/Petschko (2010), 112; Botteman/Patsa (2013), 366.

[3] Merger Remedies Study (2005), 6f.

[4] See Sect. 3.4.1.2.2.1.2 with footnotes 912ff above.

[5] Cengiz (2011), 152; Botteman/Patsa (2013), 367.

[6] See Klees (2011), 20; Schweitzer (2011), 658; Temple Lang (2011), 224.

procedure, access to the file and the participatory rights of complainants will also briefly be touched upon.

6.1.1 Limiting the Scope of Application of Article 9

As explained above, requests to limit the scope of application of the Article 9 procedure, in particular by excluding its application to novel, controversial or particularly serious cases are not convincing.[7] It is submitted that no reform is needed in that regard.

6.1.2 Access to the File

It was argued above that the concerned undertakings have a right to access to the file also in Article 9 procedures that do not involve a statement of objections.[8] Given that the existing soft-law leaves the question open or follows the contrary opinion,[9] the Commission should clarify that the concerned undertakings have such a right.[10] Moreover, it was argued above that Gerard's suggestion that the Commission should consistently provide committing firms with a full non-confidential version of the observations submitted by third parties in response to the market-test, is not convincing.[11] No reform is necessary in that regard.

6.1.3 Participatory Rights of Complainants

Botteman and Patsa have suggested to formalise the consultation of complainants by the Commission. In their view, the Commission would "strike a better balance between what the investigated company wants to offer and what the complainant wants the [Commission] to demand", if it were to introduce formal consultations into commitment proceedings.[12] It is submitted, however, that there is no need to implement this suggestion. The rights of complainants are in principle sufficiently protected through the opportunity to participate in the market test. If the Commission

[7]See Sect. 5.1.1.3 with footnotes 32ff above.

[8]See Sect. 4.1.1.2.2.2.1 with footnotes 39ff above.

[9]See Sect. 4.1.1.2.2.2.1 with footnote 25 above.

[10]See Botteman/Patsa (2013), 370; for a right of access to the file also Jenny (2015), 769f.

[11]See Sect. 4.1.1.2.2.4 with footnotes 73ff above.

[12]Botteman/Patsa (2013), 370f.

considers that there is a need for further consultation, it can already do so.[13] Given that further consultation of complainants in addition to the market test would increase the burden for the Commission and hence run counter to the objective of procedural economy, the Commission should retain the flexibility to decide whether it wants to consult a complainant in addition to the market test or not.

6.1.4 Judicial Control

Proposals to increase the judicial control of commitment decisions are among the most widespread ones. In that regard, two different suggestions can be distinguished. The first one relates to the Commission's obligation to state reasons and consists of requesting the Commission to carry out a more comprehensive analysis in commitment decisions than is currently the case, which can then be challenged before the Courts. The second suggestion is more radical: It consists of requesting to subject the adoption of a commitment decision to prior approval by the EU Courts. A different suggestion wants to restrict judicial control by excluding the rights of complainants to appeal commitment decisions.

6.1.4.1 More Detailed Reasoning and More Comprehensive Analysis by the Commission

Several commentators have proposed to require the Commission to carry out a more comprehensive analysis in commitment decisions or give more detailed reasons than is currently the case.[14] Most times, these proposals aim at strengthening judicial

[13]See Sect. 4.1.2.2 with footnote 99 above.

[14]Klees (2011), 20: "Denkbar wäre etwa, die Kommission in Art. 9 Abs. 1 VO Nr. 1/2003 ausdrücklich zur Prüfung der Geeignetheit und Erforderlichkeit abgegebener Zusagen zu verpflichten, unabhängig davon, ob alternative Zusagen der Unternehmen vorliegen oder nicht"; Cengiz (2011), 152: "[...] the Commission could accompany its commitment decisions with a proportionality analysis which would specify its concerns, the factual and economic context leading to those concerns and the proportionality of the commitments secured to those concerns". Wagner-von Papp (2012), 968: "It would already help if, in its commitment decisions, the Commission set out in abstract terms, but in detail, which legal theories of harms it is pursuing as a major premise, what legal precedent supports these theories of harm and how the remedies chosen relate to these theories of harm – why they are deemed adequate, necessary and proportionate"; Mariniello (2014), 1 and 7 has suggested publishing "the full detail of the objections addressed by the European Commission to defendants". He explains that "[t]he published commitment decision could resemble a non-confidential version of a Statement of Objections". See also OECD (2016), 64.

control by providing potential applicants and the EU Courts with a more solid basis to assess whether the remedy is justified.[15]

The call for a more detailed reasoning of commitment decisions must be approved in so far as it concerns the choice between an article 7 and an article 9 decision.[16] For the remainder, the proposals are, however, not convincing. Although a commitment decision is normally more succinct than an Article 7 decision, it typically contains a summary of the facts of the case, the Commission's legal assessment including references to existing case-law, a description of the commitments offered by the concerned undertakings and of the submissions received in response to the market test, and an explanation why the Commission considers that the commitments address its concerns in a proportionate manner.[17] It is submitted that, at least as a general rule, the commitment decisions are sufficiently detailed to enable potential applicants and the EU Courts to assess whether the remedy is justified. Moreover, it would be difficult to prescribe in abstract terms how detailed the analysis contained in a commitment decision should be. In that regard, it is worth recalling that the EU Courts have consistently held that the requirements to be satisfied by the statement of reasons depend on the circumstances of each case.[18]

Klees' proposal to require the Commission to carry out a full-scale proportionality assessment, i.e. to seek itself less onerous alternatives to the commitments that have been proposed by the concerned undertakings, must also be rejected. Such an obligation would run counter to the goal of procedural economy pursued by Article 9.[19] It is sufficient that the Commission is obliged to take into account alternative solutions that are known by it and in particular those that have been proposed by third parties.[20]

Wagner-von Papp criticises that the Commission's commitment decisions do not distinguish clearly enough between facts and law. In his view, a commitment decision should be challengeable even in the absence of a manifest error, if the theory of harm is erroneous as a matter of law. Wagner-von Papp states the following:

> The manifest error standard should only apply to the complex economic assessment that is involved in subsuming the – preliminarily assessed – facts under the major premise; there is no reason to apply the deferential standard to the framing of the major premise. The current practice of intermingling the theory of harm (the major premise) with the assessment of the facts (the minor premise and conclusion) in the section on "practices raising concerns" in

---

[15]See Cengiz (2011), 152; Wagner-von Papp (2012), 969; Mariniello (2014), 7. Differently Klees (2011), 20, who argues that the problem of limited judicial review would remain, even if the Commission were obliged to carry out a more comprehensive proportionality control.

[16]See Sect. 5.1.1.4 above.

[17]See Manual of Procedures (2012), Module 16, 70.

[18]Eg CJ, C-280/08 P (Deutsche Telekom, 2010), 131; C-494/11 P (Otis, 2012), 94; Kerse/Khan (2012), 6-011.

[19]See the opinion of AG Kokott, C-441/07 (Alrosa, 2009), 51ff; Hennig (2010a), 180f and (2010b), 448 and 450f; Messina/Ho (2011), 750.

[20]See Sect. 2.2.2.2.2.2 with footnote 102 above.

commitment decisions leads to an unjustified extension of the deferential standard to pure questions of law.[21]

This criticism is not convincing for several reasons. First, Wagner-von Papp overestimates the possibility to distinguish clearly between facts and law or between major premise, minor premise and conclusion. The boundaries between facts and law are blurry in general and in particular in the field of competition law.[22] Second, it seems mistaken to confine the manifest error standard to the assessment of facts. As explained above, the EU Courts have recognised that the Commission enjoys discretion inter alia in the context of the market delimitation, of the cost allocation necessary to carry out an AEC test, of the assessment whether a restraint is ancillary or of the application of Article 101(3) TFEU.[23] It is impossible to classify these areas exclusively as assessment of facts. Third, it is submitted that the EU Courts are capable of evaluating whether the Commission should enjoy discretion in respect of a certain aspect of a case, regardless of whether that aspect is presented in the decision as a matter of fact or a matter of law. Hence, the fear that the Commission extends its discretion by commingling facts and law appears unfounded.

6.1.4.2 Subjection of Commitment Decisions to Prior Approval by the EU Courts

The proposal to subject the adoption of commitment decisions to prior approval by the EU Courts is widespread.[24] Its proponents refer sometimes to the US Tunney Act[25] as a potential model for an increased judicial control of commitment decisions in the EU.

6.1.4.2.1 Judicial Control of Consent Decrees Under the US Tunney Act

In the US, the Tunney Act provides inter alia that consent decrees negotiated by the Antitrust Division of the Department of Justice (DoJ) may only be entered into by

[21] Wagner-von Papp (2012), 969.

[22] Schweitzer (2013), 507: "In competition law – fact intensive by nature and characterized by broad and open legal terms meant to enable the courts to translate economic theory into law – the lines between the evaluation of the facts, the interpretation of the law and an assessment whether the facts adduced suffice to substantiate a legal claim can easily blur. The frequently broad legal concepts gain their full meaning in interaction with economic theory and in their case-by-case application to a given set of situation-specific facts. The factual basis for a competition law infringement can thus easily turn into a question of law [. . .]".

[23] See Sect. 4.2.2.1.2.1.3.1 with footnotes 294ff above.

[24] See Klees (2009), 382 and (2011), 21; Schweitzer (2011), 658; Wagner-Von Papp (2012), 967; Podszun (2012), 69; see also Waelbroeck (2009), 223 and 259f; Temple Lang (2011), 224; De Bronnet (2012a), 209.

[25] 15 U.S.C.A. § 16.

the competent district court upon determination that the decree is in the public interest.[26] Prior to the passage of the Tunney Act, the US courts applied a deferential standard under which a consent decree was only refused in case of "bad faith or malfeasance on the part of the Government".[27] Congress enacted the Tunney Act in 1974 with the aim to strengthen judicial control following press reports that the DoJ had settled a case against ITT in return for financial support for the 1972 Republican National Convention.[28] However, subsequent to the passage of the Tunney Act, many US courts continued to apply a deferential standard of review.[29] In particular, in 1995 the D.C. Circuit Court overruled a judgment in which the district court had denied the DoJ's motion to approve the consent decree in a case against Microsoft.[30] In the wake of the 1995 judgment of the D.C. Circuit Court, a standard of review developed under which approval to a consent decree could only be withheld if any of the terms of the decree appeared ambiguous, if the enforcement mechanism was inadequate, if third parties would be positively injured, or if the decree otherwise made "a mockery of judicial power".[31] In 2004, Congress amended the Tunney act, again with the aim to strengthen judicial control of consent decrees. The statute of 2004 states that "it would misconstrue the meaning and Congressional intent in enacting the Tunney Act to limit the discretion of district courts to review antitrust consent judgments solely to determining whether entry of those consent judgments would make a mockery of the judicial function".[32] In its present version, the Tunney Act (15 U.S.S.C § 16(e)) provides as follows:

(e) Public interest determination

(1) Before entering any consent judgment proposed by the United States under this section, the court shall determine that the entry of such judgment is in the public interest. For the purpose of such determination, the court shall consider—

(A) the competitive impact of such judgment, including termination of alleged violations, provisions for enforcement and modification, duration of relief sought, anticipated effects of alternative remedies actually considered, whether its terms are ambiguous, and any other competitive considerations bearing upon the

[26] 15 U.S.C.A. § 16(e).

[27] See Sam Fox Publishing v. US, 366 U.S. 683 (1961), 689: "Apart from anything else, sound policy would strongly lead us to decline appellants' invitation to assess the wisdom of the Government's judgment in negotiating and accepting the 1960 consent decree, at least in the absence of any claim of bad faith or malfeasance on the part of the Government in so acting". See also Furse (2004), 6; Georgiev (2007), 1008 and D. Shapiro (2013), 14.

[28] See Georgiev (2007), 1009; Frankel (2008), 552, who also emphasises that these allegations were never proved. On the legislative history of the Tunney Act in general see Frankel (2008), 551ff; Hennig (2010a), 55ff.

[29] See Georgiev (2007), 1010f; Frankel (2008), 559ff.

[30] US v. Microsoft, 56 F.3d 1448 (D.C. Cir. 1995).

[31] See US v. Microsoft, 56 F.3d 1448 (D.C. Cir. 1995) at 1462; Massachusetts School of Law v. US, 118 F.3d 776 (D.C. Cir. 1997), at 783; US v. Pearson, 55 F. Supp. 2d 43 (D.D.C. 1999), at 45.

[32] Antitrust Criminal Penalty Enhancement and Reform Act of 2004, Pub. L. No. 108 237, tit. II, § 221(a)(1), 118 Stat. 661, 668 (2004); Frankel (2008), 567; Kipiani (2014), 458.

adequacy of such judgment that the court deems necessary to a determination of whether the consent judgment is in the public interest; and

(B) the impact of entry of such judgment upon competition in the relevant market or markets, upon the public generally and individuals alleging specific injury from the violations set forth in the complaint including consideration of the public benefit, if any, to be derived from a determination of the issues at trial.

(2) Nothing in this section shall be construed to require the court to conduct an evidentiary hearing or to require the court to permit anyone to intervene.

Despite the 2004 amendments, the US Courts continue to apply a deferential standard of review to consent decrees.[33] In the merger case SBC, the District Court for the District of Columbia confirmed that the DoJ had to be granted room "to make concessions in the negotiation process", that a court was "not permitted to reject proposed remedies merely because the court believes other remedies are preferable", that a court "should be deferential to the government's predictions as to the effects of the proposed remedies", and that the "relevant inquiry" was whether there was "a factual foundation for the government's decisions such that its conclusions [. . .] are reasonable".[34] The precise standard of review that must be applied under the Tunney Act remains to date largely unclear.[35]

6.1.4.2.2 A Model for the EU?

The proposal to subject commitment decisions in the EU to prior approval by the General Court along the lines of the model of the US Tunney act is not convincing. Gerard rightly points out that "introducing a systematic public interest review of proposed commitment decisions does not fit well into the EU framework and, judging by the limitations of that review in the US, is unlikely to deliver the expected result".[36]

[33]See Georgiev (2007), 1011; Frankel (2008), 570ff; Goldfein/Pak (2010), 213; Bueren (2011), 64 and 455 fn 2439; D. Shapiro (2013), 50; Jenny (2015), 708.

[34]US v. SBC Communications, 489 F. Supp. 2d 1, 9 (D.D.C. 2007), at 15f; Frankel (2008), 574.

[35]See Frankel (2008), 574; Areeda/Hovenkamp/Blair/Durrance (2014), 327e.

[36]Gerard (2013), 35. Bourgeois (1993), 99, raised similar concerns against the idea to subject informal undertakings under Regulation 17/62 to prior approval by the General Court: "In view of the U.S. practice, one could of course be tempted to suggest a procedure whereby such a decision is registered by the Court of First Instance of the E.C., which would then be required to ascertain whether the decision and the underlying undertaking are in the public interest. However, in the United States, the division of responsibilities between the Department of Justice and the judiciary is different. [. . .] Protection of the public interest is thus in the E.C. essentially a matter of political accountability of the Commission and should probably remain so." Sceptically also Kipiani (2014), 631: "Le contrôle juridictionnel effectué sur les consent decrees américains sur la base de l'intérêt public [. . .] comme standard de référence, fait face à de nombreuses critiques. Ce critère de l'intérêt public n'est finalement pas entièrement satisfaisant"; careful also von Kalben (2018), 446.

6.1.4.2.2.1 *The US Standard of Review of Consent Decrees Is Not Stricter Than the EU Standard of Review of Commitment Decisions*

The US standard of review of consent decrees is not stricter than the standard of review applied to commitment decisions in the EU.[37] In that regard, three points bear mention. First, also the public interest control under the Tunney Act does not categorically exclude that the content of a settlement goes beyond what the DoJ could have attained if it had successfully litigated the case.[38] One of the major points of criticism of the judicial control of commitment decisions in the EU is hence not resolved differently under the US system. Second, the US discussion about the intensity of review under the Tunney Act is to a large extent concerned with the question to what extent the DoJ may negotiate consent decrees that do not completely eliminate all existing competition concerns.[39] In that regard, the already mentioned SBC judgment states that, also after the 2004 amendment of the Tunney Act, a court "cannot look beyond the [DoJ's] complaint in making the public interest determination unless the complaint is drafted so narrowly as to make a mockery of judicial power.[40] In the EU, the General Court must control—albeit only under the Tetra-Laval standard of limited review—whether a commitment eliminates the existing competition concerns to an extent that is sufficient to bring them outside the scope of the Commission's enforcement priorities. Nothing suggests that the "mockery of judicial power" standard applied in the US is more rigid than the control of the Commission's enforcement priorities in the EU. Third, in the US, the opportunities for third parties to challenge a consent decree after its adoption are more limited than the opportunities for third parties to challenge a commitment decision in the EU.[41] This can be explained with the comparatively strong possibilities for private enforcement that exist in the US.[42]

The key difference between the two systems is not the intensity, but the quantity of judicial review: In the US, every consent decree negotiated by the DoJ is necessarily reviewed by a court, while, in the EU, commitment decisions are only rarely appealed.[43] However, in that regard, Hennig has argued persuasively that the necessary review of the DoJ's consent decrees by courts is less the result of a want to subject the adoption of a consent decree to an additional control than the

[37] Lübking/von Koppenfels (2012), 81, express the opinion that the DoJ and the FTC enjoy larger "prosecutorial discretion" when negotiating consent decrees and orders than the EU Commission when it adopts a commitment decision. By contrast, Marsden (2013), 11, seems to be of the opinion that judicial control is more rigid in the US than in the EU.

[38] See Furse (2004), 8; Hennig (2010a), 385; Bueren (2011), 64; Ginsburg/Wright (2013), 3 and passim; Gerard (2013), 27.

[39] See Frankel (2008), 573; D. Shapiro (2013), 16.

[40] US v. SBC Communications, 489 F. Supp. 2d 1, 9 (D.D.C. 2007), at 14; Frankel (2008), 573.

[41] See Lübking/von Koppenfels (2012), 81.

[42] See Georgiev (2007), 1022f; Areeda/Hovenkamp/Blair/Durrance (2014), 327d.

[43] See Gerard (2013), 27.

consequence of the DoJ's lack of power to adopt any consent decrees itself.[44] The DoJ does not have any administrative adjudication powers and acts primarily as a prosecutor, but not as a decision maker.[45] Due to the particularities of the US system, the DoJ's consent decrees can from the outset only be entered into by a court. In contrast, the US FTC can adopt consent orders itself. However, US law does not provide for a compulsory court review of consent orders issued by the FTC.[46] If an FTC consent order is challenged, the limited standard of review of administrative law applies.[47] Therefore, if the US system is at all to be taken as a model for the EU, the deferential standard applied by courts when entering consent decrees negotiated by the DoJ, the absence of a mandatory review of consent orders issued by the FTC, and the limited standard of review of consent orders issued by the FTC in case of an appeal all militate more against than for a rigid control of the adoption of commitment decisions.

6.1.4.2.2.2 The Introduction of a More Rigid Public Interest Control of Commitment Decisions in the EU Would Not Fit the Institutional Framework of the Enforcement of EU Competition Law

The deferential standard applied by the US courts when entering consent decrees does of course not exclude the introduction of a more rigid public interest control in the EU. The introduction of such a control would, however, not fit the current institutional framework of the enforcement of EU competition law. Under the current framework, the Commission holds not only investigative and prosecutorial, but also decision making powers.[48] The EU Courts are confined to a review of Commission decisions and to preliminary reference procedures. They do, however, not act as first instance decision makers. This is consistent with the general repartition of the respective functions of the Commission and the EU Courts laid down in

---

[44]Hennig (2010a), 384: "[...] weniger dem Anliegen geschuldet, eine weitere Rechtmäßigkeitskontrolle vor Erlass eines consent decrees durchzuführen als vielmehr der mangelnden Befugnis der Antitrust Division, selbst Anordnungen treffen zu können. Denn wäre ersteres der Fall, hätte man ein entsprechenden Verfahren wohl auch im Rahmen des consent order-Verfahrens der FTC implementiert".

[45]See Jones/Sufrin (2014), 20.

[46]See Georgiev (2007), 1007; Goldfein/Pak (2010), 214; Hennig (2010a), 384 and 95ff.

[47]See Jacob Siegel v. FTC, 327 U.S. 608, at 611ff: "The Commission has wide discretion in its choice of a remedy deemed adequate to cope with the unlawful practices in this area of trade and commerce. Here, as in the case of orders of other administrative agencies under comparable statutes, judicial review is limited. It extends no further than to ascertain whether the Commission made an allowable judgment in its choice of the remedy. [...] The Commission is the expert body to determine what remedy is necessary to eliminate the unfair or deceptive trade practices which have been disclosed. It has wide latitude for judgment, and the courts will not interfere except where the remedy selected has no reasonable relation to the unlawful practices found to exist"; Areeda/Hovenkamp (2014), 302e; see also Frankel (2008), 602ff, for a detailed description of the standard of review of consent orders issued by the FTC.

[48]See Wils (2004); Schweitzer (2013), 491.

Articles 17(1) TFEU, according to which the Commission acts as the executive, responsible for the application of EU law, while the role of the EU Courts is merely to control the Commission's actions. The systematic subjection of commitment decisions to prior approval by a court would change the current institutional balance to the detriment of the Commission and in favour of the Courts.

It is questionable whether the systematic subjection of the adoption of commitment decisions to a prior public interest control by the EU Courts could at all be realized without amendment of the Treaties. Article 103(2)(d) TFEU empowers the Council, on a proposal from the Commission and after consulting the European Parliament, to define the respective functions of the Commission and of the Court of Justice of the European Union in applying EU competition law. The precise scope of Article 103(2)(d) TFEU is, however, controversial. In essence, three approaches can be distinguished. According to the first one, Article 103(2)(d) TFEU enables the Council to alter the respective functions of the Commission and of the Court of Justice without further restrictions.[49] According to the second approach, Article 103 (2)(d) TFEU can only be used where the Treaties either expressly provide for a possibility to alter the repartition of the functions between the Commission and the Courts, or where the Treaties do at least not determine the repartition of those functions in an exhaustive manner.[50] Proponents of the second approach recognize that Article 261 TFEU expressly permits the conferral of unlimited jurisdiction on the Courts with respect to fines and periodic penalty payments. Hence, they interpret Article 103(2)(d) TFEU as enabling the Council to transfer the power to impose such sanctions from the Commission to the Courts.[51] Proponents of the second approach disagree, however, as regards the question whether Article 103(2)(d) TFEU allows the Council also to shift further enforcement powers besides the imposition of fines and periodic penalty payments from the Commission to the Courts. According to one view, Article 103(2)(d) TFEU must be interpreted as a mere reference to Article 261 TFEU, with the result that the Treaties must be considered to determine the repartition of the respective functions of the Commission and the Courts outside the scope of Article 261 TFEU in an exhaustive manner.[52] According to the contrary

[49]Pernice (1997), Art. 87, 25; Wils (2004), 209; Slater/Thomas/Waelbroeck (2008), 46; Waelbroeck/Merola (2010), 250 and 255f; Temple Lang (2011), 221; De Bronnet (2012a), 163ff.

[50]See Sturhahn (2009), Art. 83, 17: "Die Aufgaben der Kommission sind ebenso wie jene des Gerichtshofes bereits im Vertrag selbst weitgehend festgelegt. Durchführungsvorschriften nach Art. 83 Abs. 2 können an diesen primärrechtlichen Vorgaben nichts ändern. Spielraum für Abgrenzungen gem. Buchst. d) besteht daher nur, soweit der Vertrag ihn ausdrücklich eröffnet oder die Zuständigkeitszuweisungen des Primärrechts lückenhaft in dem Sinne sind, dass sie keine abschließenden Anordnungen treffen"; similarly Ehlermann (1997), 36; Rapp/Jung (2008), 2-16-028; Bechtold/Bosch/Brinker (2014), Art. 103, 15; Jung (2011), Art. 103, 34; Ludwigs (2014), Art. 103, 32; Stadler (2014), Art. 103, 33; Schröter (2014), Art. 103, 52.

[51]See Sturhahn (2009), Art. 83, 18; Jung (2011), Art. 103, 34; Ludwigs (2014), Art. 103, 32; also Booß (2011), Art. 261, 8; Cremer (2011), Art. 261, 5.

[52]Jung (2011), Art. 103, 34: "Durchführungsvorschriften nach Art. 103 können diese Aufgabenverteilung nur gestalten, sofern *die Verträge organisationsrechtliche Lücken* lassen. Dies ist lediglich im Bereich von *Sanktionsentscheidungen* der Fall. [...] Im Ergebnis verweist

view, the Treaties do not determine the repartition of the respective functions of the Commission and the Courts in the enforcement of EU competition law in an exhaustive manner. Proponents of this view argue, for instance, that the power to adopt merger control decisions could be transferred from the Commission to the EU Courts.[53] Finally, according to the third approach, even the transfer of the power to impose fines or periodic penalty payments from the Commission to the Courts would necessitate an amendment of the Treaties.[54]

Which of the described approaches is preferable shall not be decided here. The systematic subjection of the adoption of a commitment decision to a public interest control by the EU Courts does in any event not appear advisable, even if it had the necessary support for an amendment of the Treaties or if no such amendment were required. In fact, the exercise of a meaningful public interest control would, on the one hand, require profound changes in the institutional set up of the EU Courts. First, as explained above, under the current framework, the control exercised by the EU Courts is mostly confined to pleas in law raised by an applicant. Since commitment decisions are generally less likely to be appealed than infringement decisions, a public interest control that would be limited to pleas in law raised by an applicant would not entail the desired increase in judicial review. Rather, in order to be meaningful, such a control would have to be exercised by the competent court of its own motion. Second, under the current framework, the General Court makes only limited use of the investigative powers laid down in the third chapter of the Rules of Procedure. A public interest control of commitment decisions exercised by a court of its own motion would, however, in turn require a more intense use of investigative powers than is currently the case. Third, under the current framework, the judges that deal with competition cases are not specialised. By virtue of Article 254(2) TFEU, their mandates run only for a period of 6 years and are not necessarily renewed. However, it appears at least doubtful whether a public interest control exercised by a non-specialised court of its own motion would bring about a significant improvement. Fourth, the systematic subjection of the adoption of a commitment decision to prior approval by the EU Courts would significantly increase the workload of the

daher Art. 103 Abs. 2 lit. d) nur auf Art. 261"; Stadler (2014), Art. 103, 33: "Bei Vorschriften nach Art. 103 Abs. 2 Buchst. d) kann es sich [. . .] nur noch um die Aufgabenverteilung zwischen beiden Organen bei der Überprüfung von Sanktionsentscheidungen der Kommission durch den Gerichtshof handeln. [. . .] Art. 103 Abs. 2 Buchst. d) verweist also im Grunde nur auf Art. 261"; similarly Schröter (2014), Art. 103, 52.

[53]Sturhahn (2009), Art. 83, 18: "Untersagungsentscheidungen im Bereich der Fusionskontrolle dürften zwar keine Zwangsmaßnahmen i. S. d. Art. [261 AEUV] darstellen. Soweit rechtspolitisch teilweise gefordert wird, die Untersagungsbefugnis nach US-amerikanischem Vorbild von der Kommission auf den Gerichtshof zu verlagern, um eine Trennung zwischen den für Ermittlung und den für die Festsetzung der Rechtsfolgen Zuständigen zu schaffen, ergibt sich aus dem Primärrecht jedoch auch kein Hindernis für eine solche Regelung. Das Rechtsstaatsprinzip gebietet eine derartige Aufgabenverteilung zwar nicht, steht ihr aber auch nicht entgegen".

[54]Montag (1996), 436; Ehlermann (1997), 36; Stadler (2014), 33; see also Andreangeli (2007), 620, and (2008), 238.

already over-burdened General Court. Reform would hence also be needed to deal with this increased workload.

On the other hand, even if the necessary institutional changes were accomplished and the public interest control of commitment decisions were carried out of its own motion by a newly created specialised competition court with sufficient capacities, there would still not necessarily be a significant improvement. Certainly, the judges controlling the commitments would be less exposed to a potential prosecutorial bias than the Commission. However, this would not prevent the judges from approving insufficient or overbroad commitments because they succumb to the advantages that commitments display in terms of procedural economy.[55] Furthermore, even if commitments were systematically subjected to prior approval by a court, they would still be based only on preliminary assessments. Their precedent value would hence remain reduced when compared to the one of a decision reached in an adversarial manner. The problem that a consensual dispute resolution does not produce the positive externalities of adjudication cannot be resolved simply by subjecting the consensus of the litigating parties to approval by a court.

6.1.4.2.3 Exclusion of the Right of Complainants to Appeal Commitment Decisions

Inspired by U.S. experiences, Georgiev has argued that complainants should not be granted a right to appeal commitment decisions. In support of his argument, he emphasises the need to make the Article 9 procedure attractive for the investigated companies and the Commission. Moreover, he is of the view that "cases where a complainant is dissatisfied with the decision of the antitrust authority [. . .] could be adjudicated more effectively through a focused private action for damages rather than through a lengthy court proceeding reviewing the basis for the competition authority's decision".[56]

Georgiev's suggestion is not convincing. Despite all efforts to strengthen private enforcement, the enforcement of EU competition law continues to depend to a much greater extent than in the US on public authorities and in particular on the Commission.[57] Against that background, the right of complainants to challenge a commitment decision constitutes a valuable safeguard against the risk that the Commission closes a case by accepting insufficient commitments. The public interest in the

---

[55]See Bueren (2011), 996 with fn 5302, who mentions that an EU Court involved closely with settlement procedures would have the same incentives to save resources as the Commission.

[56]Georgiev (2007), 1022f.

[57]See Schweitzer (2014), 345: "In Europa bleibt die öffentliche Durchsetzung [. . .] auch mit der Richtlinie für wettbewerbsrechtliche Schadensersatzklagen dominant. Der Fokus der Richtlinie liegt auf Follow-on-Schadensersatzklagen bei Hardcore-Verstößen gegen Art. 101 AEUV, nicht auf einer autonomen privaten Durchsetzung des Wettbewerbsrechts insgesamt, und auf dem Schutz der öffentlichen Durchsetzung vor negativen Rückwirkungen privater Schadensersatzklagen. Die Richtlinie sichert im Ergebnis die Vorherrschaft der öffentlichen Durchsetzung in Europa ab".

correct enforcement of competition law by the Commission constitutes at least one—if not even the paramount—justification for the attribution of such a right.[58] Even if the individual interest of a complainant were sufficiently protected through possibilities of private enforcement, this would still leave the public interest in a right of complainants to challenge commitment decisions unaffected. This interest cannot be outweighed by potential efficiency gains resulting from an increased attractiveness of the procedure for the investigated companies and the Commission.

6.2 Reform Proposals Relating to Article 7 Decisions

Several reform proposals aim at improving the Article 9 procedure indirectly by changing the conditions for Article 7 decisions.

6.2.1 *Market Test*

It was submitted above that there is no need to extend the necessary conduction of a market test provided for by Article 27(4) Regulation 1/03 also to remedies adopted on the basis of Article 7.[59]

6.2.2 *Increasing the Commission's Flexibility?*

Wagner-von Papp has suggested allowing the Commission "to adopt remedies in the infringement procedure that go beyond the merely backward looking termination of the infringement". His suggestion aims primarily at making the infringement procedure more attractive for the Commission in order to avoid the disadvantages of commitment decisions in terms of legal certainty.[60] Also Hjelmeng sees a "potential for more flexible use of Article 7".[61]

It is, however, submitted that de jure Article 7 offers the Commission already sufficiently broad powers to address competition concerns in an effective manner. According to the approach that was defended throughout the present work, Article 7 permits the Commission not only to terminate on-going infringements, but also to address imminent infringements, to eliminate the causes of future anticompetitive

[58] See more generally for the instrumental attribution of individual rights in order to enforce public law the references in Sect. 5.1.4.4.1.3.4 with footnote 189 above.

[59] See Sect. 4.1.3.3 with footnotes 138ff above.

[60] Wagner-von Papp (2012), 966.

[61] Hjelmeng (2013), 1036.

conduct and to eliminate the subsisting effects of past anticompetitive conduct. Wagner-von Papp's suggestion predicates on the false premise that Article 7 confines the Commission to backward looking termination orders.[62] The greater flexibility of the Article 9 procedure regarding the scope of the adopted remedies does not result from the fact that Article 9 enables the Commission to make binding particular types of remedies that could not have been imposed under Article 7. Rather, the greater flexibility is a consequence of the facts that Article 9 relieves the Commission of the burden of having to prove the infringement to the standard required under Article 7 and that Article 9 allows the Commission to accept remedies that go beyond what it could have imposed under Article 7, if the concerned undertaking has not offered any less onerous alternative solutions and subject to the observance of the rights of third parties. These two deviations of the Article 9 procedure from the Article 7 procedure are justified precisely by the consensual nature of commitment decisions. They cannot be transferred to the Article 7 procedure, which is characterized by its unilateral nature. Against this backdrop, it appears neither necessary nor appropriate to enlarge the Commission's powers under Article 7 any further.

It is true that de facto the Commission does currently not fully exploit the powers it has under Article 7.[63] This reluctance merits approval. Due to their unilateral nature, Article 7 remedies are exposed to a higher risk of being ineffective or of interfering in an unwarranted manner with the concerned undertaking's freedom to conduct its business. Information asymmetries and resistance from the concerned undertaking make the unilateral design and implementation of a remedy against the will of the concerned undertaking a difficult enterprise that is prone to error. Similar considerations also seem to underlie the Merger Regulation. Under the latter, the Commission is from the outset not allowed to impose unilateral injunctions in order to make a notified concentration compatible with the common market. The Commission can only either prohibit the notified concentration in its entirety or accept commitments offered voluntarily by the parties.[64] Unlike the Merger Regulation, Regulation 1/03 does not subject the conduct of undertakings to prior approval by the Commission. The Commission does hence not dispose of the same leverage as under the Merger Regulation to induce the concerned undertakings to cooperate. This explains why Regulation 1/03 must grant the Commission the power to impose unilateral injunctions. Although the power to impose unilateral injunctions is hence necessary under the system of Regulation 1/03, this power should nevertheless be used only cautiously.

[62]See Sect. 3.3 with footnote 137 and Sect. 3.3.1.3.2.1 with footnote 165 above.

[63]See Sect. 3.3 with footnote 139 above.

[64]See Sect. 1.1.3 with footnote 31 above.

6.2.3 Relationship Between Commitment Procedures and Fines

Various reform proposals have been made as regards the relationship between commitment procedures and fines. On the one hand, there are two suggestions that seek to combine the benefits of a commitment procedure with the possibility to impose a fine by enabling the Commission to take the cooperation of the concerned undertakings into account to a greater extent in the context of infringement procedures.[65] In that regard, commentators suggest either to extend the scope of application of the settlement procedure to non-cartel cases or to revise the fining guidelines. On the other hand, it has been proposed to reinforce the separation between the possibility to impose a fine and the commitment procedure by barring the Commission from imposing a fine subsequent to the issuance of a preliminary assessment or to the publication of a market test notice.

6.2.3.1 Extending the Settlement Procedure to Non-cartel Cases?

Botteman and Patsa have suggested addressing some of the disadvantages of the Article 9 procedure by extending the settlement procedure to more than just cartel cases. They argue that the "dichotomy – infringement/fine versus no infringement/no fine – [. . .] may not capture all the enforcement situations that may arise".[66] In their view, extending the settlement procedure to more than just cartel cases would enable the Commission to "send a deterrence signal through the finding of an infringement with a (reduced) fine, while at the same time providing a quick fix to the identified competition concerns".[67] This suggestion is, however, not persuasive.

6.2.3.1.1 The Reasons for the Restriction of the Scope of Application of the Settlement Procedure

According to the heading of Article 10a Regulation 773/2004 and to the Commission's Notice on the conduct of settlement procedures,[68] the settlement procedure is currently applicable only in cartel cases.[69] Former Commissioner Kroes[70] and

---

[65] See also the criticism of Georgiev (2007), 1024f, according to whom the "statutory limitation" that Article 9 decisions can be used only in cases where fines are not appropriate imposes a "distortionary effect on antitrust enforcement in the European Union".

[66] Botteman/Patsa (2013), 374.

[67] Botteman/Patsa (2013), 368.

[68] Notice on the conduct of settlement procedures (2008), 1.

[69] See Hennig (2010a), 293f; Bueren (2011), 573; Brenner (2012), 31; Heltemes (2014), 12.

[70] Kroes (2007), 4.

members of the Commission's services[71] have advanced two reasons for this restriction of the scope of application of the procedure. On the one hand, they see an increased scope for procedural economies in cartel cases. In that regard they argue that procedural burdens, in particular those brought about by the right to access to the file, are exacerbated in the handling of cartel cases due to the multiplicity of parties and languages involved and to the jurisdictional issues cartel cases raise. On the other hand, they see an increased likeliness to reach a settlement in cartel cases. In that regard they argue that cartel cases do usually not involve much dispute as regards the substantive qualification of the incriminated practice as infringement of the competition rules. Cartel cases are said to concern mostly the factual prove of the participation in the cartel and the level of the fine, but not issues intrinsic to other antitrust cases such as the market delimitation or the balancing of anti- and pro-competitive effects. For the latter reason, settlement discussions in cases outside the area of cartels are considered to delay rather than accelerate the procedure.[72]

Already during the Commission's consultation prior to the introduction of the settlement procedure, it was argued that the procedure should not be limited to cartel cases.[73] To date, some commentators continue to criticise the restriction of the scope of application of the procedure.[74] They can rely in particular on the practice in France and Germany, where the respective equivalents of the EU settlement procedure are not limited to cartel cases.[75] Other voices in the literature are more careful: They see at least no urgent need to expand the scope of application of the EU settlement procedure.[76] Which of the two opinions is preferable from a general point of view shall not be discussed here. It is submitted that in any event a need to expand the scope of application of the settlement procedure cannot be inferred from the shortcomings of the Article 9 procedure. As will be shown immediately below, on the one hand, the settlement procedure and the commitment procedure follow different objectives. The former can therefore not serve as a substitute for the latter. On the other hand, an expansion of the scope of application of the settlement procedure would not significantly mitigate the shortcomings of the commitment procedure.

[71] Metha/Centella (2010), 400f.

[72] For a presentation of the Commission's reasons for restricting the scope of application of the settlement procedure see also Hennig (2010a), 294f; Bueren (2011), 575; Heltemes (2014), 13f.

[73] See Bueren (2011), 988 and Heltemes (2014), 15, with references.

[74] See Hennig (2010a), 294f; Heltemes (2014), 15.

[75] See Bueren (2011), 70 and 81; Botteman/Patsa (2013), 368 fn 103 with references.

[76] Bueren (2011), 989; Brenner (2012), 32.

6.2.3.1.2 Different Objectives of the Commitment Procedure and the Settlement Procedure

The commitment and the settlement procedure share the features that both require cooperation of the concerned undertakings and that both pursue the goal of procedural economy. However, apart from that, both procedures pursue different objectives and follow a different logic.[77] The essential difference between the commitment and the settlement procedure has already briefly been touched upon above[78]: Whereas an Article 9 decision renders binding a commitment to behave in a certain manner, the settlement procedure leads to the finding of an infringement pursuant to Article 7 and to the imposition of a fine pursuant to Article 23(2) Regulation 1/03. This difference in the outcome of the two procedures manifests their different objectives. The major goal of the commitment procedure is to align conduct that raises concerns for the future with the competition rules. By contrast, the settlement procedure aims at punishing past anticompetitive conduct in cases where an alignment with the competition rules does normally not make sense, because cartels can only be prohibited outright and participants of a cartel usually stop their illegal practices anyway as soon as these are detected.[79]

Three further differences should be emphasised. First, a settlement rests on a full investigation of the case.[80] The Commission engages into settlement discussions only once it has gathered sufficient evidence to process the case under the standard procedure.[81] The intention of the settlement procedure is not to provide a shortcut for the regular investigation of the facts. Rather, it is meant to streamline the adversarial stage of the procedure by relaxing the exigencies that apply to access to the file, to the statement of objections and to the final decision.[82] By contrast, an Article 9 decision does not necessarily rest on a full investigation of the case. The procedure merely requires a level of investigation that is sufficient to enable the Commission to

---

[77]Similarly Richter (2012), 540f; Kellerbauer/Ortiz Blanco/Jörgens/Centella (2013), 10.120.

[78]See Sect. 2.1.3 with footnote 8 above.

[79]See Metha/Centella (2010), 398f: "Possible commitments to terminate cartel behaviour normally consist of simple abstention from contracts, exchanges of information and concerted or agreed action. As a rule, cartels are interrupted from the moment that parties become aware of the Commission investigation. Moreover, since cartels are multilateral infringements by nature, they are unlikely to terminate through individual unilateral commitments to act or abstain from acting (that would require all members to unilaterally decide to defect from the cartel"; Colombani/Kloub/Sakkers (2014), 8.715: "Article 9 [. . .] provides for decisions with commitments, intended to conclude an investigation by an acceptable engagement by parties to alter their commercial practices and bring them in line with the competition rules. [. . .] In the case of cartels, however, the only possible remedy is an immediate halt to the illegal behaviour".

[80]See Metha/Centella (2010), 407f; Laina/Laurinen (2013), 303; Colombani/Kloub/Sakkers (2014), 8.714 and 8.717; sceptically Bueren (2011), 584f, who emphasises that in the absence of institutional checks it is likely that the Commission will in reality investigate cases which are going to be settled to a lesser extent.

[81]Laina/Laurinen (2013), 303; Colombani/Kloub/Sakkers (2014), 8.717.

[82]See Colombani/Kloub/Sakkers (2014), 8.714 together with 8.722.

raise concrete competition concerns in a preliminary assessment.[83] Second, in a settlement decision, the Commission does not impose a fine that has been proposed by the undertakings. The Commission only informs the concerned undertakings in advance about the range of the fine it intends to impose.[84] The concerned undertakings can then decide whether they want to acknowledge their liability in order to receive a reduction of the fine. By contrast, in the commitment procedure it is up to the undertakings to offer commitments to the Commission. The Commission does not first indicate the most intrusive, still proportionate remedy and then only impose a less intrusive one as reward for the cooperation of the concerned undertaking. Third, unlike an Article 9 decision, the Article 7 decision that is adopted subsequent to a settlement facilitates private damages claims, because the finding of an infringement is binding for the national courts.[85]

Against this backdrop, it becomes clear that the settlement procedure is no substitute for, but only a complement to the commitment procedure. Even if the scope of application of the settlement procedure were expanded, the Commission would probably not address cases under the settlement procedure that would otherwise have been resolved under the commitment procedure. In fact, if a case is resolved by means of a commitment, the avoidance of the finding of an infringement and of a fine are precisely the incentives that spur the cooperation of the concerned undertaking as regards the design and implementation of the remedy. These incentives would be significantly reduced, if the case were resolved by means of a settlement instead. Moreover, as explained above, at least the Commission assumes that settlement discussions outside the cartel area would delay rather than accelerate the procedure, due to the higher substantive complexity of non-cartel cases.[86] Under the Article 9 procedure, the risk of a delay of the procedure is at least not as important. For the concerned undertakings, it is easier to accept even controversial or novel theories of harm, given that commitment decisions do not involve a finding of an infringement.

6.2.3.1.3 No Significant Mitigation of the Disadvantages of the Commitment Procedure

Even if an expansion of the scope of application of the settlement procedure led to the adoption of settlement decisions instead of commitment decisions, this would not significantly mitigate the disadvantages of the commitment procedure. In fact, the settlement procedure is exposed to criticism that is comparable to the one levied at

[83]See Metha/Centella (2010), 397.

[84]Article 10a(2)(d) Regulation 773/2004; Notice on the conduct of settlement procedures (2008), 16; Kellerbauer/Ortiz Blanco/Jörgens/Centella (2013), 10.134; Colombani/Kloub/Sakkers (2014), 8.720.

[85]Ratliff (2010), 310; Metha/Centella (2010), 399; Hennig (2010a), 337.

[86]See Sect. 6.2.3.1.1 with footnote 72 above.

the commitment procedure.[87] It is broadly accepted that appeals against settlement decisions are possible de jure,[88] but de facto excluded.[89] In view of the concerned undertakings' acknowledgement of their liability, appeals against settlement decisions are generally considered to have only limited chances of success.[90] Moreover, settlement procedures predicate on a restriction of the rights of defence of the concerned undertakings.[91] In particular, the concerned undertakings do not enjoy the full right of access to the file. They are in essence confined to access to the evidence used to determine the envisaged objections.[92] Also the participatory rights of complainants are restrained when compared to the normal adversarial infringement procedure.[93] Unlike in the Article 9 procedure, there is no market test that provides for a control by third parties.[94] The lack of checks of settlement decisions is said to expose the settlement procedure to the risk that the Commission adopts decisions that go either too far or not far enough.[95] Finally, it has been emphasised that an expansion of the scope of application of the settlement procedure beyond cartels would lead to a loss of the positive externalities of adjudication in areas where clarification of the law is needed.[96]

6.2.3.1.4 No Necessity to Extend the Scope of the Settlement Procedure Given the Existence of Other Means to Combine an Infringement Decision with a Cooperative Solution Regarding the Remedy

Extending the scope of the settlement proceeds to non cartel cases appears also unnecessary to combine an infringement procedure with a cooperative solution regarding the remedy. On the one hand, the Commission has the possibility to foster

[87] See in particular Waelbroeck (2009), 241ff.

[88] See the Notice on the conduct of settlement procedures (2008), 41.

[89] Eg Wils (2008), 340; Soltész/Von Köckritz (2011), 263f; Whish/Bailey (2012), 264; Brenner (2012), 311; Laina/Laurinen (2013), 311. See also Laina/Bogdanov (2014), 717 and 722, who report that out of 14 settlement decisions adopted until July 2014, only one has been appealed to the General Court: see GC, T-98/14 (Société Générale, pending).

[90] Wils (2008), 348; Waelbroeck (2009), 256f; Hennig (2010a), 381; Bueren (2011), 918ff; Kellerbauer/Ortiz Blanco/Jörgens/Centella (2013), 10.154; Colombani/Kloub/Sakkers (2014), 8.722.

[91] For the details of the access to the file and hearings in settlement procedures see eg Kellerbauer/Ortiz Blanco/Jörgens/Centella (2013), 10.138ff.

[92] Article 10a(2)(b) Regulation 773/2004; Notice on the conduct of settlement procedures (2008), 16; see also Laina/Bogdanov (2014), 720.

[93] Article 6(1) Regulation 773/2004 provides that, in cases where the settlement procedure applies, complainants do not receive a non confidential version of the statement of objections, but are merely informed in writing of the nature and subject matter of the procedure; see Bueren (2011), 629.

[94] Waelbroeck (2009), 258; Brenner (2012), 314.

[95] Brankin (2011), 167f; Gamble (2011), 451; Brenner (2012), 312.

[96] Bueren (2011), 989: "Verständigungen im Bußgeldverfahren würden die nötige Fortbildung des materiellen Rechts noch stärker behindern, als es durch Verpflichtungszusagen bereits geschieht".

cooperative solutions by imposing an obligation on the concerned undertaking to submit proposals regarding the remedy.[97] On the other hand, as will be explained in the following section, the fining guidelines provide already for a sufficient possibility to take account of the adoption of a cooperative strategy regarding the remedy by a concerned undertaking.

6.2.3.2 Revision of Fining Guidelines to Take Cooperation of Undertakings into Account?

Lugard and Möllman have made a suggestion that resembles the one of Botteman and Patsa to extend the settlement procedure to non-cartel cases. Lugard and Möllmann have proposed that the Commission should revise its Guidelines on fines in order to allow the cooperation of an investigated company to be taken into account as a mitigating factor to a greater extent. In their view, "efficiencies obtained under the commitment procedure could be preserved" this way "while allowing a greater consideration of third parties' interests".[98]

Under Regulation 17/62, the Commission adopted several infringement decisions in which it granted a reduction of the imposed fine or even abstained completely from imposing a fine in exchange for undertakings given by the concerned companies.[99] Although it seems to have taken a while until a similar decision was adopted under Regulation 1/03, the ARA decision[100] shows that cooperation with the Commission regarding the remedy can still be rewarded with a reduction of the fine.

The Commission's current Guidelines on fines provide that both a termination of an infringement upon intervention by the Commission and an effective cooperation with the Commission constitute mitigating factors that may reduce the amount of a fine.[101] It is true that these two mitigating factors are applied restrictively. The termination of an infringement will only be taken into account as a mitigating factor, if it was prompted by the Commission's intervention. No reduction will be granted, if the concerned undertaking puts an end to its illegal behaviour of its own motion.[102] Also the termination of manifestly anticompetitive practices, in particular cartels,

---

[97] CJ, C-6/73 (Commercial Solvents, 1974), 45; see eg COMP/40.208 (ISU, 2017), 338ff; COMP/39.740 (Google Search, 2017), 694 and 702; COMP/39.813 (Baltic Rail, 2017), 392 and 394ff; see also Sects. 3.3.1.4.1.1.2.2.4 and 3.3.1.4.2 above.

[98] Lugard/Möllmann (2013), 11.

[99] OJ 1985 L 85/1 (Woodpulp, 1984), 149; OJ 1988 L 65/19 (Hilti, 1987), 103; OJ 1988 L 284/41 (Napier Brown, 1988), 85f; OJ 1992 L 366/47 (Distribution of railway tickets by travel agents, 1992), 112; COMP/37.685 (GVG, 2003), 164; see also OJ 1993 L 20/1 (Ford Agricultural, 1992), 23; Temple Lang (1993), 368f; van Bael (1995), 241; Rachwol (2010), 26; Hennig (2010a), 340.

[100] COMP/39.759 (ARA, 2017); for a discussion Wollmann (2017), 167.

[101] Guidelines on the method of setting fines (2006), 29.

[102] Sauer (2013), 11.63, rightly explains that "[w]here the undertaking terminated its participation prior to the intervention by the Commission, this is sufficiently taken into account through the (lower) factor for duration".

does not constitute a mitigating factor.[103] A non-contestation will only count as effective cooperation, if it is useful to the Commission. This is not the case, if the non-contestation is ambiguous or where the Commission already possessed sufficient elements to establish the facts in question.[104] Despite this restrictive application, it is submitted that the current Guidelines on fines provide already for a sufficient possibility to take account of the cooperation of a concerned undertaking and of the alignment of its practices with the competition rules upon intervention by the Commission. A revision of the Guidelines does not appear necessary. In that regard, it should also be recalled that the list of mitigating factors provided for in the Guidelines is in any event not exhaustive. In ARA, the Commission relied on point 37 of the Guidelines, according to which the particularities of a given case may justify departing from the methodology specified in the Guidelines, in order to grant ARA a 30% reduction of the fine for its cooperation regarding, in particular, the adoption of a structural remedy.[105]

6.2.3.3 Prohibition to Impose a Fine Subsequent to the Issuance of a Preliminary Assessment?

Gerard has made a proposal that differs from the two just discussed suggestions in that it does not seek to combine the advantages of a commitment procedure with the possibility to impose a fine, but to relieve the commitment negotiations even further from the threat of the imposition of a fine. Gerard has suggested that the Commission should be barred from imposing a fine once it has issued a preliminary assessment, or, where a statement of objections has already been issued, once the Commission publishes a market test notice. His suggestion aims primarily at strengthening the voluntariness of commitment offers as safeguard against disproportionate decisions. In support of his argument, Gerard relies inter alia on the last sentence of Recital 13 Regulation 1/03, according to which commitment decisions are not appropriate in cases where the Commission intends to impose a fine.[106] The idea to strengthen the voluntariness of commitment offers as safeguard against disproportionate decisions by relieving the concerned undertaking of the threat of a fine seems at first blush tempting. Nevertheless, for the following reasons the proposal is not convincing. In Google Search, the Commission hence rightly rejected the argument that it could no longer revert to the article 7 procedure after having negotiated and market tested three different sets of commitments.[107]

[103]Sauer (2013), 11.63(i) with references.

[104]Sauer (2013), 11.63(iv) with references.

[105]COMP/39.759 (ARA, 2017), 161f. For a more detailed presentation of the decision see also Sect. 3.4.1.2.1.2.1 above.

[106]See Gerard (2013), 34f; Jenny (2015), 768, is of the same opinion.

[107]COMP/39.740 (Google Search, 2017), 123ff.

First, a prohibition for the Commission to impose a fine subsequent to the issuance of a preliminary assessment or to the publication of a market test would only decrease, but not fully eliminate the pressure for the concerned undertaking to offer a commitment that corresponds to the Commission's demands. From the perspective of the concerned undertakings, the threat of a fine would remain until the issuance of the preliminary assessment or until the publication of the market test notice. Even thereafter, the threat of a finding of an infringement with the resulting facilitation of follow-on actions would remain.

Second, there is always a risk that commitment negotiations fail after the issuance of a preliminary assessment or after the market test. Neither of the two procedural steps expresses a definitive position of the Commission on the appropriateness of a commitment proposal. Certainly, the Commission issues a preliminary statement only once it is convinced that the commitment negotiations have a basic chance of success.[108] Moreover, the Commission publishes a market test notice only if it is convinced that the commitment prima facie addresses its competition concerns.[109] However, these circumstances do not mean that the issuance of a preliminary assessment or the publication of a market test notice could be understood as a definitive position of the Commission on the appropriateness of the commitment proposal. At the stage of the preliminary assessment, the concerned undertaking has normally only outlined the main elements of the envisaged commitment proposal to the Commission.[110] The actual commitment offer is submitted only after the issuance of the preliminary assessment.[111] Also at the stage of the market test, the Commission may still have doubts as to the appropriateness of the commitments that the market test is envisaged to clarify.[112] Moreover, the market test may reveal new aspects that demonstrate that the commitment is inappropriate. Changes to a commitment may hence be necessary as a consequence of the market test.[113] If the concerned undertaking does not submit a commitment that prima facie meets the Commission's concerns or if the undertaking is not willing to carry out the amendments that become necessary subsequent to the market test, the negotiations will fail.

---

[108]See Best Practices (2011), 121: "Once the Commission is convinced of the undertakings' genuine willingness to propose commitments which will effectively address the competition concerns, a Preliminary Assessment will be issued"; Manual of Procedures (2012), Module 16, 23: "Once the case team is convinced that the commitments informally proposed by the undertaking may address the competition concerns and that the undertaking is seriously interested in submitting adequate formal commitments, it should propose to draft a Preliminary Assessment".

[109]Best Practices (2011), 129; Manual of Procedure (2012), Module 16, 55.

[110]Manual of Procedure (2012), Module 16, 22.

[111]Best Practices (2011), 126; Manual of Procedure (2012), Module 16, 39.

[112]Manual of Procedure (2012), Module 16, 53: "Once the case team considers the commitments offered are adequate to address the competition concerns, it should draft a note to the Competition Commissioner to ask for his/her approval to market test the commitments [...]. The note should also draw attention to any areas where doubts remain as to the appropriateness of the commitments that the market test is envisaged to clarify".

[113]Best Practices (2011), 133; Manual of Procedure (2012), Module 16, 67.

In such a case, the Commission must have the possibility to revert to the Article 7 procedure.[114]

Third, if the Commission reverts to the Article 7 procedure subsequent to the failure of commitment negotiations, the imposition of a fine depends on whether the case merits a fine or not, and not on the question whether the Commission was willing to enter into commitment negotiations before. By commencing commitment negotiations, the Commission does not decide that the case in question does in any event not merit the imposition of a fine. The eligibility of a case for a fine and for the Article 9 procedure are not mutually exclusive. If a case is in principle eligible for a fine, the Commission must balance the factors that militate for the fine against the factors that militate for the commitment procedure. The commencement of commitment negotiations can hence mean that the factors that militate for the commitment procedure, namely the simplification of the procedure, a swifter resolution of the competitive concerns and a more effective implementation of the remedy, offset the factors that militate for the fine, namely in particular the need to deter. Where this is the case, the failure of the commitment negotiations eliminates the factors that outbalance the need to impose a fine. The imposition of a fine hence becomes necessary again subsequent to the failure of the commitment negotiations. The last sentence of Recital 13 Regulation 1/03 does not call into question the conclusion that the commencement of commitment negotiations does not imply a definitive decision whether the case merits a fine or not. As explained above, according to the view defended here, this sentence has the purely declaratory meaning that the Commission cannot adopt commitment decisions that involve fines.[115] Even if recital 13 were construed more narrowly, as a substantive exclusion of particularly serious infringements from the scope of application of the Article 9 procedure, this would not imply that the respective scopes of application for commitment decisions and decisions imposing fines do not overlap. Rather, a grey area of cases that merit the imposition of a fine, but that are also eligible for the commitment procedure, would remain. The conclusion that neither the issuance of a preliminary assessment nor the publication of a market test notice imply a definitive decision that the case does not merit a fine is further supported by the fact that the Commission can revert to the Article 9 procedure even after it has issued a statement of objections that indicates the Commission's intention to impose a fine.[116] The latter possibility would, however, not fit a model like the one that seems to be suggested by Gerard, in which the Commission would be forced to take a definitive position as regards the question whether a case merits the imposition of a fine or not already at an early stage of the procedure.

Fourth, the implementation of Gerard's suggestion would conflict with the current procedure of the adoption of commitment decisions. As is apparent from

[114]See Best Practices (2011), 133.

[115]See Sect. 5.1.1.1 with footnote 12 above.

[116]See Sect. 5.1.1.1 with footnote 6 and Sect. 5.1.1.2 with footnote 18 above.

the Manual of Procedures, the issuance of a preliminary assessment[117] and the publication of a market test notice[118] constitute acts that are adopted by the Competition Commissioner by way of empowerment. By contrast, the final commitment decision is adopted by the College of the Commission.[119] If the issuance of a preliminary assessment or the publication of a market test were to bar the Commission from imposing a fine, the Competition Commissioner could restrict the rights of the College of the Commission. In the Manual of Procedures, the Commission emphasises that during the discussions on potential commitments no final position may be taken on their appropriateness in order not to forestall the decision of the College of the Commission.[120]

Fifth, a prohibition for the Commission to impose a fine subsequent to the issuance of a preliminary assessment or the publication of a market test notice would open the door for an abuse by the concerned undertaking. The latter could initially signal a willingness to cooperate with the Commission in order to avoid the imposition of a fine. After the issuance of the preliminary assessment or the publication of the market test, the concerned undertaking could assume a more antagonistic attitude and let the negotiations fail, without having to fear that the Commission imposes a fine. In that regard it should be recalled that commitment offers can be withdrawn until the adoption of the final commitment decision.[121]

6.2.4 *Reform of the Procedure Before the EU Courts*

6.2.4.1 Increased Judicial Review of Infringement Decisions and Fines?

Several commentators have linked the risk that the Commission uses the Article 9 procedure to extract overbroad remedies to an alleged absence of a sufficient judicial control of infringement decisions and fines. In essence, it is argued that in view of the weak standards of judicial review of infringement decisions and fines, the Article 7 procedure does not constitute a genuine alternative for the concerned undertakings. The alleged lack of judicial control of infringement decisions is thus said to undermine the voluntary nature of commitments as a safeguard of their proportionality.[122] In particular Gerard therefore calls for an increase of the intensity

[117]Manual of Procedures (2012), Module 16, 26, 29 and 31.

[118]Manual of Procedures (2012), Module 16, 53.

[119]Manual of Procedures (2012), Module 16, 21 and 73; Hennig (2010a), 221.

[120]Manual of Procedures (2012), Module 16, 21.

[121]Manual of Procedures (2012), Module 16, 10; Temple Lang (2006), 283; Ortiz Blanco/Jörgens/Kellerbauer (2013), 13.11.

[122]See Muguet-Poullennec/Barbier de la Serre (2010), 40: "Dès lors que la Commission dispose d'une grande marge d'appréciation pour constater des infractions et imposer des amendes, l'alternative à la proposition d'engagements, c'est à dire l'imposition d'une amende, est-elle toujours abandonnée de façon volontaire? Est-il pleinement réaliste de considerer que l'entreprise

of review exercised by the EU Courts in appeals brought against infringement decisions. In his view, this would "restore infringement proceedings as a credible alternative to the negotiated route for firms willing to litigate the Commission's concerns or objections, and as a source of law capable of providing stable guidance".[123]

The current repartition of the respective functions of the Commission and the EU Courts in the context of infringement decisions and fines has already for a long time been the subject of criticism. Claims that the intensity of the review exercised by the EU Courts over infringement decisions should be increased[124] or even that the first instance decision about the existence of an infringement or the imposition of a fine should be transferred from the Commission to the existing EU Courts or a newly created specialised competition court[125] continue to be raised. An in-depth discussion of this criticism is beyond the scope of the present work.[126] For the present purposes, the following remarks must suffice: It shall not be disputed here that an effective judicial control of infringement decisions and fines is paramount to preserve the voluntary nature of a commitment offer as a safeguard for its proportionality. However, according to the view defended here, the EU Courts exercise already an effective control of infringement decisions and fines, even if they subject their review of "complex assessments" to certain limits.[127] Against this background, it is submitted that the current opportunity for an investigated company to insist on an infringement decision, if necessary accompanied by a fine, and to challenge the latter before the EU Courts constitutes already an alternative to the offering of a commitment that is sufficient to preserve the voluntary nature of the commitment as a safeguard of its proportionality. An increase of the intensity of the review exercised

poursuivie s'engage toujours volontairement si ne pas s'engager résulte en une décision aux effets particulièrement délétères et sur laquelle le Tribunal n'exercera qu'un contrôle restreint? La seule manière de garantir pleinement la liberté qu'ont les entreprises à proposer des engagements consiste donc, pour les juridictions de l'Union, à assurer un contrôle approfondi des décisions constatant une infraction et imposant une sanction". Similarly Gerard (2013), 11ff, 28 and 35f; Waelbroeck/Frisch (2013), 683; Jenny (2015), 766f. See also, albeit in a slightly different context, Dunne (2014), 425: "the significant margin of discretion granted to the Commission in respect of its economic assessments suggests that even weak cases pursued under [Article 7] might survive judicial review"; Wollmann (2017), 168f, who points out that in COMP/39.759 (ARA, 2017), ARA cooperated with the Commission and proposed a structural remedy only due to its fear of the marginal review exercised by the General Court.

[123]Gerard (2013), 35; similarly Waelbroeck/Frisch (2013), 683; more carefully Muguet-Poullennec/Barbier de la Serre (2010), 44: "[. . .] la rigueur du contrôle exercé par les juridictions de l'Union sur les décisions de la Commission constatant une infraction et imposant une sanction apparaît comme une condition essentielle du libre consentement exprimé dans la procédure d'engagements".

[124]Eg Forrester (2011b); Gerard (2010); Temple Lang (2011), 212f; Waelbroeck/Frisch (2013).

[125]See only Waelbroeck (2009), 223; Temple Lang (2011); Möschel (2011); De Bronnet (2012a).

[126]See for a further discussion the references in Sect. 4.2.2.1, footnote 233 above.

[127]See Sect. 4.2.2.1.2.1.3.2 with footnote 318 above. The intensity of the judicial control required as regards the imposition of a fine is well illustrated by CJ, C-99/17 P (Infineon, 2019), 191ff.

by the EU Courts over infringement decisions and fines or even a transfer of the first instance decision about the existence of an infringement and the imposition of a fine to the Courts or a newly created competition court appear therefore not necessary.

6.2.4.2 Speeding Up Court Procedures?

Podszun has argued that the voluntary nature of a commitment offer is sometimes called into question less by the threat of fines than by the length and bureaucracy of the procedures before the EU Courts. In his view, speeding up the procedure before the EU Courts would remove some of the pressure on the concerned undertakings to opt for the Article 9 procedure.[128] Podszun abstains, however, from making any more precise proposals how the procedure before the EU Courts should be accelerated.

There are already several mechanisms that aim at mitigating the problems of lengthy court proceedings before the General Court: For instance, applicants can apply for interim relief[129] or for a treatment of their case under the expedited procedure[130]; a case may also be given priority over others[131]; the pages of written pleadings are subject to maximum amounts.[132] Nonetheless, with an average of around 4 years,[133] the duration of appeals in competition cases was considerable between 2009 and 2013 and constituted probably an additional incentive for a concerned undertaking to offer a commitment instead of litigating a case. In some cases, the Court of Justice has found the length of the procedure before the General Court to be excessive and in contravention of the principle of effective legal protection laid down in Article 47 Charter.[134]

There was widespread agreement that the duration of appeals in competition cases before the General Court ought to be reduced. The means to achieve this goal were, however, a matter of discussion.[135] The more radical reform proposals comprised the establishment of a specialised EU competition court on the basis of Article

[128] Podszun (2012), 64: "Dass ein Drohpotential überhaupt besteht, liegt zum Teil weniger an den zu fürchtenden kartellrechtlichen Sanktionen, als vielmehr an den langwierigen und aufwendigen Verfahren, die ein Unternehmen betreiben müsste, um letztlich doch Recht zu bekommen. Eine Verkürzung und Entbürokratisierung von Gerichtsverfahren würde die Nötigungssituation entschärfen".

[129] Articles 278f TFEU and 104ff Rules of Procedure of the General Court.

[130] Article 76a Rules of Procedure of the General Court.

[131] Article 55(2) Rules of Procedure of the General Court.

[132] Practice directions to parties before the General Court, 15.

[133] According to the Annual Report of the Court of Justice (2013), 182, from 2009 until 2013, the average duration of competition procedures was between 46.2 and 50.5 months.

[134] Eg CJ, C-385/07 P (Duales System Deutschland, 2009), 188; C-58/12 (Gascogne, 2013), 96.

[135] See for the discussion about the reform of the General Court eg House of Lords (2007); House of Lords (2011); Court of Justice (2011); Van der Woude (2012); Sharpston (2013); Meij (2013); Montag/Hoseinian (2013); Jenkins/Bushell (2015), 13.

257 TFEU; the formation of specialised competition chambers within the General Court; an increase of the number of judges at the General Court[136]; a reduction of the workload of the General Court in other areas than competition law.[137] In 2007, the European Union Committee of the UK House of Lords advised against the establishment of a specialised EU competition court for merger cases.[138] In 2011, the Court of Justice took position against the establishment of a specialised court in the field of intellectual property and proposed instead to increase the number of judges at the General Court by 12.[139] However, subsequently 28 Member States could not agree on the procedure for the nomination of 12 new judges.[140] Ultimately, it was decided to abandon the Civil Service Tribunal and to double the number of judges at the General Court, into which the Civil Service Tribunal will be reintegrated as of autumn 2016.[141] The extent to which this will really speed up competition cases remains to be seen[142]; the latest annual report of the Court of Justice seems to indicate a reduction of the length of competition appeal procedures before the General Court.[143]

Less radical proposals for improvement concern in particular an abolishment of the reports for the hearing, which are currently used as an objective summary of the case that enables the parties to check that their arguments have been properly understood and serves as a starting point for the discussion during the oral hearings[144]; an effort by the parties to increase the "brevity and pertinence"[145] of their written pleadings[146]; an effort by the Member States to ensure that members of the General Court are appointed timely and not replaced too often.[147] In July 2015, the new rules of procedure of the General Court entered into force, that strive inter alia to increase the overall efficiency of the Court.

[136]Pursuant to Article 19(2) TEU, the General Court shall include at least one judge per Member State. Article 254(1) TFEU provides that the number of judges of the General Court shall be determined by the Statute of the Court of Justice.

[137]Van der Woude (2012), 124f, has suggested in particular to introduce a registration fee for appeals in trademark cases; to transform the procedure before the Ombudsman into a precondition for any appeal in access to documents cases; and that EU institutions should abstain from conferring jurisdiction in contractual matters to the General Court by virtue of Article 272 TFEU.

[138]House of Lords (2007).

[139]Court of Justice (2011).

[140]Meij (2013); Eggers/Karpenstein (2013), Art. 257, 8.

[141]For a brief overview of the reform see Hoffmann (2016).

[142]For a criticism of the reform see Dehousse/Marsicola (2016).

[143]According to the Annual Report of the Court of Justice (2018), 255, the average length of competition appeals went from 45,8 in 2014 to 21,6 in 2017 but reincreased to 38,3 in 2018.

[144]See Ortiz Blanco/Jörgens (2013), 1.110.

[145]See Brinker (2014), 82, who attributes the "bonmot" that "the essence of a lawyer is brevity and pertinence" to Bellamy, former judge at the General Court and later President of the UK CAT.

[146]Sharpston (2013), 454.

[147]See Opinion of AG Sharpston in C-58/12 (Gascogne, 2013), 89; Sharpston (2013), 454; Jenkins/Bushell (2015), 13.

Although the described efforts and achievements to reform the organisation of the General Court could or—where carried out—will probably reduce the duration of competition procedures before the General court to a certain extent, it should be borne in mind that there are limits. Competition cases are complex. Moreover, the EU Courts are multilingual jurisdictions where translation is necessary between the respective language of procedure and French, the working language of the EU Courts, and where the judges have to deliberate and write the judgments in a language which is not their mother tongue. If a high standard of review is to be maintained, the treatment of competition cases by the General Court will hence inevitably take time and resources.[148]

Irrespective of the extent to which future reforms will result in an acceleration of competition proceedings in court, it is submitted that such an acceleration would in any event only have a rather limited impact on the frequency with which concerned undertakings opt for the Article 9 instead of the Article 7 procedure. Although it is true that the duration of an appeal against an infringement decision will play a certain role in the considerations of the concerned undertaking, the major incentives for the latter to opt for the commitment path remain the avoidance of an infringement decision that facilitates follow-on actions, of a fine, and of the litigation costs. It is doubtful, however, whether the litigation costs of a concerned undertaking would be significantly reduced simply through an acceleration of the court procedure.

6.3 Miscellaneous

Finally, four further reform proposals merit discussion that concern directly neither the Article 9, nor the Article 7 procedure. They relate to an increased use of the informal closure of procedures and of interim measures and to the strengthening of the administrative decision making process and of private enforcement.

6.3.1 Increased Use of Informal Closure of Procedures?

Despite the introduction of the Article 9 procedure, the Commission continues its earlier practice of closing procedures informally subsequent to the alignment of a competitive practice with the competition rules.[149] It is broadly accepted that

[148]Forrester (2011a), 191; Sharpston (2013), 453.

[149]See eg IP/04/1314 (Hollywood Studios, 2004); IP/05/195 (OMV, 2005); IP/05/710 (E.On, 2005); IP/05/519 (Fifa, 2005); IP/06/139 (Philips CD-R-Licenses, 2006); IP/06/302 (BMW, 2006); IP/06/303 (GM, 2006); IP/07/122 (DeBeers, 2007); IP/08/22 (iTunes, 2008); MEMO/09/549 (IPCom, 2009); IP/09/515 (Mastercard, 2009); IP/10/1175 (iPhone, 2010); IP/11/842 (Boehringer Ingelheim, 2011); Hennig (2010a), 355ff; Bueren (2011), 477ff; Ortiz Blanco/Jörgens/Kellerbauer (2013), 13.03 fn 9.

Regulation 1/03 does not exclude this way of dealing with a case.[150] The possibility to adopt a commitment decision provided for by Article 9 does not mean that the Commission is obliged to adopt such a decision instead of closing a procedure informally.[151]

It could therefore be argued that the Commission should reduce the amount of commitment decisions in favour of an increase in the amount of informal closures of the procedure. Indeed, Klees has emphasised that the informal closure of procedures remains an option for the Commission. He appears to be of the opinion that, in view of the absence of a decision that adversely affects the concerned undertakings, the extraction of an overbroad remedy by the Commission gives rise to less concern in the context of the informal closure of a procedure than in the context of Article 9.[152] Wagner-von Papp has underlined that a premature commitment decision may in some cases be worse than a simple closing of the file, because a commitment decision de facto shields the concerned undertaking against enforcement by national competition agencies and private parties.[153]

It is submitted, however, that neither of the two arguments constitutes a convincing reason to resort to the informal closure of a procedure instead of adopting a commitment decision. An overbroad remedy does not become less worrying because it is not incorporated in a formal decision. The risk that the competitive process is stifled because the concerned undertaking complies with an overbroad commitment exists regardless of whether the commitment is made binding pursuant to Article 9 or whether the commitment is merely given in consideration of the informal closure of the procedure. The possibility for the Commission to reopen the proceedings, find an infringement and impose a fine in case of non-compliance with the informal undertaking entered into vis-à-vis the Commission will normally constitute a sufficient incentive for the investigated company to comply also with an informal undertaking.[154]

---

[150]But see Kipiani (2014), 50, who states that the use of the informal closure of the procedure should remain limited to exceptional cases ("La référence aux engagements informels post procédure d'engagements, si elle peut s'avérer utile dans certaines circonstances, doit rester marginale").

[151]See Wils (2006), 363; Klees (2009), 376, and (2010), 693; Hennig (2010a), 355; Jones/Sufrin (2011), 1130; Bueren (2011), 4756f; Ortiz Blanco/Jörgens/Kellerbauer (2013), 13.02.

[152]Klees (2010), 693: "Bevor man sich aber im Interesse der Verfahrensökonomie und einer effektiven Kartellrechtsdurchsetzung von tragenden Grundsätzen des Kartellrechts verabschiedet oder sie bis zur Unkenntlichkeit verstümmelt, ist zu berücksichtigen, dass die Kommission mit der formlosen Einstellung eines Verfahrens nach der Abgabe geeigneter (aber möglicherweise zu weit gehender) Zusagen eine weitere Option zur schnellen Lösung von Wettbewerbsproblemen an der Hand hat [. . .]. Die formlose Einstellung mag zwar mit gewissen Nachteilen verbunden sein [. . .]; sie hat aber gerade den Vorteil, dass die Kommission hier mangels belastender Entscheidung weitergehende Freiheiten genießt". Bueren (2011), 477, points out that an Article 9 decision is more burdensome for the concerned undertaking than an informal closure of the procedure.

[153]Wagner-von Papp (2012), 954.

[154]Temple Lang (2006), 295, suggests that a fine imposed subsequent to the violation of an informal commitment would be higher than it would otherwise have been.

Moreover, nothing suggests that the informal closure of a procedure shields the concerned undertakings less than a commitment decision against enforcement by national competition agencies and private parties. Compared with an informal closure of the procedure, the adoption of a commitment decision displays the benefits of increased transparency, the right for third parties to participate in the market test, the required consultation of the Advisory Committee, and the possibility for the Commission to enforce the commitment without having to prove an infringement. The major advantages of an informal closure of the procedure are the procedural efficiencies that are generated if the Commission can abstain from the preliminary assessment, market test, consultation of the Advisory Committee, and from drafting a commitment decision. The respective costs and benefits of an informal closure of the procedure and the adoption of a commitment decision must be balanced according to the circumstances of the case at hand. A general statement that the informal closure of a procedure is preferable to the adoption of a commitment decision and that the Commission should make an increased use of the informal closure of procedures instead of commitments can, however, not be made.

6.3.2 *Increased Use of Interim Measures?*

Lugard and Möllmann have suggested an increased use of interim measures as an alternative to the commitment procedure. In essence they argue that also interim measures would satisfy the need for a speedy restoration of competition on the market.[155] This proposal is not convincing.

The Commission sometimes issued interim orders under Regulation 17/62.[156] It has, however, to date not adopted a single interim decision on the basis of Article 8 Regulation 1/03.[157] This can be explained, on the one hand, with the cumbersome procedural requirements that must be met to adopt an interim decision.[158] These requirements are essentially the same as those of an ordinary Article 7 procedure: Before the Commission can adopt an interim decision, it must formally open

---

[155] Lugard/Möllmann (2013): "[. . .] if the concern of the Commission [. . .] is to put an end as swiftly as possible to the infringement, one may legitimately ask why it has so far never made use of interim measures under Article 8 of Regulation 1/2003. Indeed, it has been argued that interim measures may very well address the necessity of a prompt reaction to safeguard competition on markets" (7); "In addition to taking interim measures seriously, revamping Article 9 proceedings could very well be compensated by [. . .]" (11).

[156] For an overview of the Commission's practice prior to the entry into force of Regulation 1/03 see eg Sauer/Ortiz Blanco/Jörgens (2013), 14.01.

[157] Commission's staff working document accompanying the report on the functioning of Regulation 1/03, COM(2009)206 final, 111; Sauer/Ortiz Blanco/Jörgens (2013), 14.01; De Smijter/Sinclair (2014), 2.117. Critically Temple Lang (2013), 13ff.

[158] See Sauer/Ortiz Blanco/Jörgens (2013), 14.13: "The heavy procedure, which makes a swift response to an urgent problem rather difficult, probably explains why the Commission has not yet made use of its powers under Article 8"; similarly Lowe/Maier-Rigaud (2008), 609.

proceedings and inform the concerned undertaking of its prima facie objections, the factors demonstrating urgency, and the measures it intends to impose. It must grant access to the file, allow the concerned undertaking to submit written observations, and, upon request, conduct an oral hearing. The interim decision is not adopted by way of empowerment, but by the College of the Commission after consultation of the Advisory Committee.[159] On the other hand, the Commission's reluctance to use interim measures can be explained[160] with the fact that interim measures cannot be applied for by complainants[161] and that the Commission considers the competition authorities and courts of the Member States to be better placed to deal with interim orders.[162]

Regardless of whether the Commission should in general make increased use of interim decisions,[163] it is submitted that interim decisions do not constitute an adequate substitute for commitment decisions. First, the substantive conditions for the adoption of an interim decision are stricter than those for the adoption of a commitment decision. In that regard, in can be left open whether the fact that Article 8 Regulation 1/03 requires a "prima facie finding of infringement" whilst Article 9 requires a "preliminary assessment" means that the Commission's obligation to instruct the file reaches further under the former provision than under the latter.[164] The substantive conditions for an interim measure are in any event stricter than those for a commitment decision because the adoption of an interim measure requires proof of "urgency due to the risk of serious and irreparable damage to competition". Furthermore, unlike a commitment decision, an interim decision may only contain a remedy that is of a temporary and conservatory nature.[165] It appears hence doubtful whether remedies that are difficult to reverse, such as the divestiture of a part of a business, could be imposed on the basis of Article 8 Regulation 1/03.[166] Second and even more importantly, interim measures are characterised by their unilateral

---

[159]I follow the description of the procedure in Sauer/Ortiz Blanco/Jörgens (2013), 14.12f.

[160]See Commission's staff working document accompanying the report on the functioning of Regulation 1/03, COM(2009)206 final, 111; De Smijter/Sinclair (2014), 2.117.

[161]Commission Notice on the handling of complaints, 80.

[162]Commission Notice on the handling of complaints, 16 with fn 18.

[163]See Lowe/Maier-Rigaud (2008), 610: "[. . .] there is scope for an increase in the use of interim measures in antitrust procedures in appropriate cases".

[164]De Bronnet (2012b), Art. 9, 7, is of the opinion that the Commission's obligation to investigate reaches less far under Article 9 than under Article 8 inasmuch as the former provision does not require the Commission to take a definite stance as regards the legal qualification of the practice. For a discussion of the question see also Hennig (2010a), 135ff, who is however of the opinion that the Commission's obligation to investigate under Article 8 Regulation 1/03 can serve only as a minimum benchmark for the Commission's obligation to investigate under Article 9; Lowe/ Maier-Rigaud (Sect. 3.1.3.1.2, footnote 58 above).

[165]Lowe/Maier-Rigaud (2008), 600; Jones/Sufrin (2011), 1091; Sauer/Ortiz Blanco/Jörgens (2013), 14.05 and 14.18; Breit (2014), Art. 8, 8.

[166]See Sauer/Ortiz Blanco/Jörgens (2013), 14.05 fn 26; Breit (2014), Art. 8, 8.

nature.[167] Since they are adopted against the will of the concerned undertaking, they do not display two major advantages of a commitment decision: The more effective implementation of the remedy due to the undertaking's cooperation and the reduced risk of an appeal. That commitment and interim decisions are not substitutes, but at best complements, is also confirmed by a glance at the French practice: As explained by Schweitzer, in France "commitment decisions frequently follow up on interim measures imposed by the French Autorité de la concurrence [. . .] – sometimes even after litigation on the interim measure in court".[168]

Even if interim decisions were to be considered as an equivalent substitute for commitment decisions, an increased use of the former instead of the latter would only partially mitigate the disadvantages of commitment decisions. Certainly, the adversarial nature of interim decisions would to a certain extent provide a greater safeguard against overbroad remedies. In view of the likeliness of appeals, the use of interim decisions would not cause the same dearth of judicial precedents as the use of commitment decisions. Nonetheless, the risk of the emergence of double standards would remain, as, unlike ordinary infringement decisions, interim decisions predicate only on a "prima facie finding of infringement" and the review of the Courts is restricted accordingly.[169]

6.3.3 Strengthening the Independence of the Administrative Decision Making Process?

For quite some time, various alternatives to transferring the adjudicative function from the Commission to a court have been discussed in order to address the criticism that is levelled at the adoption of antitrust decisions by the Commission, an institution that is not only political but combines also investigative and prosecutorial with adjudicative functions. The alternatives have in common that they leave the power to take the first instance decision in antitrust cases within the sphere of the administration. At the same time, they all strive to strengthen the independence of the administrative decision-making. For this purpose, they seek, on the one hand, to separate the adjudicative from the investigative and prosecutorial powers. On the other hand, they aim at insulating the administrative decision making from the political influence of the College of the Commission. The proposals that have been

[167] But see Temple Lang (2006), 294, who points out that "interim measures in practice often need to be discussed and negotiated".

[168] Schweitzer (2012), 16, with references. See also Kipiani (2014), 90ff.

[169] See GC, T-23/90 (Peugeot, 1991), 21, where the General Court held that in order to examine the legality of an interim measure, it had to assess whether the Commission was entitled to make a prima facie finding of an infringement. If an application for a suspension of an interim measure is made pursuant to Article 278 TFEU, the President of the General Court examines only whether the concerned undertaking can demonstrate a prima facie illegality of the Commission's interim measures decision. See Sauer/Ortiz Blanco/Jörgens (2013), 14.20.

made[170] stretch from transferring the investigative and prosecutorial powers to an independent unit[171] over the further strengthening of the role of the Hearing Officer[172] and the establishment of a separate adjudication panel[173] to the creation of a EU competition agency,[174] preferably with separate units for the investigation of a case and the decision-making.[175] The strengthening of the independence of the administrative decision-making has also been discussed as a palliative for the shortcomings of the Article 9 procedure.[176]

In particular members of the Commission often defend the current institutional set-up. They argue that the Commission's independence from national and political interests is greater than that of national authorities. Moreover, the currently existing delegation of the investigation of a case and of the managing of due process to DG COMP is considered to constitute a "solid guarantee of the integrity and impartiality of investigations and their conclusions, while reserving all key decisions on cases

[170]For a good overview and discussion see Temple Lang (2011), 213ff; also Wesseling (2000), 168ff; Waelbroeck/Merola (2010), 237ff.

[171]Andreangeli (2008), 240ff, suggested that the investigative and prosecutorial powers should be transferred to an independent unit along the model of OLAF; the decision making powers would remain with the College of the Commission.

[172]Wernicke (2009), cited in Temple Lang (2011), 215 fn 25; Killick/Dawes (2010), 212, suggest that the independence of the Hearing Officers should be strengthened by detaching them from the Commissioner responsible for competition and granting them a status similar to that of the Legal Service. Moreover, they propose that Hearing Officers should be "the primary decision maker in relation to all procedural issues such as confidentiality or legal professional privilege claims". See also Jones/Sufrin (2011), 1081.

[173]Forrester (2009), 840ff; Riley (2010), 201; Nazzini (2012), 1001f: They all suggest in essence that the drafting of the final decision should be conferred on a panel that is separate from the unit charged with the investigation and prosecution of the case; the College of the Commission would retain the power to endorse or reject the draft by reasoned decision that would be subject to judicial review.

[174]The discussions about the creation of a European Competition Agency date back at least to the 1960s. The 1965 Treaty merging the institutions of the then three European Communities provided that that the location of a potential future European Competition Agency was to be in Luxemburg. The discussions peaked in the mid-1990s, when in particular Germany was pressing for the establishment of a European Competition Agency in order to shield the enforcement of EU competition law from unwanted political influence. For summaries of the debate see eg Rodger (2000), 308; Andreangeli (2008), 239f; Monti (2007), 400f and 419; Temple Lang (2011), 220; von Kalben (2018), 430ff, all with further references.

[175]See Temple Lang (2011), 219.

[176]See Ehricke (2008); Hennig (2010a), 385. Already with a view to the Commission's commitment practice under Regulation 17/62 Bourgeois (1993), 101, stated that there was "something to be said for entrusting the negotiations of an undertaking to an official other than the official investigating the case". At the same time, he rightly opposed the suggestion made by Van Bael (1986), 84f, to entrust separate entities with the negotiation of a commitment and the adoption of an infringement decision in case the commitment negotiations failed as "needlessly cumbersome". Both Van Bael and Bourgeois argued also in favour of the strengthening of the – then more limited – mandate of the Hearing Officer to oversee the adoption of informal commitments.

and policy for the college of Commissioners as a whole".[177] The creation of a European Competition Agency is rejected in particular for the reason that it would isolate the enforcement of the competition rules applicable to private undertakings,[178] which would be transferred to the Competition Agency, from the enforcement of the competition rules applicable to states,[179] which would remain with the Commission, and from the broader regulatory context.[180] The understanding underlying this argument is that the competition rules applicable to undertakings cannot be enforced in a pure and dogmatic legal manner. Rather, they are considered to leave room for assessment and discretion allowing for their alignment with other policies of the EU.[181] Also the less radical proposals to strengthen the role of the Hearing Officer or to establish separate adjudicative panels are viewed with a sceptical eye. It is considered that the creation of an "administrative law judge" according to the US model would blur the institutional balance between the Commission and the EU Courts and moreover protract the decision-making process.[182]

It is submitted that the strengthening of the independence of the administrative decision-making is in principle preferable to the alternative of transferring the power to take the first-instance decision to a court.[183] Certainly, the examples of some Member States and of the US and the increasing role of private enforcement also in the EU demonstrate that judges are in principle capable of deciding competition cases equally well as administrators. Nevertheless, increasing the independence of the decision-making within the executive would correspond better to the historical development of public enforcement of competition law in the EU than transferring the decision-making to the judiciary.[184]

At least at first blush, the Commission's opposition against increasing the independence of the decision-making process on the EU level appears to create a certain tension with the Commission's criticism of the lack of independence of several

---

[177]Lowe (2008), 1.

[178]Articles 101 and 102 TFEU and merger control.

[179]Article 106 TFEU and state aid.

[180]Van Miert (1996); Lowe (2008), 1f.

[181]Van Miert (1996), 3; Wesseling (2000), 172.

[182]Kellerbauer (2013), 14: "Die Schaffung eines "*administrative law judge*" nach US-amerikanischem Vorbild, der die Gesamtheit der rechtlichen und tatsächlichen Grundlagen einer Verwaltungsentscheidung in unabhängiger Stellung prüft, würde einen Fremdkörper in das EU-Wettbewerbsverfahren einführen, der letztlich die Grenzen zu den Unionsgerichten verwischen und die abschließende Entscheidungsfindung erheblich verzögern könnte".

[183]In that direction also Nazzini (2012), 1001f. In favour of transferring the decision-making power to a court Waelbroeck/Merola (2010), 256; Temple Lang (2011), 221ff.

[184]See also Commission, Ten Years of Antitrust Enforcement under Regulation 1/2003, SWD (2014) 231/2, 10f: The majority of the Member States have in the mean time opted for an administrative enforcement model, where a single administrative authority investigates a case and takes enforcement decisions subject to judicial control. About half of the Member States that follow the administrative model separate the decision-making from the investigation. Only few Member States operate a judicial model, where an administrative authority carries out the investigation and then brings the case before a court for a decision on substance.

national competition authorities.[185] Moreover, it seems doubtful whether the often-advanced argument that the Meroni-doctrine precludes the delegation of any substantial decision-making powers from the College of the Commission without amendment of the Treaties[186] is still valid under the Treaty of Lisbon.[187] Nonetheless, for the purposes of the present work, a detailed analysis of the described proposals to strengthen the independence of the administrative decision-making is not necessary. Regardless of their general desirability and feasibility, it is submitted that all of the described proposals would mitigate the disadvantages of the Article 9 procedure in any event at best to a limited extent. The reason for this has already been explained above in the context of the discussion of the proposal to subject the adoption of commitment decisions to prior approval by a court: Nothing suggests that decision makers with a greater degree of independence would not equally succumb to the advantages that commitments display in terms of procedural economy.[188]

6.3.4 *Strengthening Private Enforcement?*

Some commentators have alluded to private enforcement as a corrective to the disadvantages that are linked to the use of the Article 9 procedure by the Commission.[189] The underlying idea seems to be that opportunities for effective private enforcement lead to adversarial litigation before the courts of the Member States, which can in turn request a preliminary ruling from the Court of Justice. While this idea shall not be fundamentally called into question here, two clarifying remarks shall be made.

On the one hand, the current efforts to strengthen private enforcement on the EU level relate mostly to the facilitation of private damages claims.[190] The new directive adopted in 2014 covers only damages actions[191]; it focuses on follow-on actions.[192] However, damages actions occur only rarely outside the area of cartels.[193] The

[185]See Commission, Ten Years of Antitrust Enforcement under Regulation 1/2003, SWD(2014) 231/2, 12-40; Italianer (2014).

[186]See Wesseling (2000), 173f; Forrester (2009), 840; Waelbroeck/Merola (2010), 238f; Temple Lang (2011), 219 with 216; Nazzini (2012), 1002 fn 175; Temple Lang (2013), 20.

[187]As was explained above (see Sect. 3.5.3.2.2.1.1 with footnotes 1334ff), the Meroni-doctrine has evolved over time. It does not preclude the delegation of decision-making powers as long as these are sufficiently circumscribed. The Treaty of Lisbon acknowledges in Article 263 TFEU that decision-making powers may be conferred on bodies, agencies and offices of the Union.

[188]See Sect. 6.1.4.2.2.2 with footnote 55 above.

[189]See Schweitzer (2012), 19; Podszun (2012), 69.

[190]Peyer (2012), 331f; Rodger (2014), 8.

[191]See Directive on antitrust damages actions, N° 2014/104/EU.

[192]Louis (2014), 90; Schweitzer (2014), 336 and 345.

[193]Schweitzer (2014), 336.

current efforts to strengthen private enforcement in the EU concern hence mostly cases that are from the outset not eligible for commitment decisions.[194] These efforts will therefore not mitigate the disadvantages of the Commission's use of the Article 9 procedure to a significant extent.

Certainly, it could be argued that private enforcement should then be encouraged precisely outside the area of secret cartels. Whether this is really necessary appears, however, questionable. Recent empirical studies have shown that there is "remarkably more [private enforcement in the EU] than had been previously imagined"[195] and that the vast majority of it consists of cases that do not involve damages claims.[196] A significant amount of it can be expected to fall outside the area of cartels,[197] so that it concerns cases that are eligible for commitment decisions. Thus, it can be assumed that there is already a significant amount of private enforcement that ensures "a continued development of competition law doctrine not only through administrative practice, but also through the courts".[198] This conclusion is also confirmed by the considerable amount of preliminary reference cases outside the cartel area that have been decided by the Court of Justice in the last years.[199]

On the other hand, it should be borne in mind that a strengthening of the rights of private parties to bring actions in competition cases before the national courts does not necessarily lead to more adversarial litigation. Reasons of procedural economy are not only of concern in administrative procedures. They also play an important role before national courts. It can be assumed that a large percentage of private competition cases is concluded with a settlement.[200] Articles 18 and 19 of the new directive on antitrust damages provide for rules that aim at facilitating the use and increasing the effectiveness of consensual dispute resolution.[201] It could even be argued that the risk of settlements that are undesirable from the perspective of the public interest is greater in civil law procedures before the national courts than in administrative procedures before the Commission. In fact, in civil law procedure before national courts there is no public interest control at all that could prevent a settlement. A civil law judge cannot rely on the public interest in setting a precedent to prevent private parties from settling. This is different for the Commission, which

---

[194]See Sect. 5.1.4.5.2 with footnote 216 above.

[195]Rodger (2014), 85f; see also Peyer (2012), 338: "The level of competition law litigation observed in Germany is evidence against the widespread underdevelopment assumption with regards to the number of proceedings brought".

[196]Rodger (2014), 125.

[197]Peyer (2012), 357, mentions that less than 10% of litigated German private enforcement cases relate to cartels.

[198]Schweitzer (2012), 19.

[199]See the references in Sect. 5.1.5.2, footnote 255 above.

[200]Rodger (2014), 13f: "[. . .] the reality is that the overwhelming majority of private disputes, including competition/antitrust disputes, settle out of court before a final judgment on the merits"; see also, with regard to the UK, Rodger (2008).

[201]See also Recital 48ff of the Directive on antitrust damages actions, N° 2014/104/EU.

can in principle decline a commitment offer for the reason that it is necessary to adopt an infringement decision in order to clarify the law.

Against this background, it is hence submitted that private enforcement does already at the present stage constitute a certain corrective to the commitment procedure. At the same time, the frequent use of the commitment procedure by competition authorities does, as such, not justify a further strengthening of private enforcement.

6.4 Conclusion on Reform Proposals

Summing up, at the time of writing there seems to be no or at least no urgent need for reform. Most of the discussed reform proposals are not convincing. This applies in particular to the often-advanced suggestion to subject the adoption of commitment decisions to prior approval by the EU Courts. In the view defended here, the Commission should clarify that the concerned undertakings have a right to access to the file also in Article 9 procedures that do not involve a statement of objections. Besides that, only the further strengthening of the independence of the administrative decision-making and the acceleration of competition procedures before the General Court constitute areas that may merit further reflections. However, while change in these two areas may well be pressing for other reasons, the modest shortcomings of the Article 9 procedure do not create an urgent need for reform. This conclusion applies all the more since neither the further strengthening of the independence of the administrative decision-making nor the acceleration of competition procedures before the General Court would significantly mitigate the shortcomings of the Article 9 procedure: Also a more independent administrative decision maker would probably succumb to the advantages that commitment decisions display in terms of procedural economy and the acceleration of competition procedures before the General Court would at best modestly decrease the incentives for the concerned undertakings to offer commitments.

Two final remarks bear still mention. Both concern the temporal relativity of the present work and the fact that the conclusion defended here relates only to the status quo of the Commission's commitment practice: On the one hand, it must be acknowledged that the constant criticism of the Commission's practice may in the past very well have provided a useful safeguard against a development that might otherwise have given rise to more serious concerns. On the other hand, the conclusion that there is presently no need for reform does not lower the need for a vigilant observation of the Commission's future practice. However, it is submitted that the focus should in the future lie less than in the past on the overall system and more on the individual decisions adopted by the Commission.

Bibliography

Andreangeli (2007): Toward an EU Competition Court: "Article-6-Proofing" - Antitrust Proceedings before the Commission?, World Competition 2007, 595
Andreangeli (2008): EU Competition Enforcement and Human Rights, 2008
Areeda/Hovenkamp (2014): Antitrust Law. An Analysis of Antitrust Principles and Their Application, Vol. II, 4th edition, 2014
Areeda/Hovenkamp/Blair/Durrance (2014): Antitrust Law. An Analysis of Antitrust Principles and Their Application, Vol. IIA, 4th edition, 2014
Bechtold/Bosch/Brinker (2014): EU-Kartellrecht. Kommentar, 3rd edition, 2014
Booß (2011): in: Grabitz/Hilf/Nettesheim (Eds.), Das Recht der Europäischen Union
Botteman/Patsa (2013): Towards a more sustainable use of commitment decisions in Article 102 TFEU cases, JAE 2013, 347
Bourgeois (1993): Undertakings in E.C. competition law, in: Slot/McDonnell (Eds.), Procedure and Enforcement in EC and US Competition Law, 1993, p. 90
Brankin (2011): The first cases under the Commission's cartel-settlement procedure: problems solved?, ECLR 2011, 165
Breit (2014): in: Schröter/Jakob/Klotz/Mederer (Eds.), Europäisches Wettbewerbsrecht, 2nd edition, 2014
Brenner (2010): Wer freut sich, wenn zwei sich nicht streiten?, WRP 2010, 1333
Brenner (2012): Das Vergleichsverfahren der Europäischen Kommission in Kartellfällen, 2012
Brinker (2014): Brevity and Pertinence, NZKart 2014, 81
Bueren (2011): Verständigungen – Settlements in Kartelbußgeldverfahren, 2011
Cengiz (2011): Judicial review and the rule of law in the EU competition law regime after Alrosa, ECJ 2011, 127
Colombani/Kloub/Sakkers (2014): Cartels, in: Faull/Nikpay (Eds.), The EU Law of Competition, 3rd edition, 2014
Court of Justice (2011): Letter from the President of the Court of Justice to the President of the Council: Draft amendments to the Statute of the Court of Justice of the European Union, Council Doc 8787/11, available online
Cremer (2011): in: Calliess/Ruffert, EUV/AEUV, Kommentar, 4th Edition 2011
De Bronnet (2012a): Plädoyer für eine Reform der Aufgabenverteilung zwischen der Kommission und dem Gerichtshof der EU bei der Anwendung der Art. 101 und 102 AEUV in Einzelfällen, ZWeR 2012, 157
De Bronnet (2012b): Europäisches Kartellverfahrensrecht. Kommentar zur VO 1/2003, 2nd edition, 2012
Dehousse/Marsicola (2016): The Reform of the EU Courts (II). Abandoning the Management Approach by Doubling the General Court, Egmont Paper 83
De Smijter/Sinclair (2014): The Enforcement System under Regulation 1/2003, in: Faull/Nikpay (Eds.), The EU Law of Competition, 3rd edition, 2014
Dunne (2014): Commitment decisions in EU competition law, JCLE 2014, 399
Eggers/Karpenstein (2013): in: Grabitz/Hilf/Nettesheim (Eds.), Das Recht der Europäischen Union
Ehlermann (1997): Decision Making at the Centre, in: Ehlermann/Laudati (Eds.), Robert Schuman Centre Annual on European Competition Law 1996, 1997
Ehricke (2008): Die Doppelmacht der Kommission in Wettbewerbssachen - ein Plädoyer für die Etablierung einer eigenständigen und unabhängigen EG-Wettbewerbsbehörde, WuW 2008, 411
Forrester (2009): Due process in EC competition cases: a distinguished institution with flawed procedures, ELR 2009, 817
Forrester (2011a): A challenge for Europe's judges: the review of fines in competition cases, ELR 2011, 185
Forrester (2011b): A Bush in Need of Pruning: the Luxuriant Growth of "Light Judicial Review", in: Ehlermann/Marquis (Eds.), European Competition Law Annual 2009, 2011

Frankel (2008): Rethinking the Tunney Act: A Model for Judicial Review of Antitrust Consent Decrees, 75 Antitrust L. J. 549 (2008)
Furse (2004): The decision to commit: some pointers from the US, ECLR 2004, 5
Gamble (2011): "Speaking (formally) with the enemy" - cartel settlements evolve, ECLR 2011, 449
Georgiev (2007): Contagious Efficiency: The growing reliance on U.S.-style antitrust settlements in EU law, 2007 Utah L. Rev. 971
Gerard (2010): EU Antitrust Enforcement in 2025: "Why Wait? Full Appellate Jurisdiction, Now", CPI Antitrust Journal December 2010/1
Gerard (2013): Negotiated remedies in the modernization era: the limits of effectiveness, available online
Ginsburg/Wright (2013): Antitrust Settlements: The Culture of Consent, Concurrences 2013/2, 56
Goldfein/Pak (2010): Negotiated Antitrust Settlements: Some Perspectives from U.S. Defendants, in: Ehlermann/Marquis (Eds.), European Competition Law Annual 2008, 2010, p. 205
Heltemes (2014): Settlements im europäischen und deutschen Kartellbußgeldverfahren, 2014
Hennig (2010a): Settlements im Europäischen Kartellverfahren, 2010
Hennig (2010b): Die Bedeutung des Verhältnismäßigkeitsgrundsatzes bei der Annahme von Verpflichtungszusagen durch die Kommission nach Art. 9 VO (EG) Nr. 1/2003, ZWeR 2010, 440
Hjelmeng (2013): Competition Law Remedies: Striving for Coherence or Finding New Ways, CMLR 2013, 1007
Hoffmann (2016): Der Gerichtshof der Europäischen Union – re-organisiert, EuR 2016, 197
House of Lords (2007): House of Lords European Union Committee, 15th Report of Session 2006–07: An EU Competition Court, available online
House of Lords (2011): House of Lords European Union Committee, Fourteenth Report of Session 2010-11: The Workload of the Court of Justice of the European Union, available online
Italianer (2014): The Independence of National Competition Authorities, Speech given in December 2014, available online
Jenkins/Bushell (2015): Justice Denied or Simply Delayed? Consequences of Excessive Delay at the EU's General Court, JECLP 2015, 3
Jenny (2015): Worst decision of the EU Court of Justice: The Alrosa judgment in context and the future of commitment decisions, Fordham Int'l L.J. 2015, 701
Jones/Sufrin (2011): EU Competition Law, 4th edition, 2011
Jones/Sufrin (2014): EU Competition Law, 5th edition, 2014
Jung (2011): in: Calliess/Ruffert, EUV/AEUV, Kommentar, 4th Edition 2011
Kellerbauer (2013): Das neue Mandat des Anhörungsbeauftragten für EU-Wettbewerbsverfahren, EuZW 2013, 10
Kellerbauer/Ortiz Blanco/Jörgens/Centella (2013): in: Ortiz Blanco (Ed.), EU Competition Procedure, 3rd Edition, 2013
Kerse/Khan (2012): EU Antitrust Procedure, 6th edition, 2012
Killick/Dawes (2010): DG COMP and the Hearing Officers Publish Detailed Explanations on How they Conduct Antitrust (and certain aspects of merger) Proceedings, JECLP 2010, 211
Kipiani (2014): Les engagements en matière de pratiques anticoncurrentielles. Analyse des droits français, européen et américain, 2014
Klees (2009): Das Instrument der Zusagenentscheidung der Kommission und der Fall E.On – Ein (weiterer) Sündenfall, WuW 2009, 374
Klees (2010): Freie Bahn für die Kommission in Kartellverfahren bei Anwendung des Art. 9 VO Nr. 1/2003, RIW 2010, 688
Klees (2011): Die Zusagenpraxis der Europäischen Kommission in Kartellverfahren – Eine kritische Analyse, EWS 2011, 14
Kroes (2007): Assessment of and perspectives for competition policy in Europe, Speech 07/722, 2007, available online
Laina/Laurinen (2013): The EU Cartel Settlement Procedure: Current Status and Challenges, JECLP 2013, 302

Laina/Bogdanov (2014): The EU Cartel Settlement Procedure: Latest Developments, JECLP 2014, 717

Louis (2014): Promoting Private Antitrust Enforcement: Remember Article 102, in: Lowe/Marquis, European Competition Law Annual 2011, 2014

Lowe (2008): The design of competition policy institutions for the 21st century – the experience of the European Commission and DG Competition, CPN 2008/3, 1

Lowe/Maier-Rigaud (2008): Quo vadis antitrust remedies, in: Hawk (Ed.), Annual proceedings of the Fordham Competition Law Institute 2007, 2008, p. 597

Ludwigs (2014): in: Grabitz/Hilf/Nettesheim (Eds.), Das Recht der Europäischen Union

Lübking/von Koppenfels (2012): Effektive Durchsetzung des EU-Wettbewerbsrechts und Verfahrensgarantien – Die Kommission zwischen Gestaltungsmacht und Rechtsbindung, in: Immenga/Körber (Eds.): Die Kommission zwischen zwischen Gestaltungsmacht und Rechtsbindung, 2012

Lugard/Möllmann (2013): The European Commission's Practice Under Article 9 Regulation 1/2003: A Commitment a Day Keeps the Court away?, CPI Antitrust Chronicle, March 2013(3)

Mariniello (2014): Commitments or prohibition. The EU antitrust dilemma, Bruegel Policy Brief, 2014/01, available online

Marsden (2013): The Emperor's Clothes Laid Bare: Commitments Creating the Appearance of Law, While Denying Access to Law, CPI Antitrust Chronicle, October 2013 (1)

McGeown/Orologas (2013): You made a pledge, then keep your promise: Article 9 commitments decisions in European antitrust law, CPI Antitrust Chronicle, March 2013(3)

Meij (2013): Courts in transition: Administration of justice and how to organise it, CMLR 2013, 3

Messina/Ho (2011): Re-establishing the Orthodoxy of Commitment Decisions under Article 9 of Regulation 1/2003: Comment on Commission v Alrosa, ELR 2011, 737

Metha/Centella (2010): EU Settlement Procedure: Public Enforcement Policy Perspective, in: Ehlermann/Marquis (Eds.), European Competition Law Annual 2008, 2010

Möschel (2011): Fines in European competition law, ECLR 2011, 369

Montag (1996): The case for a radical reform of the infringement procedure under regulation 17, ECLR 1996, 428

Montag/Hoseinian (2013): The forthcoming reform of the General Court of the European Union – Potential Specialization within the General Court, in: Hawk (Ed.), Annual proceedings of the Fordham Competition Law Institute 2012, 2013

Monti (2007): EC Competition Law, 2007

Muguet-Poullennec/Barbier de La Serre (2010): La procédure d'engagements en droit de l'Union: à la recherche du juste équilibre entre efficacité administrative et protection des entreprises, RLC 2010 n° 25, 36

Nazzini (2012): Administrative Enforcement, Judicial Review and Fundamental Rights in EU Competition Law: A Comparative Contextual-Functionalist Perspective, CMLR 2012, 971

OECD (2016): Commitment decisions in antitrust cases, OECD Policy Roundtables, 2016, available online

Ortiz Blanco/Jörgens (2013): in: Ortiz Blanco (Ed.), EU Competition Procedure, 3rd Edition, 2013

Ortiz Blanco/Jörgens/Kellerbauer (2013): in: Ortiz Blanco (Ed.), EU Competition Procedure, 3rd Edition, 2013

Pernice (1997): in: Grabitz/Hilf (Eds.), Das Recht der Europäischen Union

Peyer (2012): Private Antitrust Litigation in Germany from 2005 to 2007: Empirical Evidence, JCLE 2012, 331

Podszun (2012): Paradigmenwechsel in der kartellbehördlichen Befugnisausübung. Grundlagen, Gefahren, Grenzen, ZWeR 2012, 48

Polster/Petschko (2010): Nach Microsoft und E.On: Auf dem Weg zu Strukturpolitik duch die Europäische Missbrauchskontrolle?, ÖZK 2010, 108

Rachwol (2010): Kartellrechtliche Zusagenentscheidungen nach Art. 9 Verordnung Nr. 1/2003, 2010

Rapp/Jung (2008): in: Hirsch/Montag/Säcker (Eds.), Competition Law: European Community Practice and Procedure. Article-by-Article Commentary, 2008
Ratliff (2010): Negotiated Settlements in EC Competition Law: The Perspective of the Legal Profession, in: Ehlermann/Marquis (Eds.), European Competition Law Annual 2008, 2010, p. 305
Richter (2012): The settlement procedure in the context of the enforcement tools of European competition law - a comparison and impact analysis, ECLR 2012, 537
Riley (2010): The modernisation of EU anti-cartel enforcement: will the Commission grasp the opportunity?, ECLR 2010, 191
Rodger (2000): Competition Policy, Liberalism and Globalization: A European Perspective, 6 Colum. J. Eur. L. 289 (2000)
Rodger (2008): Private enforcement of competition law, the hidden story: competition litigation settlements in the United Kingdom, 2000-2005, ECLR 2008, 96
Rodger (2014): in: Rodger (Ed.), Competition Law Comparative Private Enforcement and Collective Redress across the EU, 2014
Sauer (2013): in: Ortiz Blanco (Ed.), EU Competition Procedure, 3rd Edition, 2013
Schröter (2014): in: Schröter/Jakob/Klotz/Mederer (Eds.), Europäisches Wettbewerbsrecht, 2nd edition, 2014
Schweitzer (2011): Verpflichtungszusagen im Gemeinschaftsrecht, in: Albach/Bechthold (Eds.), Recht, Ordnung und Wettbewerb, Festschrift zum 70. Geburtstag von Wernhard Möschel, 2011
Schweitzer (2012): Commitment Decisions in the EU and in the Member States: Functions and Risks of a New Instrument of Competition Law Enforcement within a Federal Enforcement Regime, available online
Schweitzer (2013): Judicial review in EU competition law, in: Lianos/Geradin (Ed.), Handbook on European Competition Law. Enforcement and Procedure, 2013, p. 491
Schweitzer (2014): Die neue Richtlinie für kartellrechtliche Schadensersatzklagen, NZKart 2014, 335
Shapiro, D. (2013): Lessons from SEC v. Citigroup: The Optimal Scope for Judicial Review of Agency Consent Decrees, available online
Sharpston (2013): Effective Judicial Protection through Adequate Judicial Scrutiny – Some Reflections, JECLP 2013, 453
Slater/Thomas/Waelbroeck (2008): Competition law proceedings before the European Commission and the right to a fair trial: no need for reform?, GCLC working paper 04/08, available online
Soltész/Von Köckritz (2011): EU cartel settlements in practice - the future of EU cartel law enforcement?, ECLR 2011, 258
Stadler (2014): in: Langen/Bunte (Eds.), Kartellrecht, Volume 2, 12th edition, 2014
Sturhahn (2009): in: Loewenheim/Meessen/Riesenkampff (Eds.), Kartellrecht. Kommentar, 2nd edition, 2009
Temple Lang (1993): Air Transport in the EEC – Community Antitrust Law Aspects, in: Hawk (Ed.), Annual proceedings of the Fordham Competition Law Institute 1992, 1993
Temple Lang (2006): Commitment decisions and settlements with antitrust authorities and private parties under European antitrust law, in: Hawk (Ed.), Annual proceedings of the Fordham Competition Law Institute 2005, 2006
Temple Lang (2011): Three Possibilities for Reform of the Procedure of the European Commission in Competition Cases under Regulation 1/2003, CEPS Special Report, available online
Temple Lang (2013): The strengths and weaknesses of the DG Competition Manual of Procedure, JAE 2013, 1
Van Bael (1986): The antitrust settlement practice of the EC Commission, CMLR 1986, 61
Van Bael (1995): Fining a la carte: the lottery of EU competition law, ECLR 1995, 237
Van der Woude (2012): Judicial Reform and Reasonable Delay, JECLP 2012, 123
Van Miert (1996): The proposal for a European competition agency, CPN 1996/2, 1

Von Kalben (2018): Verpflichtungszusagen im EU-Wettbewerbsrecht. Eine Untersuchung der Funktionen und Grenzen von Verpflichtungsbeschlüssen nach Art. 9 VO 1/2003 unter besonderer Berücksichtigung des Energiesektors, 2017

Waelbroeck (2009): The development of a new "settlement culture" in competition cases. What is left to the Courts?, in: Gheur/Petit (Eds.), Alternative enforcement techniques in EC competition law. Settlements, commitments and other novel instruments, 2009

Waelbroeck/Frisch (2013): Après l'arrêt Menarini: l'impact de la Convention européenne de sauvegarde des droits de l'homme et des libertés fondamentales sur les procédures en droit de la concurrence, in: Govaere/Hanf (Eds.), Scrutinizing internal and external dimensions of European law. Les dimensions internes et externes du droit européen à l'épreuve. Liber amicorum Paul Demaret. Vol. II (2013), p. 663

Waelbroeck/Merola (2010): Towards an optimal enforcement of competition rules in Europe. Time for a Review of Regulation 1/2003?, 2010

Wagner-Von Papp (2012): Best and even better practices in commitment procedures after Alrosa: the dangers of abandoning the "struggle for competition law", CMLR 2012, 929

Wernicke (2009): In Defense of the Rights of Defence: Competition law procedure and the changing role of the Hearing officer, Concurrences 2009, N° 3, 1

Wesseling (2000): The Modernisation of EC Antitrust Law, 2000

Whish/Bailey (2012): Competition Law, 7th edition, 2012

Wils (2004): The Combination of the Investigative and Prosecutorial Function and the Adjudicative Function in EC Antitrust Enforcement: A Legal and Economic Analysis, World Competition 2004, 201

Wils (2006): Settlements of EU Antitrust Investigations: Commitment Decisions under Article 9 of Regulation No. 1/2003, World Competition 2006, 345

Wils (2008): The Use of Settlements in Public Antitrust Enforcement: Objectives and Principles, World Competition 2008, 335

Wollmann (2017): ARA Foreclosure: A Step Towards Consent Decrees in EU Antitrust Proceedings, JECLP 2017, 167

Chapter 7
Summary of Key Findings

The Commission's use of commitment instead of infringement decisions is criticised for three reasons: The relaxation of the link between harm and remedy; the relaxation of procedural safeguards; and the negative impact on legal certainty. In the view defended throughout the present study, most of the criticism is not justified. There is no need for reform.

I. The link between harm and remedy is only modestly relaxed.

1. Article 7 vests the Commission with broad and flexible powers. The latter provision allows the Commission in particular to adopt remedies that are prescriptive and prospective[1]; to address on-going and imminent anticompetitive conduct[2]; to eliminate the causes of future anticompetitive conduct[3]; to eliminate subsisting effects of past anticompetitive behaviour[4]; and to impose ancillary obligations to ensure the effective implementation of a remedy.[5]

2. Article 9 entails only a modest risk that the Commission adopts remedies that go beyond what it could have imposed under Article 7. In particular, the Alrosa judgment of the Court of Justice can and must be interpreted restrictively: The Commission may only make commitments binding that go beyond what it could have imposed under Article 7 provided that the interests of third parties are respected and provided that the Commission is not aware of any less burdensome alternatives that are manifestly equally effective.[6]

---

[1]See Sect. 3.3 with footnotes 137ff above.

[2]See Sect. 3.3.2 with footnotes 590ff above.

[3]See Sect. 3.4.1.2.1.2 with footnotes 846ff above.

[4]See Sect. 3.3.4 with footnotes 600ff and Sect. 3.4.1.1.4 with footnotes 820ff above.

[5]See Sect. 3.5 with footnotes 1155ff above.

[6]See Sect. 2.2.2.2.2 with footnotes 86ff above.

K. Reiter, *Market Design Powers of the European Commission?*, Munich Studies on Innovation and Competition 13, https://doi.org/10.1007/978-3-662-60711-4_7

3. An assessment of the Commission's commitment practice against the normative benchmark of Article 7 does not reveal any concrete indicia that the remedies adopted on the basis of Article 9 go systematically beyond what the Commission could have imposed on the basis of Article 7. This applies in particular to the often-criticised so-called "structural" remedies.[7] Excessive Article 9 remedies remain the isolated exception rather than the general rule.

II. The procedural safeguards are only modestly relaxed.

1. The adoption of a remedy on the basis of Article 9 instead of Article 7 curtails the rights of the concerned undertakings, complainants, and other third parties during the administrative procedure only moderately. In particular, the concerned undertakings have a right to access to the file, notwithstanding the fact that a full exercise of this right will in practice normally be waived.[8] The interests of complainants and other affected third parties are in the context of Article 9 protected by the mandatory conduction of a market test pursuant to Article 27(4) Regulation 1/03.[9]

2. As far as judicial review is concerned, the conditions for the admissibility of actions against Article 9 decisions are not more restrictive than the conditions for the admissibility of actions against Article 7 decisions.[10] The scope of judicial review of Article 9 decisions is influenced by the slightly less strict requirements regarding the substantive and procedural requirements of the adoption of such a decision. Apart from that, the adoption of an Article 9 instead of an Article 7 decision does, however, not entail an additional relaxation of the scope of judicial review.[11]

III. There is at most a modest negative impact on legal certainty. The most valid concern remains that the use of commitments does not entail the positive externalities of adjudication. However, this concern appears less alarming than is often contended, in particular in view of the considerable amount of case law outside the cartel area that continues to be produced by the EU Courts in annulment and preliminary reference procedures.[12] Moreover, all potential disadvantages of the Article 9 procedure in terms of legal certainty must be balanced against an important advantage: The fact that commitments result in precise and enforceable obligations without sacrificing the concerned undertakings freedom to choose how to stop the infringement in question.[13]

IV. There are no viable alternatives. In particular the suggestions to exclude the application of the Article 9 procedure in novel, controversial or particularly serious

[7]See Sect. 3.4.2 with footnotes 946ff above.

[8]See Sect. 4.1.1.2.2.2.1 with footnotes 24ff above.

[9]See Sect. 4.1.2.1 with footnotes 75ff above.

[10]See Sect. 4.2.1.1.1 with footnotes 165ff above.

[11]See Sect. 4.2.2.1 with footnotes 232ff above.

[12]See Sect. 5.1.5 with footnotes 218ff above.

[13]See Sect. 5.2.1 with footnotes 267ff above.

cases[14] or to subject the adoption of a commitment decision to prior approval by the EU Courts[15] are not convincing.

V. Overall, the modest relaxation of the link between harm and remedy and of the procedural safeguards and the modestly negative impact on legal certainty must be accepted in view of the consensual nature of commitments, the goal of procedural economy that underlies the Article 9 procedure and the lack of viable alternatives.

[14]See Sect. 6.1.1 with footnotes 7ff and Sect. 5.1.1.3 with footnotes 32ff above.

[15]See Sect. 6.1.4.2 with footnotes 24ff above.

The manufacturer's authorised representative in the EU is Springer Nature Customer Service Centre GmbH, Europaplatz 3, 69115 Heidelberg, Germany. If you have any concerns regarding our products, please contact ProductSafety@springernature.com

Printed and bound by CPI Group (UK) Ltd, Croydon, CR0 4YY
23/09/2026
02221535-0008